M000309705

SAM BASS
&
GANG

Samuel Bass in Dallas, Texas, ca. summer 1876.
(Courtesy Robert G. McCubbin, Jr., El Paso, Texas.)

SAM BASS

&

GANG

by

RICK MILLER

STATE HOUSE PRESS
Austin, Texas
1999

Copyright © 1999
by Rick Miller
All Rights Reserved

Library of Congress Cataloging-in-Publication Data

Miller, Rick, 1941-
Sam Bass & gang / by Rick Miller.
p. cm.
Includes bibliographical references (p.   ) and index.
ISBN 1-880510-65-0 (alk. paper)
ISBN 1-880510-66-9 (pbk. alk. paper).
ISBN 1-880510-67-7 (limited deluxe)
1. Bass, Sam, 1851-1878.
2. Outlaws—Texas Biography.
3. Brigands and robbers—Texas Biography.
4. Texas Biography.
I. Title. II. Title: Sam Bass and gang

F391.B287M55 1999
364.1'552'092—dc21   99-34248
[B]

Printed in the United States of America

cover design by David Timmons

First Edition

STATE HOUSE PRESS
P.O. Box 15247
Austin, Texas 78761

TABLE OF CONTENTS

The World of Sam Bass and Gang

INTRODUCTION

&

ACKNOWLEDGEMENTS

By 1878 Texas was returning to some degree of normalcy after the anguish and confusion of Reconstruction. The era of the Texas gunfighter was over—the notorious John Wesley Hardin and Bill Longley had both been nabbed in the summer of 1877—and law enforcement in the state had stabilized and, for the most part, was back in the hands of competent men. A reconstituted Frontier Battalion, since known as the Texas Rangers, although still concerned about diminishing Indian depredations, had shown its ability to deal with various outbreaks of violence and outlawry throughout the state. Stability had returned to Texas and the citizenry was caught up in the normal pursuits of farming, ranching, trade, and community-building. In Austin, the state capital, the Democrats had returned to power and the outlook for Texas was generally promising.

For a few months in 1878, however, the swift, repeated raids of Sam Bass and his gang on the railroads of the state electrified Texas, and a law enforcement response was marshaled at a level never before seen. The Frontier Battalion, aided by local officials, met the challenge, and before the hunt was over five of the nine known members of the Bass gang were dead, two were in prison, one escaped to meet justice elsewhere, and one disappeared. It was a statewide manhunt that would be unequaled in the state's history, and it established the fact that law and order had returned after the turmoil of Reconstruction.

Sam Bass became an immediate object of notoriety in Texas, assuming a "Robin Hood" mantle as the facts of his exploits became clouded in myth and legend. Today one can still hear rumors of outlaw gold stashed by Bass in some cavern or cave, and of someone's great-grandmother who reportedly gave him sanctuary as he rode to escape the pursuing posse. Within weeks of Bass' death, two biographies went to press for quick commercial profits, and a song about the bandit and his exploits further popularized his myth.

Four books have come to be the mainstay of the Sam Bass saga. In August 1878 *The Authentic History of Sam Bass and His Gang*, written by Denton County Judge Thomas Hogg, was rushed into publication. It competed for sales in depots up and down Texas railways with *The Life and Adventures of Sam Bass, the Notorious Union Pacific and Texas Train Robber*, which was written by an unknown author and published by a Dallas newspaper. Both small books quoted contemporary newspaper acounts of the Bass pursuit, many of which have not survived in any collection today. The account by Hogg, however, deserves greater credence because Judge Hogg led one of the many posses that scoured the Denton County countryside and probably personally knew the outlaw and members of the gang. He also had access to Jim Murphy, the "spy" who directed the rangers to Round Rock and the ultimate demise of Bass and his gang. Hogg used Murphy's accounts to give his book a more authoritative basis. Many of Murphy's accounts, especially the account of the trek of the gang from North Texas to Round Rock, are not available anywhere else.

In 1880 Dallas newsman Charles Martin penned *A Sketch of Sam Bass*. This book relied primarily on the two 1878 books but also introduced some new information on "Arkansas Johnson," one of the gang members, and hinted at two "novices" involved in the Eagle Ford train robbery. But it was not until 1936 that a serious effort was made to pin down a definitive account of Sam Bass. Wayne Gard, a Dallas newspaperman who subsequently wrote some important books on frontier history, included in his *Sam Bass* the results of his diligent research into the life of the bandit, including personal contact with surviving oldtimers from Denton County who recollected the Bass days. Since then a number of books about Bass have been published, but for the most part they were sloppily researched, added nothing that was new, and relied primarily on Gard and the 1878 books.

This book attempts to flesh out the Bass story further,

hopefully correcting the mistakes of earlier efforts and cutting through the mythical to find the basic facts that will tell the Bass story and set the record straight. There were many people, both major and minor, who played a role in this story, and an effort was made where possible to flesh them out as well. The reader who just wants to read the story of Sam Bass should skip the endnotes; they provide the sources on which I relied as well as biographical information on the names mentioned. The endnotes are for other researchers who may want to take the Bass story further; they won't have to "reinvent the wheel" by wasting time looking for the same information. Also, if I have misconstrued information, I certainly want it corrected in some other forum.

Several years of research effort were invested in this book, but many, many folks contributed to that effort, and the book would not be possible without their help. First and foremost are the members of the National Association for Outlaw and Lawman History, Inc. ("NOLA"), who share with me a deep desire that the real story of these fascinating gunfighters be told. NOLA members who provided invaluable input, and who have been good friends, were Elvis N. Allen, Fruitvale, Texas; Larry D. Ball, Jonesboro, Arkansas; Kent Biffle, Dallas, Texas; Stanley V. Bowen, Arlington, Texas; Donaly E. Brice, Lockhart, Texas (a mainstay at the state archives); James A. Browning, Charleston, South Carolina; Mike Cox, Austin, Texas; Robert K. DeArment, Sylvania, Ohio; Jim Earle, College Station, Texas; Harold L. Edwards, Bakersfield, California; Robert R. Ernst, Stillwater, Oklahoma; Gary Fitterer, Kirkland, Washington; Clell Furnell, Sedalia, Missouri; Steve Gragert, Stillwater, Oklahoma; David Johnson, Zionville, Indiana (who shared his home for a week); Warren Johnson, Allen, Texas; Robert G. McCubbin, Jr., El Paso, Texas; Leon Metz, El Paso, Texas; Chuck Parsons, Yorktown, Texas (who kept my mailbox interesting); Gary and Jeri Radder, Alamo, California; Nancy B. Samuelson, Eastford, Connecticut; Ida Saunders, El Paso, Texas; Glenn Shirley, Stillwater, Oklahoma; Robert W. Stevens, Dallas, Texas; Larry J. Walker, El Paso, Texas; and C.B. Wilson, Dallas, Texas.

Others who provided most important assistance, and to

whom I am truly grateful, were:

Arkansas: John L. Ferguson, Arkansas History Commission, Little Rock; John Wampler, Arkansas Historical Association, Fayetteville.

California: Erich Baumann, Tujunga; Robert J. Chandler, assistant vice president, Wells Fargo Bank, San Francisco.

Illinois: Glenn V. Longacre, archivist, National Archives-Great Lakes Region, Chicago.

Indiana: Wayne Bass, West Baden; Boone County Public Library, Lebanon; Helen Burchard, Lawrence County Historical-Genealogical Society, Bedford; Mary Dunn, Mitchell; Helen Henderson, Mitchell; Alma Herbert, Lawrence County Circuit Court Clerk, Bedford; Helen Horstman, Jennings County Public Library, North Vernon; Indiana State Archives, Indianapolis; Indianapolis Public Library; Lebanon Public Library; Debby Jarrett, Boone County Clerk's Office, Lebanon; Linda Jeffries, Vigo County Clerk's Office, Terre Haute; Harold R. Johnston II, deputy prosecuting attorney, Vigo County, Terre Haute; John Lynch, Mitchell; Patricia Mansard, Vigo County Clerk's Office, Terre Haute; Sue Medland, Mitchell Community Public Library; Chief of Police Joseph M. Newport, Terre Haute; Debbie Ottinger, Boone County Clerk's Office, Lebanon; Jeff Routh, Bedford; Terre Haute Public Library; Don Tatlock, Jackson County Historical Society, Seymour; and Dustin Tolliver, Bedford.

Kansas: Wanita Cook, Gove County District Clerk, Gove; Ellis County District Clerk, Hays; Janet Johannes, Ellis County Historical Society, Hays; Hays Public Library; Labette County District Clerk, Parsons; Ann Werth, Ellis County Historical Society, Hays.

Minnesota: Cecilie Gaziano, Minneapolis.

Mississippi: Barbara Tweedle, Bolivar County deputy chancery court clerk, Rosedale.

Missouri: Audrain County Historical Society, Mexico; Rose M. DeLuca, reference supervisor, National Archives-Central Plains Region, Kansas City; Susan McCormack, Missouri State Historical Society, Columbia; Mary Jane Scott, Audrain County Circuit Court Clerk, Mexico; Alta Webb, Mexico.

Nebraska: Dr. Lloyd Ambrosius, Department of History,

University of Nebraska, Lincoln; Paul J. Eisloeffel, Nebraska State Historical Society, Lincoln; Thelma Lyons, Fort Kearney Genealogical Society, Kearney; Linda A. Wagamon, Nebraska State Historical Society, Lincoln; Katherine Wyatt, Nebraska State Historical Society, Lincoln.

New York: Stephen J. McArdle, Albany County Hall of Records, Albany.

North Dakota: Jim Benjaminson, Walhalla; Chuck Walker, Pembina.

Pennsylvania: H.T. Crown, Historical Society of Schuylkill County, Pottsville

Texas: Sam Akins, Grapevine; Atascosa County District and County Clerks, Jourdanton; Bastrop County District and County Clerks, Bastrop; Bee County District and County Clerks, Beeville; Bexar County District and County Clerks, San Antonio; D. August Boto, Austin; Linda M. Brainard, Kingsland, Texas; Pat Brown, Argyle; Calhoun County District and County Clerks, Port Lavaca; Beth Paschal Carruth, Lewisville; Clay County District and County Clerks, Henrietta; Collin County District and County Clerks, McKinney; Cooke County District and County Clerks, Gainesville; Anita Cowan, Denton; Dallas Public Library, Dallas; Denton County District and County Clerks, Denton; Denton Public Library; Barbara Chapman Elliott, San Angelo; Jerry Ferrell, Kemp; Fort Worth Public Library; Frio County District and County Clerks, Pearsall; Cindy Mayes Gage, Denton; Gainesville Public Library; Goliad County District and County Clerks, Goliad; Guadalupe County District and County Clerks, Seguin; Holly Hervey, collection management assistant, Denton County Historical Museum, Denton; Jeff Jackson, Lampasas; Mary Elizabeth Jiminez, District Clerk, Victoria County, Victoria; Vickie Jones, Southwest Collection, Texas Tech University, Lubbock; Karnes County District and County Clerks, Karnes City; Roane Lacy, Jr., Waco; LaSalle County District and County Clerks, Cotulla; Ruth Leatherwood, Mesquite; Natalie Massengale, Denton; McMullen County District and County Clerks, Tilden; Montague County District and County Clerks, Montague; Nueces County District and County Clerks, Corpus Christi; Michelle L. Moreland Orlando, San Antonio; Parker

County District and County Clerks, Weatherford; Gaylon Polatti, artifacts curator, Dallas Historical Society, Dallas; Barbara Rust, archivist, National Archives-Southwest Region, Fort Worth; San Antonio Public Library; San Patricio County District and County Clerks, Sinton; Ruby Schmidt. Granbury; Gail Schramm, Tarrant County District Clerk's Office, Fort Worth; Emma Jean Schulle, District Clerk, Caldwell County, Lockhart; Christina Stopka, librarian/archivist, Texas Ranger Hall of Fame, Waco; Vada Sutton, Bell County Clerk, Belton; Karen Thompson, Austin; Nita C. Thurman, Denton; J. Clark Tucker, Garland Genealogical Society; Gail M. Turley, District and County Clerk, Goliad County, Goliad; Victoria County District and County Clerks, Victoria; Eddie Williams, reference specialist, Texas State Library, Austin; Williamson County District and County Clerks, Georgetown; and the Wise County District and County Clerks, Decatur.

Wyoming: American Heritage Center, University of Wyoming, Laramie.

In addition, the following professional researchers were able to use their valuable skills in turning up important information: Teresa L. Blattner, Fulton, Missouri; Daniel Davis, Laramie, Wyoming; John Davis, Bellevue, Nebraska; Ruth Priest Dixon, Mitchelville, Maryland; Aimee L. Harvey, Lincoln, Nebraska; Weldon I. Hudson, Fort Worth, Texas; and Kathryn F. Schumann, Valley Center, Kansas.

Finally, all of you who choose to read this book owe as much a debt of gratitude as I do to Dr. Nora Stafford, chair of the English Department, Mary Hardin Baylor University in Belton, Texas, and Erik Mason, editor for State House Press, for taking this manuscript in their capable hands and making it literate. Without them and Spellcheck, the story of Sam Bass would still not be told, at least not literately. And, as always, an effort such as this means time spent away from the others in my life, especially my wife, Paula, who truly understands my passion for the Old West. I owe all of them a big dinner.

-I-
INDIANA BEGINNINGS

Sam Bass was born in Indiana, it was his native home;
And at the age of seventeen young Sam began to roam.
Sam first came out to Texas, a cowboy for to be—
A kinder-hearted fellow you seldom ever see.[1]

And so begins one of a number of versions of the "Ballad of Sam Bass," likely composed not long after Bass' death in July 1878. In life Sam Bass forged a criminal career in the space of about a year in Nebraska and Texas, first as a cattle thief, then as a stagecoach robber, then as a train robber. In the last five months of his life, Bass electrified the entire state of Texas with four quick (and relatively unprofitable) train robbery attempts, setting in motion one of the largest organized manhunts in the state, then or since, which climaxed with Bass' death in Round Rock, Texas.

It was then that the myths and tales began to be passed down from generation to generation, resulting in today's popular image in Texas of a "Robin Hood" rather than of a train robber and thief. Today, driving south on Interstate 35 and entering the city limits of Round Rock just north of Austin, the first prominently and proudly displayed sign announces the exit to "Sam Bass Road." Each summer the community's "Round Rock Days" celebration features a hellzapoppin' gunfight in the downtown streets to recall the violence in 1878 that helped put Round Rock on the map.

The legend of Sam Bass, like that of his criminal counterparts Jesse James and Billy the Kid, has been established and perpetuated in one way or the other through the years by various media with considerable artistic license. Numerous books and articles have cursorily attempted to deal with the Bass legend, usually only making it worse. In a 1949 Universal-International movie, *Calamity Jane & Sam Bass* written and directed by George Sherman, Howard Duff starred as the illit-

1

Exit sign on Interstate Highway 35 in Round Rock, Texas.
(Author photo).

erate farm boy from Indiana who comes to Denton, Texas, intent on being a rancher, and who acquires the "Denton Mare," the fastest horse in Texas. By unfortunate circumstance, the horse is intentionally poisoned before a race, and Texas cattlemen's money recklessly bet on the mare by Sam and his companion, Joel Collins, is lost. This drives a well-meaning but misguided Sam into outlawry in order to pay back the cattlemen. The Bass gang is aided by, of all people, Calamity Jane, played by Yvonne DeCarlo. Motivated by a reward, Jim Gordon (listed as Murphy in the credits) lures Bass into an ambush. Mortally wounded, Sam drags himself back to Denton, Texas, in the vain hope of seeing his beloved "Denton Mare" one more time, but he dies in the arms of the lovely Calamity Jane.

In a 1951 Columbia Pictures movie *The Texas Rangers*, however, Sam Bass is portrayed as the menacing terror of Texas who arrogantly defies the Texas Rangers by recruiting a gang of marauders composed of John Wesley Hardin, Butch Cassidy, the Sundance Kid, Dave Rudabaugh, and Duke (rather than King) Fisher. George Montgomery plays outlaw Johnny Carver, the fastest gun in Texas, who is recruited from the state prison by Major Jones of the rangers as the only man with the ability to go into the Little River area of Central Texas and set up an ambush of the Bass gang. Carver relies on his wits to carry out the mission, lures Sam and his gang into attempting the robbery of a train heading into Round Rock, stymies them until the rangers can ride to meet the gang, then, of course, kills Bass and wins the heroine. Artistic license strikes again and the myth of Sam Bass as either a misguided hero or an evil villain remains unresolved.

The real story of Sam Bass begins in the lush farming country of Lawrence County, in south central Indiana, which saw an influx of newcomers from the Carolinas and other states in the early part of the nineteenth century. In 1823 Sam Bass' grandfather, John Bass, aged twenty-five, a blacksmith and farmer, and his young wife Sarah Fender Bass, fifteen, moved their family to Marion Township in Lawrence County, near what would be the town of Mitchell. John returned briefly to North Carolina in 1824 but returned to Lawrence County in 1826. He was remembered as "a Whig and a Republican, and an industrious, respected man."[2] Among John's and Sarah's five sons and five daughters was Daniel, who was born in North Carolina on May 3, 1821.[3] The 1850 Lawrence County census listed Sarah Bass as forty-one years old, and court records confirm that she was the mother of Daniel; thus it is likely that she gave birth to Daniel around the age of thirteen. On March 19, 1831, John Bass purchased 180 acres in Lawrence County from John Maxwell for $130.[4] In 1850 John and Sarah Bass still had six of their children living with them at home.[5]

The Sheeks family was also moving into Indiana at approximately the same time. Sam Bass' other grandfather, George Sheeks, a cabinet maker who arrived as early as 1816,[6] was a native of Rowan County, North Carolina, and his wife Elizabeth Canotte Sheeks was born about 1780 near Hagerstown, Maryland. Both of German origin, they were married in Wayne County, Kentucky. In the spring of 1816 they moved to Orange County, Indiana, near Orleans, where they stayed long enough to farm only one crop. In January 1817 they finally settled on Rock Lick Creek in the Marion Township of Lawrence County, where they established a new farm and raised their family of six sons and six daughters.[7] According to Wayne Gard in his 1936 book *Sam Bass*, George Sheeks was one of the thirteen original voters in the first township election in August 1817 and was a Jeffersonian Republican. There was an Indian village near the Sheeks homesite, and often the family entertained Indian visitors who became quickly disgusted when offered sauerkraut, reflective of the family's German heritage, as a gift of food.[8]

George Sheeks engaged in farming and accumulated considerable property, becoming one of the wealthiest men in the county before he died in 1842, followed by his wife in 1856.[9] One of their daughters, Elizabeth Jane Sheeks, named for her mother, was born in Lawrence County on December 17, 1821, the next to the youngest of the Sheeks children.[10]

Daniel Bass courted Elizabeth Sheeks, in between the demands of farm life, and on October 22, 1840, they were married.[11] According to Gard, the ceremony took place at the home of Elizabeth's brother, David Sheeks, who also performed the ceremony.[12] The first two children born to Daniel and Elizabeth Bass died in infancy,[13] but they went on to have eight children who survived. According to the 1860 Lawrence County census and court records,[14] George W. Bass was the oldest, born about 1845, followed by Euphemia (July 20, 1847), Clarissa (October 2, 1849), Samuel (July 21, 1851),[15] John L. (July 24, 1853), Mary (June 23, 1855), Sarah (September 2, 1857), and Denton (December 4, 1859).[16]

Less than two miles south of the Bass farm, the town of Mitchell was platted in 1853 and named for Ormsby MacKnight Mitchel (the second "l" in the town's name is the result of a clerical error), who had been graduated from West Point in 1829 along with Robert E. Lee, and who was a Cincinnati lawyer who surveyed the town. As early as 1851 the New Albany & Salem Railroad ran through the Juliet community north of where the town would be located. This railroad was reorganized in 1857 as the Chicago, New Albany, & Louisville Railroad, popularly known as the "Monon Route." Sam Bass' uncle, George Sheeks, became the first postmaster in 1854 and was county treasurer from 1856 to 1858. By 1859 Mitchell was the site of two depots for both the Chicago, New Albany line and for the Baltimore and Ohio Railroad, bringing considerable prosperity to the town. A part of that prosperity also produced a multitude of saloons on Mississippi Avenue, and the small town earned the longlasting moniker of "Saloon City."[17]

Gard wrote that Daniel Bass' farm, while not a large one, was nevertheless adequate for the growing family. The frame farmhouse had three downstairs rooms and one room upstairs. The timber in the surrounding countryside supplied ample boards for construction and for firewood, and the crops they farmed ranged from corn and oats to wheat, hay and potatoes. Through various land transactions in the 1840s and 1850s, Daniel Bass gradually acquired up to 320 acres, selling some of them in 1852 to the New Albany & Salem Railroad whose tracks bordered the eastern edge of the farm. However, there is some indication that Daniel Bass' farm production was not always sufficiently abundant to sustain his family. Periodically he would borrow money, such as one hundred dollars borrowed from Kip Brown on December 25, 1860, and another hundred that he and his brother John borrowed from Mary Finger on April 15, 1862.[18] There is no record that young Samuel Bass and his brothers and sisters experienced anything out of the ordinary as children on the farm, helping their parents with chores, perhaps occasionally attending a nearby school (although Sam did not learn to read and write), working in the fields, and visiting with the wealthier Sheeks family.

By 1855 there were 833 children old enough to attend school in Marion Township, ranging from five to twenty-one years of age. The community built by subscription a small brick schoolhouse in 1856 on the east side of Mitchell, and the first term was taught in the winter of 1856-1857 by E.M. Baldwin. A graded school was later established in Mitchell in 1869.[19] Gard wrote that Sam occasionally attended a school near the Woodville switch close to the Bass farm, but work on the farm did not allow much time for education.[20] A successful farm required dawn-to-dusk labor, and it may fairly be concluded that Sam's life was a hard one but no different than that of any other farm boy.

As the clouds of civil war threatened to envelope the nation, a calamity struck the family when Sam's mother, Elizabeth, died on June 3, 1861.[21] Various accounts have her dying while giving birth to her youngest son Denton, but he was over a year old at the time. It is possible, of course, that her death could have resulted from complications related to that birth. She was buried in what became the Sheeks family cemetery on a corner of her brother David Sheeks' farm. Likely, Euphemia, fourteen, and Clarissa, eleven, Sam's older sisters, filled the void left by their mother's death and attempted to help their father by assuming a larger responsibility for the domestic chores of the household.

Grave marker of Elizabeth Sheeks Bass, mother of Sam Bass, in Mitchell, Indiana. (Author photo).

After several months of mourning, Daniel Bass briefly courted a widow, Mrs. Margaret A. Newkirk, the former Margaret Seibert who had married Lauson B. Newkirk in Lawrence County on April 6, 1851.[22] That union had produced two children, Robert and Mary, known as Bob and Molly, but Newkirk died sometime before 1860. The widow and her children boarded at a hotel in Mitchell.[23] Gard describes the widow as a "plump, auburn-haired woman, with a reputation for piety and with a little money from the estate" of her late husband.[24] She and Daniel Bass were married on March 13, 1862, and she and her two children moved in with the large Bass family.[25] The piety of his new bride must have had a positive effect, for it was reported that Daniel joined the Methodist church shortly after the marriage.[26]

In the meantime the Civil War had become a fact, and North and South began to recruit their armies. Captain Columbus Moore of the 16th Indiana Regiment rode into Mitchell on July 14, 1862, to raise a company of one hundred men for three years' service. Meeting under a large beech tree on Main Street, Company D was quickly organized, and the new unit promptly marched to the nearby home of Mrs. Silas Moore, who presented the soldiers with a homemade flag. Filled with the glory of the moment, Captain Moore proudly declared that he personally would see that the flag would never be dragged in the dust.[27] Among the eager recruits who received an advance twenty-five dollar bounty was eighteen-year-old George W. Bass, Sam's older brother, described in his enlistment record as born in Lawrence County, 5'6" tall, dark complexion, dark hair and eyes, and whose occupation was that of farmer.[28] On August 30, 1862, barely a soldier for six weeks, George fell, mortally wounded, at the battle of Richmond, Kentucky, and was buried in an unmarked grave. His uncle, David Sheeks, also lost a son, John W., who was colorbearer for Company D,[29] although it is unknown if his death occurred in this battle.

Coupled with this second tragedy in the Bass family in little more than a year is evidence that Daniel Bass' health was failing even as his oldest son was enlisting in the Union army. An affidavit included with a pension application filed years later in 1889 by Denton Bass, based on his brother George's brief military service, stated that Daniel had been suffering from consumption.[30] Despite his illness, however, in 1863 his wife Margaret delivered Daniel another son, Charles, adding to the crowding of the farmhouse.[31]

Daniel Bass died on February 20, 1864, at the age of forty-two years and nine months. His widow ordered a marble grave marker from Glover & Eades, for which $28.25 was paid from Daniel's estate.[32] Apparently Margaret decided not to remain with the Bass family nor to assume the responsibility for children other than her own three. On March 7, 1864, Daniel's brother, Solomon Bass, a farmer and blacksmith who lived on a farm adjoining that of Daniel, was appointed as the administrator of his brother's estate, and Margaret relinquished her right to serve as administratrix.[33] Since the probate of her first husband's estate was still before the court, Margaret was appointed on May 23 as guardian of her three children, Robert and Mary Newkirk, and young Charles Bass.[34]

To pay off the debts left behind by his brother, Solomon Bass conducted a public auction of personal property and livestock from the Bass farm on March 31, 1864. The remaining Bass children, including thirteen-year-old Samuel, had gone to live with their prosperous uncle David L. Sheeks, who filed for and was formally appointed by the court as their legal guardian in May 1864, at the request of Euphemia, Clarissa, and Sam, and of their grandfather, John Bass.[35] Everything but the land and buildings was sold at the auction, including farm tools, household items, furniture, and sheep and hogs. Among the purchasers was widow Margaret Bass, who bought a hoe, some brown yarn, a Franklin stove, a mat, and a desk. Sam's grandfather and other immediate members of the Bass family also bought items, all of which represented the life the children had known up to this point. Euphemia bought a bedstead and bedding for thirty dollars as well as a side saddle for five dollars, her surety being an uncle, John L. Dodson. Sam, backed by his uncle John Bass, Jr., bought a new saddle for seven dollars and paid four dollars cash for a large bull calf. The auction realized a total of $1,535.50, all of which was placed in trust under the control of David Sheeks on behalf of the children.[36]

As court-appointed guardian, David Sheeks now assumed responsibility for his sister's seven remaining children. A partition suit was filed to divide the 175.75 acres of Bass property between the seven children and Margaret and Charles. On January 5, 1865, the court awarded a 1/12-interest to each of the seven Bass children and 5/12 to Margaret and Charles.[37]

Although four of the Bass children went to live with their uncle David Sheeks, the youngest three, Mary, Sarah, and Denton, lived with their grandfather, John Bass, at least temporarily. He was paid $26.30 out of Daniel's estate for boarding the three children from March 4 to April 17, 1865. The three attended a school taught by Susanna Pace, who was also paid $5.70 out of the estate in June.[38]

Two years after Sam and his brothers and sisters had settled into a new life with their uncle, a singular event occurred that might have had some influence on young Sam Bass. At about 6:30 p.m. on Saturday, October 6, 1866, the eastbound Ohio & Mississippi train was pulling out of the Seymour, Indiana, depot, a little over forty miles northeast of Mitchell, when two masked men slipped into the express car and held it up for thousands of dollars in money and jewels.[39]

David L. Sheeks, uncle of Sam Bass.
(From Dorothy Alice Stroud,
My Legacy for Mitchell, Indiana.)

The first recorded train robbery in the United States, it generated widespread public interest, and a young, impressionable farm boy such as Sam Bass was certain to have heard about the crime. Within days of the robbery, detectives arrested brothers John and Simeon Reno and Frank Sparks for the robbery. A second train robbery near Seymour was committed almost a year later on September 28, 1867, by Charles Walker Hammond and Michael Colleran, both of whom were soon apprehended and subsequently sent to prison. Although almost two years had passed after the first robbery, community outrage over the crime continued to roil, and in July 1868 Frank Sparks was taken from the clutches of Pinkerton detectives and lynched. In December of the same year, Simeon Reno and his two brothers, Frank and William, were also forcibly taken from their cells at the New Albany jail by vigilantes and hanged.[40] The lynching undoubtedly also made some impression on the young Sam Bass.

Almost twenty, Euphemia Bass married carpenter John Beasley, who farmed property adjacent to that of David Sheeks, on February 14, 1867.[41] Seventeen-year-old Clarissa followed suit by marrying Abner Horsey on March 21, 1867,[42] and their sister Mary would reportedly later marry Abner's brother, George Horsey.[43] This left Sam, almost sixteen, as the oldest of the five children remaining with their uncle. Given that Sam Bass would remain illiterate, he was apparently not attending much school, if at all, and instead worked on his uncle's farm and other of his uncle's enterprises such as the sawmill.

There is no definitive record of Sam Bass' development into a young man during this period. David Sheeks continued to prosper, entered into the dry goods business in town with Anselm Wood, reportedly owned six thousand acres of land, and remained a well-respected member of the Mitchell community. In addition to the twenty-two children he would ultimately sire, Sheeks was credited with being a benevolent man who provided care for children without parents or means of support.[44] Gard says that Sheeks built an addition to his house by the Christmas of 1864 to accommodate the arrival of the Bass children. He was well-liked by the community and proved a most hospitable host, although Gard says that he was strongly opposed to card playing. He proved also to be a most energetic and efficient manager of his various enterprises, producing abundant crops and ample business profits. Again according to Gard, Sheeks, though a moral man personally, was nevertheless only a nominal Baptist, and Sam Bass, who had become a Methodist shortly before his father's death, was equally uninterested in regular attendance and long sermons.[45] Kept busy working for his uncle with very little time devoted to school, the strictures of farm life should have been a disciplining influence, but there is evidence that the prospect of a life as a farmer stirred some restlessness in Bass as he drew close to his majority. Although it is pure speculation, perhaps a growing curiosity about other lifestyles and habits helped fuel this adolescent rebellion and led the young farmboy to sneak away from his duties occasionally to frequent the low dives of Mississippi Street in nearby Mitchell.

Bass' sister Sarah, who was called Sallie, was later paraphrased as saying that for several years after their father's death, Sam's "character was spotless, but mixing in bad company, and the indulgence in the vain glory of the world, gradually led him into paths of sin, and gave him a rambling disposition."[46] Another contemporary account written shortly after Bass' death, and perhaps exaggerated for melodramatic effect, also pointed to his dissolution.

[I]f Sam ever had opportunities he neglected them, and we find him at an early age turning his attention in the direction of his untimely and disgraceful end. He gained a passion for cards, horse-racing and revelry, and sought the acquaintance of the most abandoned and desperate characters of both sexes. He was of a roving, restless disposition, and soon cut himself loose from all restraint....[47]

Without identifying his sources of information, Gard presents a picture of a young man, shy with girls but a quick friend to other young men, who was fascinated with tales of the legendary Daniel Boone. Desirous of going to Texas and herding cattle, Gard says, Sam Bass was dissatisfied with his life working for his uncle, who kept after him about petty gambling. Also, David Sheeks treated him like a minor ward rather than as a young man and didn't pay him a regular wage for his efforts. Bass wasn't due his full inheritance until 1872, when he would be twenty-one, and, according to Gard, Sheeks did not regularly pay him any of his share of the rent due from his father's farm. The daughter of Texas Sheriff William Egan would relate years later that one of Bass' sisters told her that Sheeks worked Sam and one of his own sons unmercifully, that Sheeks did not believe in education, and that he never allowed the two boys to go anywhere. The two rebelled, although Sheeks' son left only briefly and returned to his father's home while Sam moved on.[48]

According to family tradition, there was a shouting confrontation in the fall of 1869 between nephew and uncle after young Bass came in late asking for his share of the inheritance money. Sheeks allegedly picked up a hickory chair and advanced on his nephew who, smaller than his uncle, fled out the door and through a nearby orchard.[49]

Absent evidence to the contrary, it is probably fair to assume that the facts fall somewhere within the two extremes of absolute dissolution and the exuberance of a youth who yearned for freedom from familial restraint, eager to pursue a fantasy of adventure on the far-flung frontier. It is also not unreasonable to assume that, filled with such notions of high adventure, perhaps colored by the excitement generated by the Reno brothers' daring train robbery near his home (but ignoring their fate), as well as by a taste of dissolution, Sam Bass was ready to leave behind his Indiana roots and the allegedly strict control exercised by his uncle. Whatever the reason or motivation, the decision was made and a determined Sam Bass left to seek a new life elsewhere.

-II-
DENTON COUNTY, TEXAS

Accordording to his sister Sarah, Bass left Lawrence County in the fall of 1869 aboard the O & M Railroad and headed for the metropolis of St. Louis. One of the contemporary accounts, in this case probably more dramatic than factual, stated that Bass "left his home on a tour of dissipation and speculation, and after considerable rambling and association with that class of humanity that comported best with his own uncultivated mind and coarse instincts,"[1] decided to leave St. Louis. For whatever reason, possibly because the industry of the city was overwhelming for an illiterate country boy, Bass decided to move on and took passage on a Mississippi steamboat to Rosedale, Mississippi. This most likely occurred in 1870.

Rosedale was a small river port town in Bolivar County, halfway between the mouths of the White and Arkansas rivers. Originally a river landing known as Abel's Point, the spot became a plantation known as "Rosedale" and was soon a small settlement; by 1870 there were 9,732 living there.[2] Perhaps because he had no money, Bass apparently took a job there for nearly a year in the mill of a man named Charles.[3] The experience in his uncle's sawmill must have been of help in quickly becoming established but, according to his sister, while at Rosedale "he became an expert in card playing, dissipation, and revolver shooting." Unfortunately, there is no mention of either Bass or a man named Charles in local records, including the census, but a major landowner in Bolivar County, Charles Scott, helped establish an oil mill and a number of cotton gins and sawmills for the county's flourishing construction.[4]

Those who were familiar with him said that Bass knew nothing about firearms when he came to Texas,[5] and it is probably fair to conclude that Sarah Bass' description of her brother's activities was speculation based on what she knew of his life in Indiana and perhaps exaggerated to explain his subsequent criminal career. It is equally fair to surmise, however, that young Bass likely again strayed from the moral teachings of his family while in Rosedale.

Gard says that Bass took up with an unnamed older man with whom he prepared to leave Rosedale in the late summer of 1870 "to try life on the plains." Thomas Hogg, who wrote *Authentic History of Sam Bass and His Gang* within weeks of Bass' death, believed that Bass did not leave Mississippi until 1872, but the exact year is uncertain.[6] Before the two left Rosedale, they met the Mayes family, consisting of Robert, his wife Elizabeth, and two sons who were returning to their home in Denton County, in north Texas, after a two-year visit with relatives in Mississippi. Bass and the other man asked to accompany them.[7] Mayes, according to Gard, maintained a small hotel and livery stable in the town of Denton, although the 1880 Denton County census lists his occupation as that of a miller.[8] Perhaps it was the similarity of the name of Denton County with his younger brother's name which appealed to Bass, but at any rate the party was soon headed for the state of Texas, and Sam may have felt that his youthful fancies for adventure were about to become reality.

Robert Mayes was born in Kentucky about 1830,[9] but further information about his origins is not known. His two sons were Robert and Elijah Scott Mayes, who went by "Scott" and who would become one of Bass' bosom companions while in Denton County and who would also become the target of law enforcement as an accessory to Bass' crimes. Born on June 6, 1858, in Missouri, Scott Mayes was about thirteen years old when he met the twenty-year-old Bass in Mississippi.[10]

The Mayes party, traveling in wagons while Bass and his companion were on horseback, ferried across a flooded Mississippi River and encountered difficulty in climbing the steep, muddy banks on the Arkansas side where there was no longer a landing. Helped by ferry workers, Bass and the other men pushed the wagons up the steep bluff. The group then had to take a roundabout way because of swampy areas and unsafe roads, stopping in Hot Springs where "it was some sort of celebration day for Negroes," perhaps Emancipation Day. They rested, Mayes and his wife took their sons into town and bought them new linen suits, then the party continued on its way until it reached Denton in Texas.[11]

Located some thirty miles north of Dallas, Denton County's fertile soil provided prime farming and ranching country. The county has three distinct physiographic divisions: the western Grand Prairie, suitable for wheat farming; the Black Prairie to the east with its greater variety of crops, especially cotton; and, sandwiched between the two, the Eastern Cross Timbers, a heavily wooded area characterized by red sandy soil. The Elm Fork of the Trinity River courses through the east central part of the county, continuing south through Dallas County to join the Trinity which flows to the Gulf Coast. Other major creeks crisscross the county, helping nourish in their floodplains thick growths of almost impenetrable trees and underbrush. Denton County had originally been a part of the Peters Colony, an organization that had requested a large portion of northern Texas and received a land grant in 1841 from the Republic of Texas. In 1846, after Texas entered the Union, Denton County was formally organized; the newly organized town of Denton was selected as county seat in 1856 although it was not incorporated until 1866. Noted cattleman John S. Chisum had ranched in the county during the 1850s, and by 1870 there were over seven thousand people living there. The decade of the 1870s saw a spurt of growth that led to over eighteen thousand citizens by 1880.[12]

According to Scott Mayes, who was interviewed in 1930 before his death in 1937, Bass and his companion rode on west of Denton where they lived and worked through the winter and spring of 1871.[13] The various accounts of Bass' early employment in Denton County are conflicting as to chronology. One account has him first working at the Lacy House, an imposing, white, two-story frame hotel on the northeast corner of Denton's town square, operated by Sarah E. Lacy, the widow of Charles Christian Lacy, formerly the county surveyor.[14] In 1870, one of Sarah Lacy's boarders was Denton grocer Clay Withers who would play a major role in Bass' life a few years later.[15] Bass is supposed to have worked for Mrs. Lacy doing general work around the hotel and stables for about eighteen months, "giving entire satisfaction and greatly endearing himself to the good lady of the house by his kind and obliging disposition and his excellent conduct." He is then supposed to

The Lacy House Hotel, Denton, Texas.
(Courtesy Denton County Historical Museum).

have gone to work briefly for a man named Wilkes.[16]

Gard, more in accordance with Scott Mayes' account, says that Bass and his companion first went to work for rancher Bob Carruth, on Denton Creek some fourteen miles southwest of Denton, where he stayed through the winter and spring of 1871. In this version, Bass quickly became disenchanted with the hard work involved in ranching, and there also remained a very real Indian threat not too far to the west.[17]

Another account, written shortly after Bass' death, says that Bass went to work as a teamster and "general roustabout" for Thomas J. Egan, for whom he worked about one year.[18] Bass may have worked for one or all of these folks after he arrived in Denton County, but there is no question that he finally went to work for Tom Egan's son, Denton County Sheriff William Franklin Egan, known to some as "Dad" or "Uncle Bill." Much like the alleged friendship between Billy the Kid and lawman Patrick Garrett, who would ultimately shoot down the New Mexico outlaw, a friendship grew up between Bass and "Dad" Egan, who had arrived in Denton County from Kentucky in 1859 and, after service in the Civil

Sarah Lacy, seated second from left, with her family. To her right is her
son W.D. Lacy who witnessed the Mesquite train robbery in April 1878.
(Courtesy Roane Lacy, Jr., of Waco, Texas).

War, been elected sheriff in 1869.[19]

Bass went to work for Egan on his Denton place, a house
and barn on twelve acres of land supporting a garden, a melon
patch, and a few cattle and horses.[20] Virginia Egan, daughter of
the sheriff, would say years later that Bass did the "outside
work" and that he was hired to attend to the horses and "work
about the place as a hired hand." She recalled that her mother
told her that Bass was quiet and never used bad language nor
cursed around the house.[21] Egan himself said that Bass was a
sober, industrious young man while he worked for his family.
On occasion he would give Bass considerable sums of money to
go to Dallas or other nearby communities to purchase lumber
and supplies.

> His habits of economy were so great that his
> employer found fault with him for starving him-
> self and [his] team. He never would wear a suit
> of clothes that cost more than five dollars. In all
> his service he was very much devoted to his
> employer's interests. He was also retired and

William F. Egan,
Sheriff of Denton County, Texas.
(From Wayne Gard, *Sam Bass*.)

quiet in his disposition, never was absent from
home in the evening or away on the Sabbath
unless sent upon an errand. His only companion was a little boy, who taught him to write
and assisted him in his efforts to make a man of
himself.[22]

It was no secret to Bass' acquaintances that he was
"intensely ignorant and wholly illiterate," unable to read a
word nor even write his name.[23] The "boy" referred to above
was Charles H. Brim, born March 22, 1858, near Clarksville,
Texas, to Thomas J., a house carpenter, and Sarah E. Brim, who
lived four households from the Egans.[24] Virginia Egan said that
her mother would sometimes read letters to Bass that he had
received from relatives in Indiana and would answer them for

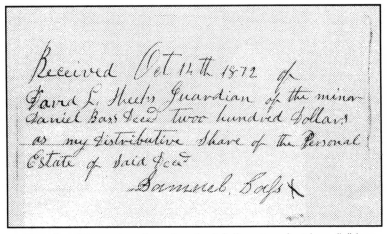

Guardianship receipt of two hundred dollars signed with an "x" by
Samuel Bass, October 14, 1872.
(Probate Records, Lawrence County, Indiana.)

him. Bass would spend his Sundays around the Egan barn with
teenaged Charlie Brim, who would also read and answer his letters, as well as read books to him. Gard said that Bass recipro-
cated by teaching Charlie the gambling card game of "seven-
up."[25]

The guardianship over Daniel Bass' children by David
Sheeks had continued in Indiana. Sheeks was required to make
a regular accounting and disbursements of the modest profits
realized through rent of the Bass farm on behalf of the children
still subject to the guardianship. Bass' older sisters, now having
reached their majority and married, no longer received any part
of the inheritance. On May 3, 1870, Sheeks reported to the
court that Samuel and his brother John were each due $151.81,
while Denton, Mary, and Sarah were to receive lesser
amounts.[26] Sheeks filed another accounting as guardian on
October 14, 1872, reporting that Sam and John Bass were each
due $199.65, and the guardianship file contains a receipt from
Samuel Bass dated October 12 for two hundred dollars as "my
distributive share of the Personal Estate of" Daniel Bass, which
is signed with an "x,"[27] but Bass apparently had not actually
received the money. Perhaps it was for this latter disbursement
that, with the help of Charlie Brim, Bass made the following
attempt at eloquence in a letter penned to his uncle from

Denton on October 27, 1872.

> Dear uncle I have just received your kind
> missive and was very glad that you have been so
> very kind to me in sending me the amount you
> have I am still doing very well and have the best
> hopes for my self and friends.
>
> I am at work for the Sheriff of this County
> and he tells me that it would be best for me to
> have you to send me a check on some bank in
> St. Louis Mo. and he will pay me the money for
> it without a percent of charge.
>
> In the first place there is no express office
> nearer here than Sherman Texas.
>
> There fore through the advise I have I have
> concluded have you to send me a check on
> some bank either in St. Louis or Austin Texas.
>
> You will pleas write as soon as you get this
> and oblige me.
>
> My respects to you and all relatives and
> friends.
>
> > humbly your relative
> > Samuel Bass to D.L. Sheeks[28]

Apparently Uncle David was not as responsive as Bass desired. Bass had plans for his future that depended on receipt of the inheritance money, which was not immediately forthcoming. On December 8, 1872, Bass and Charlie Brim again teamed up and sent the following letter to Sheeks.

> Dear uncle - I have taken the opportunity
> of writing to you one more and stating to you
> that I am well and enjoying good health and
> hope that this letter may find you one and all
> enjoying the same good blessing.
>
> I signed that receipt that you sent me
> directly on the reception of it and have waited
> patiently for a reply from you but have never
> got any word about it.
>
> I have given up all hope almost of hearing

any thing more about it.

That land that I had engaged and promised to pay $3.00 three dollars per acre It has since been sold for $5.00 per acre since I written to you.

I am agoing to buy some land here yet providing that I raise the money that I want to make the undertaking.

The rail road will be here soon The supposition is that it will be here by the first of May next sure.

Land and property is a going up every day in price. One can get land very cheap farther west in advance of the road.

I desire you to send me the money very much if you have not sent it yet.

I want to go West in the spring.

I hope that you wil write to me so soon as you get this and if you have not send the money, tell me why you have not sent it.

Give my respects to all Friend and relations.

Tell them all to write to me.

I remain is [sic] ever your affectionate relative,

Samuel Bass[29]

There is no record that Bass ever bought any land.

Although a newspaper in 1878 stated that Bass served as a deputy to Egan,[30] such was not the case. According to an acquaintance, Johnny Hudson, his duties were only those of the ordinary hired hand: tending to the livestock, milking the cow and similar activities. During the falls and winters of 1874 and 1875, Egan sent Bass south of Denton to cut and haul firewood for the Egan home. Richard E. "Dick" Cobb worked for Judge J.E. Carroll, whose farm adjoined that of Egan, and joined Bass in the firewood search.[31] Cobb recalled having a good time visiting with Bass and remembered him then as a "nice, quiet boy."[32] Egan loaned out Bass to other farmers and ranchers, and Bass helped build fences on additional land that Egan bought. The sheriff also had a small freighting business, and

Sam found himself driving to such nearby centers of commerce as Sherman, in Grayson County, and Dallas where the newly constructed Houston and Texas Central Railroad brought needed supplies from southern parts of the state. It was during these frequent trips, Gard wrote, that Bass became familiar with the landscape and roads—a knowledge that would later serve him well.[33] Bass was an almost daily sight in Denton, reins in hand to one of Egan's wagons and teams, driving through the streets "with that same imperturbable, downcast look which ever characterized him."[34]

By 1874 the twenty-three-year-old Bass had matured into a young man. Because of his subsequent criminal activities, his physical description was noted by various observers. Thomas Hogg, who knew Bass personally, certainly did not ascribe a heroic visage.

> [H]e was quite as poor a prospect for a hero as ever blossomed into notoriety. He was about five feet eight inches in height, dark sallow complexion, dark hair, and brown or hazel colored eyes. He had a thinly scattered black beard, which habitually appeared about a week old. He was stooped in his shoulders, and wore a downcast look, more a look of embarrassment than of villainy. He rarely spoke, except when under the influence of whiskey, and when he did, his words were drawled out with a shrill, nasal twang that was devoid of melody and exhibited a total absence of refinement. He was dull in all but trickery, but be it said to his credit he was a faithful and trustworthy servant.

Hogg recalled that Bass would not look into the eyes of a person addressing him, but instead would gaze no higher than "the central button on the second party's shirt front." However, once under the influence of whiskey, Bass "was rather garrulous, and though not quarrelsome, was easily aroused to pugnacity."[35]

In an interview in 1895 the noted Texas Ranger Lee Hall, who participated in the final shootout with the Bass Gang, recalled Bass as about five feet seven inches, stoop-shouldered, with "a sort of Roman nose, a Jewish caste of countenance," weighing about 135 pounds, with brown or black hair and brown or hazel eyes.[36] When Bass was fleeing the Union Pacific train robbery in Nebraska in September 1877, the description given out to law enforcement agencies was "quite young and boyish looking," 140 or 150 pounds, dark complexion, black hair that was cut short, and a thin, black moustache that was "not very stiff." The description noted his "very white teeth," and that he showed his front teeth when laughing. He was described as a "slow talker and don't talk much," and it was stated that he "drinks very little and does not use tobacco."[37]

At the time of Bass' death in July 1878, the *Galveston Daily News* opined that he would be "a good looking man anywhere," with "large, expressive dark eyes," and that he was

> stoop shouldered; very quick in his movements; of swarthy complexion; black thin moustache; straight hair, black beard, heavier on the jaw than the chin; his head bends forward; eyes turns [sic] downward; his voice is thin and shrill, and he talks no more than he is obliged to.[38]

Well established in Denton County by 1874, Bass likely tired of the routine of working for "Dad" Egan, the restlessness spawned in Indiana apparently unfulfilled. As he went about his chores and drove through the county, he met a variety of young men, a number of whom who would play prominent roles in his criminal career. Young Scott Mayes remained a close friend, and others such as Bob and Jim Murphy, sons of old-time settler Henderson Murphy, came to be regular acquaintances. Probably the one man who would have the most profound impact on his future as a sort of evil mentor was a fellow Hoosier, Henry Underwood.

According to his wife, Underwood was born in Jennings County, Indiana, on January 10, 1846,[39] although another account has him born in the year 1847[40] and his grave marker shows January 11, 1848. Of Henry Underwood's early life, little is known. At the height of his notoriety in Texas, it was said that his father was a respectable farmer and miller and that the family occupied a "position of high esteem among their neighbors" in Jennings County. His parents were supposedly strict Baptists and Henry was reared "under good influence." His education was described as quite limited, but he could read and write legibly.[41]

On November 15, 1863, Henry Underwood enlisted in Company A, 122nd Indiana Infantry Regiment, commanded by a Captain Brasher, giving his age as eighteen, although he could not have been any older than seventeen, perhaps sixteen.[42] Underwood would later complain that in March 1865, while at Kingston, North Carolina, where the company ended up at the end of the war, he incurred both epilepsy and "catarrh of the head," and that on July 1, 1865, in Charlotte, he permanently injured the third finger of his left hand while unloading barrels of pork.[43] A later prison record would describe Underwood with his "3rd finger on left hand bent down into the palm of hand."[44]

The first recorded character flaw in Henry Underwood made its appearance at the end of his military career. Underwood had been absent on detached service to Greensboro, North Carolina, since July 13, 1865. On October 31, 1865, having returned to his unit at Raleigh, the army private left camp without permission, then entered the Raleigh home of Elizabeth Taylor and "did create a disturbance and riot breaking the furniture" belonging to Taylor. For this imprudent action, he was placed under arrest by the military authorities and charges were preferred against him for being absent without leave and rioting. The records reflect only that he was mustered out of the army at Raleigh, North Carolina, on January 8, 1866.[45]

Henry Underwood likely returned to the family farm in Jennings County after his discharge. Henry C. Hall and Charles C. Hall, two brothers who knew Underwood between 1866 and 1871, stated that they lived in the neighborhood with him and saw him almost every day. They remembered Underwood's regularly complaining of the catarrh in his head that he claimed had been incurred while in the service.[46]

Farm life apparently didn't agree with Underwood, and he next showed up in Labette County, Kansas, in 1871 with Nathan, his older brother born on January 26, 1844,[47] who had also served in the Union Army in the 37th Indiana Infantry Regiment.[48] On January 11, 1872, Henry Underwood married sixteen-year-old British-born Mary Ann Emery at the home of her parents.[49] Mary Underwood would later say that Henry labored as a farmer, living a quiet, steady life, without engaging "in dissipation or reckless adventuring." To later rumors that Underwood had killed a man in Kansas, his wife vigorously protested, alleging that he was never in a "difficulty" prior to going to Texas.[50] The protestations of Underwood's wife notwithstanding, all was not stable and calm in Labette County. On April 19, 1872, the grand jury indicted

Nathan Underwood, brother of Henry Underwood.

Henry and Nathan Underwood for the "unlawful taking, stealing, and carrying away [of] certain bedding and household furniture and clothing" belonging to a Rebecca Jones on February 1, 1871, over a year earlier. Sheriff G.W. Franklin arrested Henry on June 6, 1872, and he promptly posted a three hundred dollar bond. Nathan Underwood, however, was never located and was not arrested on the charge. Henry's attorney, F.A. Bettis, filed a motion to quash the indictment, alleging that the charge was based on insufficient facts, and on July 1, 1872, the motion was sustained and the charge was dropped.[51]

Shortly after this incident, likely having worn out his Kansas welcome, Henry and his wife moved to Denton County in Texas, where he was employed "hauling fuel for market" and freighting with a team between Denton and Dallas. Judge Hogg claimed that Underwood was on his best behavior for about a year after he moved to Texas, and others in Denton County who knew Henry Underwood, while recognizing him as a "bad character—a malefactor and a renegade from justice," also saw a number of virtues in him. He paid his debts promptly and made an honest living after coming to Denton. "He was true to his attachments and would go to any length to accommodate a friend. He was courteous and warm-hearted when sober, and idolized his wife and children with the devotion of a true and dutiful husband and parent." Hogg remembered Underwood as five feet nine inches tall, dark complexioned, with very small black eyes "which look from their sockets as though the apertures were too small." He usually sported a dark moustache and was described as being "quick and nervous in his movements.[52]

> He has a laughing, rollick some disposition while free from anger, but is quick tempered and daring to resent an affront. His voice is very shrill and loud when he is excited. With the courage of a lion he combines the cunning of a fox. Ever ready for adventure and often unscrupulous in the means to be employed, yet he is not cruel or bloodthirsty in his disposition....[53]

In May 1881 Indiana's list of convicts in prison described him as five feet, eight inches tall, 171 pounds, dark complexion, dark brown eyes, and black hair, with a bent third finger on his left hand.[54]

After Underwood had been in Texas about a year, "he began to form evil connections, and soon fell into gambling and dissipation," most frequently found in saloons in the company of other sordid characters. Underwood would periodically engage in honest enterprise, if only to raise a little money for his family, "but his general course was downward, until he became somewhat noted for recklessness."[55]

By 1874 Henry Underwood, in the course of his downhill slide, had made the acquaintance of Sam Bass, and their close relationship began to form with fateful consequences for Bass.

-III-
THE DENTON MARE

In 1874 Sam Bass was living and working in Denton County, and tax records show he owned four horses worth fifty dollars each. Henry Underwood owned two horses and two cows.[1] At about this time, Bass discovered his passion for horse racing. "Scrub racing," usually between two horses on homemade quarter-mile tracks, was a common, frequently festive pastime throughout Texas, more often than not the scene of horse swapping, spirited betting and heavy drinking. Not uncommonly, farmers and ranchers would camp out at the rural racetracks after considerable travel from their homes.[2] The exciting world of horse racing was a notable departure from the daily grind of farm life.

One horse, the bay yearling Steel Dust which had been brought as a colt to Texas from Kentucky in 1844, gained renown throughout the state for his dazzling speed in such matches. He soon developed into a well-muscled stallion, word spread about his sprinting ability, and his legend was insured with a victory over the noted Monmouth in McKinney, Texas, in 1855. An injury later the same year, coupled with progressive blindness, forced the stallion's retirement from racing, but there remained a great demand throughout the state for Steel Dust's services as a sire in hopes of colts endowed with equal speed. Sometime in the 1860s Steel Dust is believed to have died, although no reliable accounts have survived.[3]

Around the fall of 1874, Sam Bass was lured by the dream of exciting riches he might attain with a racehorse, but he did not have enough money saved. He teamed up with Armstrong "Army" Egan, the twenty-four-year-old younger brother of "Dad" Egan, and the two pooled their funds to purchase a gray mare.[4] The mare, two years old and reportedly containing strains of blood from Steel Dust, was purchased from Mose Taylor, of the

Little Elm community on the McKinney road, after the two young men saw the horse tied near the Denton courthouse. The young horse was named Jennie, although the inspiration for that name was not "Dad" Egan's daughter, Virginia, as was later asserted, because Virginia Egan was not born until several years later.[5]

Sheriff Egan was not happy about either the acquisition of the speedy mare or the involvement of his younger brother; he well knew that association with the type of bad company that thrived in the milieu of racing would only lead to trouble. Egan insisted that Army give up his interest in the horse.[6] According to Gard, the sheriff advanced Bass $130 to buy out his partner and even let him keep the mare in his barn temporarily.[7] Bass supposedly consulted Alvin C. Owsley, a twenty-year-old Denton attorney and teacher who had received a law license in 1875. According to Owsley, recalling the event many years later, he handled the matter between the parties although Bass neglected to pay his twenty dollars legal fee.[8]

Bass turned out to be a good judge of horseflesh. Jennie quickly established herself as one of the fastest horses in Denton County, and in races outside the county she became known as the "Denton Mare." Gard said that Luther Clark, who had been a cowboy on Randolph Paine's ranch near Pilot Knob, a small hill a few miles southwest of town, rode as Bass' jockey for the horse's first race and whipped the competition handily. Clark was about the same age as Bass, born in Mississippi to William and Helen Clark who also had a ranch in Denton County.[9] For the mare's second race, according to Gard, a skinny black jockey rode Jennie to an even more impressive victory. The jockey, Charley Tucker, who called himself Dick Eidson because he had been raised by prominent racing man Reece Eidson, appeared to have a good feel for the horse, and Bass retained him as his regular rider.[10]

In Indiana, Margaret Bass filed suit in May 1874 against the children of Daniel Bass on a claim of $429.60 related to a land title problem with the Bass property. Subpoenas were issued for four of the children, including Sam. Curiously, the Lawrence County sheriff filed a return of the subpoenas showing that he personally served them in Lawrence County on September 11,

Guardianship receipt of $78.39 signed December 5, 1874 by Samuel Bass, but with no "x". (Probate records, Lawrence County, Indiana).

1874, to both Euphemia and Samuel Bass,[11] although there is no information that Bass ever returned to Indiana after he left in 1869. David Sheeks filed a final guardianship accounting for 1874 on December 12. He declared that "Samuel Bass is of full age and lives in the State of Texas," and asked that he be discharged as his nephew's guardian. He filed a voucher that $78.39 had been disbursed to Bass. A receipt dated December 5, 1874, and signed "Samuel Bass" acknowledged that the amount had been paid as the "remainder of my distributive shair" of the estate of Daniel Bass.[12] Perhaps this sum went toward the purchase of the Denton Mare.

Although the chronology is almost impossible to establish, there have been various accounts of Bass' experiences in racing his horse, most of them unsubstantiated recollections of old men provided scores of years later. Jim Gober, who would become Potter County's first sheriff, recalled seeing a match race in Denton County in the summer of 1875 between Bass' horse and the mare of Tom Spotswood, of Collin County, who would later be tried as one of Bass' accomplices. The Denton Mare won the race by a nose, as declared by race judges, and a number of the two hundred men present who disputed the

29

decision quickly became violent. Gober's father removed him from the fracas in a hurry.[13] The incident was illustrative of the "bad company" that Sheriff Egan knew would come with involvement in gambling and horse racing, and he gave Bass an ultimatum to give up the horse or give up his job with the Egan family. Bass chose the mare, ending some eighteen months of employment with the sheriff.[14]

One of Bass' later jockeys, Johnny Hudson, told of a race in Denton where the horse "Rattler," owned by Buck Tomlin of Tarrant County, was brought in to run a match race against Jennie. Because it was well known that Bass' horse always seemed to win with Eidson aboard, Tomlin and his supporters objected to the jockey. A confident Bass relented and Harry Hayes was selected to ride Jennie. Rattler won the day and beat the mare, which apparently missed Eidson's skilled touch. Gard describes Hayes as a handy man for Scott Mayes, who was supposed to have opened a saloon and bowling alley in Denton.[15] J.A. Brooks, who would become a noted Texas Ranger captain, would recall that as a young man he also ran a race against Bass' horse somewhere west of Bolivar in northwestern Denton County.[16]

According to Gard, Eidson preferred to ride Jennie bareback, dabbing a smear of molasses on the horse's back rather than using a saddle. All the jockey had to do was pat the horse on the neck at the end of the race to get her to stop. Bass had Eidson start the horse from a small dirt mound built up at the start of the race; if anyone objected, he would allow the other horse a slight lead at the start. Bass raced the mare in various match races around the area, sometimes winning as much as five hundred dollars and, when no money was on the table, even racing for stakes composed of wagons, buggies, other horses, or clothing.[17] By this time Henry Underwood was helping to train and race Jennie, sharing in the winnings as Bass' new partner. Thus, Sheriff Egan's concerns for Bass' future were increasingly confirmed.

Jockey Johnny Hudson[18] recalled a race that would become a prominent part of the Bass legend. After Jennie had won a race at the Head of Elm community near St. Jo in Montague County, Bass, Hudson and several others headed for another race at Fort Sill across the Red River in the Indian Territory. When Jenny won a six hundred-yard match race against a pony backed by Indians, the judges declared that the mare "had a start that exactly equaled her length, or lead," so a second race was set up several days later at eight hundred yards, a distance that the Indians thought was beyond Jennie's range.

Bass suspected a double-cross and instructed Hudson to ride Jennie across the finish line, then keep going until he was across the Red River and back in Texas. Their wagon and extra horses had already been sent on ahead before the race. Bass and other men with him, perhaps including Underwood, would bring along any horses won from the Indians. Jennie won handily, and Hudson rode on to Texas where he joined the wagon. Bass and the others soon rode up with the prize horses and the party set up a camp. On the next day two federal marshals heading up a posse rode into the camp and demanded back the horses that had been won, claiming that the Indians were poor losers and that the return of the horses was the only way to appease them. Bass refused and threatened a "battle to the death." The marshals suggested a compromise of the four best horses but Bass again refused, and the marshals, threatening legal action, returned to Fort Sill empty-handed.[19] According to Gard, the Indians had refused to turn over the ponies so Bass and others stole them and hightailed across the river.[20]

Many tales about the Denton Mare have been passed down that cannot be verified. The family of Meredith Hart (Bud) Rayburn recalled that he was a thirteen-year-old rider for Bud Schillings of Hood County. Schillings had a mare called "Blaze," but in an early race in Denton, Jennie proved the fastest. Rayburn claimed that Blaze later bested Jennie at a race at Nolanville in Bell County in which the Denton Mare was the stake. An angry Bass threw his hat on the ground, cursing, and Rayburn claimed he felt sorry for him and returned ownership of the horse along with fifty dollars. Supposedly, Blaze and Jennie met again at Nolanville a few years later, and Rayburn passed himself off as a drunken bum and altered his mare's appearance so that Bass did not recognize her. Again, Blaze is supposed to have bested Jennie for a large stake.[21] This account more than likely reflects an exaggeration further complicated by the passage of years.

A better documented episode in Bass' racing career occurred when Bass agreed to a match race with a horse owned by Marcus Milner, a former constable of Parker County.[22] The horses at stake by each of the contestants were held in a nearby pen outside Denton. Milner's pony beat Jennie, but an infuriated Bass claimed that there was a faulty start and the judges became confused about what had happened. During the confusion Bass turned the stake horses out of the pen and taunted Milner to help himself. Early the next morning, Milner and his companions seized the horse staked by Bass and rode quickly for Parker County.[23]

Bass engaged Denton City Marshal Bill Fry,[24] who took temporary leave from his job, and the two men went to Parker County in pursuit. Bass and Fry located four of Milner's party and Bass' horse at a dance in Parker County. Fry pretended to have legal papers authorizing his seizure of the pony and they took possession, promising to meet Milner the next day at the court of a local justice of the peace to determine the matter. Unable to locate the judge immediately, Bass and Fry then rode into the county seat, Weatherford, and made a criminal complaint of theft against the four men. Fry recalled that Bass was afraid the men would ride after him and Fry to kill them. Armed with a warrant, and meeting the four men at the justice court the next day as scheduled, the county sheriff arrested the alleged horse thieves.

Milner was forced to file a civil lawsuit in a Denton County justice court to regain the horse, and it took several trips by him and his attorney before he finally prevailed. Bass, aware that Milner had already incurred expenses in trying the suit that surpassed the total value of the horse at stake, appealed the case to district court. Milner offered some compromise of the matter, but Bass shrugged off the compromise and referred Milner to Bass' own attorney. When Milner was unable to pay his attorney's fee and lost his legal representation, Bass won the lawsuit with a default judgment. According to Gard, Bass executed a note to his own attorneys for their fees, his tortured signature appearing as "Sam B Ass." Bass did not honor his note and had no resources to seize when the attorneys obtained a judgment against him.[25] Unfortunately, no court record of this legal episode could be located.

Bass' lifestyle during this time appeared to take a turn downward, and it was apparent that his companions provided no encouragement for improvement. Both Henry Underwood and his brother Nathan were active cattle rustlers in the area in 1875. In Hamilton County, Nathan Underwood was indicted on May 21 for theft, and in July he was indicted in Menard County for theft of cattle which had also occurred in May. Declared a fugitive, Nathan was described as being from Hood County, rather dark complexioned, with dark brown hair, "sleepy looking," round shoulders, and weighing about 140 pounds. Nathan fled North Texas and surfaced in Lincoln County, New Mexico Territory, in the spring of 1877 as a member of a band of horse thieves.[26]

Henry Underwood was equally busy. In mid-August 1875 two men named Hickey and May who grazed their cattle in Denton County learned that about seventy head had been stolen and driven toward Sherman, in Grayson County. The two men went to Sherman and, with the help of the sheriff and two deputies, went looking for the stolen cows. At John Lindsay's place about twelve miles from Sherman, they spotted the cattle in the possession of Underwood, Joe Horner and a man named Loury. The three rustlers fled, and Hickey and May drove the cattle back to Denton County.[27] As far as is known, Underwood was never arrested for this episode. Horner, his brother and a third man later held up the Comanche bank in January 1876, for which Horner served time in the Texas penitentiary. He then escaped, fled Texas, and emerged as Frank Canton who would be a respected lawman in Wyoming and Oklahoma into the twentieth century.[28]

Bass and several other young men attended a country dance in Denton County sometime during this period. According to an account, a fiddler known as Pomp Rose imbibed freely with several other men; a fight ensued during which knives and pistols began appearing in the crowd. A deputy sheriff, Tom Gerren, tried to quiet the crowd but was himself threatened. According to Gerren, Bass came to his side and helped extricate him from the threat. The woman who owned the house was enraged at the row and ordered everyone out, making "threatening demonstrations" toward Bass, who had a knife in his hand. Bass vainly tried to tell her that he had nothing to do with the disturbance and was trying to calm it down, but the woman kept coming toward him and Bass finally had to warn her that he would cut her throat if she touched him. Someone inflicted serious stab wounds on Rose during the melee, and Bass and others were reportedly arrested for the assault but later released for lack of evidence.[29]

On another occasion, Bass and Underwood had been in Denton and were leaving town for their camp on Hickory Creek six miles away, Bass balancing a large watermelon on his horse as he rode. The horse became unruly and the watermelon fell to the ground and burst. Both Bass and Underwood cursed the bad luck. About a half dozen black men lounging at a nearby street corner had a hearty laugh at their expense. Enraged at the impertinence, Bass and Underwood dismounted and began pelting their audience with rocks and brickbats. One rock scored a direct hit on the head of Albert Williams, knocking him to the ground. Thomas Hogg, a Denton lawyer who had his office nearby, witnessed all of the black men scampering away except for Sterling Johnson, held at bay by Underwood who wielded a club and threatened to knock off his head. Drawing back the club, Underwood hissed, "I've a good notion to knock your damn head off! Sterling, if you wasn't a good nigger I'd kill you, damn you!" Some men rescued him from Underwood's threats, and Underwood and Bass left Denton at full gallop. They returned a little later and Deputy Tom Gerren, whom Bass had rescued at the dance fracas, attempted to arrest Underwood, who ran as Gerren fired at him. Bass and Underwood returned to their cow camp then retreated into the Hickory Creek bottoms, eluding a pursuing posse. According to Hogg, it was shortly after this that Bass and Underwood took Jennie and left for other parts of Texas.[30]

The chronology remains unclear, but it appears that Bass, Underwood, and Johnny Hudson subsequently traveled to the vicinity of San Antonio to continue their racing activities. It is probably about this time that Bass and Underwood made the acquaintance of Joel Collins, a meeting that would be of momentous consequence for Bass.

Joel Collins was born in Dallas County in 1848, his parents having settled a few miles northeast of the small village of Dallas in the White Rock Creek area three years earlier where they worked hard on their farm and established themselves in the Dallas community.[31] In November 1860 when the Dallas County Agricultural and Mechanical Association held its second annual five-day fair, Joel Collins, almost twelve, received mention for his efforts in the "Boys' Equestrian Ring."[32] Only a few years later Joel was with his older brother Joe in Calhoun County on the Texas coast learning the cattle business.[33] Joe Collins' 1869 Calhoun County holdings amounted to 675 acres and twenty horses, and in 1870 was two hundred acres, eighteen horses, and twenty cattle.[34]

Joe remained in the cattle business throughout south Texas and became well known among cattlemen. His base of operations changed from Calhoun County to Atascosa County, where he was indicted on March 20, 1871, for gaming, to which he pleaded guilty on that date.[35] In nearby Karnes County, Joe Collins ran into more problems with the law. On November 3, 1871, he was acquitted on a November 1870 indictment alleging that he had committed an assault with intent to kill in that county. He was indicted again on November 6, 1872, for theft of a hog, but a jury acquitted him on that charge in March 1874. In March 1877 he would be indicted again for assault with intent to murder and subsequently acquitted in March 1879.[36] In spite of these occasional problems, Joe Collins rode on a number of trail drives north from south Texas to the railhead cattle towns of Kansas, quite often accompanied by brothers Joel and Billy.[37] In June 1873 Billy Collins reportedly killed "one of his Mexicans" while on a trail drive in the Indian Territory.[38]

Joel Collins appears to have been just as much of a free spirit as his brothers. He was described as dark complexioned, with black hair and beard, about 5'11", and found to be affable, with a "pleasing address," and "decidedly handsome."[39] The first record of any violence in his life occurred in mid-April 1870 at Kemper City in Victoria County some twelve miles southwest of the town of Victoria. According to sketchy details, a Hispanic man named Bedal Rosalees, or Rosinler, somehow interfered with Joel while he was taking cattle across the Guadalupe River. Collins protested and Rosalees pulled a knife, threatening him, whereupon Collins shot him down.[40] He was indicted for murder by the grand jury on September 17, 1870, but a jury acquitted him on September 26.[41]

In addition to working for Allen & Poole, a prominent Galveston firm, from 1868 to 1870, Joel Collins took a herd of one thousand cattle to Kansas in 1870 for Choate (J. Monroe Choate of Karnes County) and Bennett. The following year he took another herd north for P.T. Adams, and again in 1873 for noted cattleman James D. "One-Arm" Reed, both times splitting the profits with them. In 1874 Collins bought a herd from Bennett and Akard, partly on credit, but the cattle market took a downturn and the quality of his beeves meant a reduced price, forcing him to sell the herd to a Chicago buyer at a loss.[42] Bartholomew cites a *Wichita Beacon* report describing a horse race in Kansas between Joel Collins and a John McEwen which Collins lost.[43] During this time there is also a possibility that Joel Collins tended a bar in Dallas, an allegation that was made by Henry Underwood in 1877.[44] Collins was well known at Wichita, Kansas, beginning in 1873 when he came north on various drives,[45] and there has even been a suggestion that his brother Billy ran a saloon in Wichita.[46]

Perhaps stung by his cattle loss in 1874, Collins changed occupations in 1875. On April 1 he and Joseph Lowe, more popularly known among Texas gamblers as "Rowdy Joe," paid $1,521.70 for the interest of A.J. Kern in the Commercial Saloon at 14 Commerce Street in San Antonio, including fixtures, and renamed it the Stock Exchange.[47] Their establishment has been described as a "combined variety show, saloon and gambling house."[48] Rowdy Joe Lowe and Collins had both been indicted in Caldwell County on January 9, 1875, for "exhibiting a gaming bank," along with noted gunfighter Mannen Clements, a cohort of John Wesley Hardin, who was cited for "unlawfully playing at a game with cards." Lowe and Collins were again indicted for the same thing on January 11, and Collins yet once more on January 15. On that same day, they pleaded guilty and were fined in each of the cases.[49]

Although this information is incomplete, it nevertheless does appear that Lowe and Collins were in the saloon and gambling business together in Caldwell County prior to April when they began to operate the Stock Exchange saloon in San Antonio.

On September 9, 1875, the two partners were again indicted in Luling, the county seat of Caldwell County, Collins for play-ing cards in a public place and Lowe for permitting card-playing in a "house under his control." There is no explanation about the existence of a saloon in Luling run by Lowe and Collins in addition to the other one in San Antonio. Collins pleaded guilty and paid a ten dollar fine and costs on April 13, 1876, but Lowe failed to appear for his April 1876 court date, as did his sureties, Joel Collins and H.W. Bennett.[50]

As 1875 ended, the players were in place for the next chap-ter in the saga of Sam Bass.

The only authenticated photograph of Sam Bass, standing (left) with John E.
Gardner to his left. Seated are Joe (left) and Joel Collins. This photograph is
believed to have been taken in Dallas, Texas, in the summer of 1876.
(Courtesy Robert G. McCubbin, Jr.)

-IV-
BLACK HILLS CRIME

I n late 1875 or early 1876, Bass left Denton County
with his racing mare and made his way to bustling San
Antonio in central Texas. According to Gard, he was
accompanied by Henry Underwood and jockey Johnny
Hudson,[1] but there is some reason to doubt Underwood's presence in San Antonio because of events in Denton County
where, at about two o'clock in the morning of Thursday,
December 23, 1875, the courthouse and most county records
were destroyed in a massive fire, despite the presence of a heavy
rain. The only buildings spared on the north side of the public
square were Sarah Lacy's hotel, the post office and news depot,
and the O.K. Saloon. The Parlor Saloon belonging to W.R.
Wetsel and Henderson Murphy was lost, as were a number of
other businesses. It was immediately and widely believed that
the fire was a result of arson, although others thought that fire-
crackers might have produced the conflagration.[2]

County offices and any records that survived were transferred to a Presbyterian church until a new courthouse could be
built. However, the church also sustained a fire, destroying most
district court records, and suspicion immediately focused on
Underwood. He was indicted for arson and kept in jail, both in
Denton and, beginning in March 1877, at Gainesville in Cooke
County to the north, for about six months. When the evidence
was determined to be insufficient, the charge was finally dismissed on July 25, 1877, by Denton County Attorney Emory C.
Smith. Underwood resented the rough handling that he
allegedly received at the hands of Sheriff Egan and his deputy,
Tom Gerren, and that resentment would translate into considerable hostility toward the two men.[3] Obviously, if Underwood
was in jail for a portion of 1876 and early 1877, he may not have
been with Bass in San Antonio.

Once in San Antonio, Bass met saloonkeeper Joel Collins.
While their early association is sketchy, contemporary accounts

indicate that Collins saw in Bass and the mare an opportunity for financial gain. Perhaps the saloon business had palled on him, or perhaps the relationship with Rowdy Joe had become difficult. Collins, "a man of reckless habits and great shrewdness," and Bass teamed in an enterprise that lasted several months and was inelegantly described as follows.

> They formed a co-partnership in horse-racing and monte-dealing—Sam playing the part of horse trainer and judge of race stock for others whom he would encourage to run their stock against his mare in the hands of Collins, when it would pay the firm to do so, thus victimizing those confiding in his judgment and honesty. Joel manipulated the monte bank and bet on the race mare. In this way they plied their double trade between San Antonio and Mexico, often crossing over the Rio Grande for the purpose of going through the sportive or festive greaser, whom to fleece was not thought a very grave transgression.[4]

Bass was supposed to have related one incident in which he had persuaded a wealthy San Antonio Hispanic man of his ability to judge horseflesh. Bass and Collins planned to swindle the old man, but their mark grew suspicious and went to Mexico, carrying some forty thousand dollars with him. Bass attempted to follow and hold up the man, but could not locate him and returned emptyhanded to San Antonio.[5]

There is only a minimal record of their presence in San Antonio. The fair grounds in the city, as in Dallas and other Texas communities, were often the scene of match races accompanied by lively betting. On Saturday, March 25, 1876, a "very sprightly gray mare from the northeast portion of the State, owned by a Mr. Collins" was entered in a half-mile race against "Joe the Laborer," a bay stallion belonging to a man named Draper, and "Rolla," a black stallion belonging to a man named Lewis. The betting favored Jennie, but Joe drew the pole position and Jennie was on the outside. The race started at the half-mile pole, and a hollar of "go" started them off. Joe and Jennie ran neck and neck, but at the finish Joe pulled ahead by about a length, winning the dash in fifty-one seconds.[6] Two weeks later on Saturday, April 8, Jennie redeemed herself by coming in forty yards ahead of "Crowell," a chestnut stallion, in a time of 53 1/2 seconds.[7]

Despite their racing successes with the mare, Bass and Collins apparently decided to pursue a new calling. One account has a dispirited Bass complaining to Collins that the mare was no longer lucrative; another account has them going through their money by spending it on "women and wine."[8] Whatever their motive, they decided to go into the cattle business and allegedly staked a small down payment on $30,000 worth of cattle to transport to northern markets from the counties southwest of San Antonio.[9] On April 22, 1876, Collins sold to C.D. Fenley for six hundred dollars his one-half interest in what was now the "Occidental Saloon."[10]

The fate of the Denton mare is unknown, but it is likely that the horse was sold. One family has asserted that an ancestor, widowed freighter Columbus Bingham of Bertram in Burnet County, ran into Bass and Collins and decided that the mare would make a good scout horse for his four sons on freighting expeditions.[11] The family also asserted that Bingham and Jenny were present at Round Rock when Bass was mortally wounded, and that Bass finally signed a receipt for the purchase price with a pointed stick dipped in his own blood.[12] The family's assertion is highly unlikely; a horse with Jennie's record was far more valuable for racing, and she was likely sold to another sporting man.

It is quite possible that Joe Collins, who had a residence in San Antonio prior to April 1876,[13] helped his brother and Bass pull the herd together, since he had an excellent reputation among cattlemen, and he even may have gone on the drive with them. They purchased the herd on credit, a common arrangement in which drovers, after selling the cattle in Kansas, would return and pay off those who had provided the cattle for the herd, keeping a fee as their profit.

Additional hands hired to help take the cattle north included cowboy John Gardner, thirty-two, of Atascosa County, Texas, who had been on cattle drives to Kansas with Joel and

Billy Collins almost every year since 1872.[14] It is possible that Bill Potts, another cowboy and an experienced badman, also accompanied them north from San Antonio. Several contemporary newspaper accounts indicate that Potts, who was from Pottsville, Pennsylvania, and well known in Wichita, Kansas, had gone to Texas and returned to Kansas with the Collins-Bass herd.[15] The Texas Rangers' "List of Fugitives" described him as twenty-eight to thirty years old, about 5'8" or 5'9" tall, weighing about 145 to 150 pounds, with light brown hair, light beard and moustache, and a missing front tooth. He had a tattoo between the thumb and first finger of his right hand, and another of a dancing girl on his right arm. Potts was known to use the alias names of Bill Heffridge and Bill Heffery.[16]

Bill Potts was a familiar character in Kansas, Texas, and the Indian Territory. In April 1872 he stole a gelding in Ellis County, Texas, for which he was indicted the following May.[17] Henry Underwood would also recall that Potts had been a barkeeper in a saloon in Dallas run by Joel Collins.[18] Potts was better known in Wichita, however, although the record is spotty. Stuart Lake, in his biography of lawman Wyatt Earp, termed "Billy Helfridge" as a member of a Texas band of gunmen in a cow camp outside Wichita that included the notorious John Wesley Hardin, Joe and Billy Collins, and a number of other Texans who featured significantly in Texas' Sutton-Taylor feud.[19] Lake, unaware that Potts and "Helfridge" were likely the same person, also alleged that both Bill Potts and Earp were deputy city marshals in Wichita in 1874.[20] Unfortunately, Lake did not cite any sources for this information, and he very likely confused Bill Potts with William Botts, a special or extra policeman in Wichita in 1875.[21]

Potts was better remembered in Wichita for his criminal activities. In October 1875 he and two black men stole two large wagons and eight yoke of oxen from a man named Saunders, for whom they worked at Fort Sill in the Indian Territory. They drove the stolen wagons and oxen back to Wichita, where the city marshal, Mike Meagher, received a wire naming Potts as the thief. With the assistance of deputy marshal John Behrens, Meagher arrested Potts and the two black men in Wichita on November 5. The three prisoners were subsequently released on a habeas corpus writ but were rearrested on a state warrant for the same offense and jailed again.[22] The disposition of the case is unknown. Whether or not he went on the cattle drive from Texas with Bass and Collins is unknown, but Bill Potts would join them in their crimes in the Black Hills.

Collins and Bass pulled their herd together. One account says that it was composed of five hundred steers,[23] while another asserts that 150 head were bought from Joe Collins and 350 to 650 more were purchased from other cattlemen.[24] Another member joining the drive may have been Jack Davis, about whom little is known.[25] One assertion was that Davis also used the name of Jack Reed and came from Fort Smith, Arkansas. Described as about thirty years old, 5'11", 190 pounds, six feet tall, stoop-shouldered, inclined to curly hair, a man who talked and drank a great deal and who had a habit of walking with his hands behind his back,[26] Davis would join Bass and Collins in the Black Hills.

The entrepreneurs started their herd north toward Dallas County. The date is unknown but, at the earliest, was in the summer of 1876 because Joe Collins and his brother Billy were registered at the Lamar Hotel in Dallas on June 12, 1876.[27] Interestingly, a herd of twenty-eight hundred was taken through Fort Worth in early June by "Collins & Kennedy for Ellison & Deewees."[28] Bass would later tell lawmen that a photograph was made of him, Joe and Joel Collins, and John Gardner "at old man A.G. Collins's house."[29] This photograph, with the Collins brothers seated and Bass and Gardner standing behind them, was likely made when the herd was taken north and is the only authenticated one of Bass, although a number of photographs of other men incorrectly identified as Bass continue to be used today.[30]

At about this time an unusual episode occurred, described in Reed and Tate's *Tenderfoot Bandits* quoting a family story, in which Bass had convinced a Dallas man named John West to sell his wife's prized horse to him for three hundred dollars, which West did without his wife's knowledge. When West realized how much his wife loved the horse he had sold to Bass, he urged Bass to return it. Bass took pity on him and instead agreed to "steal" the horse so that West would be off the hook, but

West's father-in-law allegedly heard about the scheme and, armed with a shotgun, staked out the horse. West warned Bass off, as the story goes, but did not repay him the three hundred dollars.[31] Subsequently West received a penciled letter from Richardson, just north of Dallas, dated August 10 and postmarked Dallas.

> Richardson Tex Aug 10 76
> Mr Coat thief
> Jim Crosby & the old man wants to know where you got that checked OCoat you wore when you was down in our neighborhood[.] Jack Jackson says you stole it at Thomson's & bro[.] winter is coming on now you had better come down and mak another draw Steal another pistol, Shoot in to old man Conly house and Steal some more[.] jeneraly you are considered the damist thief that was ever in the neighborhood[.] we all want you to do the Stealing for the neighborhood[.] Crosby says he wants you to Steal another pistol from him
> Yours Truly
> Sam Bass
> Kiss my Ass[32]

This letter was followed a month later by a postcard with a September 9 postmark.

> Mr. John West Sir Dan Whitfield says Thompson has Plenty of coats now if you will come down you can get some good ones as the weather is getting cool[.] he says also Jackson Jackson has let the cat out of the wallet about you Shooting in to old man Conoly House[.] he says he is going to prosecute you for it[.] The neighbors advise him to do so
> Bass & Co[33]

Reed and Tate, accepting the story about the horse as true,

speculate as to the meaning of these communications, concluding that a sarcastic Bass is making veiled, cryptic references to the failure of West to pay back the three hundred dollars. Speculating that "the old man" is Joel Collins' father and that "Conoly" is actually "Collins," Reed and Tate identify the other names as close friends or relatives of West's father-in-law. Without more documentation, however, especially given the fact that Bass was illiterate, the meaning of these communications will have to go begging. A plain reading of the letter and postcard, if they are from Bass, hints at matters other than reneging on a horse deal; Bass does not seem to be sufficiently complex for such elaborate sarcasm.

Leaving Dallas County behind, the men drove their cattle north across the Red River and into Indian Territory toward Kansas where railheads were gradually moving to the west, leaving one infamous cowtown after another in their wake. The actual destination of the Collins-Bass drive is not certain. Hogg wrote that the cattle were taken to northwest Kansas and sold there, and Bass on his deathbed talked of going to Kansas with John Gardner.[34] However, another of the 1878 accounts holds that after they arrived in Kansas, Bass and Collins had others take the cattle on to Sidney, Nebraska, while they took the train northward to meet the cattle when they arrived.[35] Gard says that the cattle were driven to Dodge City but, once there, Collins decided that he could get higher prices for them further north. Accordingly, he sent the herd on north and subsequently sold it for eight thousand dollars.[36] This is somewhat confirmed by a report that Collins had "come up the trail" to Dodge City, then went on to Ogallala, Nebraska.[37] Al Sorenson, an Omaha newspaperman, wrote in 1877 that Collins drove the cattle to the Black Hills where they were sold.[38] Contemporary newspaper accounts seem to confirm that the cattle were driven "up from Texas early in the season" to the Black Hills and sold to a northern rancher.[39] Yet another account alleges that the cattle were driven to Deadwood in Dakota Territory and sold there.[40] John Gardner claimed that he and Collins "bought two hundred fat cows, horses and wagon at Ogallala and drove them to Deadwood,"[41] indicating the possibility that the first herd may have been sold in Kansas and the proceeds used to purchase more at Ogallala.

However they got there, Bass, Collins, and Davis finally found themselves in the Black Hills in late 1876 with cash in their pockets, variously estimated to be from five to eight thousand dollars.[42] They decided to stay in that area and keep the cattle money rather than return to Texas and repay the ranchers who had trusted them. They are supposed to have first established themselves at Deadwood in the Dakota Territory. With tongue in cheek, one anonymous correspondent gave this description of the teeming mining town.

> Deadwood . . . is a lively town of two thousand inhabitants. Of course,...it is the central camp, where all the gambling, fighting and business is done. Everything goes on a grand rush night and day. There is no regularity about anything. A man opens a place of business and makes lots of money, then he gets prospecting fever, starts for the gulches and shuts up his shebang. We have no municipal government at all. Every man thinks he's Mayor of the town. When a place is closed up it means that the owner is out digging, has been killed in a fight, or is off on a spree. Every once in a while the boys call a mass meeting, draw up resolutions, etc., and decide to incorporate the town and have a board of aldermen; but at the end of the week nobody knows what has become of the resolutions or the aldermen. We start a new city government every two weeks and burst one.
>
> Saloons all over the place, and whiskey four bits a drink. They put two barrels up on an end, nail a board across for a bar, and deal it out. A miner who wants to treat pours some gold dust on the barrel head and says: "Set 'em up." They never weigh the dust. Sometimes a man won't put down enough dust, but they never say a word; and if he's a little tight and pours out ten or fifteen dollars worth, they never mention it.

They have three faro banks running all the while. They don't use checks for the boys; when they won a pile of checks they threw them all over the place, and some were too drunk to handle them. So the checks got played out. Now a man puts a little gold dust in a dollar greenback and it goes for two dollars. Ten dollars worth of dust in a ten dollar greenback goes for twenty dollars and so on. They never weigh dust at all, but guess the amount.

Every man carries about fourteen pounds of firearms hitched to his belt, and they never pass any words. The fellow that gets his gun out first is the best man, and they lug off the other fellow's body. Our graveyard is a big institution, and a growing one. Sometimes, however, the place is right quiet. I've known times when a man wasn't killed for twenty-four hours. Then perhaps they'd lay out five or six a day. When a man gets too handy with his shooting irons and kills five or six, they think he isn't safe, and pop him over to rid the place of him. They don't kill him for what he has done, but for what he is able to do. I suppose that the average deaths amount to about one hundred a month; but the Indians kill some.[43]

On August 2, 1876, the noted gunfighter and former lawman James Butler "Wild Bill" Hickok had been assassinated in Deadwood as he sat in a saloon playing cards.[44]

In this chaotic, lawless, get-rich-quick environment, the Texas cowboys likely ran through their cattle proceeds quite quickly. According to Sorenson, Collins invested some of the cattle proceeds in a dance hall in Deadwood, "a dive of the very lowest grade, and the resort of the very worst and most dangerous characters in the Black Hills."[45] Tom Hogg described it as a "dwelling" costing some $3,500 which Collins furnished in "elegant style" and in which he installed as proprietress his mistress, a "lewd siren" or prostitute known as Maude.[46] There were reportedly other prostitutes to service the miners.

One author in 1939 claimed to have talked with a man named Anse Tippie who told him that he and Collins had been partners at Potato Gulch, some twenty miles west of Deadwood, in a grocery and saloon business.[47] Hogg said that, in addition to the dance hall in Deadwood, Collins set Bass up to freight supplies between Deadwood and Cheyenne, in Wyoming Territory. Upon Bass' return from his first trip, his expenses exceeded revenues by sixty dollars, an inauspicious beginning for a new enterprise. Collins then set Jack Davis off with a wagon and team and $250 to see if he could make a go of it, but Davis returned without any money.[48] There is also an account that Collins and Bass invested in a quartz mine with high hopes of striking it rich. Bass supposedly wrote Underwood back in Denton that they had been offered four thousand dollars for the mine, but they refused to sell when they had the opportunity, convinced they would be wealthier. Bass' letter reflected a rather happy-go-lucky attitude, and he told Underwood that they would be coming back to Texas in the fall of 1877 when he would be able to pay off his creditors.[49]

But success was denied them, and the more sordid side of Collins' character helped thwart his pursuit of wealth. It was alleged that he was an accomplished "trickster" and that he swindled both a man named W.W. Wells out of six hundred head of cattle and the Texas cattle partnership of Akers & Bennett out of three hundred cows.[50] What money the Texans did come up with was likely squandered on loose living. Collins' whorehouse could not be sustained; the freighting business was a bust; and it is fair to assume that the expectations for the quartz mine were dashed. Collins, Bass and Davis began to look at other, less legitimate pursuits.

About this time, they became associated with other men of like ilk—men ready to break the law if their honest pursuits proved unproductive. Red-haired Robert McKimie was the illegitimate son of Rose McKimie from Rainsboro in Hamilton County, Ohio. Raised by an aunt, McKimie had a restless spirit, and at the age of fourteen he went to Columbus where he somehow enlisted in the regular army. He quit the army, likely deserting, and wrote his aunt that he was in the cattle business in

Robert "Little Reddy" McKimie.
(From Bridwell, *Life and Adventures of Robert McKimie*.)

Kansas, but he may have already been part of a gang of rustlers. He was reportedly a member of a gang of stage robbers in Utah, finally being apprehended and prosecuted and sentenced to fifteen years in the penitentiary for murdering a man in the southern part of the state. During his escape with another convict, Jack Williamson, a guard was killed by one of the men.[51] McKimie moved his base of operations to Denver, then in 1875 was in Cheyenne where he worked as a "utility man" for B.L. Ford at the Inter Ocean Hotel in Cheyenne. Ford finally fired McKimie for his impudence and the red-haired escapee departed for the Black Hills where he was known as "Reddy" and "Little Reddy From Texas." Deadwood Sheriff Seth Bullock arrested him for stealing a horse in Wyoming and offering it for a ridiculously low price in Deadwood, but he was not prosecuted. He stayed in Deadwood, gambling and occasionally getting lucky. In February 1877 he joined Collins, Bass and Davis, ready to make some real money.[52]

Another red-haired companion to join the embryonic outlaw gang was James F. "Jim" Berry,[53] described as 5'9" or 5'10", 180 pounds, sandy or red hair with a little gray in it, a sandy beard and moustache with a long chin beard. He had a red, florid complexion, blue eyes, talked a great deal, and when he was drinking his full round face became quite red.[54] He was reportedly a member of Bloody Bill Anderson's guerilla troop, associated with the infamous Quantrill's raiders in Missouri during the Civil War, when Anderson and his men were in Glasgow, Missouri, to rob Thompson & Dunnica's bank in 1864. Anderson seized Col. B.W. Lewis to hold him for ransom, but because Anderson was quite intoxicated, Berry had to handle the negotiations, which resulted in payment of nearly seven thousand dollars in gold.[55]

Berry married Mary E. "Mollie" Craighead and by 1875 they had six children and were living on a rented farm at Nine Mile Prairie Township in Callaway County;[56] however, envisioning the sort of wealth that a farmer could not achieve, Berry left his family about 1875 for the Black Hills. At North Platte, in Nebraska, he maintained a grocery store with a partner named Garrison or Garretson. The business folded quickly after they swindled a prominent man out of money that he had posted with them for the purchase of goods.[57] Berry, too, was in Deadwood in February 1877 when Collins, Bass, Potts, Davis and McKimie began pulling together their new scheme.

Another new member of the forming group is a mystery figure. Not much is known about the man called Tom Nixon, who worked as a blacksmith in the Black Hills during the summer of 1877. The Pinkerton Detective Agency would allege that he used an alias of "Tom Barnes" and described him as 5'7" or 5'8", 145 to 150 pounds, about twenty-five years of age, blue-gray eyes, with light hair and whiskers. His beard was not heavy or long but he wore a long, neat moustache.[58] Another member was James F. "Frank" Towle, about whom also little is known.[59]

The plan, very simply, was to rob stages. The Cheyenne and Black Hills Stage Company had been running durable six-horse Concord coaches between Cheyenne and Deadwood, an approximately 290-mile route, since September 1876.[60] The rich red coaches had three cushioned seats inside to accommodate up to nine passengers. Two more passengers could sit on the front boot, and on top were two more seats that could hold six to nine passengers, the front one called the "dickey seat," and the rear one the "China seat" where oriental passengers were relegated.[61]

Bass would later say that they attempted to rob only seven stages, although he also said that he, Davis and Nixon were the only ones involved.[62] However, the Black Hills were inundated with would-be road agents, and many more than seven attempts were made on coaches during the spring and summer of 1877. The first task at hand for the gang was to steal some good saddle horses, and the men set forth in groups of two to find themselves sturdy mounts. Bass and Davis found two good horses just outside Deadwood and made off with them. Several days later, however, the owner of the horse taken by Davis came upon the gang in camp along the main road into Deadwood. When he saw his horse, he demanded its return. Davis quickly claimed that he had traded someone for the horses and had even thrown in an extra twenty dollars. He insisted that, if he had to give up the horse, the owner should pay back at least half the money. The man didn't have any money, but Davis returned the horse anyway.[63]

Collins, the acknowledged leader of the fledgling band, chose the evening of Monday, March 25, 1877, for the gang's criminal debut. As the Cheyenne and Black Hills coach rumbled through Whitewood Canyon, about two-and-a-half miles from its Deadwood destination, it came upon five men walking along the road ahead. As the coach pulled up to them, they wheeled and revealed themselves to be masked and armed. The robbers were Collins, Bass, McKimie, Towle, and either Berry or Potts. They reportedly had spent the evening sharing several bottles of whiskey while awaiting the arrival of the coach and had been about to give up and return to Deadwood. They ordered driver Johnny Slaughter to halt, but the team of horses shied at the sudden movement of the men and unexpectedly jumped to one side. A blast erupted from McKimie's shotgun, and Slaughter was instantly killed, twelve of thirteen buckshot said to have formed a perfect circle above his heart. The unrestrained horses pitched and Slaughter's body tumbled to the ground. Another passenger, Walter Iler, a representative of the Iler Distilling Company in Omaha, received a flesh wound in an arm and hand, and another passenger named Smith suffered a hole through his coat but was not injured.

The coach continued on about a half mile, the frightened horses eager to escape, but they became badly tangled in the harness and could not proceed further. Equally unnerved, the five bandits ran off up an adjacent hill and into the timber. Iler managed to get the harness straightened out and drove the coach on in to Deadwood, leaving Slaughter's body in the road. A party was sent out to retrieve the body, and Slaughter was taken to the hotel in Deadwood until his father, J.N. Slaughter, the city marshal of Cheyenne, could come for the body.

Johnny Slaughter had lived in Cheyenne for seven or eight years, was highly esteemed by those who knew him, and had been assigned the particularly rough route to Deadwood because of his dependability. A memorial service was held for him in Deadwood at the Grand Central Hotel on March 27; then the body was taken to Cheyenne where a second funeral service was held on April 4 at the Congregational Church, with a forty-carriage procession to the cemetery. His fifty-four-year-old mother had also died four days after him on March 29 and they were buried together.[64]

The death of Slaughter had been unexpected; the gang had not intended to hurt anyone unless forced to defend themselves. Their anger was directed at "Reddy" McKimie, perhaps more for losing any loot on the stage than for killing the driver. Collins seriously considered killing him, but the gang instead decided to let him leave.[65] McKimie briefly joined a gang led by Dunc Blackburn and Clark Pelton in the Hat Creek area and was involved in another driver shooting, but he subsequently returned to Ohio where he purportedly attempted an honest life. When he was tracked down and arrested in January 1878, McKimie claimed that Joel Collins had shot Slaughter.[66]

TERRITORY OF DAKOTA

A Proclamation.

Five Hundred Dollars Reward.

EXECUTIVE OFFICE,
Yankton, Dakota, April 13, 1877.

WHEREAS, It has been represented to me that on the night of the 25th of March last, some person or persons unknown, attacked the stage of the Cheyenne and Black Hills Stage Company, near Deadwood, in the county of Lawrence, in this Territory, killing John Slaughter, the driver; and

WHEREAS, The person or persons committing the said murder have fled, or so concealed themselves that the officers of the law have been unable to make arrests and bring them to justice; Now, therefore,

I, JOHN L. PENNINGTON,

Governor of the Territory of Dakota,

By virtue of the authority vested in me by the Laws of the said Territory, do offer a reward of

FIVE HUNDRED DOLLARS,

for the apprehension and delivery to the Sheriff of Lawrence County, or the confinement in any jail or prison, so that he, the said Sheriff of Lawrence County, may get them, of the person or persons who killed the said John Slaughter.

Done at Yankton, the Capital of the said Territory, this, the 13th day of April, in the year of our Lord one thousand eight hundred and seventy-seven.

JOHN L. PENNINGTON.

By the Governor:

GEO. H. HAND,
Secretary of Dakota.

Reward poster from the Dakota Territory offering five hundred dollars for the capture of the murderers of stagecoach driver Johnny Slaughter. (Courtesy Robert G. McCubbin, Jr.)

53

On suspicion, Sheriff Bullock arrested Frank Towle the day after the robbery, but there was no evidence that would justify holding him.[67] On September 13, 1878, Towle was shot to death during an attempted stage robbery, and when his hidden body was finally located in December, driver Boone May cut off his head in order to prove his claim to an outstanding reward.[68]

Their first attempt at stage robbery having fizzled, the Collins gang regrouped to try again.

-V-
STAGECOACH AND TRAIN ROBBERY

I t is next to impossible to determine which of the numerous stagecoach robberies that occurred in the Black Hills between March and September 1877 were those of the Collins gang. The lure of quick riches compelled a number of men to opt for a shortcut, and stagecoach robbery was seen by them as preferable to the bonewearying toil of mining ore from the ground. When coaches were not available, any traveler or herd of stock made suitable targets. On March 30, 1877, six days after the fiasco that resulted in Johnny Slaughter's death, two armed men stopped Edward Moran on the stage road five miles from Deadwood. Tying him to a tree, they relieved him of $260 in gold dust, some cash, and a watch.[1]

The spring and early summer of 1877 saw sufficient bad weather to make the stage roads almost impassable, so coaches were often canceled or delayed. Thus, there were no robberies until the evening of June 1 when three armed men sought to rob the Cheyenne and Black Hills stage just north of the Hat Creek station, one hundred miles south of Deadwood. When the well-armed coach passengers climbed out to the ground and ordered the three to leave, however, the would-be robbers promptly fled. Amazingly, the passengers were criticized.

We flatter ourselves that we are not especially vindictive, but we cannot help saying that it would please us to see those passengers come into town naked and penniless. They allowed three of the worst men in this country to ride away unharmed, after having threatened the lives of the timid fellows on the coach, when they should have shot them down like dogs. We care not who these passengers are, but denounce them for their cowardice and hold them up to the contempt of all brave men....[2]

A freighter, F.M. Darling, was robbed by several men a few days later after he had made a run to Deadwood and was returning to Cheyenne. He gave up fourteen dollars in gold dust, a watch and chain, a rifle and pistol, then the outlaws went through his wagons and took all of his provisions. One robber gave back his watch before they left.[3] The next stagecoach robbery occurred about 8:30 on the morning of June 14, twenty-five miles north of the Hat Creek station. As the stage came through a narrow ravine, two men with blackened faces jumped up in front of the coach and ordered it to halt. When ordered to throw down the treasure box, the messenger threw down an empty decoy box, leaving the loaded box hidden on the stage. The robbers left with the empty box.[4]

A rage over the continuing robberies and other crimes began to build throughout the area. On Tuesday, June 19, horse thieves A.J. Allen, thirty-five, Louis Curry, twenty-nine, and James Hall, nineteen, were captured and jailed at Rapid City, about thirty miles southeast of Deadwood. The next evening, a party of men took them out of the jail and hanged them.[5] The lynching led to only a brief respite in criminal activity.

At about ten o'clock on the evening of Monday, June 25, as the stagecoach from Deadwood headed south toward the Cheyenne River, the curtains of the coach were tightly buttoned and the four passengers slept. As the team struggled to pull the stage out of a slight gully, two armed men appeared on each side of the coach, ordered the driver to halt, and herded him into the coach with the passengers. One of the robbers tried to open the treasure box, being carried from Custer, which was riveted to the iron work of the coach. The robbers gave up after laboring over the box for about an hour.

Frustrated, the robbers ordered the driver and passengers out of the coach and robbed each of them. Garrett Crystal, a freighter, lost seven hundred dollars in cash and a gold watch. Ex-Denverite Alex Francis handed over three hundred dollars to the two men, and a miner from Potato Gulch named Irwin lost $198. F.B. Reed surrendered $120 and a gold ring. It was estimated that the two robbers escaped with money and jewelry totaling about $1,400.[6]

The next night, June 26, the outlaws were a little better prepared. Close to the same place, as the stage crossed the Cheyenne River at about ten o'clock in the evening, the wide-awake passengers talked about the possibility of the stage's being held up again. About two miles from the river, Hawley the driver and Roberts the messenger were confronted by two armed men who commanded them to halt the stage. Almost instantly, the rifle held by one of the robbers discharged, and Hawley was struck glancingly on the left side, a painful but not serious wound. A passenger, Pierce, fired his Spencer rifle from the coach at one of the robbers, "a big ugly looking fellow" who was profane, but Roberts demanded that he stop firing or else they would all be killed.

Five masked men surrounded the coach and ordered everyone to the ground with their hands held high. With the exception of a robber called "Charlie" by the others, the bandits did not appear to have a plan for the use of bogus names, so one would call to another "Come here, you, man with the shotgun." With two robbers standing watch, two others went through the passengers' pockets taking money and watches. "Charlie," whom the passengers took for the leader, admitted that he had shot the driver but that it was accidental. The fifth robber unsuccessfully struggled with the treasure box using a hatchet. After a short discussion about turning around the coach and returning to the last station to find tools, the gang forced Roberts to hand over some gunpowder that he had, placed it in the keyhole of the box, lit a paper fuse and blew off the lock. They placed the sacks and packages of gold into an ore sack and returned some of the weapons they had taken from Roberts and the passengers. Before the five bandits left and headed south with an estimated forty pounds in gold worth about $12,800 and $1,200 in personal property taken from the passengers, they admitted they had tried to rob the stage the night before and described how they swore when they opened the empty box.[7]

With these two back-to-back robberies, the Cheyenne Daily Leader became apoplectic. "It should...be the business of the people on both ends of this route to rid the country at once of such monsters. Hemp is the proper and unfailing remedy."[8] Unfazed, the robbers stopped the stage for the third night in a row at about the same spot, on June 27, and escaped with two treasure boxes, although this time the passengers were not disturbed. The road agents arrogantly instructed the driver to tell the stage line owners to send along a pair of gold scales the next time. "Dividing dust with a spoon is not always satisfactory," they declared, and the treasure boxes should be carried loose in the coach to save them trouble. The next morning, a cavalry detachment left Fort Laramie in pursuit, and the *Cheyenne Daily Leader* fumed, "the people must rise and summarily end the career of road agents and horse thieves, after which ineffective officials will be deposed."9

It was later learned that the three rapid-fire robberies on the Cheyenne River were pulled off by the Duncan Blackburn and Clark Pelton gang, which had been joined by "Reddy" McKimie. McKimie was the "Charlie" who shot Hawley, and he would later admit that it was he who killed Slaughter.10 The stage company became resigned to the fact that, as long as "treasure" was going to be carried along the stage routes, "these robberies must be calculated on and anticipated in running a stage line over a country so sparsely settled and offering such temptations to desperate men."11

At about midnight on Tuesday, July 10, a coach eastbound from Deadwood to Sidney, Nebraska, was stopped near French Creek by five masked men, but the robbers found no passengers and an empty treasure box, which they reportedly opened with a skeleton key. Cursing the driver, the robbers asked him when the next coach to Deadwood would be coming then sent him on his way. The driver warned the oncoming coach, so it went to a nearby ranch not far from the holdup point and the passengers spent the night in hiding, hoping to spring an ambush. The robbers, suspicious, circled the area and signaled to each other with whistles but did not venture close to the coach. One of the passengers, George Caruthers, urged his companions to open fire on the bandits, but they refused to do so, "fearing they might hurt somebody."12

Four masked men struck on Friday, July 13, stopping a coach on the Sidney route at a point about three miles north of Battle Creek about seventy miles south of Deadwood. They took watches, jewelry and money from the passengers and ransacked their baggage as well as the treasure box. The gang also took a set of dentist's equipment, remarking that they might want to start a tooth-pulling business in Omaha once they were through with a career of robbery. The bandits expressed regret that more gold dust and bullion was not being shipped on the stages and announced they were soon going to change their tactics because they were aware there were other methods by which gold dust was being shipped east. Bragging, they asserted they were "determined to levy a tribute on the dust going out of the Hills, and that there was no force that could be organized that could capture them."[13]

Although cavalry troops were stationed at various points along the different stage routes, the robberies continued unabated. On Tuesday evening, July 17, a stage southbound from Deadwood was stopped and, although the treasure box was empty, the passengers were forced to give up their personal valuables. On the same evening, about a dozen thieves stampeded and stole about seventy horses and mules from a camp of freighters near Crook City, not far from Deadwood.[14]

On the next evening, the southbound coach from Deadwood was stopped near the Cheyenne River by five men with handkerchiefs over their faces. The passengers were lined up and compelled to remove their boots, coats and pants, after which a thorough search was made of each of them. The robbers took about fifty dollars, arms and clothing. The coach resumed its trip and was stopped again twelve miles later by four more robbers who took the passengers' remaining arms and their blankets. On that same evening, the northbound stage was stopped and the passengers yielded thirteen dollars.[15] The coach from Deadwood was stopped again on the evening of July 23 by six men near the Cheyenne River; there was no treasure aboard, but the robbers relieved the passengers of about twenty dollars, arms and some bedding.[16]

The volume of attacks on coaches led to an increased number of army patrols along the routes and even engendered bolder reactions by drivers and messengers. On July 25 one messenger, a former eighteen-year-veteran soldier named Smith, was near the Cheyenne River and spotted several men on the river bank by the road. He opened fire on them, not caring whether they were ranchers, herders, hunters or bandits, and the men returned the fire until the coach was out of range.[17]

As August came on, stage robberies had become practically

a way of life. One correspondent, no doubt a robbery victim, described his impressions of road agent activities.

> But if you want a sensation—something new in life—you can have it from the "road agents," the highwaymen who infest the road from Cheyenne to Deadwood, and constantly stop the coaches after gold dust and greenbacks, passing up and down.
>
> To be aroused out of one's sleep at midnight, after the moon has gone down, in a desolate sandy plain, to hear the words "Halt! Stand and deliver!" and simultaneously therewith the clicking of five Spencer rifles, as they are cocked; to peer out of the window and see by the front lights of the stage five tall wiry-looking gentlemen in dominoes, with their Spencer rifles brought to bear on driver and passengers in deadly aim; to hear your driver respond in the Black Hills vernacular— "Halt? You bet I will!"—to listen as the road men bid the express messenger "hold up his hands and come down;" to hear this tall masked gentleman, with long rifle, come to the stage window and in a voice as musical and soft as a woman's say: "Gentlemen will please leave their arms in the coach and descend one by one, and pass to the front for examination;" to get out one by one, five great strapping passengers, leaving their arms in the coach; to have your baggage all taken out and examined, and then stand up and have the same soft-toned gentleman in domino feel your pockets, examine your wallet, take its contents not leaving a penny; to take off your boots and stockings at his gentle command, lest something may be there concealed; to give up your gold watch and chain, and, to surrender that beautiful revolver, your companion for many years, to have Dick Turpin, after doing all this, gently say: "Well, old fellow, I think I know you, what's your name?" (very imperatively) and then, to give him that name on compulsion, sir—then, after all the robbing to eat peaches with the gentleman of the road, to be marched back in single file to your seat in the coach, and as the horses dash away

in the dust to realize that a man has been robbed so gen-
tlemanly, so pleasantly, by one of his old clients and
friends from Salt Lake, is what you cannot find at
Saratoga or New York, but what did happen to GEO.
C. BATES.[18]

Again on the night of August 11, 1877, the southbound
coach from Deadwood to Sidney was stopped between Rapid
Creek and Buffalo Gap, and the passengers turned over about
twenty dollars.[19]

According to G.W. Mills, a cowboy for the Ellison &
DeWees outfit who had left Texas with a herd in March 1877
and arrived on August 1 in Ogallala, Nebraska, on August 20
he went to the Gass House, a hotel, to get paid and to pay his
respects to his employer, cattleman J.F. Ellison, who was staying
there and was ill.[20] Ellison was an old friend of the Collins
brothers, and Mills says that while there he was introduced to
both Joel and Joe Collins.[21] Although Mills wrote this account
many years later, it is possible that he did meet Joel Collins, but
it is unlikely that Joe Collins was there.

Five robbers stopped the Sidney coach from Deadwood on
the evening of Thursday, August 23, above Buffalo Gap, firing
at the coach before they called out for it to halt. The division
superintendent of the stage line, Ed Cook, was in the coach and
was shot through an ear. The passengers were ordered out and
told to raise their hands. One passenger eager to respond did so
with five hundred dollars in his hand, but because of the darkness the robbers never noticed it. Although there was about one
thousand dollars in possession of the passengers, the outlaws
seized only about twelve dollars and left hurriedly. The next
morning Cook personally led a posse after them, but the group
turned back when it came upon a large band of Indians.[22]

Just exactly which of these robberies were perpetrated by
Collins, Bass and company is not known. Bass would take back
to Texas with him stories of dismal failure at stage robbing. The
fruits of one robbery was eleven dollars and, in another, instead
of a teeming treasure box they were only offered a dozen peaches
by the driver. In another robbery, according to Hogg's *Authentic
History*, the take was only thirty dollars. Jack Davis was

supposed to have become so perturbed that he berated the passengers, "You are the darndest set of paupers I ever saw. What are you traveling for if you don't carry any more money than that? Why, darn it, we fellows will starve if you don't get to doing better!" To make matters worse, the pitiful pleading of one passenger even coaxed the robbers into giving back a dollar to each passenger so they could buy breakfast.[23]

Because of the frequent robberies, more and more precautions were taken to deter them and to minimize any losses. Securely bolted treasure boxes could not be removed from the stagecoaches, and passengers now deposited their money or valuables at one end of the stage line and, taking a receipt, drew it out at the other end.[24] Thus, the profitability of stage robbing diminished and, added to the heat now being generated by local lawmen and the army, the risk was correspondingly greater. The Collins-Bass gang had not been very successful at the business to begin with; it was obvious to the gang that a new approach had to be taken before winter came on again.

Who originated the idea of robbing a train is not known. Train robbing was no longer a novel idea; in 1866 the Reno brothers had pulled off the first one, not far from Bass' Indiana home, and a second one there a year later was accomplished by Charles Walker Hammond and a companion. Jesse and Frank James were believed to have led a gang in the robbery of a train at Adair, Iowa, in July 1873, followed by others at Gads Hill, Missouri, in January 1874, again at Muncie, Kansas, in December 1875, and at Otterville, Missouri, in July 1876.[25] Anse Tippie, who was supposed to have been a partner of Joel Collins in a grocery and saloon business at Potato Gulch, west of Deadwood, claimed that the train robbery plot was concocted in the back room of the saloon.[26]

According to Hogg, the scheme was discussed at Collins' place at Deadwood by Collins, Potts, Berry and Nixon. There are some accounts that hold that Collins had been able to maintain a facade of respectability, occasionally appearing at the Red Cloud and Spotted Tail agencies posing as a cattleman.[27] Collins decided that the gang might have a good chance of locating a large quantity of the gold being shipped from San Francisco east over the Union Pacific road. Bass and Davis, who were camped about twelve miles away, were summoned to Deadwood. When the two reached Collins' place, Maude was supposed to have excitedly warned them, "You fools! You'd better leave here at once. The soldiers are thick around here and they'll get you sure. They've just run Joel and the other boys off."[28] If the story about Maude's hysteria is true, it would appear that Collins and his men were already suspected of being criminals, but there is no contemporary account to corroborate this.

The gang assembled in Ogallala, Nebraska, on the South Platte River. Sorenson says that in late August, Collins and Maude left Deadwood on a Cheyenne and Black Hills stage. Leaving Maude in Sidney, Collins went on to Ogallala, where he met the other five men.[29] Between them, they had their mounts, a pack mule and forty dollars in cash.[30]

Ogallala was a small village, 340 miles west of Omaha, with no more than 150 residents. Two hotels, two or three stores, and nine or ten saloons greeted cowboys bringing cattle for shipment on the Union Pacific. The townsfolk, not unlike those of the Kansas railhead towns, were not surprised by the occasional rowdiness of the Texas drovers. Collins was well known here.[31] Cowboy J.H. Cook would recall that Collins and his men made camp about one hundred yards west of the Rooney Hotel in Ogallala. Cook told Collins that he had met him in Kansas; Collins remembered him and replied that he and the riders with him had just delivered a herd to the Black Hills. Cook spent some time in their camp, meeting the other men, and even loaned seventy-five dollars to Collins for gambling. Cook and Jim Berry became good friends, although Berry was much older. One day Cook was in the Rooney Hotel talking with Collins when some cowboys enthusiastically fired their sixshooters. This frightened several women in the hotel and Collins calmed them.[32]

It was now September, and the gang settled in to observe the operations of the train and to scout out the surrounding area, looking for a site along the railroad that would offer the best prospects for escape. They finally settled on Big Springs, a small, less-populous watering station some eighteen miles downriver from Ogallala and only a few miles north of the Colorado-

Nebraska state line. Small and isolated, and located near a large natural spring, the station consisted of a depot, the railroad agent's house, the water tank, and a house for railroad section hands.[33] George W. Barnhart was the station agent and telegraph operator at this lonely outpost, which had served as a landmark for both the Pony Express and overland stage routes.[34]

On Monday, September 24, a man named Allen was in Ogallala and saw Collins making preparations to leave.[35] On that same evening, Collins reportedly purchased several seamless grain sacks and some twine, along with a supply of provisions, which he prepared as a pack load for a pony.[36] While in Ogallala, Berry went to the store of M.F. Leach to buy a pair of boots on credit. Leach refused, familiar with how Berry and Garrison had cheated people a year or so earlier, so Berry fetched Collins to pay for the boots.[37]

On Tuesday evening, September 18, 1877, the eastbound Union Pacific train was making its run toward Omaha and Chicago from San Francisco. In addition to the engine, there were first and second-class coaches, two Pullman sleeper cars, express and baggage cars, and a director's car of the Central Pacific Railroad, occupied by Central's President Leland Stanford and his family. It was a clear, moonlit night, and the passengers were in their berths.[38] George W. Vroman, the engineer,[39] was making good time and had passed through Cheyenne that afternoon at three o'clock.[40]

Sometime before ten o'clock, Collins led Bass, Davis, Berry, Nixon and Potts to station agent Barnhart's office at Big Springs, and two of the men with revolvers in each hand surprised the agent. As Barnhart stared down the barrels of the weapons, the masked men ordered him to tear up his telegraph instruments. He had the presence of mind to try to deceive them by pulling up his sounder, which would not render the instrument useless, but the outlaws were not fooled and compelled him to hand over the relay to them.[41] Barnhart had the impression that the robber giving him instructions might be a telegraph operator because of his apparent familiarity with the instrument.

The robbers then forced Barnhart to hang a red light outside, signaling the train to stop for mail or passengers, and they also had him ready his mail sack as he usually did. In Cheyenne, night dispatcher A.J. Borie, a twenty-three-year old Ohioan, went off duty at 10:30, telling his brother who relieved him that the local wire between Cheyenne and North Platte was open and that the trouble must be at Ogallala.[42] The masked men took their places and waited. According to one account, Collins and Potts were assigned to capture the engineer and fireman.[43] It wasn't a long wait until the train pulled into the Big Springs depot at 10:40 p.m., and Engineer Vroman shut off the steam, reversing the engine. As the train slowed, he saw a man in the ditch on the side of the track pointing a rifle at him. The man called out, "come down out of that," but Vroman, thinking it was a joke, stooped to pick up a piece of coal to toss at the man. A rifle ball whizzed past his head, striking a tallow can hanging behind him. Vroman then saw another man up on the tender behind the engine, also aiming a rifle at him. Realizing it was no joke, the engineer sprang through the window of the cab, ran along the footboard toward the front of the engine, climbed over the boiler and hid behind the dome. A third man aimed his revolver at the fireman and ordered him off the engine and to the ground. The riflemen converged on Vroman, and he surrendered and joined the fireman as a prisoner.

Conductor M.M. Patterson waited as the train slowed for the Big Springs depot, unaware of the activity at the engine. He sprang off the train and started for Barnhart's office. As he started up the steps leading to the station platform, two masked men, each carrying a pair of revolvers, intercepted him and ordered him to throw up his hands. Seeing that one of the masks worn was the lettered portion of a flour sack, Patterson also thought it was a joke and continued to walk on. One of the men snarled, "We'll show you that this is no laughing matter," and pulled the trigger of a revolver just inches from the conductor's head. The cartridge miraculously failed to fire, and Barnhart, who was being guarded nearby with Vroman and the fireman, called out to him, "this is business." Patterson threw up his hands and joined the other prisoners, who were guarded by Berry and Nixon. A black porter followed Patterson off the train and also treated the orders to halt and throw up his hands as a joke. Barnhart and Patterson instinctively ducked to get out of the line of fire if the robbers shot the porter, but when the porter realized that the masked men were serious, he "wilted" and quickly handed over six dollars to the robbers, compelling Patterson to laugh.[44]

In the express car messenger Charles Miller had been asleep for about fifteen minutes of his customary short nap when he was not busy on the run between Julesburg and North Platte. After the train stopped, he was awakened by a private signal rapped on the express car door by station agent Barnhart, who was closely guarded by the armed robbers. According to one account, the robbers had first accosted the baggagemaster, a man named Bland who directed them to the express car and then casually retreated into the baggage car to enjoy a cigar while the robbery continued. Barnhart was then hustled away as Miller arose and looked out the door window. He noticed the red light and opened the door slightly. Bass and Davis, who had been standing out of sight, forced the door open and thrust their revolvers in Miller's face.

Bass and Davis took Miller's pistols and searched him for additional weapons. The robbers broke into the flimsy way safe and took $458 in currency. However, the through safe, which was sturdier and could only be opened at the train's originating point or its ultimate destination, was bolted to the iron work of the express car directly under the folding berth used by Miller, and the combination was known only to agents at Ogden, Cheyenne and Omaha. Jack Davis pointed his revolver at Miller's head and ordered him to open the through safe. As the pistol touched his face, Miller instinctively pushed it away and told them that he was unable to do so. The robber threatened, "you will, will you?" and forcefully struck Miller on the mouth with the cocked pistol, cutting his upper lip and gum, and the blood flowed down across his chin. The bandit continued to pistolwhip the messenger, producing almost a dozen cuts on his head and ear, all the time cursing the hapless man and ordering him to open the safe. Miller was thrown to the floor of the car, then was pulled to his feet and thrown down again over a chair. Wracked with pain, he continued to protest that he could not open the safe and pleaded for them not to kill him. Finally, overcome, he begged them to kill him to stop the vicious beating.

On the platform, Conductor Patterson could hear Miller's cries and called out that Miller did not know the combination and could not open the safe. The men guarding Patterson told him to be quiet, but he explained how the through safe worked. One of the robbers then went to the express car and told the robbers there. The bloodied Miller was removed from the express car and taken to where the other prisoners were being guarded.

While Miller was being subjected to the brutal attack, other robbers were searching through the express car, breaking into boxes but finding no valuables. After Miller was taken away, they found three heavy iron-clad boxes. One of the robbers went to Miller on the platform and asked him what they contained. He said that from the weight he supposed that they contained castings. An axe was used to break open one of the boxes, and the robbers were delighted to discover a cache of newly minted twenty-dollar gold eagles being shipped east from the San Francisco mint. Although in a normal run the gold shipments from San Francisco would total anywhere from $200,000 to $500,000, there was a total of only $60,000 in gold coins on this shipment. Forty thousand dollars of the amount was consigned to Wells, Fargo & Company in New York and $20,000 to the New York National Bank of Commerce. The robbers deliberately refused to take 535 bars of silver that were lying all over the floor of the express car and over which they frequently tripped. The bars were worth $682,476 and weighed over one hundred pounds each so were too heavy to haul off. On the platform, one of the robbers took Patterson's gold watch and about fifty dollars in fare money but overlooked one hundred dollars in his wallet.[45]

W.F. Erdman, the news agent in the first-class coach of the train, heard the pistol shot fired at Vroman as the train reached the station then heard a quick succession of shots. He went to the door of the car and was confronted by a masked man with a revolver who told him to throw up his hands, which he promptly did. At the robber's direction, Erdman went back into the car, and, while two masked men stood at each end of the car, a fifth robber carrying a revolver and a lantern started down the aisle relieving passengers of money and valuables.[46]

As the train had pulled into the station, the passengers in one of the sleeping cars had been aroused by the unusual activity. An attorney, Guthrie Smith, was in the next-to-last coach and raised the window in time to see Conductor Patterson's being escorted at gunpoint and telling the robbers, "Upon my honor, as a gentleman, I protest that I do not know the combination of that safe." Smith and the other passengers realized that a robbery was in progress. The men in Smith's car hastily dressed, locked the door leading into the coach, then huddled together and inventoried their arms: three pistols. Several Englishmen in the car wanted to attack the robbers, but the others demurred. A little girl in the car was awakened by the commotion and, on being told that robbers were holding up the train, told her mother, "Well, I've got no money, have I, mamma?" The robbers did not enter their car.[47]

From his first-class coach, former Omaha councilman Merrick Cummings stepped out onto the platform to talk with another passenger, Andrew Riley. Four masked men rushed up with cocked revolvers and ordered them back into the car "damned quick." As Cummings reentered through the car door, the robbers fired twice at Riley, grazing his left hand and cutting a hole through his coat sleeve, and another shot damaged the door frame. After the robbers took two silver watches and twenty-seven dollars from him, Riley quickly went back into the car. The robbers followed them, loud and abusive, and one fired off a shot to show that they meant business. One of the robbers hollered, "Hold up your hands, every son of a bitch, and keep still; we want your money, but will give each man $10 back, and we won't hurt a man unless he makes a break. We've killed one man and don't want to kill any more, but your money we will have; so, damn you, keep still and give it up—all of it, quietly!"

With one man at each end of the car, the other two went down the aisle relieving passengers of valuables and money. A New York drummer named Morris or Norris was told to "stand up, hold up your hands, and keep your damned mouth shut!" They took from him $480, a $300 gold watch, and a railway ticket to Chicago. The next man had only one arm, and the robbers refused to take anything from him. The robbers approached a post trader, A.T. Feay, and searched his person three times without finding anything, not realizing that he had over four hundred dollars concealed in his coat sleeve while his hands were in the air. Cummings watched the robbers from his seat, his hands in the air, occasionally bringing them down for some relief. He put his pocket book containing four hundred dollars behind a lady's work basket on the floor, then somehow was able to move four seats back unnoticed and hide his watch and chain behind a valise on the floor. He had only about ten dollars on his person. When he saw the robber holding up the passengers in the other aisle go by him, ahead of the robber working his aisle, Cummings simply moved to a seat across the aisle and was never touched by the robbers. When the robbers finished with the car, they ordered the passengers not to move then left.[48]

The accounts are not clear, but it is likely that the gang robbed more than one coach. It was later reported that a man named Harris was robbed of $450 and a watch, but before he thrust his hands in the air he pulled six hundred dollars from his pocket and threw it down on the seat beside him, and that money was overlooked by the thieves. The second-class coach was not bothered, although in that car a miner quickly placed a money belt containing $11,000 around the waist of his baby and kept only twenty dollars to hand over to the robbers if they came in. No women on the train were bothered.[49] John H. Brophy, a former sheriff of Albany County in Wyoming Territory, sleepily entered the passenger coach from the sleeper and was promptly relieved of six dollars in loose change. Fortunately, Brophy had left his gold watch, a diamond pin and twelve hundred dollars with his wife in the sleeping car, which was locked behind him.[50] Another passenger, Dan Fretwell of Sidney, was well known to wear an enormous diamond pin, and one of the robbers asked, "Where's that pin of yours, eh?" The robbers refused to take silver watches, sneering that they didn't want any "snides."[51]

The robbers attempted to enter the sleeping cars but found them secured against invasion. In the distance a train whistle sounded, alerting the robbers to an approaching freight train, Number Ten, and they ceased their attempts to get into the sleeping cars. Conductor Patterson asked the robbers if he could go out and flag the train, and a guard was sent with him.

As he passed the sleeper, Patterson coughed loudly hoping to alert the passengers inside, and the guard ordered Patterson back to the station. A robber that Patterson thought was the gang's leader asked him to open the sleeper, but the conductor denied that he had a key and suggested that it would be best for them to send for the porter. Again, Patterson asked permission to flag down the oncoming train.

With a robber accompanying him, Patterson again set out carrying a white light to the rear of the train. When they were abreast of the special car on the end of the train carrying Mr. and Mrs. Stanford, the robber instructed Patterson to go on to the end of the train and flag the approaching freight, threatening to shoot him if he went further. Patterson climbed on the rear platform of the Stanford car and softly rapped on the glass door, alerting the occupants to the robbery and advising them to hide their valuables. Taking a red lamp from the rear platform and putting it under his coat, he then jumped to the ground and walked up the track a short distance. He dropped the white light and jumped from the track into a side ditch, trying to avoid being shot, and ran toward the approaching train thinking that it could back up to Julesburg where help could be obtained. Since there was a steep grade toward Julesburg, the train was too heavy to make backing up a practical idea. The train stopped and, after Patterson held a quick conversation with Conductor Strong and others during which it was ascertained that there were no firearms aboard, proceeded back toward the depot where the other train was stopped.[52]

While Patterson was making his way to the freight train, the robbers realized that it was time to leave. They threw water on the engine fire and ordered Vroman to empty the water tanks. The engineer dallied in this task, trying to gain time, and told the bandits that he would be unable to get up steam for at least two hours. Satisfied, the robbers took their loot to the horses hitched behind the depot and rode off. Shortly after the six men had left, Vroman fired up the engine and was ready to move the train within a few minutes. Barnhart went into the station house and rewired his telegraph instrument, and at about midnight the Cheyenne dispatcher received this message.

Robbed passengers. Guess they got $100,000 off the train. They started north. Don't send me anything. Can't take it. Instrument destroyed. Patterson, Conductor No. 4, Big Springs.[53]

While the passenger train continued on eastward, the freight engine was detached and Patterson, who had found his watch where the robbers had dropped it, rode with the engine to Ogallala where he telegraphed a more detailed account of the holdup to both Cheyenne and Omaha.

Train 4 was robbed at Big Springs by from 10 to 15 men. They had the agent captured, a red light out for orders and telegraph instrument out. When I came out on platform to get orders two men with a revolver in each hand told me to throw up my hands. They already had the engineer, firemen [sic] and express messenger captured. They got $65,000 in coin and $458 in currency from the express car. They only went through the passengers on the first-class coaches, when freight No. 10 came along and frightened them off. They got $1,300 cash, four gold watches and a ticket to Chicago from the passengers. Miller, express messenger, was bruised about the head but not seriously. They made the agent knock at the express car door. The express safe with combination lock is safe with its contents. A man named Morris lost a gold watch, ticket and $480 in money. I was back flagging No. 10. They sent a guard with me part way, and then put fire out in passenger engine. M.M. PATTERSON, Conductor.[54]

Word of the robbery went out in all directions. Joel Collins and his men had made a large haul in an almost successful robbery—almost successful because several men, including the wounded Andy Riley, had recognized Joel Collins through his mask. Riley had become well acquainted with Collins in the fall of 1876 when Collins and Bass arrived in the Black Hills with cattle. Just a few days before the robbery Riley had run into Collins again at Ogallala, where Collins was posing as a cattle dealer. Another passenger had also met Collins sometime earlier while doing business at an Indian agency, and he, too, recognized Collins on the train.[55] The hunt for the gang would soon begin.

-VI-
DEATH AT BUFFALO STATION

T he news of the Union Pacific robbery made head-
lines around the country. The train finally
reached Omaha about 5:30 Wednesday morning,
September 19.[1] E.M. Morsman, superintendent of the Union
Pacific Railroad Express Company, immediately issued notice of
a ten thousand dollar reward for the capture of the robbers and
return of the money. "Pro rata of the above reward will be paid
for any portion of the money so returned, or for the capture of
any of the robbers."[2] The loss from the robbery had come at a
difficult time for the Union Pacific. Railroad Superintendent
S.H.H. Clark, a New Jersey native who lived in Omaha with his
wife and son, commiserated about a bridge collapse along the
rail line that would require funds for the building of two spans;
now the loss of sixty thousand dollars added to the financial
impact.[3] On September 20, Union Pacific Treasurer Henry
McFarland in Boston urgently wired Union Pacific President
Sidney Dillon in New York inquiring as to how much loss the
company would suffer. Dillon responded, giving him the details
he had learned from Superintendent Clark, and expressed his
concern that if the robbers were familiar with the country, they
would be difficult to catch.[4] Large posters proclaiming the
reward were hastily printed and distributed along rail and stage
lines.[5]

The railroad sought the assistance of the army to hunt down
the robbers. On the day after the robbery, at Camp Robinson in
the far northwest part of Nebraska, just three weeks after the
Sioux chieftain Crazy Horse was stabbed to death there,
Lieutenant Colonel Luther P. Bradley ordered Lieutenant J.F.
Cummings to lead forty-two enlisted men of the 3rd Cavalry
southeast from the post with four days' provisions to look for
any "suspicious characters" who might be the train robbers. The
patrol returned to the post emptyhanded on September 23 after

traveling seventy miles.[6] Also on September 19, at about 11:30 in the evening, a sergeant and five privates left the post at North Platte and headed for Big Springs, although General R. Williams, assistant adjutant general of the Department of the Platte, was critical that the patrol left so late.[7]

In the early hours after the robbery, Collins and his five men, "armed to the teeth and splendidly mounted," rode into Ogallala where they briefly camped with the cowboys of a cattle herd readying to head south. They had buried the money in the sand on the banks of the South Platte River between Big Springs and Ogallala.[8] Collins gave out the story in town that they had recently sold a herd and were all planning to return to Texas, riding with the herd that had just left and helping it to reach the Kansas Pacific railroad line two hundred miles south of Ogallala. The news of the robbery was the main topic of conversation, and Collins was supposed to have remarked that if he had not agreed to go on with the herd, he would have liked to go after the robbers himself if the Union Pacific was going to pay a reward.[9]

The gang remained in town for about twenty-four hours, buying provisions, blankets and clothing for their departure. Leaving Ogallala on Thursday, September 20, the six robbers rode south and caught up with the herd, stopping only briefly along the way to pick up the buried coins. They stayed with the herd for just a few days, making only about forty-five miles, then left the herd and rode rapidly off.[10]

A posse led by Sheriff Bradley from North Platte rode from the Big Springs station shortly after the robbery and discovered the gang's trail. About ten miles from the station they found one of the boxes that had held the gold coins, half of an old handkerchief, an old pocket book, and a tobacco box.[11] Another account stated that the posse found empty coin bags and a brace of pistols.[12] On September 22, railroad superintendent E.M. Morsman filed a formal criminal complaint with Cheyenne County, Nebraska, Justice of the Peace James Green. The complaint charged Collins and eight unknown men with the train robbery, and arrest warrants were handed over to Douglas County Deputy Sheriff David E. Burley for execution.[13]

M.F. Leach, the detective-merchant from Ogallala, had been hunting near Big Springs when the robbery took place and learned about it the day after it occurred. He went to the Big Springs station, talked to Barnhart, then consulted with Superintendent Morsman who had come to Ogallala to conduct his own investigation. Morsman was satisfied that the robbers had been "loafing around" the town just before the robbery and decided to employ Leach to continue the investigation, aware that he had some detective experience and was familiar with the countryside.

Leach looked at some of the handkerchiefs or material that had been used as masks, then followed the trail of the gang from Big Springs to Ogallala, where he found the gang's deserted camp near town. Looking around, he found more pieces of handkerchief and observed the print of a heavy boot with the bootmaker's initials made by heavy nails in the sole. In Ogallala he located where the handkerchiefs had been purchased by Collins. He now knew who some of the outlaws were since he recognized the prints as coming from the boots he had sold to Berry.[14] He asked the Union Pacific for some men to help him track the robbers, but was refused.

Riding back to the deserted camp, Leach again began to follow the gang's trail. Estimating that he was at least twenty-four hours behind the robbers, he raced his horse and finally came upon their camp in a thicket about 11:00 p.m. on Saturday night, September 22, on the Republican River within a few miles of the Kansas border.[15] Newspapers had speculated that the gang had originally split up into three pairs after leaving Ogallala and then reunited on the Republican River to plan their next move. According to Leach in an 1877 account, the next thing he did bordered on the insane: he sneaked into the robbers' camp.

Leach said that when he found the camp, he recognized Collins and Berry among the six men sitting around a campfire counting the money. In another account by him in 1895, he said that he found the men asleep, then took his horse back to the north side of the river where he staked it. Leach said that he actually sneaked into the sleeping robbers' camp between two and three o'clock Sunday morning and verified that the gold was in a seamless bag lying beside one of the men. Feeling the coins through the fabric, he briefly entertained the idea of dragging the loot out of the camp, but it was far too heavy and he would have awakened the men. He returned to his horse to obtain a knife, and when he went back to the camp he found that the man lying next to the bag had shifted position and was now sleeping with his arm over the gold. Leach returned to his horse to await the gang's next move.

Later that morning, Leach climbed a cottonwood tree and watched the robbers saddle up and ride south. He mounted and rode up the river until he found a ranch and persuaded a cowboy to take a "letter in cipher" to the railroad company reporting that the robbers seemed to be heading toward Buffalo Station on the Kansas Pacific line. The courier reached the Platte River that night but was unable to cross because of a heavy rainstorm and the darkness. The next morning, Monday, September 24, the cowboy crossed and rode on to Ogallala where he delivered the message to railroad officials. Leach had continued to follow the gang on Sunday and found their next camp on Beaver Creek where the storm and darkness had forced them to halt. He again staked his horse on the opposite side of the creek, waded across, and crept up to within two hundred feet of where the men were sitting in a circle dividing the gold. Collins had a saddleflap across his knees and was stacking the gold in six separate stacks. Each robber sewed up his share of the money in trouser legs. Leach claimed that he overheard them discussing stopping at Buffalo Station before going on to Dallas for more train robbing in Texas, where it would be "easy and safe work."

The six men exchanged the locations where they could later be reached. Collins then suggested that since one of them might be caught and decide to squeal, they should take an oath that under no circumstances would any of them be taken alive. The men stood in a circle around the fire and, with bare heads and raised hands, solemnly swore the oath. When they finally lay down, Leach returned to his horse to await daylight.[16]

At the same time back in Ogallala, a letter dated September 24 was reportedly forwarded to Collins at Ellis, Kansas, on the Kansas Pacific line. The letter, however, apparently intended to help him, would not come to light until after Collins' death.

J.J. COLLINS FRIEND
I have herd that Leech has follard you and said that yoe have robe that train at Big Springs[.] I think St Clare is the man that said yoe ware the partie that Rob it—and they sent Leech to hunt yoe up[.] if I was yoe I wood Come back and kill the sun of a bitch and kill[;] if yoe will I give a good horse to ride off[.] Joe send Sam back. I will help helpe yoe off be sheure and kill Leech if yoe Can git a good c[h]ance for he and St. Clare is the two men that said that yoe ware the man that don it[.] kept this to yoe self and write me and I will write yoe and kept yoe posted.

I am you friend
S.R. M___s[17]

The writer of this letter was the subject of some indignation among the good citizens of Ogallala. A check of the 1880 Douglas County (Omaha) census reveals a Scottish stonecutter by the name of John St. Clair, but whether this is the person referred to is unknown. There is no known connection to Collins or Bass by anyone named St. Clair.[18]

The next morning, Tuesday, Leach followed the gang south into Kansas. A little after dark, he reached Sappa Creek where a widow kept a house where cowboys could stop and get something to eat. Riding toward the house, Leach was within fifty feet when he spotted Collins and Berry walking around a corner. Whirling his horse, he spotted two more members of the gang, then raced for a ford across the creek but found himself riding through the outlaw camp. Davis fired at him as he sped by and raced north, aware that the gang had mounted and was pursuing him. His horse tired quickly, so Leach stopped in an arroyo patched with brush, tied down his horse's ears to keep him from whinnying, and quickly fixed up a barricade with old logs behind which to hide. The gang members rode to within one hundred feet of the hidden detective but didn't spot him and returned to their camp.

Undaunted, Leach followed them back through a fog to

their camp then, sensing that they had turned around and were coming toward him, rode out into the darkness and let them pass. He returned to the widow's for something to eat, but she was reluctant to admit him until he convinced her that he was not a badman. She told him that she had baked biscuits for the gang, but the men had fled when they spotted Leach. After finishing a meal, Leach followed the fleeing robbers south to Prairie Dog Creek, where the gang divided into pairs of two and rode off in different directions.[19] For the time being, Leach lost the gang's trail, but he would follow Jim Berry into Missouri several weeks later.

In the meantime, the press was speculating as to who might be responsible for the robbery. A Kansas City newspaper surmised that a brother-in-law of the notorious Younger brothers, now prisoners in the Minnesota state penitentiary after the ill-fated 1876 Northfield bank robbery attempt, had organized the train robbery to raise funds to finance a breakout of his famous relatives. Another supposition was that Jesse and Frank James, along with Civil War associate John Garrett, might be responsible.[20] In Ogallala, one hapless individual, whose story of being a stock owner from Deer Trail hunting stray cattle did not hold much strength with officials, was arrested as a suspect in the train robbery and taken to Julesburg, Colorado.[21]

Although early patrols sent out after the robbers had by now returned to their posts, the army had not backed off. On September 25, after having at last heard from Leach that the gang was headed south in the direction of Buffalo Station or Ellis, Superintendent Clark in Omaha immediately wired telegrams to Fort Hays in Ellis County, Kansas.

Robbers with plunder have been discovered near Young's ranch Republican River. There are six of them. One party now making south. Send Sheriff and strong party from Ellis north to intercept them, and if Gen'l Pope calls for special train, furnish it at our expense. Please also use your own judgment in helping to catch the thieves. Ten thousand dollars reward will be paid. Act promptly as the party will soon separate. Answer quick.

A second telegram the same day continued to stress the urgency.

They camped at Young's ranch night before last and left there early yesterday morning twenty-fourth inst. Six in party. Had plunder with them, well armed. There is no mistake about it. It is thought they will strike your road Thursday. Collins, Ned, and James Berry are their leaders, the other three unknown. It will require good force to capture robbers and it is thought best to send posse north to intercept them before they separate which will be soon.[22]

At 3:00 p.m., Tuesday, September 25, General George Crook, commander of the Department of the Platte headquartered at Omaha, ordered General John H. Pope, commanding the Department of the Missouri at Fort Leavenworth, to assist the local authorities.

Have received positive information that party who robbed Union Pacific train are now on Republican river travelling south and will reach Kansas Pacific rail road some time on Friday, possibly sooner. It is probable that they will cross rail road in vicinity Ellis station – not certain. Will you please send out parties from posts on line of rail road and have them arrest them. Party is composed of six men and still have their plunder with them. A Mr. Burley from Omaha[,] deputy sheriff[,] is now at Ellis and knows the men. They are well armed. Have been pursuing them by troops in this department, but they have eluded pursuit.[23]

General Pope, in turn, telegraphed instructions to posts thought to be in the probable vicinity of the robbers' path of flight. Captain Duncan McArthur Vance, who commanded Fort Hays, was ordered to send a patrol from the post west along the Kansas Pacific line toward the small town of Wallace, in far western Kansas almost to the Colorado border. Another order was telegraphed to Captain William George Wedemeyer at Fort

Wallace, about eighteen miles south of Wallace.[24] Wedemeyer then ordered Captain Peter M. Boehm of the 4th Cavalry to head eastward by rail with twenty-four enlisted men; he left half of his detachment at Buffalo Station and proceeded on to Ellis.[25] As far south as Texas, Captain Wirt Davis led a detachment of 4th Cavalry soldiers out from Fort Elliott to see if they could intercept any of the robbers.[26]

In Kansas, Ellis County Sheriff George W. Bardsley[27] was away from the county seat of Hays City when he received word of the manhunt for the robbers and of the reward offered by Union Pacific. He quickly arranged with J.O. Brinkerhoff, superintendent of the Kansas Pacific Railroad, to have an engine, a tender and a cattle car placed at the sheriff's disposal. Bardsley then telegraphed A.D. Gilkeson at Hays City to recruit men, horses and provisions for a posse and to have it meet him in Hays City at 6:00 p.m. Bardsley also requested that O. Branham, telegraph operator and railroad agent in Hays City, send one of Bardsley's deputy sheriffs to request that Fort Hays commander Captain Duncan Vance loan the posse military arms and ammunition for the pursuit of the train robbers thought to be headed their way. Vance had not yet received the telegram sent by General Pope when the deputy sheriff arrived with Bardsley's request. The captain sent a reply to Branham agreeing to provide the arms if Branham would be responsible for them. A wagon sent from Hays City delivered fifty-caliber Springfield Rifles to the telegraph office.[27] About an hour after the rifles had been picked up at Fort Hays, Bardsley, having returned to Hays City, personally delivered to Captain Vance the telegram from General Pope, ordering a patrol to be sent out, which had come through agent Branham. Vance immediately directed Second Lieutenant Leven C. Allen of the 16th Infantry to go to Buffalo Station, some sixty miles to the west, with a non-commissioned officer and nine privates.[28]

After the confrontation with Leach, Collins and his men realized that an intensive manhunt was being mounted across state lines and that their escape direction was now known. Rather than staying together, they had a better chance of escaping by splitting up. Collins and Potts left the Prairie Dog Creek camp on Tuesday, September 25, and rode south toward

Lieutenant Leven C. Allen, commander of the soldiers who killed Joel Collins and Bill Potts at Buffalo Station, Kansas. (Courtesy National Archives and Ruth Priest Dixon).

Buffalo Station on the Kansas Pacific line. Berry and Nixon headed east for Berry's home in Missouri, and Bass and Davis set out in a slightly different direction south toward Texas. Each of them carried his share of the loot; Collins and Potts used a third horse as a pack animal to carry the trousers containing the gold inside a flour sack.

At Fort Hays, Lieutenant Allen ordered Corporal William M. Eddy to ready himself and nine men with .45-caliber breech-loading carbines and ten days' rations to start to Buffalo Station that afternoon. The nine privates in the detail were William Graff, Charles F. Sloan, Hiram A. Doliver, Francis Toohey, D.G. Walker, Benjamin F. Simmons, Octavous A. Shindlebower, Joseph Ayers, and musician Frank Rust. In the company's orderly room the men drew their carbines and ammunition, then went to the stable to saddle up. The hastily formed patrol rode to Hays City where its twelve horses and mules and equipment were loaded onto the cattle car that Bardsley had arranged with the Kansas Pacific. The posse Bardsley had requested from Hays City had failed to materialize, and Lieutenant Allen said that he and the sheriff discussed the operation. Allen later stated that the two agreed to cooperate but that the military was not placing itself at Bardsley's disposal. However, Bardsley later claimed that the soldiers were preparing to ride to Buffalo Station on horseback and that he offered the use of the special car provided by the railroad. There is evidence that Bardsley, believing that Corporal Eddy was in charge of the soldiers, did not meet Allen until after the special train was enroute to Buffalo Station.

At about 6:00 in the evening of Tuesday, September 25, with stock and equipment loaded, Bardsley, Corporal Eddy and the nine privates, and reportedly Sheriff Bradley of North Platte and a "Denver detective" clambered atop the cattle car, and the train set off for Buffalo Station. Several of the army's rifles were overlooked and left behind in the telegraph office. While Lieutenant Allen rode with the engineer, Private Francis Toohey, a nineteen-year veteran, Graff, and other soldiers engaged Bardsley in conversation atop the cattle car. At one point Toohey had to request the sheriff to point his rifle muzzle in a direction other than at him. Bardsley's mind was clearly set on the reward offered by the Union Pacific, and the soldiers would later recall that he promised them an equal share if they caught any of the robbers. When the train reached Ellis, a box car was added to the small train, and the party transferred to that car for the rest of the trip. At about midnight, they pulled into Buffalo Station and set up camp.[29]

Buffalo Station was located on the north side of the tracks in a desolate stretch of the Kansas plains in Gove County. The Kansas Pacific line had laid rails through there in the spring of 1868, one of a number of stations with sidetrack, well, and water tank that had been located approximately every fifteen miles. A major cattle trail running north and south was to the east of the station and had been the site of a number of cattle drives over the years. Early occupants at the station were railroad employees and occasional buffalo hunters; the nearest settlers were on Beaver Creek some seventy or eighty miles to the north, and the lonely station had great difficulty keeping a station agent there any longer than about six months. Finally in 1869, William A. "Bill" Sternberg, who had learned telegraphy

Left: Gove (Buffalo Station), Kansas, as it appears today.

Bottom: The approximate site of the deaths of Joel Collins and Bill Potts at Gove (Buffalo Station), Kansas. (Author photos).

at the Manhattan, Kansas, Agricultural College, agreed to take the job if the railroad would provide a boxcar so that he could lay in a stock of goods for trade with passing hunters and Indians. He also used the car as both an office and a residence. The first post office was established there in August 1873 and named Gove Hill. By 1877 Sternberg had been joined by James L. Thompson, a thirty-six-year old cattleman and farmer who ran a store in the basement of the railroad section house and was postmaster. He had living with him his wife, Lydia, two children, and his seventeen-year-old sister. By 1877 Buffalo Station boasted a barn and corral, water tank and windmill, in addition to the station office with a platform and a section house.

Sternberg supplemented his monthly salary of sixty-five dollars by killing buffalo and antelope and shipping the meat to cities in central and eastern Kansas. He used the section handcar with a fifteen-foot sail to soar up and down the track until he located buffalo crossing the tracks. To lure antelope, he rode out onto the prairie and picketed his unsaddled horse with a red blanket across its back, then he read until curious antelope came within range of his rifle. When settlers began to encroach, he found a market for the buffalo bones brought to the station by the settlers for shipment.[30] Years later, Sternberg would recall receiving a telegram on September 20, 1877, from Union Pacific express superintendent Morsman.

To All Agents and Operators: Last night the Overland Express No. 2 was held up at Big Springs, Nebraska, the express car broken into and robbed of a large sum of money and the messenger brutally beaten. It is believed the robbery was perpetrated by six cowboys under the leadership of Joel Collins, as they have suddenly disappeared from one of the cow camps in the vicinity. The horses they rode carried the pot hook brand. As Collins was from Texas, it is thought they will ultimately head southward. A reward of ten thousand dollars will be paid for their capture, or a pro rata amount for the capture, dead or alive, of any one of them. Post conspicuous notices.[31]

When Bardsley and the soldiers disembarked from the train on their arrival, they tied their stock to a fence of the corral and to wagons and immediately found a place to bed down, most sleeping near a haystack about 100 to 150 yards from the station house. Shindlebower fed his horse before lying down for the night. Private Sloan, posted as sentinel about 2:00 a.m. with instructions to halt anyone advancing and to report if he saw anyone coming or going, was relieved two hours later by Shindlebower. Bardsley stayed some distance from the soldiers on the south side of the tracks.

Before daylight on Wednesday, a thick fog covered the station and most of the soldiers began to rise after a brief rest. Lieutenant Allen read to Corporal Eddy and some of the men the description that he had of some of the bandits, mentioning Collins' name, and told them that it was reported that one of the robbers was riding a "claybank" or yellowish-brown horse with a peculiar heartshaped counterbrand. He ordered Hiram Doliver to take D.G. Walker and ride northeast until they struck the Saline River, follow that for nine or ten miles looking for sign of the robbers, then return to the station by noon. Taking Private Rust and a civilian, Lieutenant Allen headed west to scout along the railroad, leaving the remaining soldiers at the station under Eddy's command. Allen was confident that any members of the gang who came to the station would be identified and arrested by Eddy and his men, and it was important to see if the robbers made any effort to go around the station undetected.[32] At about seven o'clock, storekeeper and postmaster James Thompson rode south into the fog from the station to gather up some horses and return them to the corral.

By about 8:30 the men remaining at the station had eaten, and the fog continued to be heavy. On the station platform Bill Sternberg and Corporal Eddy, listening for a train that was running late, were joined by privates Toohey, Graff and Shindlebower. Sloan was still sleeping after going off guard duty; Simmons and Ayers were likely up and about, preparing for their day and the return of the two patrols at noon.

Joel Collins and Bill Potts slowly rode through the fog, the buildings of Buffalo Station becoming visible only when they were within a hundred yards or so. Collins, sporting a four-inch black beard and wearing a buttoned-up waterproof coat, rode a yellowish-brown horse, the brand of a heart counterbranded with another one. Potts was astride a bay pony and leading a smaller brown horse with a pack on its back. All three animals were weary from the long trek. No doubt surprised at the presence of soldiers, the two outlaws had no choice but to proceed as if nothing were wrong. They rode up to the station platform and Collins greeted the men standing there; Toohey returned the greeting. Eddy and Graff left the platform, and Eddy noticed Collins' horse and the unique brand. Collins volunteered that he and his companion had been up north with a herd of cattle and were now on their way home. The soldiers walked over to alert Sloan, Simmons and Ayers of the possibility that the two strangers might be part of the train robbers. Toohey told Eddy that he thought they were the wanted men, and the soldiers prepared to saddle their mounts. At the platform, Collins asked Sternberg about watering their horses and if there was a store at the station. The agent directed them to Thompson's store in the basement of the section house.

Collins dismounted, handing the reins of his horse to Potts and telling him to find a place to camp. Potts rode 150 yards down the north side of the track to wait but made no effort to set up a camp. He dismounted while the horses grazed. Station agent Sternberg, just as suspicious as Corporal Eddy, locked the door to his office and followed Collins over to the section house about fifty yards to the rear of the station house. They entered the house, then came out and went down into the cellar where Thompson, who still had not returned from gathering horses, kept his store. Thompson's "hired girl," Jennie Humphrey, holding a lamp, did not know the prices that Thompson charged and suggested to Collins that he wait until her employer returned shortly. Collins said that they would have to come to some agreement and that he would pay her enough to satisfy Thompson. He bought some canned fruit and an old coffee pot worth ten cents, but he agreed to pay seventy-five cents for it.

Collins unbuttoned his rubber coat and retrieved a long black leather pocketbook to pay for the items, at the same time pulling out an envelope or piece of paper that had "Joel Collins,

Ogallala, Nebraska" inscribed on it. Sternberg impulsively asked him if his name was Joel Collins, and without hesitating Collins admitted that it was. Collins asked why the soldiers were at the station, and Sternberg replied that they were a regular, permanent guard assigned there to protect the station and railroad from Indians and deserters. Afraid that Collins suspected him because he had asked about his name, and only briefly entertaining the thought of finding a club and braining the desperado as he climbed out of the cellar, Sternberg made some excuse and hurried out of the cellar to find Sheriff Bardsley. Collins paid for the items, left the cellar and rejoined Potts. The two mounted their tired ponies, crossed the tracks and headed east toward the cattle trail, then turned south. They had been at the station about thirty minutes, trying not to show concern about the soldiers, and were now trying to ride off as leisurely as possible. Sternberg later claimed that he ran and obtained his Sharp's rifle along with some ammunition, but that Bardsley refused to allow a civilian in his posse.

Sheriff Bardsley had been sleeping on a bed made from a tarpaulin and blankets when Sternberg came to tell him of the two men and the paper with the Collins name on it, but Corporal Eddy had already roused the sheriff and was expressing his opinion that the men were two of the robbers and should be arrested. Reportedly, Bardsley offhandedly commented that he didn't think they were the men, although this would be an unusual response if Sternberg had told him about Collins' admission about his name. Eddy replied that it would do no harm to arrest and search them to be sure, threatening that his men would do it anyway. When Sternberg told Bardsley about his conversation with Collins, the sheriff asked where the two men were. As Eddy pointed them out, Collins rode back toward them and called out to ask how far it was to water. Sternberg replied that it was about six miles to the first creek. Collins thanked him and rejoined his partner. Eddy again urged that the men be checked out; Bardsley, in spite of his reported reservations, agreed and went to saddle his horse.

Thompson, returning to the station with his horses, encountered the two riders, who left the trail to meet him. Thompson vaguely recognized Collins, who called out, "Isn't this Mr. Thompson?" Thompson told him that he had the advantage and that he could not recall his name, and Collins, without giving his name, replied that he was one of Texas cattleman Seth Mabry's men and that they had met two years earlier. Collins told him that a friend named Gardner had recommended that Collins call on Thompson. Thompson knew that a Gardner had been Mabry's foreman, and he noted that their horses bore Mabry's band, with which he was familiar.

When Thompson asked Collins what he could do for him, the outlaw replied that he was in pursuit of a murderer named Shorty Stevens who had killed one of his friends while camped on the Platte River. He asked Thompson if he could find water in Big Creek if he stayed on the cattle trail, and the storekeeper told him that the Hackberry, some twelve miles distant, was the closest water where he could camp. Thompson suggested that they should stay at the station since their horses looked tired, and that while there they could help him brand some cattle. Collins declined, saying that they wanted to be in Dodge City by nightfall the next day.

As the three sat on their horses talking, Bardsley led his horse to the sidetrack where he began to saddle the animal. Collins spotted the sheriff's movements and asked Thompson who he was. Thompson identified Bardsley as the Ellis County sheriff. More suspicious, Collins now asked if the soldiers were regularly stationed there, and Thompson said they were not; that there was "a little excitement up now over a train robbery." Collins inquired further as to what they were doing about the train robbery, and Thompson said, "not much but telegraphing so far." Showing Collins a telegram that he had from the chief of the Rocky Mountain Detective Association that described Joel Collins, by name, Thompson told Collins that if he had mahogany hair and whiskers he would go and get his .44 and take him in. Thompson still did not know Collins' name. Collins handed back the telegram and confidently pronounced that the robbers had gone north into the Black Hills. Thompson looked at Collins, decided that he didn't fit the description, bid the two goodbye and began to move again toward the station. Collins and Potts continued on south, but as Thompson started to leave, Bardsley rode up and said,

"Good morning, who are these fellows?" Thompson told him what they had said, then rode on toward the station with his horses as Bardsley rode up to Collins and Potts, calling out "hello there." The two horsemen stopped again to talk with the sheriff for several minutes about the man that they said they were looking for. Collins told the sheriff that his name was Collins and that he used to be from around Wichita. They briefly talked about mutual acquaintances in Wichita. Bardsley then returned to the station, and Collins and Potts leisurely resumed their journey southward.

At the station, Thompson conversed with Sternberg, and when he was told that one of the men was Joel Collins, he recalled meeting him before. Thompson, however, expressed his belief that they were only cowboys, not train robbers, which caused Private Shindlebower to unsaddle his horse.

Information as to what happened next is conflicting. Both Sternberg and Bardsley would state that the conversation with Collins and Potts confirmed the sheriff's suspicions, if indeed he really had any, and that Bardsley returned to the station to obtain the soldiers' assistance in their capture. Corporal Eddy and the other soldiers, on the other hand, would later testify that Bardsley returned and told them that the two riders were not any of the men that they were seeking. Disgusted with the sheriff, Eddy allegedly told his men to mount up and that they would ride out and search them. Thompson later recalled that Bardsley returned and asked him what he had observed about the men, and after hearing what he had to say, the sheriff said that he had a notion to go out and search them. Thompson told him that if the men were all right, it would do them no harm, but that he thought that the sheriff was on the wrong track. Strangely, Sternberg, even though he claimed that Collins identified himself, would later testify that he, too, scoffed at the idea of their being train robbers. Regardless of this conflict, however, the soldiers had saddled their horses and mules, and Bardsley decided that, indeed, it would do no harm to bring back the two men for more investigation.

Bardsley started after Collins and Potts at full gallop, followed closely by Corporal Eddy and Private Ayers. Graff and Sloan, and Shindlebower after resaddling his mount, rode after them, but Simmons was left on foot because his mule had been taken by Allen on patrol. By this time Collins and Potts were about two hundred or more yards south of the tracks. According to Corporal Eddy, when the first three riders caught up with Collins and Potts, Bardsley said, "I would like you men to come back to the station with me."

"What for?" replied one of the men.

"Oh, nothing much; you answer a description I have of a man, and I want you to come back to the telegraph dispatch, though I do not think you are the men," the sheriff responded. Casually, the two consented and turned their horses back toward the station, Collins saying something to the effect that they were cattlemen and not the ones they were looking for. Bardsley rode in front of the two, and Eddy and Ayers rode behind them; the other soldiers were still riding toward them. No sooner had they turned their horses than Collins gave a "significant look" at Potts and reached for his revolver.

According to Eddy, he called to Collins to "drop that" and leveled his carbine at him, but Collins turned in his saddle and aimed his pistol at the two soldiers behind him. Ayers immediately fired, but his horse fell and tossed him to the ground. Bardsley apparently also fired at Collins, who was dismounting when Eddy also fired at him. He staggered a few steps with a revolver held head high, but threw it on the ground and fell to his knees, calling out "Hold on, boys, I am shot through." He attempted to pull off his coat but , with one hand out of a sleeve, slowly began to sink. Bardsley's horse had shied at the shooting, and the sheriff found himself afoot on the ground. Sloan, who had not been able to keep up when the party went after the robbers, rode up on a mule and shot Potts off his horse, killing him instantly. Shindlebower also rode up, and it is possible that other soldiers fired at Potts while he was drawing a pistol. Sloan dismounted to reload his carbine and join in the fight with Collins, but the robber, on his knees, fell over on his side and was dead. An excited Bardsley shot at Potts' dead body, missing and almost hitting Ayers, hollering, "Shoot the son of a bitch; he is playing possum on you!"

Bardsley later testified at an inquest that after he had turned his back to Collins and started back for the station,

Collins pulled a pistol. The sheriff said he pulled his .32 caliber Smith & Wesson pistol and fired twice at the outlaw but missed him both times. As Collins threw his leg over his saddle horn and dismounted, Bardsley said that he was distracted by his frightened horse. He then saw Collins pointing his pistol and fired one shot, hitting the outlaw, who fell.[33]

Private Toohey, joining his companions, jumped from his horse and took the excited pack horse under control. He felt the weight of the pack and called out that he had the gold. Bardsley rushed up, threw the pack containing two old heavy seamless flour sacks to the ground, and opened them to reveal overalls in which gold coins were sewn up. "We've got the money, boys! We've got the money, boys!" Bardsley excitedly shouted. He called out for someone to ride to the station and send a telegram that the two robbers had been killed and that they had the money. One of the soldiers rode furiously back to the station, waving his cap and shouting that the robbers had been killed. Sternberg and Thompson climbed into a spring wagon and headed for the scene.

Eddy and Bardsley searched the bodies of the two dead robbers and their horses, finding more gold and currency, including a small leather bag containing about $250. The only other item found on Collins was a roll of copied poems, dedicated to him by a young woman, one of which was entitled "Will You Love Me When I'm Old?" Potts had no information on him. Leaving the bodies on the ground, the party started back to the station. Bardsley and others took turns carrying the heavy gold and finally transferred it to Graff's mule and then to Thompson's wagon to be carried back to the station. Eddy then directed Graff and Simmons to retrieve the bodies and the two soldiers, again accompanied by Thompson in his wagon, returned to the site of the shooting, retrieved the bodies, and placed them in an old dismounted boxcar south of the track. The gold was taken to the telegraph office where it was weighed by Thompson. A brief telegram was quickly dispatched to Hays City, "Have killed Collins and his pal. Have two sacks of gold; can't tell how much, about eighty pounds."[34] A total of $19,456.67 in gold, silver, and currency was recovered by Bardsley and the soldiers from the dead robbers. Clearly elated by the turn of events, Bardsley personally guarded the gold until it could be handed over to the proper officials, and one account says that for a time his joy was such that he shouted and acted like a wild man. With his coat off, sleeves rolled up, and two pistols thrust in his belt, the sheriff did not move out of sight of the sack of gold except for a brief dinner with Thompson.[35]

Lieutenant Allen, Private Rust and the civilian returned to Buffalo Station from their patrol about eleven o'clock that morning and learned of the shooting. Allen dispatched Sloan and Simmons to find Doliver and Walker on patrol to the east. Simmons rode Collins' horse, and the two soldiers found the patrol within a mile of the station and returned as directed. In the meantime, a dispute arose between Bardsley and Allen over the items that had been taken from the robbers. After Allen had inventoried the articles captured, he had to convince Bardsley, who was wary of giving up his claim for the reward, to sign a receipt and formally take charge of the items. Bardsley argued that since Allen had never had possession of the loot, he could not very well turn it over to the sheriff. That afternoon, Brinkerhoff of the Kansas Pacific took charge of the gold on behalf of the Union Pacific and signed a receipt for Bardsley, although the sheriff really wanted to hold onto the money until the reward was paid.[36]

At two that same afternoon, Allen led his men to the southeast to see if more robbers could be intercepted. The infantry soldiers were unaccustomed to extended horseback riding and had very little experience on the prairie. Indeed, Private Sloan had only enlisted on September 19, one week earlier. They camped Wednesday evening on Hackberry Creek, then spent the next day scouting to the north of the Smoky Hill River but found nothing of the robbers. One of the horses gave out in the afternoon and was abandoned. The troop did not return to Fort Hays until early on the morning of September 29.[37] While Allen and his men patrolled the vicinity around Buffalo Station, other military detachments and civilian law enforcement officers throughout Kansas searched diligently for any sign of the remaining train robbers.[38]

An inquest over the bodies of Collins and Potts, who was still unidentified, was commenced on Thursday, September 27, by attorney Charles W. Talmadge, the county coroner, who had traveled to Buffalo Station on the midnight train with a hastily assembled jury in response to a telegram from Bardsley. By the light of a dim candle, the jury examined the bloody, dirt-covered bodies lying in the old boxcar covered with blankets. Talmadge noted that each man had been shot once through the left breast, Collins' wound being within half an inch of the nipple, the ball passing through and exiting near the backbone just below the shoulder blade. Collins also had a slight flesh wound on the left shoulder. Talmadge noted that the bullet hole in Collins was a small one, perhaps from a .32 caliber pistol (although Eddy and Graff would later testify that they thought it was .45 caliber, and Eddy said that he had inserted a .45 cartridge into Collins' wound). Talmadge inserted a cartridge in the wounds of both bodies, determining that Potts had been shot with a larger caliber weapon, probably .45 caliber. Testimony was taken from Sternberg and Thompson; then the jury returned to Ellis on the train, taking the bodies with them.[39]

A large crowd awaited the train in Ellis, and the bodies of the two robbers were laid out for viewing. One member of the inquest jury, Morgan Cox, a hotelkeeper in Ellis, had known Collins in Wichita between 1872 and 1874 and easily identified him, as did a Jimmy Price of Ellis. A number of Texans present also recognized Collins, but no one recognized his partner although there was some speculation that his name was Bass.[40] There are several accounts of how Potts was finally identified. In one account, Talmadge, desirous of identifying the body, determined to have all of the "erring women" of Ellis brought to view the bodies, thinking that the "wild, reckless men of the plains" would be known to them. A Mrs. Anna Lang reportedly viewed the unidentified body and immediately uttered a piercing cry and loud sobs, recognizing him as William Potts whom she had married in Pottsville, Pennsylvania, many years before. He had deserted her some time back, and by coincidence she was now a prostitute living near where he was killed. She was able to confirm his identity by the India ink tatoos on his hand and arm.[41]

In another account, a Mrs. Jacobs viewed the body and exclaimed that it was her husband and, like the version featuring Mrs. Lang, confirmed the presence of tatoos on him. The

93

The former site of the train depot at Ellis, Kansas, where the bodies of Joel Collins and Bill Potts were delivered for an inquest. (Author photo).

widow of a man named Jacobs, a recorder of deeds at Wichita who had died a drunkard, she had then married Potts. However, she had left him eighteen months earlier when she had learned that he already had a wife in Pennsylvania.[42]

On October 9 and 10, Coroner Talmadge took additional testimony about the shooting of Collins and Potts. Bardsley testified, as did privates Ayers and Sloan. The jury concluded that Collins was shot through the heart by Bardsley, and that Sloan killed Potts with a carbine shot through the left breast. The bodies were buried in the Ellis vicinity, and Talmadge submitted a bill in the amount of $174 for his services and expenses.[43] The personal effects of Collins and Potts had already been grabbed up by several persons. Anthony W. "Tony" Waits, a detective from Ogallala, Nebraska, who had come to Buffalo Station with an army patrol from Fort Wallace, ended up with Collins' pistol, his needle-case, and the horn-string by which Collins' lariat had been secured to his saddle. Waits vowed to use Collins' sixshooter to "plug" some of the other robbers.[44]

The chapter on Collins was not quite finished, however. The news of his death had flashed across the country, and in Dallas his heartbroken, disbelieving parents retained Guthrie & Brown, a prominent law firm in Topeka, Kansas, to investigate

94

their son's killing. The Collins family contended that he had gone to the Black Hills with a large number of cattle and had written that he had sold them for twenty-five cents a pound, nearly twenty thousand dollars in gold, and was starting on his way home. They believed that a study of his movements would establish that he could not have been near Big Springs at the time of the robbery, and the fact that he had "amassed a great deal of property at San Antonio by dealing in cattle" was surely enough to place him above suspicion. His actions at Buffalo Station were attributed to those of a man with a large amount of money on him who thought he had fallen among thieves and was determined to resist to the end. The *Hays City Sentinel* was quick to refute the idea that Joel Collins was an innocent man and described witnesses who had seen him in the vicinity of the robbery, the mintage of the coins that he was carrying, his being in company with a notorious badman, and the presence of soldiers in uniform.[45] In Cheyenne the story was also dismissed because of evidence that Collins had been in Ogallala without a cent and that "his character while in Deadwood was very bad."[46]

Claims for the reward were promptly made to Union Pacific by Bardsley and Allen and the soldiers. In fact, the soldiers were told by higher command that they were "clearly entitled to a portion at least" of the reward offered.[47] The pro rata amount was determined to be $3,242.76, and on October 1 the railroad paid Bardsley fifty dollars but withheld the rest until proper distribution could be determined. Bardsley filed a lawsuit in the U.S. Circuit Court for the District of Nebraska on April 17, 1878, contending that it was solely by his "labor, skill, planning, calculations, information, and knowledge" that Collins and Potts were captured, and asked for the full amount. He also demanded an additional $250 for his efforts from September 26 until September 30, during which time he was on constant scout for other robbers. Lieutenant Allen and the other soldiers responded that they were present on behalf of the United States government and that they were responsible for the capture and asked that they receive $2,927.49 as their share of the reward. It was their contention that all parties were fairly entitled to just under three hundred dollars each. After depositions were taken of most of the participants, a jury on May 19, 1879, awarded $2,250 to Bardsley and $1,002.76 to all of the soldiers, for some reason omitting D.G. Walker.[48]

Two of the six gang members had been killed within a week of the robbery. The manhunt continued.

-VII-
THE LAW IN PURSUIT

T he Union Pacific Railroad Company, elated at the partial success of the robbery investigation, received the gold recovered from Collins and Potts and sent on $19,440 in gold coins to Ham Brothers, a brokerage in New York, to sell for the company. The coins were sold on October 3, and the railroad realized $20,011.05 after the brokerage's commission. The railroad had already sent a check in the amount of sixty thousand dollars to the Chemical National Bank of New York on September 22 to pay for the gold taken.[1]

The manhunt was intensified by the capture and killing of Collins and Potts. Tony Waits, the detective from Ogallala, rode with Captain Peter Boehm's Fort Wallace detachment after it left Buffalo Station on Wednesday evening, September 26. A day and a half later the patrol reached the Cimarron Station on the AT&SF line some 110 miles to the south. Captain Boehm enlisted a gang of railroad section men and a hand car and continued on to Dodge City. Waits then received a telegram from Kingley, forty-two miles to the east, advising him that two men who might be the robbers were there. Taking a few Dodge City residents with him, Waits took a train and was there very quickly, but the suspicious men were only some cowboys. On his return to Dodge City, another telegram was waiting stating that two men, believed to be Berry and a man named Reed, were at Great Bend ninety miles to the east. Again, the men turned out to be transients only too glad to be on their way after being locked up all night. Back at Dodge City, a telegram from Union Pacific superintendent Morsman instructed Waits to report to Superintendent Clark at Omaha if he had no additional information to check out in Kansas, so Waits left for Nebraska.[2]

On Wednesday, October 10, in Texas, Major John B. Jones, who commanded the Frontier Battalion (Texas Rangers), sent a letter to the commanders of the ranger companies instructing them to keep a sharp lookout for the Union Pacific robbers. He enclosed a copy of a telegram received from Superintendent Morsman that gave the descriptions of William Heffridge alias Bill Heffery, Sam Bass, Jack Davis, James Berry and Tom Nixon.[3] Since the origin of some of the bandits was believed to be Texas, the railroad officials obviously believed that Texas would be their likely destination.

Jim Berry and Tom Nixon left the gang at Prairie Dog Creek in Kansas and headed for Berry's home in Callaway County in eastern Missouri. Leach was on their trail, having overheard the gang discuss where they would be headed, and was close behind them.[4] According to Sorenson, Leach stayed around Buffalo Station and Hays City in Kansas for a few days, then went to Omaha to consult with railroad officials. Accompanied by some other men, he made his way to Fulton, the county seat of Callaway County, and staked out Berry's home, which was in a more desolate part of the countryside.[5]

Berry stepped off the train at Mexico, Missouri, on Friday, October 5, with a pair of saddlebags thrown across his arm. His hair was shoulder length and matted, his beard was unkempt, and he was shabbily dressed. He strolled over to a hotel and registered under his own name, unaware that his identity as one of the robbers had already been flashed across the country. A porter lifted the pair of saddlebags that Berry had carried with him and thought they must be full of horseshoes.[6] Nixon, who had arrived on the train with Berry, proceeded on with his share of the loot to Chicago on the C&A Railroad, perhaps continuing on to Canada.[7] Never positively identified, "Tom Nixon" disappeared into historical oblivion.

The next morning Berry went to the three banks in Mexico, selling nine thousand dollars in gold coins for the same amount in currency, and opened an account at the Exchange Bank with a deposit of about $1,600. As a cover story, he claimed that he had sold a mining claim in the Black Hills to a man from California. With his pockets full of cash, Berry promptly went on a spree before he returned home, beginning with a haircut and shave. On the street he ran into two young men whom he had known in the Black Hills and treated them to a drink, flashing his large roll of bills. He boasted of having struck it rich, but his two young friends remembered distinctly that their red-haired companion had been broke just a few short weeks before.

Berry wore a revolver in plain view, but the local authorities hesitated to arrest him because he obviously did have a sizable amount of money to protect. They were also probably aware of his service with "Bloody Bill" Anderson, and that he had three brothers who could be dangerous on occasion. Word of the money was all over town. Berry stayed in town several days drinking and gambling and losing much of his money. His extravagance cost him: to one old mining acquaintance he gave $250 as a gift; he bought drinks all around; he ordered a fine suit of clothes at Morris Blum's dry goods store in Mexico, promising to pick it up later; and he paid $390 for groceries that he had sent to his home in Callaway County. Finally, on Sunday evening Berry left Mexico for his home and family.[8]

The following Wednesday, October 10, someone spotted Berry at tiny Williamsburg near where he lived and notified Union Pacific officials. Superintendent Morsman immediately responded with a telegram that same day to Colonel A.B. Garner of the Missouri, Kansas & Texas Railroad advising that Berry, "an old resident of Callaway County," was one of the Union Pacific robbers, that he had been seen at Williamsburg, and that the railroad was offering a five hundred dollar reward and ten percent of any money recovered.[9] The previous Union Pacific reward had been withdrawn, apparently in light of the claims of Bardsley and the soldiers. Berry had a singular reputation in the area as a ne'er-do-well of questionable honesty, seldom having as much as even fifty dollars at one time. His selling of nine thousand dollars in freshly minted twenty-dollar gold pieces did not correspond to what was known about him. According to Sorenson, a suspicious express agent in Mexico wrote to Superintendent Morsman about Berry and the money, and Morsman immediately responded that Berry was one of the wanted train robbers and advised him of the reward that had been offered. Morsman then traveled to Mexico from Omaha and consulted with Audrain County Sheriff Harry Glasscock, entreating him to go after Berry.[10]

Glasscock and a companion quietly slipped into Callaway

County and made a surprise raid upon the Berry farm, but the outlaw was not there.[11] Berry, now aware that there were people looking for him, decided to lie low. Sheriff Glasscock was not aware of Leach's presence in the area, nor apparently was Morsman, and Leach did not know that Audrain County officials were also after Berry. Leach had consulted with the Callaway County sheriff and, with several other men, had reconnoitered around Berry's farm. In fact, Leach would later recall that he was in hiding in some woods when he saw two men, one of whom he later learned was Glasscock, peering into Berry's stable. But Berry remained out of sight.[12]

On Saturday, October 13, Glasscock returned to Mexico and discussed his failed scout with Morsman. They were convinced, as was Leach, that Berry had not departed the area. Morsman boarded the train to return to Omaha,[13] and at about 6:30 p.m. Glasscock went to eat some dinner. Shortly after 7:00, R.T. "Bose" Kasey went into the store of Morris Blum and Son[14] to pick up the suit of clothes ordered by Jim Berry the Saturday before, but Blum refused to give him the suit until Kasey paid the thirty dollars still owed, as agreed with Berry. Someone sent word to Sheriff Glasscock about 7:30 that Kasey was trying to pick up Berry's suit, and he left his meal and hid around the corner from Blum's store at Kabrich's Hall.

The sheriff watched Kasey leave the store then followed him to Wallace & McKamey's livery stable. Close to the stable, Glasscock encountered John Carter and recruited him to come along. As Kasey paid for his horse and started to mount, the sheriff grabbed him by the collar and thrust a pistol to his head, threatening to shoot if he moved. When Kasey was reluctant to tell the sheriff what he knew about Berry, Glasscock ordered two more horses saddled and tied Kasey to his horse. Then he and Carter led Kasey's horse to a secluded spot south of town and halted while Glasscock went to raise a small posse.

Joining Glasscock and Carter were John T. Coons, a Kentucky-born, thirty-three-year-old who would later be the Mexico city marshal,[15] Bob Steele, who had been city marshal,[16] and a young man named Moore. The three newcomers came to the posse mounted and carrying double-barrelled shotguns loaded with buckshot. Glasscock again demanded that Kasey tell him where Berry was, but the prisoner said that he had not seen Berry since the red-haired outlaw had told him that he could have the suit. Kasey's response was not sufficient, and the barrels of five weapons were pointed at his chest. The men threatened to kill him if he did not lead them to his house or if he led them into a trap. The frightened man agreed to take them to his house "if it would do any good."

The group started out and rode in the darkness into Callaway County. About three o'clock Sunday morning, October 14, they stopped at the farm of James Armstrong. Glasscock, concerned that Kasey was merely leading them around in the darkness, explained what they were doing and asked Armstrong, who knew the area and could show them where Kasey lived, to join them. Armstrong begged off, saying that he did not know where Kasey lived. Shortly afterwards the posse arrived within one-half mile of Kasey's place, about three miles south of Shamrock. Taking Kasey off his horse, they once more tried to persuade him to give up Berry's whereabouts, to no avail. They tied him up again and staked out Kasey's farm. Glasscock left Steele to guard Kasey and posted Carter and Coons on the north side of the house and stable while he and Moore took the south and west sides. The sheriff's instructions to the posse were, "Boys, if you see him, halt him; if he shows fight, shoot him down; if he runs, shoot him in the legs. Catch him at all hazards." The men hunkered down in the thicket surrounding the farm and waited, listening intently for any sound.

After about half an hour, Glasscock heard a horse "nicker" about a half mile off. Glasscock and Moore crept toward the noise, going about three hundred yards along a creek until they reached a fence. In the darkness they were able to detect fresh horse tracks along the fence line. Glasscock quietly climbed over the fence and hid once more in the thicket, listening. He heard a horse snort about fifty yards off and crawled about twenty steps toward the sound then rose to his knees. About forty yards off he could make out the back of a horse, so he took off his hat and carefully moved about twenty yards closer and saw a man he presumed to be Berry unhitch the horse from a tree then lead him roughly in Glasscock's direction toward water. Berry had just arisen from a bed of blankets on the ground.

Glasscock cocked both barrels of his shotgun, ran about twenty yards to within about twenty feet of Berry, and ordered him to halt. Without hesitating, Berry ran and Glasscock fired, the charge flying harmlessly over the fugitive's head. Lowering his barrels, Glasscock released a second blast of buckshot, and seven or eight pellets hit Berry's left leg below the knee. Berry fell head-long down an embankment, coming to rest against a small sapling with his revolver wedged in its scabbard so that the outlaw could not easily draw it. Glasscock leaped for him and grabbed the pistol away from Berry's grasp, thrusting it in his own belt. A later allegation that the buckshot entered the leg below the knee and ranged upward, one pellet coming out below the groin, hinted that Berry had been shot while lying on the ground. The posse claimed that Berry had stumbled just before being shot, which would explain the trajectory of the pellets.

Berry asked Glasscock to finish him off because he did not want to live. The sheriff told him that he didn't want to kill him. Moore came up, and Glasscock called for the rest of the posse to assemble. In the wounded outlaw's belt they found five packages each containing five hundred dollars (with one thirty-five dollars short); an additional $304 was in his pocketbook. They also located a gold watch and chain, and in the area they found a dress coat, three overcoats, and "comfort." They took Berry to Kasey's house where Mary Kasey made breakfast as the sun came up. One man was sent to Williamsburg to find medical assistance, and Dr. T.M. Maughas returned to dress Berry's wound. It was this doctor who noticed the trajectory of the pellets.

After breakfast Glasscock and Moore rode over to Berry's farm to see if they could find any more of the money. Not telling thirty-two-year-old Mollie Berry what had happened, the sheriff asked her if she knew where her husband was. She replied that she had not seen him for four or five days and thought that he might have left the country. When Glasscock showed her Berry's watch and chain, one of the children said, "Oh, I thought that was Papa's." Glasscock now explained that her husband had been shot. She asked if he had been taken alive, and when the sheriff told her that he had, she responded, "I never thought he would be taken alive. He has said a great many times he would never be taken alive." She began to cry, and the sobbing extended to the three little girls and little boy with her. A search of the farmhouse turned up no money, but the two lawmen noticed that it was well stocked with provisions for the winter: numerous hams, sacks of flour and coffee, kegs of molasses, and many other supplies.

The sheriff returned to Kasey's place to find his men sitting around and talking with bystanders. A group of some fifteen people had gathered, drawn by the news of Berry's capture. Allegations would be reported in a local newspaper that threats were muttered among the bystanders and that there was talk of a rescue, but in actuality no relative of Berry was in the crowd and the people were merely curious. James Muir approached Sheriff Glasscock and offered to take Berry back to the town of Mexico for $2.50, but the lawman declined and arranged for a wagon.[17]

Berry, in a great deal of pain, was taken that evening to Mexico and placed in a room at the Ringo House. Glasscock summoned Dr. Samuel N. Russell[18] to attend to Berry, and Dr. Thomas P. Rothwell, forty-five,[19] arrived to assist him. Doctor Russell did not think that the wounds were too serious and administered chloroform to ease the pain. On Monday afternoon, October 15, Berry told a reporter for the *Mexico Ledger* that he was confident he would survive the wound. The sheriff planned to take him to Omaha as soon as the wounded man could travel, but gangrene set in that evening and there was no way to save the outlaw's life.

On Monday evening, Berry confessed to Glasscock and a Union Pacific express detective, J.H. Gaines, that he was one of the six men who had robbed the Union Pacific train. He adamantly expressed his lack of remorse for having been involved and named Joel Collins as the leader. Berry refused to talk about any of the gang members who were still alive. He also refused to say where the rest of the money was, only that it was where the family would get the benefit of it although they did not now have it. His brother-in-law, James Craighead of Fulton, was with him.

In his last hours the doctors tried to make Berry as comfortable as possible, although he was feeling considerable pain. A Dr. Lacy prayed with him several times during the night, but Berry paid him no attention. Once when Lacy had left his bedside and gone out of the room, Berry asked,"Who in the hell was that?" When told that he was going to die, Berry believed it was a ploy to scare him into saying more about his criminal activities, and he hooted at the idea of death. Sheriff Glasscock waited in attendance on the dying man, and Berry seemed to harbor no ill will toward him.

Early Tuesday morning, October 16, a man named Jones arrived with a buggy to transport Mrs. Berry to Mexico to see her husband, but at 12:40 p.m. Jim Berry died peacefully. Only hours earlier Virginia Berry, his seventy-three-year-old mother, had preceded him in death. Berry's sister and friends arrived from Martinsburg on the 3:00 train, too late to see him alive. At 3:30, Dr. Russell, also the Audrain County coroner, summoned a jury of six men, including John Coons, which found that Berry was killed by eight gunshot wounds in the left leg inflicted by a shotgun in the hands of the sheriff, "a necessary act in the discharge of his duty." At about four o'clock Mrs. Berry finally arrived, surprised to find her husband dead.[20] That same afternoon, unaware of Berry's death, the governor of Missouri issued a warrant for Berry based on a requisition from the Nebraska governor, ordering the delivery of the prisoner to Deputy Sheriff Dave Burley who was to take him to Cheyenne, Nebraska, for trial.[21]

At about two o'clock the next afternoon, under threatening weather, Jim Berry and his mother were buried next to his father, Caleb, in the Liberty Church Cemetery. The brief ceremony was held with a closed coffin, his body not being deemed presentable for his "five beautiful and interesting children." His wife, at the request of a doctor, had been returned to her home, and Berry's sister had to rush to the bedside of another dying relative in Martinsburg.[22]

Too late to be in on the capture of Berry, M.F. Leach was interviewed by the *Mexico Ledger* on Tuesday at the depot as he prepared to leave. Surprise was expressed at Leach's appearance.

He was a short, wiry-looking little fellow, dressed in a very outlandish manner. He had on an old pair of shoes, almost worn out pants, a new hat and a loose coat with the tails cut off. The only thing in his appear-

The Liberty Cemetery, Callaway County, Missouri,
where Jim Berry was buried, as it appears today.
(Courtesy Teresa Blattner, Fulton, Missouri).

ance that would strike a casual observer, was that bril-
liancy of his eye. He had an eagle eye surely; under his
coat he had a long "45" calibre pistol with two belts full
of cartridges. He was evidently "fixed" for any body.

A total of $2,769 had been recovered from Berry, making
the reward a total of $776. The posse met with the sheriff, and
it was agreed that each of the possemen would take $100, while
the sheriff would get $376.[23]

As with Sheriff Bardsley, Glasscock did not escape contro-
versy. An anonymous writer to a local newspaper took great
exception to the sheriff's essentially kidnapping Kasey, "a peace-
able law abiding citizen," with a pistol to his head, accusing the
sheriff and his posse of forgetting the law in their avid pursuit
of a reward. Further, the anonymous author alleged that Berry
was killed for the reward, killed before he could be tried and
convicted in a court. Reference to the strange trajectory of the
shotgun pellets again brought into question how the arrest
actually occurred.[24] This complaint led to the filing of a lawsuit
for damages of twenty thousand dollars against Glasscock by

Berry's wife later in October, alleging that the shooting and delay in medical attention was inexcusable.[25] There is no record of the lawsuit's outcome.

The Union Pacific Railroad brought suit against the three Mexico banks that had accepted the nine thousand dollars in gold coins from Berry, alleging that they had been informed soon after the transaction that the coins were stolen. The Mexico banks had shipped the gold to banks in St. Louis, where it was sold off before those banks could be notified.[26]

Francis Brandon, public administrator of Callaway County, appointed by the court to take charge of Berry's estate, filed an inventory with the court two years later, on September 2, 1879, showing that the estate totaled $4,450.82. This included the $1,600 on deposit in the Exchange Bank at Mexico, $2,465 found in his belt, three hundred dollars in his pocket book, four dollars in Fulton "scrip," and $81.82 from the sale by Glasscock of his horse and saddle. All of this was attached by the court pending the outcome of a lawsuit by the express company against Berry's estate. Mollie Berry had moved her family to Fulton in October 1877. On September 19, 1879, the Circuit Court of Macon County, Missouri, finally found for the express company against Berry's estate in the amount of ten thousand dollars, ordering the assets to be turned over to the express company.[27]

In the meantime, the hunt for the remainder of the train robbers continued. On October 18 in Omaha, Douglas County Deputy Sheriff David E. Burley swore out an affidavit formally alleging the robbery of the train by the six men, "together with certain others whose names" were unknown. Attached to the affidavit was a copy of the complaint filed by Superintendent Morsman on September 22 in Cheyenne County, Nebraska. Burley alleged that Nixon, Davis and Sam Bass had fled Nebraska and were believed to be in Texas.[28]

Sam Bass and Jack Davis, the remaining pair, continued south and were likely oblivious to what had happened to the others. Their route took them across desolate reaches of the Kansas prairie and, according to Hogg, they used their bags of gold as pickets for their horses when they camped and rested. In some small settlement, they allegedly swapped one of their horses for an old buggy. They hid the gold in the bottom of the buggy, then hitched the remaining horse to the buggy and leisurely continued on. A squad of soldiers camped at a creek, no doubt on alert for sign of any of the train robbers, asked Bass and Davis if they had seen two armed men on horseback and leading a pack pony. The two said that they had not but had paid no attention to the various persons they had seen along their route. They said that they were farmers from western Kansas whose crops had failed and that they were now on their way to eastern Kansas, maybe Missouri, to find work. In another account, allegedly given later by Bass, the two told the soldiers that they were also in pursuit of the robbers and hoped to nab a part of the reward.

The ranking soldier of the squad told the two that they were looking for two express robbers named Bass and Davis and gave them a description and where they could contact him if they spotted the robbers. Bass and Davis earnestly agreed to keep an eye out then pitched a camp nearby for the evening. For their supper and breakfast, they even borrowed some of the soldiers' utensils. The next morning Bass and Davis continued on, pledging to the soldiers that they would watch out for the wanted men. In another account, they rode with the squad for four days before they parted and continued on through the Indian Territory to Texas.[29]

By November at the latest, Sam Bass was back in Texas. In one account, he and Davis passed through Denton County and went on to Fort Worth. Davis is supposed to have gone on to New Orleans, and Bass allegedly went north to Cooke County where he made a camp at Cove Hollow on Clear Creek in the extreme southwestern portion of the county, just above the line with Denton County. This spot, a deep, wild, overgrown ravine which would become a regular hideout for Bass, was near Bob Murphy's ranch and not far from the small town of Rosston.[30]

Another contemporary account had Bass using the name of Sam Bushong and returning to Denton County after he and Davis separated in Cooke County north of Denton. Davis allegedly went on to New Orleans but returned to Texas and met Bass when he suspected that detectives were closing in. The two then were supposed to have gone to Fort Worth where Jim Murphy, son of oldtime Denton settler Henderson Murphy and brother of Bob Murphy, exchanged four thousand dollars of the gold coins for greenbacks and Davis left again.[31] The Murphy family, especially Jim, would come to play a regretfully significant role in Bass' future.[32] Bass would later tell Ranger Major John Jones, while dying, that Davis had gone on to New Orleans but had returned to Denton in the latter part of April 1878 to persuade Bass to go in with him to buy a ship.[33]

Apparently concerned that the manhunters would track him to Texas, Bass stayed out of sight. But it had to have been a lonely existence, and he put out feelers to some of his old friends he thought he could trust. One of these was twenty-one-year-old Francis M. "Frank" Jackson who lived in Denton with his sister, Maranda, and her husband, Benizett A. Key, a tinsmith. Orphaned with his brothers and sisters when he was eight years old, Frank Jackson was supposed to have grown "like a wild weed, uncultivated and uncouth," but nevertheless he was of "kind disposition and was not adverse to labor; yet susceptible to evil impressions, full of blood and impetuous." He had acquired the rudiments of an education and could read and write legibly. However "this did not comport with his restless nature, and he soon broke through the thralls of moral restraint to seek the haunts of vice, and associate with rough characters, and was often at nights seen about saloons and billiard tables, places whose influence upon the young or old is anything but elevating." He was about six feet tall, cleanshaven, with a tawny or sunburned complexion, dark hair, and "rather blue eyes." He was said to wear a sort of "devil-may-care expression," and "his look was either that of an impudent stare or vacant gaze," and he looked younger than he actually was. "There was nothing attractive about his appearance and very little that was positive. No man could read him – none divine from his exterior what lurked beneath." Jackson, who had established that he could be a tough adversary when he killed Henry Goodall in 1876, would prove to be one of Bass' closest comrades.[34]

Sam Bass made contact in November with his old friend, coming into Denton to Key's tin shop after dark and asking Jackson to drop what he was doing and come with him. Bass pulled one thousand dollars in gold from his belt and emptied the coins into his hat, cajoling, "Now just lay down them tin-

The Denton, Texas, square in the 1870s. Ben F. Key's tinshop is in the
center. (Courtesy Denton County Historical Museum.)

North side of the Denton Square, in the 1870s.
(Courtesy Denton County Historical Museum).

ner's tools and go with me and I'll insure that you get plenty of this." Jackson hesitated, and Bass thrust a handful of the coins at him, promising to pay him one hundred dollars per month. Jackson reportedly continued to hesitate, and Bass had to visit him three times before the young tinner finally yielded to the glowing picture of life as a bandit that Sam painted, although his sister Maranda pleaded with him not to go.[35]

In addition to recruiting Jackson, Bass renewed his friendship with Henry Underwood, and the three were frequently together. Since being released on the arson charge in early 1877, Underwood had moved his wife and children from Denton to the small town of Bolivar in the far northwestern corner of Denton County.[36] Bass told Jim Murphy that he had a lot of money, and that while in the Black Hills he had located several rich lodes that he sold for "big money" and had also continued his success in horse racing. In mid-November, Bass purchased two horses from Jim Murphy, and he and Jackson and Underwood prepared for a trip south to San Antonio to spend some of the Union Pacific money and to have a good time. Bass may have still had ideas of venturing into legitimate pursuits, such as ranching or the cattle business; it had not been many years since he had expressed a desire to buy land in the west.[37] Bass, Underwood and Jackson reportedly rode to Fort Worth where they bought new clothes and firearms then headed south.[38]

While Bass may have forgotten about the lawmen on his trail, they had not forgotten about him. Express company detectives J.H. Gaines and T. E. Kennedy had gone to Texas in October, establishing their headquarters in Fort Worth. Tony Waits followed a few weeks later to help identify any of the men if they were caught. They nosed around Fort Worth and picked up what they thought was the trail of Bass and Underwood, whom they mistakenly thought was Tom Nixon.[39]

In Denton County several sheriffs from surrounding counties, no doubt lured by the promise of the Union Pacific reward, met to confer about strategy. Sheriff William C. Everheart of Grayson County, aware that Texas Governor Hubbard had issued warrants for Bass and Tom Nixon at the request of the Nebraska governor, was keenly interested in starting on their trail right away.[40] One of the lawmen to whom Everheart talked was a

Denton County deputy sheriff for "Dad" Egan, Thomas E. Gerren, who would prove to be one of the most controversial men involved in the chase after Sam Bass, the same Tom Gerren whose life had reportedly been saved by Bass and who had fired at Underwood after the assault on "Parson" Johnson. Gerren was not a well-liked man in Denton County, and the trouble in which he periodically found himself seemed a reflection of some character flaw on his part.[41] His trustworthiness among other lawmen would be seriously questioned, especially after repeatedly bragging that he had "slept with" Sam Bass for two years.

At the late November meeting in Denton, it was learned that Bass and "Nixon" might have gone to San Antonio, although Gerren and Everheart would dispute which one of them told the other. Everheart wanted Denton Deputy Riley Wetsel to go with him to help identify the parties. However, it was Everheart and Gerren who joined up in Fort Worth with detectives Gaines, Kennedy and Waits, who were convinced that Underwood was Tom Nixon. Gerren, however, was later credited with saying that he personally knew Underwood could not have been involved in the Union Pacific robbery because he knew Underwood had spent the night at Jim Hall's ranch in Denton County on September 16 or 17. The deputy must certainly have informed his companions of that fact. The five took the train to San Antonio, arriving there about 6:00 p.m. on an evening in the first week of December. After taking hotel rooms, they immediately spread out to look for their prey and learned that the men they were looking for had arrived in town on horseback some two hours before they arrived.[42]

Everheart said that he and Waits saw Underwood on the street talking to some other men, but rather than arrest him right then, Everheart suggested that perhaps they had better return to the hotel, where he had a warrant for Underwood for cattle theft. If Underwood was arrested for cattle theft rather than for being "Nixon," his confederates might present themselves to try to have him released. Gerren would claim, however, that he had found Underwood but, before he could arrest him, Everheart demanded the warrant then went personally to talk with Underwood and released him without executing the arrest warrant. Gerren claimed that Everheart later told him that he

Texas Ranger
J.L. "Lee" Hall.
(From Raymond,
Captain Lee Hall of Texas.)

wanted to wait until the gang was all together; instead, Underwood disappeared with Bass and Jackson.[43]

Detective Gaines sent a telegram to Lieutenant J.L. "Lee" Hall, commander of the Texas Ranger Special Troops, and Hall left Austin on December 5 for San Antonio.[44] Telegraphing from Austin to Ranger Sergeant A.L. Parrott at Cuero to meet him, Hall reached San Antonio to find that the suspected robbers had been there two days earlier but, because of the "mismanagement" of the investigation, had not been arrested, and no one knew what direction they had taken. Hall nosed around during the day and developed information that led him to believe that the men had gone to Uvalde. Parrott and two rangers reported to him in San Antonio on December 7. That evening Parrott was walking down a San Antonio street with Everheart looking for any of the Bass party when a prostitute, later alleged to be a "mistress" of Nathan Underwood, called to them from across the street, "Where is Tom and Tony?" The two crossed to talk to her. When Everheart pretended that he didn't know who "Tom" was, she replied, "That is too thin." She said that Gerren, who had visited her, had told her who Everheart was. She pulled open Everheart's vest, exposing the pistols he was carrying, telling him that Gerren had told her he would have his weapons there. She talked about Joel Collins, Bass, and the others and offered to tell where they had gone for $150. Gerren would later label this story as false.[45]

A.L. Parrott was a unique Texas Ranger about whom little is known. An itinerant photographer, he joined Captain Leander McNelly's ranger unit at Burton, Texas, on July 26, 1876, and was mustered into the reorganized Special Troops on March 2, 1877. By the end of the month he was a corporal under Lieutenant Hall and a sergeant by May.[46] Parrott would later swear that Gerren flashed a roll of twelve hundred dollars in San Antonio, although Sheriff Egan had given the deputy only three hundred dollars in expense money for the trip. The innuendo, strengthened by Gerren's statements of friendship with Bass, was that he had been bought off and had warned the bandits. Gerren would respond that the presence of the lawmen in San Antonio had been revealed to the undesirable element there by Richard G. "Dick" Head, Jr., of Caldwell County, at the time the general manager for the extensive cattle business of Ellison, DeWees & Bishop of San Antonio, although there is no explanation about Head's involvement in the episode.[47]

On December 7 Lieutenant Hall told a San Antonio newspaper that he was on his way to Corpus Christi to join his men, but that evening he and five men, including Everheart, headed toward Castroville. There they learned that five men they thought were the ones they were after had come through two days earlier saying they were on their way to Uvalde to buy cattle. The next day the lawmen were in the vicinity of Uvalde and heard that the men had continued on west. Unfortunately, another party of men with similar descriptions had come through at the same time, and the lawmen mistakenly followed them to Fort Clark. When they realized their mistake, they returned to Uvalde and found that Underwood and Bass had tried to buy some cattle at a ranch six miles east of the town then had headed for Frio City. Hall turned the detachment over to Sergeant Parrott and returned to San Antonio, then to Cuero. Parrott learned that the men they were pursuing had gone north and were supposed to be at a specific place in

Denton County on December 27. Taking one ranger, he and the detectives left for Denton County.[48]

Ranger Lieutenant Pat Dolan, who commanded Company F at Camp Wood on the Nueces River in Real County, wrote Major John Jones on December 12.

> About a week ago three of the Omaha train robbers passed through Uvalde traveling West Sam Bass-Jack Davis-Tom Nixon by name[.] there were four other men with them[.] they were seen to count ($19,500.00) nine-teen thousand five hundred dollars in '77 Gold in Fort Worth[.] paid for all purchases in 77 Gold there and on their route they avoided Austin and San Antonio[.] all the above information I learned from a Mr. Farmer a Deputy sheriff of Tarrant co who trailed them to Uvalde where he and the Deputy sheriff of Uvalde co joined and came to my camp and asked assistance[.] I let them have Sergt. R. Jones and seven men.[49]

The next day Dolan again sent a telegraph to Jones stating that three of the "Omaha train robbers" were supposed to be in the neighborhood of Eagle Pass or had crossed into Mexico. On December 10, Dolan had sent out Sergeant Jones with seven men, accompanied by Deputy Farmer from Tarrant County and the deputy from Uvalde County, and the scout covered some 275 miles before it returned to camp on December 21.[50] This message may have been what brought Hall back to San Antonio on December 15, perhaps to confer about the troublesome train robbers.[51]

Bass would later say that he, Underwood and Jackson were in San Antonio "on a general carousal" for a good time and did not know that Gerren and Everheart were after them. He said that Jackson did run into Gerren on the street one day, but they did not leave on account of the officers. Gerren also claimed that while he and Everheart were out on the street, Jackson spot-ted them, mounted his horse, and alerted the remainder of his party hidden in a wagon yard.[52]

Bass had eluded capture again, but the lawmen were not about to give up.

-VIII-
HOLDUP AT ALLEN STATION

B ass, Underwood and Jackson, unaware of the chaos among the lawmen that their jaunt to San Antonio and the countryside west of there had caused, rode leisurely north toward Denton County. Perhaps in need of some excitement, the three hatched the idea of robbing a stagecoach. They stopped in the bottoms of Mary's Creek, which flows southeasterly from Parker County into Tarrant County, at a spot about nine miles west of Fort Worth, and waited by the road for the Concho stage which ran between Cleburne and Fort Worth.

At about one Saturday morning, December 22, 1877, the eastbound stage finally made its appearance. Recent heavy rains and the resulting high water had delayed its schedule.[1] Inside the coach were only two passengers, English-born drummer George Mellersh, forty-one,[2] and Charles F. Shield, twenty-three, a merchant from Coleman County.[3] As the stagecoach slowly rumbled through the muddy creek bottoms, the three bandits called out to the driver to halt and ordered the passengers at gunpoint to get out of the coach. While Underwood and Jackson covered him, Bass ordered Mellersh and Shield to hand over their valuables. The two men surrendered about twenty dollars each, but Mellersh had both three hundred dollars and a fine gold watch hidden in his trousers. Mellersh was apparently a gifted salesman and implored the road agents to leave him with at least enough money to eat breakfast. Generously, Bass returned one dollar to each of the men. The bandits made a comment that there should be a law prohibiting "such poor trash" from traveling then allowed the stagecoach to continue its journey. As in the Black Hills, Bass and his companions thus continued to be less-than-unsuccessful at the stagecoach robbing business.

The three rode after the coach to Fort Worth, where they stayed overnight. Three "suspicious looking parties" were seen at the El Paso Hotel after daylight, but because there was no means of identifying them, the local officers chose not to disturb them.[4]

Bass, Underwood and Jackson left Fort Worth on December 23 and likely went on to the hideout at Cove Hollow. With Christmas nearing, Underwood went to spend some time with his family, at that time living in Wise County immediately to the west of Denton County.

Everheart and Waits, in the meantime, had returned from the pursuit to Fort Clark and rejoined Gaines and Kennedy in San Antonio, as well as Sergeant Parrott and a ranger identified as John McNally.[5] Gaines and Kennedy, who had remained behind in San Antonio, had picked up information that Underwood's party had gone north to Sherman in Grayson County, not far from the border with the Indian Territory. The detectives and rangers arrived in Sherman on the evening of Saturday, December 23, and there learned where Underwood's family was staying in Wise County. The party rode westward on horseback all day Monday and arrived within five miles of Underwood's place about four in the morning on Christmas day. The men set up camp to rest until that evening, intending to catch their unsuspecting prey with his family.[6]

Underwood arrived at the Wise County house at about eleven o'clock on the morning of Christmas day. He found that, in addition to his family, there were others there and a wedding was scheduled for that evening. The groom and the preacher had not yet arrived, and preparations were made for the ceremony and celebration. The mood was jovial; no one suspected the proximity of the lawmen.

At about five o'clock that evening the lawmen, in one report accompanied by a "Deputy Hardy" of Wise County, decided to make their move and saddled up as darkness began to fall. They rode down the road toward the house at a dead run, stopping within a half mile of the house, hitching their horses and proceeding the rest of the way on foot. By now it was nearing seven o'clock and the wedding party, still awaiting the arrival of the groom and preacher, was having a lively dance to the tune of a local fiddler. The lawmen quietly surrounded the house and, when all were in place, called out to the people in the house and Underwood to "come out and give up." About a dozen men and women flew out of the house, but Underwood, armed with a Winchester rifle and a pistol, ran upstairs and barricaded himself.

Outside, no one would acknowledge Underwood's presence in the house, but the lawmen, fiercely brandishing their weapons, threatened to burn down the house. When they went so far as to throw a few gallons of coal oil on the house, the members of the party acknowledged Underwood's presence. The lawmen called out to Underwood who, through a window, refused to surrender, afraid that they would hang him. Underwood denied that he was Tom Nixon, but Everheart told him that there was a man with him, Waits, who would swear that Underwood was one of the train robbers. Underwood surveyed his situation, determined that there was no escape, and finally relented, telling them he would come down when it was daylight. The lawmen agreed, settling in for the remainder of the night to guard against an escape attempt.

While the lawmen were waiting, they heard the sound of approaching horses. Waits and Deputy Hardy, not sure who would be coming, went to the road to greet the three newcomers. As the first rider approached the officers in the darkness, they called out "Halt! Throw up your hands!" The lead rider halted, but in the darkness the officers thought they saw him reaching for a weapon and leaped for cover behind a nearby wagon. The other two riders unhesitatingly whirled their horses and raced for safety. The lead rider had briefly said something in response to the command, but then he turned his horse to make a dash for it and the officers sent six rifle balls after him. Waits and Hardy returned to the house, only to encounter the sobbing bride who had recognized the preacher's voice. Her future husband had been one of the three riders, who must have thought that they were amidst thieves and murderers.[7]

The next morning, as promised, Underwood came downstairs and surrendered. He was handcuffed and taken to Sherman, where the party arrived at eleven o'clock Wednesday evening. At seven Friday morning, December 28, Underwood started north on the train, closely guarded by detectives Gaines, Kennedy and Waits. Close to midnight on Saturday they arrived in Omaha, and Underwood was temporarily held in the city jail.

Underwood, interviewed the next morning by reporters, stoutly denied that he was Nixon or that he had ever been in

Ogallala. He admitted that he knew Nixon by reputation but said that Nixon was a Canadian. Underwood said that he had met Joel Collins and Bill "Heffridge" in Dallas, where Collins had a saloon and Heffridge was barkeeper. He also admitted meeting Sam Bass near San Antonio and riding north with him one day. Underwood said that he did not know what had become of Bass, but that Bass had money with him; however, it was currency, not gold. He claimed that he refused to surrender to the lawmen because he knew there was a warrant for him for carrying a pistol, and he was afraid that the men would hang him.

M.F. Leach arrived in Omaha and also interviewed Underwood on Sunday morning. After a long talk with the prisoner, Leach told the press that Underwood greatly resembled Nixon "except perhaps in the eyes." Underwood's eyes were black while Nixon's were blue, he said. Also, Nixon was cleanshaven except for a small moustache and was neat in appearance. He described Underwood as having a heavy moustache and a slovenly appearance. But Underwood's "motions, his gait, the shaking of his head, etc., are the same as those of Nixon." Leach was not convinced that this was Nixon, but Waits believed it was.

Union Pacific Assistant General Superintendent James T. Clark, a forty-six-year-old Ohioan, made available his private car, and at noon Sunday Underwood was taken from Omaha to Ogallala accompanied by Clark, Waits, Deputy Sheriff Dave Burley and M.F. Leach. Although it had been planned to keep the prisoner in Omaha for a few days, railroad officials were concerned that a writ of habeas corpus would be filed to gain his release before he could be positively identified as Nixon.[8]

On Monday, December 31, after a stop in Ogallala where no one came forward to identify him, Underwood was taken before a justice of the peace at Lodge Pole in Cheyenne County. He was bound over for trial at the next term of court at Sidney in February, and his bail was fixed at an astounding $100,000. The judge ordered him to be confined initially in the Dawson County Jail at Plum Creek, not far from Kearney, because jails west of there were not considered secure enough.[9] On January 5 Underwood was transferred to the Buffalo County Jail at

Kearney.[10] Simultaneously, *Hands Up!*, a book written by Al Sorenson, city editor of the *Omaha Daily Bee*, was published by the news agency of Barkalow Brothers, which detailed the Union Pacific robbery and its aftermath up to the death of Berry. The book was released for circulation by newsboys on trains, and it was anticipated that thousands would be sold.[11]

In Texas, Bass and Jackson moved their headquarters from Cove Hollow in Cooke County to the cross timbers below Denton, a densely wooded region known as Green Hills on Hickory Creek. People who lived in the area were acquainted with the two, who certainly treated the local residents civilly, and these folks could be counted on to provide harbor if danger was present. There were rumors that Bass had been involved in the Union Pacific robbery, but there being no evidence other than rumor nor any warrants for him in the hands of the authorities, no active measures were taken to apprehend him. This said, the following contemporary account was probably closer to the truth.

> A freebooter, with ten thousand dollars in ready cash at his command, is apt to prove a great demoralizer to any community not steeled in moral integrity. As he passes here and there among his friends and neighbors, with a pocket full of gold pieces which he deals out with a free hand, buying without pricing and loaning without hesitation, he soon becomes such a convenience and desideratum that men of easy morals and scant conscience do not care to see him driven out of the country or lugged off to jail.[12]

Perhaps because of the gold, a number of stories about Sam Bass in the Denton area would be told many years later, some based in fact and others in myth. Johnny Hudson said that Scott Mayes often took gold coins from Bass to convert into currency. Mayes once asked Hudson to go with him to a creek near the county jail where he hid six hundred dollars in gold given to him by Bass that Mayes was not able to convert but was afraid to be caught with. He looked to Hudson for some advice as to what to do, but Hudson had no suggestions. The money was left down by the creek and they returned to Mayes' saloon and pool business, and Hudson never found out what happened to it.[13]

Mayes, almost twenty, owned his own saloon and bowling parlor in Denton, located two blocks west of the square. There is some evidence, however, that out of friendship Bass was behind the purchase and let Mayes run it for him. Mayes' father, Robert, would tell a newspaper in April that "Scotty" Mayes "keeps a saloon for Sam Bass."[14]

Bass and Jackson camped around Green Hills for about six weeks, one night again at Cove Hollow, then returned to their Hickory Creek camp. They stopped in Denton at about eleven o'clock at night in front of Tom Wheeler's[15] saloon and called out to him for a bottle of whiskey. Wheeler brought Bass and Jackson the bottle they requested, but Wheeler had a keen memory and reminded Bass that he owed him three dollars for drinks that he had four years before. Bass paid off the amount, commenting that he had plenty of money now; then he and Jackson, in a fit of exuberance, rode leisurely off while firing their pistols in the air.

They were spotted by Deputy Tom Gerren, who ordered them to halt. Replying with a volley from their pistols, Bass and Jackson sped off with Gerren in hot pursuit. A "lively skirmish" ensued until Gerren ran out of ammunition, and the two free spirits returned to their camp in the breaks of Hickory Creek.[16] Actually, this episode of Gerren's chase is contrary to the reputation that Gerren had among the townsfolk. Both Bill Fry and Scott Mayes talked of the boys' having a good laugh when Bass would run a "windy" on Gerren. If Bass were in some fight or other disturbance and the law was notified, Mayes said that Gerren would always wait until Bass had been gone about a half hour before starting after him. Of course, he would return empty-handed saying that his horse had given out.[17] Likely because of the fiasco between Gerren and Sheriff Everheart in San Antonio, coupled with the general dislike of the man around Denton, Sheriff Egan fired Gerren as his deputy at the end of December.[18]

Another episode allegedly involving Bass concerned an attempt to hijack a merchant carrying a payroll, although the time period is unknown. According to this tale, retail drygoods merchant Henry Hill[19] was building a gin in Denton County and went to Dallas for money to meet his payroll and other expenses. He returned from Dallas to Lewisville, where the railroad ended, and retrieved his horse from the livery stable for the ride to Denton. The plan was for Bass and two local brothers, John and Harvey Slade,[20] to wait in heavy timber north of Lewisville and intercept him.

As Hill rode toward Denton, the three would-be robbers called for him to halt and deliver. Instead Hill spurred his horse and made a run for it, the bandits in pursuit. One shot downed Hill's horse, and he jerked off his saddle bags and ran for cover at a nearby cabin. Rather than risk being seen, the three road agents gave up the chase and rode off.[21] No documentation to corroborate this story could be located.

Another uncorroborated episode attributed to Bass occurred in Dallas. According to this story, related in 1948, Bass had ordered a pair of boots from Dallas bootmaker O.P. Levlon shortly before Levlon got into a dispute about his "loud talking" with a Dallas policeman who lived nearby. The officer threatened to run him in; Levlon replied that the officer wasn't man enough and, by the way, why didn't the officer come over and pick up Sam Bass when he was there? The policeman threatened to shoot Bass on sight. When Bass came to pick up his boots, Levlon sent his son, with Bass' permission, to notify the officer, but the policeman didn't come. The next day, when the officer denied he had received the word, the bootmaker called him a liar and the fight was on. He beat the officer badly, as the story goes, and the family had to move to Arkansas for three years before they could return.[22] The date of this incident, if it occurred, is unknown.

Bass and Jackson, tiring of camp life interspersed with occasional evening trips into Denton, decided on another stage robbery. Returning to Mary's Creek on the Tarrant-Parker County line on the morning of Saturday, January 26, 1878, they picked a spot in a branch about a mile west of Mary's Creek and the stage station near there. Wearing handkerchiefs over their faces with eye holes cut out, they waited for the Weatherford and Fort Worth stage. A young man walking westward along the road to Weatherford descended a small ravine only to be confronted by the two masked men, who jumped out from behind some thick brush and leveled a rifle and a pistol at him. He was ordered off the road, and they threatened that if he uttered any sound or tried to make a break, they would riddle him with "peanuts and corn." They told their prisoner that they planned to rob the stage but they bore him no ill will and the delay in his trip would be only temporary.

Very shortly the stage could be heard coming toward them from Fort Worth. It was a beautiful morning and, with good roads all the way, the driver cracked his whip with authority and the horses moved spiritedly. Aboard were five passengers: Dr. Styles Kennedy of St. Louis Springs, Michigan; G.W. Clements of Tuscaloosa, Alabama, who had moved to Texas; Valentine Werner of Fort Worth, who had designed the Tarrant County Courthouse; Benjamin S. Williams, a thirty-two-year-old Mississippi-born farmer from Breckinridge in Stephens County; and a man named LeCompte from Leavenworth, Kansas. Williams rode outside the coach next to the driver.

As the stage rounded a steep bank and had to slow, Bass and Jackson stepped out and demanded that it halt. The driver pulled up the horses and the passengers were ordered out. Williams climbed down to the ground, but the driver was allowed to remain in his seat. Werner stepped out of the coach first, imploring them, "For God's sake, don't shoot." LeCompte, right behind him, repeated that request, followed by Kennedy and Clements. Bass lined up the five and hurriedly searched them. Werner gave up a gold watch and thirty-five dollars, while Clements gave up a new Elgin watch with a hunting case, and Dr. Kennedy surrendered a ladies' watch. The two robbers reportedly stole between four and five hundred dollars. Williams told them that he was only a hard-working man, and Bass returned five dollars to him so that he could pay hotel bills. However, the joke was on Bass because Williams had four hundred dollars stuffed into a glove that he carelessly carried and which Bass overlooked. The robbers even asked the driver to contribute if he could.

The passengers were ordered back aboard the coach, and the driver started the horses on their journey once more. After

the coach had traveled a hundred yards or so the robbers disappeared, no doubt mounted and headed north. Williams, who
had been a deputy sheriff in Hunt County, Missouri, opined
that one of the robbers might be a Missouri robber named
Hopkins that he had once jailed there. In Weatherford, suspicion focused on a man named Sogden or Soden, an escaped
robber from Fort Worth, whose sister lived only seven miles
from the robbery scene.[23] According to Hogg, Bass and Jackson
realized only seventy dollars from the robbery plus the three
watches, but Bass was said to have remarked, "Well, this is the
best haul I ever made out of a stage, and I've tapped nine of 'em
so far. There's mighty poor pay on stages, generally, though."[24]

Bass and Jackson returned to their Hickory Creek camp
south of Denton then went to Cove Hollow. They decided to
see if they could do better with the stage running between
Sherman in Grayson County and Gainesville in Cooke County
north of Denton. Riding to Sherman, they traced the stage
route westward to Gainesville, selecting a likely holdup site
about twelve miles east of Gainesville between Callisburg and
Whitesboro. For some reason they backed off from any robbery,
and Bass was quoted as saying, "The dung got up in my neck
and I didn't strike it." Perhaps the meager returns for such a
risky enterprise caused him some hesitation. The one successful
criminal enterprise in his experience was the Union Pacific robbery, and very likely he and Joel Collins had discussed train robberies in Texas. Bass and Jackson seriously considered robbing a
train and began to cast about for some more men to help them
pull it off.[25]

The capture of Underwood as Tom Nixon did not deter others from coming after Bass. The Union Pacific reward was a
great lure. Even as Underwood languished in the Kearney,
Nebraska, jail, two would-be detectives in Dallas joined forces in
December and hatched a scheme to track down Bass. William
"Billy" Scott was a twenty-four-year-old former Dallas deputy
sheriff;[26] the other young sleuth was E.W. "Jack" Smith about
whom little is known but who apparently bankrolled the
scheme.[27] Scott and Smith knew of the close relationship
between Bass and Joel Collins' family and fully expected that
Bass would seek out the family for assistance. Their plan was for

Scott to become friends with the Collins family and ingratiate himself until he could learn what they needed to know.[28] It would take a few months before the effort would pay off.

In January, according to Reed and Tate, Bass allegedly took pen in hand (or someone took pen in hand for him) and sent two more postcards to the hapless John West in Dallas. Both postmarked January 31, 1878, the first card said,

> You coat thief you thought I was gone but I come again your time is at Hand the pinchers is made to pull your nails your days are numbered your time of shooting in Houses is over you must atone for it you shal have Justice ant be afreid Iv been gone but I've come again prepare thy carcass for an unknown world your time is near at hand
>
> Sam Bass

The second card was equally threatening.

> _____ you _____thief Weas again I'v come at time to destroy prepare thyself for thy days are finish the sentence is assessed you know the ground you stand on remembers that justice overtakes ___ all learn it well Steal slowly die
>
> Sam Bass[29]

Bass and Jackson looked around for men they thought suitable to be a part of their gang of train robbers. One of the first was Seaborn or Seaburn "Sebe" Barnes,[30] a young Texas-born cowboy who worked in Denton for potter Augustus H. "Gus" Serren.[31] Not much is known about Barnes' background, but he was of a "wandering disposition," according to Hogg, who described him as

> rather slender of build, light complexion, had a large prominent nose of the Roman "variety," dark hazel eyes overhung by rather a heavy brow. The upper portion of his face was broad, while from his cheek bones downward it receded rapidly, leaving the region of his mouth

and chin disproportionately narrow. His neck was
unusually long, and his throat marked with a huge
Adam's apple. With such a physiognomy his appearance
could not fail to be remarkable, and it is said that
withal he was not ungainly or unhandsome. He was,
however, like all of Bass' confederates, illiterate and
rough in his demeanor. . . .[32]

Two years earlier Barnes had been acquitted of assault to
murder by a Fort Worth jury; like Frank Jackson, he was disposed to the adventure promised by joining Bass' fledgling
gang.[33]

Another member recruited at this time into Bass' circle was
Tom Spotswood, a widower with a glass right eye who had reportedly killed men in Missouri and Texas and who lived in Denton
County.[34] Apparently ready to add train robbing to his repertoire
of crimes, he joined Bass, Jackson and Barnes in laying their
plans. Up to this time there had never been a full-fledged train
robbery in Texas, although there had certainly been thefts from
express and baggage cars. Three masked men in June 1875 had
boarded the Houston & International train at Houston intending to seize the express car safe, but the railroad vice president
was on board and "throttled" the leader of the gang, a man
named Brooks, and the other two were also captured.[35]

The gang scouted around North Central Texas for a likely
target and settled on the tiny station at Allen in Collin County,
about eight miles southwest of McKinney and twenty-five miles
north of Dallas. The small community had been established in
1870 by a purchasing agent for the Houston and Texas Central
Railway and named two years later for former Texas Attorney
General Ebenezer Allen, who helped promote the railroad. It
acquired its own post office in 1876.[36]

On the evening of Thursday, February 21, 1878, Bass and
his men camped near Allen. He sent Spotswood into the small
town to find out the exact time the train would arrive.
Spotswood went into thirty-one-year-old A.J. "Bud" Newman's
saloon, passing himself off as a "sporting man" and asking
where in town he could gamble. He asked Newman casually
when the southbound train would arrive and was told about

The site at Allen, Texas, of the former depot of the Houston & Texas
Central Railroad, where Bass and his gang committed the first successful
train robbery in Texas on February 22, 1878. (Author photo).

eight o'clock in the evening.[37]

On Friday night the southbound Train No. 4 of the
Houston & Texas Central, composed of two or three sleeping
cars, a passenger car, a mail car and an express car, with 175
passengers, left Denison in Grayson County about an hour
late. The county's sheriff, Bill Everheart, was in Sherman recovering from a bout with rheumatism that kept him confined to
his room for several weeks.[38] Aboard one of the sleeping cars
was Major J. Waldo, the general freight agent for the H&TC, a
forty-six-year-old Texan who lived with his family in Houston, as
well as Oscar G. Murray, a thirty-one-year-old nephew of
Superintendent George Nichols, who was from Connecticut
and who was the general freight agent for the Galveston,
Houston & Henderson Railroad. Officials also aboard from
other railroad lines were J.C. McCoy, an official of the
International & Great Northern Railroad, and John Newman,
a twenty-five-year-old, German-born mail route agent for the
Texas and Pacific Railroad who lived in Houston next to the
household of Major Waldo. After a stop in McKinney, the train

continued south to Allen and pulled into the station at about nine o'clock.[39]

No sooner had the train stopped at the station just to the east of the small town, where Dishon Street stopped at the railroad tracks, than an unmasked man armed with a sixshooter climbed up in the engine cab and told engineer William Sullivan and the fireman to step off. The fireman was directed to the rear of the express car while Sullivan was held under guard near the engine. At the express car one of the robbers told the fireman, "Partner, we don't wish to hurt you or any one else; all we want is money out of this car, and we are going to have it." Inside the express car was messenger James L.A. Thomas, who had the door open for a delivery to Allen. The first he was aware of the robbery attempt was when a voice called out through the open door, "Throw up your hands and give us the money." At first Thomas thought it was a joke, but he was quick to see the men were serious. He pulled a pistol, fired a quick shot at the robber on the ground, and retreated from the open door back into the car, taking cover behind some boxes and firing three more shots. The robber returned the fire with a shot, missing the messenger. Thomas believed that he hit the robber.

In the mail car the route agent heard the shots and looked out the door to see the bandits at the express car. One of the robbers fired a shot in his direction, and he immediately closed up his car and put out the light. The robbers fired three more shots into the express car without effect. Frustrated, the robbers threatened to set the express car on fire, but Thomas stayed inside with his pistol aimed at the opening. The bandits ordered engineer Sullivan back into the cab and, after the cars behind the express car were disconnected, had him pull the rest of the train, with the express car, forward some sixty feet. With the engineer back on the ground under guard, the other robbers again called on Thomas to come out or they would burn him out, promising not to injure him if he gave up. Thomas had only one cartridge left in his pistol, and his cartridge box was in open view of the robbers so he couldn't get to it. He finally was compelled to surrender, and two men leaped up in the car and disarmed him. Thomas noticed that the unmasked robber with a revolver pointed at him had a strange right eye that was larger than his left one.

In the sleeping cars Conductor Brown heard the gunfire, briefly stepped off the train, then alerted the railroad executives and other passengers of the holdup. Their immediate thought was to hide their watches, money and other valuables. They then made an effort to gather weapons but could find only one toy pistol. It was determined later that there was only one pistol among all of the passengers. Major Waldo started to leave the sleeping car and walk to the express car but returned to hide the watch that he was carrying. One passenger, Maryland-born Will Apperson, thirty,[40] a saloon keeper at the Crutchfield House Hotel in Dallas, tried to rouse some of the other passengers to resist, but without weapons none of the passengers was disposed to show fight. Reportedly, but quite unlikely, it was said that one of the robbers rushed through the passenger coach to intimidate the passengers and dissuade then from resisting by hollering that there were from fifty to sixty robbers.

Aboard the express car, with Spotswood's cocked pistol pointed at him, Thomas unlocked the safe and stepped back while Bass removed six or seven packages of money, overlooking two packages of gold consigned to San Antonio. Not searching the car any further, the two robbers jumped to the ground then sat by the track and opened two of the packages that contained silver coins. One of the robbers expressed the idea of going through the passenger cars, but the others decided not to do anything more. The robbers were satisfied with the coins in the two sacks and returned Thomas' unloaded pistol and lantern to him. One man, later believed to be the gang's leader, took all of the money, walked around the engine, then ran off on foot in a westerly direction toward where the horses were hitched, followed by the others.[41] Once the four bandits had ridden off, the train was recoupled and resumed its journey toward Dallas.

As the train pulled into Union Depot in Dallas and passengers started to get off, an unidentified plainclothed officer, probably a Dallas policeman, directed that they get back on the train because he was looking for some criminal that he expected to be on the train. The alarmed passengers, thinking that perhaps more robbers were at hand, once again stuffed money and watches into their boots and other hiding places.[42] It is not clear whether or not the actions of the officer were in response to the following telegram sent after the robbery, likely from Allen, to the city marshal of Dallas, William F. Morton.[43]

> Train No. 4 was robbed at Allen tonight by a party of six men. Express car robbed. See conductor of train and get particulars.
>
> T.A. Quinlan
> Engineer and Superintendent

This was followed by another telegram at about midnight advising Marshal Morton that a special car would be made available for him by 1:00 a.m. to carry men up the railroad to start pursuit. Marshal Morton and some policemen headed for Allen and tried to find a trail, but their initial search turned up nothing. The authorities initially speculated that the Allen robbers were the same men who had rescued a Louisiana murder suspect being taken to Fort Worth from Weatherford on Thursday afternoon.

J. MacCulloch, an agent for the Texas Express Company, sent out a description of Spotswood, who was labeled as the leader of the gang, "...about thirty-five years old, five feet eleven inches high, light blue eyes, right eye disfigured and larger than the left, fair complexion, light colored mustache and chin whiskers of three or four weeks growth, light long hair, rode a gray pacing pony." Another man, who rode a "fine bay, fast walking horse," was described as about six feet tall, about thirty years old, no whiskers, dark mustache, hair and eyes, and a very swarthy complexion.[44]

On the day after the robbery, Texas Governor R.B. Hubbard wrote the H&TC Railroad that he was offering a five hundred-dollar reward for the arrest and conviction of each of the six robbers alleged to have been at Allen.[45] Both the HT&C Railroad and the Texas Express Company also offered a five hundred-dollar reward, bringing the reward total to nine thousand dollars.[46] Perhaps influenced by the response of the railroad and the express company, Governor Hubbard immediately upped the state's reward offer to one thousand dollars per robber.[47] At the same time, the governor sent Captain Lee Hall to Houston to confer with railroad officials and to arrange for transportation of rangers to the north to start pursuit.[48]

The initial reports of from six to twelve robbers exaggerated the number of bandits who held up the Allen train. Major John Jones later confirmed that there were four robbers: Bass, Jackson, Barnes and Spotswood, and Bass himself allegedly confirmed there were only four men.[49] When Bass and his men finally stopped after leaving Allen, they had a chance to get a closer look at their loot, unaware that they had missed the HT&C payroll train by a few hours. Newspapers reported that the gang took a total of $1,470 in cash—$910 from Thomas that belonged to the railroad, $500 belonging to C.P. Smith of Dallas, $60 owned by R. Perkins of Round Rock—and a package of papers worth $1,400 on consignment to S.W. Lomax or John Hays in Fort Worth.[50] A later indictment stated that the bandits took $1,600 in cash— a sack containing $140 in silver, a package containing $55 in silver and $1,405 in currency—and the papers worth $1,400.[51] Bass would later be attributed as stating that the four equally split $1,280.[52]

While Texas officials scrambled to respond to the startling robbery, Bass, Jackson and Barnes returned to their Hickory Creek camp south of Denton, and Spotswood returned to his family at Pilot Point in northeast Denton County. The three camped for several days to see if anyone would come after them, then rode to the hideout at Cove Hollow in Cooke County. Bass traded his worn horse with Jim Murphy, giving him an additional twenty dollars for the difference in value.[53] The money actually realized in the Allen robbery would not go very far, after being split four ways, but the yield certainly exceeded any of Bass' stage robberies.

-IX-
THE HUTCHINS ROBBERY

L ee Hall went to Houston and directed Sergeant
Parrott and four men, including James E. Lucy,[1] to
meet him there on Monday, February 25. The
next morning Parrott and the four men took a train north to
Allen to begin their investigation. From Allen the rangers went
to nearby McKinney where the express company provided
horses for their scout.[2]

Even before the rangers had begun to organize their investigation, however, Texas Express Agent W.K. Cornish,[3] tena-
ciously protective of his company's assets, immediately left his
Dallas office when he heard about the robbery and went north
to Allen. Recruiting express messenger James Thomas to ride
with him, the two rode west after the trail of the robbers. About
eighteen miles from Allen they ran into a man who had sold seventy-five cans of feed corn on Saturday to a man who fit the
description of one of the robbers and who was accompanied by
another man called "Charlie." Cornish and Thomas likely
learned at this time that the man's name was Spotswood. With
this information they rode on to Denton to alert the local
authorities.[4]

At two o'clock on Tuesday afternoon, February 26,
Cornish, Thomas and their Denton posse, which included
Deputy Sheriff George W. Drennan, a twenty-eight-year-old
Kentuckian,[5] went to where Spotswood lived with his family in
the bottoms of the north fork of Elm Creek. Hiding in the
dense undergrowth until daylight on Wednesday, they rushed
the house only to find that Spotswood had left for Cooke
County, north of Pilot Point. Cornish, Thomas and Drennan
rode on to Pilot Point in northeastern Denton County, planning to get fresh horses there before pushing on to Cooke
County. As the three walked from the livery stable, they saw
Spotswood riding into town in a wagon with a small boy beside
him. With cocked pistols aimed at him, Spotswood immediately

surrendered, his son crying hysterically as a result of the sudden rough commands of the armed men.

Although Spotswood was now cleanshaven, Thomas had no difficulty in identifying him as the robber who had held him at gunpoint. Spotswood stoutly denied that he was involved in the robbery, and his captors found only eleven dollars and change on him. At about three o'clock in the afternoon Spotswood was taken to McKinney, where the party arrived Wednesday night, and saloonkeeper Bud Newman and others who saw him on the night of the robbery also identified him. On Thursday morning, February 28, a bond of $2,500 on a charge of robbery was set at a preliminary hearing, and he was locked up in the Collin County jail. Should he make bail, the authorities had readied a second warrant charging him with assault with intent to kill because of his involvement with the shooting at Thomas during the robbery.[6]

The train robbery led to statewide reflection upon the methods of investigating such crimes. The *Dallas Daily Herald*, which felt that open robbery by common criminals was less objectionable than robbery by large corporations, called for a law that would require express and stage companies to underwrite a strong guard to escort money shipments, the guard to be organized by the state. Even better, the newspaper implored, the state should organize a "sufficient and competent corps of detectives, who would pervade the haunts" of such robbers.[7] As an interesting coincidence, but unrelated to the Allen robbery, on Saturday, March 2, a group of Denton County citizens met at Elizabethtown in the southwest part of the county near the Tarrant County line. Concerned about "certain organized bands of thieves, villains and cut-throats running at large" stealing horses and committing other crimes, the men formed a vigilante group known as "The Gold-Backs" to work with the civil authorities to apprehend and punish horse thieves especially. Captain of the group was Peter Clay Withers, who had been partners with Henderson Murphy at their saloon in Denton.[8]

When Bass heard about Spotswood's arrest, he was disgusted that Spotswood had tried to return too soon to his home, which was only some fifteen miles from Allen.[9] On March 5, Captain Hall telegraphed Adjutant General William Steele that Ranger Jim Lucy had been instrumental in arresting Spotswood, although he didn't say how. He said that the prospect for the arrest of "the others" was good and that the rangers had them located but did not have sufficient evidence to make an arrest.[10]

Although there was yet no idea that Bass was responsible for the Allen robbery, several area lawmen contacted Governor Hubbard's office about the existence of a formal requisition on Texas by Nebraska for Bass, Jack Davis and Tom Nixon for the Union Pacific robbery. Superintendent Morsman had apparently sent telegrams to local officials stating that Grayson County Sheriff William Everheart had state warrants for their arrest and that Nebraska's requisition was on file in the Texas governor's office. Of course, the telegrams emphasized the pending reward. Fort Worth City Marshal Timothy I. "Long-Haired Jim" Courtright requested warrants, as did former Denton County Deputy Sheriff Tom Gerren. The governor was not aware of any such requisition in Austin.[11] On March 14 Ranger Jim Lucy telegraphed the adjutant general from Sherman that he and the other rangers had just returned from scouting Denton County and thought that they had the "parties" located.[12]

In the meantime, Bass, Jackson and Barnes laid low, waiting to see if the lawmen would be coming after them. The furor over the train robbery died down within several weeks, and friends kept them posted as to what was being said in the newspapers. They lounged in the camp on Hickory Creek and soon became bored. Barnes was sick, leaving just Bass and Jackson to plan a new venture. In mid-March they rode back into Dallas County, then followed the H&TC line nine miles south from Dallas to the small station at Hutchins. The community at Hutchins had been settled around 1860 and had become a trading center for settlers along the west bank of the Trinity River. The town was named for H&TC promoter William J. Hutchins when the railroad came through in 1872, the same year it obtained a post office. The town had only about twenty-five buildings, including two or three stores and two railroad depot buildings.[13] The two outlaws observed the lay of the land around the station, the train schedule, and may have even considered pulling a robbery by themselves.[14]

Bass and Jackson returned to their camp in Denton County

A group of Texas Express Company employees, including
Henry "Heck" Thomas (seated center) and Sam Finley (standing left).
(Courtesy Glenn Shirley, Stillwater, Oklahoma).

and found that Barnes had recovered from his illness and was
ready to go. It had only been twenty-four days since the Allen
robbery. On a foggy Monday night, March 18, just before the
arrival at Hutchins of the southbound H&TC train at ten
o'clock, Bass, Jackson and Barnes dashed into the station office
and overpowered the agent. After going through his pockets,
they waited. As the train pulled into the depot, and even before
it stopped, Jackson leaped upon the tender box and pointed his
weapon at the engineer and fireman. When one of them asked
what he wanted, Jackson was supposed to have responded, "We
want money-that's all-and there's no use kicking."

"All right, go ahead, it's no skin off our backs!" was the reply.

The bandits rounded up the station agent, the engineer, the fireman, a black man named Bright Reese who assisted the station agent, and two Dallas tramp printers who had been hitching a ride on the front of the locomotive. Using the six prisoners as a shield, and perhaps recalling the gunfire they had drawn from the express car at Allen, the three robbers moved on the express car. The route agent in the mail car, R. Terrell, was stepping up to the door to throw out a mail bag when a robber ran up pointing a pistol at him. Terrell jumped back, slammed the door shut, and called out to the express messenger that robbers were on the platform. Terrell then put out the light in the car and concealed the registered letter bag and his watch, but he left out five registered packages so that the robbers, if they gained entry, would think that this was all there was.[15]

The express messenger Henry A. "Heck" Thomas,[16] a cousin of express agent James Thomas, would later become a noted lawman himself in the Indian Territory. As the robbers with their human shield came up to the express car, Thomas shut the door and secured it, then extinguished the lights. According to a statement later attributed to Thomas, when the Allen robbery occurred Thomas realized that he also could be held up and prepared some decoy packages that he kept in the way safe. With the robbers now banging on the express car door with axes, Thomas quickly hid four thousand dollars in the stove, leaving a little silver in the safe, and prepared to do battle. As the robbers hacked at the express car door and Thomas aimed his pistol, waiting, the hostages between him and the robbers called out, "Don't shoot; you'll kill us!" Thomas lowered his pistol, unlocked and opened the door, and one of the robbers entered the car. This bandit was later described as about 5' 8", light moustache, twenty-five or twenty-seven years old, "had a care-worn, sallow look," and certainly fit the description of Sam Bass. He found only $384, and the robbers moved on to the mail car where Terrell made no resistance. Here they took five packages containing a total of $232.80.

One of the passengers in a sleeper car, E.L. Ranlett, a twenty-eight-year-old whose father operated a powder and shot warehouse in New Orleans, was almost asleep when a boy ran through the car crying that the train was being robbed. Two other passengers were an army lieutenant, Courtney, and Bingham Trigg, a thirty-eight-year-old Missouri-born lawyer from Austin. The six or eight men in the sleeper scrambled to hide their valuables in every nook and corner. Some of the trainmen called for arms among the passengers. A crowd of men with a few pistols were in a forward car, waiting for the robbers to leave the express car and fully expecting them to come into the passenger cars. The conductor hurriedly sent a brakeman to a nearby house where he borrowed a shotgun and returned to the train.

When it appeared that the robbers had completed looting the express car, one of the passengers opened fire on them even though they had a human shield. The robber in the express car leaped out, and the gang returned fire in the direction of the passengers. A rear car brakeman fired with a double-barrelled shotgun, but only succeeded in hitting Expressman Thomas with a pellet in the neck and another one just under the left eye. It was estimated that some thirty or forty shots were exchanged, but the only other injury was a gunshot wound to the knee of one of the itinerant printers, a man named Edgar. The three robbers retreated, dropping the unopened mail packages they had taken, and headed for the nearby woods where their horses were waiting. They rode off without pursuit.[17]

Some citizens in Hutchins formed a posse but were unable to find the robbers' trail. A telegram to authorities was sent out by the express company and Marshal Morton in Dallas had his officers mount up. He placed guards at the bridge over the Trinity River, at fords in the river, and on all main roads leading into the city, then sent the mounted police out to scour the countryside. Express agent Cornish caught a train to Hutchins so he could personally follow the trail of the robbers.[18] Morton's men returned to Dallas on Tuesday morning, having failed to find any sign of the gang.[19] On Wednesday, March 20, Morton arrested a vagabond, J.H. Himan or Hammond also known as Fakir Joe, because on the morning of the robbery he had been seen in the vicinity of Hutchins. He was later released.[20]

The superintendent of the Texas Express Company, C.T. Campbell, a forty-four-year-old Virginian who lived in Dallas,[21] ordered upwards of three armed guards to be placed in the express cars of all night trains, "fully equipped and armed with the most effective weapons."[22]

One Dallas man concerned about the two train robberies decided that it was time for him to take some action, and he would subsequently be selected to lead a company of rangers against Sam Bass and his men. City Recorder Junius "June" Peak had already accrued an admirable reputation as a deputy sheriff and as city marshal.[23] After the Allen robbery June Peak resigned his position as city recorder and hired on as a detective for the Texas Express Company. Taking with him James McGinley, a thirty-three-year-old Irish stonemason, he quietly left Dallas on March 19, the day after the Hutchins robbery. The two rode into Denton County to gather information on the train robbers. McGinley was somewhat of a notorious character around Dallas who had distinguished himself in June 1870 when, unarmed, he captured the assassin of the city's mayor.[24]

After a few days of exploring the dense thickness of the cross timbers of Denton County, Peak realized that he would need a guide and hired a sixteen-year-old boy named Tommy Stout. One afternoon Peak, McGinley and young Stout stopped at the place of farm laborer Green Hill for water and some rest.[25] Peak did not realize that Hill was an old sporting companion of Sam Bass. Hill, thirty, lived in Denton County with his wife, Sarah. His older brother, Monroe Hill, forty-four, who also farmed in Denton County, had been indicted in June 1874 in Parker County for an 1872 murder there.[26] As Peak and McGinley rested in front of Hill's house, three men rode by, well armed, and Hill told them that it was Bass, Jackson and Barnes, likely headed for Bob Murphy's place. Peak mounted, leaving McGinley behind, and rode after the trio until they turned off the road.

Riding back to Hill's place, Peak told the Stout boy to go to Murphy's place and see if Bass and his men had been there, and if not to stay there for the night then meet him at daylight at Rocky Ford, a small creek nearby. Stout did as instructed and found that the Bass party had not been there. After Stout went to bed, Bass, Barnes and Jackson rode up to Murphy's place, followed shortly by Green Hill. They told the boy that they had

Junius "June" Peak as a young Confederate soldier.
(Courtesy Robert W. Stephens, Dallas, Texas).

Junius "June" Peak. (From Wayne Gard, *Sam Bass*).

been watching him with Peak and McGinley and suggested they did not want to hurt him so he ought to go on home; if he kept riding through the timbers with the two men, he was likely to be killed. The next morning, Stout met with Peak and McGinley, told them what had been said and, as suggested, went home. Peak was now convinced that Green Hill and the Murphys, if not accessories to the train robberies, would at least harbor the gang and provide them with supplies.[27]

Peak went to Pilot Point, where he sent a telegraph to Cornish about what he had found and asking him to send help to make an arrest. Ranger Jim Lucy was in Dallas when the telegraph was received and immediately headed for Denton County. Deputy Sheriffs John W. Spencer[28] and Ashton G. Pryor[29] also left Dallas to go to Denton. Peak, McGinley, Spencer and Pryor failed to spot the robber gang again and returned to Dallas on Sunday, March 24.[30] Others, however, saw the gang, because it was reported that the "festive Sam Bass . . . scouted through" Denton on Wednesday, March 20, firing his pistol as he went, no doubt celebrating the small haul from Hutchins.[31]

The apparent belief among many in Denton County that Sam Bass was not one of the Union Pacific robbers had begun to erode, although folks were slow to make the connection between him and the recent Texas train robberies. But even now, Bass, Jackson and Barnes were thought to be behind the recent attacks, and local newspapers began to treat them as the perpetrators. Sheriff Egan began to consider various plans to nab him, and to assist him he employed Denton deputy sheriff or jail guard William T. Minor.[32]

Egan kept his plan a secret between him, Minor, some deputies, and the U.S. Commissioner in Denton, Alex Robertson.[33] The scheme was for Minor to infiltrate Bass' camp, gain his confidence, and then either lead the gang into a trap or provide Egan with an opportunity to capture them. Minor became fast friends with Scott Mayes, who freely talked about his friendship with Bass, and Mayes reportedly took him on several visits to the outlaw camp.[34]

In early March Henry Underwood, still languishing in the Kearney, Nebraska, jail while authorities pondered whether or not he was Tom Nixon, decided that it was time to leave and broke out. Details are sketchy, the only detailed account being one provided by Hogg likely as a result of stories later told by Underwood. In jail with him were two other prisoners, Manly Caple and a man known as Huckston who went by "Arkansas Johnson." According to Hogg, Huckston's wife had brought the prisoners a bucket of butter that had a false bottom. Hidden in the bucket was a supply of steel saw blades. Underwood also procured an old shoe that someone had kicked off in the cell area. From the sole of the shoe he removed a steel shank that he converted into a saw. A prisoner who had been jailed for some minor offenses was released but left Underwood with additional saw blades and some nitric acid which Underwood used to "soften" the steel bars of the cage in which they were confined. It took about three weeks to break through, Underwood reportedly hiding his tools each day in a small hole in the wall of his cell that was covered by a paper containing jail rules. The cuts in the bars were covered with a dark-colored soap.[35]

According to *Life and Adventures of Sam Bass*, Bass had arranged for one hundred dollars to be sent to Underwood shortly after he was jailed in Nebraska. Underwood was supposed to have provided a released prisoner seven dollars to procure some means of escape. The man returned with a file. Using the file and a watch spring, it took six weeks for Underwood to break through the iron bars.[36]

Finally at about two o'clock on the morning of March 12 or 13, 1878, the prisoners were through the bars and ready to flee. The three men—Underwood, "Arkansas Johnson" and Caple—scrambled through a barbed-wire fence surrounding the jail, appropriated some horses from a stable belonging to a local judge, and headed south for Texas.[37] According to statements attributed later to Underwood, the prisoners were rather skimpily clad for the cold weather. What happened to Caple is unknown, but Underwood and Johnson stuck together. The two had only fifty cents between them, which they promptly spent for whiskey at the first crossroads grocery they came to. In Kansas they broke into an "old lady's larder" and appropriated a cooked and dressed turkey which lasted them for several days. They stole and begged their way back to Texas, arriving in Denton County seventeen days after they had broken out of the jail.[38]

The origins of "Arkansas Johnson" are vague. According to

Life and Adventures of Sam Bass, his true name was John McKean from the Knob Noster community in Johnson County, Missouri. However, Martin in *Sketch of Sam Bass* identified him as an Irishman named Huckston who had viciously murdered a family in Arkansas, although there is no information to corroborate either claim.[39] Johnson was described as a man of heavy build, about 5'8" tall, approximately thirty-five years old, with a ruddy complexion, blue eyes, and light hair. His beard was a "sun-burnt brown," but he was readily distinguished by numerous smallpox scars that pitted his face. According to Hogg, "He was a man of few words, but was truculent as a Comanche, and entirely repulsive in his general appearance and bearing. From the best information that can be obtained of him he was a veritable brute in all but form. . . ."[40]

In the meantime a widespread search for the train robbers continued, and strangers in the Dallas area found themselves suddenly confronted as suspicious characters; a number of "wild arrests" were made based on "reckless reasoning." On Monday, March 25, a "squad of armed men" with Springfield rifles was spotted on the northbound train through Dallas, and it was rumored that the men were soldiers in civilian dress who were on their way to Denton County to look for the robbers.[41] In Ellis County south of Dallas, a man named Samuel West was arrested on suspicion of being one of the robbers. According to reports, he appeared to know a great deal about the train robbery at Hutchins, giving the names of several men that he alleged were the robbers, but no one knew how much stock to put in his statements.[42] Mysteriously, on March 30 Dallas Marshal Morton advertised for the anonymous person who sent him a card to recontact him for an interview, promising not to "arrest or molest him" and to provide protection that he was seeking.[43]

On Sunday, March 24, Tom Gerren, apparently on his own authority, arrested Charles D. Hewitt, a twenty-seven-year-old Texan from Pilot Point in Denton County, alleging that he was involved in the Allen robbery. Hewitt was admittedly a close friend of Tom Spotswood, living only four miles from him. However, Hewitt claimed that he was home on the night of the robbery and could prove it. On March 26 Gerren took his prisoner from Dallas to McKinney, where Spotswood was being held. Hewitt was allegedly identified in Allen as being one of the train robbers, and Gerren returned him to jail at Dallas on March 27.[44] There is no further record of what happened to Hewitt, but he was not charged with any train robbery.

Ranger A. L. Parrott wrote Captain Hall on March 30 from Grayson County on Sheriff Everheart's stationery.

> Dr Sir: Still we toil in hopes of a future reward. We have gained points sufficient to have an idea who the parties are or 2 of them at least. Who the others are we have not yet decided. Parky and Wagner are the ones we have detected. They were seen with Spotswood the morning after the first robbery going in the direction of Hill Town before day. Parky & Wagner lived at Hill Town till a short time before the robbery. They moved west but was seen in the section of Hill Town by other parties about that time. Parky's home is now sixty miles west of Fort Worth and has a sister living on Grape Vine Prairie. I was down there and found that he had been at his sister's about the time of the last robbery. I know the man he is living with west of Fort Worth. We can get other corroborating evidence. Wagner, I don't know his whereabouts. He is in that country some where. Think of starting aft[er] him Parky soon. Corwin has come in; will send him back. We have done lots of riding. Hope it will not always be a failure. There has been several innocent parties arrested. I want the right one before I arrest. It's nearly impossible to get Sam Bass for Tom Gerren who is the damndest rascal of the town. He brags of seeing and knowing all of Basses movements and says he can't be taken out of Denton so long as he is there, etc. McMurray is on the sick list. Had a chill and nothing serious. Please send my money as soon as received care of Everheart.
>
> Give regards to all of the boys.
>
> Respectfully yours,
>
> A.L. Parrott[45]

In Austin, railroad officials alarmed by the two quick train robberies contacted Governor Hubbard and Adjutant General Steele looking for state assistance in the crisis. The governor reminded them in a March 26 letter of an 1871 Texas statute prohibiting the carrying of a pistol on or about the person, saddle or saddle-bags unless on one's own premises or place of business, while "traveling," or unless in fear of imminent deadly attack.[46] The governor pointed out that the carrying of rifles, shotguns, carbines and muskets on passenger or freight trains was perfectly legal and suggested that "short double-barrel shotguns (fitted to be strapped to the shoulder) and cavalry carbines" were more suited to resisting highway robbers than sixshooters. He pledged to offer suitable rewards for such criminals as a means of supporting the civil authorities.[47] A report sent to the governor from Dallas on March 27 tallied the armament available to the two local militia units in that town: the Lamar Rifles had sixty .50 caliber Remington rifles, as did the Stonewall Greys.[48]

Adjutant General Steele, addressing the crime problem more broadly, advised the railroad officials that he would urge each grand jury throughout the state, in addition to hearing evidence, to make note of the physical descriptions of alleged criminals so that they could be identified. Court clerks were to send these descriptions of indicted felons to the adjutant general, and he would semi-annually publish a list of these fugitives. Recognizing that "arbitrary and unjust acts" committed by the state police set up during Reconstruction had created a "deepseated prejudice to the name of state police," Steele nevertheless urged that something of that sort was necessary and that a law could remove the "objectionable features" of such a statewide detective force under legislative oversight.[49]

Another Denton County lawman, William Riley Wetsel,[50] who had been in the saloon business with Henderson Murphy, conceived his own idea to find out about the Bass gang, although his activities would lead Peak and others to believe that he was a friend of Bass. With the approval of Sheriff Egan and U.S. Commissioner Robertson, in the latter part of March Wetsel rode from Denton to Bolivar in the northwest part of Denton County on Clear Creek, only a few miles from the Bass hideout at Cove Hollow. Wetsel was ostensibly going there to serve some civil process for the district court. He contacted Jim

Murphy at his place and told him that he wanted to see Bass and wanted Murphy to take him to Bass' camp. At night Murphy led the deputy to the outlaw camp in a field behind Murphy's place in the bottom of Clear Creek. Bass, Jackson and Barnes were asleep on a single blanket with another blanket for cover but did not get up when the two men arrived.

The five men talked for awhile, Seaborn Barnes cajoled Wetsel into a poker game the next day, and Wetsel and Murphy returned to Murphy's place. The next morning Wetsel returned to the camp and a daylong poker game began. That evening the party went into Bolivar and continued the game there. Wetsel, who would later report that Barnes and Jackson were not very good card players but that Barnes "made it warm and worried him considerably," ended up winning only about ten or fifteen dollars. All during the game Wetsel attempted to draw them out about the train robberies, but they knew he was a lawman and kept their mouths shut.[51]

While the game was in progress on Saturday, March 30, two more men rode in to join the party. Billy Collins arrived with Billy Scott, who had developed a plan with Jack Smith to go after the Bass gang and who had ingratiated himself with the Collins family in Dallas. Scott quickly became close friends with Billy Collins, the older brother of Joel Collins who had been with his brothers in the cattle business in Calhoun County.[52]

Billy Collins had an ulterior motive for accompanying Scott to seek out the Bass camp. In early January 1878, along with his younger brother Henry, Samuel J. Pipes and Bruce Brazil,[53] he was arrested in Dallas County for seriously assaulting a man named Mays by striking him in the head with a pistol, apparently during a period of rowdiness at a dance the young men attended in the Duck Creek area northeast of Dallas. All but Brazil were arrested and released on bond. Their cases were set for trial in the county court in Dallas on February 20 but, although subpoenas were issued, none of the state's witnesses showed up. One of the state's witnesses was Charles Lafayette Nash, an uncle of Sam Pipes. Because the defendants demanded that their cases be disposed of that day, the prosecuting attorney, Robert E. Cowart, agreed to recommend that they be punished for a lesser assault, which the court did. Both Henry and Billy

Collins were fined five dollars and court costs. On the same date, complaints were made in a justice court against the Collins brothers for carrying concealed weapons, although there is no record of the disposition of those cases.

Nash later showed up and demanded witness fees, even though he did not appear when summoned. When these were denied, he and others caused a letter to be printed in the *Dallas Commercial* complaining of County Judge R.H. West, who had presided, and prosecutor Cowart. West took umbrage at the accusation that he had "soiled the judicial ermine" and filed a lawsuit on March 27 against the parties and the newspaper, alleging slander. Cowart, seeing a great deal of humor in the attack on him, defended Judge West's integrity and asserted that a jury would likely have found the defendants guilty of the lesser offense since it was difficult to determine who was the more culpable aggressor. Thirty-nine Dallas attorneys also came to Judge West's defense. Judge West attended a town meeting on March 17 in Mesquite, to the west of Dallas, where he had to defend himself against some of his accusers.[54]

With this background, Billy Collins looked for the Bass camp with Billy Scott and with the idea of getting Bass and his men to come to Duck Creek for revenge on the farmers who had pressed charges against him, brother Henry and Sam Pipes. Collins and Scott believed that the gang would be in the vicinity of the Murphy place and secured a letter to Bob Murphy from a Denton lawyer. They then found the Bass camp and were greeted cordially, although the men there apparently had no interest in avenging Collins' troubles in Duck Creek.[55] Neither Scott nor Wetsel was aware that the other man was "spying" on the Bass gang with the intent to get information to the authorities, and Scott would subsequently identify Wetsel as one of Bass' sympathizers. During his stay with the gang Scott suggested that they might rob a Dallas bank or a Weatherford bank, his idea being to set a trap.[56]

While the gang and their visitors were engaged in conversation and card playing, Jim Murphy rode into the camp and called Bass to one side. Gleefully, Bass announced that Underwood had returned to Texas and saddled up to ride out to meet him. He returned later that Saturday evening having been unable to find Underwood. The next day, Sunday, March

31, the party relocated to Bob Murphy's barn for a continuation of the poker game. Henry Underwood and Arkansas Johnson rode in and were greeted with a great deal of enthusiasm by Bass. Wetsel had in his pocket a warrant on Underwood for cattle theft and felt compelled to read it to Underwood and ask him to post a bond. At first Underwood refused but then agreed if Bob and Jim Murphy would be his sureties. Bass had reservations and called Underwood aside and convinced him that he should not submit himself to the courts. Underwood told Wetsel that he had changed his mind but might surrender in a week or so. Bass and Underwood then rode off together.[57]

Scott Mayes was continuing to keep Bass and his men posted on activities occurring in and around Denton. As April made its appearance, Mayes gave information to the gang about a Polish grocer in Denton, Paul Agus, forty-eight, who supposedly kept a large sum of money, perhaps as much as $2,500, in a trunk in a room over the store. A plan was hatched to have Mayes lead the gang to Agus' room on some pretended business, then get the drop on him. Mayes would pretend to be terrified and would be "overwhelmed" by the gang, alerting the authorities after the gang had a chance to get away. Sheriff Egan somehow heard about the plot and planned to lie in wait in order to nab the whole gang. When some rangers and detectives arrived in Denton on the evening prior to the planned robbery, Bass called it off.[58]

Another scheme apparently concocted about this time with Mayes' help was another attempt to rob Henry Hill, the Denton and Little Elm drygoods merchant who had foiled the attempt by Bass and the Slade brothers to rob his payroll near Denton. Allegedly Hill was in possession of a large amount of money that belonged to him and Sam Davis and Tom Sublett, two of his neighbors. Mayes was to go to Hill with fifty and and one-hundred dollar bills and ask him to change them. When Hill opened his safe, Mayes would be able to tell if there was enough money there to make a robbery worthwhile. This plan was allegedly thwarted by the untimely appearance of lawmen in the vicinity. The gang also supposedly abandoned a plan to take Sheriff Egan into custody by a ruse and loot the sheriff's safe of any collected tax monies.[59]

147

As if two spies in the Bass camp weren't enough, Denton deputy Bill Minor, working for Sheriff Egan, would later say that he accompanied Mayes about this time to just north of Denton to meet with Bass, Jackson and Billy Collins. Supposedly Bass paid five hundred dollars to Mayes and gave "a pile" to Collins. Minor said that he went with Mayes to Mayes' saloon and saw the money there that Bass had given him.[60]

In camp Bass decided it was time to strike another train. This time he selected the small station at Eagle Ford just west of Dallas. However, as these plans were being laid, the authorities were finally moving. On Monday, April 1, the *Dallas Daily Herald* printed a statement by Alex Cockrell of Denton[61] that he had recently talked with Bass and that Bass, while admitting the Union Pacific robbery, steadfastly denied having any involvement in the Texas robberies. Bass boasted that he had a lot of the Union Pacific money left and that "the authorities will have to get up early in the morning to catch him."[62] No doubt such a boast by Bass was incentive enough for the various lawmen to begin even more serious efforts to ferret him out.

-X-
RESISTANCE AT MESQUITE

The community of Dallas settled down somewhat from the alarm of the Hutchins robbery, and on Tuesday, April 2, William F. Morton succeeded in being reelected city marshal.[1] But Bass and his men were planning once again to disrupt the city. The next target was a different railroad line, the Texas and Pacific, which ran east-west through Dallas, intersecting the H&TC tracks. Bass had bid goodby to Billy Scott and Billy Collins, telling them that when they heard of another "excitement," they should return and they could pull some operation together.[2]

The small town of Eagle Ford, six miles west of Dallas at a shallow part of the West Fork of the Trinity River, had first been settled in 1844 by Enoch Horton and his family. The name came from the discovery of an eagle's nest in the area. A post office existed there from 1858 until 1866, but the community grew rapidly when construction on the Texas and Pacific railroad stopped there in 1873 because of an economic depression, and it remained the terminus for the railroad until construction resumed in 1876. Cattle pens were built, and the site became an important livestock shipping point. However, with the resumption of railroad construction and completion of the line to Fort Worth, Eagle Ford decreased in importance and by 1878 was primarily an agricultural shipping point.[3]

According to Hogg, after the Hutchins robbery Frank Jackson began having doubts about life as an outlaw. The values he had learned as a child were being discarded as he caught himself being drawn deeper by Bass into a life that would know no peace. The pleas of his brothers and sisters to leave Bass and straighten out his life sometimes brought him to tears. He pledged to them that he would quit the bandit life, but when he declared that intention to Bass he was told it was too late and that he would be hung if he ever turned himself in. Jackson yielded to Bass and resigned himself to whatever fate held for him as a train robber.[4] Green Hill later related an incident occurring at the Hickory Creek camp when Bass and Jackson were alone. Jackson had built a small cage out of twigs in which he kept a woodpecker that he called "Old Honest Eph," the name Bass was called while in camp. Jackson referred to the cage as the Denton jail and goaded the bird with a stick, enraging the noisy animal. "This is the way Old Hub [Denton jailer Willis Hubbard Bates] will do Old Eph when he gets him in jail. Stand around there, you blasted train robber!" Reclining on his elbow, Bass retorted, "The hell; you'll be in there a darned sight before I will, yet."[5]

As the time grew close for the raid on Eagle Ford, Underwood declined to go and said he needed to be with his family after his involuntary absence in Nebraska. Seaborn Barnes was sick again and unable to ride. Jackson, still muddling over the situation he was in, told Bass he did not want to go on this trip. Bass mulled it over and decided that if Underwood, Barnes and Jackson stayed behind in Denton County while the robbery was pulled off, it might deflect suspicion from Bass as being responsible for the raids. Bass said that he knew two "good ones" in Dallas who could step in, so he and Arkansas Johnson headed to Dallas County.[6]

Bass recruited two "novices" to join him and Johnson for the Eagle Ford job.[7] These two men were never identified in contemporary newspaper accounts, but it is possible that they were Matthew Gray and James Tyler, both indicted by a federal grand jury in 1880 for being involved in the Eagle Ford robbery. Gray, whose uncle had been sheriff of Denton County, was apparently a rambunctious sort and had recently been remanded to the custody of the Cooke County sheriff pending trial for an unknown crime committed in Denton County but was now out on bond.[8] Little is known about James Tyler. When he was arrested in 1881, he told a newspaper reporter that at the time of the Eagle Ford robbery he was laid up about six miles from Denton after being thrown and injured by a horse. He said that he knew Underwood and Barnes slightly but had never met Bass.[9]

Around midnight of Thursday, April 4, the eastbound Texas

and Pacific train pulled up to the platform of the Eagle Ford depot and station agent E.L. Stevens, a twenty-seven-year-old Ohioan,[10] prepared to leave his office to greet the train. As he walked out on the platform, he saw a man with a mask covering the lower part of his face step around the corner with a pistol in his hand, followed by two other similarly masked and armed men. The first man held Stevens at gunpoint as the train slowed for the station.

The engineer, a man named Smith, and his fireman were taken prisoner when the train finally stopped and were marched to the platform and held with Stevens. One of the robbers was stationed near the passenger coach, apparently to prevent any interference by would-be heroes. Conductor E.W. Campbell was the next to be taken prisoner and was lined up with the others along with Ely the baggage checker. Benjamen Franklin Caperton, the baggagemaster, opened the door to the baggage car to receive packages but was immediately confronted by one of the masked men, who shoved a pistol in his face and, mistaking him for the express agent, demanded what money he had. Caperton calmly asked the gunman to remove the pistol from his ear, which the bandit did, and the baggageman pointed out where the express car was. Caperton was then escorted to where the other prisoners were being guarded and was relieved of his watch.[11] A passenger named Wilson stepped off the train and blundered into the group of prisoners on the platform, and one of the bandits hollered, "Fall into line, Wilson, damn you, fall into line." Wilson could not recognize the voice.

One of the bandits ordered agent Stevens to go to the express car, pretend that he was alone, and ask to be admitted. Aboard the express car was express agent J.H. Hickox and guard Clarence E. Groce.[12] Suspecting a holdup, the two men locked the door from the inside and extinguished the light. Hickox told Stevens that the only way that they would get the door open was to break it open. Bass went to the engine tender and picked up a heavy stick of wood, then returned to the express car and battered the door with it. The bandit called out to the express messenger that he would give him two minutes to open the door.

Unexpectedly, without any further prompting or resistance, Hickox unlocked the door and admitted Bass. Groce was relieved of his Smith & Wesson pistol, and Hickox was compelled to open the way or "local" safe in which valuables were often kept for transportation between stations. The bandit handed Hickox a note written with a lead pencil that, bizarrely, indicated that June Peak had been involved with this same gang in the Hutchins robbery, although no one later believed that this was true. Hickox and Groce were ordered out of the express car and lined up by the others. The bandit went through the express safe and found about fifty dollars, unaware that the express companies now thought it was too risky to keep cash in the express cars and were transporting money through anonymous passengers on the coach.

The bandits turned their attention to the mail car, where William W. "Billie" Carr had also locked himself in and extinguished the light, hastily hiding registered packages. When the outlaws threatened to burn the car, he relented and opened the door. The robber who entered the car searched it and took twenty-seven packages containing a total of $233.95.[13]

Bass was satisfied that there was no large amount of money aboard the train. When Conductor Campbell alerted him that the train was now running late, Bass told the prisoners they could lower their hands when the bandits were out of sight but not to make a sound nor try to shoot at them. Bass warned them that they had a lot more men surrounding the station and would signal them if necessary. The four robbers then slowly backed away, their cocked weapons held ready. Reaching their horses, they raced off in a northeasterly direction.[14]

The train crew waited until the robbers were well away, then Conductor Campbell, still trying to avoid any noise as instructed, went over to Engineer Smith and whispered that they should get the train moving again. The train moved on to Fort Worth.[15]

Colonel George Noble, general superintendent of the Texas and Pacific Railway,[16] happened to be staying in Dallas at the time and received a telegram informing him of the Eagle Ford robbery. He promptly notified local officers, and a posse led by June Peak started in pursuit almost immediately. The *Dallas*

Daily Herald labeled the spate of robberies as disgraceful and called for the state and express companies to offer sufficient rewards and for the railroads to arm their trains.[17] The stories also spread that Bass and his men could not be captured in Denton County so long as they had friends there to help them hide. The governor was called on to give Captain Hall enough men "to whip the robbers and their friends." The state press vilified Hickox and Groce, "Had the guard and messenger made good use of their weapons...two of the robbers, at least, would never have rode away in the darkness again." Both men were suspended from duty because the express company did not believe that they "acted very bravely or discreetly" during the robbery.[18] A variety of would-be detectives, motivated by potential reward or a need for adventure, joined lawmen in looking for the robbers.[19]

En route to Denton County, the four bandits stopped to split the paltry amount of loot that had been taken. According to Hogg, the two "novices," with one robbery under their belts, were already "sick of the business and expressed their determination to abandon that mode of life." Bass and Johnson decided to delay their return to Denton County and were supposed to have remained in Dallas County for a few days. While there, with the assistance of some old friends in the Duck Creek area, they made the acquaintance of some new friends who might be of help in future jobs.[20] Reportedly on Friday night, during a foray into Denton to celebrate, the gang got the drop on some unnamed officer and had their temporary prisoner join them in a drink. Bass was also supposed to have left a friend with a twenty-dollar gold piece.[21]

That same day a party led by Texas Express detective Sam Finley with detective James Curry, who was supposed to know Bass by sight, telegraph operator Ed Smith, former Dallas policeman William Edwards and others set out to find the trail of the Eagle Ford robbers. They struck the trail and followed a roundabout path through prairie and timber, bringing them within two miles of Lewisville in Denton County. They camped there for the night and employed a local man to help guide them through the countryside. On Saturday morning the party resumed the hunt, finally turning towards Denton.

Riding in the timber about three miles below Denton, near the farm of Robert H. Hopkins who would later follow Egan as Denton County sheriff, they saw two unattended horses hitched in the woods just off the main road. Thinking that the animals might belong to Captain Hall's rangers, but nevertheless taking no chances, they spread out and moved toward the horses. Finley and Curry rode directly toward the horses, but as they neared a shot came from the woods at Curry, who returned the fire. The two dismounted and called to the others to try to go around to the rear of the unseen assailant. Finley was tying his horse to a tree when he spotted a man he later thought was Frank Jackson standing behind a tree and taking aim at Curry. Finley threw the reins to the ground and was aiming at Jackson when a second man, later identified as Henry Underwood, warned, "Look out, Frank!" Jackson quickly put the tree between him and Finley, who barely caught a glimpse of the second man taking cover behind a tree.

Jackson called out and asked why they were shooting at them, and Curry asked him the same question. Jackson said he had merely shot at a rabbit that had jumped up between them. Finley, unsure of whether or not these were innocent men, called to them to step out and identify themselves. They refused, telling the posse, "You go away; we don't know you." Finley stepped out and exposed himself, asking them to also show themselves. Again they refused, "No, you go away; we don't want to see you." Finley called to Curry and asked him if any of the men were Bass and he replied, "No." Finley walked over to where his horse was grazing, and one of the two strangers asked him what he was going to do. Finley responded that he would let him know in a few minutes, then led his horse over to where Curry was standing. Curry again assured him that neither of the men was Bass, and Finley was now more convinced that they were not the men they were after. After a few more efforts to persuade the men to identify themselves, Finley and his party pulled back and watched each of the two men saddle his horse while the other stood guard, then ride off in the woods. When the two riders were about 350 yards off, they stood up in their stirrips, waved their hats, and cheerfully called for them to "come on." With that amount of a lead, the subsequent chase was futile. Thus ended what turned out to be the first of many encounters and skirmishes that lawmen would have with Sam Bass and his men.

Finley took his posse into Denton where Tom Gerren told them that Bass and four or five of his men, all armed with Winchesters, were at a mill about three quarters of a mile from town. When Finley asked Gerren to accompany them he refused, saying, "No, Sam Bass is a friend of mine and I will do nothing against him."[22]

What happened next is disputed. The following account was reportedly included in a *Denton Monitor* story about the encounter with Jackson and Underwood.

> Continuing on to Denton they [Finley and party] stopped at the Lacy House on Saturday afternoon (once the home of Bass), and while there the notorious Sam Bass and a number of his associates appeared on the outskirts, and according to one statement rode into the city. They had heard that the Dallas party were looking for outlaws, and were anxious to know if they were the men whom they sought; if so, they would like to have them come out and try to take them. Messengers galloped back and forth between the excited and defiant crowd and their friends in the city. Finally, later in the evening, Bass and company sent a messenger to the Dallas men to inform them that they would remain in sight of them for two hours and a half, and challenging them to come out and fight. They stood near the residence of John L. Lovejoy, Jr., in the suburbs of the city, plain to the view of the public square. More than a hundred saw them.[23]

Finley reported that after it was learned that Gerren refused to assist his party, some Denton citizens became indignant, armed themselves, and went to the mill where they found that Bass and his men had fled. Finley said nothing about Bass' throwing down the gauntlet as described by the *Monitor*.[24] Likewise Thomas Hogg, ever protective of Denton County, adamantly denied that it ever happened, saying that there were no messengers and Bass was never seen in the city. Hogg did say that the Dallas party refused to go with Egan and his posse to check the mill and refused to loan Egan's men any of their weapons.[25]

In yet another account, the *Monitor* story is accepted as accurate and, because the Bass party was larger than Finley's group, Finley allegedly decided not to go after them without additional help. Denton City Marshal George Smith was then supposed to have attempted to raise a posse to check out the mill but ended up riding out himself to check out the place, followed shortly by a few sheepish men. Finding no one at the mill, Smith and the men returned to Denton. Sheriff Egan was supposed to have agreed to go out if the Dallas men would loan them their weapons, but this was refused. Also, Egan reportedly had some concerns that the Dallas posse had no warrants for the outlaws and was only looking for men who fit whatever description they were able to garner from those present at Eagle Ford who actually saw the robbers. Although Bass might have been suspected of being involved in the train robberies, the *Denton Monitor* summed up the local attitude.

> There is no charge against any of this party, in Denton county, except Henry Underwood. That is for carrying a pistol, and it is not believed he can be convicted on evidence. And it is not believed here that any of this party participated in the train robbery at Eagle Ford, at Allen or at Hutchins. Certain it is that they were here on Thursday night of last week when the Eagle Ford train robbery occurred.[26]

The fact that Frank Jackson and Seaborn Barnes remained behind may have worked to give Bass and Johnson an alibi. Finley said that because he needed a "superior force" he telegraphed to Dallas for help. At about 10:00 p.m. on Saturday, the Texas Express agent at Dallas received a telegram from Pilot Point in Denton County that Bass, Jackson and Underwood were there in the bottoms of the Elm Fork. A rumor rapidly spread that the gang had been confronted near Lewisville, in Denton County, and that gunfire had been exchanged until the attacking party, lacking sufficient force, backed off. Marshal Morton took police officer J.C. Arnold, plus James McGinley and another man named Walton, and left on horseback that evening to see if they could assist.[27] Captain Hall had also been staying in Dallas for a few days, but left Friday night "for the frontier."[28] When June Peak, Marshal Morton, James McGinley and police officers Arnold and Waller arrived in Denton, they scouted around Denton for some miles but failed to find any trace.[29]

While Finley and his men were experiencing frustration, Sheriff Egan's spy Bill Minor had set out on the evening of Saturday, April 6, accompanied by Scott Mayes, to locate Bass' camp. They rode south until they arrived at Green Hill's place and were introduced to Billy Collins. Not gaining any information as to Bass' whereabouts, the two started back toward Denton. As luck would have it, they ran into Bass and Jackson and rode with them to the outlaw camp on Hickory Creek, where Collins had also arrived. Minor and Mayes spent a little time with the outlaws then rode back to Denton.[30]

The next day, Sunday, ex-deputy Tom Gerren decided that he would look for the Bass camp and visit the outlaws in order to learn what they were doing. No doubt he still had a reward in mind. Egan argued with him that it would be a foolish thing to do and that they would kill him, but Gerren went anyway and ran into Bass and Jackson a few miles south of Denton near the main road to Dallas. While they did not treat Gerren roughly, they were suspicious of him and did not freely discuss their affairs. When Gerren noticed burly Arkansas Johnson squatting down by a tree with a cocked Winchester pointed in his direction and asked who the man was, Bass replied, "Oh, he's a feller that stays around here." Realizing his danger, Gerren decided that it was time to leave and did so. Hogg later observed that, regardless of what Gerren had done before to hinder the pursuit, he was now legitimately trying to work covertly to bring Bass and his men to justice.[31]

Gerren and the others were not aware, even as they rode all over Denton County looking for the bandit, that Bass and his men were already planning another train robbery; Bass was discussing with Underwood, Barnes, Jackson, Johnson and Billy

Collins his idea to hit the Texas and Pacific at Mesquite, east of Dallas.

Dallas City Marshal Morton left Finley's party in Denton County and returned to Dallas on Monday, April 8.[32] On that same day Bass and his men rode to Dallas County and camped in the bottoms of White Rock Creek, near Billy Collins' place some twelve to thirteen miles east of Dallas. While in camp, Bass reportedly met some of the local youth attracted to the daring outlaw, all chafing for some of the adventure. Bass would later tell Jim Murphy that nine of these youth joined him, Barnes, Jackson and Underwood. Among the young men visiting the camp was Billy Scott, still working with Jack Smith to trap the Bass gang, and it may have been that he had originally gone to Collins' place to get more information, unaware that Bass would be there.[33]

Two of the young men recruited by Bass for the Mesquite robbery were Albert G. Herndon and Samuel J. Pipes. Herndon, about twenty, was no stranger to trouble, having been exposed to a raucous experience with a stepfather and having been arrested along with Belle Starr's brother in 1875 for carrying a pistol. Also arrested for other minor charges in 1876, his brushes with the law reflect a young man with a wild streak, a good candidate to be attracted to the adventure offered by Sam Bass. He was about 5'8" tall, 150 pounds, "well made," with dark brown hair and a light brown moustache dyed black.[34]

Sam Pipes came from a similar mold. He had already shown his wild side when he was arrested in January 1878 along with Billy and Henry Collins for an assault at a dance at Duck Creek and for carrying a pistol the following month.[35] In addition to his Dallas County misdemeanors, Pipes was sought by the Texas Rangers for theft in Llano County, although he was likely never arrested for that charge.[36] Pipes, who was balding, was about 5'10" tall, 175 pounds, with black hair, moustache, and eyes.[37] Herndon and Pipes, both young farmboys with a reckless side, eagerly looked forward to their first serious foray into crime although they would later claim that they were intoxicated when they ran into Bass' camp and were recruited.

On Tuesday, April 9, the *Dallas Commercial*, allegedly at the insistence of express company businessmen, made a demand on the state government to do something about the crime wave. Concluding that the investigation pointed only to Denton County as the headquarters of Bass, Underwood and Jackson, the editor demanded that the state take a more responsible role.

The fastness in which these highwaymen have each time successfully taken refuge is an extensive tract of woodland, full of undergrowth and very difficult of ingress. It is described as a place where a man could live for a year and nobody ever see him. This forest contains many log cabins standing among the trees and in such isolated places that nothing but a long search can discover them. It is believed that there are many good people among the inhabitants, but fear of their desperate neighbors compels them to keep their lips closed.

But many of the people are thought to be more or less in sympathy with the gang. Their houses are always open to them, and when compelled to stay in the woods, they carry them meals and act as spies for them. A detective fully acquainted with the character of the people says there are women among them who would ride fifty miles in a night to warn one of the gang of approaching danger. It is said, too, that they have couriers scattered through all the neighboring country, who keep them constantly informed of every movement of the authorities. Some of these couriers are supposed to be here in Dallas, and constantly act as spies to gather and report the sentiments of the people....

Detectives can do no more, for they have traced the robbers to their hiding place, and can almost name the guilty parties. The local authorities are powerless to capture the robbers, therefore the matter should at once be taken in hand by our State authorities and a sufficient force should be sent into Denton to arrest the guilty parties or drive them out of the country....[38]

On the same day, Governor Hubbard received a telegram from acting Postmaster General Thomas J. Brady in

Washington, D.C., who asked for the cooperation of Texas officials with postal authorities in tracking down the robbers who had violated the U.S. mails, suggesting "the propriety of a proclamation of outlawry against them."[39] As this thought was being shared with the governor, Bass dispatched Billy Collins to ride to Mesquite, a small station on the Texas and Pacific railroad thirteen miles east of Dallas,[40] and investigate its potential for another robbery. Collins returned to the outlaw camp optimistic that the small station would be a suitable target for the gang. The only thing out of the ordinary was the presence of a group of convicts being used to improve the road at Mesquite. On March 20 two of the convicts had attempted to run off, and one was killed by shotgun fire. Tuesday evening the gang stealthily moved to the vicinity of the station there, but the evening train had already come through so the outlaws returned to their camp near Duck Creek.[41]

On Wednesday, April 10, a group of executives from various major Texas railroads and representatives of various express companies called on Governor Hubbard to consult about preventing future robberies. They met at the Raymond House in Austin and on hotel stationery drafted a resolution offering the resources of the corporations to assist the state. In return they asked Hubbard "to extend to us all legal means at his command to the extent of providing a sufficient force for the future protection of the passengers and property entrusted to us for transportation."[42]

On Wednesday evening, a clear, moonlit night just five days after the Eagle Ford robbery and forty-seven days after the Allen robbery, the Bass gang once more stealthily made its way to Mesquite. Billy Scott managed to keep from being included in the robbery scheme, and Bass told Billy Collins to stay home, although he wanted to go along. Bass did not want too large a party, perhaps anticipating that the amount of loot they recovered could not be profitably split between more than a few participants. Henry Collins did not want to go at all, likely concerned about beefed-up railroad security, and even tried to talk Sam Pipes out of going.[43] Making their way to Mesquite were Bass, Underwood, Jackson, Johnson, Barnes, Pipes and Herndon, although Jim Murphy would later say that he was told that Billy Collins and Scott were also along.[44]

The darkness covered the movements of the gang as they hitched their horses in trees behind the railway station, likely leaving one of the newer members of the gang to guard them. Nearing the station, they waited until 10:40 p.m. when the westbound T&P No. 1 slowed as it approached the station. In the engine were engineer Jim Barron and fireman Tom Mooney, who stood a gigantic 6'8" and weighed 180 pounds.[45] Jake Zurn, the station agent,[46] stepped out onto the platform to greet the train. Another special train, carrying fifty-seven prisoners of the convict road crew under the charge of T.W. Taylor, was preparing to leave a side track where it was standing about a hundred yards from the station. Guards saw some men climb over an embankment and run up behind the railroad station.[47]

Zurn was confronted by a masked man who thrust a pistol at him and ordered him to hold up his hands. The other bandits fired several pistol shots in the air to enforce their shouted orders for the train to stop, and Barron brought the train to a complete stop after a brief effort to restart the train. He and Mooney were ordered down from the engine by Jackson. Somehow Mooney was able to walk away and ended up out on the prairie south of the train but was finally halted by one of the robbers. On the way back to the station with his hands raised, he tripped in a hog-wallow. Barron and Mooney joined Zurn as prisoners on the platform, and all three were ordered to keep their hands raised.[48] Agnes Zurn, who lived above the station with her husband, came out on the platform, but when she saw what was happening and was told to raise her hands, she made a dash back inside the station. A volley of shots struck the door as she closed and locked it behind her. An account many years later asserted that she pulled money out of the station drawer and hid it.[49]

A passenger, Daniel J. Healey, who was night clerk and telegraph operator at the Windsor Hotel in Dallas, was returning from a short trip that day to Terrell. When the train arrived at the station, he stepped onto the platform even before the train stopped in order to visit with Zurn, a good friend of his, but saw a number of men step up out of the shadows onto the platform. One of the men covered him with a pistol and ordered him to raise his hands and come with him, backing slowly while Healey followed the gunbarrel. The masked man cursed him for walking too slowly. When Barron made an attempt to restart the engine before the robbers captured the engineer, the robber was distracted and Healey managed to take one hundred dollars from his vest pocket and stuff it in his boot. He raised his hands quickly as the robber once again focused his attention on his prisoner, but even though he obeyed the gestures of the menacing pistol, someone struck him on the head from behind with a pistol, stunning him. Healey called his unseen assailant a coward. When his guard was again distracted, Healey fled and the robber ran after him, firing as he went, but finally gave up the pursuit. Healey ran to the convict train and hid under it. The next day Healey's hat was found on the track with a bullet hole through it.[50]

As the train was pulling into the Mesquite station, the conductor, Jules Alvord,[51] heard its whistle and stepped with lantern in hand from the sleeper car to the rear platform of the preceding car. He heard gunfire from the direction of the engine and guessed that a holdup was in progress. A masked man stepped up and cursed him, ordering him to step down. Pulling a small, double-barreled derringer from his pocket, Alvord fired a shot at the robber. Two other bandits fired at him, and he retreated back to the sleeper to retrieve a larger pistol that he had stored there.

Followed by Hart Collins, an employee of the Texas & Pacific, and John W. Delaney, passenger agent for the Texas & Pacific,[52] both of whom were unarmed, Alvord resumed the gunfight with three of the bandits. He believed later that one of his shots hit a bandit wearing brown overalls and a broad-brimmed hat who had a heavy black moustache that came down over his mask. The man had staggered back against a lumber pile before being helped away. One bullet grazed the small of Hart Collins' back and another grazed Delaney's face, although neither shot broke the skin.

One of the bandits fired at the conductor, and the Winchester's ball slammed into Alvord's left wrist and came out through a large exit hole near the elbow, shattering his arm. Another shot tore out the side of his hat above the brim. The wounded Alvord jumped down to the ground and took cover under the car, emptying his pistol at the outlaws. One of his adversaries was heard to comment something to the effect that it would be a shame to kill such a brave man. Weakened by pain and the loss of blood, Alvord managed to reboard the train on the second-class coach, where he found the passengers flat on the floor, but then he decided to go back to the sleeper to have his serious wound bound up. As he stepped between cars, several more shots were fired at him and he ducked back into the coach. He called out and asked what they wanted, identifying himself as a passenger. The bandits replied "we want money," cursed him, and fired again. He made it into the sleeper where he bound his arm with a torn sheet and laid down.

There were two men traveling to Fort Worth in the sleeper with their wives, one of whom had concealed his considerable cash in various hiding places in the car. Hastily dressing, this man told the weakened Alvord that he had a pistol and asked if he should have a go at the robbers. Alvord suggested that he stay in the car and shoot only if the robbers tried to enter.[53]

Another passenger on the train was William D. Lacy, son of Sarah Lacy who had once employed Sam Bass.[54] Currently a dry goods merchant in Ozark, Arkansas, and traveling to Denton with his wife and daughter, he raised a shade of the car window to see what the shooting was about and a shot was sent in his direction.[55]

At his residence about a quarter of a mile west of the station, Mesquite merchant Jim Gross heard the gunfire, retrieved a pistol, and headed in the direction of the excitement. As he approached near enough to see what was going on, he discreetly dropped the weapon in the weeds, but a robber spotted him and asked what he had been holding. He responded that it was a stick because he was afraid of dogs. The robber sent him back to fetch the weapon then had him raise his hands. When he had to scratch his nose, a robber obliged by scratching his nose for him with his own pistol. He was lined up with the other prisoners. Another nearby Mesquite resident, Mrs. August Tosch, who with her husband had only recently immigrated with their children from Prussia to become Texas farmers, heard the shooting but refrained from waking her snoring husband for fear he would become involved.[56]

John T. Lynch, supervisor of the convict train during the Mesquite train robbery, as a Dallas policeman in the 1890s. (Photo in possession of author)

At the convict train, Healey finally climbed out from under the car under which he had hidden about twenty minutes earlier. He contacted some of the convict guards, who were having problems controlling some very restive prisoners, and they discussed the ongoing robbery. One of the guards, Fluellen, also identified as Finellen, went down the side track toward the station but retreated back to the special car after exchanging fire with a robber.[57] Later, Fluellen and two other convict guards, Henning and John T. Lynch, approached the train on the side opposite the Mesquite station and were stopped by two robbers. When the guards announced that they had no intention of interfering but just wanted to see what was going on, the robbers told them they had no objection so long as they kept quiet.[58]

Aboard the combined baggage, express and mail car, the baggagemaster was Ben Caperton, who had lived through the Eagle Ford robbery only five days earlier. The express messenger was Spofford Curley, sometimes identified as Kerley, and the mail agent was fifty-two-year-old William C. "Uncle Billie" Towers of Texarkana.[59] There were also two guards on board, Jack Allen and J.G. Lynch. The lights on the baggage and express ends of the car had been extinguished as the train approached Mesquite, and when the train stopped Caperton opened his door and immediately saw one of the masked robbers step from behind the depot building, jump from the platform to the ground, and start for the express car. He doused the handlight that he was carrying and hollered a warning of the bandits' approach to Curley, Towers and the two guards.

Curley rushed down the narrow aisle in the car and past mail agent Towers, telling him to stay away from the door. Curley grabbed a muzzle-loading double-barreled shotgun, and Caperton also procured a shotgun. Through a door window Caperton could see one of the robbers standing about twenty yards away, and he opened the door quickly and fired both barrels. Guards Allen and Lynch emptied a shotgun and two sixshooters in an exchange of gunfire with the robbers. While the firing continued, Curley hid two packages containing about $1,500. During a lull in the firing, the robbers were able to crawl under the express car, preventing any more shooting by those inside. The robbers called out and asked if the occupants preferred opening the door and coming out or forcing the robbers to separate the car, pull it down the track, and set it on fire.

The group huddled in the car, decided to fight it out with the outlaws, and announced their intention to the robbers. They heard one of the robbers order another to bring the kerosene oil can from the engine and "see what the damn sons of bitches could be made to do with a little fire." The robber continued to threaten to burn them out and shoot them as they fled the flames. The oil was poured all over the car and the robber, probably Bass, announced that he would count to fifty. If they did not then open the door, he would apply a match. The counting commenced, slowly reaching twenty-five. The guard Lynch had reloaded his shotgun and crept forward to the door, shooting down towards the coupling from where the voices appeared to be coming. No fire was returned, but the robber asked them if they were going to open the door.

"Don't be in such a damn big rush; give us time to counsel

Benjamen Franklin
Caperton, baggage mas-
ter at both the Eagle
Ford and Mesquite train
robberies. (Photo in
possession of author).

a little," Curley responded. Bass continued counting: thirty . . .
thirty-five . . . forty. At some point—the accounts range from a
count of twenty to as long as five or six minutes after the count
of fifty—another hurried consultation led to a decision by the
inhabitants of the car to surrender. Leaving their weapons in the
car, they opened the side door and jumped to the ground, raising their hands. Bass crawled into the car and searched it. Not
finding any cash, the outlaw began looking through small packages and boxes, throwing them to the floor as he looked.
Caperton suggested that he ought to be careful because there
might be eggs in some of the boxes; sure enough, Bass dropped
a box with a half-dozen goose eggs in it and laughed.

The robbers overlooked what had been hidden and
obtained only about $150 from the express portion and four
registered packages containing a total of $12.50 and a gold ring.
Outside the car Bass began to search the prisoners, but when he
came to Caperton he said, "Why, you old bald-head! You
haven't a cent; I robbed you just a week ago." True to form, Bass
failed to find the month's pay that the baggageman had in his
watch pocket. Bass looked at Towers and stated that he was too

old to be robbed, but he took cash and valuables from the remaining prisoners. Curley lightheartedly asked for a receipt from the robbers. The prisoners were then marched some distance from the train and, at the insistence of some of the prisoners, Bass returned fifty cents or a dollar to each of them for a meal. Their mission completed, the robbers mounted up and rode off.[60]

It was a disaster for the outlaws. Not only was the booty garnered a paltry sum, but it would also be alleged that Barnes was wounded four times, three in the right leg and once in the left thigh, all flesh wounds. A small caliber bullet went through Jackson's shirt, barely striking his right shoulder, then fell down his sleeve into his hand.[61] Sam Pipes was wounded on his left hip.[62]

When the gang was gone, the trainmen walked back to the train but no one was in sight. Caperton boarded the second-class coach and announced that the robbers had left, and passengers began to appear from under the seats. He saw one man retrieve a wallet that he had hidden in the waistband of a child. A passenger agent crawling out from under his seat had no response when Caperton reminded him of an earlier statement that he would like to see a gang hold up any train that he was on. The wounded Alvord turned the train over to Caperton.[63] Both Curley and Alvord sent brief telegrams about the robbery, then the train proceeded to Dallas.

The train arrived in Dallas about midnight and Alvord was removed to a room in the Windsor Hotel. Dr. L.E. Locke[64] was called in to treat his badly wounded arm and believed that the arm could be saved.[65] In the meantime, Alvord was being widely praised for his pluck and determination in the fight with the robbers. At about 2:30 in the morning, Sam Finley led out another posse out to pick up the trail at Mesquite, and another party under W.K. Cornish also went in pursuit.[66] Bass and his men had finally met bona fide resistance, and the countryside was up in arms. The Mesquite robbery would prove to be the "straw that broke the camel's back," and now nothing would be spared to track him down.

Major John B. Jones, commander of the Frontier Battalion.
(Photo in possession of author)

-XI-
TEXAS RANGERS TAKE CHARGE

Texas was in an uproar over the train robberies. In Austin on Thursday, April 11, Governor Hubbard increased the reward to one thousand dollars for each man arrested and convicted for the train robberies. However, he declined the suggestion of railroad and express officials to put a guard of rangers on each train; he questioned its legality and worried that it would also overextend the manpower of the Frontier Battalion.[1] No sooner had the Mesquite robbery been reported to Austin than Adjutant General Steele dispatched Major John Jones to Dallas, telling him instructions would follow by mail.[2]

Steele told Jones that he thought the governor was going to authorize the use of the Frontier Battalion to go into Denton County after the robbers. He proposed to use Captain Dan Roberts' Company D, with detachments from the companies of Lieutenant N.O. Reynolds and Captain Neal Coldwell. The railroad officials had promised him a special train on twenty-four-hour notice, and Steele believed he could have the force organized in Austin in ten days. Jones was to "post" himself "in a legal manner to arrest as many felons as possible," especially the train robbers.[3]

Major John B. Jones now stepped to the forefront to direct the pursuit of the Bass gang.[4] He stood in contrast to the popular image of a Texas Ranger as "a tall fellow of massive build with long locks flowing over his shoulders, a full beard, a weather-beaten face wearing an expression of devil may care recklessness," and sporting a battery of sixshooters and a savage sheath knife. One rather florid report described Jones, no doubt embarrassing him.

By birth and education a gentleman, and by profession a lawyer, this daring chief of the lawless border as

169

he appears on our streets and as a guest in the best houses, is a small man scarcely of medium height and stature, whose conventional dress of black broadcloth, spotless linen and dainty boot on a small foot, would not distinguish him from any other citizen, while in his quiet, easy manner, almost free from gesticulation, his soft and modulated voice, his grave but genial conversation, one would look in vain for the marks of a frontier bravo.

If his face were consulted one would see a mask of bronzed [sic] seasoned and embrowned by a semi-tropical sun and by the war of wind and weather and the storm of battle. Quiet, serious, but always ready to smile, determination, resolution, self-possession and intrepidity would be seen in every feature, and especially in the firm mouth and dark eyes with their steady concentrated gaze; but it would require a good deal of penetration to see in this quiet, affable gentleman the leader of the celebrated Texas Rangers and the hero of many a daring assault and wild melee, and the bulwark of the border and the terror of the frontier forayers.[5]

Unaware of the preparations being made, the governor and state authorities were roundly criticized again by the *Dallas Daily Herald* in its Friday, April 12, edition for failing to send a strong detachment of rangers after the Allen robbers. The railroad and express companies were also accused of being derelict because they had not heavily armed their trains nor provided guards nor had arms available for passengers to help defend the trains. "Let General Steele and Governor Hubbard forget legal and executive formalities and the red tapery of Austin for a few days, and make a manly and vigorous effort to catch and punish the train robbers...." In sympathy with the "quiet people" of Denton County who were unable to contend with the armed robbers, the editor observed, "They rely upon the authorities, and anxiously but hopelessly turn their eyes toward Austin, but help cometh not."[6]

All sorts of lawmen and would-be detectives were flocking to Dallas, eager for the glory and reward of nabbing Bass and his gang. The Texas and Pacific Express Company retained the noted Pinkerton Detective Agency, and William Pinkerton and some of his agents came to Dallas to join in the hunt. Operative Tony Waits was installed as an employee in Tom Wheeler's saloon in Denton, supposedly working closely with ex-Deputy Tom Gerren and Grayson County Sheriff William Everheart.[7]

Several posses from Dallas under the command of Sheriff Moon and Marshal Morton, and June Peak and Sam Finley, spent the better part of Thursday, April 11, scouring the coun-tryside around Mesquite but found no trace except for a carbine and a shotgun a half mile west of the station.[8] Rumors about the gang abounded: parties in Dallas were keeping the gang posted as to law enforcement measures; a gang was spotted south of Dallas between Hutchins and Ferris, apparently primed to attack a train there. The posses returned to Dallas Thursday evening.

The superintendent of the Texas and Pacific at Marshall in East Texas urgently telegraphed Colonel E.G. Bower in Dallas and asked him to bring some of that city's organized militia to Mesquite for protection against another rumored robbery. Bower and Peak called up a force composed of members of the Stonewall Greys and the Lamar Rifles and, armed with rifles furnished by the railroad, left the city at about eleven o'clock Thursday evening on a special train. At about the same time, U.S. Marshal Stillwell Russell[9] arrived in Dallas to begin his investigation and to consult with local authorities. The west-bound passenger train that was headed for Mesquite was briefly delayed at Forney until the militia could arrive. After the arrival of the militiamen at Mesquite, a telegram was received that six robbers had been seen at Corsicana at sundown. Bower and Peak took a few men to investigate that report while the remain-ing militiamen reboarded the train and headed back west to Fort Worth to respond to a rumor of robbers there.[10]

Now there was no doubt that Bass and his gang were responsible for the train robberies, or that the gang repeatedly sought refuge in Denton County. As one newspaper put it, "the thick woods and brush in the southern portion of Denton county affords a safe retreat." It was alleged that Denton author-ities had confessed their inability to capture the outlaws and, because of unfortunate statements by Tom Gerren that he had "slept" with Sam Bass, it was generally thought that perhaps the officials were not inclined to do their duty.[11] Sheriff Everheart was quoted as believing that some of the local officers in Denton were in league with the bandits.[12] Texas Express detective Sam Finley told a Fort Worth reporter after returning from scouring the Denton County countryside, "I found Bass is known by everybody, and two-thirds of the people are indebted to him for personal favors, and those who are not are afraid to expose his whereabouts." He claimed that Sheriff Egan had told him that he was afraid to go after Bass because it would be certain death. It was Finley's opinion that the officials were either linked to the outlaws in some way or afraid to do their duty.[13]

The statewide focus on Denton County ruffled some local feathers. County Judge Thomas E. Hogg[14] bristled and, on behalf of his community, responded in letters to various editors.

Mr. Editor - In justice to the fair name of Denton county, please state that the rumors about lawlessness here and connivance at crime by our county officials are absolutely false. Life and property are as safe here as in Vermont. Sam Bass and his crowd, said to be train robbers, are understood to be perambulating about in the cross timbers, but they are molesting no one, and as there has heretofore been no papers here against them, no one has felt patriotic enough to molest them. Bass and his crowd are on the dodge, however, and may be robbers and probably are, yet be they so or not, they are not robbing here, and they are not disturbing the public peace. So let all persons concerned about Denton county understand, once [and] for all, that the rumors about disorder here, are lies; that a man has only to come here to find them so and so pronounce them. All we ask for is a fair trial. Let any man come to Denton and if he does not say that he never saw better order anywhere, then I will acknowledge that I know not what good order means.

THOMAS E. HOGG[15]

To the editor of the *Dallas Daily Herald*, Judge Hogg said that "the rumors afloat about Denton county being a refuge for train robbers, and her people harborers of malefactors, are all stuff of the thinnest fabric." Only Henry Underwood had a warrant against him for cattle theft, but there was no legal process for the rest of the gang. "So long as they molest no one, it is hardly reasonable that anybody is going to arrest them or try it on vague rumors."[16] Another letter signed by Hogg and other Denton County officials defended Sheriff Egan, based on the fact that no one had provided him with any legal papers for the train robbers and thus he was not authorized to raise a posse to go after them. They recognized that it would take a small army to go after Bass.[17]

One correspondent, who wrote from Denton on April 11 and who claimed to have encountered a polite Sam Bass four miles south of town on April 6 carrying a Spencer rifle, two Colt revolvers and a knife, said that the gang largely roamed in the cross timbers south of Denton between Pecan and Cooper Creeks. However, according to him, the gang would frequently come into Denton at night "to play ten-pins, drink, and have a good time generally." Bystanders heard both their protestations of innocence of the robberies and their oaths never to be taken alive. There was a rumor that Bass was the true owner of Scott Mayes' saloon, and townsfolk speculated about Bass' gold and where it might be buried. This correspondent, too, came to the defense of the good citizens of Denton County who felt powerless to confront the heavily armed band.[18]

The widespread criticism did not fall on deaf ears. Steele, after consulting with Governor Hubbard on Friday, April 12, wrote Major Jones that the decision had been made to raise a force of thirty new rangers as part of the Frontier Battalion, but only for one month. He instructed Jones to muster the unit into service and see to their supplies. Steele would have preferred to send more experienced men after Bass, but "the object is to make arrests where it is claimed that the civil authorities are powerless on [the] Elm Fork of [the] Trinity and elsewhere."[19] The passenger trains running on the Texas and Pacific lines and the Houston and Texas Central at night were now well guarded, and Winchester rifles were shipped to Dallas by order of the adjutant general in Austin for use by express companies and local authorities.[20]

Texas Adjutant General William Steele.
(Courtesy Chuck Parsons, Luling, Texas).

Deputy U.S. Marshal Walter P. Lane[21] went to Denton on Saturday, April 13, to remedy the problem of the local authorities' not having any legal process to justify a pursuit of the Bass gang. Appearing before U.S. Commissioner Alex Robertson, he swore out a complaint against Bass, Underwood, Barnes and Jackson for the Mesquite robbery. Warrants were issued for their arrest and placed in Egan's hands.[22] No one except Robertson was aware of Egan's scheme to have Bill Minor ingratiate himself with Bass and his men.

On Monday, April 15, Captain Hall wrote the adjutant general from San Antonio offering to lead some of his men from the Special Troops after the robbers. "I have no doubt if I was

174

able to pursue them long enough I could catch or kill some of them."[23] But Major Jones had other ideas. He was in Dallas on the fifteenth telling the newspapers that he was not there after the train robbers but had only come there to purchase supplies for his men at Coleman City.[24]

Jones huddled with June Peak and discussed the new ranger company with Peak at its command. Peak assented, and on April 16 Jones wrote Steele requesting that Peak be appointed a second lieutenant to command a detachment of Company B of the Frontier Battalion at Dallas.[25] Jones described Peak as "the best man that can be gotten for the position....He has been raised here, is very popular, is regarded as a terror to evil doers, is a man of fine courage, active, energetic, and efficient in arresting violators of the law."[26] Anticipating the governor's approval, Jones went ahead and issued a special order appointing Peak and assigning him to duty. Jones followed up his letter with a wire. "Commission Junius Peak second lieut. this date to command detachment Co. B. Will enlist men for thirty days. Cannot be done secretly."[27] Peak resigned his position with Dallas as City Recorder. The Board of Aldermen accepted his resignation and promptly abolished the office, assigning the duties to the mayor.[28]

Peak's appointment was made by Governor Hubbard, and on Wednesday, April 17, the *Dallas Daily Herald* announced that he was raising a company of thirty men.[29] Gathered in Dallas now were a number of key officials who were consulting with one another as to the best strategy to nab the train robbers. U.S. Marshal Russell and U.S. District Attorney Andrew J. Evans[30] were staying at the Windsor Hotel where Jules Alvord was still recovering. Grayson County Sheriff Everheart had a room at the LeGrand Hotel, as did Ranger A.L. Parrott and express agent Sam Finley.[31] There would be considerable problems in the days to come with organizing the various entities prowling the countryside after Bass. It was about this time that Billy Scott and Jack Smith approached Major Jones and advised they would provide him information about the Bass gang and the train robberies in return for a share of any rewards. It was quickly agreed that the two would receive two-thirds of any reward for each train robber who was convicted.[32]

Peak turned his attention to recruiting his ranger detachment, after first selecting deputy sheriff Thomas S. "Tom"
Floyd[33] and A.W. Mixon[34] to be his sergeants. Floyd, a member
of the Stonewall Greys with a reputation as a crack shot, agreed
to be Peak's second in command and was mustered into the
detachment on Wednesday, April 17. Peak was familiar with the
background of former Deputy United States Marshal and
policeman Adrian Worth Mixon, who was mustered into Peak's
unit as a fourth sergeant on the same day. A third key member
of Peak's detachment was Tom Rice, appointed as a third corporal on April 17. He had been a constable but, in one manhunt, had been criticized for allowing a suspected rapist to
escape custody. In spite of this, Peak must have seen qualities in
him that made him essential to the pursuit of Bass.[35]

Attracting young men to the new ranger detachment did
not prove to be much of a problem, for they were drawn easily
to the allure of frontier adventure, largely as an escape from the
dull routine of farming. However, finding the caliber of recruit
that could actually face up to the danger of tracking down dangerous criminals was another matter. Setting up camp on the
fair grounds three-quarters of a mile east of Dallas, Peak and
Floyd interviewed applicants while Major Jones visited Denton
County again, returning on Thursday night, April 18. Like others, Jones expressed his concern that both Denton County
deputy Wetsel and ex-deputy Gerren would aid the gang.[36]

In Austin a very nervous Adjutant General Steele advised
Jones that he had ordered Captain Dan Roberts to move his
company to Burnet County, where he would be more centrally
located, and had called for five men from Captain Neal
Coldwell's company to come to Austin to guard the state treas-
ury. The approximately one million dollars there was guarded at
night by "Old Man Warren" and seldom by any guards in the
daytime. Steele also mentioned that the governor had received a
letter from Sheriff Egan saying that he did not require any assistance in executing writs in his county and that he had not been
called upon. Steele suggested that Jones place writs for the Bass
gang in the sheriff's hands, likely unaware that this had already
been done.[37]

Peak had thirty men signed on by Saturday, April 20.[38] One of the new recruits, smarting at his dismissal and the public censure, was J.H. Hickox, the express messenger at Eagle Ford two weeks earlier. The rangers were issued new Winchester rifles, for which they each had to pay twenty-seven dollars, and relocated to a camp at the place of a woman named Knight, about four miles northwest of Dallas, in preparation for the ride into Denton County. Peak had already sent Sergeant Mixon to Denton County on Friday with one private, and they returned on Sunday after riding about sixty miles.[39]

Billy Scott and Jack Smith, who would be described as two of the Bass gang's "confidants," conferred with Jones and Peak about Scott's contacts with the Bass gang, identifying all of the gang members, including Pipes and Herndon, as well as those who had provided any support for the gang.[40] The plan was to obtain federal warrants for all of them and take them into custody. By denying Bass and his men any sanctuary among his friends, the gang could more easily be tracked down.

On the letterhead of Denton law firm Welch, Piner, & Austin, Tom Gerren mailed a letter on Friday, April 19, to Governor Hubbard, no doubt with one eye on the reward.

> Since the 1st day of January 1878 there has been several Rail Road and Express Cos. robed [sic] in this part of the state and I have been trying to find out who has been doing it and at last have succeeded, but am unable to make the arrest as they number from 10 to 15 in gang and armed with the best of arms and a good many of the people here are harboring them and they are doing the most of there [sic] crimes in Dallas County and the people here don't feel much interest in it, and if they wanted to arrest them they have no arms here to do it with. As to who I am refer you to Judge J.A. [sic] Carroll, F.E. Piner, Capt. Hall & our Sheriff.

Governor Hubbard, well aware from reading the *Galveston Daily News* who Gerren was and of the suspicion about him, politely responded that he would "consider" his letter. Adjutant General Steele sent a copy of the letter to Major Jones to "ascertain about the man and if his information is worth anything."[41]

Telegrams were exchanged between Major Jones in Dallas and Marshal Russell in Tyler concerning the approval of the arrest warrants by federal judge Thomas Duval.[42] Jones wanted Judge Duval to order arrests by telegraph rather than making warrants returnable to Tyler. Russell telegraphed Peak the authority to make arrests on Sunday, April 21,[43] and warrants were obtained from George R. Fearn,[44] the federal commissioner in Dallas.

At about ten on Sunday evening, April 21, Major Jones and Lieutenant Peak, with twenty rangers, quietly rode out of their camp and headed northeast of town into the Duck Creek area. By daylight Monday morning the lawmen had surrounded the house of Albert Collins, and Peak knocked at the door. Henry Collins opened the door with a pistol in his hand, but he recognized Peak and invited him inside. Pipes, with Billy Scott lying beside him, was asleep and awoke to find himself surrounded by several heavily armed rangers. Taking Pipes into custody as one of the Mesquite train robbers, the rangers then rode about a mile to the residence of Thomas J. Jackson,[45] another uncle of Sam Pipes, where Albert Herndon was arrested before he could eat breakfast. The two prisoners were hustled off to the county jail in Dallas, and crowds formed to try to get a glimpse of the suspects. Both young men exuded confidence that they could prove an alibi for the night of the Mesquite robbery.[46]

Jones telegraphed Russell of the arrests, and Deputy U.S. Marshal William Anderson was dispatched to ferry the prisoners to Tyler where the federal court was located.[47] The names of Billy Scott and Jack Smith as informants were being kept secret, but both were quietly enlisted into Peak's detachment on May 1. Pipes and Herndon were first charged before a justice of the peace for a state charge of assault with intent to murder, and bail of five hundred dollars was set. When family members began efforts to get the two released, Sheriff Moon served a second warrant on them for state charges of robbery, resulting in an additional $750 to the amount of bail. At the same time Major Jones went before Commissioner Fearn to swear out warrants for federal charges of mail robbery.[48]

On Tuesday evening Scott Mayes was the next Bass associate to be arrested. The day before, he and a deputy city marshal of

Denton identified as J. Minor[49] had come to Dallas on some business, likely in support of Bass. The two had visited various Dallas gun stores inquiring about the prices of Winchester rifles. Mayes bought some zinc flasks and ordered some checks to be printed for his saloon. Peak and several rangers caught up with Mayes at the depot of the Dallas and Wichita Railroad as he started to board for a trip back to Denton. A few days earlier James McGinley had sworn out a federal complaint against Mayes for harboring and abetting the mail robbers at Mesquite, and Fearn had issued a warrant for his arrest.

Mayes was carrying a Smith & Wesson .38 revolver, as well as "a lot of police whistles." The newspaper described Mayes as five feet in height, of muscular build and heavy set, weighing about 140 pounds. The reporter was impressed by his "dark, piercing eyes." Peak was of the opinion that the two men had come to Dallas to spy for Bass and buy ammunition for the gang. The media was well aware of the role that Mayes played as a courier and informant for Bass. An order was obtained from Judge Duval to send Mayes on to Tyler, and he was kept separate from Pipes and Herndon. The prisoner was quite indignant at this "outrage" perpetrated upon him and insisted that he did not want to be placed in the train robber category.[50]

At the same time Tom Rice and two rangers who had left their Dallas camp on Monday, returned from Denton County. Sheriff Egan had arrested John Skaggs,[51] a black man who was known to have carried notes to and from the Bass camp in Denton County and who was described by some as Bass' confidential servant. Egan turned him over to Rice and his rangers, who then rode back to Dallas on Tuesday.[52]

Jones and Peak prepared to turn their prisoners over to federal marshals to be transported to Tyler. Jones wired Marshal Russell that Mayes would be sent on Wednesday, April 24, but that Pipes and Herndon were still being held under state charges, and if they gained bail on those charges, he would send them on to Tyler under Judge Duval's order.[53] At eight o'clock Wednesday morning Mayes was sent on by train to Tyler in the custody of deputy U.S. marshals William H. Anderson[54] and Forsythe. Just missing him was his father, Robert, who had come from Denton with Deputy Marshal J. Minor. He confirmed that his son kept a saloon for Sam Bass, then the concerned father proceeded to Tyler.[55]

Unexpectedly, however, Pipes and Herndon not only gave bail on their state charges, but Commissioner Fearn also released them Tuesday evening on $2,500 bail on the federal charges. The sureties on their bonds were Thomas Jackson, John McCommas[56] and Benjamin Fleaman, a son-in-law of Amon McCommas and Herndon's uncle.[57] Public comment on such a small bond for suspected mail robbers facing a life sentence was quick to form.[58] Major Jones was shocked. On Wednesday morning he wired the news to Marshal Russell in Tyler.

> Commissioner has released Pipes & Herndon on bond. The whole business is spoiled unless they can be rearrested at once and [held] for some weeks in confinement at Tyler under Judge Duval's order. Pipes is said to be one of those wounded. Was not examined. Can you telegraph order to Anderson to rearrest them at once.[59]

Russell immediately consulted with U.S. Attorney Evans and sent his instructions to Jones.

> Am much astonished at action of Commissioner as he has no authority to bail in felony cases when the federal court is in session. Tell Anderson to get the warrant from Commissioner & rearrest Pipes and Herndon as the action of the Commissioner is void and bring them forthwith without any delay. The District Attorney agreed with me and is provoked that the Commissioner has so acted. If he cannot get the old warrant, have another affidavit and warrant and arrest them. See Anderson tonight.[60]

On Thursday afternoon Major Jones left Dallas on the westbound Texas & Pacific, confident that Pipes and Herndon would be quickly back in custody. He had received a telegram that day from J.M. Henderson in Fort Worth that five hundred dollars in 1877 twenty-dollar gold pieces had been deposited there.[61] As Jones was leaving, more express detectives were pouring into town along with other would-be detectives. Several men in "rough frontier costumes" rode through the city, and on Tuesday evening the horse of one of them stumbled, throwing the rider, and his false whiskers fell off. He snatched them up, remounted his clumsy steed, and rode on out of town.[62]

Pipes and Herndon appeared before Justice of the Peace Edward C. McLure on Friday morning, April 26, for arraignment on the pending state charges. Prosecutor Robert Cowart requested that the matter be continued because the state's witnesses were not present. Their attorney, Hickerson Barksdale,[63] agreed to postpone the case until Monday. As Pipes and Herndon left the courtroom, Deputy U.S. Marshal William Anderson stepped forward and placed them under arrest again for mail robbery. They were immediately taken before U.S. Commissioner Jeremiah M. Hayes, and a ranger had to be posted at the door to keep the office from becoming too crowded.

Barksdale registered a protest and claimed that Hayes had no jurisdiction since another commissioner had already set bond. Cowart, summoned by Marshal Russell to act as prosecutor in the hearing, explained that so long as the federal court was in session in Tyler, no commissioner had authority to take a bond for such felony offenses. The only recourse, he said, was to detain the defendants. Commissioner Hayes announced a bond of fifteen thousand dollars on each of the prisoners, which Pipes and Herndon could not possibly post, and they were taken back to jail, crestfallen.

That afternoon friends and relatives joined to pledge the total bonds of thirty thousand dollars, including Elisha[64] and John McCommas, John H. Cole, A.G. Collins, Thomas J. Nash, Ben Fleaman and W.E. Daniels, a thirty-two-year-old farmer from Alabama.[65] Barksdale asked that the two prisoners be returned to court from the jail in order that their bonds could be posted, it being his understanding that Marshal Russell had left instructions at the jail that no one but a federal officer could handle the prisoners, and no federal officers were present. Deputy Anderson came into the court and asked to speak privately to the commissioner. Commissioner Hayes told

Barksdale that Anderson had refused to go get the prisoners, and the lawyer asked that the court order the county's jailer to bring over the prisoners. The order was given and delivered to County Jailer H.B. Dean, but he refused to present the prisoners under the instructions of Marshal Russell to hand them over only to a federal officer. To reinforce Russell's instructions, Anderson and a detective went to the jail and stood in the doorway to make sure that the prisoners were not removed until Russell said they were to be moved.

The sureties waiting to post their bonds were outraged and Barksdale worked to calm them down. In the meantime, the authorities were not losing any time. At about four o'clock that afternoon, while the defendants' friends were roiling, Pipes was brought from his cell to the sleeping room of one of the guards for a physical examination by Dr. Albert A. Johnson. An agitated Pipes protested his innocence, but he was directed to remove his shirt. The doctor noticed a bandage, and when it was removed he found a gunshot wound on Pipes' left hip. Pipes first claimed that it was only a boil then said that "one of the boys" accidentally shot him one night, but he didn't report it because he didn't want his friend to be arrested. When Pipes was returned to his cell, a guard heard him tell Herndon, "Well, we are gone up now—they have found it."

Concerned about an attempt to rescue the prisoners, rangers and federal officers took Pipes, Herndon and Skaggs at about eight o'clock that evening to the district courtroom to await delivery of the warrant from Tyler. Pipes and Herndon laid on the floor while Skaggs sat and ate some bread and cheese provided by the rangers.[66]

Jones had returned to Dallas and sent a telegram to Adjutant General Steele advising him of the situation. "I cannot produce the evidence in court here, but can bring it before grand jury at Tyler....If they can be kept in jail think I will be able to catch others. If these are released it is doubtful....Went to Fort Worth yesterday. Found some of the seventy-seven gold. Another link in the chain against certain parties whom I am investigating."[67] Jones was still relying on Scott and Smith to gain more information on the Bass gang and was not ready to reveal their identities in open court.

Shortly after ten o'clock the heavily armed party took their three prisoners to the Texas and Pacific depot to await the east-bound train for Tyler. Deputy U.S. Marshal Walter Johnson had come in on the westbound train with the warrants from Tyler. The three prisoners were hustled aboard and were soon on their way.[68]

Media combat broke out on several fronts about this time. The *Galveston Daily News* reported that Bass had friends in Denton County who watched and even questioned any strangers that visited there, reporting every move to Bass. "It is said he has six men, regularly employed, who receive $60 gold each, per month, besides their drinking free."[69] The *Denton Monitor*, feeling the need to defend the reputation and good name of the county's citizens, published its umbrage at what other newspapers had been saying, especially the Dallas papers, accusing them of having "slandered and vituperated the whole country."[70]

Even more bizarre was the warfare that broke out in the pages of Texas newspapers between Grayson County Sheriff William Everheart and former Denton deputy Tom Gerren. It began with a letter from Everheart printed in the *Sherman Register* on April 24. Everheart discussed his meeting with Gerren in December, asserting that he told the deputy that the Union Pacific robbers had gone to San Antonio. The sheriff claimed that while in San Antonio, Gerren had told the mistress of a brother of one of Bass' men why Everheart was there. He also claimed that when Gerren returned to Denton, he flashed a huge roll of fifty and one hundred-dollar bills in front of Deputy U.S. Marshal Walter Johnson, claiming that Bass had given it to him for being his friend. Gerren was also supposed to have told Ranger Jim Lucy and June Peak that he had given Everheart away in San Antonio.[71]

When Gerren saw the letter, he claimed that it was he who had told Everheart where Underwood was, and that he was not aware at the time that Bass was the same Bass named as a Union Pacific robber. He denied ever saying that he received any money from Bass, although he admitted knowing Bass. Gerren pledged to "make it hot for his maligners."[72] Through the *Denton Monitor* in May, Gerren formally responded to the sheriff, calling him a "perjured villain" and a liar and slanderer and claiming that Everheart accompanied him to San Antonio. He alleged that Everheart talked to Underwood and Bass there, and that Tony Waits declared his intention to swear that Underwood was Tom Nixon, even though he knew that Underwood was in Texas when the Union Pacific robbery occurred. He said that Everheart lied about the prostitute and that he had never flashed any money in front of Walter Johnson. He averred that Sam Bass was no longer a friend of his and that Everheart arrested Underwood only to obtain the reward.[73]

Everheart was quick to reply. In a letter published in the *Sherman Register* on May 13, he noted that the issue boiled down to who was to be believed. He included an affidavit by Cooke County Sheriff M.M. Ozment swearing that Everheart knew that Underwood had gone to San Antonio before conferring with Gerren. Ranger Sergeant A.L. Parrott affirmed that a prostitute in San Antonio told him and Everheart that Gerren had told her about them. He also stated that Gerren flashed a large roll of bills. Deputy Marshal Johnson swore that Gerren told him that he gave Everheart away to keep him from getting the reward and that the deputy had flashed a roll of bills, inferring that the money came from Bass for his friendship. Finally he included an affidavit by Ranger Jim Lucy that Gerren had given Everheart away.[74] The conflict ultimately died down, although Gerren's credibility was never restored, even with his vigorous denials.

Now, with Mayes, Pipes, Herndon and John Skaggs in jail, the manhunt after Bass and his men had demonstrated the commitment of the rangers to track them down and capture or kill them.

-XII-
CLOSE PURSUIT

P eak and his men prepared for the major campaign after Bass in Denton County. On Friday, April 26, Albert Collins, father of Joel, Billy and Henry, came to Dallas to express to a newspaper his mortification at Pipes' being arrested at his residence.[1] Jones sent a telegram to Adjutant General Steele asking him to arrange railroad transportation for him and the rangers. "It is required every day." Railroad executives were quick to pledge transportation at any hour of day or night for the pursuit.[2]

That same evening a Dallas prostitute, Maude Dunbar, sent for City Marshal Morton to come to her Jackson Street residence because Bass and Jackson were there. Morton and his officers responded quickly but were told the outlaws had just left. Maude Dunbar, born to French parentage in Kentucky about 1859 and who had been a prostitute in Dallas as early as 1876,[3] knew Bass personally, and Morton found her to be very excited.[4]

On Saturday Marshal Russell wired Jones in Dallas of the arrival of the prisoners in Tyler. Jones, concerned that the defendants would seek a habeas corpus hearing in Tyler to win their release, urged Russell to postpone it at all costs until Scott and Smith could appear before the federal grand jury.[5] For the present, however, he was not ready for their identity to be revealed. Billy Scott was back in contact with Bass in Denton County. Meeting at Green Hill's place, Scott proposed that the gang rob the Gaston & Thomas bank in Dallas. Scott returned to Dallas, purportedly to work out the details of the raid but actually to contact Jones and Peak to lay the trap. According to Martin, Billy Collins did not trust Scott and warned Bass that Scott was a spy and traitor. Jones was not keen on the idea of a bank robbery attempt because of the danger of an innocent person's being hurt.[6]

It was reported that a total of $1,800 in newly minted

California twenty-dollar gold pieces had turned up in north central Texas, especially Dallas.[7] It was also rumored in Dallas that Bass had sent a note to Peak asking for a meeting under truce and that Peak had answered the note, but no one knew the substance of the response. Tom Gerren would later turn up with Peak's note, which Peak had sent to Scott Mayes for delivery to Bass. However, when Mayes was arrested the note was left with Green Hill, from whom Gerren retrieved it. The note essentially promised Bass that he would not be arrested or harmed if he should meet under a truce, and it warned him that Peak would have rangers in Denton, but not for the purpose of arresting Bass.[8]

With Peak's men finally ready to ride, Major Jones sent a letter with Peak on Sunday, April 28, to be handed to Sheriff Egan in Denton County.

> Lieut. Peak has warrants for the arrest of Bass, Barnes, Jackson, Underwood and Johnson, alias "Arkansas."
>
> He will make an effort to arrest them on Tuesday the 30th and I write to request you to assist him in finding them and effecting the arrests.
>
> He will be at Capt. Swishers, eight miles below Denton at daylight Tuesday morning and I will be glad if you will meet him at that time and place with [him] three or four *good* men who know the country well where these parties are said to be hiding.
>
> These outlaws must be arrested or driven from the country and, as I do not believe they can be caught in "traps," I know of no other way to accomplish the desired object except to make a drive for them through the woods, scour the country thoroughly when they will certainly be caught or be forced to leave the country.
>
> I hope and shall expect that you, as well as all citizens of Denton County, will render us all the assistance in your power to rid the country of these out-laws. Would have communicated with you in regard to this matter sooner but have not been ready to do anything until now.

I hope you will go with Lt. Peak yourself, as I am extremely desirous to have some county official with the party, but if you cannot possibly go you must send him *four good men* to act as guides.

I would come with Lt. Peak and his men but am compelled to go to Tyler to appear myself and to produce witnesses before the Federal grand jury in order to procure indictments against these men and some whom I have already arrested. I am informed by Marshall [sic] Russell that the grand jury will adjourn in two or three days and if the indict-[sic] are not found within that time it cannot be done during this term of court.

It is of the utmost importance that these movements be kept profoundly secret.[9]

However, Egan was not waiting for the rangers. The county had been stung by the criticism it had received and was embarrassed by the presence of Bass and his men. On Sunday morning the sheriff was advised that Bass, Underwood, Jackson and one other man, probably Barnes, were seen in the woods about three miles south of Denton. Egan quickly rounded up a posse of eight to ten men and rode out. Arriving at the place where the gang had been seen, Egan split up his men in an attempt to surround the outlaws, but Bass and the outlaws spotted the posse and, with Bass yelling defiance, the gang opened fire and a gunbattle ensued. The robbers rode quickly off in the direction of Denton and a running battle ensued until their horses outdistanced the posse after about a mile. All the lawmen had to show for the effort was a saddle blanket left behind by the outlaws.[10] Bass and his men, one of them riding a badly wounded horse, intercepted an old man on a horse and demanded that the old man turn his horse over to them. When he refused, they drew their weapons and took the horse at gunpoint. The man reported that one of the gang had been shot in the face and was bleeding badly,[11] although it was likely a scratch from a tree limb incurred during the hasty flight through the thick underbrush.

Egan placed Deputy Riley Wetsel in charge of part of the posse and sent him in one direction while the sheriff took the remainder of the posse in another. The posse had been increased by the voluntary enlistment of several farmers from the area,[12] but it was soon determined that the hastily summoned posse's ammunition was depleted and the men returned to Denton Sunday night.[13] Alex Cockrell and two others spotted Bass later that morning about four miles from Denton and gave chase, firing at the fleeing band, but the bandits were mounted on superior horses and were soon out of sight.[14]

While Peak and twenty-seven rangers were making their way to Denton County on Sunday, and while Egan was engaged with Bass, Major Jones served a federal subpoena that day on Billy Scott, his most important witness, to appear before the grand jury. The two took the train together for Tyler.[15] At the same time Billy Collins, interviewed by a newspaper, defended Pipes and Herndon, saying they had been at his place at the time of the Mesquite robbery and had been preparing to go west with him on a cattle drive. Collins said that Pipes' bullet wound was made by a small pistol at his house.[16] Shortly after this, Collins was himself served with a federal attachment and taken into custody by Sergeant Mixon and two rangers, to be turned over to federal officers and taken to Tyler on Monday.[17]

Peak and his rangers arrived in Denton early Monday morning, April 29, and consulted with Sheriff Egan. Egan had a posse of thirty men ready to ride, having impressed weapons and horses for the pursuit. Even the four horses used to pull the stage between Denton and the terminus of the Dallas and Wichita Railroad were taken up, leaving the driver to hunt for another team. Egan and his posse rode out, and Peak took his unit into the field.[18]

While Peak and Egan were leading their men around Denton on Monday, Sheriff Everheart and his posse, which included Sergeant Parrott and others of Captain Hall's command, rode to check out Jim Murphy's place in northwest Denton County. Bass and his men were nearby and spotted the posse approaching their camp on the other side of the deep canyon through which a branch of Clear Creek flowed. Aware that the gang had ample time to escape and confident that the distance across the canyon, approximately five hundred yards, would prove too much for accurate gunfire, Bass taunted the posse to stand and fight like men, launching a shot in their direction. During the ensuing exchange of gunfire, Parrott calmly aimed his rifle and shot cartridges out of Bass' gunbelt.

At this Bass screamed, "They've hit me at last, boys. Let's get away from here." The gang rode quickly off, assured that the posse would be unable to pursue across the canyon at that point. The fleeing bandits stopped at Murphy's place, where Underwood's wife and family were staying, and gave her one hundred dollars, then doubled back. Through Bass' spyglass they watched Everheart's posse scouring the countryside for them.[19]

On Monday evening Wetsel was riding with Denton Constable A.R. McGintie[20] north of Bolivar, about thirteen miles northwest of Denton. They saw a group of five men and rode after them. The group fled east and lost the two pursuers when it became dark,[21] but on Tuesday the pursuit continued. Early that morning Wetsel and McGintie followed the trail of the fleeing gang to the Clear Creek bottom behind a field belonging to William Whitehead, a crippled forty-three-year-old farmer from Arkansas.[22] Joined by Whitehead, they followed the trail on foot and came upon Bass' camp just as the outlaws were leaving. Whitehead and McGintie returned to Whitehead's farm for their horses while Wetsel continued to follow the gang through the thick Clear Creek morass. When he reached a clearing beyond the creek, he was joined by Whitehead and McGintie and they continued to follow the outlaws' trail.

At about eight o'clock that morning they found that the gang had settled into a new camp at the farm of Hardin Carter,[23] about four miles northeast of Denton, to feed their horses and to eat breakfast. Wetsel sent a courier to Denton to inform Egan. The sheriff in turn rounded up six men—Tom Yates,[24] Jack Yates,[25] Alex Cockrell, Charley Hart,[26] Finley Grissom[27] and Dode Fain—who quickly gathered what arms they could and rode to join Wetsel, McGintie and Whitehead. On their arrival, the men were deployed around the campsite.

Wetsel saw the men eating breakfast about 150 yards in front of Carter's place. He quietly rode up to Carter's house and was talking with Carter about the gang when they spotted him.

Bass and his men quickly saddled their horses and rode off, Bass ordering, "To Clear Creek bottom, boys!" Wetsel fired a shot in the air to alert the posse, then dismounted and opened fire on the fleeing men. Whitehead, Jack Yates and Grissom also dismounted to fire at the outlaws. Egan led the remainder of the men in pursuit in another running gunbattle for about a quarter mile until the outlaws, who had been yelling and firing, managed to enter the woods and turn southeastward toward the Elm Fork bottom. The gang left behind blankets, overcoats and other small items.

When Egan and his men again struck the gang's trail, word of the chase was received in Denton and about fifty more armed citizens joined the hunt. At the end of daylight Egan lost the trail in the Elm swamp. He left a dozen men to look for the trail and returned to Denton to organize the rapidly building corps of new recruits for posses. The men left behind in the swamp split into two groups to watch two houses; the group led by Tom Yates actually encountered the gang briefly in the darkness but did not know who it was until the gang had again dispersed.[28]

On the morning of Tuesday, April 30, the posse under Tom Yates joined with Peak's men to track the outlaw trail on foot through the Elm Fork bottoms, but Bass and his men had scattered and the posse lost the trail. By now Denton's streets resembled a military camp as citizens armed and mounted themselves to help the sheriff and the rangers. The best information indicated that the robbers were sticking to the swampy, overgrown area between the Elm Fork and Hickory Creek south of Denton. Peak and his rangers camped about seven miles south of town on the Dallas road in the area where the gang was believed to be hiding.

Egan divided his growing force into several squads, making the former county seat of Alton his headquarters for purposes of communications. Tom Hogg, the county judge, led one squad toward Alton to watch a crossing on Hickory Creek, while Egan and other squads scoured the area between the two creeks. Some 150 men were now split between the forces of Peak, Egan and Everheart, who was in the northern part of the County.[29]

Judge Hogg had with him I.D. Ferguson,[30] Robert

McIlheny,[31] A.E. McMath,[32] William Davis, and two men named Drake and Bryant. As they rode toward Alton, they ran into a man named Thomas at Robertson's Mill who told them he had seen fresh horse tracks that morning heading into the swamps of Hickory Creek below the Alton crossing. Thomas showed them where the tracks were, and Hogg and his men could see that the horse had been led into the thick briars and underbrush. McMath and Davis were left with the posse's horses while the remainder of the men followed the trail on foot about one and a half miles until they reached Hickory Creek.

They stealthily crossed the creek and found themselves within sixty yards of Henry Underwood, who spotted them and jumped out of sight. The party rushed through the thick brush, down and out of a steep ravine, to where he had been standing. Ferguson spotted a horse and raised his weapon, but the horse moved out of sight. Since there were only five poorly armed men, it was not thought prudent to charge the better-armed gang. Word was sent to Egan, and he responded with about thirty men to scour the area. Bass' camp, now deserted, contained all of the gang's bedding, cooking utensils and provisions as well as two saddled horses that belonged to Bass and Jackson. Apparently, the bandits abandoned the rest of their horses some distance from the camp and struck out on foot until they could steal other horses near Denton. The two saddled horses were taken to Denton and kept at the Work brothers' stable.

Egan and his men rode for miles around the swamp, although many places were almost impenetrable, and were joined by Peak and his rangers. Lawyer Alvin Owsley,[33] accompanied by Ed Wilson[34] and others, found a shawl hanging from a limb of a tree in a hollow near the place of Warren Jackson, Frank's brother. In the shawl was a bucket containing food.

As the different groups rode through the countryside during the day looking for Bass, there were inevitable mistakes. On one occasion Tom Gerren, W.S. Kirksey and John Work[35] charged and fired at a group of riders who turned out to be some of Peak's rangers.[36] By the time the sun fell Tuesday evening, the gang had eluded capture and the posses regrouped for a new search the next day.

Early Wednesday, May 1, a rumor flew through the streets of

Dallas that Peak had been shot during an encounter with Bass.[37] That afternoon Jones went to the terminus of the railroad in Denton County and met with Peak for an update. Billy Scott and Jack Smith formally went on the ranger payroll as members of Peak's detachment. At Duck Creek U.S. Deputy Marshal C.V. Fraley[38] arrested E.D. Walton[39] and John P. Price[40] on an attachment from Tyler, and they were to be taken there on Thursday morning.[41]

In Tyler on Wednesday the federal grand jury returned indictments against Bass, Underwood, Jackson, Pipes, Herndon, Barnes, Johnson and Billy Collins for robbing the mails at Mesquite on April 10. Named as accessories who aided the robbers were Green Hill, Henry Collins, Scott Mayes, Robert Murphy, Riley Wetsel, Ben A. Key, Warren Jackson and Monroe Hill.[42] Warrants were issued to arrest those not yet in custody. The next morning Herndon, Pipes, Mayes and Billy Collins appeared "cool and jocular" during their arraignment before Judge Duval in Tyler. They asked for time to get their witnesses to Tyler but wanted their trials to be held as soon as possible. The judge granted them a few days, and U.S. Attorney Evans announced that he was ready for trial in all cases.[43]

A crowd gathered in Dallas on Thursday afternoon, May 2, when Mixon, Tom Rice and Bob Williams brought in new prisoners, including Green Hill, Bob Murphy, Bill Minor and Peter J. Mullin, a young Denton lawyer who was supposed to be distantly related to the Collins family,[44] although charges against him would later be dropped. They were held at a hotel until they could be taken to Tyler the next morning.[45] Turning their prisoners over to federal marshals, Mixon and the two rangers returned to the field to try to find Henry Collins.[46]

Peak and twenty rangers, accompanied by Egan with a large posse, left Denton at about eleven o'clock Friday morning. They had information that Bass and his men might be making for a particular house in Wise County and rode to try and intercept them.[47] Jones' plan to make it too hot both for Bass to stay in the confines of Denton County and for those who aided him in any way, was resented somewhat in Denton County. "Scores of the best citizens were dragged from their homes as witnesses who knew nothing more about Bass and his gang than the man in the moon, and kept from their business and families, at Tyler, for weeks. It was, in truth, an evil day for Denton and she paid dearly in every way for the presence of these bandits."[48]

Reports over the next several weeks as to the whereabouts of Bass and his men were many and conflicting. A farmer in Denton County named Hoffman noticed a trail of shelled corn leading from where sacks of the corn had been stolen at his place. He followed the trail into the woods until he came to an abandoned campsite. Figuring that it was Bass' campsite, he returned to his farm and forgot about it. He said he later met Bass on the road and the bandit paid him a twenty-dollar gold piece for the corn.[49]

Another farmer butchered a cow for Bass and had a neighbor boy, Shelton Story,[50] take it to some men camped in the Denton creek bottoms. Story hitched the meat behind his fine new saddle, of which he was quite proud, and rode to the camp of the men where the beef was handed over. One of the men suggested that he trade his new saddle for a broken-down one. Not wanting to argue with the heavily armed men, Story let the exchange of saddles occur without protest and rode home heavyhearted. But when he arrived home and unsaddled his horse, he found six twenty-dollar gold pieces in the saddle pockets and was able to outfit himself in even finer fashion.[51]

On Friday morning, May 3, Grayson County Sheriff Everheart and his posse, including Ranger Jim Lucy and a man named J.W. Phillips,[52] moved in on the farm of Henderson Murphy and arrested him along with his son Jim, Monroe Hill, and brothers Jack and Tom Burshon. Jim Murphy later claimed that Everheart took a horse from him and never returned it. The five were taken to Sherman by detective Pat Connell for transfer to Tyler. Posse member Charley Hart was brought into Denton with a gunshot wound in his right foot, although it is unknown how he received that wound.[53]

Anticipating that Bass and his men might be trying to make their way to Wise County, Peak, Egan and some of their men rode to Decatur, the Wise county seat. Peak sent a telegram to Major Jones that he had information that Bass might have gone to Jack County and asked how far he should follow them. Jones instructed him to follow them as long as he kept trace of them.[54]

The next morning, Saturday, May 4, in Clay County to the north, Sheriff Thomas W. Gee[55] was serving papers in the southwestern part of the county, about twenty-five miles from the county seat of Henrietta, when he saw three riders emerge from some timber. At first they did not notice the sheriff, but when they did, about fifty yards away, they halted and drew their revolvers. Gee immediately dismounted, aimed his rifle over his saddle at the riders and ordered them to come forward. They in turn called out to him as to his business, and the four men remained in a standoff. Finally the three men slowly rode off to the west, weapons drawn. Gee held his fire because he was outnumbered. When he gave the description of the men, it was believed they were Bass and two of his gang.[56]

Corporal W.C. Lewis and nine men of Peak's command returned to Dallas from Wise County on Sunday, May 5. Sergeant Mixon and the rangers with him remained camped near Dallas, awaiting orders, joined by another Ranger, Gaston Hardy, who had arrived at the camp the night before from Denton because he had come down with typhoid fever. Mixon and Deputy U.S. Marshal Fraley made another stab at serving a warrant on Henry Collins in Dallas County, but his mother told them that he had left "upon advice of friends."[57] Major Jones shared with the newspapers his opinions of whom he thought was involved in each of the Texas train robberies, and he declared that Bass was "the absolute chief, and pays the expenses out of the gold he got by the Union Pacific robbery."[58] It was reported that a woman in the northwest part of Wise County recognized Bass, Underwood and Jackson as being three of five men who stopped at her place for water.[59]

Bass and his men had dropped out of sight, and various posses roamed through Denton and Wise Counties looking for them. On Tuesday, May 7, Ranger Lieutenant G.W. Campbell of the regular Company B ordered a scout to help in the search for the Bass party. Sergeants J.E. Van Riper[60] and Charles M. Sterling[61] took eight men from Camp Sibley to try to intercept the bandits, believed to be coming from Clay County. Sterling and Van Riper split their squads, searching in different directions in the Wichita and Archer County vicinity. Corporal J.E. Smith and E.W. Jordan were also sent on a separate scout.[62]

Tom Gerren, described as an "acting deputy sheriff" of Denton County, was still on the trail. On Tuesday evening he brought two prisoners to Dallas, en route for Tyler. One was a counterfeiter, Levi Breeding, and the other was William Day, a Denton County farmer suspected of being an accomplice of Bass. Gerren admitted he was not an officer but was "acting at the request of the Tyler authorities as any citizen may."[63] On that same day Major Jones came to Dallas from Austin, intending to stay in north Texas for about ten days.[64] Marshal Russell also arrived in Dallas from Sherman with Monroe Hill and Henderson and Jim Murphy, intending to take them to Tyler the next day before they could be released on habeas corpus.[65]

That night in Dallas, two of Peak's men, L.S. Hart and Bob Williams, engaged in a spree and shot off their pistols near the Central depot. Local police took them into custody, and when they were admitted to bond, their pistols were turned over to Sergeant Mixon.[66]

According to Hogg, Bass and his men had never left Denton County but had remained in the Hickory Creek bottom while posses roamed through the countryside trying to pick up some clue as to their whereabouts. On Tuesday, May 7, they stealthily left their hiding place and made for Stephens County to the west.[67]

Major Jones continued to share some of his information with the newspapers. According to him, Bass and his men had intended to rob a Weatherford bank in Parker County but had then decided to rob a Dallas bank, likely at Billy Scott's suggestion. They had then thought about heading for Kansas to avoid detection.[68] Everheart briefly returned to Sherman on May 8, admitting that no one knew where Bass was right now. While in Denton a few days earlier, Everheart and Gerren accidentally found themselves eating dinner at the same table, but no words or gunfire were exchanged. Everheart expressed considerable frustration at the disorganized fashion in which the variety of bands of lawmen and would-be lawmen criss crossed the countryside, blundering into each other far too frequently.[69]

By Saturday, May 11, Ranger Lieutenant G.W. Campbell

had concluded that Bass had either turned south toward Stephens County or gone from Clay County north into the Indian Territory. The squads under Van Riper and Sterling had found no sign of the gang's trail, and cowboys that they had encountered had not noticed any movements by strangers through their country. The rangers returned to their camp after traveling 417 miles on horseback.[70] In Dallas Major Jones received a telegram from U.S. Attorney Andrew Evans that he now needed Billy Scott and Jack Smith to return to Tyler as his most important witnesses against all of the men now being held in custody for grand jury action.[71] At the same time Peak sent a telegram to Colonel E.G. Bower in Dallas, trying to get in touch with Major Jones. He had received information that Henry Underwood was in Stephens County and would await Jones' orders.[72] In Coryell County, far to the south, a man named Julius Hegler was arrested by rangers as a suspect in the Allen robbery.[73]

Everything was in readiness in Tyler for the trial on Tuesday of Pipes and Herndon. Other prisoners were filing affidavits to the effect that they could not afford to hire attorneys. The defense attorneys' request of the court that the prisoners be allowed to be present when any witnesses for the government were questioned was refused by Judge Duval, who told the attorneys they could talk to their clients and to the witnesses separately.[74]

The May 12 *Dallas Daily Herald* reported an unusual story it thought might be related to the Bass gang. Several weeks earlier a woman had arrived in Dallas from Denton and taken a room at the Crutchfield House. On her first night, two men dressed in frontier garb called on her about midnight and one stayed with her that night. About five the next morning the man who had stayed the night came down to the desk and paid the woman's bill with a gold coin. When asked, he denied that the woman was his wife but told the landlord, "You just let her stay here, for there is plenty of this sort of stuff to pay for it," shaking a purse with gold coins in it. Dissatisfied, the proprietor notified the woman that she would have to leave and she departed that evening.

Dallas Marshal Morton heard about the woman and

searched for her, finally locating her in the southeastern portion of the city. Another woman living nearby had become interested in this visitor from Denton and was able to give Morton the information that the Denton woman had identified herself as Malinda Carter and that two men visited her every night around midnight, leaving before dawn. Morton caused any mail to her to be monitored and finally intercepted a letter from McKinney.

> Three Miles from McKinney in the Brush
> Dear Mollie - Tony brought your message through all right, and I was glad to hear that you were washing your way through all right. There are five of us, and another with us that you don't know, and it will do no good to put his name on paper. "Old well boys" jaw is doing all right, and we will make it yet, if the woods are full of them. Don't you be so scared about me, but steer your way through like the brave woman you are, and all will yet be good. We will leave Denison on our left, and make for the C.N. Put up a pitiful mouth to old General Cabell, and get a ticket to Denison, where you will see Jim, who will send you to Caney, where you must wait until we can come after you.
> Your own, F.

Morton resealed the letter and returned it to the post office to await delivery to the woman, but she had left Dallas the day before, and no one knew where she had gone.[75] There is no information as to who this woman was or whether this was a letter from Frank Jackson. There was speculation that she might be related to Hardin Carter of Denton County, whose son would become involved with the Bass gang, but a diligent search has failed to turn up anything further on her identity.

On the evening of Sunday, May 12, leaving Tom Floyd and some men in Wise County, Peak and the rest of his contingent returned to Dallas and went back into camp four miles from town on the Dallas and Wichita Railroad. Apparently because of the note that Peak had sent to Bass in response to a request for a parley, Tom Gerren had sworn out a complaint against

Peak in Denton for being an accessory to the train robberies. The complaint was labeled as ridiculous and Gerren's credibility sunk even lower.[76] Gerren himself had been attached as a witness and was now being kept in Tyler. Billy Scott and E.W. "Jack" Smith, having testified before the grand jury in Tyler, were reassigned to Lieutenant G.W. Arrington's Company C, although they would not report until their duties with Peak were completed.[77]

Unable to leave Tyler, Gerren, now apparently appointed as a deputy U.S. Marshal, wrote a letter to Governor Hubbard on Monday, May 13, using some of Marshal Russell's stationery.

> I wrote you some time ago refurring [sic] to the robberies that have been committed by unknown parties in Dallas County on the Rail Roads. I state to you now as I did then that I know who the parties are that have been doing the robbing and can furnish evidence to convict them if they were arrested, and have spent 250.00 in trying to arrest them but am unable as they number from 10 to 15 in gang. If you want them arrested and will give me a position and 15 good men, I will arrest them & deliver them without any reward from the State of Texas. We have 6 principals arrested and in jail here now but Bass & Co. are still at large.
>
> I am held here at present as a witness against them. I don't want a position any longer than to arrest the parties and I am personally acquainted with all of the parties that I want - Though I will not work unless I can get good pay for it. I will refur [sic] you to F.E. Piner of Denton as to who I am and what I want to do.
>
> If Your Excellency should think this worthy of an answer, I would be pleased to hear from you.

Hubbard had his secretary, Thomas Harkin, forward Gerren's letter to Major Jones in Dallas for whatever he wanted to do with it.[78]

Jones received a telegram from Marshal Russell stating there was no warrant for Peak based on Gerren's complaint and asking the major to come to Tyler the next day, Tuesday the fourteenth, after instructing Deputy U.S. Marshal Anderson to hurry up and serve the subpoenas for the upcoming trial of Pipes and Herndon.[79] In Tyler on Tuesday, the trial did not begin because defense attorneys were requesting additional time for their witnesses to arrive there. William Pinkerton was in attendance, and it was now anticipated that further delay would force the criminal cases to be continued and transferred to the federal court in Austin for trial.[80]

Major Jones, back in Dallas on May 13, was provided with a letter purportedly written to Sam Bass in care of Tom Gerren by a man named Eugene Campbell. He sent the letter to Lieutenant Arrington of Company C, directing him to check out Campbell as a man to whom Bass and his men might turn for help and who might even be Nixon or Davis, the Union Pacific robbers. On May 21 Arrington responded to Jones that Campbell was a stage driver between Concho and Brownwood, had formerly been a ranger in Company D, had once lived in Denton County and known both Bass and Gerren two years earlier, and had written them after reading about them in the newspapers. Arrington said that he did not fit the description of either Nixon or Davis.[81]

While the status of the trial in Tyler was still up in the air, Peak was faced with the end of the thirty-day term of his ranger detachment and its disbandment. On Thursday, May 16, Scott Mayes and Henderson Murphy and his two sons were all released on bail, one condition being that they remain in Tyler. A partner of Bob Murphy, Charles Cannon, acted as a surety on the bonds of the Murphys. Billy Collins was unable to get out of jail because of an excessive bond that had been set.[82]

Rethinking the original plan, Jones and Steele were able to preserve some of Peak's ranger detachment. On Friday, May 17, Jones ordered Peak to discharge sixteen of his men because the thirty-day enlistment term had expired, but the remainder would be kept in state service for a few weeks more to continue the pursuit.[83] Retained with Peak were Sergeant Floyd, corporals Tom Rice and W.C. Lewis, and privates R.H. Armstrong, Thomas R. Bailey, H. Britt, James W. Bruton, Harry C. Cammack, R.C. Darsey, J.H. Hickox, C.E. Tucker, Theo. J. Whitley and Robert E. Williams. In addition, Jack Smith and

Billy Scott were added to Peak's unit.[84] State budget problems were forcing other economies, and Jones was also forced to dismiss Lieutenant Campbell and all but Sergeant Van Riper and five of the regular Company B command on May 18.[85]

In the meantime nothing had been heard from Bass since April 30, and the general belief was that he and his men had successfully escaped from the area, perhaps into the Indian Territory. Given the number of lawmen who had joined in the chase, some of the press around the state continued to be critical of the efforts to track him down. "There is reason to believe that the want of harmony among the different parties and the over anxiety to make the capture and obtain the reward had much to do with the unsatisfactory results."[86]

The next day Major Jones responded to Gerren's May 13 letter to Governor Hubbard, making his attitude about the former lawman very clear.

> Sir - Your communication of 14th inst. enclosing letter of T.E. Gerrin [sic] to His Excellency Gov. Hubbard, received.
>
> In reply I have to say that I have no confidence whatever in Mr. Gerrin and would not trust him in any way or for any purpose. He has admitted to several parties privately that he "gave Sheriff Everheart away" in San Antonio and that he made money by doing so, his only excuse for this being that Everheart did not "tote fair" with him. He admitted this to Marshall [sic] Russell and then proposed to assist in catching Bass and to my astonishment was taken into Russell's service. My opinion of Mr. Gerrin is that if you promised Gerrin $500 to catch a criminal and he should get him into custody, he would release him for $600 rather than turn him over to you for $500. In other words that he would serve the man who paid him the most without regard to truth or honesty. For these reasons I have held no communication with him. Besides this I have information which satisfies me that Bass himself has lost confidence in Gerrin and would not put himself or his friends in his power.

I do not believe that Gerrin ever knew who the parties were that committed the train robberies in Texas or that anyone else knew who they were, except their friends and the party from whom I got my information about them, until after the first two, Pipes and Herndon, were arrested and all of them indicted by the U.S. Grand Jury at Tyler & I do not believe that Gerrin knows anything of Bass whereabouts now.

I was told on the 18th of April by some of the best citizens in Denton that they did not believe Bass and his party had anything to do with the train robberies. The efforts that were being made to capture Bass at that time were only on account of his having robbed the express on the U.P. railroad last fall, and there was no complaint against Jackson and others except for harboring and protecting Bass, for during which it was said that Bass was paying them stipulated wages.

Pipes and Herndon were never accused of having any connection with the robberies until they were arrested and even then many good people here thought them innocent. Public opinion has undergone a great change since these parties were arrested and of course there are plenty of people to come forward now and say "I told you so" and "I knew it.". . . .

Jones also advised the governor that Colonel E.G. Bower in Dallas was being employed to assist Evans in prosecuting the train robbery suspects.[87]

Free on bond in Tyler, Jim Murphy was struck by a sense of guilt that his father, a respected old settler of Denton County, had been embarrassed by his arrest solely because of the relationship between his sons and the Bass gang, he having done nothing worse than perhaps feeding them. His sense of duty to his father far outweighed whatever obligation he felt to the robbers, and he had no compunction about what he did next. He approached Deputy U.S. Marshal Walter Johnson and June Peak about the feasibility of his joining the Bass gang and setting up the outlaws for capture. Major Jones was advised of Murphy's proposal and summoned him to his hotel room in

Tyler. With Johnson and Peak present, they had a long talk about the scheme and the obvious danger. Jones left the room to consult with U.S. Attorney Evans, promising Murphy that he would do the best he could, and expressed his opinion that Evans might agree. Thirty minutes later Jones returned and said that the case against him could be dismissed if Murphy did what he said he would do.

The plan was for Murphy to leave town secretly before court met, and it would be announced that he had run off and forfeited his bond, although Evans would protect Cannon, the bondsman, from any loss. Murphy would then make his way back to Denton, join the Bass gang, and as soon as possible maneuver them into a position to be captured. He was to stay in communication with Jones, Peak or Johnson, whoever was most convenient. He was not to mention the arrangement to another soul. If he were to be rearrested, the lawmen would have him released again. The case against him would be dismissed if Murphy did all within his power to nab any of the gang. If he made a good faith effort, but failed through no fault of his own, he would receive credit for his attempt at the time of trial. Also, he was to have a share in any reward, including all of Jones' share if Jones was able to be present at the gang's capture.

Murphy pleaded with Jones to have the charges against Henderson Murphy dismissed, and the major promised to talk to the district attorney about it.[88] On May 21, U.S. Attorney Evans reduced the agreement to writing.

> 1st, whereas James Murphy stands indicted as an accessory in robbing U.S. mail in several causes now pending in U.S. District [Court] at Tyler, and whereas I believe public justice will be best subserved thereby, I, Andrew J. Evans, U.S. Attorney for the Western District of Texas, bind the United States as follows:
>
> 1st, if the said Murphy should leave Tyler, I will protect him and his bondsmen at this term of the court.
>
> 2nd, if the said Murphy shall be instrumental in securing the arrest and delivery to the U.S. Marshal of the Western District of Texas, of all or any one of the

following principals (in this order, Bass, Jackson, Underwood, Barnes and Johnson) in said indictments, then all prosecutions are to be dismissed as to said Murphy, growing out of his acts as accessory to the said principals; to be done upon certificate of Major J.B. Jones.

3rd, in case the said James Murphy shall use all reasonable and possible means in his power to capture the said Bass and his above named associates, and if Major J.B. Jones will certify to such facts to the U.S. District Attorney, then the said Murphy is to have the relief named in section 2 above, although he may be unsuccessful.

A.J. Evans

U.S. Attorney[89]

In addition, charges against Henderson Murphy were to be dropped. The officials warned Murphy that he had better not deceive them. It was decided to have Peak keep his men at Dallas so that Murphy would know where he was. Upon hearing from Murphy, Peak was to move promptly to apprehend the bandits. If it was more convenient to contact Deputy Marshal Johnson, the deputy would then contact Peak.[90]

Witnesses poured into Tyler on Monday, May 20, for the trial of Pipes and Herndon that was to begin that day. Billy Jackson, Frank's brother, was there and commented that Bass and his gang would eventually be caught; it was only a matter of time. As to his brother Frank, he was "his own man" and would have to be responsible for his own actions.[91] The next morning the case against Pipes and Herndon was called in Judge Duval's court. Evans announced ready for trial, but the attorneys for the two defendants, Hickerson Barksdale and Sawnie Robertson of Dallas,[92] requested a delay, alleging that two members of the grand jury had been disqualified. After that motion was overruled, Judge Duval also denied a request to transfer the case to the U.S. Circuit Court. Exceptions to the indictment were also overruled. However, when the defense attorneys pleaded the absence of material witnesses and asked for a continuance, Judge Duval reluctantly granted the continuance, but solely because one of their witnesses, Arzelia Shipley, the sister of Billy and Henry Collins, was sick and could not attend court. The case was postponed until the court met at Austin in the latter part of June, and the prisoners were ordered transferred to Austin to await trial.[93]

On Wednesday, May 22, Jim Murphy jumped bond and left Tyler as agreed. According to his affidavit, he was back in Denton that night. In Hogg's account, he stopped briefly in Mineola to have his beard shaved off so that when the train arrived in Dallas he was not recognized and was able to walk past the waiting policemen. His bondsman, Cannon, not in on the secret, immediately sent a telegram to Marshal Morton in Dallas. Police officers, assisted by Express officer Sam Finley, searched the incoming train without success. It was believed by then that Murphy exited the train at Terrell.[94]

Murphy reached Denton that evening and hired a horse from Work Brothers' stable for the ride to Wise County where his family lived. On the way the horse ran into a barbed wire fence and threw Murphy, who hurt his neck. The horse ran off and Murphy lay on the ground until daylight. He was finally able to start walking but fortunately ran into a woman friend in a buggy who gave him a ride to his father's house at the head of Hickory Creek. Murphy found a horse here and rode on to Wise County, where he stayed for two days before returning to Denton County. He waited about two weeks in the timber below Denton looking for Bass and his gang.[95]

On the evening of Friday, May 24, all of the prisoners at Tyler were placed in irons, two by two, and taken by Marshal Russell and his deputies to the train depot for transfer to Austin. Relatives and friends were there to say goodby. A.G. Collins bid goodby to his son, Billy, reducing the train robber to tears.[96] The Bass gang was on the run, and Bass had fifty-eight days to live.

-XIII-

Running Gunbattles

Tom Floyd and his ranger squad spent the better part of Wednesday, May 22, scouring Dallas County for Henry Collins. Speculation was that the elusive fugitive had fled the country, but the rangers had run across at least one abandoned campsite that they believed was his. Other witnesses against the Bass gang, Charles A. Allingham,[1] J.W. Taylor, Charles L. Berry[2] and John Ailer,[3] were brought from northwestern Denton County to Dallas en route to Tyler.[4]

Jim Murphy roamed between the Hickory Creek bottoms and his old stomping grounds in far northwestern Denton County and near the family homestead in southwestern Cooke County. Staying alert for any lawmen who might come snooping around, he looked to find and make contact with Bass. His father returned home and told him his own case had been dismissed but that Jim's bond had been forfeited. The son comforted the father with news of what had been promised by Major Jones and Andrew Evans.[5]

The six train robbery suspects—Pipes, Herndon, Billy Collins, Green and Monroe Hill, and John Skaggs—arrived in Austin on Saturday, May 25, along with two counterfeiters, and were conveyed in irons from the depot to the Travis County Jail in an omnibus. The entourage, complete with heavily armed guards, attracted considerable attention as it passed up Congress Avenue. The prisoners soon found themselves enclosed in a row of cages in a large room, stripped to the waist and perspiring heavily in the heat. Sheets of plate iron provided a floor, and only a blanket or quilt was available for a bed. Among the sixty or so prisoners was the notorious gunman John Wesley Hardin, awaiting trial for a murder in Comanche County.[6]

The whereabouts of Bass and his men did not remain secret for long. In Stephens County, west of Fort Worth and Mineral

Wells, a woman who lived near Caddo Creek told a deputy sheriff named Freeman[7] that she had seen men who answered the description of the train robbers. The gang had been camped for about two weeks in the mountains in the eastern part of the county, about fifteen miles from Breckenridge, believed by the authorities to be provided supplies by a brother-in-law of Frank Jackson who lived nearby. Freeman, taking an unknown ranger from Shackelford County and two others, Buck Amis[8] and Perry Paschall,[9] rode to investigate. On finding that it likely was the Bass gang, the ranger returned to his Shackelford County camp, and Freeman and the others returned to Breckenridge.[10]

In Breckenridge an alerted Sheriff Berry B. Meaders[11] had Freeman and Deputy James M. Hood[12] round up a posse to take up the pursuit, and they set out for the bandit encampment on Sunday evening, May 26. At about midnight Meaders sent back to Breckenridge for reinforcements, and about twenty new volunteers with about as many old shotguns were organized.

The next day, before the reinforcements from Breckenridge could arrive, the posse ran into the gang near a store on the Palo Pinto road, about thirteen miles east of Breckenridge. About forty shots were exchanged in the rain, three of the outlaws' dismounting and firing from behind trees. The bandits remounted, one of their horses possibly wounded, and retreated about two miles back into the mountains. The gang, better armed than the pursuing posse and better oriented to the lay of the land, was not too concerned and camped Monday evening in the trees and thickets near King Taylor's store. The sheriff and his men camped about a half mile away on the prairie.[13]

Bass *did* have an ally in Stephens County, but not Jackson's brother-in-law as believed by the lawmen. Perry King Taylor was a brother-in-law of Joel, Henry and Billy Collins, and lived in Stephens County where he and his wife farmed and also ran a store.[14] In the meantime Lieutenant G.W. Campbell in Shackelford County, ready to disband part of his ranger company under Major Jones' order, received information of the fight in Stephens County. On Monday, May 27, Corporal J.E. Smith left camp with the sixteen dismissed rangers to catch up with Sergeant Van Riper and his men, already on the way.[15]

Palo Pinto Sheriff J.T. Wilson received a telegram on

Monday afternoon from lawyer William Veale,[16] a member of Meaders' posse.

> Big Caddo Crossing
> May 27, 1878
>
> Dear Tom - The devil is to pay here, sure enough. Bass and his gang of train robbers are now supposed to be within a mile of this place. They ride through the country in daylight openly and defiantly, and are splendidly armed and mounted. Berry asked me to write to you a line and urge you to come to his assistance.
>
> The robbers have relatives in the neighborhood, who will not do anything towards their capture. Berry wants you to bring with you about two day's rations.
>
> In haste, yours
> WM. VEALE[17]

Sheriff Wilson[18] was not able to lead a posse personally, but he sent ten men under Deputy Sheriff James L. Owens[19] to the area some thirty miles west of Mineral Wells. Meaders and his men had found themselves confronted by the outlaw gang, which had control of the high ground with excellent arms. Realizing that an assault on their position would likely produce certain casualties, Meaders had backed off until reinforcements could arrive.[20]

Early Tuesday morning, May 28, Deputy Owens and his men joined with Sheriff Meaders, as did Lieutenant Campbell with eighteen rangers. They also welcomed the arrival of Shackelford County Sheriff William R. "Bill" Cruger[21] and his deputy, former Texas Ranger William C. Gilson.[22] The lawmen spent the day combing through the mountains looking for signs of the gang but were unable to pick up the trail. In the meantime Bass and his men had gone on about four miles further to the east and stopped at the store of John McKasson, a sixty-six-year-old Ohioan who lived there with his wife and daughter.[23] Purchasing eight dollars' worth of provisions, a cocky Bass left word for his pursuers that the outlaws would "stand their ground and give them a desperate fight, and that they did not propose to be bulldozed." The gang tried to swap off one of its horses, and the storekeeper noticed that each man had a Winchester and a pair of sixshooters.

Perhaps as many as eight farmers who lived in the area had been summoned to arm themselves and join Meaders' posse. Intent on reward and glory, the farmers trailed the gang from McKasson's store, but Bass and his men surprised and captured them. Taking them to King Taylor's store, Bass treated them to bottles of beer until the farmers were quite intoxicated. A member of the gang remarked that they were not petty thieves and interfered with no private citizen. Holding out a handful of twenty-dollar gold pieces, the bandits told their attentive audience that this was what the sheriff and his posse wanted.[24]

The rumor spread to Fort Worth and other cities that certain persons in Stephens County had carried baskets of provisions to the gang and kept it informed of the movements of the lawmen.[25] This was apparently what a thoroughly disgusted Lieutenant Campbell discovered when he and his rangers finally arrived, according to his report.

Reached Sergt. Sterling's scout. Sergeant reports that his fight with Bass was a mistake as he had not been able to overtake the robbers, but that on the 27th the sheriff of Stevens [sic] County with a posse had attacked the robbers and were repulsed and drew off. The robbers captured eight of the posse and disarmed them. Two thirds of the citizens in that country openly boast that they are friends of Bass and his confederates. Bass was informed that the Rangers had been seen out in the country. The robbers drew off to the mountains where Sergt. Sterling followed them, but could not overtake them owing to the ruggedness of the country. After pursuing them around and over the same mountains for two days, drew off N.W. about 15 miles leaving spys [sic] to watch Bass and announced to the citizens his intention of giving up the chase and returned to camp in order to let the excitement die out and get Bass located again. It is the intention of the robbers [to stay] in the country as they openly boast that it is the best country they have found and they intend to stay as the majority

208

of the citizens will assist them in any emergency. Not less than 250 persons from adjoining counties were endeavoring their capture, but without success owing to the ruggedness of the country.[26]

By Friday, May 31, after finding no sign of the outlaw gang, Sheriff Meaders terminated his pursuit and returned to Breckenridge. Campbell and Van Riper had already returned to their camp on Thursday, leaving Sergeant Sterling on a scout with the nineteen rangers who volunteered to ride with him, even though most of them were scheduled to be dismissed the next day, the last day of the month. Once the chase was abandoned, one of the volunteer rangers, Jim McIntire, later said that he took their equipment to Dallas and turned it over to Peak.[27] But Sergeant Sterling and four men of Company B with fourteen dismissed rangers continued the pursuit.

Sterling and his men remained concealed in the mountains around Cedar Creek in Stephens County to see if Bass might still be there and show himself. On June 2 they received word that Bass was camped about sixteen miles northeast of them, but they just missed him. Following the trail east back to Denton County, the party of rangers rode to Black Springs, eighteen miles from Jacksboro, on June 5, camping within a mile and a half of the outlaws. The day before, Bass had paid twenty dollars in gold for ammunition and provisions and held a brief conversation with a mail carrier who ran across them, but the bandits rode out during the night of June 5 before an attack could be mounted by the rangers. The lawmen trailed the gang through the mountains for three days until their horses gave out, and Sterling and his four men returned to camp on June 9. Some of the volunteer rangers, however, found fresh horses, and Sterling resumed the chase with them on June 10.[28]

In the meantime, on Major Jones' recommendation, June Peak was promoted to ranger captain, commencing June 1. Jones told Adjutant General Steele that he was "an energetic, efficient and faithful officer whose services I can use to better advantage in my command with the rank of Captain than Lieutenant." Jones ordered Peak to stay in the Dallas area until further orders, no doubt waiting to hear something from Jim

Murphy.[29] On Wednesday, May 29, Peak led ten men on a scout unrelated to Bass, looking for horse thieves in a thicket in the southeastern portion of Dallas. Finding nothing, they returned to camp. Peak's movements were noted by the local press, which believed the activity was related to the hunt for Bass, but a ranger stated that Peak had no orders to move from his camp at the present and that no one had any idea if and when they would move.[30]

In the Hickory Creek bottoms below Denton, Jim Murphy learned of the gunbattle in Stephens County. He left word with folks in the area to tell Bass to come to his place near Rosston, then returned home.[31] Texas lawmen were waiting for the next appearance of Sam Bass. Near San Antonio Captain Hall had a detachment of five men surveilling the ranch of Henry Underwood's brother, Nathan, in hopes the Bass gang might try to slip out of North Texas and make its way there for refuge.[32] At about this time Bass and his men apparently split up briefly. Just after the fight on Caddo Creek, Bass and one of the bandits rode up late one evening to the ranch of the widow Mahala Roe, fifty-one, seven miles west of Palo Pinto. Staying with her were her daughters, Semerimis E. Maddox, thirty, and Martha F. Maddox, twenty-two, both married to brothers who were off helping to build a church at Slaughter Valley.

According to Gard, the two strangers rode up and asked to stay there that night. Telling the men they were assumed to be gentlemen, the women had them stable their horses in the barn and fed them dinner. The five talked for about an hour, then the men were shown to a spare bedroom for the night. Concerned about the men, one of the women retrieved an axe and a hoe from outside. The family shotgun was empty, and the women realized that the shells were in the bedroom where the men were. Mrs. Roe bravely went to the room, knocked, and was told to come in. Knives and guns spread all over the bed added to the women's fright, and Mrs. Roe said, "I think you gentlemen should turn those weapons over to us for the night." Bass politely declined, pleading their own safety, but he allowed her to carry out the shotgun shells. The women stayed up all night without event. The next morning, after eating breakfast, the men saddled up, thanked Mrs. Roe, and paid her a twenty-dollar gold piece.[33]

The Maddox farmhouse in Palo Pinto County where Sam Bass and a
member of his gang spent the night after fleeing Stephens County.
(From Clark, *The Palo Pinto Story*.)

Bass and his men were reported seen in a number of places
simultaneously. On Sunday, June 2, Bass and five men stopped
at a store in Young County, on Dillingham's Prairie, run by a
man named McIntosh. The bandits stayed there until about
9:00 p.m., some of them standing guard outside while Bass
made purchases.[34] On Tuesday, June 4, a report was received in
Jacksboro that Bass was in the northern part of Palo Pinto
County and headed eastward. Sheriff L.L. Crutchfield[35] of Jack
County hastily organized a small posse and rode southeast
through a soaking rain into Wise County in an unsuccessful
effort to intercept the outlaws.[36]

On Tuesday morning Billy Collins was returned to Dallas
from Austin. His bond had been a stiff $15,000, but his attor-
ney, Hickerson Barksdale, had arranged for six relatives to stand
as sureties: John H. Cole, A.G. Collins, John McCommas, B.F.
Fleaman, Arzelia Shipley and Thomas J. Jackson, as well as a seventh person, E.L. Huffman.[37] They swore that they were worth
a collective total of $79,000. The bond had been approved by
Commissioner Fearn in Dallas, and Collins was released from
custody.[38]

Lawmen were convinced that the pressures placed on the Bass gang had forced it to seek more hospitable climes, perhaps toward Mexico. But Bass, in a move that would become part of his legend, returned to Denton County. On Wednesday June 5, he was spotted near the farm of a man named Burnett on Denton Creek about nine miles northwest of Denton. A courier was sent to Elizabethtown to alert Denton deputy Clay Withers, who led a posse back to where Bass had been spotted and scoured the creek bottoms until darkness fell. Withers sent A.E. Allen[39] off to Denton to alert Sheriff Egan as to Bass' presence, but in the rain Allen lost his way and did not arrive there until nine Thursday morning.[40]

Meanwhile, about twelve miles west of Denton, Bass and his gang, including Henry Collins, confronted Stephen "Tweed" Christal, who was related by marriage to Collins and who had once lived in the household of John and Arzelia Collins Shipley.[41] They asked him for breakfast, but Christal refused to provide them any assistance and told Henry Collins that he ought to be ashamed of himself for running with Bass. Christal told them he had no desire to travel to Tyler on their account. Rebuffed, the gang rode off and camped the rest of the day in the area.[42] About 3:30 Thursday morning the gang was spotted riding by a Baptist church headed toward Denton.[43] About thirty minutes after sunrise on Thursday, June 6, Bass, Underwood, Jackson, Barnes, Johnson and Charles Carter rode into Denton from the timber, riding near where the new county jail stood, and quietly rode up to the Work Brothers' livery stable. Charlie Carter, the twenty-year-old son of Hardin Carter, had joined up with the gang[44] but had not previously been known to be associated with Bass. He had been seen in Denton the night before when Denton City Marshal George W. Smith[45] and a deputy named Murray tried unsuccessfully to arrest him on a warrant for cattle stealing.[46] John Work, who had ridden at least once in a posse led by Tom Gerren and had even fired on the Bass gang on April 30, was asleep in the stable loft, a double-barreled shotgun within reach. The night before he had alerted the stable hostler, Charles McDonald,[47] that he wouldn't be surprised if Bass tried to come into Denton and retake the two horses that Egan had captured on April 30. At about one o'clock in the morning someone had rapped on the stable door wanting to put up two horses, but a spooked McDonald refused to open the door. He put on his clothes and stayed up the rest of the night, taking a short nap before dawn.

When the sun rose, McDonald was inside the stable cleaning up. Suddenly Bass and four of his men, pistols drawn, pushed open the door and rode into where McDonald was working. Underwood remained outside on his horse to keep a watch. Bass demanded his horses, but McDonald played dumb. "What horses?"

"Get them horses quick or I will shoot you," menaced Bass. McDonald refused and Jackson struck him over the head with his pistol, again threatening to kill him if he didn't get the horses. Bass cautioned Jackson not to hurt the stableman. McDonald told Bass that he hadn't put the horses in there and he wasn't going to take them out.

Ordering McDonald not to move, Bass directed Jackson and Carter to dismount and find the horses. The outlaws took two saddles, one belonging to the Work brothers and the other to Alex Cockrell, then rode north out of Denton leading the saddled horses behind them. Witnesses recalled hearing Underwood laugh raucously and proclaim, "Damn 'em! We'll show 'em they can't steal anything from us that we can't get back!" The gang rode by Sheriff Egan's house and called out to the slumbering lawman, "Get up; the country's full of thieves!" According to Gard, Egan's son John, eight, was headed toward the barn with a hired girl to do the milking when Bass rode by. Giving the boy a friendly wave, Bass called out "Hello, little Pard!" Egan's wife refused to wake her exhausted husband, but he was roused when some pursuing townsmen stopped by the house.

McDonald immediately awakened Work then ran into the street giving the alarm "Bass! Bass!" But the outlaws were already several hundred yards away and, even though about fifty men went in pursuit, the gang's trail was lost.[48] Deputy Riley Wetsel's small posse, following Bass' trail, arrived in Denton from farmer Burnett's place on Denton Creek just after the excitement had occurred then joined Egan, who led the chase. The gang stopped three miles north of Denton but spotted the pursuers and escaped into the Clear Creek bottoms, their flight aided by a recent rain and swollen streams.[49]

Egan spent all of Thursday looking for Bass. A Dallas man named Bancum told the *Dallas Daily Herald* that he was returning from Denton to Dallas when he encountered Bass and two men on the road. Bass had apparently been drinking. Bancum knew Bass, and as they passed he asked the outlaw how he was. Bass stopped and rode up to him, producing two pistols. He told Bancum that he did not know him and asked him if he wanted to arrest him. Alarmed, Bancum said that he did not. Bass said that if he wanted to arrest him, he could have a pistol, extending one to him but keeping the other cocked and aimed at the traveler. Bancum finally convinced Bass that he did not want to arrest him, and the outlaw leader put his pistols away. He asked Bancum what people thought of him and Tom Gerren, and the response was "not very well." Bancum said Bass was mounted on a "fine gray mare with a full Mexican rig." He carried a Spencer rifle and two ivory-handled, silver-mounted revolvers. According to Bancum, Bass demonstrated how he ran from posses, leaning first on one side of the horse to shoot, then the other. The other two men with Bass only watched, and when the conversation was over the three rode off quickly leaving Bancum to continue his journey.[50]

Fort Worth City Marshal Jim Courtright and a deputy, A.N. "Ab" Woody,[51] left the city as part of a posse headed by Tarrant County Sheriff John M. Henderson,[52] after the two received a ten-day leave of absence from the city council. Henderson and Courtright subordinated their personal and political rivalries to the pressing threat of Bass and company riding south into Tarrant County.[53]

At about nine o'clock the next morning, Friday, Egan and two members of his highly unorganized posse spotted the gang about five miles north of Denton and gave pursuit but, lacking sufficient manpower and adequate horses, were forced to draw back when the outlaws rode into the thick Elm Fork bottoms.[54] It rained heavily all day. That evening the gang boldly rode within a mile of Denton and stole two more horses belonging to citizens named McDade and Dixon.[55] The bandits then disappeared back into the darkness.

George Washington Smith,
Denton city marshal wounded by
the Bass gang.
(Photo in possession of author.)

Bass and company turned up Saturday morning, June 8, near Pilot Knob, a small but prominent hill about six miles southwest from Denton, where they stopped at a nearby farmhouse and gave an elderly lady a twenty-dollar gold piece in exchange for a dozen eggs. From the top of the steep hill, they had a good view of the surrounding countryside while they ate breakfast. Still recruiting men to join in the manhunt, Sheriff Egan had earlier dispatched Deputy Clay Withers[56] and four men— F.M. Murphy, Tom and Jack Yates, and City Marshal George Smith—to look for the gang. They

A view of Pilot Knob, six miles south of Denton, Texas. (Author photo).

215

struck the gang's trail about two miles from Denton and followed it to Pilot Knob. As Withers and his small posse approached the gang opened fire; in the ensuing gunfight Smith's horse was hit in a leg and the marshal received a slight wound in the right hip. The battle was brief and the robbers retreated, holding off the posse with heavy gunfire.[57]

Withers sent couriers back to Denton and Elizabethtown to find reinforcements, and the wounded Smith also returned to Denton. Bass and his men spotted one of the couriers, James Martin, headed for Elizabethtown. Suspecting his purpose, they chased after him, firing and calling on him to halt. Martin was riding a mule and had no choice but to stop. Bass and the six men with him—Underwood, Jackson, Barnes, Johnson, Henry Collins and Carter—confronted Martin about his mission, which he admitted. The bandits ordered him to surrender his new saddle as well as thirty cents in his pocketbook. Bass cut his bridle to pieces, turned the mules loose, and slapped Martin's jaw and told him to go home.[58] The gang then rode into the timber to hide and rest their horses.

Later that morning Withers and his remaining men again rode up on the gang and dismounted as another firefight broke out. About twenty-five shots were exchanged before the outlaws once again retreated and left the posse behind. Sheriff Egan and additional men arrived from Denton before noon to join Withers in the search. Bass led his men south toward the small town of Alton then, after riding about a mile, ducked back into the thicket again in hopes of eluding his pursuers.

Egan raced his posse south in pursuit, passing the spot where Bass and company had ducked into the woods. Two of Egan's posse bringing up the rear, Jesse Chinn[59] and Gillis Hammett,[60] spotted the outlaws among the trees and called out to Egan. The bandits opened up on the two possemen and rode back the way they had come, then headed east toward a place known as Bullard's or Ballard's Mill. For over two miles Egan's posse chased after the fleeing gang, catching up with them at a small prairie clearing. About twenty of the posse continued to pursue them in a running gunbattle that extended about a mile and a half, deputies Wetsel and Withers in the forefront firing as they rode. However, no one was hit.[61]

The lawmen were now a very serious menace which Bass and his companions, mounted on superior horses, looked to escape. The heavy rains had left the ground quite soft, making it even more difficult to hide their trail. The chase continued in the noonday heat with no rest for either side. At one point as the gang ranged through the wilderness between Denton and Fort Worth, it stopped at Davenport's Mill to purchase some peaches and crackers at the store of Harding Throop.[62] The storekeeper was waiting on some ladies when Bass walked in to ask for the provisions. Throop told Bass to wait just a minute while he finished with the women, but Bass impatiently declared, "Look here. I'm in a hurry and I want you to wait on me. I am Sam Bass." That's all it took for Throop to leave his female customers and attend to the needs of the outlaw chief.[63]

The posse again came upon the gang, shots were exchanged, and the outlaws hastily retreated back to the east then to the north.[64] Darkness provided a respite for both of the exhausted parties, and Egan had his posse go into camp on the outlaws' trail about twelve miles south of Denton on Hickory Creek.[65] Riley Wetsel and Tom Gerren had become separated from Egan's posse and nervously rode through the darkness looking for the sheriff's camp. As they approached the camp, they mistook it for Bass' camp and opened fire. In the ensuing gunbattle Wetsel was wounded in the calf by Alex Cockrell and had to be taken back to Denton for medical care.[66]

Following Major Jones' instructions, June Peak had kept his men in their Dallas camp waiting for word from Jim Murphy, who had yet to make contact with Bass. But with reports coming in on the desperate flight of the Bass gang from Egan's determined posse, and while the running gunbattle was occurring between Denton and Tarrant counties, Peak sent two men to Denton County on Saturday to gather information about what was happening. Swollen creeks between Dallas and Denton made travel quite difficult. Peak apparently received more information and, without waiting for the return of the scout, took ten of his rangers to Denton. His wagons and equipment followed on Monday.[67]

The search for Bass resumed Sunday morning, June 9, as Egan and his posse followed the gang closely, finding their trail within an hour of leaving camp. Two trackers from Elizabethtown named Medlin and Stein had joined the posse and were able to follow the gang with amazing ease and speed. At one point the trail indicated that the gang had split up then joined together again. At about eleven o'clock, in the bottoms about eight miles south of Denton near the farm of Frank Jackson's brother, David Warren Jackson, the lawmen came upon the gang eating in camp. The posse was within sixty yards of the outlaw camp before its members were spotted and a short fight broke out. Alex Cockrell and John Work both had their horses shot out from under them as the outlaws took cover in the underbrush, and Work was wounded in the shoulder. Outnumbered, the gang fled from the fight through the tangled thicket, leaving behind one of the horses taken from the Work Brothers' stable in Denton, the saddle taken from James Martin, and their camp baggage and provisions. It was reported that either Underwood or Henry Collins was riding behind Jackson. In addition, citizens who saw the gang told the pursuing posse that both Collins and Carter had been wounded.[68]

The sheriff sought to find their trail again. In the meantime Bass and his men had ridden up to farmer Reuben Bandy's[69] place. They spotted a horse tied to a fence that belonged to fourteen-year-old John Hyatt,[70] and Underwood seized the horse, telling the boy that he wanted to borrow the pony for a while. The gang headed back to the Elm Fork bottoms with the sheriff in close pursuit.[71] Egan and his men lost the gang's trail on the McKinney road about six miles east of Denton, but they did receive information that the gang now consisted of six rather than seven men. Fort Worth Marshal Courtright and his deputy Ab Woody, who had killed a horse during the ride from Tarrant County, now joined Egan.[72]

On Sunday evening, Courtright and three men—Denton deputy sheriff John Carroll,[73] Ab Woody and Jack Yates—rode near the farmhouse of Charles Gray.[74] They spotted the Bass gang with Frank Jackson riding in front, and Courtright mistook Jackson for Richard B. "Dick" Coleman, a Denton carpenter.[75] The marshal called out to Jackson, alerting the gang to the posse's presence. Jackson wheeled his horse and scrambled into the underbrush, followed closely by the rest of the gang, and they disappeared again into the Elm Fork bottoms.[76]

The gang headed to the northwest part of Denton County, near Bolivar, arriving there early Monday morning. Bass paid fifty dollars for more provisions for his men as well as a considerable amount of ammunition, their stockpile having been depleted over the last three days. The storekeeper objected to selling to Bass so the sale was consummated at gunpoint. Bass told the storekeeper to ask the posse to give the gang a short rest because they had not slept for three days and nights. Egan received word of the gang's new location but arrived in Bolivar after they had left.

At about noon a posse led by Grayson County Sheriff Everheart, which included Deputy U.S. Marshal Walter Johnson and a deputy sheriff from Cooke County named Parish, encountered the gang on Pond Creek near the Denton-Cooke line. The outlaws were in camp preparing to eat when the posse rode up at full speed. Abandoning all of their equipment, Bass and his men hastily mounted their horses and raced away, firing as they fled. A desperate chase ensued, but the gang was able to reach the Clear Creek bluffs about twelve miles to the west and Everheart's posse gave up the pursuit. A witness to the pursuit said that the gang was riding seven abreast, maintaining a furious pace, while the sheriff's posse was three to four hundred yards behind, strung out in single file trying to keep up.[77]

Sometime Monday a man named Dawson left Denton with the intent of joining Egan's posse but was intercepted on the road by Bass and his men. They searched him for legal papers, but finding none they held a mock trial. The gang finally returned his pistol to him and told him to hurry along or he would be too late, but he was forced to swap saddles with one of the gang before they let him go on his way.[78]

On Monday evening Bass and his men went to Bob Murphy's place near Rosston. It would later be believed by lawmen that the gang picked up ten fresh horses from him, but Murphy would say that he encountered Bass Tuesday morning while riding and that Bass took only one animal from him. Murphy said that Bass had claimed he never intended to leave Denton County alive, but if the lawmen persisted in hunting him down he would make it warm for them. Bass supposedly boasted that he had never robbed a man in the world but that the railroads owed him a living and he intended to get it out of them. Very few thought that Murphy was telling the truth about the horse,[79] but the quotes were vintage Bass. Bass was also quoted as saying he did not want to hurt any Denton men but would defend himself. He intended, however, to get four men if he could—Tom Gerren, Riley Wetsel, Billy Scott and Jack Smith—because they had "stood in with him and then went back on him."[80]

June Peak and his men arrived in Denton on Monday evening and had their horses shod the next morning before taking the trail after Bass. The rangers rearrested Scott Mayes in Denton on Tuesday morning. It was believed that Mayes, even though out on bond, was still delivering provisions and liquor to the outlaws.[81] Peak and his men briefly joined Egan's posse, then the two groups separated and set off in different directions. There were a number of posses now in Denton County looking for the gang: Peak, Egan, Withers, Everheart, Tarrant County Sheriff Henderson, and Fort Worth Marshal Courtright. Bass had few places to hide with impunity.

On Tuesday evening, June 11, Peak and some of his rangers came upon Bass in the Hickory Creek bottoms, headed for the Elm Fork bottoms. A few shots were exchanged, but the rangers were not as familiar with the terrain as the outlaws and Bass escaped again. It was believed that Charley Carter was wounded in a leg on Sunday, although he later claimed it was an accidental gunshot that was bandaged by a woman in the area.[82] With darkness Peak and his men set up a camp until morning, but Bass took the opportunity to ride northwest into Wise County.

Peak and his men followed the gang's trail into Wise County on the next day, joined by a posse led by Wise County Sheriff George W. Stevens.[83] Along with this group was another posse, composed of Denton deputy John Carroll, William P. Withers of Denton[84] and Tarrant County deputy John Stoker,[85] which had become separated from Egan's posse and took it on themselves to follow Bass' trail westward until they ran into Peak's group.[86]

Wise County Sheriff George W. Stevens.
(From Cater, *Pioneer History of Wise County*.)

Bass and his men went into a camp on Salt Creek, about seven miles southwest of the small community of Cottondale in southern Wise County and about ten miles southwest of Decatur. The town had only had a post office since 1875 and, as the name implied, had cotton at the center of its industry.[87] While the bandits relaxed for the first time in several days, their horses were roped together in a grassy area some distance from the camp, restoring their energy as they grazed. The combined posses of Peak and Stevens suddenly rode up on the camp, and caught the lounging outlaws by surprise. The lawmen immediately dismounted, crossed the creek which had high bluffs on both sides, and opened a withering fire. The surprised outlaws fired a few shots at the attackers, but their priority was to get to their horses. The surprise was so complete, however, that the posse stood between them and their mounts, and the only feasible escape was into a dense thicket nearby.

Arkansas Johnson's horse was hitched to a nearby tree and Johnson went to mount him. One account had him picking up a blanket off the ground to saddle his horse when he was shot. Another account had him mounted when Tom Floyd jumped to the ground from his horse, cocked his Winchester, then turned over on his back to rest his rifle on his raised knees and fire a single shot. The bullet entered just above Johnson's left nipple and the outlaw fell instantly to the ground, dying almost immediately. Peak and Underwood exchanged shots and Peak, fearing that the robbers might reach their horses, ordered his men to shoot at the gang's mounts. Two of the gang's horses were killed and four others were captured.

The gang scrambled on foot into the thicket, and some of the posse urged Peak to attempt either to surround or enter the thicket after the gang. It would be alleged that Bass stopped Jackson from shooting at one of the rangers they saw from a hiding place in the thicket. Concerned that some of his men might be killed, Peak declined to enter the thicket and ordered the men to set up a camp. Disgruntled lawmen, upset that the opportunity to nab Bass once and for all had been lost, grudgingly followed Peak's orders. Sheriff Stevens rode to Decatur to summon a coroner for an inquest over Johnson's body.

That evening Arkansas Johnson's body was buried where it fell. In his pockets were thirty-five cents. John Stoker took possession of Bass' horse and Johnson's rifle, as well as a set of field glasses abandoned by the robbers, then reportedly left the posse.[88] The zenith of the saga of Sam Bass had been reached. His gang had disintegrated, and he had barely a month to live.

-XIV-
TRAITOR IN THE GANG

B ass and the members of his gang scattered after the Salt Creek fight. Underwood, apparently deciding that any future with the outlaws was too risky, struck out on his own. He passed the place of a Doctor Young and, in conversation, "expressed supreme disgust for Bass and the intention to leave him and the country."[1] Likely he headed for Bob Murphy's place in order to contact his wife. With the strong presence of various posses all over North Texas, coupled with the near misses the gang had experienced in the last several days, Underwood was ready to shake Texas dust from his boots and head for safer climes.

The others—Bass, Barnes, Jackson, Henry Collins and Charlie Carter—fled through the night in a heavy rain to south-eastern Wise County. Catching their breath, they then headed back toward Denton on Friday evening. One of the gang stole a horse belonging to a man named Payne Holt,[2] and the others also procured horses along the way. Sheriff Stevens took his posse back to Decatur, but Peak and his men followed Bass' trail until losing it about fifteen miles from Denton. Peak was accompanied by N.L. Jenkins, a noted Indian scout called "Buffalo Bill" who formally enlisted in Company B on July 1.[3]

Once in Denton, Henry Collins and Carter also decided to set off on their own and tried to put as much distance as they could between themselves and the remnants of the gang. Young Carter, injured and weary, sought sanctuary in the vicinity of his father's place, vowing to Hardin Carter that if he survived this trouble he would follow the straight and narrow for the rest of his days.[4] Peak and his men went into camp outside Denton and conferred with Sheriff Egan. All they could do was sit and wait until Bass made the next move.[5] On June 19 the rangers moved their camp to Lewisville.[6]

Jim Murphy had returned home to the Cove Hollow area

after leaving word with friends around Denton County for Bass to come to his place. The account of Bass' movements from this point forward is derived exclusively from statements directly attributed to Murphy. However, as will be seen, the chronology is confused.[7] On Saturday, June 15, Bass and Jackson rode by Murphy's place. Barnes' whereabouts are unknown. Since Murphy had visitors, the two did not stop but signaled him by raising their hats and rode on to find a secure camp nearby. Murphy excused himself and found Bass and Jackson on Clear Creek. Bass chided Murphy for having been in jail, or "playing checkers with his nose," and invited him to join the gang. Murphy expressed interest but told Bass that perhaps the right thing to do was to face the music and get back to a normal life. Weighing the two options, Murphy finally agreed to join him if Bass would wait and let him thresh his wheat on Sunday. Bass gave Murphy fifty dollars to take to Rosston for change and they agreed to meet on Monday.

Apparently Murphy at this point contacted Deputy U.S. Marshal Walter Johnson to alert the lawmen that what was left of the Bass gang was camped near him. Johnson and Sheriff Everheart headed in that direction with a posse and inadvertently ran into the outlaws, who scurried away. Everheart himself then made contact with Murphy, but Murphy had never met the sheriff and disclaimed any knowledge of Bass. Everheart assured him that he was "full partners" with Johnson, and Murphy finally told the sheriff that Bass and Jackson would be at a corner of his field that night when he would carry some food to them. Everheart mulled over the opportunity, then decided that the darkness would present too many problems and that he would rather have them in an open space in daylight. Murphy told him of the plan for him to join the Bass gang and likely again pledged to get word to the lawmen.

Murphy met Bass and Jackson on Monday, June 17, then sent word to Clay Withers that the outlaws were headed to camp just above Bolivar. Bass told Murphy of a scheme to go into Denton that night or the next to steal fresh horses from Bill Mounts' stable, and Murphy passed on this plan to Withers. The next morning, Tuesday, Bass, Jackson and Murphy rode to Bolivar, purchased some ammunition and baked bread, then returned to the Hickory Creek bottoms near Lone Elm where they camped for the night.

On the morning of Wednesday, June 19, the three rode through the bottoms to Bob Murphy's field where they could see hands plowing the field. They ate breakfast there then rode out to see if they could find Billy Jackson, Frank's brother, and trade some horses. They went to a high point known as Bush Knob and decided to wait and see if they could spot Billy Jackson with his herd of cattle. While waiting, the three engaged in some target practice with their pistols. When lunchtime rolled around and Billy Jackson had not shown, the three returned to the Hickory bottoms for something to eat.

After lunch Bass sent Murphy to the C2 Ranch to see if Billy Jackson was camped there. Murphy found Jackson and told him that his brother wanted to see him, then returned to the Bass camp behind Bob Carruth's field. Late that afternoon the camp was visited by two boys—Gus Egan, Sheriff Egan's brother who had just turned seventeen,[8] and Alonzo Carruth, eighteen, the son of Bob Carruth.[9] Bass was glad to see them and joked about starting a sheep ranch next to the Carruth place. Near sunset Wednesday evening Bass, Jackson and Murphy rode over to Billy Jackson's camp where Murphy's brother, John, was also with him. Frank Jackson asked his brother for a reliable horse, Old Ben, which he took, although Billy was afraid that it would get him into trouble with the law. Jim Murphy also took a fresh horse from his brother, who had the same misgivings as Billy Jackson. The trio then rode off laughing and went to Medlin's Point on the Decatur Road, about a mile and a half from Denton, where they rested until midnight.

Bass, Jackson and Murphy rode to William Mounts' place[10] in the darkness and stopped outside his gate. While Murphy stayed on his horse keeping watch, Bass and Jackson sneaked into Mounts' stable and took a dark bay horse that belonged to a man named Hugh Davis[11] and a saddle. There were no lawmen to stop them, and they rode east from Denton to the Elm Fork Bottom where they set up camp just at sunup, Thursday morning, June 20. The three caught a quick fifteen-minute nap, then moved on across the Elm Fork where they had breakfast and rested, this time for several hours. Several riders' passing by on the nearby road led Bass to decide that they had better relocate to a better-hidden site. By noon they were near Hilltown and stopped to eat some corn that they had stolen. They rode out again that afternoon and headed into Dallas County. The plan was to leave Denton County and all of the lawmen and seek new targets elsewhere.

When it became dark, a steady drizzle obscured their way and they became lost. They stopped at the place of a farmer named Burton about ten miles from Dallas. Under Bass' instructions, Murphy told the farmer that his name was Paine, that he was from Wise County, and that he had met two of Peak's rangers and was helping them track some stolen livestock. The three shared supper with the farmer and talked about Sam Bass. Burton was of the belief that Bass had been cheated by the railroad out of a large amount of money, perhaps justifying the robberies. Bass pleaded ignorance, saying only that the outlaw chieftain apparently had many friends.

On Friday morning the three rode on east to the village of Frankfort in Dallas County where they had one of the horses shod, and Bass bought a large amount of candy. While waiting, they encountered a poor farmer who bemoaned his failure at making any money and muttered that perhaps he ought to start robbing trains. Bass suppressed a chuckle and traded candy to the farmer for some peaches. The three rode on again and stopped for lunch about two miles east of Frankfort. While they were there, some horses and mules belonging to a man named Oby became inquisitive and came over to check out the trio; the bandits briefly considered stealing them.

Riding into the Duck Creek area northeast of Dallas, Bass left Jackson and Murphy and rode alone to Billy Collins' place, staying gone about two hours. Jackson and Murphy rode on. About two miles east of the spot where he had left the two, Bass returned to meet them. Riding with him were Henry Collins and two men Murphy did not recognize. Murphy later said that he heard one of the strangers cursing Murphy's name and suggesting to Bass that he kill Murphy. An alarmed Murphy turned to Jackson, who promised that he would look out for him and not let them hurt him. Bass told the party that they were going to ride and pick up Seaborn Barnes, and the six rode out. One of the strangers left them shortly after they started out.

As they rode along, Murphy was quite concerned about the cool treatment he was receiving from Bass, Collins and the remaining stranger, known to him only as Jake, and looked again to Jackson for assurance. Jackson told him he did not know why the others were acting that way. Murphy tried to put up a brave front. They heard a whistle as they approached a church in a creek bottom. Bass returned the whistle. and when another whistle sounded they rode toward it. Barnes came out from the bushes and shook hands with all but Murphy. He told Bass that he had been concerned about them because there was news that one of the Murphy boys was going to give him away.

Apparently Jim Murphy's service on behalf of the rangers was not the best kept secret. The *Sherman Register* had just reported that Deputy U.S. Marshal Walter Johnson had confided to a "certain indiscreet friend" that a friend of Bass had "given him away" and was trying to induce him to return to Denton with the intention of leading him into the clutches of Sheriff Everheart.[12] The *Register*'s story was reprinted in the Saturday, June 22, *Fort Worth Daily Democrat* which, on July 2, 1878, over a week later in a report of a false story of an encounter with Bass, would also indicate that a spy named Murphy was working for the lawmen. Murphy had every reason to fear that his true mission had been uncovered and that Bass would order his execution.

Seaborn Barnes expressed no trust in Murphy, stating that a marshal had telegraphed Fort Worth that Murphy was going to lead them to rob a bank there, a trap to nab the entire gang. He urged Bass to kill Murphy on the spot, and Bass appeared to agree. Thinking fast, Murphy spoke up and admitted that he did have an agreement with Major Jones but never had any intention of carrying it out. His whole intent in entering the agreement was to take advantage of any opportunity to get away before he went to the penitentiary. He promised that if they would let him live, he would take the lead in anything they tried. The story sounded plausible to Frank Jackson, and he defended Murphy to Bass and Barnes, stating that he had known Murphy for a long time and did not think that he would give them away. Jackson then said that if they killed Murphy, they would have to kill him also. Barnes pulled his pistol, ready to carry out the threat, but Bass stepped in and, although still unconvinced of Murphy's innocence in the matter, decided for now to trust Jackson's feelings. He ordered Barnes to leave Murphy alone. Bass and Barnes would watch Murphy closely, looking for any sign that he might betray them.

The party then rode on, a sullen Bass and Barnes riding together while Jackson, Murphy, Henry Collins and the stranger rode along quietly. Murphy rode with Jackson, staying close for the protection that Jackson had promised. They rode through swampy creek bottoms for the rest of the day, stopping in a clearing about midnight and resting until daylight.

The next morning, Saturday, June 22, the gang shared breakfast, then Henry Collins and the stranger, Jake, decided to move on. Bass urged Jake to ride with them, but he declined and rode off with Collins. The four remaining men rode on, camping that night in the bottoms of the East Fork of the Trinity River. The mosquitoes swarmed all over them, compelling Jackson to build a small fire near his head. As he slept, the fire consumed his hat and the tail of his coat, providing all of them with a good laugh. In the morning Jackson rode bareback to a nearby farmhouse and bought a hat from a boy, telling the farmers that they were cattlemen headed east to buy cattle. Jackson's cover story upset Bass—their rough appearance reflected anything but cattle buyers—so the gang rode out quickly toward Rockwall.

While Bass and the others were fleeing the intensive manhunts in Denton and surrounding counties, Fort Worth City Marshal Jim Courtright and Ab Woody returned from Denton County to Fort Worth on Saturday night and declared that Bass and his men were hidden in the thickets near Denton. Courtright claimed to have thwarted a plot by Bass to rob a Fort Worth bank, apparently during the hectic chase sequence between Denton and Fort Worth. He said that he had recovered the horse belonging to Payne Holt that had been taken after the Salt Creek fight. Courtright and Woody then returned to Denton County on Sunday morning to resume the manhunt.[13] Peak and ten men left their Lewisville camp on Saturday on a four-day scout for some sign of the gang, having heard rumors that the outlaws were at Cove Hollow.[14] In fact, numerous rumors that Bass was still in Denton County kept the rangers and other lawmen hopping around from spot to spot. On Wednesday, June 26, in Denton, Deputy U.S. Marshal Bill Anderson arrested Frank Jackson's brother, David Warren Jackson, and Ben Key on warrants charging complicity in the train robberies, but each gave a two thousand-dollar bail.[15]

Bass, Jackson, Barnes and Murphy headed for Rockwall on Sunday, June 23. Bass led them gingerly across the bridge spanning the East Fork of the Trinity River over which the rainswollen water flowed as high as the sides of their mounts. They reached Rockwall about four o'clock that afternoon, camping outside the small town.[16] Barnes was dispatched to the town to purchase some canned fruit, eggs and salmon.

About fifty yards from their camp stood an ominous, silent gallows and, while Murphy and Jackson began preparations for cooking supper, Bass walked over to inspect the structure. It had been constructed in anticipation of the hanging of a murderer named George Garner, but on the eve of his execution Garner was visited by his wife who smuggled in poison for both her and him to cheat the hangman. When the poison did not work on her, Garner hung her by the neck with the bale of a bucket then killed himself by suffocation, filling his mouth and nostrils with strips from his clothing. The sight of the gallows depressed Bass, "Boys, that makes me feel bad. That is the first one of them things I ever saw and I hope it will be the last."

Barnes returned to camp with the provisions and the four men ate. They then left camp and rode through Rockwall, stopping at a store to purchase some yeast and a sack of salt. They camped for the night about two miles east of town, but because it was so dark when they went into camp, it was not until daybreak on Monday, June 24, that they realized they had camped next to a house, risking discovery. They quickly saddled up and rode out southeast, arriving one mile south of Terrell at about four in the afternoon. Murphy was exhausted and quickly fell asleep beneath two small blackjack trees.

As Murphy slept, Bass and Barnes continued the debate as to whether or not to kill him. Barnes was adamant that Murphy had to die. Bass agreed and the two drew their pistols, but

Jackson again intervened, insisting that they would have to kill him first. Again, reluctantly, the guns were holstered, and the decision was once more postponed.

Leaving Barnes with Murphy, Bass and Jackson rode into Terrell to buy some clothing, crackers and canned peaches. They discussed the idea of holding up a bank there and looked around town. On Tuesday morning they returned to town for a better look but, according to one of Murphy's accounts, they spotted "an old acquaintance and very desperate character," Billy Reed, who did not recognize them. Afraid that Reed might give them away, they did not speak to him. In another account, Murphy said that Bass and Jackson returned to camp saying that they did not think "we could make it" in the bank. Murphy proposed looking at other banks and choosing the easiest. They decided to look elsewhere for a suitable bank target, and the four men mounted up and rode south to Kaufman where they set up another camp.

Bass sent Barnes and Murphy into Kaufman to look at the banks and to buy some fruit. They found no bank but bought a new suit for Murphy and had shaves. Marion P. "Chunk" Porter,[17] a clerk at Cates' Dry Goods Store, had just opened the store and was sweeping the plank sidewalk outside. According to a story told by Porter years later, the outlaws came to his store, ordered a wool suit, and paid him with two twenty-dollar gold pieces. When Porter opened the safe for change, revealing a full cash drawer to the two strangers, one of the men advised him that he shouldn't allow everyone who came along to see how much money was in the store safe. Taking the suit, the men then left,[18] Murphy leaving his old clothes there to alert Everheart or any other lawman trailing them.

The next morning, Wednesday, June 26, Bass, Jackson and Murphy rode back into Kaufman, where Bass and Jackson also had shaves. Murphy took the horses to a blacksmith to be shod then put them in a stable to be fed. The three walked around the town, finally entering a store on the east side. A large safe was in a back room. Bass, apparently unaware of the money that was in the Cates' store safe, decided to see if there was enough money to justify robbing the place. He asked for change of a twenty-dollar bill and looked over the storeowner's shoulder when he opened the safe, but there was barely enough to change the bill. The men returned to their camp and spent the rest of the day and evening eating peaches, relaxing, and listening to Bass tell stories of his adventures.

The four men broke camp Thursday morning and rode toward Ennis further south in Ellis County. They camped that night between Chambers Creek and the Trinity River. The next morning when they approached a river crossing, the water was high and the ferry cable had snapped. Bass and Barnes crossed the stream in a skiff while Jackson and Murphy tried to persuade the horses to swim across, but the animals only went part of the way and turned back. Bass and Barnes returned to their side, and they went into another camp. Bass went to a nearby farmer's house where he bought some watermelons, and the four spent the day eating the melons. Here Murphy's chronology breaks down. He stated that it was Thursday, July 4, but obviously a week has been lost and it can only be surmised that Murphy's memory failed him as to the amount of time it took to go from camp to camp.

In Collin County Tom Spotswood went on trial before District Judge Joseph Bledsoe at McKinney for the Allen train robbery. After twelve men were picked on June 28 for the jury, James Thomas was the principal witness for the state. He testified that Spotswood had not been masked during the robbery of the express car and that he had ample opportunity to see the bandit's face while Spotswood kept him covered. His glass eye was especially noticeable, he said, and even with the nervousness generated by having a cocked revolver in his face, Thomas said that he could not be mistaken. Bud Newman, the saloon keeper, also testified that Spotswood had come into his establishment the day before the robbery, passed himself off as a sporting man looking for some gambling action, and inquired as to when the southbound train would arrive in Allen.

Spotswood's attorney put the defendant's brother, Bill Spotswood, and a second man, John McCastlin, on the stand to establish an alibi, claiming that Tom Spotswood had slept at his brother's Denton County home at Little Elm on the night of the robbery. But McCastlin testified that he and Bill Spotswood were chopping wood for fence rails on February

23, thus refuting the alibi. Two other witnesses, Cicero Cullen and Andrew Johnson, testified that they also met Bill Spotswood and McCastlin in the woods the morning after the robbery, and that Bill Spotswood and the other man told them they had not slept at home the night before because they were unable to get across the creek.

On July 2 jury foreman E.H. Bowlby handed over the jury's verdict of guilty, and Spotswood's punishment was assessed at ten years confinement in the penitentiary at Huntsville. Spotswood's attorney immediately set into motion an appeal of the verdict. As Spotswood was taken back to his cell from the courtroom, he passed Thomas and lunged at him, striking the expressman until he was pulled off.[19]

Prior to trial Dallas City Marshal Morton had arrested Spotswood's brother, John, and Ira Jones at Pilot Point in Denton County for also being involved in the Allen robbery. They were transported to jail at McKinney, but there is no record that they ever stood trial.[20]

The trial of Sam Pipes, Albert Herndon, Monroe Hill and Bob Murphy, docketed to commence on July 2 in the federal court in Austin, was taking shape. Witnesses and attorneys converged on Austin to make their preparations. On Tuesday, July 2, the government, represented by U.S. Attorney A.J. Evans and Austin attorney W.M. Walton, announced that it was not yet ready for trial, and Judge Duval reset the trial to begin the following Friday.[21] Arriving at the same time were June Peak with the prosecution's two most important witnesses, Billy Scott and Jack Smith, as well as Sheriff Egan and Tom Gerren. In town also were railroad employees Julius Alvord, recovering nicely from his wound, William Carr, William Towers and Spofford Curley.[22]

The hunt for Bass continued in North Texas. Prior to leaving for Austin, Peak had conducted a brief scout for Underwood and Henry Collins in Dallas County but found nothing.[23] John Stoker and A.J. Bryant returned to Fort Worth reporting that all was quiet in Denton County.[24] In Peak's absence Tom Floyd took nine men and scouted south of Denton on July 3, returning to camp without discovering anything.[25] Sheriff Everheart finally returned to Grayson County from Denton on Thursday, July 4, having suffered a thorn in one eye from riding through the thick undergrowth. He reported that Bass and fifteen men were still in Denton County being aided by his friends.[26]

On July 5, when Bass, Jackson, Barnes and Murphy broke camp, they returned to the flooded crossing above Ennis and helped the ferry employees stretch rope across the stream. Late that evening, charged only half fare because of their help, they rode into the stream bottoms where they stayed with a local farmer, passing themselves off as cattle buyers from Wise County. The next morning, Saturday, July 6, the four men continued to ride south to Ennis. On the road they encountered a talkative school teacher who irritated the four men, but they couldn't get him to leave them. They stopped to buy some watermelons and Bass treated the schoolteacher, who had started to count the melons to determine how much he owed. Finally they parted from the teacher by turning off the road before they got to Ennis.

Stopping about a mile from Ennis and setting up a camp, Jackson and Barnes stayed behind while Bass and Murphy rode into the town. The two put their horses in a livery stable and went for dinner. The local bank did not appear to be an easy one so they decided not to attempt it. A generous Bass purchased a cartridge belt for Murphy and bought himself a pair of small saddle pockets lined with cashmere goat skin. They then returned to the camp.

The four moved southwest the next day for Waco. At about one on Sunday afternoon, they stopped about a mile south of town and set up another camp. Bass sent Jackson and Murphy into town to look at the banks. Both men stabled their horses, ate dinner in a restaurant, had shaves, then walked around town. At one bank they changed a five-dollar bill and saw that the bank had a good supply of gold and greenbacks. The bank looked promising to Jackson, but Murphy raised the question of how safe the escape route might be. Reporting back to Bass at camp, Jackson was enthusiastic about the bank, but Murphy suggested that Bass should go check it out himself. Just before dark the men moved their camp closer to Waco.

In the morning Bass and Jackson went back into Waco. By

the time they returned to camp, Bass had decided to take the bank after resting their horses at a spot five or six miles west of town on the other side of the Bosque River. They rode back through Waco, and as they passed through the western portion of town Bass directed Murphy and Jackson to purchase enough bacon, lard and coffee to last them until they were ready to rob the bank. Murphy suggested to Jackson that they first check out the escape route from the bank, trying to point out dangers that might discourage the robbery attempt. Jackson was not dissuaded. Back at camp Murphy tried to point out the dangers to Bass, but he was determined to carry through the plan. Murphy became very quiet and serious, leading Bass to believe that he truly thought it was too dangerous. When they awoke the next morning, Bass contemplated Murphy's concerns and changed his mind, telling him that they would go wherever Murphy said. Relieved, Murphy suggested that they should go to Round Rock in Williamson County and rob the bank there. Apparently with the distance they had put between themselves and Denton County, Murphy appeared to be more trustworthy.

They ate dinner and saddled up, riding back to Waco. Jackson and Barnes went on to their former camp south of the city while Bass and Murphy stopped off at the Ranch Saloon for some beer. Bass obtained change for the last twenty-dollar gold piece he had left from the Union Pacific robbery, commenting in rather cavalier fashion that there would be more.[27] The four stayed in their camp for a short while then left during the night. Barnes had returned to Waco and stolen a bay mare with white hind legs and a broken rib, which caused a protuberance on the animal, then caught up with the rest of the gang on the road south to Belton. Barnes went on ahead, leaving his old horse with Murphy and instructing him to sell the pony at Belton for what he could get.

The gang reached Belton in Bell County on Saturday, July 13. Sitting astride the Chisholm Trail along the banks of the Leon River, Belton was a well-known stop for cowboys going to and from cattle markets. Murphy was able to sell Barnes' horse to a blacksmith for twenty-five dollars, with which they bought canned fruit and jelly. He gave a bill of sale to the purchaser using his own name in hopes that it might come to the attention of lawmen. They camped just south of town, across the Leon River, on a small hill where they ate dinner. Looking over the town, Bass ruled out an attempt on the Belton bank, observing, "I would hate for them Belton fellows to get after us for they are bad medicine....These Bell County fellows are different material."

Perhaps Bass was familiar with some of the violence that had occurred in Bell County in recent years. On June 4, 1874, a mob of men had surrounded the Bell County Jail while the sheriff was absent in Waco. Forcing the jailer to surrender the keys, the mob proceeded to shoot to death nine prisoners in a cell on the lower floor. The motive for the lynching was apparently a lack of effective law and order in the county, thus a need for vigilante justice.[28] More recently, in June, a mob of men had approached a farmhouse in northern Bell County near Troy and shot to death a man and a fourteen-year-old boy, apparently because an elopement had been planned.[29]

A little over a month earlier on May 31, Belton merchant J.M. Embree had written Governor Hubbard complaining of lawlessness in the town and asking for a squad of six rangers for "a month or so." Belton Mayor W. H. Estell, on June 3, sent Hubbard a second letter citing disturbances by a "lawless element" in the community and stating that the city marshal was unable to deal with it. Repeated threats by this element had forced the resignation of the deputy city marshal, and now the marshal was ready to quit. Estell asked for a detachment of six to eight rangers.

Responding to Embree's letter, Major Jones sent a letter on June 4 to Mayor Estell saying that he currently had no men that he could send, but he was awaiting some rangers bringing prisoners to Austin and would send some of them. He followed this up with a letter on June 7 to the mayor advising that Corporal Warren and five men were being sent but could not remain in Belton very long. The rangers arrived the next day, much to the surprise of many leading citizens, and the mayor was criticized locally for sending for the lawmen. Mayor Estell promptly sent a letter to Major Jones the next day advising that the sheriff had now offered his cooperation to the city marshal, as had other citizens, that the marshal had hired a new deputy, and, well, the rangers weren't needed anymore. The rangers returned to Austin, but on June 10 an anonymous person sent a lengthy letter to Major Jones reciting the 1874 shooting of the prisoners, the lynching of two horse thieves, and the rescue from the jail of two posse members who had been arrested for killing a Mexican prisoner in their custody. The letter asserted that those who told Major Jones there was no need for rangers were the very ones against whom the rangers were needed.[30]

Clearly Belton was not a peaceful community in which four armed men could attempt a bank robbery without considerable risk of a quick, armed response. The town's bank was in the rear of a store and, from a bank robber's perspective, hard to get at. Bass instead set his sights on Round Rock to the south in Williamson County. In the meantime, given a five-dollar bill to change, Jim Murphy was finally able to break loose from the scrutiny of the gang long enough to write a few short lines to Deputy Marshal Johnson and Sheriff Everheart that the gang was headed for Round Rock to rob the bank and for God's sake to come at once. This was mailed at the Belton post office located in the Avenue Hotel only a block east of the county courthouse.

The four men rode south from Belton and reached Georgetown in Williamson County, thirty-three miles to the south. They camped near town, resting for a day. Jackson and Barnes went into Georgetown so that one of them could have a boot repaired. Chamberlain, the city marshal, thought they looked suspicious and went into the shop to check them out. A deputy sheriff, Milt Tucker,[31] stood at the door to back him up. Since the lawmen had no evidence as to who the men were, other than their suspicious appearance, they decided to investigate them no further. The two bandits returned to their camp where Bass and Murphy waited.[32]

While Bass and the others were in camp at Georgetown preparing to ride south to Round Rock, the federal trial of Pipes, Herndon, Monroe Hill, Scott Mayes and Bob Murphy commenced. Billy Collins was also supposed to be on trial, but he had jumped his $15,000 bond and did not show up in Austin. When Judge Duval convened court on Friday, July 5, the parties announced ready, a jury was selected, and trial began

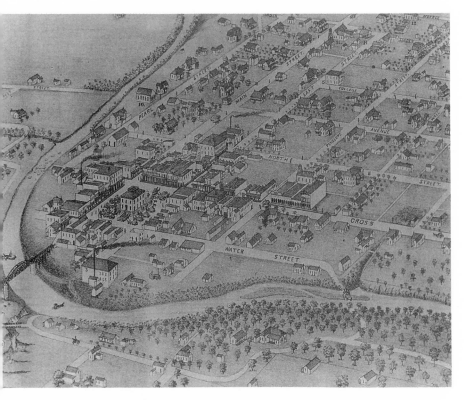

A view of Belton, Texas, at about the time of Sam Bass and from
where Jim Murphy was able to send a message to lawmen.
(Courtesy Belton Public Library).

on Saturday morning. The attorneys for the defendants—
Hickerson Barksdale and George W. Chilton[33]—questioned the
court as to the legality of trying accessories before the principals, Bass, Underwood, etc., were convicted.

When court convened on Monday, July 8, Judge Duval
ruled that the trial would proceed. Prosecutor Evans began his
case, his first witness being Billy Scott who testified that he and
Jack Smith had conceived the idea last December, before the
Texas train robberies, to nab Bass and any other Union Pacific
robbers. Scott made friends with the Collins brothers, which
led to meeting Bass and his associates over several months, but
he never had an opportunity to set them up for a trap. He identified Pipes and Herndon and reported damaging conversations
with them regarding their association with Bass. Scott also gave

important testimony against Billy and Henry Collins.

Julius Alvord testified about the Mesquite robbery but was unable to identify any of the defendants as being involved. Over a hundred witnesses had been subpoenaed to Austin, and the trial continued with additional testimony. On Tuesday Dr. Albert Johnson testified as to the wounds he found on Pipes, but court had to adjourn because one of the jurors was sick. Scott's testimony again on Wednesday, July 10, about his agreement for a share of any rewards upon the conviction of any of the outlaws, led the *Austin Daily Democratic Statesman* to opine that his mercenary interest reflected badly on Scott's credibility. This editorializing prompted the *Evening State Gazette* to come to Scott's defense, and the *Statesman* had to admit that it had taken its account of Scott's testimony from defense attorneys Barksdale and Chilton, who had placed a partisan twist on it.

The next morning, Thursday, the newspaper incident led to a physical altercation between Barksdale and A.J. Evans, and both lawyers were fined fifty dollars by Judge Duval. Major Jones then testified as to how Pipes and Herndon came to be arrested, and he was followed on the stand by Sheriff William Egan. Evans rested the government's case on Friday morning after testimony by Peak, Gerren, lawyer James G. Eblin of Dallas,[34] and Dallas farmer Sloan Jackson.[35] The defense began presenting its witnesses that afternoon, trying to present alibis for Pipes and Herndon. One of the defense witnesses was Maggie Caton, a granddaughter of A.G. Collins,[36] who sought to establish an alibi for her uncle, Billy Collins, and testified that all of the defendants were at her father's place during the Mesquite robbery. Interestingly, Collins' wife, Sallie, was present at the trial but did not testify.

On Wednesday, July 17, the jury returned a verdict of guilty against Pipes and Herndon but acquitted Monroe Hill, Mayes and Bob Murphy. The two convicted train robbers were each sentenced by the jury to ninety-nine years in the penitentiary, although Judge Duval changed the sentence to life imprisonment. They were returned to the Travis County Jail until they could be transferred to the state penitentiary at Huntsville and a subsequent move to some facility contracting with the federal government. The other three defendants, although acquitted of being accomplices in the Mesquite robbery, were rearrested on another charge and promptly gave bond for their appearance. Green Hill and John Skaggs remained in the Austin jail.[37] To add insult to injury, on July 17 while the jury was finding against Barksdale's clients, his home in Dallas was burglarized that night by three men who took a trunk purportedly containing gold coins, his fee for the train robbery cases.[38]

Likely oblivious to the ongoing federal trial in Austin, Bass, Jackson, Barnes and Murphy remained in camp near Georgetown. On Tuesday, July 16, Murphy was able to mail a second note, this time to Major Jones in Austin, warning that they were headed to Round Rock to rest their horses for several days before robbing a bank or a train. Again he urged them "for God's sake to be on hand and prevent it." The letter also expressed Murphy's concern that if the rangers did not prevent the robbery, he would have to help the gang or else the gang would kill him. Just as Murphy mailed the letter, Bass came into the postoffice and asked what he was doing in there so long. Murphy responded that he was trying to talk a man out of his newspaper. The man took the hint, although probably not sure why, and threw down the paper and told them he would loan it to them but could not sell it. Unsuspecting, Bass remained while Murphy read him some of the news on one page. They returned to camp, and that day the four men rode the ten miles south to Round Rock where they camped on the west side of the older portion of the town. Bass was eager to scout out the town and finally carry out another bold robbery.

Ranger Vernon Coke Wilson, who was dispatched by Major Jones to notify Lieutenant N.O. Reynolds to bring men to Round Rock. (Courtesy Harold L. Edwards, Bakersfield, California).

Ranger Lieutenant N.O. Reynolds ca. 1875. (Courtesy Chuck Parsons, Luling, Texas.)

-XV-
SHOWDOWN AT ROUND ROCK

ettlers had found the land north of Austin along Brushy Creek to be suitable for crops, and their presence in that area traced back to 1839 when conflict with Indians was still a concern. Williamson County was created and organized in 1848, largely through the efforts of Judge Robert McAlpin Williamson, popularly known as "Three-Legged Willie" because one leg had been crippled and bent back since childhood, forcing him to use a pegleg and to have three trouser legs to accommodate them. Judge Williamson was one of the very first ranger commanders.[1]

A large table-shaped stone sat in the middle of Brushy Creek about sixteen miles north of Austin where the Chisholm Trail crossed near the rock, and the small community of settlers became known as Round Rock in 1854. Its first choice of a name, Brushy Creek, was not acceptable to the post office. The Greenwood Masonic Institute was established here in the late 1860s, attended for one day by no less notorious a figure than John Wesley Hardin. In 1876, however, the International & Great Northern railroad laid its tracks some distance east of Round Rock, so the community gradually shifted toward the railroad and the south bank of Brushy Creek. Platted by the Texas Land Company, "New" Round Rock was formally incorporated in the fall of 1877, and the old townsite became largely abandoned. By the time the Bass gang arrived in the area, the relocated community had approximately a thousand citizens, a dozen businesses and professional offices, several hotels, a broom factory and a lime plant.[2]

Bass and his three companions camped about a quarter of a mile west of Old Round Rock, about two miles from "New" Round Rock, on the San Saba road. Murphy was quoted as saying that they pitched their camp on Sunday, July 14, but that is likely a day or so earlier than their actual arrival, and Bass would say that they arrived on Tuesday, July 16.[3] The next night after their arrival they pitched a new camp about a mile closer to the town, south of a graveyard and near the houses of some black families. It later would be claimed that Bass hired Mary Matson, a black girl who lived in one of the houses, to "parch" coffee and cook biscuits for them, for which she was paid a dollar.[4] The gang bought some provisions and feed for their horses at the nearby store of Livingston M. Mays[5] and J.M. Black, located in Old Round Rock near Brushy Creek. The first telegraph line from Georgetown to Round Rock had gone to the Mays & Black store. Mays, who started the store, had refused to join the immigration eastward to the new townsite[6] although the partners purchased a lot there.

The plan was to rest and graze the horses so that the gang would be ready for a quick getaway from a bank robbery on Saturday, July 20, at 3:30 p.m., after receipts for the day had been deposited. Murphy pretended that his horse was "nearly broken down," trying to buy time for the rangers to reach Round Rock. Bass and Jackson rode into Round Rock to take a look around. When they returned to camp, Bass complimented Murphy on his choice of targets, "We can take that bank too easy to talk about."[7]

The target of the Bass gang was the Williamson County Bank located on the north side of Georgetown Avenue, now Main Street, on the third lot west of Lampasas Street on the east end of the block. Originally M.D. Miller had operated Miller's Exchange Bank both on this site and in Georgetown, but in June 1878 when Miller retired, it was leased by William S. Peters and his brother, Porter G. Peters, for the Williamson County Bank.[8]

The next morning after Bass and Jackson had checked out the bank and returned to camp, Barnes and Murphy went into Round Rock to look for themselves, changed a five-dollar bill at the bank, then had shaves. Barnes was enthusiastic about robbing this bank and expressed a desire to do the job that very day if the horses were rested. By now Murphy had been accepted fully into the group. Bass detailed the plan: on Saturday afternoon he and Barnes would go on foot into the bank, the four leaving their horses hitched in an alley behind the bank. Barnes would ask for change in silver for a five-dollar bill, at which time Bass would "throw down" on the banker. Barnes would then dramatically jump over the counter to gather the money. Murphy and Jackson would stand guard at the door to handle anyone who came into the bank.

Murphy felt that if he could somehow get into Round Rock on Friday or Saturday morning before the holdup, he would be able to contact Major Jones and tell him the plan.[9] On Friday afternoon, July 19, the gang planned to make another trip into Round Rock to buy some tobacco and take one more look around.

In a letter to Major Jones sent on July 16 from Denton County, Captain Peak informed him that nothing had been heard in several weeks in that area from Bass or his men and it was thought that they had left that part of the country. Peak was confident that Jim Murphy was still with the outlaw gang.[10] Jones, however, had received the letter from Murphy and was now desperately trying to round up a sufficient force of men. On Thursday, July 18, he sent a succinct telegram to the agent of the International and Great Northern Railroad, which had a stop at Round Rock, to "guard trains against robbers."[11]

Knowing that he did not have enough rangers in Austin to take with him to Round Rock, Jones dispatched Corporal Vernon Coke Wilson,[12] who commanded the small squad of rangers at the state capitol, to ride to Lampasas to summon Lieutenant N.O. Reynolds and a squad of rangers from their camp there. No telegraph communication to that area existed at the time. After sending Wilson to Lampasas, Jones then sent the other rangers of the squad, Dick Ware,[13] Chris Connor[14] and George Herold,[15] on ahead to Round Rock early Thursday morning to await his arrival.[16] They were to stable their horses and stay out of sight but to be alert for any suspicious men who might be the Bass gang.

Wilson, who had a fine voice, played the guitar with skill and was a nephew of former Governor Richard Coke, headed for the Austin stable where his horse was kept. However the horse had been relatively inactive for several months and had grown fat and soft. Wilson nevertheless unmercifully sped his horse the sixty-five miles toward Lampasas, arriving there by daylight Friday morning. The spent horse was overheated and died. Wilson was shocked to find that Lieutenant Reynolds had moved his troops to San Saba, so the ranger caught an outgoing stagecoach and, after a delay of time that left him fuming, reached San Saba. He quickly obtained a horse at the livery stable and raced one mile to Reynolds' camp on the San Saba River, arriving about 7:30 Thursday night. The exhausted ranger promptly reported to Lieutenant Reynolds and passed on Major Jones' orders, then briefly rested.[17]

The rangers in Reynolds' camp had just completed supper and their horses had been fed and tied up for the night, but Wilson's frantic arrival excited the camp. Hearing Jones' orders, Reynolds summoned his sergeant, Charles L. Nevill,[18] and directed him to have eight men with the best horses prepare for a hard ride to Round Rock. Nevill rounded up James B. Gillett, the brothers John R. and William Lawrence Banister, Henry W. McGhee, Abe Anglin, David L. Lygon, William Derrick and an unknown ranger. Horses were saddled, mules packed, and cartridge belts filled as the rangers hurriedly prepared to leave. Reynolds had been ill and was not in shape for a wild horseback ride, so two pack mules were hitched to a light spring hack to carry him. At sunset, within thirty minutes of Wilson's arrival, the party was ready to leave. Reynolds took his seat in the hack, throwing in some blankets for Wilson who had not slept for over thirty hours and who laid down in the wagon to rest on the way.

The eleven rangers set off at a fast trot, a pace that would be maintained for most of the 110-mile trip. They rode into Lampasas County where Jack M. Martin, a merchant in the small community of Senterfitt just west of Lometa, heard them pass through in the night and later told a customer that hell was to pay somewhere because the rangers had passed his store on a dead run. As dawn broke on Friday morning, July 19, the rangers stopped for breakfast at the San Gabriel River, fifteen miles south of Lampasas. The weary horses were provided oats while the lawmen wolfed down bread, bacon and coffee; Reynolds gave them only thirty minutes before they had to be on their way again. In the saddle once more, the intense July heat began to wear down both the riders and their mounts, and they could not make as good a time as they had during the night.[19] There would be no more stops until they reached Round Rock, forty-five miles away, and hopefully a fight with the Bass gang.

Major Jones prepared to go from Austin to Round Rock after noon on Thursday. He received a telegram from the Round Rock telegraph operator, Holman T. Ham,[20] that a young man with a smooth face and a tall white hat had just inquired as to when the train would arrive for Austin.[21] On the streets of Austin Jones ran into Maurice B. Moore, a former ranger and now a Travis County deputy sheriff.[22] He asked Moore if he could go with him to Round Rock for two or three days, and Moore agreed, "if the pay is good." At about one that afternoon the two men met at the train depot and boarded for the short ride north to Round Rock, during which Jones briefed Moore of the expected presence of the Bass gang.[23]

Arriving at Round Rock, Jones immediately went to the post office, maintained in a corner of Henry Koppel's store on the southwest corner of Georgetown and Mays Streets, hoping to find a message from Jim Murphy, but there was nothing.[24] Jones' rangers had left their mounts in the livery stable of Henry Highsmith,[25] located on the north side of Georgetown Avenue just west of the Williamson County Bank. The ranger commander stopped in the Williamson County Bank and warned William Peters that a bank robbery was anticipated but the rangers would attempt to capture the bandits.[26] Understandably, Peters would be reported as "greatly alarmed and agitated."[27] Jones then sent a telegram to Captain Lee Hall in Austin that the Bass party was probably in the area but was also possibly in Austin. He directed Hall to notify the Travis County sheriff and a man named Creasy but to maintain secrecy.[28] Checking into the Davis Hotel a block west of the livery stable on Georgetown Avenue, Jones established his room as a command post.

During the day Scott Mayes, Harry Hayes, John Skaggs, Green and Monroe Hill, and one other, all just released from custody in Austin, drove through Round Rock on their way home, stopping only long enough to purchase some supplies and watermelons. They were unaware of Bass' presence but were nevertheless closely watched by the rangers.[29]

Jones was up early on Friday morning and positioned himself at the telegraph office, waiting for Reynolds' arrival with his
men. Ware, Connor and Herold were placed at strategic posi-
tions in town, keeping their eyes open for suspicious men. He
wired the adjutant general in Austin, "Parties answering
description of Bass and Collins were here night before last. I
have spies in the country around. Robbers may have gone to
Austin...."[30] This was followed by another telegram asking
Steele to send Captain Lee Hall on the one o'clock train,[31] perhaps concerned that Reynolds would not arrive in time. Jones
was not aware that Jackson and Murphy had come into town
that morning to look around. Bass was concerned that two cowboys he had seen might be rangers, but at about eleven o'clock,
satisfied that all seemed in order, the two returned to the outlaw camp.[32]

In Austin, Travis County Sheriff Dennis Corwin[33] placed a
heavy guard on the county jail in case Bass decided to try to rescue some of his friends imprisoned there. Concerned that the
communications from Murphy might have been a ruse by the
Bass gang, Jones consulted with Everheart and asked him and
Deputy U.S. Marshal Walter Johnson to stay on guard in
Austin against such an attempt.[34] Lee Hall, who was in attendance at the state Democratic convention in Austin as sergeant-
at-arms, was told by Adjutant General Steele to go to Round
Rock. Hall arrived by train in Round Rock about two that afternoon and, after consulting with Jones, telegraphed his lieu-
tenant in Austin, John Armstrong, to bring some men to
Round Rock. Jones had earlier called for stable keeper Henry
Highsmith and Williamson County Deputy Sheriff A.W.
"Caige" Grimes,[35] both ex-rangers, to meet him at his hotel
room, and Hall arrived in time to meet with them.[36]

Grimes had earlier been asked by Jones to find two citizens
familiar with camping places and have them scout around the
outskirts of town late Thursday and see if they could spot any
strangers. Highsmith would later recall that the purpose given
by Jones was to locate some "bad men," and when asked who,
Jones declined to reveal who the bad men were. Contemporary
news accounts reflect only that Jones took Highsmith and
Grimes "into his confidence."[37] According to Captain Hall in

Williamson County Deputy Sheriff A.W. "Caige" Grimes, killed at Round Rock. (Courtesy Robert W. Stephens, Dallas, Texas)

1895, Maurice Moore was also at the meeting, and Grimes and Moore were told to go down on the street to look for suspicious characters and report them to Jones and Hall.[38] Thus there is some substance to the claim that Grimes and Highsmith did not know that the Bass gang was believed to be coming to Round Rock. Likely Hall's memory was faulty concerning Moore's presence, but Moore certainly understood that the Bass gang was believed to be on its way.

The two Round Rock citizens, Wayne Graham[39] and By Asher,[40] had volunteered on Thursday to explore the outskirts of town to see if they could spot any suspicious men. They reported to Jones on Friday that they had not located any unusual camps.[41] Surprisingly, Bass and his men had come to Round Rock several times, visiting the bank at least twice, but apparently no one suspected them. Not having heard anything more from Murphy, Jones was concerned that the gang may have chosen to bypass Round Rock and go on to Austin. Neither could he rule out that they might try to hit another train.

As the hot July afternoon wore on with no sign yet of Reynolds and his men, the rangers settled in for a wait. Because he felt that Barnes and Jackson might recognize him, Hall suggested to Jones that he should remain indoors and keep a watch for the gang from his hotel gallery. Exhausted from his ride, however, Hall pulled off his boots and laid down on his bed.[42] While Jones went back to the telegraph office, Dick Ware was posted in German-born Henry Burkhardt's[43] barber shop just

247

east of Henry Koppel's store and across the street from the bank. Deputy Sheriff Grimes, Highsmith, and a man named Mitchell were sitting in front of Highsmith's barn in the middle of the block.[44] Rangers George Herold and Chris Connor were inside Highsmith's livery stable.[45] Deputy Sheriff Moore stood in front of the livery stable, near Highsmith, Grimes and Mitchell.[46]

It was about four o'clock Friday afternoon. In the livery stable was twelve-year-old Jeff Dillingham, unloading fodder that he had just sold there.[47] Benjamin Warden, a farmer from Burnet County, and his ten-year-old son James had been to Austin for supplies and were on their way back home, stopping briefly in Round Rock.[48] Not far away, Alf Dieckmann, a Prussian, was tending his small fruit stand wiping apples.[49] In front of a hardware store on the north side of Georgetown Avenue, ten-year-old David H. "Dock" Davis waited by his father's wagon holding the team's reins while his father was inside buying him a pocket knife.[50] In the sultry Texas heat, the stage was set for sudden violence and the end of the Bass gang.

At their camp Bass and the others prepared to go back into Round Rock Friday afternoon to buy tobacco and take one last look around before the Saturday holdup. Murphy had not made any contact with Jones and was likely concerned that he might be killed if the rangers were in town. As they rode toward town, Murphy stopped off at the Livingston and Mays store in Old Round Rock, ostensibly to see if he could pick up any information about the rangers, and Bass, Barnes and Jackson rode on to the new town.[51]

The three outlaws rode leisurely into the town and hitched their horses in the alley on the north side of Georgetown Avenue, near the east end a few lots west of Lampasas Street almost behind the Williamson County Bank. They walked up Lampasas Street to Georgetown, then walked west on the north side of the street, passing Moore, Highsmith and Mitchell. Grimes had moved up the street. Highsmith observed them and said, "There go three strangers." Moore looked at them closely and thought he saw a sixshooter beneath the coat of one of the men. The other two men were carrying saddlebags. Moore walked over to Grimes and told him he thought one of

Henry Koppel's store as it appears in Round Rock today.
(Author's photo.)

the men was armed. The three bandits crossed the street directly
for the corner store of Henry Koppel, giving the lawmen a hard
look. Grimes told Moore, "Let me go over and see," and the two
lawmen followed the trio to the store.[52] Williamson County
Sheriff Sam Strayhorn had instructed Grimes that any cowboys
passing through Round Rock had to "discard" their firearms
until they were ready to leave.[53] All evidence indicates that
Grimes, at least, had no idea that it was the Bass gang. Why
Moore did not pass on what he knew will never be known.

The owner of the store, Henry Koppel, thirty-seven, was originally from Germany. He and his wife, Caroline, twenty-eight,
had purchased the lot on the southeast corner of Georgetown
Avenue and Mays Street two years earlier, erecting the masonry
building in which to house their store.[54] In April he had been
elected an alderman for the town.[55] Koppel was sitting outside
his store as the three strangers walked inside.[56]

Inside, Koppel's clerk, Simon Juda, a twenty-eight-year-old
Prussian,[57] waited on the three men when they stepped up to the
counter and bargained good-naturedly for some tobacco. Grimes
entered the store first, walking up behind the men. Moore
stepped just inside the door then put his hands in his pockets

and whistled, appearing as if he were not watching the men. Juda later said that Grimes merely walked up to the men without saying anything and put his hand on the man where he thought there was a pistol. Moore said that Grimes approached them carelessly and asked one if he had a pistol, and Bass later said that Grimes asked him if had a pistol. Bass replied, "yes," and all three, figuring they had been discovered, pulled their pistols, two shooting at Grimes and one at Moore.

Grimes, his pistol still in its holster, turned and ran for the door, calling out "Don't, boys!" Barnes was right behind him, shooting. A bullet slammed into Moore's left lung, exiting from his rear left shoulder. Moore drew his pistol and fired at the man who had shot him. Acrid gunsmoke filled the store and obscured everyone's vision, but Moore and the men continued shooting. Grimes fell dead on the ground outside the store, riddled with four or five bullets. Koppel had streaked away at the first sound of gunfire and was nowhere to be seen. Moore, still firing but growing weak, retreated from the doorway. He saw the three men dart from the store through the thick gunsmoke and into the street, one of them bleeding from the arm and side. One of Moore's bullets had shot off Bass' ring and middle fingers on his right hand. Faint and sick, Moore leaned against the building and fired his last shot at the fleeing bandits.[58]

With the gunfire's echoing through the streets, the waiting rangers sprang into action. Dick Ware came out of the barber shop, spotted the three men making their way across the street, each keeping a little distance from the others, and immediately opened fire. Major Jones, who had been walking from the telegraph office at the railroad depot several blocks to the south, ran up Mays Street toward the gunfire and joined in the battle. As the robbers reached the corner building on the north side of the street, one of them took deliberate aim at Jones and sent a round over his head and into the wall of the building behind him. Ware was showered with splinters when he took what cover he could find behind a hitching post, and a round split the top of the post within inches of his head. Young Dock Davis couldn't hold on to the wagon team, but his father was able to jump into the wagon as it rushed off. The boy took cover in a nearby store.[59]

The wounded Moore, loading his empty pistol, staggered across the street to Highsmith's stable to recover his Winchester. He started to resume his pursuit when Dr. A.F. Morris[60] stopped him, warning him that if he moved any further the exertion would kill him. Moore surrendered his rifle to someone and went with the doctor and a Judge Schultz to the hotel.[61] International and Great Northern station agent J.F. Tubbs, who was missing his left hand, heard the gunfire and saw Grimes lying on the ground with a pistol beside him. He picked up the pistol, rested it on his left arm, and fired several shots at the retreating bandits. He believed that he hit one of the men.[62]

When the firing broke out, Highsmith ran back into his stable office to grab his Winchester, expecting to fire on the robbers as they ran from Koppel's store. Ranger George Herold ran by him to get his own rifle then pushed Highsmith back, telling him that he might hit innocent citizens. Herold had seen where the robbers' horses were hitched in the alley behind the stable, and he had Highsmith come with him to the rear of the stable to station themselves between the robbers and their horses. Joined by Connor, they went into the back stable yard to watch the fleeing men come down the alley, but there were so many fences to the rear of buildings along the alley, including a tall picket fence behind the stable, that they could not fire a clear shot until the men were almost immediately behind the stable.

On Georgetown Avenue, Ware, Jones and Tubbs steadily advanced on the slowly retreating bandits in a crackling exchange of gunfire. Jackson called to his comrades, "Come on! Come on!" Dieckmann, the fruit peddler, ducked from a shot above his head and took cover, scattering fruit every which way. Jones emptied his pistol. Lee Hall jumped up from his bed, put on his boots, grabbed his Winchester and ran to the street to see citizens scurrying away from the gunfire. He also saw Grimes' body in the dust outside Koppel's store. Someone running by told Hall that it was part of the Ross-Grimes feud; Round Rock's city marshal, A.G. Hall, had been shot to death in March by one of two brothers named Ross.[63] Hall saw Ware and Jones up the street but did not reach the scene in time to join in the fight.

The three robbers ran north from the corner, stopping spas-

A view of the Round Rock alley down which Bass, Barnes, and Jackson
fled, as it appears today. (Author's photo).

modically to take cover and fire at their pursuers, then started
east down the alley with Barnes and Jackson ahead of the
wounded Bass. A saloon keeper, Frank Jordan,[64] fired at them
from the back of his establishment, and they dodged and kept
running from cover to cover. Slowly they made their way toward
their horses, holding off Ware, Jones, Tubbs and others with
well-placed shots. Barnes and Jackson passed by the stable and
were about to reach their horses when Herold and Connor
opened up on them from the livery yard. Bass was not far
behind coming down the alley. Highsmith had a cartridge hang
up in his Winchester and could not fire. Two of the robbers
returned Herold's and Connor's fire. A bloodied Bass hesitated
and stopped at a horse hitched at the back of the stable. Within
fifteen feet of the wounded outlaw, Herold called out to him
not to mount the horse and to surrender; Bass snapped an
empty pistol at him with his left hand. The horse, excited from
the steady popping of gunshots, pushed Bass against the stable
fence. Herold was able to fire a shot at him beneath the horse's
neck as Bass turned to try and mount the animal.

"Oh, Lord!" exclaimed Bass as a bullet struck him. The
round entered to the left of Bass' spine, ranged up and near or

Left: Ranger Richard "Dick" Ware, whose shot killed Seaborn Barnes.
(Courtesy Robert W. Stephens, Dallas, Texas.)
Right: Ranger George Herold, as he appeared with the El Paso Police
Department, who fired the shot that gave Sam Bass his mortal wound.
(Courtesy Robert G. McCubbin, Jr., El Paso, Texas.)

through his kidney, then exited three inches to the left of his
navel. The bullet reportedly hit a cartridge in his belt, splitting,
and one-half of the bullet remained in his body, raising a question later as to who actually shot Sam Bass. Bass clung to the top
of the fence with his free hand, attempting to conceal himself
from the men in the stable yard, then made for his companions.
Jackson came back to assist him and cover his retreat toward the
horses.

As this occurred, Barnes was attempting to mount his horse.
Jones, Ware and Tubbs ran down the alley from Mays Street,
shooting as they came. Ware stopped and took deliberate aim at
Barnes as the outlaw was beginning to mount his horse. The bullet tunneled in behind Barnes' left ear and came out by the right
eye. Still clutching his pistol and saddle bags, he fell dead to the
ground. Bass had the presence of mind to pick up Barnes' saddle bags, then Jackson, returning the lawmen's fire and forcing
them to remain close to cover, used his free hand to help his
badly wounded leader mount his horse. The two raced their

horses east out of the alley, turning back west and out of town.

Jim Murphy, sitting in the Livingston and Mays store, saw Jackson and Bass fly by as they raced through Old Round Rock. Jackson was helping the weakened Bass to stay in the saddle.[65] As Bass and Jackson rode furiously across Brushy Creek, thirteen-year-old Anna Fahner was sitting and swinging her legs in the fork of a liveoak tree that served as a gatepost in front of the family's house near the road. The two bandits rode past, and Jackson called to her to run into the house, likely because any pursuers would be shooting at them. She ran toward her house, ruining her shoes and a good pair of stockings.[66]

Herold mounted Barnes' horse to take up the pursuit of Jackson and Bass, and Jones ordered the available rangers to find mounts and go after the two. Hall found a saddled horse nearby and joined Herold, along with two other men and several other citizens. Jones found an old plug of a horse in the livery stable, but it played out before he could catch up with Hall's party and he returned to Round Rock. Murphy had called to Jones when he rode by the store after Bass and Jackson, but Jones did not hear him.[67]

In the alley, the danger past, Round Rock citizens slowly emerged from cover and gathered to look at the body of the dead Seaborn Barnes. J.W. McCutcheon would recall that Barnes had one leg thrown over the other, was smoothly shaved, and was wearing a blue overshirt and new spurs. In his left rear pocket was a blue paper of fine cut tobacco.[68]

Jim Murphy rode in from Old Round Rock to find out what had happened and joined the crowd in the alley. When someone wondered who the dead man was, Murphy remarked that if it was the Bass gang, the body must be that of Barnes. When asked how they could tell, Murphy told them that Barnes had been shot four times in his legs, three in the right and one in the left, during the Mesquite robbery. When the wounds were located, the crowd started to arrest Murphy as one of the gang. Major Jones returned in time and, recognizing Murphy, stopped the crowd by identifying Murphy as one of his men.[69] Murphy was obviously relieved that his ordeal was at an end. He told a reporter, "I wouldn't go through it all again for $50,000 piled down on the floor before me—no, sir! With all the anxiety and watching I had to suffer....It's all over now and I am glad of it!"[70]

Hall and the rangers and citizens with him soon lost the trail of the fleeing bandits. Hall later declared in an 1895 interview that they found a pair of gloves, one of them bloody with the finger shot through. The trail led into rocks and cedar brakes as it became dusk. Since one of the fugitives appeared to be seriously wounded, the pursuers decided it would be best to return to town and properly organize a posse to find their trail the next morning. Darkness was not far off and their horses were nearly spent from the furious pace. The hastily organized pursuit would not be nearly as effective as one that was better armed and equipped.[71]

Lieutenant N.O. Reynolds and his men arrived about two hours after the fight, meeting some of the impromptu posses as they rode to the outskirts. Reynolds had his men set up camp while he went into town to confer with Jones. Later that evening Lieutenant Armstrong arrived from Austin with additional rangers from Hall's company. The body of the fallen Seaborn Barnes was taken to a small room used as a corn bin, not far from where he fell, and a wooden coffin was hastily put together in which to place him.[72]

On Friday evening Maurice Moore sent a telegram to his brother J.S. Moore in Galveston, and it is apparent that an analysis of the gunfight had not yet occurred.

> James [sic] Bass and two of his train robbers attacked the deputy sheriff of Williamson county and myself. They fired first, killing the deputy of Williamson and slightly wounding me. I killed one and wounded another. I am doing well and will soon be all right. Don't let mother be uneasy.[73]

Major Jones telegraphed Adjutant General Steele a report of what had happened. Then another bizarre exchange of telegrams was commenced. For some reason, perhaps expecting Billy Collins to come join the gang at Round Rock, Jones sent telegrams to Ranger Captain J.C. Sparks at Corsicana in Navarro County and the agent of the I&GN Railroad to "look out for Collins on the down train," saying that he was part of the Bass gang. Navarro County Sheriff E.E. Dunn[74] promptly arrested a man, fitting the description that Jones had given, who was carrying two sixshooters and a pair of Winchesters and claiming that he was a Grayson County deputy sheriff named J.M. Winter. Sheriff Everheart quickly confirmed his deputy's identity, saying that he had telegraphed him from Austin to come help him.[75]

After Jackson led Bass furiously out of Round Rock, they briefly returned to their camp to pick up the rifles they had left there then struck north toward Georgetown, likely figuring that any help for the rangers would be coming from Austin to the south. After they had ridden about three miles, Bass could go no further and they turned down a lane into some woods where they stopped.[76] There is no record of what the two men discussed, although popular stories would have Jackson's declaring to remain with Bass and fight to the death. Bass was supposed to have urged his companion to ride on without him and to have given him his rifle. In any event, Jackson rode on and disappeared from history.

Bass remained in the woods throughout the night, bloody and in considerable pain. He cut his undershirt into strips to help stem the bleeding. In the early morning hours, leaving his horse, he crawled from the woods to hail a black man driving a load of wood, offering money for a ride, but the frightened man refused and drove off. He then dragged himself to a nearby farmhouse for some water, and twenty-three-year-old Semantha Sherman, who lived there with her husband, John, reportedly gave him a drink, although another account says that she became frightened at his bloody appearance and ran off.[77]

Bass also encountered a group of laborers working on the Georgetown spur of the I&GN Railroad and called to them from where he was sitting beneath a live oak tree not very far from where Jackson had left him on the edge of Dudley Snyder's pasture.[78] At first the workers ignored him, but finally one old man brought him a cup of water. Bass told the samaritan that he was a cattleman from South Texas and had been shot the day before in a little difficulty in Round Rock. His arm dangling and bleeding, Bass told him, "We give them hell in the new town, but they got us some."[79]

Early Saturday morning at first light Sergeant Charles Nevill and eight men from Reynolds' squad again took up the trail after Bass and Jackson. There is some evidence that someone had come into Round Rock and informed the lawmen that he had encountered Bass. Accompanying them as guides were Williamson County Deputy Sheriffs Milt Tucker and Olander C. Lane.[80] Not many minutes after reaching the point where Hall and his men had lost the trail the evening before, the ranger

Williamson County Deputy Sheriff James Milton "Milt" Tucker. (From Shroyer and Wood, *Williamson County History*)

squad noticed a man lying under a tree not far from where the railroad was under construction. Because of the mules grazing near the man, Tucker presumed that it was a railroad worker herding the mules, and they rode on. The rangers dismounted to follow the trail on foot and quickly came upon two men who told them that the man under the tree was wounded and had been trying to hire someone to take him away.

The rangers mounted and rode back to within sixty yards of the man under the tree. Nevill approached cautiously with gun drawn and ready, ordering the man to throw up his hands, and Bass called out, "Don't shoot; I surrender." Nevill moved closer, and the wounded man identified himself as Sam Bass. Seeing the seriousness of Bass' wounds, Nevill immediately sent a courier to notify Major Jones and to bring back an ambulance and a doctor. Milt Tucker holstered his pistol and approached Bass. Bass noticed his weapon and said, "Your gun is cocked; you will shoot your foot." Tucker remedied the problem with some chagrin. Bass then asked Nevill if someone would get his horse and saddle, telling him where the animal could probably

Ranger Sergeant Charles L. Nevill (standing) and Chris Connor in 1877. (Courtesy Chuck Parsons, Luling, Texas).

be located. Tucker and two men went to look but could not find the horse. Nevill took two men to search for himself but could only find a saddle and bridle.[81]

Receiving the word of Bass' capture, Jones enlisted the aid of Round Rock physician C.P. Cochran,[82] and a wagon was summoned to bring Bass into Round Rock.[83] Before leaving town, Jones had telegraph operator Holman Ham send word to Adjutant General Steele, "Major Jones has gone to Bass seven miles in country. It is a positive fact about Basses [sic] capture."[84]

At the scene Dr. Cochran examined the outlaw's wounds and pronounced them fatal. He told Bass that he did not have long to live, and the wounded man was loaded into the wagon for the trip to town.[85] Coming through Old Round Rock, the wagon stopped briefly at the residence of Dr. Alexander McDonald so that he could examine the prisoner. Two sons of the doctor, Alec and Robert, climbed up on the wheel for a good look at the noted bad man before their father scooted them off.[86]

Back in Round Rock, Bass was taken to the tin shop of August Gloeber, a long plank shack facing east, next to the Hart House hotel on the west side of Mays street just across from the west entry of the alley in which the gang had met its fate.[87] He was laid on a plain low cot in the middle of the shack and the rangers asked the manager of the hotel, Richard C. Hart, to provide a sheet and pillow from the hotel for the bandit's comfort. Hart, who refused to allow Bass to be brought into the hotel, later billed the state for $5.20.[88] Doctors Cochran and A.F. Morris again examined Bass and confirmed that he was dying. A waitress at the Hart House, Nancy Earle, brought Bass some soup prepared by Hart's wife, but he was too weak to eat.[89] Jones also hired a black man, Jim Chatman, to act as a nurse for Bass.[90]

While the arrangements were being made on Saturday morning for the care of Bass, Dr. Morris also attended Maurice Moore and, once he determined that the deputy's wound was not a fatal one, accompanied him on the train back to Austin where he was left in the care of a close friend, Mr. Petmecky, an Austin gun dealer. Moore's mother left her home in Galveston Saturday afternoon to attend her son.[91] Barnes' body was taken without ceremony to the cemetery in Old Round Rock and buried at the far western end, near the area reserved for blacks. Jones sent a telegram to Sheriff Dunn in Corsicana that Grayson County Sheriff Everheart and his deputy, Winter, were in Round Rock,[92] then sent a telegram to Steele confirming Bass' capture. Steele promptly wired him back, "It is claimed that your dispatch is an election trick. Bring Bass here if possible. Answer." The delegates at the state Democratic convention in Austin theorized that the news might be a political ploy by Governor Hubbard and questioned whether the man captured was really Bass.[93] Jones also sent a telegram to June Peak at Dallas advising him to watch for Frank Jackson at his brother's place in Denton County, instructing him also to send scouts to Palo Pinto and Stephens Counties.[94] Sergeant Tom Floyd promptly took five men to Stephens County while Peak and one man looked for Underwood near the Slade residence in Denton County.[95]

Major Jones steadily pumped Bass for information about the gang's activities, but the outlaw was playing it close to the vest. "It is agin my profession to blow on my pals. If a man knows anything he ought to die with it in him," he told the lawman.[96] Jones stationed someone near Bass with paper and pencil to take down all of his comments, but when Bass was awake he remained guarded in his comments. He admitted to seven stage

A 44.40 cartridge from the belt of Sam Bass.
(Courtesy C.B. Wilson, Dallas, Texas.)

robberies and the Union Pacific robbery, naming Joel Collins, Bill Heffridge, Tom Nixon, Jack Davis and Jim Berry as his confederates. As to whether he had ever killed anyone, he replied that "If I killed Grimes it was the first man I ever killed."

He would not discuss who was with him in the Texas train robberies, although he admitted who was with him at the Salt Creek fight. A *Galveston Daily News* reporter was admitted to Bass' bedside on Saturday afternoon to ask him more questions. He denied knowing Pipes and Herndon, saying that he had intended on "making a raise" on the bank in Round Rock before heading to Mexico. Breathing heavily, he claimed that some of the men with him had heard on the Round Rock streets that the rangers were in town.[97] According to Ranger Jim Gillett, Bass said that he had received both of his wounds just after leaving Koppel's store, not in the alley,[98] although no contemporary accounts quote Bass as making that statement. Bass presented his pistol to Milt Tucker, according to the *Galveston Daily News*, but Ranger John Banister sent a letter to his mother on Sunday stating that Bass had given his pistol, belt and scabbard to him.[99]

In spite of the doctors' grim prognosis, Bass rallied on Saturday and felt a little better, thinking that he might recover after all. He talked briefly about his family but steered away from any discussion of religion. In Round Rock that day with his two oldest sons was the Reverend Austin C. Aten, pastor of the Round Rock Christian Church.[100] A group of citizens approached him about going to Bass and providing spiritual consolation, but the pastor did not believe in deathbed confessions and refused to go. On subsequent entreaty, however, he

The Reverend Austin
Cunningham Aten, who
attended to the dying
Bass. (Courtesy Gary
and Jeri Radder, Alamo,
California).

relented and went to see Bass and asked the wounded man if he
wanted him to pray for him. Bass reportedly said, "Well, go
ahead. I don't care. If you think it'll do any good."[101] The
Reverend Aten's second oldest son, Austin Ira Aten, would go
on to become a noted Texas Ranger.

On Saturday evening Grimes' two brothers appeared outside
the shack that contained the outlaw. According to Highsmith,
they confirmed that the doctors had said that his wound was a
fatal one. Grimly, one brother remarked, "This man must not
leave this house alive."[102] Bass did not complain about the body
wound but did express concern about the pain in his hand.

On Sunday morning, July 21, Bass still felt that he might
recover. Around eleven o'clock, however, his condition began to
deteriorate and he began to experience increasing discomfort
and pain. Jim Chatman stayed with him, tending to any request
to help make him more comfortable. The doctors remained near
but there was nothing more they could do. Bass sent for Jones to
ask if he could provide some relief, but he, too, could not help
him. Sensing that this might be the best opportunity, Jones suggested that there might be some vindication for the outlaw by
giving him the information he wanted, but Bass again declined.
At about 3:30 Sunday afternoon the doctors told Bass that death
was near, thinking that he might want to make some final state-

ment. In severe pain, Bass muttered, "Let me go." Several minutes later he spoke to no one in particular, "The world is bobbing around."

Bass lapsed into unconsciousness then took a few short gasps. His breathing simply stopped for about a minute, followed by a short jerk of his head. Then there was nothing. At 3:55 p.m., Sunday, July 21, 1878, on his twenty-seventh birthday, Texas bandit Sam Bass was dead.[103]

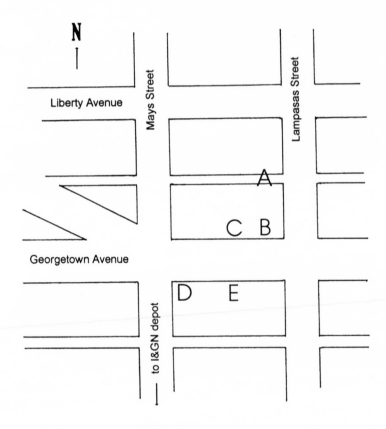

The Round Rock Shootout
July 19, 1878

A. Horses hitched   D. Koppel's store
B. Bank   E. Barber shop
C. Highsmith's stable

-XVI-

AFTERMATH

A n inquest was held after Bass' death, and speculation began almost immediately as to who actually fired the fatal shot. Major Jones believed that Dick Ware deserved the credit because Ware had been the only one beside him as they pursued the bandits down the alley. According to Gillett, all of the rangers in Reynolds' group believed Dick Ware had to have been the one, but Ware denied shooting Bass. Gillett wrote also that Herold testified he had killed Bass. The jury ruled that Seaborn Barnes was killed by Ware and that Herold fired the shot that led to Bass' demise.

Both Lee Hall and Gillett claimed years later that Bass told them he had been shot before entering the alley, thus precluding Herold from consideration, and into the next century Gillett would champion Dick Ware as the slayer of Sam Bass.[1] Maurice Moore was quoted as saying Bass was bleeding from both the hand and the side when he and his cohorts fled from Koppel's store, leading to Moore's conclusion that he had been responsible for Bass' death.[2] There is, however, no contemporary quote attributed to Bass to support Hall's and Gillett's memories, or Moore's statement, that Bass was mortally wounded anywhere other than in the alley as determined by the jury of inquest.

Another puzzle concerns the weapon Herold used to shoot Bass. In 1900 Herold, then an El Paso policeman, swore in an affidavit that he "was given credit as the one who made the shot that later killed" Bass and that a long-barrelled .45-caliber Colt single action revolver, serial number 29569 (which later had its barrel shortened), was "the gun that I had that day at Round Rock."[3] The stilted, formal language, likely written by someone else for the illiterate Herold, is a strange choice of language for the lawman, who more likely would have said simply that this was the weapon he used to kill Sam Bass. In addition, an account of the gunfight in the July 26 *Austin Daily Democratic*

Statesman hints that Herold was firing a rifle. Herold told the newspaper that as soon as he heard the gunshots, "he picked up his gun" and ultimately went to the rear of Highsmith's stable.[4] In both 1926 and 1927 Highsmith related specifically that Ranger "Terrell," as he recalled Herold's name, shot Bass with his Winchester. Gillett, who was not present in Round Rock until hours after the gunfight although he most certainly talked with the principals involved, also claimed that both Herold and Connor were firing at Bass, Barnes and Jackson with Winchesters.[5]

Major Jones wired Adjutant General Steele and asked if he wanted Bass' body brought to Austin, but Steele instructed him to have an inquest and bury him.[6] Hundreds of people had flocked to Round Rock to see the remains of the notorious desperado. On Monday, July 22, the same cart that had carried Barnes' body was used to transport that of Sam Bass. Bass' coffin was loaded onto the wagon, and two black men began the journey to the cemetery in Old Round Rock, not very far from where the outlaw camp had been. Seated atop the coffin, the two men drove past the residence of Methodist minister John W. Ledbetter,[7] who took exception to the cavalier manner in which they were conducting themselves. Ledbetter stopped them, made them climb down from the coffin, then had them drive the wagon on to the cemetery in a "more stately manner." At the cemetery the minister supervised the burial then read a psalm and said a prayer over the Bass' grave,[8] which lay next to that of his fallen comrade, Barnes.

Caige Grimes was buried some eighty yards away from the graves of his killers in the more respectable portion of the cemetery. Round Rock citizens took up a collection and presented Grimes' widow with two hundred dollars, and Jones turned over to her one of the horses belonging to the Bass gang.[9] The Houston and Texas Central Railroad also presented Mrs. Grimes with $250 in recognition of her husband's sacrifice.[10]

Jones returned to Austin by horseback on Monday evening, accompanied by Jim Murphy. He promptly fired off letters to the Texas Express Company, the Texas and Pacific Railroad, the Houston and Texas Central Railroad, the Pinkerton Detective Agency, and the Union Pacific Railroad inquiring about any available rewards for the capture of Pipes and Herndon and for

The modern grave markers of Sam Bass and Seaborn Barnes as they
appear today in Round Rock, Texas. (Author photo).

the killing of Bass and Barnes. Pipes and Herndon were formally sentenced to life terms on Monday, July 22.[11] On
Thursday, July 25, Murphy appeared in federal court before
Judge Duval and, in compliance with the agreement, U.S.
Attorney Evans asked that all charges against Murphy be
dropped. The forfeiture on Murphy's bond was set aside, much
to the bondsman's relief, and Jim Murphy was free to return home
in Denton County.[12]

Another newspaper furor erupted over who should be
awarded the credit for bringing an end to the Bass gang. The
Sherman Register complained that Sheriff Everheart had already
known of the planned robbery in Round Rock and was hidden
there "waiting for matters to develop" and that he had sent for
Deputy Winter to assist him. Holman Ham, the telegraph operator at Round Rock, a "miserable skunk," was blamed for tip-
ping off the rangers who were being given the credit—and the
rewards—for breaking up the gang. At the same time that
Everheart was disgruntled about being left in the cold, U.S.
Deputy Marshal Walter Johnson stated that he could prove that
it was he who "conceived and matured" the plan with Murphy
by which Bass was brought down, and that Everheart was never

in on the plan until June 10. An Austin newspaper, however, printed an affidavit by Jim Murphy which described what happened, concluding that Everheart had passed up a chance to confront the gang in Denton County and that Jones had seized every opportunity to capture the robbers.[13]

With regard to the rewards, the Texas and Pacific Railroad denied offering any reward for the train robbers, but the Texas Express Company and Houston and Texas Central proposed that all of the entities offering rewards should consult each other and act jointly. The governor approved the state's reward for the conviction of Pipes and Herndon, but because the budgeted reward appropriation was depleted, any payment would have to await a new appropriation by the state legislature. Accordingly, Jones authorized the claim against the state for the reward to be sold to private parties at a discount of $714, two-thirds of which was given to Billy Scott and Jack Smith.

The remainder of the reward claim on the state was sent to Colonel E.G. Bower in Dallas to be distributed to Peak and his men who were in on the two men's arrest. Of that amount, Peak's rangers received $21.25 each. In August the Texas Express Company and the Houston and Texas Central Railroad each decided to give Jones and his rangers a separate $1,000 donation, rather than a reward, but the Texas and Pacific declined to give them anything. Jones gratefully accepted the $2,000 from the two railroads, thanking them "for your kindness and for complimentary manner in which you are pleased to mention the service performed by myself and my rangers in ridding the country of the outlaws."[14] In addition, Sam Bass' Winchester rifle was located in some brush not far from Round Rock, and Major Jones gave it to Vernon Wilson in recognition of his ride to San Saba.[15] Bass' rifle scabbard was given to Maurice Moore.[16]

Another lawman, M.F. Leach, wrote Major Jones from Ogallala inquiring as to a description of Seaborn Barnes. Tom Nixon had been known to go by the name of Tom Barnes, and he wondered if they might be the same person. He also wondered if Jack Davis might not be Frank Jackson.[17]

On Friday, July 26, Lieutenant Reynolds led his men back to their San Saba camp,[18] and Sam Pipes and Albert Herndon were transported to the state penitentiary at Huntsville to begin serving their sentences until they could be transferred to a federal prison. It was reported that the two talked freely about being involved in the Mesquite robbery and that they had hoped Bass would help them escape, but they later wrote their attorney in Dallas, Hickerson Barksdale, that they never made any confession while on the way to prison, continuing to proclaim their innocence.[19]

In the meantime, the search for the remnants of the Bass gang continued in North Texas. Charley Carter had fled the Bass gang after the fiasco at Salt Creek in Wise County and it was believed that he had returned to Denton County, likely staying near the place of his grandfather, Hardin Carter. Denton City Marshal George Smith accidentally ran into young Carter one night on a side street and called out, "Charlie, is that you?" The answer was six wild pistol shots which Smith returned without effect. On Friday, July 26, express detective Sam Finley and his posse set up a watch on the road leading to Hardin Carter's house. During the evening the men twice spotted young Carter but could not get close enough to nab him. Smith hid in a corn patch directly behind the house. Toward dawn the lawmen saw a servant go out to the smokehouse, look around carefully, then call, "Come to breakfast, Charlie. Everything is all right." Carter rose from some nearby weeds and started for the house. The house was immediately surrounded by the lawmen, and the young bandit gave himself up. He was transported to Denton, where he was jailed.[20] On August 6 Finley took Carter to Austin for trial.[21]

In McKinney, in Collin County, Tom Spotswood's attorney filed a motion on Wednesday, July 24, 1878, asking Judge Bledsoe to grant the convicted train robber a new trial. It was alleged, first, that the procedures followed in jury selection and the exercise of challenges to jury panel members were not proper. Further, Spotswood complained that he should have been allowed to withdraw his announcement of ready for trial when Ira Jones was indicted on June 29, it being claimed that the indictment was solely to disqualify Jones as a witness for Spotswood. Jones and Spotswood's brother, John, had both been indicted earlier in the month by the Collin County grand jury for complicity in the Allen train robbery, and both were admitted to bail of one thousand dollars each.

More importantly, Spotswood argued that the two state witnesses, Cullen and Johnson, whose reputation for truth and veracity was alleged to be bad, were mistaken about seeing William Spotswood and John McCastlin cutting fence rails on February 23 and were thus unable to provide Tom Spotswood the alibi that he was at his brother's place at Little Elm in Denton County when the Allen robbery occurred. An affidavit was presented from McCastlin in which he blamed his erroneous testimony in the original trial on the "embarrassment and excitement he was laboring under at the time." He now said that he was working the road that day. In addition, it was alleged that state's witness Johnson had been paid by "Uncle Sam" to ride a horse at five dollars a day. Spotswood's attorney provided new alibi witnesses, as well as character references by Henry Hill (the alleged Bass target) and Harvey Slade (who had supposedly been in with Bass to rob Hill). On July 26 Judge Bledsoe granted Spotswood a new trial.[22]

The major manhunt was for Frank Jackson. Peak reported to Jones that the outlaw had been spotted eight miles south of Denton on Wednesday, July 24. Two posses led by Clay Withers and Jim McGinley scouted through the county on the lookout for the fugitive. A number of Peak's men were in camp sick and requiring medical attention, so he was unable to lead any scouts.[23] It was reported that Jackson, armed with a Winchester rifle and two sixshooters, was looking for Jim Murphy in order to avenge the death of Bass.[24]

On Monday, July 29, a posse led by Dallas Sheriff Marion Moon and Detective Lesh raided the Spotswood residence near Pilot Point in Denton County. They were able to arrest a man named Joe Davis as a train robbery suspect, but Bill and John Spotswood made a break for the nearby woods and escaped. Lesh saw a man leading horses toward the timber and took a group of men to follow him, hoping that he would lead to the Spotswoods. As they neared a ranch near Little Elm, a small gunfight ensued and the Spotswoods escaped again.[25]

Peak was convinced that both Jackson and Underwood had left Denton County for parts unknown and asked Major Jones in the first part of August to give his men something to do, "as we are becoming very restless." Jones directed Peak to move his Company B and establish a new headquarters in Coleman

County that had been formerly occupied by Company C.[26]

Jim Murphy arrived back in Denton County on August 1, staying at Peak's camp that night, and the next day he wrote Major Jones. He had pledged to Peak to continue working with the rangers in trying to locate Jackson. He complained about the horse that had been taken from him by Everheart and asked Jones to intervene with Peak to recover him.[27] Peak's opinion that Jackson had disappeared was premature. On August 9 Murphy again wrote Jones complaining about an angry Peak's refusal to return his horse, but he also informed the major that Jackson had gone to the Murphy place near Rosston and told his family that he wanted Jim's saddle horse, claiming that it would be alright with Murphy. They gave Jackson the horse, and Murphy subsequently communicated with Jackson through one of his brothers. Murphy wrote to Jones.

> Frank believes me to bee all right with him yet but dont you say anything about it. He warns me to bee ware of the Collins boyes—He believes they will kill [me] if they get a chance. Keep still. I think that I will [catch?] 2 or 4 more of the train robers after while....[28]

Jackson was seen twice in Denton after the Round Rock shootout,[29] and the elusive Henry Collins was spotted in the White Rock bottoms near the family home in Dallas County, well-armed and mounted.[30]

The notoriety surrounding the pursuit and death of Sam Bass occasioned the eruption of a number of commercial enterprises. Pete Stephenson and a man named Harrison, both of Dallas, publicly showed off what purported to be "fine photographs of Sam Bass and Arkansaw Johnson."[31] A hat claimed to have been Bass' was placed on exhibition at the El Paso Saloon in Fort Worth by C.A. Sparks, a traveling agent for Watkins & Gilliland, a wholesale hat and cap dealer. It was described as size 7-3/4, low crowned, black, with a six-inch brim that was limp, well-used with the brim's having torn loose and resewn to the crown. Sparks claimed that he was in Round Rock and that Bass had personally presented the hat to him.[32]

Simultaneously, two books about Sam Bass were raced into circulation in August. Judge Thomas Hogg of Denton County penned *Sam Bass and His Gang,* one thousand copies of which were published by the *Denton Monitor* to be sold for fifty cents each. The publishers, Geers and Dodson, promised that it was "no highly colored, half-fictitious romance, but made up of facts which may be relied on as being correct....It is hoped that this book will do much towards forestalling the mass of yellow covered trash that may otherwise flood the country—to the demoralization of the youth of our land, and the detriment of the good name of Texas abroad."[33] W.M. Leslie, with the *Dallas Commercial,* was on the road to introduce and promote *Life and Adventures of Sam Bass, The Notorious Union Pacific and Texas Train Robber.*[34] Claimed to be illustrated, the original edition of *Life and Adventures* contained only pen and ink drawings of roses at the end of each chapter and, for some reason, one of a cat, under which was printed the obtuse phase "boiling drunk."[35] Both books relied heavily on newspaper accounts, but the important contributions by Jim Murphy in Hogg's book underscore its attempt at accuracy.

Frank Jackson was not bent on revenge; he was concerned about his own well-being. On August 27 Jim Murphy again contacted Major Jones.

Well Major Jones, I received a mesage from Frank Jackson this morning—He wants to no of me if thare is any thing that he can do to get his self repreved—He ses that he will lay the plan to catch Underwood and all of the rest of the crowd if it will have him turned loose. I told him that I would right to you and see what could bee dun. He ses that he was pursuaded in to it and that he is tired of that kind of life and will do anything in the world to get repreved and I am sadisfied that him and his brother can work up a job on the hole crowd. Let me hear from you soon.

J.W. MURPHY

[Reverse] If it hadn of bin for Frank Jackson I would of bin killed shore and that is the reason that I want him repreved. So major if thar is any chance for him let me no right away an he will get to work—I haft to have a letter from you to sadisfy them that ever thing is all right—

I talk to Frank through his brother William Jackson.
What ever Billey ses I can reli on.[36]

The pursuit after Billy and Henry Collins also continued.
On August 22, using the name Bob Rogers, Henry Collins
arrived in Grayson County with his cousin, named Joel Collins
like Billy and Henry's late brother. Like his cousin, this Joel
Collins was no stranger to trouble. He lived ten miles south of
Sherman on the Houston and Texas Central Railroad, a little
over two miles east of Howe Station. On November 16, 1876,
Collins was bested in a fist fight with farmer James Hall after
claiming that Hall's cattle were in his fields. Collins then
retrieved a Navy Six revolver and found his prey driving a wagon
near a schoolhouse at Farmington. The first round from his
Navy Six failed to fire, and Hall ran toward the school house.
Collins continued firing at him, missing, as the children scattered for cover.[37]

The two Collins cousins met a man who would only be
identified by his initials, J.B.W., and he learned from them that
Rogers was really Henry Collins of the Bass gang. Henry Collins
was there to raise some money so that he could leave Texas for
Kentucky and the relatives living there who would help him. On
Monday, August 26, J.B.W. went to Sherman and passed along
his information to Grayson County Deputy Sheriff Henry
Haley,[38] Sherman City Marshal Sam Ball,[39] and others. That
afternoon Haley pulled together a posse composed of Marshal
Ball, Deputy Sheriff J.M. Winter, Sherman Policeman George
Bond[40] and Deputy Sheriff William Erwin.[41]

Just after sunup Tuesday morning, the posse quietly
approached Joel Collins' farmhouse through a cornfield. As
they came within thirty yards they saw Joel Collins in the doorway, but he spotted them at the same time and jumped back
inside. The lawmen surrounded the house. Bond raced to the
west side of the structure just as Henry Collins sprang out of the
west door, firing as he streaked for the brush that bordered a dry
spring branch nearby. Bond couldn't control his horse and
snapped off several wild shots at the fleeing man. Collins turned
and fired back, hitting Bond's horse in the jaw and causing the
animal to whirl in desperate circles, preventing Bond from making an accurate shot. Ball appeared and fired twice at Collins,

the first shot whizzing over his head and the second hitting him in the calf of his left leg, breaking both bones and exiting through his boot. Henry Collins fell to the ground, his pistol scooting out in front of him in the dirt.

Collins threw up his hands and asked them not to shoot anymore. He was taken into the house where his leg wound was washed, bandaged, and placed in a frame. Carrying Collins on a mattress, the lawmen took him to the Howe Station and brought him to Sherman, where they arrived at about 10:30 that morning. A large crowd gathered at the depot to see the wounded member of the noted Bass gang, and the officers had to push aside the crowd in order to walk Collins to the express wagon and the short journey to the county jail.

Collins was placed in a cell and given a cup of water while a reporter for the *Sherman Register* interviewed him. Collins, with blue eyes, a prominent forehead, and light fuzzy sideburn whiskers adorning his cheeks, denied any association with Sam Bass or his gang. The doctors examined his shattered leg and determined that it had to be amputated. On Tuesday afternoon Doctors Eagan and J.D. Sanders, using chloroform to sedate their patient, removed the leg just below the knee. Two hours after the operation, perhaps still under the influence of the chloroform, Collins chatted again with a reporter. He admitted that he knew Sam Bass but denied involvement with his gang. He also denied knowing the whereabouts of his brother Billy. He did, however, regret the disgrace that had been visited on his family.

Albert and Permelia Collins, Henry's long-suffering parents, came from Dallas to visit him in the Grayson County Jail on Friday evening, spending most of Saturday with him. He seemed to be recovering well until Tuesday morning, September 3, when he began to deteriorate rapidly. At eight o'clock Tuesday evening, Henry Collins died, the doctors blaming his death on an embolism. Permelia Collins' piercing cries at losing another son were heartrending, causing a crowd to gather outside the jail, and the Collins family blamed the Grayson County officials for Henry's death. Deputy U.S. Marshal Walter Johnson arranged to have the body neatly dressed, and he bought an elegant casket for the return with the Collins parents to Dallas, where Henry was buried on the family farm.[42] Only Billy Collins was left for the family to sacrifice.

While Henry Collins was dying in the Grayson County jail, Ranger Captain Neal Coldwell sent a letter to Major Jones from his post at Camp Vinton, not far from El Paso. John Gardner, the cowboy who had accompanied Bass and Collins north on the cattle drive in 1876, had approached Coldwell to offer his services to locate the Collins boys provided he received a free pass over the railroads. Jones declined the offer since Henry Collins was dead and he felt that Billy Collins had left the state. "If he can find out where William is by letter, I might then employ him to help catch him."[43]

Jim Murphy continued to correspond with John Jones, on September 6 sending a letter apologizing to the major for some insult apparently related to comments he had directed to the ranger about rewards.[44] In Williamson County the grand jury finally indicted Frank Jackson on September 20 for the murder of Deputy Sheriff Grimes.[45]

An unexpected gunfight at Lewisville in Denton County on Saturday, October 12, 1878, resurrected rumors that the brother of Seaborn Barnes and other survivors of the Bass gang had banded together to ride the outlaw trail once more, but it turned out to be a group of eight cowboys from Dallas County who had spent the day there "getting pretty well steamed up." They rode up and down the street, pistols drawn, calling for Deputy Sheriff Tom Gerren who was also in town that day.

Gerren heard about the rowdiness and walked to the cowboys' location with the intention of arresting them for carrying weapons. About forty yards away he stepped into the road and ordered the cowboys to surrender. They opened fire on the lawman, bullets whizzing around him, and he coolly advanced on them, shooting as he walked, and actually driving them back several hundred yards down the street. The cowboys retreated, reloaded, and decided to attack again but fled the town after several shots from Gerren's Winchester. The only casualties were two badly wounded horses and a flesh wound on the hip of one of the men. All during the fight Gerren smoked a cigar, and he returned from the fray wearing a broad-brimmed hat left behind by one of the cowboys.[46] This perspective of Gerren does not correspond to other images. The following month, on Thanksgiving Eve, it would be alleged that he went into Craddock's saloon on the Denton square, drank some whiskey, and picked a fight with a bystander at the bar. The man promptly knocked Gerren through the saloon door into the street, it is said, then marched Gerren back inside to fetch his hat that had dropped to the floor and kicked him back out into the street.[47]

After jumping bond rather than standing trial in Austin, Billy Collins disappeared completely. Deputy U.S. Marshal William H. Anderson somehow learned of Collins' whereabouts in Canada in early November. Collins had fled Dallas on June 27 and left a meandering trail as he sought someplace where he would be safe from arrest. On August 28 he was at Buckston, Missouri, and on September 15 he was at St. Paul, Minnesota. By September 20 he had reached Pembina, a small community located on the Dakota Territory and Minnesota borders within sight of Canada. Using the name J.W. Gale, Collins went to work as a thresher for some Mennonites and worked there until the end of the season. At some point in October he had a Pembina lawyer, Robert Walker, send a letter to his wife in Dallas, which was probably intercepted by lawmen there. In another account, Dallas Sheriff Marion Moon was credited with learning from a Hannibal & St. Joseph railroad detective, R. Davis, that Collins had been in Linn County, Missouri, then gone on to other points before stopping at West Lynn, and Sheriff Moon turned the information over to Anderson.

Around the end of October Collins took a job as a bartender for Jim White, who owned a saloon in partnership with a man named Schribner that was located on the United States-Canada border in the West Lynn community adjacent to Pembina. Schribner and White's saloon actually straddled the border, a red line drawn across the floor purportedly marking that boundary. The saloon portion was on the American side and White's sitting room and kitchen were in Canada. It would be remembered that while Collins was a big fellow and quite personable, he always positioned himself in a building so that he could see the door.

Deputy Marshal Anderson left Dallas on Tuesday, October 29, for Fargo, Dakota Territory, where he tried to get the assistance of a United States marshal. However, the federal court was in session and he was forced to go on to Pembina alone. Upon his arrival he contacted Deputy U.S. Marshal Jud LaMoure and

Sheriff Charles Brown and told them of his mission. Since Collins knew Anderson well, it was decided that LaMoure and Brown would try to arrest the fugitive at Schribner and White's saloon. Brown, a Union veteran who had been captured at Antietam and held as a prisoner of war in Atlanta, had been elected sheriff in 1875 and would serve until 1884 when he died of cancer.

The two local lawmen casually entered the saloon, ordered drinks, and chatted with Collins, trying to maneuver him into a position where they could get the drop on him. But Collins, perhaps sensing their purpose, kept up his guard, and the two decided not to risk an arrest. Another account stated that the two lawmen were unsure of the description and returned to see Anderson for better instructions. At any rate, LaMoure and Brown finally decided to leave the arrest to Anderson, and somehow Collins learned that there was a Texas lawman in the area. The next day he mentioned to Brown that he expected to "have it out" with Anderson.

On Friday, November 8, Anderson was in the Pembina post office talking with postmaster and customs officer Charles Cavileer. It was late in the afternoon and Anderson lay on a bench, apparently waiting to see if Collins would come for mail. While sorting mail, Cavileer spotted Collins through a window approaching the post office and told Anderson, "Here comes your man now." Anderson sprang to his feet, readied his sixshooter, and took a position a few feet from the door.

Collins entered the post office and Anderson ordered him to throw up his hands. Collins raised his hands but greeted Anderson and began to engage him in chatter, his overcoat open and giving him access to the pistol in a holster under his left arm. Slowly Collins began to lower his hands. Anderson cautioned him to keep up his hands, expressing a desire not to have to kill him. Collins laughed, "Oh Bill, there's no use of that; let's go and get a drink," and began to lower his hands again. Anderson ordered a bystander to take hold of Collins, and the man grabbed Collins' left arm. No longer laughing, an enraged Collins went for his pistol and Anderson fired, the bullet passing under Collins' left arm, barely scratching it, and over his hand, taking off the end of his right thumb then tunneling through his overcoat and leather shoulder holster and entering

Collins' left side a few inches above the nipple. The bullet plowed inward and upward, lodging in the lower part of the back of Collins' neck. Collins made a quick, convulsive motion, drawing himself into a knot in great pain but cocking his pistol.

As soon as he fired, Anderson ran toward a door leading to Cavileer's private quarters, and Collins fired one shot that missed Anderson and went through a window. Outside the window, seated on an open stairway were Shep Moorhead, Joe Bouvette, Ira Davis and several other youngsters, and the bullet just missed young Davis. Once inside the kitchen of Cavileer's living area, Anderson maneu-

Pembina, Dakota Territory, Postmaster Charles Cavileer. (Courtesy Charles Walker, Pembina, North Dakota, and State Historical Society of North Dakota).

vered to place a stove between him and Collins for some cover. He saw Collins was bent over and Anderson, peering through the doorway, thought the wounded fugitive was about to fall. But when Anderson exposed himself, Collins fired another shot that went through Anderson's heart.

Collins cocked his pistol again for another shot, but Anderson fell dead to the floor. In one account Collins relaxed, took one step backward, then fell dead to the floor himself. In another account, Cavileer came from behind the post office counter and pushed Collins outside through the door, where he fell dead.[48] When the news reached him, N.E. Nelson, the U.S. Commissioner in Pembina, wired Marshal Russell in Texas informing him of the tragedy.[49]

The next morning the American Express Company route agent at St. Paul, J.E. Atherton, sent a telegram about the deaths to the Texas Express Company,[50] which then notified Anderson's wife and made arrangements to bring Anderson's

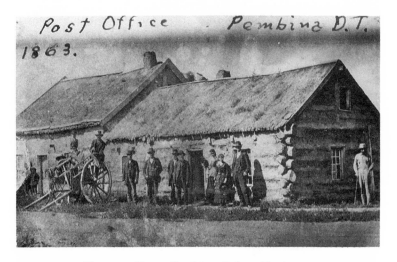

The postoffice at Pembina, Dakota Territory,
where W.H. Anderson and William Collins killed each other.
(Courtesy Charles Walker, Pembina, North Dakota, and State
Historical Society of North Dakota).

body back to Dallas. Marshal Stillwell Russell received the news in Tyler. John Cole, one of Collins' bondsmen, was told by federal authorities that proof of Collins' death must be provided the Tyler court in order to avoid a forfeiture, and on November 12 E.H. Huffman and George Waller[51] left Dallas for Pembina. In the cold, icy weather, and with the help of local officials, two cords of wood were burned over Collins' gravesite to thaw the ground. The grave was opened and Collins' velvet-covered coffin was taken out so that photographs of the body could be taken. The body was reburied and the two officials, after taking depositions about the shooting, returned to Dallas on Monday, November 25. Anderson's body had been returned to Dallas on Friday morning, November 15, and buried the following Sunday, mourned by a widow and three children.[52] All of the Collins brothers who had ridden with Bass were now dead at the hands of lawmen. Only Jackson and Underwood remained at large.

It was subsequently rumored that both Henry Underwood and Frank Jackson were in the north with Billy Collins. One news account stated that the two had been chased by federal troops from Fort Pembina only to lose their pursuers in a desolate region, but there is no corroboration of this account and it is highly unlikely.[53] The death of three sons did not end the misery for the Collins family. Because Henry and Billy Collins had failed to appear for trial, their bonds were forfeited. The bondsmen felt that the deaths of the two men released them from their obligation, but a lawsuit was instituted and judgment was rendered for the government. In December 1881, a levy having been filed against E.L. Huffman, John McCommas, B.F. Fleaman, A.G. Collins, Arzelia Shipley, Thomas Jackson and John H. Cole, the property they had pledged in support of the bonds was scheduled for sale at a public auction.[54]

Jim Murphy made no peace with Major Jones and the rangers. In January 1879 he moved from Denton to the family home near Rosston in Cooke County. He was quoted as saying that he had been swindled "by government officers" out of any share of rewards for his part in the demise of the Bass gang, except for fifty dollars that Major Jones had given him. According to Murphy, Billy Collins never participated in a train robbery, and Murphy claimed that Collins had been released at Tyler under an agreement, similar to that which Murphy had with the authorities, for the arrest of a wanted man named Davis.[55] Scott Mayes later claimed that after his release in Austin he resumed running his saloon and bowling alley in Denton. He was not bashful about his opinion of Murphy, and Mayes said that on one occasion Murphy pulled a pistol on him, forcing a bystander to take it away from him.[56]

Death came to Jim Murphy on Thursday, June 5, 1879, under bizarre circumstances. He suffered from an eye ailment common within the Murphy family which caused one of his eyes to have a downward cast. The treatment prescribed by Dr. Ed McMath was an eyewash with belladonna, a crude medicine derived from a plant that caused extreme dilation of the eyes but which was a narcotic poison. Murphy would go to McMath's drug store on the Denton square and lie on a cot while the wash was carefully administered to his eye so as not to get in his mouth. Murphy sat up to light a pipe and some of the drops inadvertently ran into his mouth and were swallowed. He quickly became sick, his body shaken by convulsions, and there was nothing that McMath could do to help him. Murphy was taken to a residence nearby and died that night, leaving a widow and several children.

Report of Murphy's death brought out claims that because Underwood and Jackson had been seen in the area, Murphy had gone to Denton for protection, even sleeping every night in the jail. "Worn out with fear and the constant strain upon his mind, he drained his bottle of eye-wash" went the description of his alleged suicide.[57] As Gard points out, the "spy hero" passed to a different reward, perhaps one more generous than the one given to him by being labeled as a traitor and turncoat.[58]

In Collin County Tom Spotswood was preparing for his second trial on the Allen robbery charge, the only member of the Bass gang to be tried in a state court. On June 25, 1879, the county attorney, P.B. Muse, applied for a continuance of the case because of absent witnesses. The following January 28 Spotswood in turn asked for a continuance for the same reason and was released on three hundred-dollar bail posted by his brother William, W.A. Gotcher and E.M. Barkley on March 12, 1880. Finally, on July 7, 1880, another jury was sworn in and his second trial began.

Prosecutor Muse presented four or five witnesses to establish Spotswood's presence in Allen on February 22, 1878. A.J. "Bud" Newman, the Allen saloon keeper, repeated his testimony. H. Clay Thomas of Coryell County and E.R. Leach had earlier told Muse that they were in Allen on the day of the robbery and recognized Spotswood. In addition, Mollie Leach Stevens was supposed to testify that Spotswood had agreed to drive her to Cooke County on February 22 but had subsequently canceled the trip. Spotswood's defense, however, presented alibi witnesses who placed him in Denton County when the robbery occurred. Caroline White said she saw him at Joe Davis' place at about 3:00 p.m. Rebecca Lasater and Thomas Callahan stated they saw William Underwood and Ira Jones at the Brewer residence in Denton County on February 23, thus the two could not have been cutting fence rails as the state contended, and they provided Spotswood's key alibi testimony. Another witness, Mack Townsley, was sure that James Thomas, the express messenger at Allen, had stated at the time that he could not swear Spotswood was the man in the express car but might have been with the gang.

On the evening of Saturday, July 10, 1880, the jury acquitted Tom Spotswood, apparently accepting as reasonable doubt the story established by Spotswood's alibi witnesses. The verdict was somewhat of a shock, and the best explanation provided was that "The most charitable view to take of the matter is that the witnesses on one side are mistaken, as both sets of witnesses appeared equally honest."[59] Spotswood left the courthouse a free man. He returned to Denton County, where in 1880 he was listed as a farmer, his household composed of his two sons, William, four, and Thomas, three, as well as his brothers William and John. On December 30, 1880, Spotswood married Mrs. Mary Connelly in Collin County. After that Spotswood's fate is unknown, although his two brothers remained in the area for the rest of their lives.[60]

Two suspected members of the Bass gang, previously unknown to the authorities, were indicted on June 16, 1880, by the federal grand jury in Tyler. It was alleged that Jim Tyler and Matthew Gray were involved in the Eagle Ford robbery on April 4, 1878. Warrants were issued for the two, and Deputy U.S. Marshal Tom Gerren looked for them in Denton County, a $1,500 reward being posted. Gerren took Gray into custody, arresting him a few days after the indictment was returned. On July 21, 1881, Gerren arrested Tyler at Scratch's Mill, twenty-five miles east of Atoka in the Indian Territory, and brought his prisoner to Denton on Wednesday, July 25, then to Dallas two days later.

Tyler promptly declared his innocence to a reporter, stating that at the time of the robbery he was injured and in bed after being thrown by a horse. He went to the Indian Territory in 1879 and had married. However, when in custody, Tyler filed a sworn affidavit for subpoenas alleging that Robert Erwin,[61] who had a farm six miles east of Denton, and Erwin's neighbor, A.M. Cochran,[62] would testify that Erwin had employed him and each could swear that he spent the night there when the robbery occurred. In this affidavit Tyler did not mention being injured. No trial was ever held. Tyler was released on bond and, despite several settings of the court case, could not be located again.[63] Gray was never prosecuted for the Eagle Ford robbery.

Other figures in the Bass saga also had their problems. By 1880 Deputy U.S. Marshal Walter Johnson, who was in on the deal with Jim Murphy, was wanted in Grayson County for carrying a pistol as well as for representing himself as a deputy U.S.

marshal after he had been decommissioned. He had been indicted twice in Dallas County for similar conduct, and he was out on a five hundred-dollar bond from Wheeler County in the Texas Panhandle for some offense after having been convicted of yet another offense there which was on appeal. In early 1880 he was arrested in Memphis, Tennessee, for carrying a pistol and alleging that he was a federal lawman. Johnson was convicted and sentenced to sixty days' confinement on President's Island, but he posted $250 bond while the case was appealed and promptly fled the jurisdiction.[64]

Another colleague of Bass, Robert McKimie of Deadwood days, was sentenced on February 18, 1879, at Hillsboro, Ohio, to four years in the penitentiary on each of two indictments for burglary. On the same day, the train carrying him to the penitentiary stopped at Chillicothe, in Ross County, and he pleaded guilty to a charge of burglary in that jurisdiction and received another two-year sentence. On February 24 McKimie was taken to Pike County where he received an additional ten-year sentence. He was wanted in Salt Lake City from where he had escaped while serving a fifteen-year sentence. He was also supposed to have escaped from a ten-year sentence in California.[65]

Scott Mayes, like others intimately associated with Bass, was also not finished with the law after his acquittal. On September 22, 1879, he was indicted in Denton County for theft of cattle, but a jury acquitted him on October 9.[66] He moved to Gainesville in Cooke County, working as a bartender in the bawdy house of Maggie Marshall,[67] and was again indicted on February 8, 1881, this time for helping Tom Ballinger to snatch $210 from M.R. Reynolds as he was riding in a hack on January 30. A jury found Mayes guilty and sentenced him to two years in the penitentiary; eleven of the jury had wanted to give him ten years but finally conceded to the one juror holding out for two years. This conviction was appealed but then affirmed on May 2, 1881, by the Court of Appeals, and he went to prison.[68]

After his release Mayes returned to Cooke County. He married Sallie Babbitt on April 25, 1883,[69] and began a wagon yard in Gainesville. Around 1892 he married again, this time to Ada Melvina Cottrell. In 1893 Mayes was indicted along with Joe Jacobs and Tom Jones for the April 5 theft by threat of seventy-five dollars from Dr. W.M. Chancellor, but on May 28 the charge was dismissed because of insufficient evidence.[70] Mayes and his second wife had two children. His son, Vernie Andrew Mayes, was a partner with his father in operating the wagon yard and as a trader until Scott Mayes died in Gainesville on June 19, 1937.[71]

Of the subsequent activities of the lawmen who pursued Bass, there was little future remaining for Major John Jones. In 1879 he married Mrs. Elizabeth Holliday Anderson, surrendering his bachelorhood of almost forty-one years. Jones replaced William Steele as Adjutant General of Texas in January 1879, at the same time holding a position as an important official in the Masonic Order in the state. In mid-1881 he became ill with what was diagnosed as an abscess of the liver and in July went to San Antonio for an operation to eliminate accumulated pus. Weakened by the operation, he returned to his home in Austin. On Monday, July 18, a second operation was attempted, but he died during the night at the age of forty-six years.[72]

Former U.S. Marshal Stillwell Russell returned to private life in 1880, resuming his life as a farmer with his wife Carrie in Smith County. On May 15, 1882, he was arrested on a federal warrant in Washington D.C., it being alleged that he had improperly deposited $6,600 of federal money in a private bank in Austin rather than a federal depository. It was also charged that he had retained $1,300 from the sale of sheep and goats seized by the United States and that he had charged the government mileage fees for transporting prisoners, even though he had a railroad pass. Released on twenty-thousand-dollars bail, he denied doing anything wrong. On July 5, 1882, Russell's trial commenced in Austin, U.S. Attorney A.J. Evans now prosecuting his former marshal. The jury acquitted Russell.[73] He was tried again by the persistent prosecutor, found guilty by a jury on April 4, 1883, and sentenced to two years in the penitentiary at Chester, Illinois.[74]

The much-maligned Tom Gerren continued as a deputy United States marshal. A daughter Willie was born to him and his wife Lutie on October 21, 1883, but died later in the decade.[75] His activities as a lawman were sparsely reported, but in October 1883 he and Ranger S.N. Piatt arrested stage robbers Dan Brock and the Terry brothers from Clay County, and in August 1885 he arrested murderer Alex Calvin in Greer County.[76] He and another man from U.S. Marshal William

Cabell's office escorted a young stage robber, Jessie Jones, to a penitentiary sentence at Chester, Illinois.[77]

On August 30, 1889, apparently no longer in the federal marshal's service, Gerren was indicted by a Denton County grand jury for robbery, but a jury acquitted him on November 16.[78] Members of the Denton community would allege many years later that Gerren was involved in the 1880s in a plot to stage a fake train robbery in order to better his job as a "railroad policeman" by capturing the "robber." Conspiring with a confederate, Gerren allegedly provided a "Bulldog" revolver to a half-witted young man, Billy Baines, then hid on the express car of the targeted

Texas Ranger Major John B. Jones, appearing frail. (From Roberts, *Rangers and Sovereignty*).

train as it chugged up Peach Orchard Hill north of Denton. When the confederate and Baines clambered aboard the train, Gerren was supposed to have shot and killed Baines, thereby stopping the robbery. The confederate left and remained unidentified. Allegedly Gerren was consorting in Denton at this time with a woman named Mary Shea, who left town when the "robbery" occurred. According to the story, Gerren was never indicted because the main witness was dead.[79] A search of newspapers did not turn up any mention of this incident. The 1860 Denton County census shows an eleven-year-old William G. Baines,[80] but there is no information linking him with the story told about Gerren.

By 1900 Gerren was reported to be a claims agent for the Santa Fe Railroad,[81] and his wife died in Denton on May 4, 1907.[82] He apparently died sometime after 1904 but before

1910, although no record could be located.

Finally, June Peak continued as a ranger captain commanding Company B. His company was posted at Fort Concho in West Texas, where marauding Indians were still a problem. In one fight that lasted from June 29 to July 2, 1879, he and his men fought Comanche and Kiowa braves, losing one ranger, W.B. Anglin. Peak resigned from the rangers on April 15, 1880, and went to New Orleans to seek employment with a coffee company. He accepted an offer to work as

Ranger Captain Junius "June" Peak, as he appeared in the 1920s. (Courtesy Robert W. Stephens, Dallas, Texas)

a contractor building and equipping supply stations for construction gangs with the Mexican Central Railroad. On November 28, 1881, in Dallas, he married Henrietta Boll, twenty years younger than he, and they returned to Mexico. Their first child, a son, was born there but died in infancy and was buried at Queretaro.

In 1884 June and Henrietta Peak returned to Texas and settled into ranching in Shackelford County. They added a son and a daughter to the family then moved back to Dallas in 1899 so that their children could have a better education. Peak worked in real estate, and from 1919 to 1924 he was superintendent of White Rock Lake in northeast Dallas. At the age of eighty-nine June Peak died in Dallas on April 20, 1934. Among his honorary pallbearers were the Texas Frontier Rangers' Association.[83]

Only two of Sam Bass' associates, Henry Underwood and Frank Jackson, continued to elude their Texas pursuers. The Sam Bass gang, which existed for less than six months, had been caught up in a maelstrom of its own making, never aware that in carrying its crimes to excessive notoriety it set in motion a statewide response that would call for nothing less than its absolute destruction. And that is what happened.

-XVII-
EPILOGUE

A fter Henry Underwood abandoned Bass and the others at Salt Creek, he realized he had to leave the state or ultimately be given away to the rangers. When he left Texas is unknown, but it is likely he first visited briefly with his family and made arrangements for them to follow him. It is known that his wife and children did leave Texas; on Tuesday, September 10, 1878, they traveled through Denison in Grayson County on their way to Indiana. Tom Gerren followed them from Denton to Sherman, hoping that Underwood would make an attempt to join them, but to no avail.[1] Mary Underwood and her three children, Mary M., Julius A. and Delila, moved in with her in-laws, Julius and Mariah Underwood, in Columbia Township in Jennings County, Indiana.[2]

Apparently fettered with a criminal disposition, Underwood did not stay out of trouble for long after returning to Indiana. On May 11, 1881, under the alias of "William Jones," Underwood was indicted in three cases by the federal court in Indianapolis, along with Isaac Haworth, John F. Holloway and James K. Rittenhouse alias James Helm, for making and passing counterfeit silver dollars and half-dollars in February.[3] Rittenhouse was the same confidence man who had posed as an Illinois detective in April 1875 to thwart June Peak's effort to arrest a swindler in St. Louis.[4] The sixty-year-old, Virginia-born Rittenhouse told the authorities that he was a painter. His wife, Missouri, lived at Osgood in Ripley County, Indiana.[5]

Bail for the four co-defendants was set at $2,500 each, and federal prosecutor Charles L. Holstein asked the district court to consolidate all of the indictments into one case number. On May 26, 1881, a jury found all of the defendants guilty. Two days later Judge Walter Q. Gresham sentenced "William Jones" to the Northern State Prison of Indiana for five years with a fine of fifty dollars and costs. Rittenhouse received a seven-year term, and Holloway three years. Haworth pleaded guilty, but because of illness his sentencing was not held until July 8 when he was sentenced to two years in prison.[6] Rittenhouse was sent along with the others to the Northern Indiana State Prison at Michigan City, but he escaped from the prison hospital at three in the morning of April 26, 1882.[7]

Still under his alias, Underwood arrived at the prison at Michigan City on the same day that he had been sentenced in Indianapolis. His prison record described him as twenty-nine years old, 5' 8", dark complexion, dark brown eyes, black hair, born in Iowa, single, literate, weighing 171 pounds, his third finger on the left hand bent down into the palm, and as having a brother, John Jones. He served almost four years of his five-year sentence and was released from the prison on April 23, 1885.[8] Although it is unknown what name Underwood used after being released, he returned to the vicinity of Boone County, Indiana, where his older brother, Gideon, was a well-respected farmer and machinist living two miles north of the county seat of Lebanon.[9]

In December 1885, eight months after Henry Underwood's release, a minor outbreak of crime in Boone County excited the citizenry. Just outside the tiny community of Mechanicsburg, in Clinton Township about eight miles from Lebanon, Israel Downing, described as a somewhat eccentric individual around fifty years old, lived with his mother and another woman, a widow named Smith, and maintained a large, productive farm. At about six on the evening of Friday, December 11, two masked men armed with revolvers burst into his house and demanded his money. One of the men wore blue overalls and a rubber overcoat, while the other wore brown overalls and a dark coat. Without hesitation Downing grabbed a chair and charged the two men. A shot went off, grazing Downing on his forehead, and he was quickly overpowered. The two women sought to interfere with the struggle, but one of the men slapped Downing's mother and both became quiet.

While one of the men kept the three covered, the other searched the house. They appeared to be familiar with their victims, even calling Downing's mother "Granny," a name by which she was commonly called. In a straw bed the robber found a sack containing eighty dollars. The two left, warning their victims that they would kill them if they attempted to follow. When Downing thought it was safe, he went to a neighbor for help. It was discovered that the robbers had escaped on horses that had been kept in a nearby grove of trees. Two local men, Lum Evans and John Campbell, were arrested on suspicion but released upon proof of an alibi.[10]

This robbery was followed three days later by a burglary of the store of John R. Beach at Mechanicsburg on the evening of December 14. The burglars took clothing goods, including flannel underwear and material, dress goods, men's and boys' suits, silk handkerchiefs, overcoats, men's boots and children's shoes, chewing tobacco, and pistol cartridges. The aggregate value of the property was $228.50.[11] Carrying the loot through the icy cold and snow to a nearby sleigh pulled by a horse, the burglars then headed toward Lebanon, where the pursuers lost the trail. Beach, who lived at the store with his wife and children, promptly offered a fifty-dollar reward.[12]

There were no clues to either crime and life in Boone County returned to normal. On March 23, 1886, Gideon Underwood and his children and their neighbors surprised his wife with a dinner in honor of her forty-ninth birthday.[13] But the authorities had learned somehow that Gideon Underwood may have been involved in the burglary of the Beach store, and on Monday, August 2, 1886, officers found goods at the Underwood farm that were identified by Beach as being taken in the burglary. A warrant was obtained for Gideon Underwood's arrest, and he was brought to Lebanon where he was released on a one thousand-dollar bond.[14]

It was rumored that Gideon's farm had been the headquarters of a notorious gang of thieves led by Tom Foster, a Ripley County horse thief who operated a livery stable in Osgood. In October 1885 Foster had been sentenced in Ripley County to three years in the penitentiary for grand larceny, but he was released on May 13, 1886, to await a new trial ordered by the state's supreme court. He was arrested again in July 1886 in Ripley County for horse theft. Foster, thirty, was a short man, 5' 5-1/2" tall, a fleshy 164 pounds, dark complexion, gray brown eyes, dark brown hair, subject to rheumatism, married, and temperate.[15]

One of Foster's cohorts, a Boone County criminal named Henry Webster who was arrested at Greensburg in late July, told the officers everything he knew about Foster and his illegal operations, as well as what he knew about the Beach store burglary. He had come to Osgood in 1884 and was given a job in Foster's stable, eventually assisting him in his stolen horse operation.[16] This information led to the discovery of the plunder on Gideon Underwood's farm, although the community was shocked and did not believe Gideon could be involved.

The officers were told who was involved and, on September 16, 1886, the Boone County Grand Jury indicted Gideon Underwood, his brother Henry, Charles Clark and Walker Hammond for the burglary.[17] Hammond was the same Charles Walker Hammond who had been responsible for the second train holdup at Seymour, Indiana, two decades earlier in 1866. The others not yet arrested, Gideon Underwood went on trial in Lebanon, but one juror's holding out for acquittal led to a mistrial on September 30, and the defendant was released on a thousand-dollar bond until a new trial could be held.[18]

Hammond and Henry Underwood were located at the Shelbyville depot on Friday, November 12, 1886. Underwood was unfortunately not detained and quickly fled the area, but Hammond was immediately returned to the Boone County jail at Lebanon while the search for Henry Underwood continued.[19]

At about nine on the morning of Wednesday, January 12, 1887, an Indianapolis second-hand dealer walked into a police stationhouse and informed Superintendent Colbert that two men were at his place offering goods at a ridiculously low price. He had slipped away by telling the men that he had to go to the bank to draw out money for the transaction. Four officers were dispatched to investigate, and they entered the store from front and rear entrances. The two suspects fought the officers but were overcome and placed under arrest.

The two men, who gave their names as Charles Brown of Texas and William Johnson of New York, had brought the clothing to the store on a two-horse sleigh, unloaded it, then taken the sleigh to a nearby stable. The men were in possession of typical burglar tools, and police suspected that the clothing was stolen but the two refused to talk. Finally someone recognized Johnson as Henry Underwood, who had been arrested for counterfeiting in Indianapolis under the name of "William Jones" six years earlier. Harry Webster was brought to Indianapolis to confirm the identification. No stranger to alias names, Underwood had used the name of Harry Clarke in Boone County, and it was by that name that Gideon Underwood had introduced him to friends. Brown was believed to be a man named John Kelly who was also a part of Tom Foster's gang at Osgood.[20]

Almost immediately the two prisoners tried to find a way to escape from jail. A jailer found Underwood trying to make a wooden key from the back of a wooden chair on Saturday, January 15. The authorities had begun to piece together Underwood's history, and newspapers dubbed him a "terror of express companies" in the southwest. Both he and Kelly were wanted in Ripley County for burglary and horse theft. The authorities also discovered a small hole in the ceiling of Underwood's cell that he had bored out.[21] The Ripley County sheriff was hesitant to take the men back to his county because the jail was not a strong one, and it was feared that a mob would make short work of Underwood. Although the items that Underwood and Kelly were trying to sell were taken in a burglary at Hardensburg and from Jennings County, where Underwood's family lived, it was decided to return Underwood to Boone County to stand trial for the burglary there.[22]

Underwood was taken to the Boone County Jail on Thursday, January 20, while Kelly was taken to North Vernon, in Jennings County, to be tried for robbery there. Apparently the horses that were in the possession of Underwood and Kelly had been stolen from Underwood's own father.[23] Underwood and Hammond went on trial in Boone County on Tuesday, February 1. Among the witnesses called by the prosecution were Harry Webster and Missouri Rittenhouse, wife of the notorious James Rittenhouse, who herself had gone to the penitentiary for counterfeiting.[24]

The jury received the case at about five on the afternoon of Friday, February 4, but deliberated until just before midnight. The verdict of guilty was quickly reached within the jury room, but the jury could not agree on the sentence. When the jury

The Boone County, Indiana, courthouse where Henry Underwood
was found guilty of burglary on February 4, 1887.
(Courtesy Lebanon, Indiana, Public Library).

came in at about ten o'clock that evening with a sentence for
each man of six years for burglary and seven years for grand larceny, the judge told them they could not sentence the accused
on each charge in the indictment, so the jury shortly returned
with a single sentence of thirteen years in prison for both defendants. Hammond was visibly stunned by the harsh sentence,
expecting a milder punishment, but Underwood remained cool
and unperturbed. On Saturday morning, witnessed by a big
crowd at the Lebanon depot, the Boone County sheriff took
them to the Michigan City prison to start their terms.[25] Gideon
Underwood was apparently not convicted of any offense and
would see another tragedy in October 1893 when his granddaughter, Tillie Magers, was shot and seriously wounded by an
ardent suitor who was not in the family favor and who promptly
committed suicide.[26]

It is interesting to note that while he was kept in the Boone
County Jail, Henry Underwood spoke to reporters for local
newspapers and was quoted as saying that after he left the Union
army, he went to Iowa where he stole horses. He also admitted
that he was involved in a train robbery in Nebraska! He did not

mention any involvement with the Sam Bass gang.[27] Both Underwood and Hammond arrived at the Michigan City prison on February 5, 1887. Oldtimers there recognized "William Jones," and he was assigned to the work he had before, that of a cooper.[28] Hammond began his thirteen-year term, even sending $1.25 to the Boone County sheriff for a subscription to the *Lebanon Pioneer*, but he would die in prison on May 8, 1890. Although Hammond was known to be dying by mid-1889, his record prevented the Indiana governor from granting him a pardon.[29]

In April 1888 Underwood began an effort from prison to obtain a pension based on his Civil War service. His attorneys, O'Connor & Prather of North Vernon, no doubt employed by members of Underwood's family, filed a claim on his behalf with the United States government claiming that he was an invalid because of epilepsy incurred in 1865, as well as "catarrh of the head" and the injury to his left hand. Affidavits were gathered from various persons, including fellow Union veterans who recalled when he waded a cold creek and took cold and when he hurt his hand. Prison employees and others swore they had seen Underwood have fits and pass out. On June 4, 1891, Underwood was approved for a monthly pension of two dollars, retroactive to April 27, 1888, because of "naso-pharyngeal catarrh." When he reapplied for a permanent disability on October 3, 1892, for the same reasons, however, the application was rejected on June 20, 1894, because "no ratable disability" was shown as required by legislation passed in June 1890.[30]

It is unknown how long Underwood remained in prison or when he was discharged, but at some point he was released. The prison experience, however, did nothing to curb his criminal tendencies. In June 1900 he was living in Vigo County, Indiana, his occupation described as "canvasses pictures," and living next to the household of James Phillips, a veterinary doctor.[31] The association with Phillips would prove another undoing for Underwood.

Phillips was an experienced horse thief, sometimes operating under the name of P.J. Monroe. He and his confederates, including Henry Underwood, operated across Indiana and into Illinois. Among other members of the theft ring were William

Edwards, who operated a wagon yard in Terre Haute, and Daniel Kelly and Charles Ferguson, and the gang regularly hung out at a saloon on the west end of the city. Late in February 1901, two horses were stolen from farmers Charles Williams and Joe McGrew, ten miles south of Terre Haute. Ferguson and Underwood were at Knightstown trying to sell the two horses on Thursday, March 7, when officers received a tip and arrested Ferguson, but Underwood escaped and returned to Terre Haute.

When the information came from Knightstown, Terre Haute police were quick to round up Underwood, Kelly and Edwards. Doc Phillips heard about the arrests and fled Vigo County. Officials from other jurisdictions appeared in Terre Haute to lay claim to the horse thieves. On Friday, March 8, Edwards, Kelly and Underwood were remanded to jail when they could not post bond after a preliminary hearing. Witnesses stepped forward and identified the prisoners as being involved in other thefts. Kelly confessed to the police about horse thefts in Illinois and Indiana, saying that he only "went along" with the other men. On Sunday, March 10, Underwood "objected very strenuously" to having his photograph taken by the police, but officers overcame his efforts to defy the camera.

Doc Phillips was finally located and arrested in Indianapolis on Thursday, March 14, when he showed up at the postoffice to pick up mail under an assumed name. He was taken to Terre Haute early the next morning. The Vigo County authorities reviewed the evidence, decided they could prosecute only Phillips and Underwood, and released Kelly and Edwards.[32] On Thursday afternoon Underwood and Phillips were each indicted by the Vigo County Grand Jury on two counts of larceny.[33]

Justice for the two horse thieves was swift. The next day, on Friday, March 15, both men appeared in court before Judge James E. Piety. Pursuant to a plea bargain with prosecutor Fred W. Beal, they waived arraignment, and each plead guilty to one of the counts against him. Judge Piety, who expressed amazement that two men in their fifties would be stealing horses, sentenced each of them to between one and fourteen years in the penitentiary. Beal dismissed the remaining charges.[34]

Underwood and Phillips arrived at the Indiana State Prison on Wednesday, March 20. Underwood's prison record reflected that he was of a "bad disposition" with "bad associates," that he smoked and chewed tobacco, voiced profanity on occasion, that his wife was not living, and that he practiced no religion. He was rejected for parole on April 1, 1902, and again on April 1, 1903, but was finally paroled on April 4, 1905, and left the prison on April 15. He would finally discharge his sentence on April 2, 1906.[35]

At the age of sixty or sixty-one, Henry Underwood left prison and moved in with his son, Julius, at Jamestown in Boone County. On Thursday, July 4, 1907, he died there of a cerebral hemorrhage, his death certificate listing him as divorced.[36]

The Vigo County, Indiana, courthouse at Terre Haute, where Henry Underwood was sentenced to prison in 1901 for horse theft. (Author photo).

Underwood's obituary kindly excluded any mention of his wild life or repeated visits to prison, reciting only his military record and that he was survived by two brothers and two sisters, his son, and his two daughters, Mrs. Barnes and Mrs. Robinett, both of whom lived in Kansas.[37] He was buried without fanfare in the local Odd Fellows cemetery. Sadly, Underwood's son would meet an untimely death when he was killed and his wife Ivy seriously injured in an automobile accident in Indianapolis in January 1929.[38]

Sam Pipes and Albert Herndon, the only associates of Sam Bass to be convicted of a train robbery, were transferred from the Texas prison at Huntsville to the Albany, New York, penitentiary, where they were received on June 16, 1879.[39] The county prison in Albany had been opened in 1846 on fifteen acres, largely built by prisoners, and by the time Pipes and Herndon arrived, had 625 cells. From the beginning prison dis-

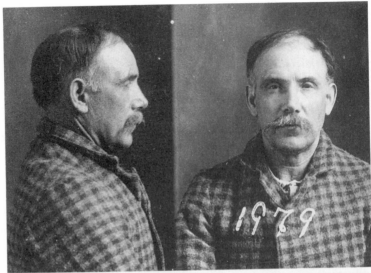

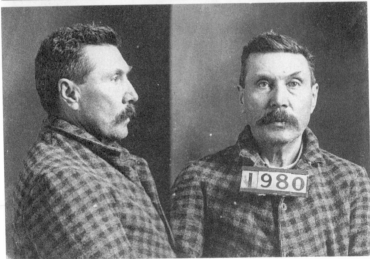

Henry Underwood (top) and Charles Walker Hammond (bottom)
as they entered the Indiana State Prison in March 1901.
(Courtesy Dave Johnson, Zionsville, Indiana,
and the Indiana State Archives, Indianapolis).

cipline centered on the "silent system," prisoners being required
to march in lock-step to and from work assignments and not permitted to converse with each other. Overseen by Superintendent
John McEwen, the prison was financially successful because of

Left: Grave marker of Henry Underwood at Jamestown, Indiana. (Courtesy James A. Browning, Douglasville, Georgia).

Below: The Albany County, New York, Penitentiary, where Sam Pipes and Albert Herndon spent eight years. (Courtesy Albany County Hall of Records).

its contracts with other counties and the United States to house their criminals. In addition to prison jobs, such as manufacture of brushes, chairs and shoes, prisoners were leased to various contractors for "remunerative wages."[40]

Less than four years after the conviction of the two men, efforts were under way to have them pardoned. On May 25, 1882, a petition signed by seventy-eight prominent Dallas County citizens was forwarded to President Chester Arthur. It was argued that Pipes and Herndon were "mere boys" at the time of the Mesquite robbery, led into the crime by older, more hardened criminals. The petition cited statements by Albany prison officials that the two prisoners' conduct was exemplary and that they were truly repentant. Among the men signing the petition were their lawyers, judges, justices of the peace, law enforcement officials and state officers. Former Texas Governor Edward J. Davis also sent a letter in support of the petition.

Opposed to any pardon was U.S. Attorney Andrew Evans, who had prosecuted the two men. He was agreeable to commuting their life sentence to ten years in prison because of their youth, but could not recommend a full pardon. Colonel E.G. Bower of Dallas, who had also participated in the prosecution, wrote the U.S. Attorney General, Benjamin H. Brewster, on their behalf, citing the strong influence that Billy Collins had exercised over the two "young farm hands." From Bower's perspective, he wrote, "Their crime, grave as it is, I believe was more the result of thoughtlessness, superinduced by orphanage & youth, than by greed, hatred of society, defiance of law, or other usual motive to crime." In January 1883, Evans revised his recommendation to five years in prison. Thomas Goree, the superintendent of the Texas Penitentiary, also urged the president to grant executive clemency.[41]

Herndon wrote a friend in Dallas in March 1884 that Pipes' health was bad and that Pipes had grown quite despondent. Herndon, on the other hand, wrote that he weighed two hundred pounds, was in excellent health, and had a position as a clerk in the prison commissary department.[42] Attorney General Brewster sat on the clemency application for a number of months, much to the consternation of the Dallas petitioners. They finally asked their congressional representative, Olin

Wellborn, to see if he could move the process forward. The Postmaster General was also opposed to a pardon. Prison Superintendent McEwen could not officially comment on the pardon application, "but as an individual citizen I would be glad to know that executive clemency had been extended in their behalf."

Edward Stair, the clerk of pardons, visited with Pipes and Herndon at the Albany prison and interviewed prison officials about them. Considering Evans' willingness to reduce the sentence to five years and the fact that by May 1884 six years of imprisonment had passed, Stair was of the opinion that a pardon "would not injure society or cause disrespect for the administration of justice." On June 17, 1884, Attorney General Brewster wrote the president that, with some reservations, he had no opposition to their pardon. But the president did not act.

In November of 1885 a disease broke out in the "short-term prison" at Albany and twenty-three sick prisoners were taken to the prison hospital where typhoid fever was diagnosed. Pipes and Herndon were both in the prison hospital at the time recovering from minor ailments. The sick prisoners were immediately isolated for treatment and they, along with additional sick prisoners, were transferred to a quarantined place in the jail. A total of 160 prisoners came down with the fever.

Pipes and Herndon, not being ill with the fever, were given an opportunity to be moved away so as not to be exposed. Instead they volunteered to act as nurses for those suffering from typhoid and remained in jail with the sick men. Many doctors refused to serve on the medical staff because of the contagiousness of the fever. Pipes and Herndon were placed in charge of a ward, on duty both day and night, and oversaw the recovery of many sick prisoners. One student, acting as an assistant on the medical staff, came down with the fever but refused to be moved to a hospital outside the prison if Pipes and Herndon could not go along as his nurses. As a result of the efficiency and fearlessness of the two prisoners, Albany Health Officer Lewis Balch and a new clerk of pardons, Alex R. Bobelet, recommended to the attorney general and President Grover Cleveland that a pardon be granted.

Pipes and Herndon finally received a pardon on February 25, 1886, having served seven and a half years of their sentence.[43] On Monday, March 1, they arrived by train in Dallas, once again in familiar surroundings. They were quoted as regarding the past "with horror" and pledged to "endeavor to merit the respect of their neighbors." They praised the "humane and reformatory manner" in which discipline was conducted at the Albany prison.[44] One of the first acts by the two as free men was to sit down together in a photographer's studio for an informal portrait. A copy of this photograph was sent to the Albany prison and medical officials there, perhaps in appreciation for how the two were treated during their incarceration.

Little is known about what happened to Albert Herndon. In 1888 and 1889 he was a clerk for Dallas grocer Henry L. McCorkle at his Elm Street store.[45] After that there is no information about him. Pipes, on the other hand, stayed around Dallas. On January 7, 1887, he and Sallie Z. Collins, the widow of Billy Collins, took out a license to marry.[46] In the last week of December 1888, Pipes was handling a pistol when it dropped to the floor and discharged a bullet into the upper portion of his leg, coming out just above the knee. Gangrene subsequently set in, and Pipes lingered until his death on Saturday, February 16, 1889. One newspaper labeled him as a "noted character."[47] Sallie Pipes continued to live in Dallas until she died at the age of seventy-eight on April 9, 1929.[48]

Curiously, the last bizarre tragedy occurring in Dallas that was related to the brief presence of Bass on the scene involved his half-brother, Charles Bass, who had run a "hightoned" cafe and restaurant in Kansas City and worked for a railroad. By about 1893 he had found his way to Dallas but was down on his luck and addicted to morphine. On December 6, 1898, he visited the home of C.L. Jones, who offered to put him in some institution so that he could cure his addiction. "I'll outlive you," was his retort. Bass lived with Walter S. Stone, who tried to take care of him, but on Thursday, December 8, his body was found in Stone's kitchen, his chest bared to reveal puncture wounds where he had injected the narcotic. His death was ruled as having been caused by an accidental overdose of morphine.[49]

Sam Bass' youngest brother, Denton, continued farming in

Samuel Pipes, left, and Albert Herndon celebrate their release from prison and arrival in Dallas in 1886 with this photograph. (Courtesy Dallas Historical Soceity).

Lawrence County, Indiana. On January 1, 1881, he married Emma Warren and they subsequently had one daughter, Lola. It was not a happy union, and Emma Bass' violent and uncontrollable temper forced a separation in August 1897 and a divorce the following year. Denton remarried Katie Tolliver and they also had one daughter. He worked for the Department of Internal Revenue, retiring after thirty-seven years of service, and died in Mitchell on December 14, 1948.[50]

The one remaining mystery of the saga of Sam Bass is the fate of Frank Jackson, the stalwart lieutenant who sought to save Bass' life amidst a hail of deadly gunfire. To this day there is only speculation. Jackson returned to Denton County briefly after the Round Rock shootout, making a tentative but futile inquiry through Jim Murphy to see if there was any chance that he might be excused by the government for his crimes. One account claimed that he hid out in Skagg's thicket some four miles northeast of Denton where Dr. R.S. Ross treated him for pneumonia.[51] Recognizing that there was no longer any sanctu-

Denton Bass, youngest brother of
Sam Bass, as an elderly man.
(Courtesy Helen Henderson,
Mitchell, Indiana, and Jeff
Routh, Bedford, Indiana.)

ary in his old stomping grounds, Jackson likely left Texas soon after the gunfight that killed Bass and Barnes. Where he went and what happened to him continues to be a matter of widespread speculation, although a fair number of people stepped forward claiming to know the answer.

In May 1881 Texas Prison Superintendent Thomas J. Goree intercepted a letter to convict J.W. Holt from Addie Wells of San Antonio. The letter commiserated about the illness of a mutual friend identified only as "Bud." Goree advised John B. Jones, now Texas Adjutant General, that he had information that "Bud" was really Frank Jackson, but there is no additional information about "Bud" or about the relationship of Holt or Wells to Jackson.[52]

Frontier Times reprinted a newspaper article in 1928 in which T.M. Willis of Abilene, a former city judge, said that he had been a friend of Jackson and that Jackson had returned to Denton County after Bass' death, stayed there out of sight for about a month, then left. Willis said that Jackson worked on an Arizona ranch under an assumed name, married and had a large family, then moved to New Mexico in the early 1920s.[53] Frontier Times even received a brief letter postmarked from Mississippi in June 1927 from a man who claimed to be Frank Jackson. Citing his age as seventy-eight, "Jackson" claimed that he was coming back to Texas soon to try to clear himself of all charges.[54] Jim Gober, who lived in Denton County with Ben Key, Jackson's brother-in-law, claimed that his brother ran into Jackson many years earlier working as a miner in Colorado.[55]

Thomas Rynning, who headed up the Arizona Rangers at

one time and who was also superintendent of the Yuma Prison in territorial Arizona, alleged that a Texan imprisoned there for train robbery under the name of William Downing was really Frank Jackson. Rynning said that he had a hunch that Downing was Jackson, so one day he hummed a verse of "The Ballad of Sam Bass." Downing gave him a "lightning look." According to Rynning, Dick Ware visited the penitentiary, saw Downing and hummed the ballad, and Downing again reacted, confirming Ware's recognition of Jackson. Rynning said that since Downing was a good prisoner, he helped him gain his release.[56] On his release Downing went to Willcox, Arizona, and opened a saloon in October 1907. Less than a year later on August 5, 1908, a drunken, raging William Downing was shot down and killed by Arizona Ranger Billy Speed.[57]

Another oldtime cowboy, Jack Thorpe, wrote that "Joe Jackson" fled to New Mexico, where he lived in cow camp after cow camp under an assumed name but known as "Jack." Friends in New Mexico were supposed to have sent feelers to Texas about a pardon for him, but their efforts were supposedly in vain because the Texas Rangers could not admit that they couldn't find him. "Jack" finally died when he was past eighty years old and was buried at Socorro, New Mexico, according to Thorpe.[58] Western writer Eugene Manlove Rhodes would become a champion of sorts for Jackson, claiming in correspondence to descendants of the Key family that Jackson had adopted an alias name, married and had several children, and entered the hardware business.[59]

The reward offered for Jackson as the sole surviving fugitive from the Bass gang led to some bizarre efforts. In February 1882 it was alleged that his whereabouts in Arizona had been determined, but efforts to track him down had failed. In New Mexico, Santa Fe City Marshal H.J. Franklin sent a letter dated February 16, 1882, claiming that Jackson was living there and inquiring about any rewards. The letter fueled additional speculation about where Jackson could be found, and it was alleged that Jackson was taken on March 29, 1882, at Las Cruces, New Mexico, after a serious gunfight in which one lawman was killed and another wounded. The prisoner was returned to Dallas on Friday, March 31, and placed in the county jail. In an interview,

"Jackson" talked about the Round Rock shootout, claiming that he and Bass had shed tears when they had to part then alleging that he had slipped into the crowd at Round Rock and brought the dying Bass a drink of water! No more was heard of this Frank Jackson because the entire incident was a hoax.[60]

According to Harry N. Graves, the prosecuting attorney for Williamson County during the administration of Texas Governor Oscar B. Colquitt from 1910 to 1915, Jackson was located in Oklahoma. Graves said that Williamson County Sheriff Sampson Connell, who was sheriff until November 5, 1912, went to Oklahoma to apprehend the fugitive, but the authorities there wanted a five hundred-dollar reward paid in advance and the sheriff returned empty-handed. Graves then stated that he went to see Governor Colquitt, who refused to grant the reward.[61] No information beyond this has yet been located but, if accurate, Graves' information could be a clue to the ultimate fate of Frank Jackson.

In 1927 noted Texas Ranger Frank Hamer, who would insure his place in ranger history as a participant in the ambush slaying of Depression-era killers Clyde Barrow and Bonnie Parker, was conducting an investigation in the Round Rock area. He somehow obtained information that Frank Jackson was then seventy-eight years old and living peacefully in New Mexico. Hamer was friends with Texas historian Walter Prescott Webb, and the two tried to correspond with the fugitive, who promptly disappeared. The Texas Adjutant General assured Hamer and Webb that far too many years had passed to consider prosecution of Jackson for Grimes' murder, so they enlisted the aid of Eugene Manlove Rhodes.

In June 1927 Rhodes urged Webb and Hamer to enlist the assistance of former New Mexico Governor James Hinkle to intercede with Jackson for them. A letter was obtained from the Texas governor assuring Jackson that he would not be arrested if he returned to Texas, but Jackson refused to reveal himself. Before Webb and Hamer could try some new tack with the aged fugitive, Jackson reportedly died.[62]

Several years later, in 1932, another effort was made by Texas officials to establish contact with Frank Jackson. Ranger William Warren Sterling, the state's adjutant general in command of all the rangers, was interested in clearing up some facts about the Round Rock gunfight. He called on retired Ranger Jim Gillett, who had ridden under Lieutenant N.O. Reynolds, and they determined to work together. On April 26, 1932, former New Mexico Governor Hinkle wrote Sterling that he thought that any information given out several years earlier about Jackson was probably not true and that Jackson was probably dead. T. S. "Stonewall" Jackson of Lubbock, Texas, claiming to be the youngest and only living of Frank's brothers, wrote Sterling that he had corresponded with Rhodes, who referred him to Sterling. Gillett read all of the books by oldtimers, such as Rynning, and concluded that they were not helpful.

With the governor ready to offer a pardon, Sterling and Gillett once again tried Rhodes, now terminally ill. Sterling's speculation, however, that Jackson was dead[63] ended the last official search for fugitive Frank Jackson. On December 21, 1936, Williamson County District Attorney D.B. Wood filed a motion to dismiss the murder indictment pending against Frank Jackson. For justification, Wood cited the fact that Jackson was aged if not dead and that even if he was alive, a conviction could likely not be obtained because witnesses to Grimes' killing were no longer alive to prove the offense or identify Jackson. The primary reason behind the dismissal was that the original indictment was desired for exhibition at the Texas Centennial being celebrated in Dallas. Until the murder case was dismissed, the indictment could not leave the district clerk's records. On the same date District Judge H.A. Dolan ordered that the case against Jackson be dismissed.[64]

With this final official act the saga of Sam Bass and his gang was relegated to the veil of myth and legend that ultimately blankets all those who defy the conventions of their time and achieve an extraordinary level of notoriety. Bass would be eulogized by a biographer as "an ignorant, vicious ruffian, who did more harm and less good, caused more sorrow and less happiness, ruined more young men and benefited fewer than any one character who has ever disgraced the State of Texas."[65] Coupled with the immediate biographies that sought to capitalize on Bass' notoriety and the brief excitement he had provided Texas, a cowboy song was written and passed from trail drive to trail drive, each recitation furthering the myth and clouding the reality.[66] In its wake would be scores of oldtimers who "remembered" some association with Bass. Stolen gold was rumored to be buried in a number of Texas counties and up and down the road between Denton and San Antonio.[67] As the legends grew, Bass evolved into a sort of amiable rogue who took on the widely disliked railroad corporations of the time and who followed the code of the outlaw by refusing to give up his companions to the pursuing lawmen.

In truth, Sam Bass was singularly unsuccessful as an outlaw except when he stumbled over the gold coins during the Big Springs robbery. Beyond that it is difficult to attribute anything to him of a positive nature. He was an illiterate crook who sought easy riches, but by being the focus of a manhunt unparalleled in the history of Texas then or since, Bass indirectly reinforced the need for an organized state police force. The diminution of both the Indian threat and the deadly menace of the bloody feuds and vigilantism that marked the state in the 1870s had generated discussion concerning the further need for the rangers and the financial cost of their activities. The successful chase after Bass postponed the budget battle for another day, an applaudable contribution by an otherwise unexceptional individual. Bass' exploits have been glamorously but untruthfully distorted to give him more credit as an outlaw than he deserves, but his is nevertheless an exciting tale that has become a significant footnote in Texas history.

> *Sam met his fate at Round Rock, July the twenty-first;*
> *They pierced poor Sam with rifle balls and emptied out his purse.*
> *Poor Sam he is a corpse and six foot under clay;*
> *And Jackson's in the bushes, trying to get away.*[68]

ENDNOTES

I. INDIANA BEGINNINGS

1. Wayne Gard, *Sam Bass* (New York: Houghton Mifflin Co., 1936), 237.
2. *History of Lawrence County, Indiana* (Paoli, Indiana: Stout's Print Shop, 1965), 296 (reprint of 1884 edition); see also 1850 U.S. Census, Marion Township, Lawrence County, Indiana.
3. Probate File, Court of Common Pleas, Lawrence County, Indiana, Box 29, File No. 6 (Estate of Daniel Bass).
4. Deed Records, Lawrence County, Indiana, Vol. C, 1020.
5. 1850 Lawrence County, Indiana (Marion Township) Census.
6. *History of Lawrence County*, 38.
7. *History of Lawrence County*, 300; 1850 Lawrence County, Indiana (Marion Township) Census, 255/255.
8. Gard, *Sam Bass*, 6.
9. *History of Lawrence County*, 300-301.
10. Gard, *Sam Bass*, 7; 1850 U.S. Census, Marion Township, Lawrence County, Indiana, 348.
11. Marriage Records, Lawrence County, Indiana, Vol. B, 236.
12. Gard, *Sam Bass*, 7, who is incorrect in stating that Elizabeth Sheeks' birthday was on October 22.
13. *Life and Adventures of Sam Bass* (Dallas, Texas: Dallas Commercial Steam Print, 1878), 3.
14. 1860 U.S. Census, Marion Township, Lawrence County, Indiana, 820.
15. Thomas E. Hogg, *Authentic History of Sam Bass and His Gang* (Bandera, Texas: Frontier Times, 1932), 7 (reprint of 1878 edition); *Denton Monitor*, 7 August 1878, as quoted in Ed. F. Bates, *History and Reminiscences of Denton County* (Denton, Texas: McNitzky Printing Co., 1918), 130; *Life and Adventures of Sam Bass*, 3; Probate File, Court of Common Pleas, Lawrence County, Indiana, Box 59, File No. 30 (David Sheeks, Guardian).
16. *Mitchell* [Indiana] *Tribune*, 16 December 1948; Probate File, Court of Common Pleas, Lawrence County, Indiana, Box 59, File No. 30 (David Sheeks, Guardian); 1860 Lawrence County, Indiana, Marion Township, Census, 820 (571/571).
17. Dorothy Alice Stroud, *My Legacy for Mitchell, Indiana* (Paoli, Indiana: The Print Shop, 1985), 3-34, 81, 86-87.
18. Gard, *Sam Bass*, 1, 7; Probate File, Court of Common Pleas, Lawrence County, Indiana, Box 29, File No. 6 (Estate of Daniel Bass).
19. *History of Lawrence County*, 227-28.
20. Gard, *Sam Bass*, 7-8.
21. Gard, *Sam Bass*, 10; David L. Sheeks and Mrs. George Lewis, Untitled Manuscript, Bedford, Indiana, Public Library; Grave Marker (Elizabeth Sheeks), Sheeks Cemetery, Lawrence County, Indiana.
22. Marriage Records, Lawrence County, Indiana, Vol. C, 285.
23. 1860 U.S. Census, Mitchell Post Office, Marion Township, Lawrence County, Indiana, 83.
24. Gard, *Sam Bass*, 10.
25. Marriage Records, Lawrence County, Indiana, Vol. D, 173.

26. *Life and Adventures of Sam Bass*, 3.

27. Stroud, *My Legacy*, 119.

28. Military Service Records (George W. Bass), Records of the Adjutant General's Office 1780s-1917, Record Group 94, National Archives, Washington, D.C. Company D was formally mustered into the 16th Indiana Infantry Regiment at Indianapolis on August 17, 1862. The soldiers immediately marched to Kentucky where Union General George W. Morgan was building a force of ten thousand soldiers in the Cumberland Gap. Confederate General Braxton Bragg, anxious to move against Morgan, directed General Edmund Kirby Smith to take his twenty thousand rebel soldiers directly to battle. Smith, however, preferred first to take Lexington, Kentucky, and learned that Union reinforcements were expected to arrive in Richmond, Kentucky, so he diverted his force. A Union cavalry unit ran into Smith's advance cavalry and retreated into Richmond, where Union Brigadier General Mahlon D. Manson was determined to make a stand, despite the fact that his command consisted of mostly raw recruits, including the 16th Indiana.

On August 30, 1862, the Confederates opened up their attack toward Richmond with an artillery barrage, and the two armies clashed outside of town. Gradually, all along the line of battle, the Union soldiers were repulsed with heavy casualties and fell back from the Confederate attack. Despite late-arriving federal reinforcements, the attack turned into a rout, and the green Union troops streamed toward Richmond. By 5:00 p.m., troops were locked in hand-to-hand combat among the tombstones of the town's cemetery. The rout continued, and the fleeing soldiers ran along the road to Lexington, running into another Confederate artillery barrage. Many of the Union soldiers dropped their arms and surrendered. A later estimate calculated that 206 Union soldiers were killed, 844 wounded, and four thousand captured, along with the seizure of ten thousand arms, nine artillery pieces, and a complete supply train. James Street, Jr., "The Struggle for Tennessee," *Time-Life Civil War Series* (Alexandria, Virginia: Time-Life Books, 1985), 45-48.

29. National Archives, Military Service Records (George W. Bass); Gard, *Sam Bass*, 10; *History of Lawrence County*, 301.

30. Pension Records, Records of the Veterans Administration, Record Group 15, National Archives, Washington, D.C.

31. Probate Orders, Lawrence County, Indiana, Vol. F, 273.

32. Probate File, Court of Common Pleas, Lawrence County, Indiana, Box 29, File No. 6 (Estate of Daniel Bass). See also Paula Reed and Grover Ted Tate, *The Tenderfoot Bandits* (Tucson, Arizona: Westernlore Press, 1988), 17, who state that Daniel Bass died of pneumonia but provide no source for that information.

33. Probate File, Court of Common Pleas, Lawrence County, Indiana, Box 29, File No. 6 (Estate of Daniel Bass); Probate Orders, Lawrence County, Indiana, Vol. F, 220; Gard, *Sam Bass*, 3. Solomon Bass was born on September 29, 1823, in Ashe County, North Carolina, and married Catherine Sheeks on March 12, 1846, in Lawrence County, Indiana. She died on October 9, 1865, after bearing thirteen children. *History of Lawrence County*, 296; 1860 Lawrence County, Indiana, Marion Township, Census (565/565).

34. Probate Orders, Lawrence County, Indiana, Vol. F, 273.

35. Probate File, Court of Common Pleas, Lawrence County, Indiana, Box 59, File No. 30 (David Sheeks, Guardian). David L. Sheeks was born in Marion Township on November 22, 1819. He became as prosperous as his father, expanding his holdings, including a sawmill, and ultimately controlling thousands of acres. On December 22, 1840, two months after the marriage of his sister to Daniel Bass, he married Cynthiana (Sylvania?) Lewis, and like his sister's family, eight children were born to them before Mrs. Sheeks died on February 24, 1856. Sheeks then married Susan Horsey on October 2, 1856, and she bore him eight additional children before herself dying on March 9, 1879. He married his third

wife Malinda Payne on July 22, 1879, who bore him at least two more children. It was said that he fathered a total of twenty-two children. Sheeks also served twice as a Lawrence County commissioner in 1870-1872 and 1878-1881. David Sheeks died on March 9, 1899, at the age of seventy-nine years. *History of Lawrence County*, 85, 300-301; Marriage Records, Lawrence County, Indiana, Vol. B, 368; Vol. F, 525; 1850 Lawrence County, Indiana, Marion Township, Census, 341 (256/256); 1860 Lawrence County, Indiana, Marion Township, Census, 97 (870/870); 1880 Lawrence County, Indiana, Marion Township, Census, 424 (85/85); Sheeks and Lewis, Untitled Manuscript, Bedford, Indiana, Public Library.

36. Probate File, Court of Common Pleas, Lawrence County, Indiana, Box 29, File No. 6 (Estate of Daniel Bass); Gard, *Sam Bass*, 3, incorrectly states that the auction was on March 30, 1864.

37. Probate Orders, Lawrence County, Indiana, Vol. F, 339.

38. Probate File, Court of Common Pleas, Lawrence County, Indiana, Box 59, File No. 30 (David Sheeks, Guardian).

39. Edwin J. Boley, *The Masked Halters* (Seymour, Indiana: Graessle-Mercer Co., 1977), 99-103.

40. Boley, *Masked Halters*, 265-73, 367-96.

41. Marriage Records, Lawrence County, Indiana, Vol. E, 9; 1860 U.S. Census, Mitchell Post Office, Marion Township, Lawrence County, Indiana, 849. John and Euphemia Beasley had three daughters by 1880. 1880 Lawrence County, Indiana, Marion Township, Census, 412 (134/139).

42. Marriage Records, Lawrence County, Indiana, Vol. E, 22.

43. Gard, *Sam Bass*, 40; *Life and Adventures of Sam Bass*, 3.

44. Stroud, *My Legacy*, 306.

45. Gard, *Sam Bass*, 13-15.

46. *Denton Monitor*, 7 August 1878, as quoted in Bates, *History and Reminiscences*, 130.

47. Hogg, *Authentic History*, 8.

48. Worth S. Ray, *Down in the Cross Timbers* (Austin, Texas: Worth S. Ray, 1947), 9.

49. Telephone conversation with John Lynch, 4 February 1997; Gard, *Sam Bass*, 13-24.

II. DENTON COUNTY, TEXAS

1. Hogg, *Authentic History*, 8.

2. Sillers, Florence Warfield, *History of Bolivar County, Mississippi* (Jackson, Mississippi: Hederman Brothers, 1948), 2, 339-40.

3. *Denton Monitor*, 7 August 1878, as quoted in Bates, *History and Reminiscences*, 130; *Life and Adventures of Sam Bass*, 4; Hogg, *Authentic History*, 8.

4. *Denton Monitor*, 7 August 1878, as quoted in Bates, *History and Reminiscences*, 130; telephone conversation with Barbara Tweedle, Deputy Chancery Court Clerk, Rosedale, Bolivar County, Mississippi, 3 October 1997.

5. Hogg, *Authentic History*, 8.

6. Gard, *Sam Bass*, 28; Hogg, *Authentic History*, 9.Scott Mayes recalled in 1930 that Bass was in Denton County by 1871. Interview of Scott Mayes by Alex Williams, 15 December 1930, Goodman-Williams Collection, Denton County Historical Museum.

7. Interview of Scott Mayes by Alex Williams, 15 December 1930, Goodman-Williams Collection, Denton County Historical Museum.

8. Gard, *Sam Bass*, 28; 1880 Denton County, Texas, Census, 20 (21/21).

9. Robert Mayes and Tom B. Wheeler were each fined $10 on May 12, 1876, for failing to appear as jurors in a lunacy trial. On February 20, 1877, Mayes was appointed the road overseer of the Denton-Bolivar road. His wife Elizabeth died on January 22, 1879, and he married Kittie Wilson on April 2, 1879. Mayes had

a total of four sons and one daughter. 1880 Denton County, Texas, Census, 20 (21/21); Commissioners Court Minutes, Denton County, Texas, Vol. A, 24, 94-95; Marriage Records, Denton County, Texas, Vol. 1, 280; Denton County Genealogical Society, *Denton County, Texas, Wills (1876-1940)* (Decorah, Iowa: Anundsen Publishing Co., 1994), 85; Grave Marker of Elizabeth Mayes, Oakwood Cemetery, Denton, Texas.

10. Certificate of Death (Elijah Scott Mayes), Cooke County, Texas, No. 30185.

11. Interview of Scott Mayes by Alex Williams, 15 December 1930, Goodman-Williams Collection, Denton County Historical Museum; Gard, *Sam Bass*, 28-32.

12. Ron Tyler, ed. *New Handbook of Texas* (Austin, Texas: Texas State Historical Association, 1996), Vol. II, 599-600; Mary Jo Cowling, *Geography of Denton County* (Dallas, Texas: Banks Upshur and Company, 1936), 61-103.

13. Interview of Scott Mayes by Alex Williams, 15 December 1930, Goodman-Williams Collection, Denton County Historical Museum.

14. Sarah Lacy was born in Mason County, Kentucky, on November 4, 1822, and married Charles Lacy in 1838 before coming to Texas. *Life and Adventures of Sam Bass,* 4; Edna Haynes McCormick, *William Lee McCormick, A Study in Tolerance* (Dallas, Texas: The Book Craft, 1952), 196; 1860 Denton County, Texas, Census, 407-08 (199/200); 1870 Denton County, Texas, Census, 120 (56/61); 1880 Denton County, Texas, Census, 19 (1/1); Gard, *Sam Bass*, 34-35.

15. 1870 Denton County, Texas, Census, 120 (56/61).

16. *Life and Adventures of Sam Bass,* 4.

17. Gard, *Sam Bass*, 33-34. Robert A. Carruth was born in Georgia in 1833 and by 1851 was farming in Fannin County, Texas. The 1860 census lists him as married to Missouri Frances Egan, and they had a one-year-old Texas-born son Alonzo. Bob Carruth moved to Denton County and by 1870 was in the retail dry goods business in Denton, living with and apparently working for merchant Henderson Murphy, although his family was not with him at the time. His family subsequently joined him in Denton County and the family is together in the 1880 census. In 1877 he was credited with owning 1,019 acres of land in Denton County. 1860 Fannin County, Texas, Census, 257 (780/791); letter to author from Mrs. Beth P. Carruth, Lewisville, Texas, 1 December 1997; 1870 Denton County, Texas, Census, 116 (14/14); 1880 Denton County, Texas, Census, 144 (335); 1877 Tax Assessment Rolls, Denton County, Texas.

18. Hogg, *Authentic History,* 9. Thomas J. Egan was an early settler of Denton County, appearing in deed records as early as 1860. Born on October 28, 1804, in Virginia, Egan moved his family to Montgomery County, Kentucky, then again in 1836 to Randolph County, Missouri, where he served as a justice of the peace. The Egan family moved once more to Denton County in January 1859, and the 1860 census lists him with his wife Nancy and their eleven children, including daughter Missouri, who later married Robert Carruth. Deed Records, Denton County, Texas, Vol. A, 454; Vol. D, 198, 228; 1860 Denton County, Texas, Census, 403 (133/134); Bates, *History and Reminiscences.* 70; *Biographical Souvenir of the State of Texas* (Chicago: F.A. Battey & Co., 1889), 274.

19. William F. "Dad" Egan was born to Tom and Nancy Egan in Kentucky on January 11, 1834, and came to Denton County with them in 1859. With the outbreak of the Civil War, Egan joined others in the area by enlisting on July 1, 1862, in a company organized by Dr. E.P. Kirby and T.W. Daugherty, and was elected orderly sergeant in what became Company A, 29th Texas Cavalry Regiment. The company was commanded by Col. Charles DeMorse, the controversial and highly political editor of a prominent Texas newspaper, the *Clarksville Northern Standard.* The unit saw battle in Arkansas and the Indian Territory, although Egan was reported "sick in quarters" in May and June of 1863.

After the war, Egan, thirty-four, married twenty-one-year-old Mary Eleanor Taylor on October 4, 1868, in Denton. Initially a farmer and store clerk, he was elected sheriff of Denton County on December 3, 1869. Sheriff Egan and his wife moved into Denton with their first child, Minnie M., where in May 1871 he purchased acreage from William H. Mounts.

Egan found on occasion that his job could be a difficult one. For example, on May 14, 1871, four of six prisoners confined in the small county jail escaped. That same month he attempted to carry out the orders of the Reconstruction government requiring militia units to be formed in each county, with leftover volunteers to be further organized by county sheriffs. According to Gard, a host of men flocked to Denton and commenced organizing units and selecting their officers, but alcohol and political turmoil dissolved the effort. The men were willing to fight Indians, but not in the name of the Reconstruction government in Austin. Egan quickly found himself filling the tiny jail with inebriated militiamen, and no militia was ever organized. On October 27, 1875, three prisoners took "French leave" from the county jail, as did six desperate inmates on August 4, 1876. National Archives, Compiled Service Records, Confederate Soldiers, Texas 29th Cavalry (DeMorse's Regt.), M323, Roll 147 (William F. Egan); *Denton Record-Chronicle*, 19 September 1921, 1; Ralph A. Wooster, *Texas and Texans in the Civil War* (Austin, Texas: Eakin Press, 1995), 197; Stewart Sifakis, *Compendium of the Confederate Armies: Texas* (New York: Facts on File, Inc., 1995), 86; Texas State Library, Confederate Pension Applications, File No. 46031 (Mary Eleanor Egan); *Biographical Souvenir of the State of Texas*, 274; Sammy Tise, *Texas County Sheriffs* (Albuquerque, New Mexico: Oakwood Printing, 1989), 155; 1870 Denton County, Texas, Census, 117 (25/25); Deed Records, Denton County, Texas, Vol. A, 43; Gard, *Sam Bass*, 35-36; *Dallas Herald*, 6, 20 May 1871, 3; *Dallas Daily Herald*, 30 October 1875, 4; 8 August 1876, 1; Reed and Tate, *Tenderfoot Bandits*, 20-23.

20. Deed Records, Denton County, Texas, Vol. A, 43.

21. Ray, *Down in the Cross Timbers*, 9; Letter from Virginia Egan to *Ace High Magazine*, 25 May 1932, Goodman-Williams Collection, Denton County Historical Museum.

22. *Life and Adventures of Sam Bass*, 4.

23. Hogg, *Authentic History*, 8.

24. 1870 Denton County, Texas, Census, 117 (22/22); *Denton Record-Chronicle*, 26 December 1941, 6.

25. Ray, *Down in the Cross Timbers*, 9; Gard, *Sam Bass*, 36.

26. Probate Orders, Lawrence County, Indiana, Vol. H, 26-28.

27. Probate Orders, Lawrence County, Indiana, Vol. I, 186; Probate File, Court of Common Pleas, Lawrence County, Indiana, Box 59, File No. 30 (David Sheeks, Guardian).

28. Letter, Samuel Bass to David L. Sheeks, 27 October 1872, courtesy of Wayne E. Bass, West Baden Springs, Indiana.

29. Letter, Samuel Bass to David L. Sheeks, 8 December 1872, courtesy of Wayne E. Bass, West Baden Springs, Indiana.

30. *Denton Monitor*, 7 August 1878, as quoted in Bates, *History and Reminiscences*, 130.

31. Interview With John Hudson by Alex Williams, 3 July 1930, Goodman-Williams Collection, Denton County Historical Association; Gard, *Sam Bass*, 36. Richard E. Cobb was born on July 8, 1857, in Bedford County, Virginia, and his family moved to Denton in 1870. *Denton Record-Chronicle*, 6 October 1939, 1; 1880 Denton County, Texas, Census, 20 (16/16).

32. Ray, *Down in the Cross Timbers*, 9.

33. Gard, *Sam Bass*, 36-38.

34. Hogg, *Authentic History*, 10.

35. Hogg, *Authentic History*, 9-10.

36. *San Antonio Daily Express*, 12 September 1895.

37. Texas State Library, "Lists of Fugitives," File Box No. 401-1160.

38. *Galveston Daily News*, 21 July 1878.

39. Hogg, *Authentic History*, 17; Charles L. Martin, *A Sketch of Sam Bass, the*

Bandit (Norman, Oklahoma: University of Oklahoma Press, 1968 reprint of 1880 edition), 64.

40. *Jamestown Press*, 12 July 1907, 1. The 1850 Jennings County, Indiana, census lists Henry Underwood as two years old. The Underwood family was prominent in Columbia Township and the county seat of North Vernon. Brothers Benjamin, John, and Julius, Henry's father, worked adjoining farms, and Henry's grandmother, Salina, lived with her married daughter, Julia Hall, on another adjoining farm. Julius Underwood was born on December 22, 1811, in Indiana and married a widow, Maria (sometimes shown as Mariah) Hall Sullivan, in 1838. Maria, the daughter of Squire Hall and Delila Underwood, was born June 11, 1816, also in Indiana, and had married Harrison Sullivan in 1830 prior to her 1838 marriage to Julius Underwood. Deed records show that Julius and Maria Underwood and their family were settled in Jennings County as early as 1841. By 1860 there were eight children on the farm with them, ranging from the oldest, Gideon, twenty, to the youngest, John, six months old. Henry was the sixth oldest of the eight at the age of twelve. 1850 Jennings County, Columbia Township, Indiana, Census, 324 (509/509); North Vernon, Indiana, Public Library, Brush Creek Cemetery Records, Campbell Township, Jennings County, Indiana; Ben H. Coke, *The Underwood Family From Madison County, Virginia* (Utica, Kentucky: McDowell Publications, 1986), 32; Deed Records, Jennings County, Indiana, Vol. H, 28; 1860 Jennings County, Columbia Township, Indiana, Census, 35 (229/228).

41. Hogg, *Authentic History*, 17.

42. National Archives, Military Service Records, Records of the Adjutant General's Office, 1780s-1917, RG 94 (Henry Underwood). Company A, 122nd Indiana Infantry Regiment mustered in at Indianapolis on December 16, 1863, and the regiment was later redesignated the following March as the 120th. The 120th played a part in the campaign against Atlanta, Georgia, in 1864, as well as the pursuit of the troops of Confederate General John Bell Hood. In 1865 it was involved in the battle at Wilmington, North Carolina, and the regiment was in North Carolina when the war came to an end. A report after the war stated that Company A saw twenty-one enlisted soldiers dying between January 1864 and August 1865, five from combat in Tennessee and North Carolina and the remainder from disease. W.H.H. Terrell, *Indiana in the War of the Rebellion* (n.p.: Indiana Historical Bureau, 1960 reprint of 1869 edition), 575; *Report of the Adjutant General of the State of Indiana* (Indianapolis, Indiana: Alexander H. Conner, State Printer, 1868), Vol. VIII, 687-89.

43. Underwood's company commander, Henry H. Robertson, later swore that in March 1865 the unit was involved in a battle at Kingston and his soldiers, including Underwood, had to wade an icy creek about four feet deep. He said that Underwood "took cold," had a "fit," and was speechless for some time, and that Underwood continued to suffer from the malady until the captain resigned in October 1865. A fellow soldier, W.H. Butler, also recalled wading the creek and that Underwood contracted a cold that affected his head and throat, stating that Underwood could not speak above a whisper even after the unit arrived in Raleigh. Another comrade, William H. Robertson, remembered that Underwood crushed his finger at Charlotte and that the hand was disabled for some time with the third finger of the left hand being crooked and stiff. National Archives, Pension Records, Records of the Veterans Administration, RG 15 (Henry Underwood).

44. Indiana State Archives, "Descriptive List of Convicts in the Northern Indiana State Prison, Near Michigan City," Vol. 3 (July 1877-May 1883), 231 (under alias of "William Jones").

45. National Archives, Military Service Records, Records of the Adjutant General's Office, 1780s-1917, RG 94 (Henry Underwood).

46. National Archives, Pension Records, Records of the Veterans

Administration, RG 15 (Henry Underwood).

47. Certificate of Death (Nathan Underwood), Bexar County, Texas, No. 21923.

48. Indiana State Archives, Army Enrollment Records (Nathan Underwood).

49. Henry Underwood and Mary Ann Emery were married by the Rev. C.V. Monfort, a day after Underwood had celebrated his birthday. His wife's parents, James and Mary Emery, had emigrated to the United States from England and by 1870 they and their five children were living in Labette County in the Mount Pleasant Township, receiving their mail through the Elston Post Office. While Mary and her brother James were born in England, Alfred, Charles, and Sarah were born in New York. Marriage Records, Labette County, Kansas, Vol. A, 119; 1870 Labette County, Kansas, Census, 50 (56/56).

50. Hogg, *Authentic History*, 17-18.

51. District Court Records, Labette County, Kansas, *State of Kansas v. Nathan Underwood and Henry Underwood*, Cause No. 217; District Court Records, Criminal Appearance Docket, Labette County, Kansas, Vol. A, 130.

52. Hogg, *Authentic History*, 18-19. The September 1871 date given for Underwood and his wife's arrival in Denton County has to be incorrect.

53. Hogg, *Authentic History*, 18-19.

54. Indiana State Archives, "Descriptive List of Convicts in the Northern Indiana State Prison, Near Michigan City," Vol. 3 (July 1877-May 1883), 231 (under alias of "William Jones").

55. Hogg, *Authentic History*, 19-20.

III. THE DENTON MARE

1. 1874 Tax Assessment Rolls, Denton County, Texas.

2. Wayne Gard, *Fabulous Quarter Horse: Steel Dust* (New York: Duell, Sloan and Pearce, 1958), 21-23.

3. Gard, *Fabulous Quarter Horse*, 26-31, 34-36.

4. Letter from Virginia Egan to *Ace High* Magazine, 25 May 1932, Goodman-Williams Collection, Denton County Historical Museum; Gard, *Fabulous Quarter Horse*, 40.

5. Gard, *Fabulous Quarter Horse*, 40-41; Gard, *Sam Bass*, 43; *IOOF Cemetery, Denton, Texas* (Denton, Texas: Denton County Historical Commission, 1989), 40; 1900 Denton County, Texas, Census, ED 46, Sheet No. 13 (236/242); *San Antonio Daily Express*, 8 April 1876, 4.

6. Letter from Virginia Egan to *Ace High* Magazine, 25 May 1932, Goodman-Williams Collection, Denton County Historical Museum; Ray, *Down in the Cross Timbers*, 79.

7. Gard, *Fabulous Quarter Horse*, 41; *Galveston Daily News*, 27 April 1878, 2.

8. Ray, *Down in the Cross Timbers*, 79; *Biographical Souvenir of the State of Texas*, 650-52; *Denton Record-Chronicle*, 27 April 1938, 1.

9. Gard, *Fabulous Quarter Horse*, 41; 1860 Denton County, Texas, Census, 431 (518/519); 1870 Denton County, Texas, Census, 131 (140/149).

10. Gard, *Fabulous Quarter Horse*, 41; Interview by Alex Williams with John Hudson, 3 August 1935, Goodman-Williams Collection, Denton County Historical Museum.

11. Probate Records, Lawrence County, Indiana, Box 50, File No. 35 (*Margaret Bass v. John L. Bass et al*).

12. Probate File, Court of Common Pleas, Lawrence County, Indiana, Box 59, File No. 30 (David Sheeks, Guardian).

13. Jim Gober, *Cowboy Justice* (Lubbock, Texas: Texas Tech University Press, 1997), 230-31.

14. Ray, *Down in the Cross Timbers*, 79; Letter from Virginia Egan to *Ace High*

Magazine, 25 May 1932, Goodman-Williams Collection, Denton County Historical Museum; Gard, *Fabulous Quarter Horse*, 41-42; *Galveston Daily News*, 27 April 1878, 2.

15. Interview by Alex Williams with John Hudson, 3 August 1935, Goodman-Williams Collection, Denton County Historical Museum; Gard, *Fabulous Quarter Horse*, 42-43; 1880 Tarrant County, Texas, Census, 89-90 (J.T. Tomlin is listed as a twenty-seven-year-old farmer from Kentucky, and S.R. Tomlin is a fifty-four-year-old farmer, also from Kentucky). In 1880 a Harry Hayes was a twenty-nine-year-old painter from Tennessee living with his wife and one-year-old son in Gainesville in Cooke County, north of Denton. 1880 Cooke County, Texas, Census, 224 (104/108).

16. C.V. Terrell, *The Terrells, Eighty-Five Years From Indians to Atomic Bomb* (Dallas, Texas: Wilkinson Printing Co., 1948), 35.

17. Gard, *Fabulous Quarter Horse*, 42.

18. Hudson was born John Allan Hudson in the Indian Territory on September 5, 1849, moving to Denton County in 1861. In 1875 he and his wife, Laura, had two children. She died in Denton on March 31, 1934, and he died there on September 9, 1936, survived by six children. *Denton Record-Chronicle*, 9 September 1936, 3; 1870 Denton County, Texas, Census, 208 (40/39); 1880 Denton County, Texas, Census, 23 (66/66).

19. Interview by Alex Williams with John Hudson, 6 January 1931, Goodman-Williams Collection, Denton County Historical Museum.

20. Gard, *Fabulous Quarter Horse*, 46.

21. Reed and Tate, *Tenderfoot Bandits*, 28-30; 1880 Hood County, Texas, Census, 66 (115/115).

22. Milner was born in Hickman County, Kentucky, on January 12, 1845. He served in Company B, 12th Kentucky Cavalry Regiment, during the Civil War, although discharged in December 1863 for "broken health and enfeebled condition." Milner came to Texas in 1869, settling in Parker County where he was briefly a constable in 1874 before resigning in November. 1880 Parker County, Texas, Census, 390 (84/84); Texas State Library, Confederate Pension Applications, File No. 20796 (Marcus Milner); Certificate of Death, Montague County, Texas, No. 61420 (Marcus Milner); Minutes, Commissioners Court, Parker County, Texas, Vol. 1, pp. 3, 13, 30; Deed Records, Parker County, Texas, Vol. 2, pp. 264, 275.

23. Hogg, *Authentic History*, 11-12.

24. William Steadman Fry was born on October 22, 1851, at Winston-Salem, North Carolina, the seventh of nine children born to Lewis M. and Rebecca Westmoreland Fry. After a few years in Tennessee, the family came to Denton County in 1859. In March 1870 Fry advertised in the *Denton Monitor* that he was "desirous of opening a correspondence with some woman with a view to matrimony," with photographs to be exchanged as soon as possible. He would not marry until September 1, 1885, when he married Lizzie Hoffmeyer. Lewis Fry died sometime between 1870 and 1880. At the age of nineteen, Fry had his minority disability removed, and he was appointed Denton city marshal in 1871. In June 1875 a tough guy named Shooler escaped after a dispute with Fry, during which Shooler pulled a deringer and wounded Fry in the foot. Fry was supposed to have served as city marshal until 1879, although George Smith was also supposed to have served in that role in 1878. However, he was also city marshal on April 26, 1888, when he was forced to kill a rapist who tried to resist after being pursued to Tarrant County. He was elected sheriff of Denton County on November 8, 1904, and served until November 1908. He was reelected sheriff on November 2, 1926, and served until he resigned in January 1928 because of a stroke. He died in Denton on September 27, 1930. 1860 Denton County, Texas, Census, 446 (736/737); 1870 Denton County, Texas, Census, 117 (26/26); 1880 Denton County, Texas, Census, 21 (36/36); Denton County Genealogical Society, Inc., *Denton County, Texas, Wills (1876-1940)*, 97; *Denton Monitor*, 19

March 1870, 2; *Norton's Union Intelligencer*, 12 June 1875; *Dallas Daily Herald*, 3 September 1885; *Dallas Morning News*, 28 April 1888, 3; *Denton Record-Chronicle*, 27 September 1930, 1; Tise, *Texas County Sheriffs*, 155; Certificate of Death (William Steadman Fry), Denton County, Texas, No. 43619; Marriage Records, Denton County, Texas, Vol. 2, 502; File No. 87.24.169, Williams-Goodman Collection, Denton County Historical Museum.

25. Interview by Alex Williams with William S. Fry, 3 March 1925, Goodman-Williams Collection, Denton County Historical Museum; Hogg, *Authentic History*, 11-14; Gard, *Sam Bass*, 44-46. Milner would be a sheep raiser in Parker County, then move to Clay County where he was granted a Confederate pension in 1912. Widowed, he died on December 25, 1936, in Bowie, Montague County, Texas. Texas State Library, Confederate Pension Applications, File No. 20796; Certificate of Death (Marcus Milner), Montague County, Texas, No. 61420; 1880 Parker County, Texas, Census, 390 (84/84).

26. Gillett, James B. *Fugitives From Justice* (Austin, Texas: State House Press, 1997), 25, 87; Frederick Nolan, *The Lincoln County War: A Documentary History* (Norman, Oklahoma: University of Oklahoma Press, 1992), 120-21.

27. *Fort Worth Democrat*, 4 September 1875, 3.

28. Robert K. DeArment, *Alias Frank Canton* (Norman, Oklahoma: University of Oklahoma Press, 1996).

29. Hogg, *Authentic History*, 14-15.

30. Hogg, *Authentic History*, 15-16; Albert Williams was forty, born in Tennessee and had at least three children at home with his wife Adaline. 1870 Denton County, Texas, Census, 127 (76/76); 1880 Denton County, Texas, Census, 4 (59/59). Sterling Johnson was also in his mid-forties and worked as a farmer and laborer, although he also served as a local preacher in the black community and was called "Parson" Johnson. 1870 Denton County, Texas, Census, 117 (24/24); 1880 Denton County, Texas, Census, 11 (178/181).

31. Albert Galvan Collins was born in Kentucky on September 12, 1803. On June 1, 1831, in Clark County, Kentucky, he married Permelia N. Foster, who was born on August 20, 1816. Between 1832 and 1837 four children were born to them: Jemima W. (31 March 1832), Arzelia O. (7 December 1833), James A. (24 October 1835) and Joseph (23 August 1837). The family left Kentucky for Missouri where they lived from 1838 to 1845 and three more children were born: Walter S. (29 December 1839), Martha E.B. (23 March 1842) and John Foster (13 February 1844). After moving to Dallas County in 1845 six more children were born to the Collins family: William O. "Billy" (10 August 1846), Joel W. (4 December 1848), Mildred Annie (4 March 1851), Albert Sanford (20 November 1853), Katie Crocket (15 September 1856) and Henry Gale (18 August 1859). Letter to Author from Mrs. Ruby Schmidt, Granbury, Texas, 14 April 1997; See also 1840 Howard County, Missouri, Census, 62; 1850 Dallas County, Texas, Census (416); 1860 Dallas County, Texas, Census, 303 (1194/1191); 1870 Dallas County, Texas, Census, 371 (449/448); Rubyann Thompson Darnall, Adrienne Bird Jamieson, and Helen Mason Lu, eds., *Dallas County, Texas: Genealogical Data From Early Cemeteries* (Dallas, Texas: Dallas Genealogical Society, 1982), 64; John Henry Brown, *History of Dallas County, Texas, from 1837 to 1887* (Dallas, Texas: Milligan, Cornett & Farnham, Printers, 1887), 71.

32. *Dallas Herald*, 7 November 1860, 3.

33. In the late 1850s, brothers James and Joe Collins left Dallas County and moved near Indianola in Calhoun County on the Texas Gulf Coast. They lived with farmer and trader James M. Foster and his wife Mary. Twenty-four-year-old James Collins became a cattle trader. 1860 Calhoun County, Texas, Census, 230 (251/211). In May 1859 James paid $1,300 to Foster for an eighteen-year-old slave girl, Emily, who was "fully guaranteed against the vices and maladies and defects proscribed by law." At the same time Joe paid Foster $1,000 for thirteen-year-old June, "a slave for life." Deed Records, Calhoun County, Texas, Vol. F, 168.

Curiously, on January 21, 1865, C.G. Napier of Bexar County sold "a negro girl named Malinda, 18 years of age," who was "warranted to be sound and healthy to date," to "J.Collins." Deed Records, Bexar County, Texas, Vol. T-1, 339.

Years before, Foster had conceived the idea of chartering ships to transport Texas cattle from Indianola to New Orleans, a short-lived project that died as Louisiana buyers placed greater restrictions on the cattle they would accept. C.L. Douglas, *Cattle Kings of Texas* (Austin, Texas: State House Press, 1989), 7. With the outbreak of the Civil War, James and Joe Collins traveled to Houston where they both enlisted on September 7, 1861, as privates in Captain John G. Walker's company, which became Company K of the Eighth Texas Cavalry, more popularly known as Terry's Texas Rangers after Colonel Benjamin Franklin Terry. Each volunteer was required to furnish a shotgun or carbine, a Colt revolver, a Bowie knife and a saddle, bridle and blanket. The army provided their mounts. Ordered to report to Albert Sidney Johnston at Bowling Green, Kentucky, the unit received a smattering of training as well as a dose of military discipline. The first battle for the unit was at Woodsonville, Kentucky, on December 8, 1861, when Colonel Terry was killed. After this the Texans participated in the battle of Shiloh on April 6-7, 1862, where Johnston was killed.

By July 1862 James Collins was a second lieutenant. At a battle at Murfreesboro on July 13, he was shot in the right arm, causing a severe compound fracture. Forced to take an extended furlough to recover, he returned to Texas and subsequently resigned his commission as an officer in the Confederate Army on May 4, 1863, which resignation was accepted on September 15. While he recuperated in Texas, the Eighth Texas fought on in Tennessee, then in Georgia. James Collins rejoined the army after recovering and by May 7, 1864, was a first lieutenant in Company K, later being promoted to captain. After the fall of Atlanta in September 1864, which the Eighth Texas helped defend, the unit joined in a retreat to North Carolina where it was finally surrendered to the Union Army by General Joseph Johnston on April 26, 1865. The war was over for the Collins brothers, although another brother, Walter, had died in a prison camp. National Archives, Compiled Service Records, Confederate Soldiers, 8th Texas Cavalry (Terry's Regiment, 1st Rangers, 8th Rangers), M323, Roll No. 49; *Dallas Herald*, 23 November 1867, 2; Thomas W. Cutrer (Introduction), *Terry Texas Ranger Trilogy* (Austin, Texas: State House Press, 1996), vii-xxvi; Stewart Sifakis, *Compendium of the Confederate Armies: Texas*, 58-60; Euroda Moore, "Recollections of Indianola," from the *Wharton Spectator*, February 1934, *Indianola Scrapbook* (Austin, Texas: Jenkins Publishing Co., 1974), 94-132; Tyler, ed., *New Handbook of Texas*, Vol. II, 805-06; Letter to Author from Mrs. Ruby Schmidt, Granbury, Texas, 14 April 1997.

The Collins brothers returned to Texas and resumed the cattle business in Calhoun County. On August 1, 1866, in Dallas, James married Mary A. Jenkins, the daughter of William Jenkins, Dallas' third sheriff in 1848-1850, and they had a son, Frank Terry Collins. Helen Mason Lu and Gwen Blomquist Neumann, eds., *Marriages, Dallas County, Texas, Books A-3 (1846-1877)* (Dallas, Texas: Dallas Genealogical Society, 1978), 15; *Memorial and Biographical History of Dallas County* (Chicago: The Lewis Publishing Co., 1892), 670, 995.

In Calhoun County James and Joe Collins, along with James Foster, entered into a partnership with noted Matagorda County cattleman Abel "Shanghai" Pierce, buying cattle in Matagorda and selling them in New Orleans. Douglas, *Cattle Kings of Texas*, 40. The tax rolls in Calhoun County reflect the consistent presence there of the two brothers between 1865 and 1867, although they did not own any real estate. Assessment of Property, 1865-1867, Calhoun County, Texas. On February 17, 1867, a second son, named for Joe, was born to James and Mary Collins, but died of yellow fever on June 1, 1867. Leonard Joe McCown, *Cemeteries of Indianola, Texas* (Irving, Texas: Leonard Joe McCown, 1979), 38. The outbreak of yellow fever also claimed the life of James Collins on July 9, 1867, and he was buried in Indianola next to his baby. It would be said of James that in matters of business he had "established a most enviable reputation for promptness, integrity and honor; his word was his bond, and its violation was never known. In his relations with his friends and associates, he was modest and retiring, affable, frank and generous." *Dallas Herald*, 23 November 1867, 2.

Joe Collins was appointed on July 29 by the court to administer his brother's estate, and an inventory of James' estate, ranging from a mule and horses to household furniture and firearms, along with claims owed the estate, totaled almost $8,000 after disbursements. Final Probate Record, Calhoun County, Texas, Vol. C, 125-26, 131-32, 468. Mary Collins and young Frank returned to Dallas where they moved in with her father. 1870 Dallas County, Texas, Census, 400 (1099/1092). She later married prominent Dallas Doctor Arch M. Cochran on January 11, 1871, with whom she would have three additional children. In 1893 she was the National Lady Manager from Texas to the Columbian Exposition in Chicago. *Memorial and Biographical History of Dallas County, Texas*, 669-70; *Dallas Morning News*, 5 August 1910; Tyler, ed., *New Handbook of Texas*, Vol. II, 180; 1880 Dallas County, Texas, Census, 42 (301/354).

Joe Collins continued in the cattle business in south Texas. In July 1867, while administering his brother's estate, he began to establish himself, buying two hundred acres of land on Chocolate Bayou in Calhoun County for $1,500 in "American metalic coin." Deed Records, Calhoun County, Texas, Vol. G, 498. Joe married Mississippi-born Artie Holliday of Victoria in 1866. Their first child, James F., named after Joe's brother, was born in December 1868. Letter to Author from Mrs. Ruby Schmidt, Granbury, Texas, 14 April 1997; J.W. Petty, *History of Victoria* (Victoria, Texas: Book Mart, 1961), 129; 1900 Goliad County, Texas, Census, Precinct 1, ED 47, 3 (60/60). By mid-1870 Joe's household, in addition to his wife and son, included brothers Joel and William, or "Billy," and Billy's wife, Martha. 1870 Calhoun County, Texas, Census, Lavaca Post Office, 361 (6/6). Martha "Mattie" Collins was born on the Guadalupe River on August 7, 1848, the daughter of Captain Arthur Swift, a veteran of the Texas Revolution. She and Billy married on October 15, 1868. She died in Dallas on January 11, 1874, after a long illness. *Dallas Daily Herald*, 13 January 1874. Billy Collins then married Sarah "Sally" Zarilda Caton in Dallas on February 25, 1875. *Dallas Daily Herald*, 4 March 1875.

34. Assessment of Property, Calhoun County, Texas, 1869 and 1870. Prominent cattleman George Saunders would recall his father selling their overstocked cattle after the Civil War to Shanghai Pierce, Foster & Allen, and Joel Collins. George W. Saunders, "Reflections of the Trail," J. Marvin Hunter, ed., *Trail Drivers of Texas* (Austin, Texas: University of Texas Press, 1985), 429. The Collins brothers worked for Allen and Poole in the partnership with Pierce, and there is some indication that Joe and Joel Collins may have periodically gone their separate ways in cattle deals during the early 1870s. Gard, *Sam Bass*, 52; Douglas, *Cattle Kings of Texas*, 42.

35. District Court Minutes, Atascosa County, Texas, *State of Texas v. Joseph Collins*, Cause No. 202, Vol. A, 296, 324-25.

36. District Court Minutes, Karnes County, Texas, *State of Texas v. Joseph Collins*, Cause No. 388, Vol. B, 177; Cause No. 595, Vol. B, 275, and Criminal Docket, Karnes County, Texas, 497; Cause No. 886, Vol. C, 177, 284-85.

37. Court records show that in 1872 and 1873 Joe Collins was in a cattle partnership with John C. Adams and Peter T. Adams, better known as "Cood" Adams and his brother of Uvalde County. Deed Records, Karnes County, Texas, Vol. W-2, 347 and 523. By 1875 Joe was on his own, as indicated by records of cattle transactions in Goliad where he dealt with James D. "One-Arm" Reed. Deed Records, Goliad County, Texas, Vol. K, 351; see also Lou Best Porter, "Sketch of Capt. James D. Reed," J. Marvin Hunter, ed., *Trail Drivers of Texas*, 690-91; Joseph G. McCoy, *Historic Sketches of the Cattle Trade of the West and Southwest* (Lincoln,

Nebraska: University of Nebraska Press, 1985), 176-77.

38. *San Antonio Herald*, as quoted in the *Austin Weekly Democratic Statesman*, 26 June 1873, 3.

39. *Hays City Sentinel*, 28 September 1877.

40. *Victoria Advertiser*, 23 March 1870, as quoted by *Flakes Daily Bulletin*, 20 April 1870, 1; *Dallas Herald*, 14 May 1870, 2.

41. District Court Minutes, Victoria County, Texas, *State of Texas v. Joel Collins*, Cause No. 913, Vol. 6, pp. 41, 58, 84.

42. *Life and Adventures of Sam Bass*, 18.

43. Ed Bartholomew, *Wyatt Earp, The Untold Story* (Toyahville, Texas: Frontier Book Co., 1963), 117.

44. *Omaha Daily Bee*, 30 December 1877, 4.

45. *Wichita Weekly Beacon*, 3 October 1877, 1.

46. Stuart N. Lake, *Wyatt Earp, Frontier Marshal* (New York: Houghton-Mifflin, 1931), 108-12.

47. Deed Records, Bexar County, Texas, Vol. 2, 289-90. Lowe, born in New York about 1845 to a transplanted English family, joined a Union artillery regiment in Missouri late in the Civil War. As early as 1868 he was running a saloon in Ellsworth, Kansas, where he earned his descriptive nickname and where he took up with his common-law wife, "Rowdy Kate" Lowe, in what was frequently a stormy relationship. Lowe and Kate moved on to Newton, Kansas, in 1871 where they established a dance hall, then again to Wichita the following year where Lowe and Joel Collins may have met. Lowe set up his new establishment in Delano, just across the Arkansas River from Wichita. In October 1873 he shot to death Edward "Red" Beard, a rival saloon competitor, for which he was acquitted by a jury. Wanted for another shooting, Lowe and his paramour fled Kansas in late 1874 for Denison, Texas, in Grayson County, where he and Kate briefly ran another saloon-dance hall before moving on to Luling in Caldwell County. Joseph G. Rosa and Waldo E. Koop, *Rowdy Joe Lowe, Gambler With a Gun* (Norman, Oklahoma: University of Oklahoma Press, 1989), 1-104.

48. Frank H. Bushick, *Glamorous Days* (San Antonio, Texas: The Naylor Company, 1934), 110.

49. District Court Minutes, Caldwell County, Texas, *State of Texas v. Joe Lowe, alias Rowdy Joe*: Cause No. 1250, Vol. D, pp. 511, 582-83; Cause No. 1276, Vol. D, p. 520; *State of Texas v. Joel Collins*: Cause No. 1266, Vol. D, pp. 513, 583; Cause No. 1292, Vol. D, 521; Cause No. 1352, Vol. D, pp. 581, 588; *State of Texas v. Manning Clements*, Cause No. 1262, Vol. D, 512.

50. District Court Minutes, Caldwell County, Texas, *State of Texas v. Joe Lowe*, Cause No. 1419, Vol. E, pp. 806, 1103; *State of Texas v. Joel Collins*, Cause No. 1410, Vol. E, pp. 806, 1076.

IV. BLACK HILLS CRIME

1. Gard, *Sam Bass*, 51.

2. *Dallas Daily Herald*, 29 December 1875, 1; *Denison Daily News*, 24, 29 December 1875.

3. District Court Civil Minutes, Denton County, Texas, *State of Texas v. Henry Underwood*, Cause No. 1480, Vol. B, 15; *Dallas Daily Herald*, 28 March 1877, 3; *Gainesville Hesperian*, as quoted in the *Denison Daily News*, 19 January 1878, 1; *Galveston Daily News*, 27 April 1878, 2.

4. Hogg, *Authentic History*, 52.

5. Hogg, *Authentic History*, 33.

6. *San Antonio Daily Express*, 26 March 1876, 4.

7. *San Antonio Daily Express*, 8, 9 April 1876, 4. Bass and Collins may have had a stable of horses in addition to the grey mare. An intriguing account of races

ENDNOTES

held at Hempstead in Waller County on June 15 and 16, 1876, refers to a grey mare, "White Sepulchre," raced by "Collins & Wear," and "Brown Dick" and "Ringneck," both entered by "J. Collins." *Dallas Daily Herald*, 15 and 16 June 1876, 1.

8. Hogg, *Authentic History*, 33; Martin, *Sketch of Sam Bass*, 12.

9. Hogg, *Authentic History*, 33.

10. Deed Records, Bexar County, Texas, Vol. 4, 405-406.

11. Reed and Tate, *Tenderfoot Bandits*, 36.

12. *Fort Worth Star-Telegram*, 3 August 1967. C.C. Bingham was born in Tennessee about 1832, had four sons by his first wife, Jane, and at least one daughter by his second wife, Isabel. 1860 Burnet County, Texas, Census, 162 (140/140); 1870 Burnet County, Texas, Census, 254 (390/390); 1880 Burnet County, Texas, Census, 148 (138/138).

13. *San Antonio Daily Herald*, 1 April 1876, 3.

14. *Dallas Daily Herald*, 17 July 1873; Personal account by John Gardner, correspondence with author from Barbara Elliott, San Angelo, Texas, 27 November 1998. John Edmund Gardner was born on May 2, 1845, in Nacatosh Parish, Louisiana, to Joseph and Martha Gardner, who had at least seven children. The family came to Texas in 1851, settling first in Goliad County, then moving in an oxen-drawn wagon to Atascosa County by 1856 where Joseph Gardner registered his "G" brand. John Gardner's obituary claimed that he was a Texas Ranger for three years during the Civil War, but there is no record of such service. He later claimed that after the Civil War he worked six years for Joel Collins helping Collins drive cattle to Indianola in Calhoun County. He set up a ranch in Frio County, establishing brands there in 1873 and 1874. According to Gardner, he "drove for Joel Collins in 1872, 73, 74, and 75."

On January 10, 1878, after his return to Texas from Nebraska, he married Cora Boone in Atascosa County, although both were then living in Frio County. On June 30, 1879, a Frio County jury found Gardner not guilty of theft of a cow, and a jury acquitted him of the theft of fifty horses on July 1, 1879. He was indicted again in Frio County on April 5, 1880, for theft of three head of "neat" cattle, but was again acquitted on April 7. In LaSalle County, Gardner was indicted on October 12, 1881, for failing to report to the commissioners court that he was slaughtering animals for market, but he was again found not guilty on October 10, 1883. Apparently his wife died, and in the late 1890s he married a Swedish immigrant, a widow, Inge or Inga. By 1900 his family was living in Tom Green County, then moved to El Paso County where he was the president of the Gardner-Moseley company, owners of a large ranch in Hudspeth County. He died on April 23, 1926. One of his sons, Joe, was a champion rodeo rider and cattle roper who was a close friend of entertainer Will Rogers. John Gardner recalled that "I lived a fast life in my young days and I thought a great deal of women at the same time. I was a particular favorite of theirs. I made it a rule through life to never turn the dark side of a woman's card up and I have seen enough to know that there is but one way to go through life and that is on the dead square in every respect." Personal account by John Gardner, Correspondence with author from Barbara Elliott, San Angelo, Texas, 27 November 1998; *El Paso Times*, 24 April 1926; Certificate of Death (John Edmund Gardner), El Paso County, Texas, No. 12948; 1860 Atascosa County, Texas, Census, 25 (194/169); 1880 LaSalle County, Texas, Census, 341 (38/41); 1900 Tom Green County, Texas, Census, ED 159, Sheet 1, Line 74 (16/16); 1910 El Paso County, Texas, Census, ED 87, Sheet 6B, Line 81 (104/106); 1920 El Paso County, Texas, Census, ED 60, Sheet 1B, Line 77 (20/20); Record of Marks and Brands, Atascosa County, Texas, Vol. 1, 62; District Court Minutes, Frio County, Texas, *State of Texas v. John E. Gardner*, Cause No. 115, Vol. A, 315; Cause No. 148, Vol. A, 323; Cause No. 154, Vol. A, 423; Deed Records, Frio County, Texas, Vol. F, 458-59; Vol. H, 103-04; Vol. I, 67; District Court Minutes, LaSalle County, Texas, *State of Texas v. John Gardner*, Cause No. 30, Vol. A2, 43, 128; Records of Marks and Brands, Frio County, Texas, Vol. 1, 115, 281.

Another cowboy, Henry Ramsdale, claimed to have come to Texas in 1876 and to have made a trail drive north with Joe Collins (rather than Joel), although he provided no details. Henry Ramsdale, "Fought Indians on the Trail," *Trail Drivers of Texas*, 37.

15. *Hays City Sentinel*, 19 October 1877, 1; *San Antonio Daily Express*, 9 October 1877, 4; *Life and Adventures of Sam Bass*, 12.

16. Texas State Library, Lists of Fugitives, Box 401-1160. In the 1850 Pennsylvania census, a nine-year-old William Potts was one of six children in the family of George and Emily Potts. George Potts was a coal merchant from New Jersey, while his wife and all of his children were born in Pennsylvania. 1850 Schuylkill County, Pennsylvania, Census, 403B (421/450).

17. Gillett, *Fugitives From Justice*, 19.

18. *Omaha Daily Bee*, 31 December 1877.

19. Lake, *Wyatt Earp*, 106.

20. Lake, *Wyatt Earp*, 108, 110.

21. Nyle H. Miller and Joseph W. Snell, *Why the West Was Wild* (Topeka, Kansas: Kansas State Historical Society, 1963), 646.

22. *Wichita City Eagle*, 11 November 1875, and *Wichita Weekly Beacon*, 10,17 November 1875, all as quoted in Miller and Snell, *Why the West Was Wild*, 38, 149-50, 493.

23. Martin, *Sketch of Sam Bass*, 13.

24. Reed and Tate, *Tenderfoot Bandits*, 64; Al. Sorenson, *Hands Up! or the History of a Crime* (College Station, Texas: Creative Publishing Company, 1982), 47-48; *Chicago Daily Sun*, 2 October 1877, also alleges that Joel Collins obtained 150 cows from his brother.

25. Hogg, *Authentic History*, 33; Martin, *Sketch of Sam Bass*, 13.

26. Texas State Library, Lists of Fugitives, Box 401-1160; Letter from M.F. Leach to Maj. John B. Jones, 27 July 1878, Center for American History, University of Texas at Austin, Transcripts From the Office of the Adjutant General of Texas, 1878.

27. *Dallas Daily Herald*, 13 June 1876, 4.

28. *Fort Worth Weekly Democrat*, 10 June 1876, 3.

29. *Galveston Daily News*, 21 July 1878, 1.

30. For an analysis of the various photographs erroneously identified as being of Bass, see Chuck Parsons, "A Sam Bass Pictorial," *The Westerner*, Vol. 7 (Fall 1987), 21-22.

31. Reed and Tate, *Tenderfoot Bandits*, 49-51. John Frederick West, the son of a Baptist minister, was born February 10, 1852, coming to Dallas from Georgia in 1872. He married Ardelia Ellen Jackson on January 26, 1877. Ellen West's first husband, John Chenault, was despised by her father who, according to the family, ran him off. Her mother sent her to an orchard to pick some peaches for a cobbler and she eloped with West. West joined his father-in-law, James Jackson, in building a general store in northeast Dallas County. Lu and Blomquist, eds. *Marriages, Dallas County, Texas*, Vol. 1, 46; *Proud Heritage: Pioneer Families of Dallas County* (Dallas, Texas: Dallas County Pioneer Association, 1986), Vol. 1, 244-45.

32. Reed and Tate, *Tenderfoot Bandits*, 52-55.

33. Reed and Tate, *Tenderfoot Bandits*, 56.

34. Hogg, *Authentic History*, 34; Martin, *Sketch of Sam Bass*, 13; *Galveston Daily News*, 24 July 1878, 1.

35. *Life and Adventures of Sam Bass*, 7.

36. Gard, *Sam Bass*, 58.

37. *Ford County Times*, as quoted in the *Hays City Sentinel*, 5 October 1877, 3.

38. Sorenson, *Hands Up!*, 48.

39. *Cheyenne Daily Leader*, 28 September 1877.

40. *Chicago Daily Sun*, 2 October 1877.

41. Personal account by John Gardner, Correspondence to author from

ENDNOTES

Barbara Elliott, San Angelo, Texas, 28 November 1998.

42. Hogg, *Authentic History*, 34; Sorenson, *Hands Up!*, 48.

43. *Weatherford Exponent*, 21 April 1877, 1.

44. Joseph G. Rosa, *They Called Him Wild Bill* (Norman, Oklahoma: University of Oklahoma Press, 1974), 297-98.

45. Sorenson, *Hands Up!*, 48; *Chicago Daily Sun*, 2 October 1877.

46. Hogg, *Authentic History*, 34; It would be stated that "Maude" later returned to Dallas and moved into a "den of infamy." It has also been speculated that she was originally from Dallas and joined the cattle drive when it came through town and perhaps rode in a wagon. In the 1880 Denton County census, a Maude Collins is listed as a twenty-two-year-old prostitute from Indiana, who had two seventeen-year-old "boarders" living with her. Several years later a Mattie Collins, alleged to be the wife of Dick Liddle, one of the members of the James Gang, was supposed to have been a paramour of Joel Collins. *Martin, Sketch of Sam Bass*, 15; Martin, *Sketch of Sam Bass*, 15; 1880 Denton County, Texas, Census, 2 (22/22); *Fort Worth Daily Democrat-Advance*, 8 April 1882, 1.

47. John S. McClintock (Edward L. Senn, ed.), *Pioneer Days in the Black Hills* (New York: J.J. Little and Ives Co., 1939), 211. A Michael Tippie, thirty-eight, a liquor seller from Ohio, was residing in Minersville, Dakota Territory, in 1880, as was twenty-five-year-old quartz miner Wesley Tippie, also from Ohio. 1880 Pennington County, Dakota Territory, Census, 108 (198/198); 124 (16/16).

48. Hogg, *Authentic History*, 34.

49. *Life and Adventures of Sam Bass*, 11.

50. *Hays City Sentinel*, 28 September 1877.

51. J.W. Bridwell, *The Life and Adventures of Robert McKimie* (Houston, Texas: The Frontier Press of Texas, 1955), 3-5.

52. Doug Engebretson, *Empty Saddles, Forgotten Names* (Aberdeen, South Dakota: North Plains Press, 1984), 155-57; *Cheyenne Daily Leader*, 22 February 1878.

53. Berry was born about 1837 in Missouri to Caleb E. and Virginia Berry, the fifth of nine children, and in 1850 the family lived on a farm in Callaway County. 1850 Callaway County, Missouri, Census, 291 (1325/1325); 1860 Callaway County, Missouri, Census, 923 (967/999).

54. Texas State Library, Lists of Fugitives, Box 401-1160.

55. *Glasgow Journal*, as quoted in *Mexico Ledger*, 8 November 1877, 2; Thomas Goodrich, *Black Flag* (Bloomington, Indiana: Indiana University Press, 1995), 146-48. According to the *St. Louis Daily Missouri Democrat*, 12 November 1864, as relied on by one author, Anderson's "orderly" was a man named Ike Berry, whom he called "Weasel." Both Anderson and Berry were intoxicated and together severely pistol-whipped and tortured Lewis, and Anderson even rode a horse over him, until the family was able to produce five thousand dollars. Lewis died, largely as a result of his injuries, on February 2, 1866. Albert Castel and Thomas Goodrich, *Bloody Bill Anderson* (Mechanicsburg, Pennsylvania: Stackpole Books, 1998), 118-22.

56. 1870 Callaway County, Missouri, Census, 438-39 (611/649); Probate Records, Callaway County, Missouri, *Estate of James F. Berry*, Bundle 6, Box 77.

57. *Omaha Weekly Herald*, 26 October 1877, Supp. 1; *Mexico Ledger*, 18 October 1877, 3.

58. James D. Horan and Paul Sann, *Pictorial History of the Wild West* (New York: Bonanza Books, 1954), 85; Texas State Library, Lists of Fugitives, Box 401-1160; *Omaha Daily Bee*, 31 December 1877, 4.

59. McClintock, *Pioneer Days*, 211; Jesse Brown and A.M. Willard (John T. Milek, ed.), *The Black Hills Trails* (Rapid City, South Dakota: Rapid City Journal Co., 1924), 245; Engebretson, *Empty Saddles*, 157.

60. Agnes Wright Spring, *The Cheyenne and Black Hills Stage and Express Routes* (Glendale, California: Arthur H. Clark Co., 1949), 88-89, 161, 185.

61. Spring, *Cheyenne and Black Hills Stage*, 88.

319

62. *Galveston Daily News*, 24 July 1878, 1.

63. Hogg, *Authentic History*, 35-36.

64. *Cheyenne Daily Leader*, 26 March 1877, 5 April 1877; Spring, *Cheyenne and Black Hills Stage*, 189-91; Brown and Willard, *Black Hills Trails*, 245-47; Engebretson, *Empty Saddles*, 157; Bridwell, *Robert McKimie*, 7-8. Brown and Willard assert that the robbery had originally been planned by a man named Charlie Barber at the Deadwood home of a man named Lee, but Barber was unable to accompany the men on the raid because he had recently shot himself.

65. Brown and Willard, *Black Hills Trails*, 247. Imagine the men's consternation if they had known that a passenger on the stage following the one they attacked, Mrs. Hattie Durbin with her baby, was on the way to Deadwood to join her prospector husband, and had been carrying $10,000 secreted in a bag. This money was for W.R. Stebbins to open a bank in Deadwood, which he did on April 6, 1877. She would recall trembling when she saw the buckshot holes that peppered the stage that preceded her. Spring, *Cheyenne and Black Hills Stage*, 192-94. General speculation as to who was responsible for the March 25 holdup attempt targeted another Black Hills bandit known as "Persimmon Bill."*Cheyenne Daily Leader*, 28 March 1877.

66. Bridwell, *Robert McKimie*, 4-5,19; *Cheyenne Daily Leader*, 30 January 1878. McKimie subsequently escaped from the Hillsboro, Ohio, jail on 11 February 1878, sparking another manhunt for him. *Cheyenne Daily Leader*, 20, 21 February 1878.

67. Brown and Willard, *Black Hills Trails*, 247.

68. Engebretson, *Empty Saddles*, 140-43.

V. STAGECOACH AND TRAIN ROBBERY

1. Spring, *Cheyenne and Black Hills Stage*, 195.

2. *Cheyenne Daily Leader*, 3 June 1877.

3. *Cheyenne Daily Leader*, 10 June 1877.

4. *Cheyenne Daily Leader*, 15 June 1877.

5. Spring, *Cheyenne and Black Hills Stage*, 209.

6. *Cheyenne Daily Leader*, 27, 28 June 1877.

7. *Cheyenne Daily Leader*, 28, 29 June 1877, 8 July 1877.

8. *Cheyenne Daily Leader*, 28 June 1877.

9. *Cheyenne Daily Leader*, 29 June 1877.

10. Engebretson, *Empty Saddles*, 55-56; Spring, *Cheyenne and Black Hills Stage*, 210; *Cheyenne Daily Leader*, 22 August 1877; Bridwell, *Robert McKimie*, 7-8.

11. *Cheyenne Daily Leader*, 7 July 1877.

12. *Deadwood Times*, 12 July 1877, as quoted in the *Cheyenne Daily Leader*, 17 July 1877.

13. *Deadwood Champion*, as quoted in the *Cheyenne Daily Leader*, 18 July 1877.

14. *Cheyenne Daily Leader*, 19 July 1877.

15. *Cheyenne Daily Leader*, 20 July 1877.

16. *Cheyenne Daily Leader*, 25 July 1877.

17. *Black Hills Daily Times* [Deadwood], 28 July 1877, 3 August 1877.

18. Letter dated 9 August 1877 from George C. Bates to the *Detroit Free Press*, as quoted in the *Cheyenne Daily Leader*, 14 August 1877.

19. *Cheyenne Daily Leader*, 17 August 1877.

20. James Franklin Ellison was born in Mississippi about 1828. He married Evelin Jaminey in Mississippi on September 13, 1849, then moved immediately to Texas. When the Civil War broke out, he enlisted in Company K, 32nd Texas Cavalry, on February 7, 1862, then became a farmer and stock raiser in Hays and Caldwell Counties. The 1880 census shows they had at least seven children. He died on December 14, 1903, in Hays County. 1880 Caldwell County, Texas,

ENDNOTES

Census, 272 (279/179); Texas State Library, Confederate Pension Applications, Files No. 8721 and 10260.
21. G.W. Mills, "Experiences 'Tenderfeet' Could Not Survive," *Trail Drivers of Texas*, 235.
22. *Cheyenne Daily Leader*, 26 August 1877.
23. Hogg, *Authentic History*, 36-40.
24. Sorenson, *Hands Up!*, 13.
25. Marley Brant, *Outlaws: The Illustrated History of the James-Younger Gang* (Montgomery, Alabama: Elliott & Clark Publishing, 1997), 90-118; Richard Patterson, *The Train Robbery Era* (Boulder, Colorado: Pruett Publishing Co., 1991), 113-15.
26. McClintock, *Pioneer Days*, 211.
27. Sorenson, *Hands Up!*, 49.
28. Hogg, *Authentic History*, 43-44.
29. Sorenson, *Hands Up!*, 49-50.
30. Hogg, *Authentic History*, 44.
31. Sorenson, *Hands Up!*, 50-53.
32. Capt. J.H. Cook, "Early Days in Ogallala," *Nebraska History Magazine*, Vol. XIV, No. 2 (April-June 1933), 92-94.
33. Bennett R. Pearce, "Night of Terror at Big Springs," *The West*, Vol. 14, No. 6 (May 1971), 20; Sorenson, *Hands Up!*, 14.
34. Pearce, "Night of Terror," 20; *Cheyenne Daily Leader*, 19 September 1877, identifies him as J.W. Barnhart.
35. *Ford County Times*, as quoted in the *Hays City Sentinel*, 5 October 1877, 3.
36. Sorenson, *Hands Up!*, 61. M.F.
37. *Mexico Ledger*, 18 October 1877, 3. M.F. Leach was born on November 24, 1850, on a farm at Tionesta, Pennsylvania. When he was fifteen he moved to Meadville where he was a hotel clerk, during which time he also learned telegraphy. Because of ill health he left in 1870 for Tennessee, where he became an engineer for the Nashville and Lebanon Railroad. Leach reportedly left the railroad to hunt "moonshiners" in the Tennessee hills. Another account stated that the existence of a large illegal whiskey operation in Kentucky led to his use as an agent, posing as a messenger boy in telegraph offices until the telegraph operators affiliated with the illegal operation could be identified and arrested. Leach then went to Omaha and on to Wyoming as a telegraph operator for the Union Pacific.
According to Leach many years later, he tired of the railroad job and became a trader among the Sioux Indians for about three years, learning their language and customs. As a government detective, he claimed to have arrested Mormon John D. Lee for his involvement in the "Mountain Meadows massacre," for which Lee was executed on March 23, 1877. Leach also claimed to have been a guide for General Crook during the Sioux wars in the mid-1870s, after which he continued to work as a detective. At the time of the Union Pacific robbery by Collins and his men, Leach had been in Ogallala for several years. *New York Times*, 24 February 1895, 9; Sorenson, *Hands Up!*, 58-59. Varying accounts also spell the name as "Leech," but "Leach" is the predominant spelling.
38. *Chicago Times*, 21 September 1877, as quoted in the *Denison Daily News*, 30 September 1877.
39. George W. Vroman was born in Fitchburg, Wisconsin, on September 27, 1841. In 1862 he moved to Lafayette, Indiana, where he worked as a fireman on the Wabash Railroad for several years, then as an engineer for five years. He arrived in North Platte, Nebraska, in January 1869 where he worked as an engineer between North Platte and Sidney until May 1881. He was married in 1874 to Mary E. Jordon of Brownstown, Indiana, and they had three children. He and his brother, W.A. Vroman, were proprietors of a sheep ranch thirty miles east of North Platte. *History of the State of Nebraska* (Chicago: The Western Historical Co., 1882), Vol. 2, 1101; *Cheyenne Daily Leader*, 21 September 1977. An "H.C.

321

Vrooman" is listed as a locomotive engineer in Omaha in the 1880 Douglas County, Nebraska, Census, 277, Line 16.

40. *Denison Daily News*, 21 September 1877.

41. *Omaha Weekly Herald*, 21 September 1877; Sorenson, *Hands Up!*, 15.

42. *Cheyenne Daily Leader*, 19 September 1877. In 1880, Borie lived in Laramie with his 20-year-old wife, F.M. from Illinois, and their one-year-old son, Guy D. His sister-in-law, Addie Dudley, nineteen, also lived with them. 1880 Albany County, Wyoming Territory, Census, 12 (202/222).

43. Hogg, *Authentic History*, 45.

44. *Cheyenne Daily Leader*, 21 September 1877; *Denison Daily News*, 30 September 1877, 6; Hogg, *Authentic History*, 45. There are two conductors named M.M. Patterson in the 1880 Laramie Census, one aged thirty-one from Iowa, the other aged thirty from New York. See 1880 Laramie County, Wyoming Territory, 181 (528/561) and 186 (623/660).

45. *Cheyenne Daily Leader*, 21 September 1877, 22 September 1877; *Cheyenne Daily Sun*, 30 September 1877; *Life and Adventures of Sam Bass*, 13; Pearce, "Night of Terror," 21.

46. *Omaha Weekly Herald*, 21 September 1877.

47. *Chicago Times*, 21 September 1877, as quoted in the *Denison Daily News*, 30 September 1877, 6.

48. *Omaha Weekly Herald*, 21 September 1877, 4, and 28 September 1877, Supp. 1; Sorenson, *Hands Up!*, 24-25, 30.

49. *Denison Daily News*, 30 September 1877, 6; *Cheyenne Daily Leader*, 21 September 1877.

50. *Cheyenne Daily Leader*, 21 September 1877; Sorenson, *Hands Up!*, 32-33. A John R. Brophy is listed in the 1880 Albany County census as a thirty-five-year-old conductor from Ireland, with a New York-born wife, Mary. See 1880 Albany County, Wyoming Territory, Census, 8 (131/143).

51. *Omaha Weekly Herald*, 21 September 1877, 4.

52. *Cheyenne Daily Leader*, 19 September 1877, 21 September 1877.

53. *Cheyenne Daily Leader*, 19 September 1877, 1.

54. *Cheyenne Daily Leader*, 19 September 1877, 1.

55. *The Commonwealth* [Topeka, Kansas], 29 September 1877, 1; *Council Bluffs Nonpareil*, as quoted in *San Antonio Daily Express*, 10 October 1877, 2; *Cheyenne Daily Leader*, 29 September 1877.

VI. DEATH AT BUFFALO STATION

1. Pearce, "Night of Terror," 23.

2. *Cheyenne Daily Sun*, 30 September 1877.

3. *Omaha Weekly Herald*, 21 September 1877; 1880 Douglas County, Nebraska, Census, 197 (63/63).

4. UPRR Collection, Nebraska State Historical Society, MS 3761, Unit 1, 1862-1880, SG8 Sec.-Treas. S2 McFarland, H., Vol. 25, p. 296 (20 September 1877); and MS 3761, SG 8, S1, Box 29, Folder 1202 (20 September 1877)

5. *Cheyenne Daily Leader*, 20 September 1877.

6. National Archives, RG 393, Records of the U.S. Army Continental Commands, 1821-1920, Fort Robinson, Nebraska, Department of the Platte, Special Orders, Vol. 2, 1877, No. 415; Muster Roll, 9th Infantry, Camp Robinson, Nebraska, Returns From Military Posts, Roll No. 1028, Microfilm No. M617.

7. National Archives, RG 94, Records of the Adjutant General's Office, 1780s-1914, Post Returns, North Platte, Nebraska, March 1875-December 1877 (September 30, 1877); Records of the U.S. Army, 1821-1920, Department of the Platte, Headquarters Records, Letters Sent, 1866-1898, Vol. 4, p. 483, Item 936 (September 21, 1877); Larry D. Ball, "The United States Army and the Big

Springs, Nebraska, Train Robbery of 1877," *Journal of the West*, Vol. 34, No. 1 (January 1995), 35.

8. Hogg, *Authentic History*, 48.

9. Sorenson, *Hands Up!*, 55.

10. *Cheyenne Daily Leader*, 28 September 1877.

11. *Cheyenne Daily Leader*, 28 September 1877.

12. *Omaha Weekly Herald*, 21 September 1877, 4.

13. Affidavit by David E. Burley, Douglas County, Nebraska, 18 October 1877 (courtesy of Robert G. McCubbin, Jr., El Paso). An Alfred Burley was Sheriff of Douglas County, Nebraska (Omaha), 1873-1875. See *History of the State of Nebraska*, Vol. 1, 695.

14. *Mexico Ledger*, 18 October 1877, 3; *New York Times*, 24 February 1895, 9; Sorenson, *Hands Up!*, 58, 61.

15. *New York Times*, 24 February 1895, 9; Sorenson, *Hands Up!*, 63.

16. *New York Times*, 24 February 1895, 9.

17. Sorenson, *Hands Up!*, 102.

18. 1880 Douglas County, Nebraska, Census, 335 (283/288).

19. *New York Times*, 24 February 1895, 9; Sorenson, *Hands Up!*, 83.

20. *Cheyenne Daily Leader*, 23 September 1877, 1; 26 September 1877, 1.

21. *Cheyenne Daily Sun*, 23 September 1877.

22. National Archives, Records of U.S. Army, 1821-1920, Letters & Telegrams Received, 1867-1889, Fort Hays, Kansas, 1876-1878, Box 6 (25 September 1877).

23. National Archives, Records of U.S. Army, 1821-1920, Letters & Telegrams Received, 1867-1889, Fort Hays, Kansas, 1876-1878, Box 6 (25 September 1877); Ball, "The United States Army and the Big Springs, Nebraska, Train Robbery," 37.

24. National Archives, Returns From Military Posts, Fort Wallace, Kansas, October 31, 1877, Microfilm M617, Roll No. 1340; Ball, "The United States Army and the Big Springs, Nebraska, Train Robbery," 37.

25. National Archives, Records of the U.S. Army, Continental Command, Department of the Missouri, 1861-1898, Letters Received, 1877 (3002-3705), Box 67, Letter 3644(2).

26. National Archives, Returns From U.S. Military Posts, 1800-1916, Fort Elliott, Texas (September 1877), Microfilm 617, Roll 346.

27. National Archives (Central Plains Region-Kansas City, Mo.), *Bardsley v. Union Pacific Railroad et al*, United States Circuit Court, District of Nebraska, Cause No. 295D (Depositions of O. Branham and Capt. Duncan M. Vance). George W. Bardsley was born on February 22, 1844, at West Wheeling, West Virginia, to English parents. After working as a cigar maker, he served in the Civil War as a private in Company K, 1st West Virginia Cavalry, from September 1861 until December 1864. It is believed that after the war he came west as a buffalo hunter and briefly served as a scout at Fort Hays in October 1868. He established himself as a saloonkeeper in Hays City in a one-story frame building proudly designated as the "Bardsley House." He also bought three lots in April 1869 on which to build a home. By September 1877 he and his wife Sarah, who was born in Ohio in 1852, had three children, although one later died in 1873. Bardsley was appointed as an Ellis County commissioner in 1874. On November 2, 1875, he was elected sheriff, at the same time opening a new restaurant and boarding house just north of the Kansas Pacific depot. "Fifty cents will buy as good a meal as ever was spread in Hays; and fifty cents will charter a bed that would even woo the wakeful Gods to slumber," he advertised.

The new sheriff was not permitted to enter office graciously. The defeated incumbent, former Deputy U.S. Marshal Jack Bridges, did not take defeat in good spirit and mounted a campaign in the courts through a series of harassment suits against Bardsley, including a suit alleging that the new sheriff had bet on a horse race. In September 1876, after receiving word from Buffalo Station railroad agent William Sternberg of the presence there of a large band of notorious horse thieves, Bardsley borrowed arms from Fort Hays, organized a posse and took a train to Buffalo Station. The posse came upon the gang in its camp and quickly arrested the bandits. One of the rustlers, "Big Ike" Cramer, was pursued and wounded, but the posse failed to nab "Chummy" Jones and "Dutch Henry." In January 1877, when Bardsley tried to relieve Texan John Connor of a pistol while Connor was in the middle of a freewheeling "jamboree," Connor took a shot at him and the sheriff wounded him in the arm with a shotgun. 1880 Ellis County, Kansas, Census, Hays City, 437 (55); Deed Records, Ellis County, Kansas, Vol. B, 219; Vol. C, 276; Application for Admission to Colorado State Soldiers' and Sailors' Home, Homelake, Colorado, No. 2068 (November 2, 1927), Courtesy Ellis County, Kansas, Historical Society; Fr. Blaine Burkey, "Sheriff George Bardsley," At Home in Ellis County, Kansas, 1867-1992 (Dallas, Texas: Taylor Publishing Co., 1991), Vol. I, 117-20; Hays City Sentinel, 6 September 1876.

28. National Archives, Records of the U.S. Army, Department of the Missouri, 1861-1898, Letters Received 1877, 3002-3705, Box 67, Letter 3703(2); Hays City Sentinel, 12 October 1877, 3; National Archives (Central Plains Region-Kansas City, Mo.), George W. Bardsley v. Union Pacific Railroad et al, U.S. Circuit Court, District of Nebraska, Cause No. 295D (deposition of Duncan M. Vance). Second Lieutenant Leven C. Allen was born in Missouri and was graduated from the United States Military Academy on June 14, 1872. He initially served at the garrison at Nashville, Tennessee, until July 1876, then was briefly assigned to temporary duties at Chattanooga, Tennessee; Mount Vernon Barracks, Alabama; Baton Rouge, Louisiana; and New Orleans. Allen was permanently assigned to "frontier duty" with Company G of the 16th Infantry at Fort Hays, Kansas, and arrived there on June 10, 1877, with his new commander, Captain Duncan Vance, and another newly assigned officer. George W. Cullum, Biographical Register of the Officers and Graduates of the U.S. Military Academy, 3rd ed. (New York: Houghton, Mifflin & Co., 1891), Vol. III, 197; National Archives, RG 94, Adjutant General's Office, Regular Army Muster Rolls, Company G, 16th Infantry, Fort Hays, Kansas, 31 December 1861 - 31 December 1877.

29. National Archives (Central Plains Region-Kansas City, Mo.), George W. Bardsley v. Union Pacific Railroad et al, U.S. Circuit Court, District of Nebraska, Cause No. 295D (depositions of O. Branham, Francis Toohey, William M. Eddy, William Graff, Hiram A. Doliver, Octavous A. Shindlebower, and Charles F. Sloan); National Archives, Records of U.S. Army, Department of Missouri 1861-1898, Letters Received 1877, 3002-3705, Box 67, Letter 3703(2); Hays City Sentinel, 12 October 1877, 3; Kansas City Times, as quoted in San Antonio Daily Express, 3 October 1877, 4.

30. Albert B. and Mary T. Tuttle, History and Heritage of Gove County, Kansas (n.p., 1982), 40-42; 1880 Gove County, Kansas, Census, Buffalo Park, 191 (129/138); William A. Sternberg, "The Big Springs Robbery of 1877," Union Pacific Magazine (December 1923), 28. Sternberg was later the Union Pacific agent at Wilson and Ellsworth, Kansas, and by 1923 was a seventy-one-year-old realtor in Tacoma, Washington.

31. Tuttle and Tuttle, History and Heritage of Gove County, Kansas, 41.

32. National Archives, Records of U.S. Army, Department of Missouri 1861-1898, Letters Received 1877, 3002-3705, Box 67, Letter 3703(2); National Archives (Central Plains Region, Kansas City, Mo.), George W. Bardsley v. Union Pacific Railroad et al, U.S. Circuit Court, District of Nebraska, Cause No. 295D (depositions of William Eddy, Francis Toohey, and Hiram Doliver).

33. National Archives (Central Plains Region-Kansas City, Mo.), George W. Bardsley v. Union Pacific Railroad et al, U.S. Circuit Court, District of Nebraska, Cause No. 295D (depositions of Charles W. Talmadge, William M. Eddy, Charles F. Sloan, William A. Sternberg, James L. Thompson, Francis Toohey, William Graff, Octavous Shindlebower). Later press accounts stated that Collins told Potts something to the effect that "By God! We will die game," but there was

no evidence such statements were made in testimony by eyewitnesses. See *Hays City Sentinel*, 28 September 1877; Hogg, *Authentic History*, 53; *Life and Adventures of Sam Bass*, 16; *Kansas City Times*, as quoted by the *San Antonio Daily Express*, 3 October 1877; Sternberg, "Big Springs Robbery," 30.

34. *The Commonwealth* [Topeka, Ks.], 27 September 1877, 1.

35. National Archives (Central Plains Region-Kansas City, Mo.), *George W. Bardsley v. Union Pacific Railroad et al*, U.S. Circuit Court, District of Nebraska, Cause No. 295D (depositions of William A. Eddy, William A. Sternberg, James L. Thompson, Francis Toohey, Octavous Shindlebower, William Graff, and Charles F. Sloan); *Hays City Sentinel*, 12 October 1877, 3; Sorenson, *Hands Up!*, 96; Sternberg, "Big Springs Robbery," 30.

36. National Archives (Central Plains Region-Kansas City, Mo.), *George W. Bardsley v. Union Pacific Railroad et al*, U.S. Circuit Court, District of Nebraska, Cause No. 295D (depositions of William A. Sternberg, Charles F. Sloan, Hiram A. Doliver); National Archives, Records of the U.S. Army, Department of Missouri 1861-1898, Letters Received 1877, 3002-3705, Box 67, Letter 3703(2).

37. National Archives, Records of the U.S. Army, Department of Missouri 1861-1898, Letters Received 1877, 3002-3705, Box 67, Letter 3703(2); National Archives, RG 94, Adjutant General's Office, Regular Army Muster Rolls, Company G, 16th Infantry, Fort Hays, Kansas, 31 December 1861-31 December 1877.

38. Captain Peter M. Boehm, who had been ordered to take twenty-four soldiers of the 4th Cavalry east by train from Fort Wallace, arrived at Buffalo Station with his men at about 6:00 p.m. on Wednesday, September 26, when they learned of the death of Potts and Collins earlier that morning. Boehm then split his unit into three detachments, sending one on to Ellis and a second with Sheriff Bardsley to investigate a report that two men had crossed the Kansas Pacific tracks at Trego Station, about halfway between Buffalo Station and Hays City to the east. Boehm accompanied the third detachment north to the Sappa River to investigate a report by Sheriff Bradley of North Platte that robbers were in that area. Anthony W. "Tony" Waits of Ogallala, Nebraska, perhaps a Pinkerton detective, was with Boehm's party when it left the Sappa and rode on to Fort Dodge, arriving there on September 29.

In the meantime, Lt. D.A. Irwin, who joined Boehm's detachment at Ellis, received a telegram on the afternoon of September 28 reporting that two men fitting the description of the robbers had eaten dinner on the 26th at a ranch on the Pawnee River, due south of the Trego Station, and had continued south from there. Irwin and the detachment searched for the suspects but without finding any trace of them, although the soldiers did hear a report that suspected robbers had crossed the Atchison, Topeka & Santa Fe line near the Ofley Station, perhaps headed toward Dodge City. National Archives, Records of the U.S. Army, Continental Command, Department of the Missouri 1861-1898, Letters Received 1877, 3717-4441, Box 68, Letter 3935(2). When Union Pacific Superintendent Morsman telegraphed Ford County Sheriff Charles Bassett at Dodge City that the robbers would likely cross the AT&SF line near Lakin in Kearney County some eighty-five miles to the west, the lawman gathered his undersheriff, William B. "Bat" Masterson, and John Webb. They took the train out on the morning of Thursday, September 27, returning the next day after finding no sign. Upon their return to Dodge City, there was another report that five men had crossed the track on Thursday morning about thirty miles west of the city. Bassett, Masterson and Webb scouted southwest on horseback to try to intercept them while Masterson's brother, Ed, and Deputy Sheriff Miles Mix went west on a train to find any information about the robbers. Nothing was found and the parties returned to Dodge City. *Dodge City Times*, 29 September 1877, as quoted in Nyle H. Miller and Joseph W. Snell, *Great Gunfighters of the Kansas Cowtowns, 1867-1886* (Lincoln, Nebraska: University of Nebraska Press, 1973), 26; Robert K. DeArment, *Bat Masterson*

(Norman, Oklahoma: University of Oklahoma Press, 1979), 85.

39. National Archives (Central Plains Region, Kansas City, Mo.), *George W. Bardsley v. Union Pacific Railroad et al*, U.S. Circuit Court, District of Nebraska, Cause No. 295D (depositions of Charles W. Talmadge, William Eddy, Charles Sloan); *Hays City Sentinel*, 28 September 1877, 12 October 1877, 3.

40. National Archives (Central Plains Region, Kansas City, Mo.), *George W. Bardsley v. Union Pacific Railroad et al*, U.S. Circuit Court, District of Nebraska, Cause No. 295D (deposition of Morgan Cox); *Wichita Weekly Beacon*, 3 October 1877, 1.

41. *Louisiana Journal*, as quoted in *Callaway Weekly Gazette*, 26 October 1877, 4. An "Anna Lang" died in Ellis on April 7, 1951, but was too young to have been the woman who identified Potts' body. See Probate Records, Ellis County, Kansas, *Estate of Anna Lang*, Cause No. 1562, Vol. 3, 606.

42. *The Omaha Bee*, as quoted in the *Hays City Sentinel*, 19 October 1877, 1.

43. *Hays City Sentinel*, 12 October 1877, 2-3. The gravesites of Joel Collins and Bill Potts could not be located in either Ellis, Kansas, or Dallas, Texas.

44. *Cheyenne Daily Leader*, 9 October 1877.

45. *Hays City Sentinel*, 19 October 1877, 4.

46. *Cheyenne Daily Leader*, 27 October 1877.

47. National Archives, Records of the U.S. Army 1821-1920, Letters & Telegrams Received, 1867-1889, Fort Hays, Kansas, 1876-1878, Box 6.

48. National Archives (Central Plains Region-Kansas City, Mo.), *George W. Bardsley v. Union Pacific Railroad et al*, U.S. Circuit Court, District of Nebraska, Cause No. 295D.

VII. THE LAW IN PURSUIT

1. UPRR Collection, Nebraska State Historical Society, MS 3761, Unit 1 1862-1880, SG8 Sec.-Treas. S2 McFarland, H., Vol. 25, 324, 340, 345; UPRR Collection, Nebraska State Historical Society, MS 3761, SG8, S1, Box 29, Folder 1202.

2. *Cheyenne Daily Leader*, 9 October 1877.

3. Center for American History, University of Texas at Austin, Transcripts From the Office of the Adjutant General of Texas, 1877, File No. 2Q400, Vol. 9(B), 127-29; Texas State Library, Lists of Fugitives, Frontier Battalion, Box 401-1160.

4. *New York Times*, 24 February 1895, 9; Sorenson, *Hands Up!*, 107; *Mexico Ledger*, 18 October 1877, 3.

5. Sorenson, *Hands Up!*, 108.

6. *Mexico Intelligencer*, 14 October 1877, as quoted by the *Hays City Sentinel*, 19 October 1877, 3.

7. *Mexico Ledger*, 18 October 1877, 3; *Mexico Intelligencer*, 14 October 1877, as quoted in the *Hays City Sentinel*, 19 October 1877, 3.

8. *Moberly Monitor*, 11 October 1877, as quoted in *Life and Adventures of Sam Bass*, 20.

9. *Hays City Sentinel*, 19 October 1877, 4; *Denison Daily News*, 13 October 1877, 1.

10. Sorenson, *Hands Up!*, 114-16. Missouri-born Harrison "Harry" Glasscock, forty, and his wife Mercy, thirty-eight, lived on a farm on Hickory Creek in Audrain County. They had two children of their own plus two adopted sons. 1870 Audrain County, Missouri, Census, Hickory Creek Post Office (77/75); 1880 Audrain County, Missouri, Census, Mexico, 137 (264/317).

11. *Moberly Monitor*, as quoted in *Life and Adventures of Sam Bass*, 20-21.

12. Sorenson, *Hands Up!*, 116-18.

13. Sorenson, *Hands Up!*, 119.

14. R.T. Kasey was born in Virginia about 1846 and farmed with his wife Mary not far from Jim Berry's place on Nine Mile Prairie in Callaway County. 1870 Callaway County, Missouri, Census, Williamsburg P.O., 400 (90/93). Morris Blum, fifty-six, was born in France and operated his store with his son Gabriel, twenty-four, also born in France. 1880 Audrain County, Missouri, Census, Mexico, 136 (242/286).

15. 1880 Audrain County, Missouri, Census, Mexico, 126 (70/71).

16. 1870 Audrain County, Missouri, Census, Mexico, 537-38 (130/118). The Robert Steele in the 1870 Audrain County census lived in his father's household in Salt River Township and is shown to be twenty-eight, Missouri-born, and a city marshal; his brothers John and David were deputy sheriffs. The 1880 Audrain County Census lists two men named Robert Steele: Robert S., a dry goods clerk in Mexico, age thirty-four, from Missouri, the other a thirty-five-year-old farmer from Canada who lived in Prairie Township.

17. *Mexico Ledger*, 18 October 1877, 3; *Mexico Intelligencer*, 14 October 1877, as quoted in the *Hays City Sentinel*, 19 October 1877, 3; *Callaway Weekly Gazette*, 19 October 1877, 2; *Fulton Telegraph*, 26 October 1877, 2.

18. 1870 Audrain County, Missouri, Census, Mexico, 555 (410/376).

19. 1870 Audrain County, Missouri, Census, Mexico, 543 (218/194). Dr. Rothwell married Carie Adams on May 10, 1865, in Audrain County, and by 1870 had one daughter, Clarina, four. See Elizabeth Prater Ellsberry, *Marriage Records of Audrain County, Missouri, 1836-1879* (Chillicothe, Missouri: Elizabeth Prater Ellsberry, n.d.), 66.

20. *Mexico Ledger*, 14 October 1877, 3; *Mexico Intelligencer*, as quoted in the *St. Louis Missouri Republican*, 22 October 1877, 2; 1860 Callaway County, Missouri, Census, 923 (967/999).

21. *St. Louis Missouri Republican*, 17 October 1877, 2.

22. *Callaway Weekly Gazette*, 26 October 1877, 3; *St. Louis Missouri Republican*, 22 October 1877, 2; *Liberty Church Cemetery*, Callaway County, Missouri, Public Library: Berry is buried next to his parents in Tier 17.

23. *Mexico Ledger*, 18 October 1877, 3.

24. *Callaway Weekly Gazette*, 26 October 1877, 3.

25. *New York Times*, 25 October 1877, 1.

26. Sorenson, *Hands Up!*, 136-37.

27. *Fulton Telegraph*, 26 October 1877, 3; Probate Records, Callaway County, Missouri, *Estate of James F. Berry*, Bundle 6, Box 77.

28. Affidavit by David E. Burley, Douglas County, 18 October 1877, Nebraska (Courtesy of Robert G. McCubbin, Jr., El Paso).

29. Hogg, *Authentic History*, 48-49; *Life and Adventures of Sam Bass*, 24-25.

30. Hogg, *Authentic History*, 24. Twenty miles from Gainesville, the Cooke County seat, Rosston was well along as a community when, on January 5, 1865, Indians from the north raided, killing nine people and stealing many horses. Four Ross brothers moved there in 1870 from Grayson County and established a mercantile store, cotton gin and a mill. By 1872 the town had its own postoffice, and the Butterfield Overland Mail passed near there as it ferried mail between Gainesville and Jacksboro. Tyler, ed., *The New Handbook of Texas*, Vol. 5, 693; Gard, *Sam Bass*, 98.

31. *Life and Adventures of Sam Bass*, 24-25.

32. A settler listed in the 1850 Denton County census, Kentucky-born Henderson Murphy was elected county treasurer on November 4, 1856, when Denton was selected as county seat. He moved to the town of Denton in 1857, next to Tom Egan on the square, and erected a log hotel, the Transcontinental, later the Murphy Hotel. He and his Ohio-born wife Ruth had at least nine children, beginning with Maranda about 1846. Robert Murphy was born about 1848 in Texas and James W. "Jim" Murphy was born about 1853.

By 1874 Henderson Murphy was a partner with William Riley Wetsel in the

Parlor Saloon next to Dr. Ross' drug store, boasting liquors of all kinds, cigars and oysters for sale, as well as sardines, crackers and canned fruits, and featuring a good billiard table. In that same year Murphy was taxed for 1,400 cattle, thirty-two horses, four lots and other property totaling $21,460. Bob Murphy continued to work in cattle and by 1870 was on his own with his wife Elizabeth and two small children, Jesse and Minerva. Jim Murphy continued to live with his parents and worked as a cowboy. Jim was described as "of quiet manner, slow gait, heavy cast of features, rather dull expresion....Underneath all he carries a comfortable ease and looks as though it would be hard to rouse his 200 pounds of flesh. He wears a red mustache and chin beard; has small blue eyes..." 1850 Denton County, Texas, Census (33); 1860 Denton County, Texas, Census, 403 (134/135); 1870 Denton County, Texas, Census, 116 (4/4; 14/14); 1880 Denton County, Texas, Census, 168 (187/187); *Galveston Daily News*, 24 July 1878, 1; *Denton Monitor*, 3 December 1874; *Denton Record-Chronicle*, 3 February 1957; *Inventory Book, Precinct No. 1 For 1874*, 57; Deed Records, Denton County, Texas, Vol. B, 100; Genealogical Records, Denton County Historical Museum, Denton, Texas.

33. *Galveston Daily News*, 24 July 1878, 1.

34. The earliest official record of Francis M. "Frank" Jackson is the 1860 Llano County, Texas, census. Reportedly born on June 10, 1856, in Llano County, he was the third child of Robert J. and Phoebe C. Jackson.

Robert Jackson was born in Tennessee about 1809 and settled with his first wife in Yell County, Arkansas, where his first child, daughter Caroline, was born about 1835. Probably widowed, Jackson remarried to Phoebe C. Barker in the mid-1840s. She was born in North Carolina about 1838 to Warren and Margaret Barker, who themselves had come to farm in Yell County via Kentucky by 1850. Robert and Phoebe's first child was daughter Mary F., born about 1846. David Warren Jackson was born in Yell County on December 25, 1849. The family moved to Llano County in the mid-1850s where a third child, Maranda A., was born in 1854 or 1855.

After the birth of Frank in 1856, the next known child was a daughter, Sarah, born about 1862, who would be called "Sallie." A final child, William Riley Jackson, was born about 1863. The tax assessment rolls for Llano County list R.J. Jackson between 1857 and 1864, showing him with 320 acres in 1857 and 1858, but apparently no land after that and owning only horses and cattle. Also on the rolls are George and William Barker, likely Phoebe's brothers. In 1864 the tax assesment entry is "Jackson, R.J. by Barker, W.," and after that there are no further entries for the Jackson family. According to Hogg, Robert and Phoebe Jackson were pious Methodists and, although listed as a farmer in the 1850 census, Robert was an industrious blacksmith. He reportedly died in 1863, followed the next year by his wife.

The orphaned Jackson children apparently returned to Arkansas where they lived with various of Phoebe's relatives. Phoebe's brother, William H. Barker, a farmer in Carroll County, Arkansas, who had six children of his own in 1870, made a home for Frank and his brother Billy, as shown in the census for that year. Hogg stated that another uncle, Joseph Barker, took the children in tow, but had limited means and could not provide the necessary attention.

For some unknown reason the Jackson children were moved to Denton County in 1871 and found homes with various families. Frank was supposed to have lived for several years with Dr. Robert S. Ross in the town of Denton. A physician, Ross was born in Mississippi on July 31, 1840, and was living in Denton by 1870 with his wife, Mary J., with whom he would have two sons and a daughter before her death on June 16, 1879. Ross owned 177 acres in 1877 and contracted with the county to treat paupers and prisoners. While living with Ross Frank was said to have performed his duties "as a hireling with fidelity...giving satisfaction to his employer."

Frank's sister Maranda married Denton tinsmith Benizett A. Key, who had his shop on the west side of the Denton square. Key was born in Ohio on September 4, 1836, and was reportedly a telegraph operator in the Union Army during the Civil War. He first showed up in Denton County deed records in April 1874. He and Maranda Jackson must have married about 1873, as by 1880 they had three children, the oldest six years old. Key was called on quite frequently to make stovepipe and other metal items, even for the county courthouse. No doubt because his sister was married to Key, and his younger sister Sallie lived there, Frank moved in around 1876, apprenticing himself to his brother-in-law to learn the tinner's trade.

The first real indication of Frank Jackson's underlying variance from his family's norms occurred in May 1876. Henry Goodall, a large, burly black man, was reportedly one of Denton County's dangerous characters. Goodall was listed in 1874 as owning three horses and ten dollars in miscellaneous property, and in the 1875 county tax rolls with two horses or mules. Goodall would be indelicately remembered as a "notorious thief and desperado,...the scourge of his own race and an incarnate insult to the public generally." About this time Jackson was working as a cowboy with Jim Murphy. Somehow he and Goodall became embroiled in a dispute involving the trade of a gun and a horse. According to Hogg, Goodall was in possession of the horse claimed by Jackson, and Jackson threatened to kill him if he did not replace the horse. After some discussion Goodall agreed to replace the horse with another one, and on May 7, 1876, they rode together out onto the prairie to find a replacement horse.

While they rode searching for the animal, they stopped to drink at a spring. Goodall took a drink first, then Jackson stooped over the spring. According to Jackson, Goodall drew a revolver, pointed it at the cowboy's head and said, "I've got you where I want you, and intend to kill you right here." Jackson leaped at the black man and the pistol discharged, the ball passing through Jackson's trousers but not injuring him. The two grappled, each now firing at the other, and a ball hit Goodall, killing him. In Hogg's account, Goodall was hit in the side, then mounted a horse to escape and Jackson pursued, shooting him in the head and killing him. Jackson returned to Denton and a rumor spread that he had cut the dead man's throat or cut off his head, but no evidence was ever established that such had occurred, and his explanation of self-defense was grudgingly accepted. While many in Denton disbelieved Jackson's version, the evidence was insufficient to bring an indictment and there is no record that he was ever prosecuted. The fact that Henry Goodall was a bad black man likely diminished the importance of his death in the eyes of prominent white citizens.

In February 1877, during a rash of thefts in Denton, a horse belonging to Jackson was stolen along with one belonging to his brother-in-law, Ben Key. The two looked everywhere for the thieves but to no avail. 1850 Yell County, Arkansas, Census, 497 (55/55), 502 (44/44); 1860 Llano County, Texas, Census, 384 (208/208); Hogg, *Authentic History*, 24-27, 29; Certificate of Death (David Warren Jackson), Montague County, Texas, No. 51905; 1870 Denton County, Texas, Census, 116 (10/10); 1880 Denton County, Texas, Census, 3 (39/39). Sarah Jackson, 18, is listed as a sister-in-law of Benizett Key, who married her sister, Maranda Jackson; *Oakwood Cemetery, Denton, Texas* (Denton, Texas: Denton County Genealogical Society, 1989), 26; Tax Assessment Rolls, Llano County, Texas, 1857-1865; 1870 Carroll County, Arkansas, Census, 66-67 (230/232); *IOOF Cemetery, Denton, Texas*, 12, 22; Tax Assessment Rolls, Denton County, Texas, 1877; Commissioners Court Minutes, Denton County, Texas, Vol. A, 10. Dr. Ross would remarry Sarah Forester in Denton County on December 22, 1881, and would die on February 8, 1890. See Vinita Davis, *Marriage Records Index, Denton County, Texas, 1875-1884* (Fort Worth, Texas: American Reference Publishing Co., 1972), 32; Deed Records, Denton County, Texas, Vol. B, 343; Letter from E.S. Key, Fort Worth, to Alex Williams, Denton, 17 August 1963 (Courtesy Jim Browning, Charleston, South Carolina); Commissioners Court

Minutes, Denton County, Texas, Vol. A, 11; *Inventory Book, Precinct No. 1 for 1874,* 93; Tax Assessment Rolls, Denton County, Texas, 1875; *Brenham Banner,* 19 May 1876, 2; Hogg, *Authentic History,* 26-27; *Life and Adventures of Sam Bass,* 38-39; *Galveston Daily News,* 27 April 1878, 2; *Denton Monitor,* 16 February 1877, as quoted in Bates, *History and Reminiscences,* 394-395.

35. Hogg, *Authentic History,* 57-58; Letter From E.S. Key, Fort Worth, to Alex Williams, Denton, 17 August 1963 (Courtesy Jim Browning, Charleston, South Carolina); Martin, *Sketch of Sam Bass,* 76.

36. *Galveston Daily News,* 27 April 1878, 2.

37. Hogg, *Authentic History,* 58.

38. Gard, *Sam Bass,* 102.

39. *Omaha Republican,* 30 December 1877, 4.

40. 1880 Grayson County, Texas, Census, 73 (251/266); 1900 Grayson County, Texas, Census, ED 89, Sheet 6, Line 84, 97-B (546); Tise, *Texas County Sheriffs,* 213; *Denison Daily News,* 19 January 1876, 3.

41. Thomas E. Gerren was born in Tennessee in December 1849 and was a deputy sheriff in Denton County by 1875. In late February 1876, it appears that Gerren was rooming at the Lacy House on Denton's square. A young "tramp printer", who had just acquired a job and worked late on his first day, was returning to his room in the Lacy House in the dark and accidentally stumbled into Gerren's room by mistake. Gerren cursed him loudly and vilely, even though it was an honest error. The next morning, Tuesday, February 29, a young man named John Patrick, who had also been known as Johnson, rebuked Gerren at the breakfast table for his conduct the night before and a heated argument developed. The argument spilled out onto the hotel porch, where Gerren cursed Patrick and drew his pistol. A struggle ensued and the pistol discharged, apparently striking Patrick. Undaunted, Patrick seized the pistol and Gerren fled upstairs to his room. Patrick went to the nearby stable, ordered his horse saddled while he stood lookout at the door with a rifle, then rode north from Denton toward Pilot Point where he was staying with a family.

A cry went up that Gerren had been shot and a group of men, bent on vengeance, pursued the wounded Patrick. A volley of shots brought Patrick down and it would later be recalled that his body had twenty-one wounds. When the townsmen found that Gerren had not been scratched, a sense of utmost shame overtook the town for some time. According to Bass' young friend Charlie Brim, Henry Underwood confronted Gerren and told him, "If I had been there, you would have had a hell of a lot harder time getting that boy murdered." It was reported in March 1876 that Gerren was being tried for the killing, but was expected to be acquitted. No court records have survived.

Scott Mayes recalled Gerren as a "brag fighter" who avoided danger if he could. City Marshal Bill Fry labeled him as "overbearing and cruel to prisoners and citizens who were afraid of him." Denton Judge Alvin Owsley told how his parents had seen Gerren ride by their house with a black prisoner arrested for hog theft who was being led on foot behind the deputy by a lariat. The prisoner snatched Gerren's pistol from him, tossed the rope around the deputy, and astride Gerren's horse, marched the deputy back the way they had come. At the edge of town he gave the hapless lawman his horse and an unloaded gun and ran off into the brush. The man surrendered to Sheriff Egan the next day and was later acquitted, the jury preferring the black man's word over that of Gerren. 1900 Denton County, Texas, Census, ED 45, Sheet 1, Line 68, 54-B (17/17); Deed Records, Denton County, Texas, Vol. A, 71; Commissioners Court Minutes, Denton County, Texas, Vol. A, 1; *Denison Daily News,* 2 March 1876, 3; 9 March 1876, 1; *Galveston Daily News,* 9 March 1876, 1; *Dallas Daily Herald,* 10 March 1876; 14 March 1876; *Brenham Banner,* 10 March 1876, 1; Interview of Charles Brim by Alex Williams, 10 July 1931; Interview of John Hudson by Alex Williams, January 1931; Interview of Richard Cobb by Alex Williams, 7 March

1931, Goodman-Williams Collection, Denton County Historical Museum; Alex Williams, "Denton County Deputy Sheriff Tom Gerren: The Bully of the Town," *Denton Enterprise*, 23 July 1972 (Vertical Files, Denton Public Library); Interview of Scott Mayes by Alex Williams, 2 December 1930; Interview of William S. Fry by Alex Williams, 11 September 1925; Interview of Judge Alvin Owsley by Alex Williams, 4 July 1930, Goodman-Williams Collection, Denton County Historical Museum; *Dallas Daily Herald*, 26 April 1878, 1; *Sherman Register*, 13 May 1878, as quoted in the *Denison Daily News*, 15 May 1878.

42. *Omaha Republican*, 30 December 1877, 4; *Life and Adventures of Sam Bass*, 25. In the 1870 Denton County census, there was a seventeen-year-old James M. Hall from Missouri who worked on the farm of Newton Hayes in Lewisville, and in the 1880 census there was a black farmer, James Hall, also from Missouri, who had a wife and seven children. See 1870 Denton County, Texas, Census, 181 (150/150), and 1880 Denton County, Texas, Census, 101 (125/125).

43. *Omaha Republican*, 30 December 1877, 4; *Omaha Daily Bee*, 31 December 1877, 4; *Sherman Register*, 24 April 1878, as quoted in the *Dallas Daily Herald*, 26 April 1878, 1; *Denton Monitor*, as quoted in the *Denison Daily News*, 12 May 1878, 1.

44. Jesse Leigh "Red" Hall was born in Lexington, North Carolina, on October 9, 1849. He moved to Texas in 1869, changing the spelling of his middle name to "Lee," and was a school teacher, then city marshal at Sherman in Grayson County. After a stint as a deputy sheriff and as sergeant of arms for the Texas Senate in Austin, he enlisted in Captain Leander McNelly's Special Force of rangers on August 10, 1876. After serving in the Nueces Strip and solving a bank robbery at Goliad, he became acting commander of the Special Force in October 1876 because of McNelly's bad health and moved to suppress the vicious Sutton-Taylor-Tumlinson feud in the DeWitt County area. In January 1877 the Special Force was reorganized at Victoria and Hall was promoted to first lieutenant. He promptly split his command to deal with incursions by bandits on the Texas-Mexico border and to run down the notorious King Fisher gang. Tyler, ed., *New Handbook of Texas*, Vol. III, 414; Robert W. Stephens, *Texas Rangers Indian War Pensions* (Quanah, Texas: Nortex Press, 1975), 39; *San Antonio Express*, 18 March 1911, 5. See also Dora Neill Raymond, *Captain Lee Hall of Texas* (Norman, Oklahoma: University of Oklahoma Press, 1982).

45. Letter From Capt. J.L. Hall to Adj. Gen. Steele, 26 December 1877, Center For American History, University of Texas at Austin, Transcripts From the Office of the Adjutant General of Texas, 1877, File No. 2Q400, Vol. 9(B), 221-22; *Sherman Register*, 24 April 1878, as quoted in the *Dallas Weekly Herald*, 27 April 1878; *Sherman Register*, 14 May 1878, as quoted in the *Denison Daily News*, 15 May 1878, 1; Raymond, *Captain Lee Hall*, 150-52.

46. Captain McNelly relied on Parrott's skill with a camera to send him undercover in the Eagle Pass area to gather information on outlaw King Fisher and his gang, and Parrott actually sold photographs to gang members. On another occasion when McNelly wanted to cross into Mexico after Mexican raiders, Parrott stripped off his clothes and swam across the Rio Grande River to find and return a rowboat, hollering back to his companions that he had found one, and in spite of the presence of enemy bandits. Texas State Library, General Service Records, File 401-167; George Durham, *Taming the Nueces Strip* (Austin, Texas: University of Texas Press, 1990), 10, 87-88, 134-35; N.A. Jennings, *A Texas Ranger* (Austin, Texas: The Steck Co., 1959), 124.

47. *Dallas Daily Herald*, 26 April 1878, as quoted in the *Denison Daily News*, 27 April 1878, 1. Richard G. "Dick" Head was born in Saline County, Missouri, on April 6, 1847, and came to Texas with his family in 1853. He was an experienced cattle drover after the Civil War and likely knew the Collins brothers. He became a prominent cattleman in Caldwell County. Hunter, *The Trail Drivers of Texas*, 734-36; James C. Shaw (Herbert O. Brayer, ed.), *North From Texas* (College

Station, Texas: Texas A&M University Press, 1996), 53, 93 n.20.

48. Letter From Capt. J.L. Hall to Adj. Gen. Steele, 26 December 1877, Center for American History, University of Texas at Austin, Transcripts From the Office of the Adjutant General of Texas, 1877, File No. 2Q400, Vol. 9(B), 221-22; *San Antonio Daily Express*, 8 December 1877, 4.

49. Letter From Lt. Pat Dolan to Major John Jones, 12 December 1877, Center for American History, University of Texas at Austin, Transcripts From the Office of the Adjutant General of Texas, 1877, File No. 2Q400, Vol. 9(B), 196.

50. Telegram from Lt. Pat Dolan to Major John Jones, 13 December 1877, Center for American History, University of Texas at Austin, Transcripts From the Office of the Adjutant General of Texas, 1877, File No. 2Q400, Vol. 9(B), 200; Texas State Library, *Results of Operations of State Troops Since August 1, 1876, to December 31, 1881*, Vol. I, 255.

51. *San Antonio Daily Express*, 15 December 1877.

52. Hogg, *Authentic History*, 58; *Denton Monitor*, as quoted in the *Denison Daily News*, 12 May 1878, 1.

VIII. HOLDUP AT ALLEN STATION

1. *Fort Worth Daily Democrat*, 23 December 1877, 4; Hogg, *Authentic History*, 63.

2. George Mellersh was born in England in 1836 and emigrated with his family to Tennessee in 1850, where they farmed. After his father's death in 1853, Mellersh was involved in steamboating on the Mississippi River, then in 1855 served as an orderly sergeant in the 9th Tennessee Infantry, fighting Indians in Washington Territory. He returned to Tennessee in 1858, worked in the mercantile business, and married Elizabeth James on November 24, 1858. With the coming of the Civil War, he served as the captain of Company E, 154th Senior Tennessee Infantry Regiment. During the battle of Shiloh he recaptured his unit's battle flag. After the war, when three of their children had died in both Memphis and Newcastle, Pennsylvania, Mellersh and his wife moved in 1873 to Dallas, where he operated a tannery. They were the parents of a total of eleven children. He subsequently became a traveling salesman, or drummer, for several wholesale grocery houses, coal interests, agricultural implements, and clothing firms. A writer of poetry, Mellersh became known as "The Drummer Poet." After his first wife died, Mellersh married Mrs. Mollie Powers, of Terrell, Texas. He died in Dallas on August 12, 1910. *Dallas Morning News*, 13 August 1910, 14; *Proud Heritage: Pioneer Families of Dallas County*, Vol. I, 163-64; Certificate of Death (George Mellersh), Dallas County, Texas, No. 15026.

3. Charles F. Shield was born in December 1854 in Mississippi. He and his second wife, Mary E., married about 1877 or 1878 and subsequently had at least twelve children. Shield was in the dry goods and grocery business in Coleman County but later turned to farming. He died on December 17, 1911, from a gunshot wound. 1880 Coleman County, Texas, Census, 529 (136/136); 1900 Coleman County, Texas, Census, ED 22, Sheet 15, Line 1, 203-A (141/155); 1910 Coleman County, Texas, Census, ED 128, Sheet 11-A, Line 5 (194/198); Certificate of Death (Charles F. Shield), Coleman County, Texas, No. 25859.

4. *Fort Worth Daily Democrat*, 23 December 1877, 1,4; Hogg, *Authentic History*, 63.

5. *Denison Daily News*, 29 December 1877, 3; *Omaha Republican*, 30 December 1877, 4. John McNelly, the nephew of noted Ranger Captain Leander McNelly, served in his uncle's company from July 25, 1874, until January 20, 1875. Chuck Parsons, *"Pidge," A Texas Ranger From Virginia* (Wolfe City, Texas: Henington Publishing Co., 1985), 126. Ranger service records reflect that a "John McNally" was a Texas Ranger Sergeant and Lieutenant in S.A. McMurray's

Company B from September 1, 1885, through February 28, 1886, but there are no records under that name reflecting earlier service. See Texas State Library, Adjutant General Service Records, Frontier Battalion, Box 401-162.

6. *Omaha Republican*, 30 December 1877, 4.

7. *Omaha Republican*, 30 December 1877, 4; 1 January 1878, 4; *Omaha Weekly Herald*, 4 January 1878, 2; *Kansas City Journal of Commerce*, as quoted in *Hays City Sentinel*, 4 January 1878, 2; Hogg, *Authentic History*, 59.

8. *Omaha Republican*, 30 December 1877, 4; 1 January 1878; *Omaha Weekly Herald*, 4 January 1878, 2; *Omaha Daily Bee*, 31 December 1877, 4; 1880 Douglas County, Nebraska, Census, 55 (1/1)

9. *Omaha Weekly Republican*, 5 January 1878, 3; *Omaha Daily Bee*, 2 January 1878; *Sidney Telegraph*, 12 January 1878, 3.

10. *Denton Record-Chronicle*, 9 December 1964, 3.

11. *Sidney Telegraph*, as quoted by the *Omaha Daily Bee*, 31 December 1877, 4.

12. Hogg, *Authentic History*, 63-64; *Life and Adventures of Sam Bass*, 25-26.

13. Interview With John Hudson by Alex Williams, 6 January 1931, Goodman-Williams Collection, Denton County Historical Museum.

14. Interview With Scott Mayes by Alex Williams, 2 December 1930, Goodman-Williams Collection, Denton County Historical Museum; *Dallas Daily Herald*, 25 April 1878, 4.

15. Thomas B. Wheeler purchased the saloon, including two billiard tables, a stock of groceries and leather contained in the building, and bar fixtures and furniture on October 28, 1876, for $1,500 from T.W. Cobb. There is some indication that he was running a saloon on the Denton square in December 1875 when the courthouse burned down. In the 1880 Denton County census, there are two Thomas Wheelers. The most likely one was Thomas B. Wheeler, miller, who was born on October 27, 1851, in Tennessee, and died in Denton on July 26, 1925. He and his wife also kept a boarding house. The other Thomas Wheeler, twenty-three, born in Mississippi, was a farmer. His wife, Dolly, twenty, was from Mississippi, and they had a one-year-old son. 1880 Denton County, Texas, Census, 5 (84/84), 131 (134); Commissioners Court Minutes, Denton County, Texas, Vol. A, 24; Cemetery Records, Denton County Historical Museum; Deed Records, Denton County, Texas, Vol. J, 64-65; *Denison Daily News*, 29 December 1875.

16. Hogg, *Authentic History*, 64-65.

17. Interview With Scott Mayes by Alex Williams, 2 December 1930; Interview With William S. Fry by Alex Williams, 11 September 1925, Goodman-Williams Collection, Denton County Historical Museum.

18. *Dallas Daily Herald*, 26 April 1878, 1; Interview With William S. Fry by Alex Williams, 11 September 1925, Goodman-Williams Collection, Denton County Historical Museum.

19. Henry Hill was born about 1835 in Virginia, and was a retail drygoods merchant in Denton County by 1870. At that time he and his wife, Mary A., had one son, Lewis, nine, born in Texas. By 1880 Hill was a farmer and he and his wife still had just the one son, but there is an indication that another son, Henry Hill, Jr., was born to them. That son married Effie George in Denton on January 4, 1881. In Collin County in 1883, Hill bought 109 acres from William D. Spotswood, the brother of Tom Spotswood. 1870 Denton County, Texas, Census, 173 (45/45); 1880 Denton County, Texas, Census, 175 (105/105); Deed Records, Collin County, Texas, Vol. 65, p. 56; Denton County Genealogical Society, Inc., *Denton County, Texas, Wills*, 63; Marriage Records, Denton County, Texas, Vol. 2, p. 9.

20. John Slade was born about 1849 in Mississippi to William Slade, a South Carolinian born about 1805. Harvey Slade, John's brother, was born March 5, 1852, also in Mississippi. William Slade was in Denton County by the late 1850s where the family farmed. Denton County marriage records reflect that an "H. Slade" married Alice Aldridge on December 27, 1877. Harvey Slade died on February 18, 1879. 1870 Denton County, Texas, Census, 140 (265/284); 173

(45/45); 1880 Denton County, Texas, Census, 175 (105/105); Deed Records, Denton County, Texas, Vol. R, 185; Davis, *Marriage Records, Denton County*, 34; *Abandoned Cemetery Records* (Denton, Texas: Benjamin Lyon Chapter, Texas Daughters of the American Revolution, 1996), 27; Davis, *Marriage Records, Denton County*, 34 (Vol. I, 176).

21. Interview With Will Clark by Alex Williams, 10 February 1931, Goodman-Williams Collection, Denton County Historical Museum.

22. Kenneth Foree, "Sam Bass Rides Right Up Main Street," *Dallas Morning News*, 3 March 1948. O.P. Levlon was born on December 27, 1844, in Sweden. His original name was Peterson. When he arrived in Minnesota in 1863 and enlisted in the Union Army, he changed his name to Leaflawn because he liked the sound of it, but it came out as Levlon in his broken English. Levlon came to Dallas in 1871 and set up shop as a bootmaker. Actually, Levlon had better reasons not to like the Dallas police. He was married in Dallas in August 1874 to Eva Rice, originally from Missouri. In April 1876 an infant child born to them died under mysterious circumstances. The case was considered by the Grand Jury, but apparently with no indictment. He claimed that he was carrying the child on his way home, which he set down on the ground when he was challenged to a fight. The child died six weeks later from some illness. *Dallas Daily Herald*, 27, 28 July 1876. In a different matter, Levlon brought charges of an unknown nature against two Dallas officers in July 1881, but they were found to be false and malicious, and a number of witnesses swore that they would not believe Levlon on oath. *Dallas Daily Herald*, 17 July 1881, 6. Levlon died on December 27, 1930. Death Certificate (O.P. Levlon), Dallas County, Texas, No. 53086; *Dallas Daily Times Herald*, 28 December 1930, Sec. 3, 7.

23. *Fort Worth Daily Democrat*, 29,30 January 1878, 4; *Weatherford Exponent*, 2 February 1878, 3; *Dallas Daily Herald*, 29 January 1878, 1; *Denison Daily News*, 30 January 1878, 1; 1880 Stephens County, Texas, Census, 473 (342/342).

24. Hogg, *Authentic History*, 66.

25. Ibid.

26. William "Bill" Scott was born on January 17, 1854, in Walker County, Texas, to James E. and Mary M. Scott. By 1870 the Scott family was in Dallas County where the elder Scott was a miller. James Scott later became Dr. Scott, a planter and physician in Somervell County. His daughter, Emily, was married to prominent Dallas lawyer E.G. Bowers. After Bill Scott and E.W. "Jack" Smith tried to lay a trap for Bass, Scott was mustered as a private into June Peak's Company B of the Frontier Battalion on May 1, 1878. In November 1878, he was shown as a corporal in Peak's unit. In August 1879 he was a private in Capt. G. W. Arrington's Company C and first corporal the following November. He was a private in Capt. J.L. Hall's Special Forces in May 1880, and then under Capt. Thomas L. Ogleby, being promoted to corporal by November 1880. In November 1883 he was a sergeant in Lt. Joseph Shely's Company F, and a lieutenant by August 1885 under Captain Shely. Scott was commander of Company F as a lieutenant in August 1885, and the following year was captain. In 1886 he led a campaign against fence cutters in Brown County, and in March 1886 was shot through the left lung during a gunbattle with the Conners gang in Sabine County. On December 13, 1887, he married Georgia Lynch. Captain Scott mustered out of ranger service on April 30, 1888, and engaged in railroad contracting in Mexico, where he was once seriously stabbed by a group of Mexicans. He retired to San Antonio where he died on November 12, 1913. *San Antonio Express*, 13 November 1913, 15; 1870 Dallas County, Texas, Census, 435 (1556/1549); Texas State Library, Adjutant General Service Records, Frontier Battalion, Box 401-171; Robert W. Stephens, *Texas Ranger Sketches* (Dallas, Texas: Robert W. Stephens, 1972), 134; 1870 Dallas County, Census, 435 (1556/1549); *Galveston Daily News*, 30 April 1878, 1.

27. *Evening State Gazette* [Austin, Texas], 11 July 1878, and Letter from

Brewster Cameron to David B. Parker, 18 July 1878, as found in file at National Archives II (College Park, Maryland), RG 204, Office of the Pardon Attorney, Pardon Case Files 1853-1946, Record J, pp. 93-118, Box 155;

28. *Galveston Daily News*, 9 July 1878, 1.

29. Reed and Tate, *Tenderfoot Bandits*, 118-119.

30. Letter to Author from Cecilie Gaziano, Minneapolis, Minnesota, 29 April 1997. Ms. Gaziano has done some painstaking research on Seaborn Barnes' origins, and the information she relied on comes from Yalobusha County, Mississippi, land patents, deeds, tax records, will abstracts, marriage records, as well as records from Cass and Tarrant Counties in Texas. It is believed that Barnes' parents were John S. and Martha Barnes. John Barnes was born in Alabama about 1813, and on February 28, 1835, in Yalobusha County, Mississippi, married Martha "Patsy" Cannon, born about 1817 in Pendleton District, South Carolina, to Carter C. and Sarah "Sallie" Latimer Cannon. Three daughters, Sarah J., Rhoda A. and Mary E., were born to John and Martha Barnes in Mississippi. By the early 1840s the Barnes family was in Cass County, Texas, where at least five more children were born to themBMary E. about 1841, Emeline Tennessee about 1843, Berry Henderson about 1846, Martha F. about 1848, and Seaborn, probably about 1852 or 1853.

Reportedly John Barnes was an officer in the Mexican War, then returned to his farm in Texas. One account says that John Barnes was a sheriff and tax collector for Cass County, but there is no record of an official by that name in either Cass County or Marion County, which was formed from Cass County in 1860. The patriarch of the Barnes family reportedly died when Seaborn was an infant, around 1853 or 1854, when John Barnes' name ceased to be listed on Cass County tax rolls, although Martha Barnes continued to be listed. Martha Barnes then reportedly moved her family to central Tarrant County, east of Fort Worth, near what would be the small community of Handley. Handley was developed in 1876 with the coming of the Texas and Pacific railroad. It appears that Seaborn Barnes' mother died in Tarrant County in 1874 or earlier. See also the 1850 Cass County, Texas, Census, 727 (98/103). Seaborn's brother, Berry, can be found twice in the 1880 Tarrant County Census, p. 76A (40/42) and p. 250B (23/23). His sister, Emeline Tennessee, married Martin V. Digby in Dallas, later moving to Bell County, Texas (and shaving a few years off her age). See 1880 Dallas County, Texas, Census, 244 (115/123); 1900 Bell County, Texas, Census, ED 21, Sheet 3, Line 41 (41/44); 1910 Bell County, Texas, Census, ED 1, Sheet 16A (227/227); and 1920 Bell County, Texas, Census, ED 25, Sheet 7B, Line 89 (810/161/197); Tyler, ed., *New Handbook of Texas*, Vol. 3, 440; "'Truest' Story of Death of Sam Bass," *Frontier Times*, Vol. 11, No. 2 (November 1933), 88-91.

31. Augustus H. "Gus" Serren was born about 1829 in New York. He is shown as living in Denton County as early as 1858, earning a living as a potter, about five miles south of Denton. He married his wife, Esther F., and by 1870 they had three children, John L., James, and Mary F. In 1874 tax rolls showed him with only livestock. He reportedly died on January 6, 1874. Hogg, *Authentic History*, 30; 1870 Denton County, Texas, Census, 124 (45/45); *Inventory Book, Denton County, 1874*, 235; Deed Records, Denton County, Texas, Vol. O, 533; Genealogical Records, Denton County Historical Museum.

32. Hogg, *Authentic History*, 30.

33. Gard, *Sam Bass*, 108; District Court Minutes, Tarrant County, Texas, *State of Texas v. Seaburn Barnes*, Cause No. 692, Vol. A, 62.

34. Born about 1850 in Missouri (probably Henry County) to Robert and Sarah Ann Bradley Spotswood, Thomas A. Spotswood was the second of at least nine children in the family, including younger brothers William D., born on February 17, 1853, and John Cleveland, born January 6, 1856, at Calhoun, Missouri. 1870 Henry County, Missouri, Census, 949 (1198/1198); certificate of Death (William D. Spottswood [sic]), Denton County, Texas, No. 5779;

Certificate of Death (John Cleveland Spotswood), Clay County, Texas, No. 1717. How Spotswood lost his right eye is unknown, although it may have been a war injury. He enlisted in Missouri as a Confederate soldier in Company D, 11th Infantry (Hunter's Regiment) on July 3, 1862. After a thirty-day furlough commencing April 4, 1863, he was captured at Little Rock, Arkansas, on September 11, 1863, by the 62nd Illinois Infantry Regiment. His record noted that he "deserted the rebels," likely meaning he preferred to be a Union prisoner of war rather than continue fighting for the Confederates. National Archives, M322, Compiled Service record of Confederate Soldiers Who Served in Organizations From Missouri, 11th Infantry, Sn-Z, Roll 161; letter to author from Ruth Priest Dixon, Mitchellville, Maryland, 9 March 1997. There is some confusion as to the unit in which Spotswood served because Hunter's Regiment has also been attributed as the Missouri 2nd Infantry Regiment, later desiganted as the 8th Infantry regiment on April 1, 1863. See Stewart Sifakis, *Compendium of the Confederate Armies: Kentucky, Maryland, Missouri, the Confederate Units and the Indian Units* (New York: Facts on File, 1995), 116.

According to an early Missouri newspaper, Spotswood moved to Sedalia, Missouri, after the war, gaining a reputation as a carousing drunk, "ever ready to use the knife, pistol or bludgeon." Reportedly on an August 30, likely in 1870, an argument ensued between him and a carpenter, John J. Jones, over who would escort a prostitute home. The 1870 Pettis County census lists a carpenter named John Jones who was born in Missouri about 1842. Jones apparently won out, and as he was walking away with the "soiled dove," Spotswood came up from behind and killed him with a blow to the head with a slung shot fashioned from a rock and a handkerchief. Spotswood fled to a stable loft, but was captured and arrested. He was granted a change of venue to Saline County, but a friend posing as a drunk had himself arrested and placed in jail, bringing with him files and saws that enabled Spotswood to escape. *Sedalia Democrat*, as quoted in Hogg , *Authentic History*, 71-73; 1870 Pettis County, Missouri, Census, 595 (543/565).

It is believed that Spotswood then went to Calhoun in Henry County where his relatives lived and began to prepare to leave the state. Before he left, however, he decided to settle accounts with a young Calhoun merchant named Edmonson with whom he had experienced a difficulty at a party a few years before. Late one night he reportedly shot and killed the storekeeper from ambush as Edmonson was entering his store. Spotswood immediately left Missouri for Texas, settling in the vicinity of McKinney in Collin County. In 1871 he was reportedly implicated in the killing of two black men there, then arrested on a warrant from Missouri and returned to Saline County for trial. However, because key witnesses could not be located, Spotswood was acquitted and he quickly returned to Texas. *Sedalia Democrat*, as quoted in Hogg, *Authentic History*, 73; The 1860 Henry County census lists a Virginia-born merchant, William E. Edmondson, and of his four children, there are two sons: James H., 13, and William P., 9. Either William or James had to have been Spotswood's victim. Another account says that Spotswood was taken by change of venue to Benton County, Missouri, in the fall of 1874, when he was acquitted. See *Dallas Daily Herald*, 1 March 1878, 1.

Spotswood and his brothers Bill and John subsequently lived in Denton County. Tom Spotswood married Rosanna Miller in adjacent Cooke County on October 18, 1874, and they apparently had two children, William and Thomas, although she died prior to 1878. Spotswood's children lived with Elijah Brewer and his family in Denton County. Denton County tax assessment rolls from 1874 to 1877 reflect that none of the Spotswood brothers owned any land. Tom Spotswood's propensity for trouble was reflected in four unknown criminal offenses filed against him in Denton County. Norma R. Grammer and Marion Day Mullins, *Cooke County, Texas, Marriages, 1849-July 1879* (no city or publisher, 1957), 32, citing Vol. 2A, p. 177, of the Cooke County Marriage Records; 1880 Denton County, Texas, Census, 195 (445/447); District Court Records, Collin

County, Texas, *State of Texas v. Thomas Spotswood*, Cause Nos. 1500 and 1501; Tax Assessment Rolls, Denton County, Texas, 1874 and 1875; *Inventory Book, Denton County, 1877*, 238; Index, Denton County, Texas, Court, *State of Texas v. Thos. Spotswood*, Cause Nos. 1362, 1363, 1405, 1406, Vol. I, 212-13, 222.

35. *Galveston Daily News*, 18 June 1875, 1.

36. J. Lee Stambaugh and Lillian J. Stambaugh, *A History of Collin County, Texas* (Austin, Texas: Texas State Historical Association, 1958), 45; Tyler, ed., *New Handbook of Texas*, Vol. 1, 116.

37. *Life and Adventures of Sam Bass*, 28; *Dallas Daily Herald*, 1 March 1878, 1. Andrew Jackson "Bud" Newman was born on December 2, 1846, in Missouri. By 1880 he was a stock dealer in Collin County and he and his wife, Francis, had three children. He died on July 10, 1912. 1880 Collin County, Texas, Census, 6 (109/120); Alice Pitts, Wanda O'Roark, and Doris Posey, *Collin County (Texas) Cemetery Inscriptions* (Fort Worth, Texas: The Manney Co., 1975), Vol. I, 361.

38. *Dallas Daily Herald*, 22 February 1878, 3.

39. *Galveston Daily News*, 24 February 1878, 1; 1880 Harris County, Texas, Census, 111 (580 and 237/581); 1880 Galveston County, Texas, Census, 106 (7/7).

40. Will "Uncle Billy" Apperson was born January 31, 1848, in Missouri to Milton and Comelia Nowlin Apperson, and married Emma A. Gray in Dallas on February 6, 1868. In addition to being a saloon keeper, he also became a traveling representative for a St. Louis drug house. In 1894 he purchased a drug store in Dallas and subsequently retired. Apperson died on June 4, 1926, survived by a son, a daughter, and a grandson. See 1870 Dallas County, Texas, Census, 338 (289/291); 1880 Dallas County, Texas, Census, 6 (Line 26); Lu and Blomquist, eds., *Marriages, Dallas County, Texas*, 17; *Dallas Morning News*, 5 June 1926, 1; Town Plat of Allen, Texas (courtesy of Warren Johnson, Allen, Texas).

41. *Galveston Daily News*, 24 February 1878, 1; *Dallas Daily Herald*, 23 February 1878, 1; *Life and Adventures of Sam Bass*, 27.

42. *Dallas Daily Herald*, 23 February 1878, 4.

43. *Dallas Daily Herald*, 23 February 1878, 1. William F. Morton was born on February 9, 1838, in Montgomery County, North Carolina, to an eminent physician and Baptist minister, and the family immediately moved to Mississippi, where he was educated. As a young man he taught school, then was a drug store clerk at Pine Bluff, Arkansas. At the outbreak of the Civil War, he was captain of Company C, 11th Arkansas Infantry Regiment. He was captured and held as a prisoner of war in Chicago for almost six months, then was exchanged at Vicksburg. During a leave of absence in 1863 he married Emma Guice, after which he fought in the war until it was over. Surrendering at Citronelle, Alabama, and paroling at Jackson, Mississippi, he returned to farm in Mississippi for a few years, then clerking and becoming a druggist. After several years, he moved to Texas, first as a grocer in Jackson County, then, in 1873, to Dallas where he worked in a lumber company for six months before becoming a member of the small Dallas police force. Morton served a year as a regular policeman, then was deputy marshal for several years under City Marshal Junius Peak. He was seriously wounded in the groin on August 3, 1875, when he tried to arrest a man for shooting a saloonkeeper. In April 1876 Morton ran for election as city marshal and defeated Peak. He was reelected on April 2, 1878, and again in April 1880.

In February 1881 Morton's wife took their three children and went to Marshall on the train. Morton asked authorities there to detain her, and he went to Marshall and brought them back to Dallas. In June 1881 he resigned as marshal because of a $61.25 discrepancy in jail books. Morton became a special officer for six months for the Texas & Pacific Railroad, then was in charge of the Dallas County Jail for about three years. He was defeated in 1884 in another bid for city marshal. Morton was a Deputy U.S. Marshal for four years, then defeated again in the city marshal race in 1888. In 1889 he started a protective agency with A.M. Gaines, then in 1890 was elected as a constable. He was reelected as constable in

1892, but defeated in 1894. Another campaign for chief of police in 1896 ended in defeat, and the following year he was appointed transfer agent for the penitentiary, leading him to withdraw his candidacy for chief in 1898. He died in Dallas on January 28, 1910. *Memorial and Biographical History of Dallas County, Texas*, 590-91; Texas State Library, Confederate Pension Applications, File No. 14992; 1880 Dallas County, Texas, Census, 50 (443/485); City Council Minutes, Dallas, Texas, 5 April 1876, 2-3 April 1878, 10 April 1880, 16 July 1880, 25 June 1881, 19 July 1881, 9 April 1884, 4 April 1888, 8 April 1896; *Dallas Daily Commercial*, 12 April 1874, 4; 30 July 1874, 4; *Dallas Weekly Herald*, 7 August 1875, 3; 3 March 1881; *Dallas Daily Herald*, 7 November 1875, 4; 30 June 1887; *Dallas Morning News*, 8 November 1890; 12 November 1892; 28 November 1892; 15 November 1894, 10; 6 March 1898, 4; *Dallas Daily Times Herald*, 13 June 1897, 5.

    44. *Austin Daily Democratic Statesman*, 28 February 1878, 2.

    45. Texas State Library, Letter From Gov. R.B. Hubbard to Col. G. Jordan, 23 February 1878, Letter Press Book, Box 301-103, p. 652.

    46. *Austin Daily Democratic Statesman*, 28 February 1878, 2; *Galveston Daily News*, 26 February 1878, 1.

    47. Texas State Library, Letter From J.W. Swindells (acting private secretary to the governor) to Col. G. Jordan, 23 February 1878, Letter Press Book, Box 301-103, p. 654.

    48. Texas State Library, "Confidential" letter from Gov. R.B. Hubbard to Col. G. Jordan, 23 February 1878, Letter Press Book, Box 301-103; Raymond, *Captain Lee Hall*, 153

    49. *Dallas Commercial*, as quoted in the *Denison Daily News*, 7 May 1878, 1; Hogg, *Authentic History*, 69.

    50. *Galveston Daily News*, 24 February 1878, 1; 28 February 1878, 4; *Fort Worth Daily Democrat*, 2 March 1878.

    51. District Court Records, Collin County, Texas, *State of Texas v. Thomas Spotswood*, Cause No. 1501.

    52. Hogg, *Authentic History*, 69.

    53. Hogg, *Authentic History*, 70.

IX. THE HUTCHINS ROBBERY

    1.   James E. Lucy was born on May 1, 1854 or 1855, in Saint Clair, Missouri. Unlike most Texas Rangers, he attended a university, at Columbia, Missouri. He came to Texas about 1873, settling in Austin. He enlisted as a private in Lee Hall's Special Troops on July 15, 1877, but by February 28, 1878, was a member of Captain Dan Roberts' Company D. On May 31, 1879, he was listed as a private in Capt. G.W. Arrington's Company C, and in August he was a 3rd Sergeant in that company. On November 30, 1879, he was a sergeant in Lt. C.L. Nevill's Company E. He left the ranger service on February 21, 1881. Lucy married Jennie Platt in 1882 in Austin, but she died in 1885. They had one child who died, and he never remarried. After leaving the rangers, he served as Austin Chief of Police. He reportedly arrested notorious gunfighter Ben Thompson at one time. He subsequently went into the bond and surety business in Austin. At his death on July 10, 1927, he was vice president of the American Surety Company, as well as a member of the board of directors of a mortgage company. *Austin American*, 11 July 1927, 1; Stephens, *Indian War Pensions*, 65; Texas State Library, Adjutant General Service Records, Frontier Battalion, Box 401-161; 1880 Travis County, Texas, Census, 255 (91/108); Certificate of Death (Capt. J.E. Lucy), Travis County, Texas, No. 22823.

    2.   Texas State Library, Adjutant General Records, Box 401-1157-18; Raymond, *Captain Lee Hall*, 153-54.

    3.   W.K. Cornish was born about 1849 in Canada. He subsequently came to Texas, settling in Dallas, and was an agent there for the Texas Express Company

for a number of years. On June 5, 1878, he married Lida (Lydia) E. Redmon at Paris, Kentucky, and they returned to Dallas. 1880 Dallas County, Texas, Census, 29 (48/56); *Dallas Daily Herald*, 11 June 1878, 4. Cornish was no stranger to express robberies. Early on the morning of Monday, September 28, 1875, with Charles Rush driving, he was riding in a light wagon from the Dallas train depot, followed by a larger wagon driven by a black employee, after picking up packages delivered on the train. Suddenly two mounted men armed with Spencer rifles rode out from behind a pile of lumber at a lumber yard, stopped Cornish's wagon, and demanded the money bag that he had or else have the top of his head blown off. With the money in their possession the two thieves rode off rapidly. Cornish immediately raised a posse and followed their trail until the bandits took to a creek bed and eluded their pursuers. One of the robbers was later identified as William Dill who was finally captured in Jack County the following November. *Dallas Daily Herald*, 29 September 1875, 4; 8 November 1875; 4, 10 December 1875; 18 May 1876, 1. Cornish would himself experience trouble with the law when he was arrested on a federal warrant for dealing in liquors without a license. It turned out to be a misunderstanding growing out of Cornish loaning money to a firm that was accused of "rectifying" liquor by adding improper substances. *Dallas Daily Herald*, 29, 30 March 1876, 4.

4. *Galveston Daily News*, 1 March 1878, 1; *Dallas Daily Herald*, 1 March 1878, 1.

5. 1870 Denton County, Texas, Census, 144 (36/36); 1880 Denton County, Texas, Census, 77 (303/310).

6. *Galveston Daily News*, 1 March 1878, 1; *Dallas Daily Herald*, 1 March 1878, 1; *Denton Monitor*, 8 March 1878, as quoted in Hogg, *Authentic History*, 70-71, which gave Drennan the credit for identifying and capturing Spotswood.

7. *Dallas Daily Herald*, 2 March 1878, 2.

8. *Fort Worth Daily Democrat*, 17 April 1878, 2.

9. Hogg, *Authentic History*, 71.

10. Texas State Library, Adjutant General Records, Special State Troops, Correspondence, Box 401-1157-18.

11. Texas State Library, Letter From T.E. Gerren to Gov. R.B. Hubbard, 12 March 1878; Letter From T.I. Courtright to Gov. R.E. Hubbard, 12 March 1878, Extradition Records.

12. Texas State Library, Adjutant General Records, General Correspondence, Box 401-396-18.

13. Hogg, *Authentic History*, 75-76; Tyler, ed., *New Handbook of Texas*, Vol. 3, 804; Martin, *Sketch of Sam Bass*, 42.

14. Martin, *Sketch of Sam Bass*, 46-47.

15. *Dallas Daily Herald*, 19 March 1878, 1; 21 March 1878, 4; *Galveston Daily News*, 20 March 1878, 1; *Life and Adventures of Sam Bass*, 29.

16. Henry Andrew "Heck" Thomas was born January 6, 1850, at Oxford, Georgia, near Atlanta. He was allowed to be a courier in his uncle's Confederate brigade until he caught typhoid in 1863 and had to return home. His father became Atlanta's city marshal, and Thomas served as a policeman. In 1871 he married Isabelle Gray and they had two children while living in Georgia. He left the police force to go into the wholesale grocery business. The family moved to Texas, where cousin James got him a job with the Texas Express Company. In 1885 he was defeated in an attempt at election as Fort Worth city marshal, then was employed with the Fort Worth Detective Association. He subsequently became a Deputy U.S. Marshal out of Judge Isaac Parker's federal court at Fort Smith, Arkansas. During his illustrious career as a federal officer, he encountered a number of dangerous criminals, including tracking down and killing the notorious Bill Doolin in 1896. His dedication to his career led to a divorce, but Thomas remarried in 1892. He served seven years as Lawton, Oklahoma's, first chief of police, dying on August 15, 1912. Glenn Shirley, *Heck Thomas: Frontier Marshal* (New York:

Chilton Company, 1962); 1880 Tarrant County, Texas, Census, 69 (385/398).

17. *Dallas Daily Herald*, 19 March 1878, 1; *Galveston Daily News*, 20 March 1878, 1; *Waco Examiner & Patron*, 22 March 1878, 7; *Austin Daily Democratic Statesman*, 20 March 1878, 4; *Fort Worth Daily Democrat*, 21 March 1878, 4; Beth Thomas Meeks and Bonnie Speer, *Heck Thomas, My Papa* (Norman, Oklahoma: The Apache News, 1988), 12; Bonnie Stahlman Speer, *Portrait of a Lawman* (Norman, Oklahoma: Reliance Press, 1996), 26-27; 1870 Orleans Parish, Louisiana, Census, 155 (27/27); 1880 Tarrant County, Texas, Census, 69 (385/398); 1880 Travis County, Texas, Census, 255 (92/109); National Archives II (College Park, Maryland), RG 204, Office of the Pardon Attorney, Pardon Case Files 1853-1946, Record J, pp. 93-118, Box 155. Thomas would subsequently be awarded two hundred dollars by the express company in recognition of his "zeal and fidelity" at the Hutchins robbery. Speer, *Portrait of a Lawman*, 28-29; *Denison Daily News*, 26 March 1878, 2. Bingham Trigg was remembered in Austin for drunkenly terrorizing his wife by discharging his pistol in their residence two days after she had given birth in October 1875. He was the Travis County district attorney at the time. *Dallas Daily Herald*, 22 October 1875, 2.

18. *Dallas Daily Herald*, 19 March 1878, 1.

19. *Dallas Daily Herald*, 20 March 1878, 1.

20. *Galveston Daily News*, 21 March 1878, 1; *Dallas Daily Herald*, 21 March 1878, 1.

21. 1880 Dallas County, Texas, Census, 133 (91/100).

22. *Galveston Daily News*, 21 March 1878, 4; 22 March 1878, 4.

23. Junius Peak was born on April 5, 1845, in Warsaw, Kentucky, to Jefferson and Martha Malvina Reisor Peak. Jefferson Peak, who had been a lieutenant in the Mexican War, moved his family to a young Dallas community in 1855 where he built the first brick house in the county. With the outbreak of the Civil War June Peak ran away from home to the Choctaw Nation. He enlisted as a private on June 2, 1861, at Fort Arbuckle in Company I, a group of Texans from Denton County, in the First Regiment of the Choctaw and Chickasaw Volunteers. He participated in the skirmish at Round Mountain against a superior force of Cherokee and Osage Indians on November 19, 1861. When Peak's one-year enlistment expired he transferred his service to General John H. Morgan's Second Kentucky Cavalry Regiment and participated in the raid through Ohio. Peak was wounded in the leg at Chickamauga, and ended up his service in General John Wharton's Eighth Texas Cavalry.

After the war and back in Dallas, Peak was reportedly a member of the Ku Klux Klan, although the record shows only that he joined a "Conservative Party" of Dallas County that was organized in March 1868. He also became a deputy sheriff at that time. In 1869 he was a candidate for Dallas County Sheriff, but he withdrew from the race because he was absent from the state on a cattle drive. In 1870 he was a partner with John L. Fisher in a furniture business, but his preference was for adventure.

In March 1872 and again the following November he was defeated in elections for Dallas city marshal. Once more a deputy sheriff in 1874, he gained local praise in January when he single-handedly pursued some cattle thieves and recovered the cattle. In April 1874 he was finally elected Dallas city marshal, then reelected in 1875. During the course of his duties, he once went to St. Louis to bring a swindler back, but was thwarted by a confidence man named Rittenhouse who would play a later role in the life of Henry Underwood. In April 1876 Peak was defeated by W.F. Morton, and the following year he was appointed City Recorder by the Dallas city council to preside over trials of city misdemeanor cases. Tyler, ed., *New Handbook of Texas*, Vol. 5, 107-08; Stephens, *Texas Ranger Sketches*, 4-5; City Council Minutes, Dallas, Texas, 8 April 1874, 7 April 1875, 5 April 1876, 5 April 1877; W.S. Adair, "Civil War Repeated in Indian Territory," *Dallas Morning News*, 1 July 1923 (Courtesy Dallas Historical Society); *Dallas Herald*, 14 March

1868, 20 November 1869, 4 December 1869, 1 January 1870, 23 July 1870; *Dallas Daily Herald*, 10 April 1875; *Dallas Weekly Herald*, 22 July 1876, 7 April 1877, 2 March 1878; National Archives, Compiled Service Records, Confederate Soldiers, Organizations Raised Directly by Confederate Government, 1st Choctaw-Chickasaw Mounted Rifles, M258, Roll 85; Texas State Library, Confederate Pension Applications, File No. 45993; Certificate of Death (Junius W. Peak), Dallas County, Texas, No. 17089; 1870 Dallas County, Texas, Census, 413 (1293/1286); 1880 Dallas County, Texas, Census, 29 (64/81); Sifakis, *Compendium of the Confederate Armies: Kentucky, Maryland, Missouri, the Confederate Units and the Indian Units*, 197-98.

24. Martin, *Sketch of Sam Bass*, 93; 1880 Dallas County, Texas, Census, 266 (45/45); *Dallas Weekly Herald*, 30 June 1877.

25. Martin, *Sketch of Sam Bass*, 93.

26. 1870 Denton County, Texas, Census, 125 (47/47); 1880 Denton County, Texas, Census, 36 (133/139), 103 (168/168); Gillett, *Fugitives From Justice*, 110.

27. *Dallas Morning Call*, as quoted in the *Denison Daily News*, 27 March 1878, 1; Martin, *Sketch of Sam Bass*, 93-94.

28. John W. Spencer was born June 14, 1842, at Woodville, Mississippi, to a Scottish father and Irish mother. He ran away to enlist in Company F, First Louisiana Volunteers, at New Orleans on April 24, 1861. He was wounded in an engagement near Seven Pines on June 25, 1862. Spencer claimed to have fought with the Army of Northern Virginia, even witnessing the battle between the iron-clads *Monitor* and *Merrimac*. He said that he was subsequently captured during a raid in Kentucky and spent the rest of the war at a prison at Fort Delaware. However, military records state that he deserted in July or August of 1862, and he was subsequently denied a pension for that reason. He married Mollie J. Kelly on March 1, 1866, and they moved to Dallas in 1873 where he became a Dallas policeman in February 1874, although briefly suspended in May for unknown reasons. On November 6, 1875, he shot and killed a man who had been erroneously pointed out as the notorious John Wesley Hardin. Spencer served as a policeman and deputy sheriff until 1885, when he became a collector and salesman for farm implement companies. He moved to Clay County in 1890, then to Hutchins in 1900. Spencer died in Dallas on August 1, 1927. 1880 Dallas County, Texas, Census, 59 (143/150); *Dallas Morning News*, 2 August 1927, 3; Certificate of Death (John W. Spencer), Dallas County, Texas, No. 26343; City Council Minutes, Dallas, Texas, 6 February 1874, 7 July 1874; *Dallas Daily Commercial*, 21 February 1874, 4; 12 April 1874, 4; 5 May 1874, 4; *Dallas Daily Herald*, 7 November 1875, 4; Texas State Library, Confederate Pension Applications, Reject File; *Gillespie & Work's Dallas Directory, 1881-1882*, 86; Rick Miller, *Bounty Hunter* (College Station, Texas: Creative Publishing Co., 1988), 71-74.

29. Ashton G. Pryor was born in Dallas on October 29, 1847, the first child of Dr. Samuel B. Pryor and his wife Virginia. Dr. Pryor was Dallas County District Clerk in 1846-1850 and served as Dallas' first mayor in 1856-1857. Ashton Pryor served as a Dallas policeman as early as 1872, and later as a deputy sheriff, and was shown as a constable in 1881-1882. John Henry Brown, *History of Dallas County, Texas*, 89; *Dallas Herald*, 16 March 1872, 2; *Gillespie & Work's Dallas Directory, 1881-1882*, 119.

30. *Dallas Morning Call*, as quoted in the *Denison Daily News*, 27 March 1878, 1; *Dallas Daily Herald*, 24 March 1878, 4; 26 March 1878, 1.

31. *Dallas Daily Herald*, 24 March 1878, 2.

32. Hogg, *Authentic History*, 79-80; William T. Minor was born in Jackson County, Alabama, on October 2, 1845, to Joseph and Mary Lewallen Minor. During the Civil War he served as a teamster, then enlisted in Company C, 15th Texas Cavalry. His father was living in Denton County by 1864. Minor was a farmer in Denton County in 1870, but was paid in 1877 for guarding county prisoners, likely as a deputy sheriff. He may also have been employed as a deputy city

marshal in Denton. On January 18, 1881, he married Vesta A. Nowlin. He died a widower on April 17, 1926. 1870 Denton County, Texas, Census, 186 (247/255 and 248/256); 1880 Denton County, Texas, Census, 109 (263/263); Texas State Library, Confederate Pension Files, No. 29134; Certificate of Death (William T. Minor), Denton County, Texas, No. 11817; *Denton Record-Chronicle*, 2 May 1926, 3; Commissioners Court Minutes, Denton County, Texas, Vol. A, 84 and 112; Marriage Records, Denton County, Texas, Vol. 2, 53.

33. Alexander W. Robertson was born in Scotland on June 12, 1839, and his family moved to the United States in 1844, settling in Louisiana. Robertson came to Denton County about 1855, and at the outbreak of the Civil War enlisted in Company A, 29th Texas Cavalry. He was wounded during a battle in the Cherokee Nation, leading to amputation of his right leg. Robertson practiced law in Denton and never married. He died in Denton on March 1, 1926. 1880 Denton County, Texas, Census, 19 (1/1); *Denton Record-Chronicle*, 1 March 1926, 1; IOOF Cemetery, Denton, Texas, 13.

34. Hogg, *Authentic History*, 80-81.

35. Hogg, *Authentic History*, 60-61.

36. *Life and Adventures of Sam Bass*, 40.

37. Hogg, *Authentic History*, 61; *Omaha Daily Bee*, 18 March 1878, 2; *Kearney Daily Press*, 23 March 1878, 4; *Denison Daily News*, 24 March 1878, 8; *Nebraska City News*, 16 March 1878, 2; *Columbus* [Nebraska] *Journal*, 20 March 1878, 2.

38. Hogg, *Authentic History*, 61-62.

39. *Life and Adventures of Sam Bass*, 41; The 1860 Johnson County, Missouri, census lists farmer James McKean in Washington Township, near Knob Noster, with his wife Mary, twenty-seven, and two sons born in Missouri, John C., six, and James C., one. 1860 Johnson County, Missouri, Census (21). According to Martin, however, Johnson's true name was Huckston and he was an Irishman by birth. He supposedly served in the Union Army during the war and mustered out in Arkansas after the fighting was over, although there is no record of a man named Huckston or McKean serving in a Union regiment. With a little money in his pocket, Huckston was supposed to have lived the high life until broke, turning then to horse stealing and highway robbery in several counties along the Arkansas River. Martin said that Huckston spent the night with a family named Wilberforce, killing Mr. Wilberforce and his wife by crushing their skulls with a heavy iron, then chloroforming and raping their daughter. He is supposed to have rifled the house of several hundred dollars and jewelry, then fled the state to Missouri and then gone on to Kansas. Martin, *Sketch of Sam Bass*, 82-84. In 1850, the family of Samuel H. Huckson, fifty-five, is listed as living in Pulaski County, Arkansas, in the Bayou Metre Township, on the Arkansas River. Among the Huckson children are Sampson G., twenty-one; William C., nineteen; Thomas, seventeen; and H. Clay, eleven. See 1850 Pulaski County, Arkansas, Census, 365 (723/732). Like McKean and Huckston, there is no mention of a Huckson serving in the Union army. No mention of a Wilberforce could be found. Letter to Author from Ruth Priest Dixon, Mitchellville, Maryland, 6 October 1997. The skimpy Nebraska newspaper articles referring to the escape of Underwood, Caple and Huckston are the only evidence supporting Martin's version, but that does not exclude the possibility that McKean was his true name and Huckston was an alias name.

40. Hogg, *Authentic History*, 29.

41. *Dallas Daily Herald*, 26 March 1878, 4.

42. *Dallas Herald*, as quoted in the *Denison Daily News*, 24 March 1878, 1. Census records in Texas for 1880 list a Samuel J. West, twenty-five, a laborer for Cooke County farmer Thomas Clarke, and a Samuel F. West, forty-eight, who lived with his family in Parker County. See 1880 Cooke County, Texas, Census, 375 (236/236), and 1880 Parker County, Texas, Census, 466 (144/151).

43. *Dallas Daily Herald*, 30 March 1878, 4.

44. *Dallas Daily Herald*, 26 March 1878, 3; 27 March 1878, 4; 28 March 1878, 1; 1870 Denton County, Texas, Census, 157 (201/201).

45. Texas State Library, Special State Troops Correspondence, Box 401-1157-18.

46. *Galveston Daily News*, 10 April 1878, 4; *Penal Code of the State of Texas* (Galveston, Texas: A.H. Belo & Co., State Printers, 1879), 42-43.

47. *Galveston Daily News*, 10 April 1878, 4.

48. Texas State Library, Governor R.B. Hubbard General Correspondence, Box 301-100-32.

49. *Galveston Daily News*, 10 April 1878, 4.

50. William Riley Wetsel was born in Arkansas about 1848. On June 24, 1866, he married Eliza Jennie Baize (Kittrell?) in Denton County, but she died on May 30, 1869. On August 15, 1869, he married Nannie (Nancy) McCurley. In 1874 he and Henderson Murphy were partners in the "Parlor Saloon" in Denton. In 1878 he was a deputy sheriff being paid by the commissioners court for transporting prisoners. By 1880 he was shown to have seven children. He moved to the state of Washington about 1887, and was still alive in November 1904. 1880 Denton County, Texas, Census, 9 (150/151); *Inventory Book, Denton County, 1877*, 267; Tax Assessment Rolls, Denton County, Texas, 1877; *Denton Monitor*, 3 December 1874; Commissioners Court Minutes, Denton County, Texas, Vol. A, 154; *Records of Collin and Denton Counties, Texas* (Plano, Texas: Mary Shirley McGuire Chapter, Daughters of the American Revolution, n.d.), 226; Deed Records, Denton County, Texas, Vol. B, 550.

51. Hogg, *Authentic History*, 85-86.

52. Billy Collins, born in Kentucky on August 10, 1846, had one son, Arthur, by his first wife, Martha E. "Mattie" Swift. Widowed, he married Sarah Zerilda "Sallie" Caton on February 25, 1875. Sallie Collins was born March 5, 1851, in Missouri to farmer J.C. and Sophia Jane Brant Caton, who moved to Denton County in the early 1850s. Letter to author from Ruby Schmidt, Granbury, Texas, 14 April 1997; 1870 Calhoun County, Texas, Census, 361 (6/6); Lu and Neumann, eds., *Marriages, Dallas County*, 38; 1860 Denton County, Texas, Census, 406 (164/165); 1870 Dallas County, Texas, Census, 371 (449/448); 1880 Collin County, Texas, Census, 36 (8/8); Certificate of Death (Sallie Z. Pipes), Dallas County, Texas, No. 20072; *Dallas Daily Herald*, 4 March 1875, 1; *Dallas Morning News*, 10 April 1929, 11.

53. Bruce Brazil may actually be William Bruce Breazeale, a Dallas barber born January 31, 1848, in South Carolina, and a veteran of the Civil War, having fought with Company C, First (Orr's) South Carolina Rifles. 1880 Dallas County, Census, 264 (12/12); Texas State Library, Confederate Pension Applications, File No. 46932.

54. *Dallas Daily Herald*, 8 January 1878, 4; 21 February 1878, 4; 2 March 1878, 3; 7 March 1878, 4; 13 March 1878, 3; 17 March 1878, 1.

55. *Life and Adventures of Sam Bass*, 42-43; Hogg, *Authentic History*, 86.

56. *Life and Adventures of Sam Bass*, 43.

57. Hogg, *Authentic History*, 86-87; *Life and Adventures of Sam Bass*, 40.

58. Hogg, *Authentic History*, 81; 1880 Cooke County, Texas, Census, 172 (5/5).

59. Hogg, *Authentic History*, 82.

60. Hogg, *Authentic History*, 83.

61. Alexander Cockrell was born September 6, 1856, in Dallas to Alexander and Sarah Horton Cockrell, two early pioneers of Dallas County. After his father's death, Cockrell's mother was responsible for building one of the first toll bridges across the Trinity River and became one of the wealthiest women in Texas for that time. He was educated in a small private school in Dallas, then attended Parsons-Carter College as well as Washington and Lee University in Virginia. He followed various pursuits in Dallas and Denton Counties but settled into ranching twelve miles west of Dallas. In 1884 he married Etta Fulkerson and they had

five children. Cockrell was involved in various business interests in Dallas and helped organize the first volunteer fire company. He later claimed to have been a Texas Ranger in 1880 for Capt. G.W. Arrington, but there is no record in the Texas State Library that he ever enlisted in that force. He was a lifelong Mason. He died in Dallas on February 24, 1919. *Dallas Morning News*, 25 February 1919, 16; 1870 Dallas County, Texas, Census, 420 (1341); 1880 Dallas County, Texas, Census, 334 (300/310); *Dallas Daily Herald*, 13 February 1880, 8; Interview by author with Donaly Brice, archivist, Texas State Library, 1 March 1997; Certificate of Death (Alexander Cockrell), Dallas County, Texas, No. 6390.

62. *Dallas Daily Herald*, 2 April 1878, 4.

X. RESISTANCE AT MESQUITE

1. City Council Minutes, Dallas, Texas, 3 April 1878.

2. *Life and Adventures of Sam Bass*, 43.

3. Tyler, ed., *New Handbook of Texas*, Vol. II, 750; *Dallas Daily Herald*, 23 July 1874, 4.

4. Hogg, *Authentic History*, 88-89.

5. Hogg, *Authentic History*, 88.

6. Hogg, *Authentic History*, 90.

7. Martin, *Sketch of Sam Bass*, 49.

8. Matthew Gray was born in Indiana in 1852 to Samuel and Mary Gray. The Gray family was in Denton County by 1860, living on a farm adjacent to that of Samuel's older brother, also named Matthew. The older Matthew Gray had been appointed Denton County Sheriff on November 13, 1867, during Reconstruction, and served until removed in March 1869. Young Matthew Gray was arrested for an unknown offense in Denton County and a *habeas corpus* hearing was held on November 26, 1877. The court ruled for the state and Gray was remanded to the Cooke County jail under a five hundred-dollar bond. A judgment against Gray for failing to appear in court was set aside on March 22, 1878. 1860 Denton County, Texas, Census, 422 (396/399 and 397/398); Certificate of Death (Matthew Gray), Denton County, Texas, No. 24622; *Denton Record-Chronicle*, 17 July 1926, 1; Tise, *Texas County Sheriffs*, 155; Civil Minutes, District Court, Denton County, Texas, *State v. Matthew Gray*, Cause No. 2, Vol. B, pp. 53, 88.

9. *Dallas Daily Herald*, 28 July 1881, 5. Gray was arrested by Tom Gerren in 1883 on suspicion of counterfeiting but was released because the offense had occurred more than three years earlier and was barred from prosecution by limitations. *Dallas Daily Herald*, 16 September 1883, 5.

10. 1880 Van Zandt County, Texas, Census, 94 (235/281).

11. Benjamin [sic] Franklin Caperton, "Sam Bass Robbed My Train, " *True West*, Vol. 11, No. 5 (May-June 1964), 28-54. B.F. Caperton was born September 8, 1847, in Tennessee. See Certificate of Death (Benjamen Franklin Caperton), Dallas County, Texas, No. 38063.

12. Clarence Groce was born about 1850 in Georgia and lived in 1880 in the home of his sister and brother-in-law, James M. and Mary E. Born. 1880 Harris County, Texas, Census, 113 (308).

13. *Fort Worth Democrat* as quoted in the *Denison Daily News*, 10 April 1878, 4. In January 1878 Carr had been temporarily suspended by the railroad when a mail pouch was discovered cut open at Texarkana. He was immediately reinstated when no evidence was developed that he had done it. *Waco Examiner and Patron*, 8 February 1878, 1.

14. Caperton, "Sam Bass Robbed My Train," 28-54; *Life and Adventures of Sam Bass*, 30-31; *Dallas Daily Herald*, 6 April 1878, 4; 7 April 1878, 4; *Galveston Daily News*, 6 April 1878, 1; *Fort Worth Daily Democrat*, 5 April 1878, 4; 6 April 1878, 4; 13 April 1878, 4; National Archives II (College Park, Maryland), RG 204,

Office of the Pardon Attorney, Pardon Case Files 1853-1946, Record J, pp. 93-118, Box 155.

15. Caperton, "Sam Bass Robbed My Train," 28-29.

16. Colonel Noble was born in Pennsylvania about 1833 and had been in Texas for only a few years, having come from Kansas sometime after 1873. At the time of the robbery, he lived in Marshall, Texas, in Harrison County, with his wife and four children. See 1880 Harrison County, Texas, Census, 337 (357/358).

17. *Dallas Daily Herald*, 6 April 1878, 4.

18. *Galveston Daily News*, 6 April 1878, 1; *Life and Adventures of Sam Bass*, 31; *Dallas Daily Herald*, 11 April 1878, 1.

19. As an example, two brothers named Lesh had taken to the field in disguise shortly after the Hutchins robbery to see what they could turn up. They later claimed they were able to learn of the Bass gang's plan to rob the Eagle Ford train on Wednesday or Thursday night, April 3 or 4, and even informed Dallas County Sheriff William Marion Moon of the plan. The two brothers then heard about a stranger who had left a double-barreled shotgun, Navy Colt sixshooter, large knife, and considerable buckshot and cartridges at the house of Patrick Powers near Cedar Springs on March 23, telling Powers that he would pick them up on Wednesday, April 3. The two would-be detectives obtained a warrant from a justice of the peace and, just a few hours before the Eagle Ford robbery on Thursday, April 4, arrested George F. Grant as he rode along with C.W. Williams. After turning Grant over to authorities, the Lesh brothers rode to Eagle Ford but arrived too late to be of any assistance.

The next day, Friday, the court heard the evidence against Grant and promptly dismissed the charge. Williams vouched for Grant and told the court that the two of them were about to join a surveying outfit after a hunting trip to Shackelford County, and that Grant had left the armament with Powers until he could locate a loose horse in the area. Sheriff Moon, to his chagrin, admitted that the "detectives" informed him of what they had heard about a robbery at Eagle Ford, but that he was so engrossed with his duties and in a hurry to take some prisoners to the penitentiary at Huntsville that it slipped his mind. *Dallas Daily Herald*, 5 April 1878, 1; 6 April 1878, 4. A George Grant was listed in the 1880 Denton County census as a twenty-four-year-old farmer from Missouri who boarded with farmer John Petty. See 1880 Denton County, Texas, Census, 201 (17/21). Sheriff William Marion Moon was one of the more colorful lawmen in Dallas. He was born in Jackson County, Missouri, near Independence, on March 18, 1830, one of the six children of Jesse and Mary J. Gilman Moon. His family moved to Texas in 1845 and settled in what was to become Dallas County, just six miles north of the village of Dallas. His father died in November and his mother died in 1853. Marion Moon clerked in a Dallas general merchandise store from 1855 to 1857, then became a deputy sheriff and was also appointed Dallas city marshal, as well as elected to the city board of aldermen. He was a blacksmith with his brother-in-law until the Civil War broke out, then served with Company H, Third Texas Cavalry, being captured toward the end of the war. Returning to Dallas, he married a widow, Mrs. Nancy J. Knight, on December 25, 1865, and farmed until 1871. He then clerked in the Dallas hardware store of his brother-in-law until elected sheriff in 1876, which office he held until 1880. Moon received great praise for his coolness in thwarting a mob intent on lynching a black man who had seriously assaulted a police officer. He briefly tried railroad grading as a pursuit, then served as a deputy sheriff. He and his wife had only one son, who died at twenty-one, and his wife died in 1889. Moon died in Dallas on March 16, 1895. *Dallas Herald*, 10 August 1859; *Dallas Daily Herald*, 12 March 1876, 4; *Dallas Daily Times Herald*, 18 March 1895, 6; Tise, *Texas County Sheriffs*, 146; 1870 Dallas County, Texas, Census, 403 (1133/1126); George Jackson, *Sixty Years in Texas* (n.d., n.p.), 211-12; National Archives, Compiled Service Records, Confederate Soldiers, Texas Third Cavalry (South Kansas-Texas Mounted Volunteers), M323, Roll 21;

Memorial and Biographical History of Dallas County, Texas, 953-55.

20. Hogg, *Authentic History,* 92-93.

21. *Life and Adventures of Sam Bass,* 37.

22. *Dallas Daily Herald,* 11 April 1878, 4; Hogg, *Authentic History,* 93-94; *Life and Adventures of Sam Bass,* 34-35. William M. Edwards, born in Tennessee about 1844, was first mentioned as a Dallas policeman in December 1876. He was dropped from the force on April 16, 1877, but was apparently reappointed a short time later. By 1880 he was serving as a justice of the peace. See *Dallas Weekly Herald,* 16 December 1876; 30 June 1877; *Dallas Daily Herald,* 17 April 1877; 1880 Dallas County, Texas, Census, 95 (368/411); *Gillespie & Work's Dallas Directory, 1881-82,* 36. A James Curry is listed in the 1880 Dallas census as a thirty-three-year-old farmer from Mississippi. See 1880 Dallas County, Texas, Census, 329 (207/214).

23. Hogg, *Authentic History,* 95; *Life and Adventures of Sam Bass,* 34-35.

24. *Dallas Daily Herald,* 11 April 1878, 4.

25. Hogg, *Authentic History,* 95-96.

26. *Denton Monitor,* 13 April 1878, as quoted in *Life and Adventures of Sam Bass,* 34-35.

27. *Dallas Daily Herald,* 7 April 1878, 4.

28. *Dallas Daily Herald,* 6 April 1878, 1.

29. *Dallas Daily Herald,* 11 April 1878, 4.

30. Hogg, *Authentic History,* 98.

31. Hogg, *Authentic History,* 96-97.

32. *Dallas Daily Herald,* 9 April 1878, 4.

33. Hogg, *Authentic History,* 98-99; Martin, *Sketch of Sam Bass,* 54.

34. *Dallas Daily Herald,* 23 April 1878, 1; *Galveston Daily News,* 23 April 1878, 1. Albert G. Herndon was the oldest of five children born to John W. Herndon, a Kentuckian who married Mary Elizabeth McCommas, a daughter of prominent Dallas County settler Amon McCommas and born about 1840. Albert Herndon was born about 1857. John Herndon died on January 15, 1869, leaving his widow with five children and an estate worth $6,700, including 160 acres of farmland bought from her father. The widow married Dr. William P. Stone, who had four children of his own including John Stone who was one year older than Albert. 1860 Dallas County, Texas, Census, 296 (1096/1092); 1870 Dallas County, Texas, Census, 438 (1587/1580); *Proud Heritage: Pioneer Families of Dallas County,* Vol. II, 163; Texas State Library, Probate Cases, Dallas County, Texas, *Estate of John W. Herndon,* Microfilm Case No. 271.

The marriage between Mary Herndon and Doctor Stone was not happy. At some point in 1874, "badly treated" by her husband, she moved out of the family home in Hutchins with their sole child, a daughter, and moved in with a nephew named Cox, apparently leaving her other children with Stone. Stone had threatened on various occasions to take his daughter from her, and, on the evening of Friday, October 2, 1874, he, son-in-law William Garrett and son John armed themselves and rode to Cox' place. Doctor Stone demanded the child, then snatched her from her mother's arms and was starting to leave when Cox rushed out with a shotgun and ordered the men to return the child. A volley of fire from three pistols rang out and the younger Stone's bullet killed Cox instantly. The three rode off and deputies were sent after them but lost the trail. *Daily Dallas Herald,* 4 October 1874, 4. Mary Stone divorced her husband in 1875. *Dallas Daily Herald,* 27 January 1875, 4.

Doctor Stone, his son John and Garrett were indicted for murder, and both Garrett and John Stone fled Dallas County, although Garrett was subsequently captured the following May in San Antonio. The governor offered a $250 reward for young Stone's arrest. *Dallas Daily Herald,* 16 May 1875, 4; Gillett, *Fugitives From Justice,* 174. It would later be reported that John Stone, using the alias Jack Watson, was mortally wounded near Fort Duncan while a member of the gang of the notorious King Fisher. Doctor Stone left Dallas to check out the report, but there is no further information about what happened. *Dallas Daily Herald*, 16 March 1876, 4; 17 March 1876. A John Stone was reported as having shot J.T. Obenchain with a derringer in Dallas on May 25, 1875, but it is believed that this is not the same person as Herndon's stepbrother. *Norton's Union Intelligencer*, 29 May 1875, 3. By 1878 the charges against the Stones and Garrett were dismissed, and Doctor Stone died on October 13, 1886. Reed and Tate, *Tenderfoot Bandits*, 47; Texas State Library, Probate Cases, Dallas County, Texas, *Estate of W.P. Stone*, Cause No. 967, Microfilm Case No. 930.

No doubt affected by exposure to such a volatile household, Albert Herndon was indicted in Dallas in April 1875, along with Dave McCommas and Shug Shirley, for carrying pistols. Reed and Tate, *Tenderfoot Bandits*, 44, citing Cause Nos. 2893, 2889, and 2899 in the 14th District Court of Dallas County, Vol. I, 55. Shirley was a brother of Myra Maebelle Reed who had married former Quantrill guerilla Jim Reed, who was shot to death in Lamar County, Texas, in August 1874. Myra Reed, who would become notorious in the Indian Territory as Belle Starr, was herself facing an arson charge in Dallas. In June 1876 several cases filed against Herndon and John Stone, likely misdemeanors, were transferred from the district court to county court in Dallas. *Dallas Daily Herald*, 15 June 1876, 4.

35. *Dallas Daily Herald*, 8 January 1878; 21, 22 February 1878; *Life and Adventures of Sam Bass*, 44. Samuel J. Pipes was born December 10, 1856, to carpenter John F. Pipes and Isabella L. Pipes, just after they arrived in Texas from Kentucky. 1860 Dallas County, Texas, Census, 313-14 (1317/1322). Isabella, born in 1836, was the daughter of Thomas J. and Eliza Flood Nash. Thomas Nash, born October 15, 1808, had been a member of the Virginia state legislature, then brought his family to Texas in 1854, settling in the Duck Creek area near Dallas. He was elected a Dallas County commissioner in 1858 and again from 1876 to 1878. Nash's wife, Pipes' grandmother, died in 1873. *Memorial and Biographical History of Dallas County, Texas*, 508-09; 1860 Dallas County, Texas, Census, 337 (11/12); 1870 Dallas County, Texas, Census, 372 (2146/2139); 1880 Dallas County, Texas, Census, 213 (62/62); Darnell, Jamieson, and Lu, eds., *Dallas County, Texas, Genealogical Data From Early Cemeteries*, Vol. I, 190-91.

John Pipes died, and by 1868 Isabella had married J.W. Jones, a Dallas farmer born in Tennessee, bringing to the farm with her Sam, his brother John Richard Pipes and sister Mariella Pipes. A son, Perry, was born to John and Isabella Jones in 1869. 1870 Dallas County, Texas, Census, 479 (2144/2137). Sam Pipes' older sister, Sarah, married Jonathan P. Pryor in Dallas on April 3, 1870. Lu and Neumann, *Marriages, Dallas County, Texas*, Vol. I, 22.

36. Texas State Library, *Results of Operations of State Troops*, Ledger 401-1082, 163.

37. *Dallas Daily Herald*, 23 April 1878, 1; *Galveston Daily News*, 23 April 1878, 1.

38. *Dallas Commercial*, 9 April 1878, as quoted in *Life and Adventures of Sam Bass*, 32-33.

39. Texas State Library, Gov. R.B. Hubbard, General Correspondence, Box 301-100-30.

40. Mesquite was established by the Texas and Pacific Railway in May 1873, the station located between the North and South Mesquite Creeks from which the town drew its name. Residents began to populate the small community, coming from nearby farming communities such as Long Creek, New Hope, Haught's Store and Scyene. It was in Scyene that Myra Reed, the future Belle Starr, lived with her family and where the infamous Younger Brothers lived several years before. In early 1878 Mesquite had one store run by James M. Gross, a blacksmith shop, several saloons and the railway station. Tyler, ed., *New Handbook of Texas*, Vol. IV, 641-42; *Galveston Daily News*, 30 March 1878.

41. Hogg, *Authentic History*, 99; *Dallas Weekly Herald*, 23 March 1878, 4.

42. *Austin Daily Democratic Statesman*, 11 April 1878, 4; *Galveston Daily News*,

11 April 1878, 1; Texas State Library, Gov. R.B. Hubbard, General Correspondence, Box 301-100.

43. *Life and Adventures of Sam Bass*, 44.

44. Hogg, *Authentic History*, 99.

45. Caperton, "Sam Bass Robbed My Train," 29.

46. Jake F. Zurn was born in Erie County, Pennsylvania, on October 23, 1855, to a German emigrant who married in Pennsylvania. Zurn was educated there and attended a business college, learning telegraphy at night with Western Union and clerking in his father's store during the day. In 1871 he went to work for the Erie & Pittsburg Railroad as both an operator and car accountant, then in 1873 went to work for the Philadelphia & Erie. He married Agnes Lacy, the daughter of a lumber dealer, on September 5, 1876, in Warren, Pennsylvania, and in November they relocated to Mesquite as station agent for the Texas & Pacific Railway. After the April 10 robbery, he was employed by the International & Great Northern Railroad at Taylor and became joint ticket agent in 1881 when the Missouri, Kansas & Texas built its road to that point. In 1887 he was transferred to Fort Worth where he was also employed as a joint ticket agent. *History of Texas Together With a Biographical History of Tarrant and Parker Counties* (Chicago: The Lewis Publishing Co., 1895), 300.

47. *Dallas Daily Herald*, 12 April 1878, 4.

48. Caperton, "Sam Bass Robbed My Train," 54. According to one account, Mooney escaped and hid his angular frame under some trestle work until the robbery was over. *Denton Monitor*, 16 April 1878, as quoted in Hogg, *Authentic History*, 100.

49. *Denton Monitor*, 16 April 1878, as quoted in Hogg, *Authentic History*, 100-01; W.S. Adair, "Holdups Recall Sam Bass Gang," *Dallas Morning News*, 23 January 1921, III, 4.

50. Unidentified news account, as quoted in *Life and Adventures of Sam Bass*, 46-47; *Denton Monitor*, 16 April 1878, as quoted in Hogg, *Authentic History*, 100.

51. Julius Alvord was born at Pittsford, Monroe County, New York, on December 10, 1835, to Agusta Tripp Alvord and Clarinda Nichols Alvord. When about seventeen, he left home and before the outbreak of the Civil War was employed by a railroad. He enlisted as a private in Company K, 30th Illinois Infantry Regiment, at Trenton, Illinois, on September 15, 1861, serving in the Quartermaster Division as a storekeeper, then later as the regimental Quartermaster Sergeant. In 1862 he had to take a leave of absence because of chronic diarrhea, but in December 1863 he was promoted to first lieutenant and adjutant of the 30th. He was periodically ill during the last months of the war and mustered out in July 1865. Alvord subsequently worked for the Missouri, Kansas & Texas Railway, then in 1876 went to work as a conductor for the Texas & Pacific. After the robbery, he was married on January 15, 1879, at the age of forty-three, to Rebecca "Ree" Porter Turner in Fort Worth. They had one daughter, Nora Estelle Alvord, who was born on April 3, 1880. Active in the Masons and Knight Templar, as was his wife who became Grand Matron in Texas of the Order of Eastern Star, Alvord continued his career as a conductor until his death at Fort Worth on February 23, 1899. Although feeling ill in the winter weather, just a few weeks prior to his death he had shown his nature as a compassionate man when he took aboard a man with smallpox who had been abandoned on the prairie by another train. *Life and Adventures of Sam Bass*, 45; Letter to Author from Mrs. Ruby Schmidt, Granbury, Texas, 7 January 1997; National Archives, Military Records, Company K, 30th Illinois Infantry Regiment (Julius Alvord); Memorial Notice, Order of the Eastern Star, 10 March 1899 (courtesy of Mrs. Ruby Schmidt, Granbury, Texas).

52. John W. Delaney was born about 1844 in Ireland and lived in Dallas. See 1880 Dallas County, Texas, Census, 88 (164).

53. *Life and Adventures of Sam Bass*, 45-46; *Dallas Daily Herald*, 11 April 1878,

4; *Dallas Morning Call*, 11 April 1878, as quoted in the *Denison Daily News*, 13 April 1878, 1;*Fort Worth Daily Democrat*, 12 April 1878, 4; *Houston Age*, as quoted in the *Waco Examiner and Patron*, 19 April 1878, 1.

54. William D. Lacy was born June 25, 1845, in Mason County, Kentucky, to Charles and Sarah Lacy. The family came to Texas in 1852, settling first at Fort Worth then at Denton. Lacy served in the Confederate Army during the Civil War, and afterwards was briefly a cotton buyer in Arkansas, going into business at Ozark, Arkansas. He married Helen Garner there in 1867 and they subsequently had four children. Locating in Paris, Texas, he subsequently moved to Waco in 1882 where he was a bank president and involved in a number of other business enterprises. His wife died in 1886 and he married Mamie Halsell, with whom he had three children. He died in Waco on March 16, 1917. *Denton Record-Chronicle*, 17 March 1917, 6; 1860 Denton County, Texas, Census, 407-408 (199/200).

55. *Denton Monitor*, 16 April 1878, as quoted in Hogg, *Authentic History*, 103-104.

56. *Denton Monitor*, 16 April 1878, as quoted in Hogg, *Authentic History*, 101-102; Mesquite Historical Committee, *A Stake in the Prairie: Mesquite, Texas* (Dallas, Texas: Taylor Publishing Company, 1984), 67. The *Denton Monitor* wrote that Gross had approached the station and got the drop on the fireman hiding under the trestle, thinking he was a robber. He walked to the station and, when he heard a laugh, let down his guard, approached the platform, and was captured. James M. Gross was born in Tennessee in 1844, and at age sixteen enlisted in Company C, 26th East Tennessee Regiment. He was captured at the battle of Fort Donelson and later exchanged at Vicksburg, Mississippi. He served again in Company I, 5th East Tennessee Cavalry, and was again captured. After being paroled, he switched sides and served with Company E, 2nd U.S. Infantry Volunteers, and did escort duty in Kansas and Colorado. After the war he returned to Tennessee, moved to Dallas County in October 1866 where he farmed, then opened a store in Scyene. On November 17, 1870, he married Margaret B. "Maggie" Riggs and they had six children. He moved his store to Mesquite. His only brushes with the law were some local option liquor violations in 1883. *Memorial and Biographical History of Dallas County*, 864-865; 1880 Dallas County, Texas, Census, 217 (131/131); Lu and Neumann, eds., *Dallas County Marriages*, 24; *Dallas Daily Herald*, 9 September 1883. The Tosch family was listed in the 1880 Dallas County, Texas, Census, 239 (35/36). See also *Gillespie & Work's Dallas Directory, 1881-1882*, 137.

57. Unidentified news account, as quoted in *Life and Adventures of Sam Bass*, 47; Caperton, "Sam Bass Robbed My Train," 54; *Denton Monitor*, 16 April 1878, as quoted in Hogg, *Authentic History*, 101.

58. Adair, "Holdups Recall Sam Bass Gang," III, 4. John T. Lynch was later appointed as a Dallas policeman on May 24, 1898, and was still with the force in 1921. *Dallas Morning News*, 25 May 1898; 14 September 1899; and 23 January 1921.

59. Towers was born about 1826 in Georgia and married Samantha McCoy Towers in Texas. He had at least one child, William Perry Towers, who was born January 1, 1856, and later became a bookkeeper and died in Dallas on January 28, 1916. See 1880 Bowie County, Texas, Census, 44 (242/301); Certificate of Death (William Perry Towers), Dallas County, Texas, No. 858.

60. *Dallas Daily Herald*, 11 April 1878, 4; *Fort Worth Daily Democrat*, 11 April 1878, 4; 12 April 1878, 4; *Dallas Morning Call*, 11 April 1878, as quoted in the *Denison Daily News*, 13 April 1878, 1; *Houston Age*, as quoted in the *Waco Examiner and Patron*, 19 April 1878, 1; *Denton Monitor*, 16 April 1878, as quoted in Hogg, *Authentic History*, 100, 104-05; Caperton. "Sam Bass Robbed My Train," 29, 52, 54; National Archives II (College Park, Maryland), RG 204, Office of the Pardon Attorney, Pardon Case Files 1853-1946, Record J, pp. 93-118, Box 155.

61. Hogg, *Authentic History*, 105.

62. *Dallas Daily Herald*, 27 April 1878, 1.

63. Caperton, "Sam Bass Robbed My Train," 54.

64. Dr. L.E. Locke was a Dallas physician, born in Alabama about 1830. His

wife, Amelia, was also born in Alabama, and no children were living with them in 1880. His office was located at 707 Main, and they lived at Oleander and Patterson Streets. See 1880 Dallas County, Texas, Census, 75 (417/436); *Gillespie & Work's Dallas Directory, 1881-1882*, 61.

65. *Dallas Morning Call*, 11 April 1878, as quoted in the *Denison Daily News*, 13 April 1878, 1. Alvord would be presented in 1880 with a fine engraved gold watch and chain by the Texas Express Company in appreciation for his bravery. *Dallas Daily Herald*, 24 February 1880, 8.

66. *Dallas Daily Herald*, 11 April 1878, 4; *Dallas Morning Call*, 11 April 1878, as quoted in the *Denison Daily News*, 13 April 1878, 1.

XI. TEXAS RANGERS TAKE CHARGE

1. *Galveston Daily News*, 12 April 1878, 1.

2. Texas State Library, Adjutant General Records, Frontier Battalion, Box 401-1159-8.

3. Texas State Library, Adjutant General Correspondence.

4. John B. Jones was born on December 22, 1838, at Fairfield, South Carolina, and his family moved to Texas in 1842, settling first in Travis County, then engaging in sugar planting in Matagorda County. In 1857 Jones moved to Navarro County. At the outbreak of the Civil War, according to his obituary, Jones traveled to Virginia rather than join a Texas unit, then to Bowling Green, Kentucky, where he enlisted in the Eighth Texas Cavalry. He became a first lieu-tenant and adjutant of the 15th Texas Infantry then was promoted to captain. According to service records in the National Archives, however, Jones enlisted as a private on February 18, 1862, at Galveston in Captain M.D. Herring's Company B of the 15th Texas Infantry. On April 16, 1862, he was appointed an adjutant to Speight's regiment of the 15th Texas.

After the war Jones went to Mexico, then in 1867 to Brazil where he stayed for eighteen months attempting to establish a colony of American families. Back in Texas he was elected to the state legislature but was not allowed to take his seat because of Reconstruction politics. On May 19, 1874, Jones enlisted in the Frontier Battalion and by August was a major and quartermaster of the ranger force. He assumed command of the Frontier Battalion in 1875. At the time of Bass' exploits he was a deputy grand master of the Masonic Order in Texas, but he had never married. *Dallas Daily Herald*, 20 July 1881, 4; National Archives, Compiled Service Records of Confederate Soldiers, 15th Texas Infantry, M323, Roll 377; Texas State Library, General Service Records, File 401-158; *Houston Telegram*, as quoted by the *Dallas Daily Herald*, 22 December 1877, 1; Tyler, ed., *New Handbook of Texas*, Vol. 3, 986. See also Helen Frances Bonner, *Major John B. Jones: The Defender of the Texas Frontier* (Master's Thesis, University of Texas at Austin, 1950).

5. *Houston Telegram*, as quoted by the *Dallas Daily Herald*, 22 December 1877, 1.

6. *Dallas Daily Herald*, 12 April 1878, 2.

7. James D. Horan, *The Pinkertons* (New York: Bonanza Books, 1967), 370.

8. *Dallas Daily Herald*, 12 April 1878, 4.

9. Stillwell H. Russell was born about 1829 in South Carolina, one of twelve children born to William Jarvis Russell and Eleanor Heady Guthrie Russell. Prior to the Texas Revolution, Russell's father commanded the schooner *Brazoria* that bombarded the Mexicans from the Brazos River, and he was said to have fired the first shot of the Revolution. His mother was credited with molding the bullets that were fired at Anahuac on June 26, 1832. An ardent Republican, Russell ulti-mately settled in Harrison County where he was elected sheriff on November 8, 1872, and reelected on October 12, 1874, serving until he was "removed" on

February 15, 1876. He stood 6' 4" and weighed 235 pounds. On March 4, 1878, he was appointed U.S. Marshal for what was then the Western District of Texas. 1880 Smith County, Texas, Census, 307 (178/212); Tyler, ed., *New Encyclopedia of Texas*, Vol. 5, 731; *Fort Worth Daily Democrat*, 1 February 1878; National Archives, RG 60, Records Relating to the Appointment of Federal Judges, Marshals, and Attorneys, 1853-1901 (Appointment Files for Judicial Districts 1853-1905); Tise, *Texas County Sheriffs*, 245; *Norton's Union Intelligencer*, 26 June 1875, 4; Sam Acheson, *Dallas Yesterday* (Dallas, Texas: SMU Press, 1977), 377-78.

10. *Dallas Daily Herald*, 12 April 1878, 4.

11. *Fort Worth Daily Democrat*, 11 April 1878, 4; *Dallas Daily Commercial*, as quoted in the *Denison Daily News*, 11 April 1878, 1.

12. *Sherman Courier*, as quoted in the *Galveston Daily News*, 12 April 1878, 2.

13. *Fort Worth Daily Democrat*, 16 April 1878, 4.

14. Thomas Elisha Hogg was born in Cherokee County, Texas, on June 19, 1842, to Joseph Lewis Hogg and Lucanda McMath Hogg. He was raised on the family plantation at Mountain Home, near Rusk, and had a vivid childhood interest in literature, aspiring to be a writer. He started attendance at Weatherford College in 1860, but the war broke out and his father was appointed a brigadier general in the Confederate Army and ordered to report to Memphis, Tennessee, to command a Texas brigade. One of the units in that brigade, Company C, 3rd Texas Cavalry, had assigned his son, Private Thomas E. Hogg. However, before he could even receive his uniform, and after Gen. P.G.T. Beauregard had him briefly arrested for recklessly endangering a supply train, General Hogg took ill and died with his son present. This led Hogg to write a novel, *The Last Stand at Corinth*, and two poems about that battle. After the war Hogg briefly taught school at Duck Hill, Mississippi, and in 1866 married his cousin, Anna Eliza McMath. They settled near Rusk, where Hogg became legal guardian to his two younger brothers, one of whom was James Stephen Hogg who would be governor of Texas from 1891 to 1895. The farm declined, and Hogg opened a school in Rusk, at the same time studying the law. In 1871 he became a justice of the peace in Rusk and purchased the local newspaper to espouse his Democratic views. In 1873 he was admitted to the bar and moved to Denton, where he was an editor and became active in local affairs, serving as city attorney and sworn in on April 17, 1876, as county judge. Shortly after the death of Bass, he authored *The Authentic History of Sam Bass and His Gang*. He and his wife had five children. He contracted typhoid fever and died on September 27, 1880, at the age of thirty-eight, and his wife died on November 4, 1892. 1880 Denton County, Texas, Census, 31 (43/52); Tyler, ed., *New Handbook of Texas*, Vol. III, 654; *Confederate Veteran*, Vol. 14, No. 10 (October 1906), 494; IOOF Cemetery, Denton, Texas, 21; Commissioners Court Minutes, Denton County, Texas, Vol. A, 17; Denton County Genealogical Society, Inc., *Denton County, Texas, Wills*, 64.

15. *Dallas Daily Herald*, 14 April 1878, 3.

16. *Denison Daily News*, 20 April 1878, 1. See also *Galveston Daily News*, 14 April 1878, 4.

17. *Galveston Daily News*, 27 April 1878, 2.

18. Unidentified account, 11 April 1878, *Life and Adventures of Sam Bass*, 36-37.

19. Texas State Library, Adjutant General Records, Letter Press Book, Ledger 401-625, p. 55.

20. *Dallas Daily Herald*, 13 April 1878, 4; 14 April 1878, 1.

21. Walter Paye Lane was born on February 18, 1817, in Cork County, Ireland, to William and Olivia Lane. The family immigrated to the United States in 1821, settling in Ohio. In 1836 Lane left for Texas and participated in the battle at San Jacinto, where he was promoted to 2nd Lieutenant for gallantry. He served aboard a privateer in raids against the Mexican coast. While part of a surveying party in October 1838 in what is now Navarro County, he was one of six men of a group of twenty-three who barely survived a Kickapoo Indian attack, he being

seriously wounded in the leg. Lane lived in San Augustine County between 1838 and 1843 then moved to San Antonio, where he became a ranger with the famous Capt. John Hays. He served as an officer in the Mexican War, rising to the rank of major, and discovered and seized the remains of Texans killed in the ill-fated Mier Expedition. He spent four years in California as part of the Gold Rush, then joined his brother at Marshall, Texas, in running a store. In 1854 he prospected in Arizona for a while, operated a ranch and clerked, then returned to Texas in 1858. With the Civil War he was a lieutenant colonel of the 3rd Texas Cavalry then later served with the First Texas Partisan Rangers. He distinguished himself in battle and by the end of the war had been appointed a brigadier general. He returned to Harrison County after the war and resumed his mercantile business. In 1878 at the age of sixty-one, he was appointed a Deputy U.S. Marshal. He was afterwards County Treasurer and tax collector in Harrison County. Lane never married and died at Marshall on January 28, 1892. Tyler, ed., *New Handbook of Texas*, Vol. IV, 62-63; 1880 Harrison County, Texas, Census, 366 (39/42); *Dallas Morning News*, 29 January 1892, 4; National Archives, RG 60, Records Relating to the Appointment of Federal Judges, Marshals, and Attorneys, 1853-1901 (Appointment Files For Judicial Districts 1853-1905); John Henry Brown, *Indian Wars and Pioneers of Texas* (Austin, Texas: State House Press, 1988), 48-50.

22. Hogg, *Authentic History*, 107-108.

23. Texas State Library, Adjutant General Records, General Correspondence, Box 401-397-1.

24. *Dallas Daily Herald*, 16 April 1878, 1.

25. Texas State Library, Adjutant General Correspondence, Box 401-397-2.

26. Walter Prescott Webb, *The Texas Rangers* (Austin, Texas: University of Texas Press, 1982), 375.

27. Texas State Library, Adjutant General Records, Frontier Battalion, Box 401-1159-8; Special Order No. 126, 16 April 1878, Adjutant General Records, General Correspondence, Box 401-397-2.

28. City Council Minutes, Dallas, Texas, 18 April 1878; *Dallas Daily Herald*, 18 April 1878, 4.

29. Texas State Library, Special Order No. 60, 17 April 1878, Frontier Battalion, Ledger No. 401-1012; *Dallas Daily Herald*, 17 April 1878, 4.

30. Andrew J. Evans was born in South Carolina about 1832. His first wife died, leaving him with four children. He married again on October 23, 1877, in Austin to Mrs. Clara E. Stinger Weir, but she is not listed in the 1880 census when he was living with his children in San Antonio. See 1880 Bexar County, Texas, Census, 117; *The Texas Capital*, 28 October 1877, 3.

31. *Galveston Daily News*, 18 April 1878, 1; *Dallas Daily Herald*, 17 April 1878, 1.

32. *Austin Daily Democratioc Statesman*, 11 July 1878, 4.

33. Thomas S. Floyd was born in August 1849 in Union County, Kentucky, to John D. and Susan Finnie Floyd, who died in Dallas on January 1, 1875. The family moved to Texas in 1850, settling some seven miles north of Dallas. Floyd worked on the family farm, but in January 1874 was appointed as a Dallas deputy sheriff, and he gained some notice for his ability as a lawman. In July 1874 he nabbed a man named Webb who had threatened the life of a justice of the peace. In that same month word came from Mississippi of a murder warrant for J.N. Eskridge, a well-known Dallas cotton buyer. Sheriff James Barkley assigned Floyd to bring him in, and the deputy tracked the fugitive on the railroad to Troup in Smith County. Stepping from the train, he spotted Eskridge in an upstairs hotel window. Eskridge also saw him, jumped through a window on the opposite side of the building, and tried to get away. Floyd ran around the building and drew down on Eskridge. The fugitive attempted to draw a weapon and Floyd fired first, shattering Eskridge's arm. Floyd later escorted him back to Mississippi. When then City Marshal June Peak went on a hunting trip in August 1874, Deputy

ENDNOTES

Floyd was named acting city marshal until his return. He was mustered into Peak's ranger detachment on April 17, 1878, and was honorably discharged on February 29, 1880. He returned to Dallas County and life as a farmer. Floyd married Lydia Gilroy about 1883, and they had at least three children. He died in Dallas on January 29, 1917. *Dallas Daily Herald*, 14 July 1874, 4; 22 July 1874, 4; 5 August 1874, 4; 19 August 1874, 4; 25 August 1874, 4; 3 January 1875, 4; *Memorial and Biographical History of Dallas County, Texas*, 982-83; 1870 Dallas County, Texas, Census, 410 (1222/1215); 1880 Dallas County, Texas, Census, 116 (102/109); 1900 Dallas County, Texas, Census, ED 129, Sheet 6, Line 36, p. 217-A (95/95); 1910 Dallas County, Texas, Census, ED 185, Sheet 1B (580); Certificate of Death (Tom S. Floyd), Dallas County, Texas, No. 980; *Dallas Morning News*, 30 January 1917, 5; Texas State Library, General Service Records, File 401-151.

34. Adrian Worth Mixon was born at Williston, South Carolina, about 1846. He enlisted as a private at Fort Johnson in Company A, 2nd South Carolina Coast Artillery Regiment, on March 10, 1864. By 1870 he was in Texas and in January 1873 was a member of the Dallas police force, one of his fellow officers being Jim Younger, one of the infamous Younger brothers. Mixon served under City Marshal June Peak, and he also served as a deputy U.S. marshal. He was defeated by William F. Morton in election as Dallas City Marshal on April 2, 1878, just two weeks before he mustered into Peak's ranger detachment on April 17. He was discharged on May 17, 1878. In 1880 he lost another bid for Dallas city marshal and served as a deputy sheriff. Mixon moved his family to Grayson County about this time, where he died at Denison on March 8, 1930. 1880 Dallas County, Texas, Census, 61 (174/182); Texas State Library, Confederate Pension Applications, File No. 41335; Reject File, Confederate Pension Applications (Enna Mixson); City Council Minutes, Dallas, Texas, 3 April 1878; *Dallas Herald*, 4 January 1873, 3; *Dallas Daily Commercial*, 12 April 1874, 4; *Dallas Weekly Herald*, 16 December 1876, 1; Texas State Library, Adjutant General Service Records, Frontier Battalion, Box 401-164; Muster and Payroll, Detachment Company B, Frontier Battalion, 17 May 1878, Box 401-747, Folder 9.

35. Texas State Library, Adjutant General Service Records, Frontier Battalion, Box 401-169; Muster and Payroll, Detachment Company B, Frontier Battalion, 1 June 1878, Box 401-747, Folder 9; *Dallas Daily Herald*, 2 August 1876; *Dallas Weekly Herald*, 23 June 1877, 4. The Dallas police force had a policeman named Rice who was dismissed in August 1876 for accepting a five dollar bribe, but there is evidence that his name was G.W. Rice. *Dallas Daily Herald*, 2-3 August 1876, 4.

36. *Galveston Daily News*, 4 April 1878, 1.

37. Texas State Library, Frontier Battalion Correspondence, Box 401-397-2.

38. In addition, the other recruits signed up by Peak, as determined by ranger service records in the Texas State Library, were the following:

(1) R.H. Armstrong - enlisted 17 April 1878; discharged 31 August 1878.

(2) Thomas R. Bailey - enlisted 19 April 1878; discharged 30 November 1878.

(3) Celcius Putnam Bodwell (listed as "Bardwell") - enlisted 18 April 1878; born at Paris Landing, Tennessee, on August 31, 1854; may have served as a ranger from January 6 to March 6, 1874; discharged on May 17, 1878; married Cassie Strain on May 2, 1880, near DeKalb, Texas, but she died on April 26, 1904. He then married Mrs. Zella Nelson Thweatt in July 1910, but they divorced in 1920. 1880 Dallas County, Texas, Census, 52 (14/16); Stephens, *Texas Rangers Indian War Pensions*, 10; Texas State Library, Adjutant General Service Records, Frontier Battalion, Box 141-143.

(4) Hiram C. Berry - enlisted 17 April 1878; born in Alabama in approximately 1853; discharged 17 May 1878. 1880 Dallas County, Texas, Census, 23 (539).

(5) A.E. Boren - enlisted 17 April 1878; discharged 17 May 1878.

(6) H. Britt (or Brett) - enlisted 17 April 1878; discharged 31 August 1878.

(7) James W. Bruton - enlisted 18 April 1878; discharged 31 August 1878.

(8) Harry C. Cammack - enlisted 17 April 1878; discharged 18 July 1878; born

353

about 1859 in Louisiana. He was a billing clerk for the Texas & Pacific Railway in 1881, and was living in Butte, Montana, in 1927. 1880 Dallas County, Texas, Census, 32 (114/140); *Gillespie & Work's Dallas Directory, 1881-1882*, 24; *Frontier Times*, Vol. 5, No. 1 (October 1927), 48.

(9) Morgan Cammack - enlisted 17 April 1878; discharged 17 May 1878; is older brother of Harry Cammack and was born about 1850 in Louisiana. He was a railroad clerk in 1881. 1880 Dallas County, Texas, Census, 32 (114/140); *Gillespie & Work's Dallas Directory, 1881-1882*, 24.

(10) J.H. Camron (Cameron?) - enlisted 23 April 1878; discharged 17 May 1878.

(11) R. C. Darsey - enlisted 19 April 1878; discharged 31 August 1878; a Robert C. Darsey was born about 1852 in Arkansas and was a store clerk in Wise County in 1880. 1880 Wise County, Texas. Census, 159 (54/58).

(12) A.G. (Allen Gano?) Eakin - enlisted 17 April 1878; discharged 17 May 1878; born about 1853 in Texas. 1880 Dallas County, Texas, Census, 109 (618/689).

(13) Timoleon Edwin Eakin - enlisted 18 April 1878; discharged 17 May 1878; cousin of A.G. Eakin; born about 1854 in Kentucky to John J. Eakin, who immigrated to Dallas County when Eakin was three months old. He was educated at the Texas Military Institute in Austin. Eakin married Mamie Hughes of San Marcos, Texas, in June 1879 and was involved in the real estate business in Dallas. 1880 Dallas County, Texas, Census, 109 (618/689); *Memorial and Biographical History of Dallas County, Texas*, 576.

(14) Gaston Hardy - enlisted 17 April 1878; became ill with typhoid fever and was discharged 17 May 1878.

(15) L.S. Hart - enlisted 19 April 1878; discharged 17 May 1878; had been a police officer under Peak in Dallas in 1875 but the City Council refused to reinstate him. City Council Minutes, Dallas, Texas, 8 June 1875.

(16) W.C. Lewis - enlisted on 18 April 1878; promoted to corporal; discharged 31 August 1878.

(17) James McDonald - enlisted 19 April 1878; discharged 17 May 1878. The 1880 Dallas census lists a twenty-five-year-old James McDonald from Kentucky, a cook at the county poor farm. 1880 Dallas County, Texas, Census, 277 (233/235).

(18) Jerry McHenry - enlisted 19 April 1878; discharged 17 May 1878.

(19) John W. Overand - enlisted 19 April 1878; discharged 17 May 1878; born in Dallas about 1853; married Charlotte Baldwin on April 29, 1875, and they had three children; appointed a special policeman in April 1880 and was foreman of the street cleaning force; became a regular policeman, but was suspended twice in 1884 for unbecoming conduct. In 1885 he was a deputy constable and was thrown from his horse on September 25, 1886, and killed. City Council Minutes, Dallas, Texas, 22 April 1880; 16 December 1884; *Dallas Daily Herald*, 1 May 1875, 4; *Fort Worth Gazette*, 30 January 1884, 2; *Dallas Morning News*, 2 December 1885, 10 February 1886, 27 September 1886; *Gillespie & Work's Dallas Directory, 1881-1882*, 73; Lu and Neumann, eds., *Dallas County Marriages*, 38.

(20) W.A. Rainwater - enlisted 17 April 1878; discharged 17 May 1878; born about 1842 in Mississippi; enlisted as private on August 10, 1861, in Company B, 27th Mississippi Infantry; promoted to sergeant; captured in 1863 and exchanged in March 1865; died in Lampasas, Texas, on January 23, 1931. Texas State Library, Confederate Pension Applications, File No. 47023.

(21) William Scott - enlisted 1 May 1878. See biographical information in Chapter Eight.

(22) E.W. "Jack" Smith - enlisted 1 May 1878; discharged 19 August 1878.

(23) C.E. Tucker - enlisted 17 April 1878; discharged 31 August 1878.

(24) J.R. Vaught - enlisted 18 April 1878; discharged 17 May 1878.

(25) Theo. J. Whitley - enlisted 20 April 1878; discharged 30 November 1878.

(26) Robert E. Williams - enlisted 17 April 1878; discharged 15 October 1878.

(27) J.B. Wright - enlisted 18 April 1878; discharged 17 May 1878.

39. *Dallas Daily Herald*, 20 April 1878, 4; Texas State Library, Monthly Return,

Company B, Frontier Battalion, Box 401-1247-5.

40. *Life and Adventures of Sam Bass*, 50.

41. Texas State Library, Adjutant General Records, Frontier Battalion Correspondence, Box 401-1159-8.

42. Thomas Howard Duval was born on November 4, 1813, in Buckingham County, Virginia, to William Pope Duval and Nancy Hynes Duval. He grew up in Bardstown, Kentucky, and was graduated from St. Joseph's College in 1833. He studied law under Charles Wickliffe, postmaster general in John Tyler's administration, then moved with his family to Florida where he was admitted to the state bar in 1837. In 1839, back in Virginia, he married his first cousin, Laura Peyton, then began his public service career in Florida, first as circuit clerk of Leon County, then clerk ex officio of the court of appeals. In 1843 he received a presidential appointment as secretary of the Territory of Florida. Following two brothers to Texas, Duval moved to Austin in December 1845 to practice law. He served as a reporter for the Texas Supreme Court from 1846 to 1851, then in 1851 was appointed Texas Secretary of State by Governor Peter Bell. In 1855 he was a district judge, then in 1857 President Buchanan named him the first federal judge for a new Western District of Texas, which extended from Tyler to El Paso and Brownsville. Loyal to the Union, Judge Duval remained in Austin during the Civil War, working for a paltry salary in the General Land Office and as a deputy county surveyor. When a son enlisted as an officer in the Confederate Army, Duval managed to make his way to Washington D.C. and present a plan to end the war by indemnifying each state as it returned to the Union for the value of that state's slaves. He stayed in New York and New Orleans until the end of the war then resumed his position in Texas as a federal judge, surviving an impeachment attempt. On December 6, 1877, his fifteen-year-old son, Johnny, was killed when a shotgun accidentally discharged. On October 10, 1880, while visiting his daughter and her family at Omaha, Nebraska, Judge Duval died. Tyler, ed., *New Handbook of Texas*, Vol. II, 741-42; *Austin Daily Statesman*, 12 October 1880, 2; *The Texas Capital*, 9 December 1877, 3; 1860 Travis County, Texas, Census, 266 (405/405); 1870 Travis County, Texas, Census, 311 (721/796); 1880 Travis County, Texas, Census, 183 (218/253).

43. Texas State Library, Adjutant General Records, Frontier Battalion, Box 401-1159-8.

44. George R. Fearn, a Dallas attorney and U.S. Commissioner, was born on May 30, 1831, at Huntsville, Alabama. He spent his early youth in Mississippi and attended Oakland College and the Virginia Military Institute, then graduated from Harvard Law School in 1852. He organized a company in the Confederate Army. Fearn came to Dallas in 1874. He was married twice, producing at least four children, and in 1894 he was Adjutant for the Sterling Price Camp in Dallas of the United Confederate Veterans. Widowed, he died in Dallas on June 22, 1914. *Dallas Morning News*, 23 June 1914, 7; Certificate of Death (George R. Fearn), Dallas County, Texas, No. 11926; *Confederate Veteran*, Vol. II, No. 4 (April 1894).

45. *Dallas Daily Herald*, 23 April 1878, 1; *Galveston Daily News*, 23 April 1878, 1; 30 April 1878, 1. Thomas Jefferson Jackson was born September 18, 1842, to John and Eliza Brown Jackson in Jackson County, Missouri. The family moved to Dallas County in 1846. During the Civil War Jackson served in Company A, 31st Texas Cavalry, and saw service in Arkansas, Louisiana, and Missouri. On December 25, 1866, he married Mary Eliza "Mollie" Nash, the daughter of Thomas J. Nash. His sister, Hannah Lenora Jackson, married Charles Lafayette Nash in October 1865. Tom Jackson and his wife had nine children. Mollie Nash died in 1902, and he died on his farm on March 3, 1910. *Dallas Morning News*, 4 March 1910, 4; *Proud Heritage: Families of Dallas County*, Vol. I, 114-15; Certificate of Death (Thomas J. Jackson), Dallas County, Texas, No. 11324; Lu and Neumann, *Dallas County Marriages*, 16; 1880 Dallas County, Texas, Census, 168.

46. *Dallas Daily Herald*, 23 April 1878, 1; *Galveston Daily News*, 23 April 1878,

1; Texas State Library, Frontier Battalion, Company B, Monthly Return (April 1878), Box 401-1247-5; *Results of Operations of State Troops*, Ledger 401-1082, p. 139.

47. Texas State Library, Adjutant General Records, Frontier Battalion, Box No. 401-1159-8.

48. *Galveston Daily News*, 23 April 1878, 1.

49. The identity of "J. Minor" is clouded. The 1870 Denton County census lists a forty-nine-year-old dry goods merchant named Joseph Minor, who had a twenty-year-old son named James L. Minor who worked on a farm. The Minor family was likely related to Denton City Marshal Bill Minor, whose father was Joseph Minor. See 1870 Denton County, Texas, Census, 186 (247/255); 1880 Denton County, Texas, Census, 119 (47/47).

50. *Dallas Daily Herald*, 23 April 1878, 4; *Galveston Daily News*, 24 April 1878, 1; *Fort Worth Daily Democrat*, 26 April 1878, 4.

51. John Skaggs, remembered at his death as a "white man's negro," was born in Kentucky about 1850. His family was brought to Denton County prior to the Civil War as the property of Thomas Skaggs. His mother, Harriett, was remarried to a Denton black minister, William Crenshaw. Skaggs and his wife Sylvy, who was also born in Kentucky and took in washing, had five children by 1880, the oldest being Lucy, fourteen, who was born in Texas. On March 8, 1878, he was indicted in Denton County for both assault to murder and theft, but he was acquitted of the assault charge on April 4, 1879, after his federal problems resulting from his association with the Bass gang were over. In 1910 he married his second wife, Eller L., who cooked in a private home. Skaggs was illiterate and never sure of how old he was. He was proud to always vote the Democratic ticket, not because of politics but because all of the white men who were willing to post his bond when he got in trouble were Democrats, "I ain't fool enough to go back on the men who stay with me." He died in Terrell, Texas, on December 13, 1916, and was buried in Denton. *Denton Record-Chronicle*, 14 December 1916, 6; 1880 Denton County, Texas, Census, 7 (107/107); 1910 Denton County, Texas, Census, ED 81, Sheet 3B, Line 99; Civil Minutes, District Court, Denton County, Texas, *State of Texas v. John Skaggs*, Cause Nos. 1532 and 1533, Vol. B, 119, 324.

52. *Dallas Weekly Herald*, 27 April 1878; *Galveston Daily News*, 27 April 1878, 1; Texas State Library, Frontier Battalion, Monthly Return, Company B Detachment (April 1878), Box 401-1247-5; *Results of Operations of State Troops*, Ledger 401-1082, p. 139.

53. Texas State Library, Adjutant General Records, Frontier Battalion, Box 401-1159-8.

54. William H. Anderson was a native of Redmond, Kentucky, and had come to Texas from Knox County, Illinois, about 1869, engaging in cattle raising. On June 15, 1869, a William Anderson married E.C. Wheeler in Dallas. In the 1870 Dallas County census there is a William Anderson, twenty-five, a farmer from Arkansas, who is married to Celia, twenty-two, from Indiana, with a one-year-old daughter, Laura A. He was appointed a deputy U.S. Marshal in 1872. *Waco Examiner and Patron*, 15 November 1878; Lu and Neumann, eds., *Dallas County Marriages*, Vol. I, 20; 1870 Dallas County, Texas, Census, 325 (125/128); National Archives, RG 60, Records Relating to the Appointment of Federal Judges, Marshals, and Attorneys, 1853-1901 (Appointment Files for Judicial Districts 1853-1905).

55. *Dallas Daily Herald*, 25 April 1878, 4.

56. John McCommas was born in Illinois about 1828, the son of Amon and Mary Brumfield McCommas. In Dallas County he married Missouri Tucker on May 10, 1849. A farmer, he and his wife had at least nine children, including John H., born about 1857. 1860 Dallas County, Texas, Census, 299 (1135/1130); 1870 Dallas County, Texas, Census, 437 (1584/1577); 1880 Dallas County, Texas, Census, 146 (304/322); Lu and Neumann, eds., *Dallas County Marriages*, 1; Brown, *History of Dallas County*, 81-82.

ENDNOTES

57. Benjamin F. Fleaman was born about 1840 in Virginia and by 1860 was a blacksmith in Dallas County living in the household of Amon McCommas. On December 24, 1865, he married Armilda McCommas, and by 1880 they had five children on the farm. 1860 Dallas County, Texas, Census, 299 (1129/1124); 1870 Dallas County, Texas, Census, 437 (1574/1567); 1880 Dallas County, Texas, Census, 146 (311/329); Lu and Neumann, eds., *Dallas County Marriages*, 14; *Memorial and Biographical History of Dallas County*, 349.

58. *Galveston Daily News*, 25 April 1878, 1; *Dallas Daily Herald*, 25 April 1878, 4.

59. Texas State Library, Adjutant General Records. Frontier Battalion, Box 401-1159-8.

60. Texas State Library, Adjutant General Records, Frontier Battalion, Box 401-1159-8.

61. Center for American History, University of Texas at Austin, Transcripts From the Office of the Adjutant General of Texas, 1878, File No. 2Q400, p. 103.

62. *Galveston Daily News*, 26 April 1878, 1; *Dallas Daily Herald*, 23 April 1878, 4; 27 April 1878, 4.

63. Hickerson Barksdale was born about 1839 in Tennessee. He married his wife, Nannie, on April 20, 1856, and served in Company G, 13th Tennessee Regiment, during the Civil War. After the war he and his wife had three children in Tennessee; then they moved to Dallas County around 1870, where they had four more. He practiced law until his death on May 14, 1884. 1880 Dallas County, Texas, Census, 130 (37/40); Texas State Library, Probate Cases, Dallas County, Texas, *Estate of H. Barksdale*, Cause No. 738 (Microfilm No. 861); Confederate Pension Applications, File No. 1077.

64. Elisha McCommas was born in 1830 in Lawrence County, Ohio, to Amon and Mary Brumfield McCommas. The family was in Dallas County by 1844, where he helped on the family farm. In August 1849 he accompanied a gold-hunting expedition to the Wichita Mountains. In December 1850 he married Rhoda Ann Tucker. In 1862 McCommas enlisted in Company B, 19th Texas Cavalry, and served in Arkansas, Missouri, and Louisiana. After the war he resumed farming, and he and his wife subsequently had ten children. He died in Dallas County on August 22, 1903. *Memorial and Biographical History of Dallas County*, 349-50; *Dallas Morning News*, 23 August 1903, 7; Lu and Neumann, eds., *Dallas County Marriages*, 2; Texas State Library, Probate Cases, Dallas County, Texas, Microfilm Case No. 2663, *Estate of Elisha McCommas*, Cause No. 3470; Brown, *History of Dallas County, From 1837 to 1887*, 81-82.

65. *Dallas Daily Herald*, 27 April 1878, 1; 1870 Dallas County, Texas, Census, 402 (1113/1106); 1880 Dallas County, Texas, Census, 152 (414/437).

66. *Dallas Daily Herald*, 27 April 1878, 1; 28 April 1878, 4.

67. Texas State Library, Adjutant General Records, Frontier Battalion, Box 401-1159-8.

68. *Dallas Daily Herald*, 27 April 1878, 1; *Galveston Daily News*, 27 April 1878, 1.

69. *Galveston Daily News*, 25 April 1878, 4.

70. *Dallas Daily Herald*, 21 April 1878, 2.

71. *Sherman Register*, 24 April 1878, as quoted in the *Dallas Weekly Herald*, 27 April 1878.

72. *Dallas Daily Herald*, 26 April 1878, 1; *Galveston Daily News*, 26 April 1878, 1; *Denison Daily News*, 27 April 1878, 1.

73. *Denton Monitor*, as quoted in the *Denison Daily News*, 12 May 1878, 1.

74. *Sherman Register*, 13 May 1878, as quoted in the *Denison Daily News*, 15 May 1878, 1.

XII. CLOSE PURSUIT

1. *Dallas Daily Herald*, 27 April 1878, 4.

2. Texas State Library, Adjutant General Records, Frontier Battalion, Box

ENDNOTES

401-1159-8; Correspondence, Governor R.H. Hubbard, Box 301-100.

3. 1880 Dallas County, Texas, Census, 13 (296); *Dallas Daily Herald*, 15 June 1876.

4. *Dallas Daily Herald*, 28 April 1878, 4.

5. Texas State Library, Adjutant General Records, Frontier Battalion, Box 401-1129-8; 401-1159-8.

6. Martin, *Sketch of Sam Bass*, 97.

7. *Denison Daily News*, 27 April 1878, 1.

8. *Dallas Daily Herald*, 3 May 1878, 1; *Denton Monitor*, 10 May 1878, as quoted in *The Frontier Echo* [Jacksboro], 17 May 1878, 2.

9. Texas State Library, Frontier Battalion Correspondence, Box 401-397-2.

10. *Dallas Daily Herald*, 30 April 1878, 1.

11. *Dallas Daily Herald*, 1 May 1878, 1; *Galveston Daily News*, 1 May 1878, 1.

12. *Dallas Daily Herald*, 30 April 1878, 1.

13. *Dallas Daily Herald*, 1 May 1878, 4.

14. *Galveston Daily News*, 30 April 1878, 1.

15. *Galveston Daily News*, 30 April 1878, 1.

16. *Life and Adventures of Sam Bass*, 51-52.

17. Texas State Library, Frontier Battalion, Monthly Return, Company B (April 1878), Box 401-1247-5; *Results of Operations of State Troops*, Ledger 401-1082, p. 139; *Galveston Daily News*, 30 April 1878, 1; *Dallas Daily Herald*, 30 April 1878, 4.

18. *Dallas Daily Herald*, 1 May 1878, 4.

19. Hogg, *Authentic History*, 108-109; *Life and Adventures of Sam Bass*, 53.

20. Albert Robert McGintie was born on July 12, 1845, in Ohio, but the family soon moved to St. Louis where McGintie's father was a prominent surgeon. His father had been born on the Atlantic Ocean while his parents were immigrating from Ireland. McGintie left home at about the age of eighteen and came to Texas to become a cowboy. Settling in Denton, he was reported to have been a pharmacist for Dr. R.S. Ross and to have managed the Lacy House. On December 28, 1875, he married Luella B. Owsley, and on November 14, 1876, he was appointed Constable of Precinct No. 1 by the commissioners court. He broke his ankle in a buggy accident in December 1877. He was also reported to have been a deputy sheriff. He and his wife had two children. Active in the real estate and rental business, McGintie died in Denton on February 13, 1920. *Denton Record-Chronicle*, 14 February 1920, 8; Certificate of Death (Albert Robert McGintie), Denton County, Texas, No. 5240; Marriage Records, Denton County, Texas, Vol. A, 3 (Courtesy Denton County Historical Museum); Minutes, Commissioners Court, Denton County, Texas, Vol. A, 77; *Dallas Weekly Herald*, 29 December 1877, 3; 1880 Denton County, Texas, Census, 19 (2/2).

21. Hogg, *Authentic History*, 109-10.

22. 1870 Denton County, Texas, Census, 209 (51/50). Whitehead had been in Denton County since as early as 1868. See Deed Records, Denton County, Texas, Vol. F, 128.

23. Hardin "Hard" Carter was born in Arkansas about 1834 or a little later. He was in Denton County by 1857, having married his wife, Sarah, also from Arkansas. They subsequently had at least five children, and he was both a farmer and stock raiser. 1860 Denton County, Texas, Census, 446 (739/740); 1870 Denton County, Texas, Census, 119 (55); 1880 Denton County, Texas, Census, 7 (120/120); Deed Records, Denton County, Texas, Vol. B, 93; Vol. J, 299.

24. Thomas M. Yates was born in Missouri about 1847. In November 1876 the Denton County Commissioners Court paid him for guarding prisoners. On December 15, 1878, he married Ida L. Gordon. The 1880 Denton County census listed him as a lawyer. 1880 Denton County, Texas, Census, 20 (22/22); Commissioner Court Minutes, Denton County, Texas, Vol. A, 76; Marriage Records, Denton County, Texas, Vol. 1, 264.

25. Jack Yates was born about 1856 in Mississippi, and was a school teacher. 1880 Denton County, Texas, Census, 121 (460/460).

26. Charles M. Hart was born in Alabama about 1854. In April 1878 he was paid by the Denton County commissioners court for guarding prisoners. He was a farmer, and on January 6, 1881, he married Sallie Bell. On December 13, 1881, he married Ettie Dewberry. 1880 Denton County, Texas, Census, 89 (200/208); Davis, *Marriage Records Index, Denton County, Texas, 1875-1884*, 17 (Marriage Records Vol. 2, 12); Commissioner Court Minutes, Denton County, Texas, Vol. A, 178; Marriage Records, Denton County, Texas, Vol. 2, 139.

27. Finley R. Grissom was born about 1859 in Texas to George A. and Lamenda Grissom, both of Tennessee. The family came to Texas sometime after 1856 and they farmed in Denton County. He married Maud Wright on March 27, 1884, and they subsequently had at least five children. 1870 Denton County, Texas, Census, 210 (67/65); Davis, *Denton County Marriage Records*, 16 (Marriage Records Vol. 2, 358); Denton County Genealogical Society, Inc., *Denton County Wills*, 53.

28. Hogg, *Authentic History*, 110-12.

29. *Ibid*, 112.

30. Isaac D. Ferguson was born July 4, 1850, in Warren County, Tennessee (although the 1860 census lists him as fourteen years old, Denton County cemetery records list him as born in 1847, and his obituary states 1848; other census listings are consistent with the 1850 date). The family moved to Texas about 1857, and he served in Company C, 16th Texas Cavalry, during the Civil War. Ferguson moved to Denton about 1872. On December 23, 1877, he married Mary E. "Matie" Chadwell. He was a lawyer, and during his life served as Denton mayor, city attorney, county attorney, five terms as a county judge, and five years as an attorney for the MK&T Railroad. The couple had one daughter, and his wife died on November 18, 1898. Ferguson died in Denton on February 6, 1916. *Denton Record-Chronicle*, 7 February 1916, 1; 1860 Denton County, Texas, Census, 452 (827/824); 1870 Denton County, Texas, Census, 206 (8/8); 1880 Denton County, Texas, Census, 1 (5/5); Bates, *History and Reminiscences of Denton County*, 87; Davis, *Denton County Marriage Records*, 13 (Marriage Records Vol. 1, 182); *Oakwood Cemetery, Denton, Texas*, 15; Certificate of Death (I.D. Ferguson), Denton County, Texas, No. 3907.

31. Robert F. McIlheny was born on December 14, 1858, in Texas and was living in Denton County as early as 1860. He married Ella or Ellen Shelton on May 14, 1879. By the age of twenty-one, he was a physician. McIlheny died on July 23, 1884. 1860 Denton County, Texas, Census, 407 (190/191); 1870 Denton County, Texas, Census, 118 (29/29); 1880 Denton County, Texas, Census, 6 (94/94); Davis, *Denton County Marriage Records*, 25 (Marriage Records Vol. 1, 292); IOOF *Cemetery, Denton, Texas*, 14.

32. Ambrose E. McMath was born in August 1856 in Mississippi. By 1870 he was in Denton County at the age of thirteen working on the farm of lawyer Christopher Scruggs. By 1880 he was a physician in Crafton, Wise County, Texas, boarding with Robert C. Darsey. By 1900 he was a physician in Palo Pinto County, having been divorced. 1870 Denton County, Texas, Census, 127 (90/90); 1880 Wise County, Texas, Census, 159 (54/58); 1900 Palo Pinto County, Texas, Census, ED 124, Sheet 3, Line 59, p. 187 (45/45).

33. Alvin C. Owsley was born on April 8, 1856, in Johnson County, Missouri, to two practicing physicians, Dr. Henry and Dr. Louisiana Mansfield Owsley. The family moved to Austin, Nevada, then settled again in California in 1864. At the age of ten, Owsley worked as a printer's devil for the *Lakeport Times*. In 1869 he attended St. Vincent's College at Los Angeles, supporting himself by carrying a route for the *Los Angeles Star*. Graduating in 1872, he worked briefly for the *Star* but then moved to Sedalia, Missouri, to study the law. He arrived in Denton in February 1873, where he taught school until 1875 when he had his minority dis-

ability removed and began the practice of law. On April 8, 1880, he married Sallie M. Blount, and they subsequently had eight children. An examiner of teachers until 1884, he helped found what is now the University of North Texas. On 1888 Owsley was elected to the state legislature and served three terms. In 1903 he received a doctor of laws from Nashville College. He was a district judge from 1926 to 1928, and in 1934 was appointed a special Chief Justice of the Texas Supreme Court. He died on April 27, 1938, in Denton. Tyler, ed., *New Handbook of Texas*, Vol. IV, 1190; Ray, *Down in the Cross Timbers*, 77-81; *Biographical Souvenir of the State of Texas*, 650-52; McCormick, *William Lee McCormick*, 92; *Denton Record-Chronicle*, 27 April 1938, 1; 1880 Denton County, Texas, Census, 29 (14/18); Marriage Records, Denton County, Texas, Vol. I, 404; Denton County Genealogical Society, *Denton County Wills*, 98-99; IOOF Cemetery, Denton, Texas, 54.

34. Edward S. Wilson was born about 1850 in Louisiana. He lived in the boarding house of Thomas B. Wheeler in 1880 and was a grocer. Jessie L. Wilson, eighteen, apparently a brother, clerked for him. 1880 Denton County, Texas, Census, 5 (84/84).

35. John M. Work was born on February 26, 1854, in Tennessee to J.A. and Mary Work. He ran a livery stable in Denton with his brother William. They later moved their operation to Dallas by 1880. A widower with three children, he died from accidental burns in Dallas on September 28, 1929. Certificate of Death (John M. Work), Dallas County, Texas, No. 44027; *Dallas Morning News*, 29 September 1929, 2; 1880 Dallas County, Texas, Census, 6 (731/124), 10 (820/239).

36. Hogg, *Authentic History*, 112-15.

37. *Dallas Daily Herald*, 2 May 1878, 1.

38. C.V. Fraley was appointed as a deputy U.S. Marshal in 1878. National Archives, RG 60, Records Relating to the Appointment of Federal Judges, Marshals, and Attorneys, 1853-1901 (Appointment Files for Judicial Districts 1853-1905).

39. Dallas farmer Edwin D. Walton was born July 25, 1815, in Virginia, and his wife, Elvira, was from Mississippi. He died in Dallas on December 10, 1887, leaving a widow and two children. 1870 Dallas County, Texas, Census, 478 (2125/2118); 1880 Dallas County, Texas, Census, 215 (98/98); Darnall, Jamieson, and Lu, eds., *Dallas County, Texas: Genealogical Data From Early Cemeteries*, 69; Texas State Library, Probate Cases, Dallas County, Texas, cause No. 1326 (Microfilm Record 1806).

40. A twenty-four-year-old mulatto, J.P. Price, from Indiana, was listed as a headwaiter in Dallas. 1880 Dallas County, Texas, Census, 2.

41. *Galveston Daily News*, 2 May 1878, 1.

42. National Archives (Fort Worth, Texas), Indictment, Western District of Texas, *United States v. Sam Bass et al*, Cause No. 731.

43. *Galveston Daily News*, 3 May 1878, 1.

44. Mullin was born on June 29, 1849, and died in Denton on October 11, 1878. IOOF Cemetery, Denton, Texas, 7; Texas State Library, Adjutant General Records, Frontier Battalion, Box 401-1159-8; Hogg, *Authentic History*, 116-17.

45. *Dallas Daily Herald*, 3 May 1878, 4.

46. Texas State Library, Frontier Battalion, Monthly Return, Company B, Box 401-1247-5; *Results of Operations of State Troops*, Ledger 401-1082, p. 140.

47. *Dallas Daily Herald*, 3 May 1878, 1.

48. Hogg, *Authentic History*, 117.

49. Reed and Tate, *Tenderfoot Bandits*, 166-67. Robert Hoffman was a farmer listed in the 1880 Denton County census, who was born about 1846 in Tennessee. He and his wife, Mary, had five children. They had been in Denton County as early as 1870. 1880 Denton County, Texas, Census, 38 (171/181); Deed Records, Denton County, Texas, Vol. B, 430.

50. Shelton A. Story was born December 10, 1859, at Piquat, Ohio, to Isaac H. and Mary Duncan Story. The family came to Dallas County and settled in the Kit community, near present-day Irving. He was credited with building one of the first frame houses in the county, which also had the first bay window in the county. In 1880 he was a farm hand boarding with farmer William Pennington in Dallas County. He died in Dallas on June 28, 1940, leaving a wife, three sons and two daughters. *Dallas Morning News*, 29 June 1940, 2:12; 1880 Dallas County, Texas, Census, 344 (79/83); Certificate of Death (Shelton A. Story), Dallas County, Texas, No. 27488.

51. J. Frank Dobie, "The Robinhooding of Sam Bass," *True West*, Vol 5, No. 6 (July-August 1958), 9-10.

52. *Sherman Courier*, as quoted in the *Denison Daily News*, 5 May 1878, 1. A Jesse W. Phillips was a Denton County farmer, born about 1838 or 1841 in Alabama. He enlisted on March 20, 1861, at Montgomery, Alabama, in Co. F, 1st Alabama Infantry. He was captured on March 15, 1865. Phillips moved to Denton County around 1875. He and his wife Rebecca had at least four children, the two oldest born in Alabama. He qualified for a Confederate pension in September 1905. 1880 Denton County, Texas, Census, 85 (116/123); Texas State Library, Confederate Pension Applications, File No. 10908.

53. *Dallas Daily Herald*, 4 May 1878, 4; 5 May 1878, 1; Texas State Library, Affidavit of J.W. Murphy, 26 July 1878.

54. Center for American History, University of Texas at Austin, Transcripts from the Office of the Texas Adjutant General, 1878, File No. 2Q400, p. 116.

55. Thomas W. Gee was born in Kentucky about 1840. In May 1875, when the official bond of the incumbent Clay County sheriff W.H. Newsom was invalidated because of the death or insolvency of his sureties, F.N. Sherman was named temporary sheriff until a successor was appointed or elected. Gee was elected sheriff on August 2, 1875, and would serve as such until November 5, 1878. On February 15, 1880, Gee married Miss Ollie Stratton, twenty, also of Kentucky. 1880 Clay County, Texas, Census, 464 (134/137); Minutes, Clay County Commissioners Court, Vol. 1, pp. 29,33,37; Tise, *Texas County Sheriffs*, 103; Marriage Records, Clay County, Texas, Vol. 1, 67; J.P. Earle, *History of Clay County and Northwest Texas* (Austin, Texas: Brick Row Book Shop, 1963), 25.

56. *Henrietta Journal*, 11 May 1878, as quoted in the *Dallas Daily Herald*, 17 May 1878, 3.

57. *Galveston Daily News*, 7 May 1878, 1; *Dallas Daily Herald*, 7 May 1878, 1,4.

58. *Dallas Commercial*, as quoted by the *Denison Daily News*, 7 May 1878, 1.

59. *Dallas Daily Herald*, 7 May 1878, 1.

60. J.E. Van Riper is first shown in ranger records as a sergeant in Lt. G.W. Campbell's Company B on November 30, 1877. After the Bass manhunt, he became a sergeant for Peak in August 1878, and his last entry is December 31, 1878. In November 1887, he again enlisted in Company D as a ranger private, described as thirty-four years old, 5'10", light brown hair, light complexion, born in Stockton, and holding a commission as a deputy U.S. Marshal, by virtue of which he would act as a "special assistant" to the rangers. Texas State Library, Adjutant General Service Reports, Frontier Battalion, Box 401-175; Muster and Payroll, Company B, August 1878, Box 401-747, Folder 9.

61. Charles M. Sterling was born January 28, 1845, in Pennsylvania to Denton and Katie Colvin Sterling. He served in Company B from November 21, 1876, to August 31, 1878, when he was a corporal under Peak. On September 9, 1881, he married Ida Haney in Montague County (although she is also identified as Mary Louisa Haney), and they subsequently had at least eight children. In 1900 he was a saloon keeper in Montague County. He died in that county at St. Jo on October 22, 1924. Stephens, *Texas Rangers Indian War Pensions*, 103; Texas State Library, Muster and Payroll, Company B, August 1878, Box 401-747, Folder 9; Certificate of Death (Charles M. Sterling), Montague County, Texas, No. 33248; Marriage

Records, Montague County, Texas, Vol. B, 316; Probate Records, Montague County, Texas, *Estate of C.M. Sterling*, Cause No. 2415, Vol. 18, 483-488; Death Records, Montague County, Texas, Vol. 2, 74; 1900 Montague County, Texas, Census, ED 46, Sheet 5A, Line 16 (87/87).

62. Texas State Library, Frontier Battalion, Monthly Return, Company B, May 1878, Box 401-1247-5; Frontier Battalion Correspondence, Semi-Monthly Report, Company B, 15 May 1878, Box 401-1159-5.

63. *Dallas Daily Herald*, 9 May 1878, 4; *Galveston Daily News*, 9 May 1878, 4. A William Day owned one hundred acres in Denton County in 1877. Tax Assessment Rolls, Denton County, Texas, 1877.

64. Texas State Library, Adjutant General Records, Frontier Battalion, Box 401-1159-4.

65. *Galveston Daily News*, 8 May 1878, 1; *Dallas Daily Herald*, 8 May 1878, 1.

66. *Dallas Daily Herald*, 7 May 1878.

67. Hogg, *Authentic History*, 118.

68. *Galveston Daily News*, 8 May 1878, 2.

69. *Dallas Daily Herald*, 10 May 1878, 2; *Galveston Daily News*, 9 May 1878, 1; *Life and Adventures of Sam Bass*, 56.

70. Texas State Library, Frontier Battalion, Monthly Return, Company B, May 1878, Box 401-1247-5.

71. Texas State Library, Adjutant General Records, Frontier Battalion, Box 401-1159-8.

72. Texas State Library, Adjutant General Records, Frontier Battalion, Box 401-1159-5.

73. *Galveston Daily News*, 12 May 1878, 4.

74. *Galveston Daily News*, 12 May 1878, 1.

75. *Dallas Daily Herald*, 12 May 1878, 1.

76. *Dallas Weekly Herald*, 18 May 1878, 4; *Dallas Daily Herald*, 14 May 1878, 4.

77. Texas State Library, Adjutant General Records, General Correspondence, Box 401-397-3.

78. Texas State Library, Gov. R.H. Hubbard Correspondence, Box 301-100.

79. Texas State Library, Adjutant General Records, Frontier Battalion, Box 401-1159-8.

80. *Galveston Daily News*, 15 May 1878, 1; *Dallas Daily Herald*, 16 May 1878, 1.

81. Texas State Library, Adjutant General Correspondence, Box 401-397-3,4.

82. *Dallas Daily Herald*, 17 May 1878, 1.

83. Texas State Library, Adjutant General Records, General Correspondence, Box 401-397-4; Frontier Battalion, Box 401-1159-5.

84. *Dallas Daily Herald*, 18 May 1878, 4.

85. Texas State Library, Frontier Battalion Correspondence, Box 401-397-4.

86. *Dallas Daily Commercial*, as quoted in the *Austin Daily Democratic Statesman*, 18 May 1878, 2.

87. Texas State Library, Frontier Battalion Correspondence, Letter to Thomas P. Martin, private secretary to Gov. Hubbard, from Maj. John Jones, 18 May 1878.

88. Texas State Library, Adjutant General Records, Affidavit of J.W. Murphy, 24 July 1878, before Travis County District Clerk.

89. Texas State Library, Adjutant General Records, Memorandum by Andrew J. Evans, 21 May 1878, U.S. Attorney for Western District, Tyler, Texas.

90. *Life and Adventures of Sam Bass*, 72.

91. *Dallas Daily Herald*, 21 May 1878, 4.

92. Sawnie Robertson was born on October 5, 1850, to John C. and Sarah J. Goodman Robertson in Chambers County, Alabama. The family moved the next year to Jefferson, Texas, then to Henderson and Tyler. He was educated at Gilmer and studied law under Oran Roberts, who would be elected governor in 1878. Robertson married Ellen Boren of Tyler and entered into law practice with his father. He later moved to Dallas, where he practiced law with several different

partners. On October 6, 1885, he was appointed an associate justice of the Texas Supreme Court, but he voluntarily resigned after a year to resume the practice of law in Dallas. He was shown in the 1880 census with two children. Robertson died in Dallas on June 21, 1892. *Dallas Morning News*, 22 June 1892, 8; Tyler, ed., *New Handbook of Texas*, Vol. V, 619; 1880 Dallas County, Texas, Census, 104 (532/587).

93. *Life and Adventures of Sam Bass*, 67-68.

94. Hogg, *Authentic History*, 137, 169-70; *Dallas Daily Herald*, 24 May 1878, 4.

95. Hogg, *Authentic History*, 137.

96. *Galveston Daily News*, 25 May 1878, 1.

XIII. RUNNING GUNBATTLES

1. Charles A. Allingham was born June 18, 1847, in Cameron, Illinois. He served in the Union Army during the Civil War, then moved to Oregon. In the early 1870s he came to Texas and settled near Bolivar in northwestern Denton County. He became a druggist and never married. In 1886 he moved to Wilbarger County, where he became a bank director. He died at Vernon, Wilbarger County, on May 3, 1925. *Denton Record-Chronicle*, 5 May 1925, 2; 1880 Denton County, Texas, Census, 158 (13/13); Certificate of Death (C.A. Allingham), Wilbarger County, Texas, No. 26578.

2. Charles L. Berry was born about 1850 in Pennsylvania. In the 1880 Denton County census he was listed as a stock hand. 1880 Denton County, Texas, Census, 167 (184/184).

3. John Ailer was later indicted for murder in Denton County on September 17, 1879, but acquitted on October 17, 1879. Civil Minutes, District Court, Denton County, Texas, *State of Texas v. John Ailer*, Cause No., 1672, Vol. B, 362, 448.

4. *Dallas Daily Herald*, 23 May 1878, 4.

5. Texas State Library, Adjutant General Records, affidavit of J.W. Murphy, 24 July 1878, taken before the Travis County District Clerk.

6. *Austin Daily Democratic-Statesman*, 26 May 1878, 4; *Life and Adventures of Sam Bass*, 68-69.

7. Two men named Freeman are listed in the 1880 Stephens County census: farmer Thomas Freeman, thirty-four, from Georgia, and farmer James S. Freeman, forty, from Ohio. 1880 Stephens County, Texas, Census, 488 (56/56), 476 (403/403).

8. Buck Amis was born about 1840 in Texas, and farmed with his wife, Elmira, and three daughters. 1880 Stephens County, Texas, Census, 505 (63).

9. In 1880, Perry Paschall, twenty-nine, and his brother Jesse B., thirty-one, were saloon keepers in Breckinridge, both born in Tennessee. 1880 Stephens County, Texas, Census, 463 (82/82,83).

10. *Fort Worth Daily Democrat*, 2 June 1878, 3.

11. Berry B. Meaders was born about 1833-1835 in Kentucky. By 1860 he was a stockraiser in Palo Pinto County, moving later to Stephens County. He served as a first lieutenant in Company F, 31st Texas Infantry. Meaders was elected Stephens County sheriff on May 13, 1876, reelected on November 5, 1878, and resigned on August 30, 1879. He was listed as a farmer in 1880, living with his wife, Carrie, twenty-one. 1860 Palo Pinto County, Texas, Census, 336 (7/7); 1880 Stephens County, Texas, Census, 467 (178/178); Tise, *Texas County Sheriffs*, 475; *Confederate Veteran*, Vol. V, No. 4 (April 1897), 179.

12. James M. Hood was born about 1850 in North Carolina and in 1880 was married to his wife, Eva, nineteen. 1880 Stephens County, Texas, Census, 461 (6/6).

13. *Fort Worth Daily Democrat*, 2 June 1878, 3.

14. Perry King Taylor was born in Texas about 1850 to cattle broker Pleasant

Taylor. He married Annie Collins, the daughter of A.G. and Permelia Collins in Dallas on December 3, 1872, after which they moved to Stephens County. A two-year old son, King Albert Taylor, died in Dallas on February 4, 1874. 1870 Dallas County, Texas, Census, 348 (413/412); 1880 Stephens County, Texas, Census, 484 (121/121); *Dallas Herald*, 21 December 1872; *Dallas Daily Herald*, 5 February 1874; Brown, *History of Dallas County, Texas, From 1837 to 1887*, 71. A "Perry Taylor" was a Dallas deputy sheriff in 1871-1873.

15. Texas State Library, Frontier Battalion, Monthly Return, Company B, Box 401-1247-5.

16. William Veale was born about 1833 in Tennessee. A lawyer in Breckinridge, in 1880 he and his wife, Lavina, had seven children. 1880 Stephens County, Texas, Census, 463 (87/87).

17. *Palo Pinto Mountaineer*, 28 May 1878, as quoted in the *Fort Worth Daily Democrat*, 30 May 1878, 4.

18. J.T. "Thomas" Wilson was elected Palo Pinto County Sheriff on February 15, 1876. He was reelected on November 5, 1878, and served until he was shot to death in Austin on January 23, 1879, in an altercation with Sherman City Marshal Sam Ball. Reportedly there was bad blood between Wilson and Lee Hall and Sheriff Everheart because of an effort by them approximately a year earlier to arrest a cousin of Wilson's in Palo Pinto County. In Austin to attend a sheriff's conference, Wilson went on a "spree" and took offense when Ball mentioned the names of Hall and Everheart. Wilson was buried at Weatherford in Parker County. Tise, *Texas County Sheriffs*, 402; *Austin Daily Democratic-Statesman*, 24-25 January 1879, 4; *Fort Worth Democrat*, 26 January 1879, 4; *Sherman Register*, as quoted in the *Fort Worth Democrat*, 29 January 1879, 3.

19. James L. Owens was born on September 17, 1845, in Indiana (or Kansas). The 1880 Palo Pinto County census showed him to be a saloon keeper, married to the former Mary Greathouse, nineteen, and they had a three-year-old son, Jay. He was elected Palo Pinto County Sheriff on November 4, 1884, reelected on November 2, 1886, and served until November 6, 1888. He died in Palo Pinto County on August 25, 1925. 1880 Palo Pinto County, Texas, Census, 139 (276/281); Certificate of Death (James L. Owens), Palo Pinto County, Texas, No. 32639; Tise, *Texas County Sheriffs*, 402.

20. *Palo Pinto Mountaineer*, 28 May 1878, as quoted in the *Fort Worth Daily Democrat*, 30 May 1878, 4.

21. William R. "Bill" Cruger was born on May 30, 1840, to Nicholas and Elizabeth Tobert Cruger at Albany, Georgia. He moved to what was to be Shackelford County in 1874 and the county seat, Albany, was named by him for his birthplace. He served as a deputy under Sheriff J.C. Jacobs from January 7, 1875, then under Sheriff John Larn, who was elected February 15, 1876. On January 17, 1877, Cruger and County Attorney William Jeffries were involved in a saloon gunfight in which three men were killed and he and Jeffries wounded. Cruger was supported for his actions, but Larn resigned on March 7, 1877, in protest of the killing. Cruger, also a railroad contractor, was appointed sheriff on March 20. After the Bass episode, Cruger had occasion to serve a warrant on Larn and, while a prisoner in the county jail, Larn was shot to death by vigilantes on June 23, 1878. Cruger was reelected on November 5, 1878, and served until he resigned on July 20, 1880. He and his wife, the former Mary R. Boynton, had one son, Nicholas. The family moved to Princeton, Tennessee, and while serving as city marshal there on May 29, 1882, he was shot to death by a drunken prisoner that he failed to search. Tyler, ed., *New Handbook of Texas*, Vol. II, 427-28; Tise, *Texas County Sheriffs*, 462; 1880 Shackelford County, Texas, Census, 453 (21/23); *Dallas Daily Herald*, 24,25 January 1877; Leon Claire Metz, *John Selman, Texas Gunfighter* (New York: Hastings House, 1966), 58, 71-72.

22. William C. Gilson was a former Jacksboro city marshal and had been city marshal at Fort Griffin in Shackelford County. He was a deputy under Sheriff

Bill Cruger and supposedly disappeared after the killing of John Larn on June 23, 1878. *Lampasas Daily Times*, 14 July 1878; Metz, *John Selman, Texas Gunfighter*, 60, 86.

23. 1880 Stephens County, Texas, Census, 503 (22).

24. *Fort Worth Daily Democrat*, 2 June 1878, 3, 4; 8 June 1878, 2; Hogg, *Authentic History*, 122-23.

25. *Fort Worth Daily Democrat*, 2 June 1878, 3.

26. Texas State Library, Frontier Battalion, Monthly Return, Company B, May 1878, Box 401-1247-5.

27. *Fort Worth Daily Democrat*, 1 June 1878, 1; Texas State Library, Frontier Battalion, Monthly Return, Company B, May 1878, Box 401-1247-5; Jim McIntire, *Early Days in Texas* (Norman, Oklahoma: University of Oklahoma Press, 1992), 62.

28. Texas State Library, Frontier Battalion, Monthly Return, Company B, June 1878, Box 401-1247-5; *Lampasas Daily Times*, 8 June 1878, 1.

29. Texas State Library, Frontier Battalion Correspondence, Box 401-1159-4.

30. Texas State Library, Frontier Battalion, Monthly Return, Company B, Box 401-1247-5; *Dallas Daily Herald*, 31 May 1878, 4; 1 June 1878, 4.

31. Hogg, *Authentic History*, 137-38.

32. Texas State Library, Special State Troops Correspondence, Monthly Returns, May 1878, Box 401-1244-4.

33. Gard, *Sam Bass*, 155-57; Mary Whatley Clarke, *The Palo Pinto Story* (Fort Worth, Texas: The Manney Co., 1956), 90-93. The Roes were originally from Kentucky, Mahala W. Roe born about 1827 and the widow of Sanford Roe. Semerimis was born about 1848 and Martha Finis Roe was born January 16, 1856, both in Kentucky. Semerimis married Robert W. Maddox, and by 1880 they had three children, two of whom were alive during the Bass episode. Martha married Byron Newton Maddox, Robert's brother, although they had no children as of 1880. Semerimis died in Dallas County on March 1, 1916, and Martha died in Palo Pinto County on August 9, 1938. 1880 Palo Pinto County, Texas, Census, 121 (4/4); 131 (163/167); Certificate of Death (Mrs. S.E. Maddox), Dallas County, Texas, No. 6306; Certificate of Death (Martha Finis Maddox), Palo Pinto County, Texas, No. 38735.

34. *Galveston Daily News*, 5 June 1878, 1.

35. L.L. Crutchfield was born about 1845 in Texas, and in 1880 he and wife Elizabeth had two children. He was sheriff of Jack County as early as 1874, reelected on February 15, 1876, and November 5, 1878, and serving until he resigned on July 15, 1880. 1880 Jack County, Texas, Census, 15 (259/259); Tise, *Texas County Sheriffs*, 277.

36. *Frontier Echo* [Jacksboro], 7 June 1878, 3.

37. There is some conflict as to the origins of Elijah Lyter Huffman. According to his certificate of death when he died on May 29, 1913, in Tom Green County, he was eighty-five years old and had been born on September 25 to John and Susan Emonds Huffman, both of Kentucky. This would make his birth year 1828. According to a recent genealogical book, he was born in 1852 to Michael Lyter Huffman and Mildred Elinor Clore Huffman, who were married in Kentucky in 1836 and who settled in Dallas County in the 1850s. The 1880 Dallas County census lists a twenty-eight-year-old Ed Huffman who was a bookkeeper born in Tennessee. Certificate of Death (Elijah Lyter Huffman), Tom Green County, Texas, No. 11877; *Proud Heritage: Pioneer Families of Dallas County*, Vol. II, 130; 1880 Dallas County, Texas, Census, 7 (159).

38. *Dallas Daily Herald*, 5 June 1878, 4; *Galveston Daily News*, 31 May 1878, 1.

39. A. Elmore Allen was born on February 19, 1830, in Tennessee. He came to Texas about 1851, settling first in Collin County, where he married Angelina Howe in December 1858. He reportedly served in the Confederate Army. Allen moved to Decatur in Wise County, where he was a merchant in the firm of Allen & Howe. Moving to Denton, he was in the mercantile and grocery business as

Allen & Carruth, then sold his interest and took charge of the Transcontinental Hotel, likely from P.C. Withers and Henderson Murphy. The 1870 Denton County census shows a wife, Harriet A., twenty-nine, and six children. About 1874 he moved to the Elizabethtown area and began farming. In March 1878 he had been among the citizens who formed the "Gold-Backs" law and order group in Elizabethtown. He moved to Pomeroy, Washington, in 1887. Early in 1905 he returned to Denton because of failing health, and he died there on March 22, 1905. *Denton Record and Chronicle*, 23 March 1905, 1; 1870 Denton County, Texas, Census, 116 (13/13); *Fort Worth Daily Democrat*, 17 April 1878.

40. Hogg, *Authentic History*, 124.

41. Stephen R. "Tweed" Christal was born October 30, 1849, in Missouri to S.R. Christal, a master miller, and Elizabeth Christal, who were living in Denton County by 1860. He married his wife, Ida, when she was fifteen, and by 1880 they had two children. He died in Denton County on August 25, 1887. 1860 Denton County, Texas, Census, 443 (691/692); 1870 Denton County, Texas, Census, 201 (140/151); 1880 Denton County, Texas, Census, 147 (364); IOOF Cemetery, *Denton, Texas*, 19.

42. *Dallas Daily Herald*, 9 June 1878, 1; 11 June 1878, 4; Hogg, *Authentic History*, 124.

43. *Dallas Daily Herald*, 9 June 1878, 1.

44. 1860 Denton County, Texas, Census, 446 (739/740). The 1870 Denton County census lists Charles as eight years old, but he was listed as two years old in the 1860 census. See 1870 Denton County, Texas, Census, 119 (55).

45. George Washington Smith was born on January 9, 1854, at Brunswick, Missouri, his mother being originally from Denmark and his father from Kentucky. Reportedly at the age of fourteen, in 1868, he helped on a cattle drive from Palo Pinto County to the Cherokee Nation, then worked on the Morris ranch near Fredericksburg and raised thoroughbred stock. By 1876 he was in Denton County as a deputy sheriff and subsequently became city marshal. On January 19, 1879, he married Catherine C. "Kittie" Backus in Denton. He was a photographer until 1902. He moved to Sonora in Sutton County where he was postmaster for eight years. Widowed, he died on June 6, 1936. *Denton Record-Chronicle*, 8 June 1936, 1; 1880 Denton County, Texas, Census, 19 (14/14); "Sends Us a Good List," *Frontier Times*, Vol. 4, No. 10 (July 1927), 47; Marriage Records, Denton County, Texas, Vol. I, 231; Commissioners Court Minutes, Denton County, Texas, Vol. A, 81, 84; Certificate of Death (George Washington Smith), Sutton County, Texas, No. 33028.

46. *Dallas Daily Herald*, 9 June 1878, 1.

47. There is a Charles McDonald, thirty-two, listed in the 1880 Denton County census, a farmer from Mississippi, who is married to Elizabeth E. and has four children. See 1880 Denton County, Texas, Census, 100 (123/123). Another Charley McDonald married Cinthy Ganner in Denton on June 27, 1878, three weeks after the stable episode. Marriage Records, Denton County, Texas, Vol. 1, 212.

48. *Dallas Daily Herald*, 7 June 1878, 1; *Denton Monitor*, 7 June 1878, as quoted in the *Luling Signal*, 19 June 1878, 6; *Life and Adventures of Sam Bass*, 62.

49. *Life and Adventures of Sam Bass*, 62; Hogg, *Authentic History*, 125-26; Gard, *Sam Bass*, 159-60.

50. *Dallas Daily Herald*, 9 June 1878, 1.

51. A.N. "Ab" Woody was born about 1845 in Missouri. He married in Missouri sometime prior to 1868 and was in Texas in the early 1870s. A William Woody, likely a brother, also lived in Tarrant County with him. By 1880 Ab Woody was a Deputy U.S. Marshal and he and his wife had four sons. 1880 Tarrant County, Texas, Census, 42 (194/194), 44 (222/222).

52. John M. Henderson was elected Tarrant County Sheriff on February 15, 1876, reelected on November 5, 1878, and served until November 2, 1880. Tise,

Texas County Sheriffs, 483.

53. *Fort Worth Daily Democrat*, 9 June 1878, 4; Richard F. Selcer, *Hell's Half Acre* (Fort Worth, Texas: Texas Christian University Press, 1991), 105-106.

54. *Dallas Daily Herald*, 11 June 1878, 4; Gard, *Sam Bass*, 160.

55. *Dallas Daily Herald*, 11 June 1878, 4.

56. Peter Clay Withers was born in Clay County, Missouri, on May 21, 1844, the son of George W. and Susan Price Withers. In August 1863 he enlisted in Col. Benjamin Elliott's Missouri cavalry regiment and reportedly was a member of Gen. Jo Shelby's brigade and rode with the infamous Quantrill. He was reportedly wounded in action at Camden, Arkansas. Withers became a prisoner of war and was paroled at Shreveport, Louisiana, on June 15, 1865. Coming to Denton County about 1865, he settled near Elizabethtown. It was alleged that he was elected Denton County Sheriff, but there is no record of that. In 1870 he was a boarder with Charles Lacy and, on November 30, 1870, he married Sarah Elizabeth "Bettie" Lacy, the daughter of the Lacy House's owner. They never had any children but did adopt Nannie T. Withers. He owned a grocery business but sold it in 1870 to Richard B. Coleman. He served as a deputy sheriff under W.F. Egan and in March 1878 was elected captain of the "Gold Backs," a law and order group organized in Elizabethtown. Later he made a living as a saloon keeper and in real estate, serving for many years as tax assessor and collector for both the city and county. Withers died in Denton on July 16, 1917. *Denton Record-Chronicle*, 16-17 July 1917; 1870 Denton County, Texas, Census, 120 (56/61); 1880 Denton County, Texas, Census, 29 (18/22); 1910 Denton County, Texas, Census, ED 81, Sheet 1B, Line 88; Certificate of Death (Peter Clay Withers), Denton County, Texas, No. 18587; *Confederate Veteran*, Vol. XI, No. 5 (May 1903); National Archives, Compiled Service Records, Confederate Soldiers, Missouri, 9th (Elliott's) Cavalry, M322, Roll 55; Texas State Library, Confederate Pension Applications, No. 35117 and Reject File; *Denton Monitor*, 19 March 1870, 4; *Fort Worth Daily Democrat*, 17 April 1878.

57. Millard L. Cope, "G.W. Smith of Sonora Chased Sam Bass," *Dallas Morning News*, 11 April 1926, Sec. 7, 5; *Dallas Daily Herald*, 11 June 1878, 4; Hogg, *Authentic History*, 126; *Fort Worth Daily Democrat*, 11 June 1878, 4; *Galveston Daily News*, 11 June 1878, 1.

58. *Waco Examiner and Patron*, 21 June 1878, 2; Hogg, *Authentic History*, 127. Gard identifies the courier as Matt Martin. Gard, *Sam Bass*, 161-62.

59. Jesse F. Chinn was born on February 1, 1844, in the Yadkin River section of North Carolina to Elisha and Mary Stowe Chinn. Both of his grandfathers had been soldiers in the Revolutionary War. The family settled in Collin County in Texas in 1852. With the outbreak of the Civil War, Chinn enlisted in Company A, Johnson's Texas Cavalry. He was slightly wounded in battles at Cabin Creek and Fort Gibson and was paroled at Galveston in 1865. He initially lived in Dallas where, on October 28, 1869, he married T. Angie Baird in Dallas. She must have died because he married Pattie Clark in 1873 in Denton, and they subsequently had five children. A farmer and stockraiser, he died in Denton County on March 15, 1918. *Denton Record-Chronicle*, 16 March 1918, 8; *Biographical Souvenir of the State of Texas*, 170; 1860 Denton County, Texas, Census, 429 (495/496); 1870 Denton County, Texas, Census, 190 (308/321); 1880 Denton County, Texas, Census, 43 (274/295); Lu and Neumann, eds., *Dallas County Marriages*, 21; Certificate of Death (Jesse F. Chinn), Denton County, Texas, No. 11396.

60. Gillis Sire Hammett was born on May 17, 1839, in Alabama to Robert B. and Elizabeth Adams Hammett. During the Civil War he served in Company A, 29th Texas Cavalry. By 1880 he and his wife, Eliza, had two sons. A farmer, Hammett died in Denton County on April 21, 1912. 1880 Denton County, Texas, Census, 46 (315/336); Texas State Library, Confederate Pension Applications, No. 31281; Certificate of Death (Gillis Hammett), Denton County, Texas, No. 9881; *IOOF Cemetery, Denton, Texas*, 88.

61. *Dallas Daily Herald*, 11 June 1878, 4; Hogg, *Authentic History*, 126-28; Gard, *Sam Bass*, 160-62; *Fort Worth Daily Democrat*, 11 June 1878, 4.

62. Harding O. Throop was born about 1839 in Missouri. He and his wife, Narcissa E., ran the store at Davenport's Mill. In 1880 they had no children, but were raising a young orphan, Ella Vickrish. 1880 Denton County, Texas, Census, 144 (327).

63. Hogg, *Authentic History*, 129.

64. *Fort Worth Daily Democrat*, 11 June 1878, 4.

65. *Dallas Daily Herald*, 11 June 1878, 4.

66. Hogg, *Authentic History*, 128; *Galveston Daily News*, 11 June 1878, 1; *Dallas Daily Herald*, 11 June 1878, 4.

67. *Dallas Daily Herald*, 8 June 1878, 4; 11 June 1878, 4; Texas State Library, Frontier Battalion, Monthly Return, Company B, June 1878, Box 401-1247-5.

68. Hogg, *Authentic History*, 129-30; *Galveston Daily News*, 11 June 1878, 1; *Dallas Daily Herald*, 11 June 1878, 4.

69. Reuben Bandy was born about 1850 in Missouri. By 1880 he and his wife, Tennessee Taylor Bandy, who was four years older than he, had four daughters and one son. Their eldest daughter was born in Arkansas, but they came to Texas about 1869-1870. See 1880 Denton County, Texas, Census, 40 (207/222).

70. John W. Hyatt was born about 1864 to Stephen H. and Jennie Hyatt, she having been born in England. His father died sometime after 1865 and before 1870. 1870 Denton County, Texas, Census, 119 (40/41); McCormick, *William Lee McCormick*, 92.

71. *Dallas Daily Herald*, 11 June 1878, 4; Hogg, *Authentic History*, 130.

72. *Fort Worth Daily Democrat*, 11 June 1878, 4; *Life and Adventures of Sam Bass*, 63-64.

73. John M. Carroll was born about 1846 in Missouri. He was a Denton County deputy sheriff by at least January 1877. The 1880 Denton County census shows that he was an unmarried cattle trader living at Pilot Point. 1880 Denton County, Texas, Census, 52 (93/93); Commissioners Court Minutes, Denton County, Texas, Vol. A, 84, 90.

74. Charles B.H.B. Gray, the son of former Denton Sheriff Matthew Gray, was born in Indiana about 1842-1845. By 1880 he and his wife, Margrett A., had three children. 1860 Denton County, Texas, Census, 422 (396/399); 1880 Denton County, Texas, Census, 14 (242/251).

75. Richard B. "Dick" Coleman was born in Missouri about 1848. He made a living as a carpenter, even contracting with Denton County to make coffins for paupers as well as courthouse furniture. By 1880 he and his wife, Eva, had three children. 1880 Denton County, Texas, Census, 21 (45/45); Commissioners Court Minutes, Denton County, Texas, Vol. A, 33, 37.

76. *Fort Worth Daily Democrat*, 16 June 1878, 1; Gard, *Sam Bass*, 165.

77. Hogg, *Authentic History*, 132-33; *Life and Adventures of Sam Bass*, 64; *Lampasas Daily Times*, 15 June 1878, 2; *Fort Worth Daily Democrat*, 13 June 1878, 4.

78. *Dallas Daily Herald*, 13 June 1878, 1.

79. *Fort Worth Daily Democrat*, 14 June 1878, 4; *Dallas Daily Herald*, 13 June 1878, 1.

80. *Lampasas Daily Times*, 15 June 1878, 1; *Dallas Commercial*, 11 June 1878, as quoted in the *Austin Daily Democratic-Statesman*, 14 June 1878, 3.

81. *Dallas Daily Herald*, 12 June 1878, 4; 13 June 1878, 1; *Galveston Daily News*, 12 June 1878, 1.

82. *Galveston Daily News*, 13 June 1878, 1; *Dallas Daily Herald*, 13 June 1878, 1.

83. George W. Stevens was born in Lowns County, Alabama, on July 12, 1830. He married Martha McDonald in 1852 and they moved to Wise County, Texas, in 1855. His wife died in 1858 and he married Nancy Buchanan in 1860. He was remembered as an Indian fighter and an organizer of several home guard units during the Civil War. On June 9, 1869, he was appointed Wise County

ENDNOTES

sheriff under the Reconstruction Act, then was elected on December 3, 1869, and served until December 2, 1873. He returned to farming, but he was again elected sheriff on February 15, 1876, and served until November 5, 1878. Stevens had a total of eleven children by both marriages, and he died in Wise County on April 11, 1893. 1870 Wise County, Texas, Census, 506 (243/243); 1880 Wise County, Texas, Census, 121 (1/1); Rosalie Gregg, *Wise County History: A Link With the Past* (?: Nortex Press, 1975), 460; Cliff D. Cates, *Pioneer History of Wise County* (Decatur, Texas: Wise County Historical Committee, 1975), 230-33; Wise County Historical Commission, *Wise County History* (Austin, Texas: Eakin Publications, 1982), Vol. 2, 9; Probate Docket, Wise County, Texas, *Estate of G.W. Stevens, Dec'd*, Vol. 2, 632; Tise, *Texas County Sheriffs*, 549.

84. William P. Withers was born in Missouri about 1849 and likely was related to Peter Clay Withers. In 1870 he was an apprentice in Denton to printer Benjamin Sullivan and living in the household of Henderson Murphy. On September 13, 1877, he married Emma McFall. 1870 Denton County, Texas, Census, 116 (14/14); 1880 Denton County, Texas, Census, 19 (1/1); Davis, *Denton County Marriages*, 40 (Marriage Records, Vol. I, 155).

85. John Stoker was born about 1844 in Ohio. Little is known about him, but in 1875 in Fort Worth he began a business of taking a wagon to Dallas for the delivery of ice. In February 1876, when T.P. Redding resigned, Stoker was appointed by the Fort Worth city council as temporary city marshal until April elections. By 1880 he was a retail merchant in Fort Worth. 1880 Tarrant County, Texas, Census, 28 (9/9); *Fort Worth Democrat*, 24 July 1875, 3; 19 February 1876, 3.

86. Hogg, *Authentic History*, 133.

87. Tyler, ed., *New Encyclopedia of Texas*, Vol. II, 355.

88. *Life and Adventures of Sam Bass*, 64-65; Hogg, *Authentic History*, 133-36; Texas State Library, Results of Operations of State Troops, Ledger 401-1082, p. 141; Monthly Return, Company B, June 1878, Box 401-1247-5; *Fort Worth Daily Democrat*, 19 June 1878, 3; *Galveston Daily News*, 21 June 1878, 1.

XIV. TRAITOR IN THE GANG

1. *Galveston Daily News*, 21 June 1878, 1.
2. *Fort Worth Daily Democrat*, 19 June 1878, 3.
3. *Galveston Daily News*, 21 June 1878, 1; Texas State Library, Frontier Battalion, Muster and Pay Roll, Company B, August 1878, Box 401-747-9. Jenkins was described as "an immense, rawboned man..., and, no matter how cold the day, always wore his shirt open over his heavy chest of hair. He never wore undershirt, drawers, or socks...He could run half a mile, stop, and draw as steady a bead with the rifle as if he had been standing still the while...He invariably lay down to sleep with his head to the north, even if he had to sleep downhill." J. Evetts Haley, *Jeff Milton, A Good Man With a Gun* (Norman, Oklahoma: University of Oklahoma Press, 1949), 33.
4. Hogg, *Authentic History*, 136.
5. *Galveston Daily News*, 21 June 1878, 1.
6. Texas State Library, Frontier Battalion, Monthly Return, Company B, June 1878, Box 401-1247-5.
7. The sources relying directly on statements made by Jim Murphy are as follows: Hogg, *Authentic History*, 137-65; Center for American History, University of Texas at Austin, Affidavit of J.W. Murphy, 23 July 1878; *Life and Adventures of Sam Bass*, 74-77; Texas State Library, Affidavit of J.W. Murphy, 26 July 1878; *Galveston Daily News*, 24 July 1878, 1.
8. Gustave "Gus" B. Egan was born in Denton County on June 10, 1861, to Thomas J. and Nancy A. Egan. He married Mary E. Cox on December 2, 1885, and they subsequently had nine children. He was a farmer and cattle raiser in

369

Denton County for most of his life, then because of ill health turned to the real estate business from 1905 until 1915. His wife died in January 1930, and he died at his home west of Denton on January 30, 1936. 1870 Denton County, Texas, Census, 141 (275/294); 1900 Denton County, Texas, Census, ED 43, Sheet 12, Line 23, p. 28A (214/215); Marriage Records, Denton County, Texas, Vol. 2, 547; *Denton Record-Chronicle*, 30 January 1936, 5; Certificate of Death (Gus B. Egan), Denton County, Texas, No. 1624.

9. Alonzo C. Carruth was born in Texas to Robert A. Carruth on December 12, 1859. He died in Denton County on January 10, 1895. 1860 Denton County, Texas, Census, 257 (780/791); 1880 Denton County, Texas, Census, 144 (335); Cemetery Records, Denton County Historical Museum (which show him born December 12, 1869).

10. William H. Mounts was born in Virginia on April 2, 1833. He and a brother were living with their mother in Denton County by 1860. Around 1863 he married Martha E. "Mattie," and they had at least five children. Mounts was a retail dry goods merchant in Denton, dying there on May 5, 1884. 1860 Denton County, Texas, Census, 407 (178/179); 1870 Denton County, Texas, Census, 116 (1/1); 1880 Denton County, Texas, Census, 20 (27/27); Deed Records, Denton County, Texas, Vol. B, 212; *IOOF Cemetery, Denton, Texas*, 35.

11. Hugh W. Davis wrote Major John Jones on July 25, 1878, from Weatherford, Parker County, asking if the horse was in the possession of the rangers after Bass' death and whether it could be sold for him. Center for American History, University of Texas at Austin, Letter from Hugh W. Davis to Major John B. Jones, 25 July 1878. A Hugh W. Davis is listed in the 1880 Young County Census as a forty-three-year-old farmer from Mississippi, with wife Lulu R. and three children. 1880 Young County, Texas, Census, 387 (212).

12. *Sherman Register*, as quoted in the *Denison Daily News*, 21 June 1878, 4.

13. *Fort Worth Daily Democrat*, 23 June 1878, 1.

14. Texas State Library, Frontier Battalion, Monthly Return, Company B, Box 401-1247-5; Results of Operations of State Troops, Ledger 401-1082, p. 141.

15. *Galveston Daily News*, 30 June 1878, 4.

16. Rockwall was and is the county seat of Rockwall County, and a post office has existed there since 1854. The town derived its name from a mysterious man-made stone wall that was discovered when the townsite was excavated. Tyler, ed., *New Encyclopedia of Texas*, Vol. 5, p. 640.

17. Marion F. Porter was born about 1856 in Texas, and in 1880 was a store clerk living with his wife, Mollie J. 1880 Kaufman County, Texas, Census, 42 (96/96).

18. Dobie, "Robinhooding of Sam Bass," 8-10, 36.

19. District Court Records, Collin County, Texas, *State of Texas v. Thomas Spotswood*, Cause No. 1500; *Life and Adventures of Sam Bass*, 27-28; *Galveston Daily News*, 3 July 1878, 1; *McKinney Enquirer*, as quoted in the *Lampasas Daily Times*, 12 July 1878, 1.

20. *Lampasas Daily Times*, 29 June 1878, 4.

21. *Galveston Daily News*, 3 July 1878, 1; *Austin Daily Democratic Statesman*, 3 July 1878, 4.

22. *Galveston Daily News*, 3 July 1878, 1; *Austin Daily Democratic Statesman*, 3 July 1878, 4; 4 July 1878, 4.

23. *Galveston Daily News*, 2 July 1878, 1.

24. *Fort Worth Daily Democrat*, 3 July 1878, 4.

25. Texas State Library, Frontier Battalion, Monthly Returns, Company B, July 1878, Box 401-1247-5.

26. *Denison Daily News*, 7 July 1878, 8.

27. *Galveston Daily News*, 21 July 1878, 4.

28. *Colorado Citizen*, 4 June 1874, 2.

29. *Austin Daily Democratic Statesman*, 23 June 1878, 3.

30. Texas State Library, Texas Adjutant General Records, General

Correspondence, Boxes 401-397-4, 401-397-5; *Galveston Daily News*, 11 June 1878, 1.

31. James Milton Tucker was born May 2, 1843, to Lewis Grodon and Hannah Tucker in Tennessee, one of eleven children. The family moved to Arkansas, then in 1857 moved to Texas. They first lived at Leander, then Gabriel Mills in northwestern Williamson County. He served as an ordnance sergeant in the 7th Texas Cavalry. On October 7, 1866, he married Augusta Morgann Allen, and they subsequently had six children. After serving as a deputy sheriff, he was elected Williamson County Sheriff on November 2, 1880, was reelected November 7, 1882, and served until November 4, 1884. In his later years he moved to Coke County, where he died April 7, 1907, at Robert Lee. 1860 Williamson County, Texas, Census, 335 (11); 1880 Williamson County, Texas, Census, 432 (172); Mrs. Jean Shroyer and Mrs. Hazel Wood, eds., *Williamson County, Texas: Its History and Its People* (Austin, Texas: Nortex Press, 1985), 299; Tise, *Texas County Sheriffs*, 544; Marriage Records, Williamson County, Texas, Book 2, 269 (License no. 319).

32. *Williamson County Sun*, 25 July 1878, Center for American History, University of Texas at Austin, Walter Prescott Webb Collection, Box 2M275.

33. George Washington Chilton was born June 4, 1828, at Elizabethtown, Kentucky. He briefly attended Howard College at Marion, Alabama, but enlisted in Company B of Colonel John C. Hays' First Regiment of the Texas Mounted Rifles and saw service in the Mexican War. Discharged on September 13, 1846, he returned to Alabama, was admitted to the bar in 1848, and practiced law at Taladega. He moved to Tyler, Texas, in 1851 to practice law, and in 1852 married Ella Goodman. A zealous advocate of slavery, he served in Texas' secession convention and then served in the 3rd Texas Cavalry. As a colonel he served as ordnance officer for Gen. Hamilton P. Bee. After the war he was elected to the U.S. House of Representatives but was refused his seat because of his war service. Chilton died in 1883 and was buried at Tyler. 1880 Smith County, Texas, Census, 112 (73/80); Tyler, ed., *New Encyclopedia of Texas*, Vol. 2, 83.

34. James G. Eblin was born about 1849 in Tennessee and married Laura S. Work in Dallas on September 18, 1873. They had at least three children. He died in early September 1883, his funeral held in Dallas on September 8. 1880 Dallas County, Texas, Census, 95 (357/405); Lu and Neumann, eds., *Dallas County Marriages*, 32; *Dallas Daily Herald*, 9 September 1883, 8.

35. Sloan Jackson was born about 1822 in Tennessee and had been in Texas since at least 1855. In 1870 he and his wife, Elizabeth, had two children. 1870 Dallas County, Texas, Census, 371 (731/724).

36. Margaret R. "Maggie" Caton was born in late 1859 in Texas, the daughter of James Calvin Caton and Sophia J. Caton of Missouri, who lived in Denton County by 1860. In 1880 she lived in Collin County with her paralyzed father. It would appear that her sister, Sarah "Sallie" Caton, married their uncle, Billy Collins, in 1875. 1860 Denton County, Texas, Census, 406 (164/165); 1880 Collin County, Texas, Census, 36 (8/8).

37. *Austin Daily Democratic Statesman*, 7 July 1878, 4; 9 July 1878, 4; 10 July 1878, 4; 11 July 1878, 4; 12 July 1878, 4; 13 July 1878, 4; 14 July 1878, 4; *Galveston Daily News*, 7 July 1878, 1; 9 July 1878, 1; 10 July 1878, 1; 11 July 1878, 1; 12 July 1878, 1; 13 July 1878, 1; *Evening State Gazette*, 11 July 1878, as found in National Archives II (College Park, Maryland), RG 204, Office of the Pardon Attorney, Pardon Case Files 1853-1946, Record J, pp. 93-118, Box 155; *The Texas Capital*, 14 July 1878, 4; *Life and Adventures of Sam Bass*, 69.

38. *Galveston Daily News*, 19 July 1878, 4.

XV. SHOWDOWN AT ROUND ROCK

1. Karen R. Thompson and Jane H. Digesualdo, *Historical Round Rock, Texas*

(Austin, Texas: Eakin Press, 1985), 17-19.

2. Thompson and Digesualdo, *Historical Round Rock*, 26, 67-70, 75-77; Tyler, ed, *New Handbook of Texas*, Vol. 5, 697.

3. *Life and Adventures of Sam Bass*, 76; National Archives II (College Park, Maryland), RG 204, Office of the Pardon Attorney, Pardon Case Files 1853-1946, Record J, pp. 93-118, Box 155 (undated clipping from the *Austin Daily Democratic Statesman*).

4. Walter Prescott Webb, "Sam Bass, Texas' Beloved Bandit," *Dallas Morning News*, 2 January 1927, Sec. 7, 4-5.

5. Livingston M. Mays was born in Virginia about 1830. He married Hannah B. Shinn in Williamson County, Texas, on November 29, 1855, and they subsequently had at least eight children. He died in Williamson County in 1914. 1870 Williamson County, Texas, Census, 399 (367/367); 1880 Williamson County, Census, 565 (165/1650; Thompson and Digesualdo, *Historical Round Rock*, 317-19; Marriage Records, Williamson County, Texas, Book 1, p. 131 (License No. 180).

6. J.M. Black had come to Round Rock in May 1871, at the age of nineteen, to attend the Greenwood Masonic Institute. He inherited $5,000 from his father and on January 6, 1873, bought a half-interest in the L.M. Mays store. He and Mays would also operate a stone quarry and other businesses, and he owned the store outright from 1898 until 1906. Thompson and Digesualdo, *Historical Round Rock*, 318.

7. Hogg, *Authentic History*, 163.

8. *Austin Daily Democratic Statesman*, 8 June 1878, 2; Thompson and Digesualdo, *Historical Round Rock*, 264, 266. William S. Peters was born about 1828 in New York. 1880 Williamson County, Texas, Census, 558 (33/33). His brother (and in some accounts his son), Porter G. Peters, was no stranger to trouble, he having been indicted for murder on September 29, 1876, and acquitted by a jury on March 21, 1877. He married Cora Davis on December 21, 1877. District Court Minutes, Williamson County, Texas, *State of Texas v. P.G. Peters*, Cause No. 1451, Vol. 5, pp. 502, 567; Marriage Records, Williamson County, Texas, Book 4, 298 (License No. 595).

9. Hogg, *Authentic History*, 163-64; *Life and Adventures of Sam Bass*, 78; Texas State Library, Adjutant General Records, Affidavit of J.W. Murphy, 23 July 1878; *Galveston Daily News*, 24 July 1878, 1.

10. Texas State Library, Frontier Battalion Correspondence, Box 401-1159-4.

11. Texas State Library, Frontier Battalion Correspondence, Box 401-397-8.

12. Vernon Coke Wilson, a nephew of Texas Governor Richard Coke, was born about 1855 near Abingdon, Virginia, and came to Texas about 1876. He was mustered into Lt. J.M. Denton's Company A on September 23, 1876, and was still in that company in May 1877 when it was commanded by Captain Neal Coldwell. By February 1878 he had been promoted to corporal and remained in that status until he left the ranger service on December 30, 1878. He was remembered as highly educated, but green when it came to horses and firearms. He had a fine voice and sang well, in addition to playing the guitar well. After leaving the rangers he was chief of Mounted Inspectors in Arizona and New Mexico in 1885. Wilson became a special officer for the Southern Pacific Railroad in California and was shot and killed on September 13, 1892, in an ambush by train robbers Evans and Sontag. Texas State Library, Adjutant General Service Records, Frontier Battalion, Box 401-177; "Vernon Wilson," *Frontier Times* (April 1929); *Visalia Daily Delta*, 14 September 1892, and *Tulare County Times*, 15 September 1892 (Courtesy Harold L. Edwards, Bakersfield, California).

13. Richard Clayton "Dick" Ware was born on November 11, 1851, in Floyd County, near Rome, Georgia, to Benjamin F. and Mary Jane Price Ware. The family came to Texas in 1870 and settled in Dallas County. He mustered into ranger service as a private on April 1, 1876, in Lieutenant B.S. Foster's Company E, which was subsequently commanded by Lieutenant N.O. Reynolds. By

ENDNOTES

December 31, 1878, he was a corporal, then a second sergeant by August 1880 in Captain Ira Long's Company B. He became a first sergeant, then was discharged from ranger service on February 1, 1881, having been elected the first sheriff of Mitchell County on January 10, 1881. He was reelected five times and served as sheriff until he was defeated by one vote on November 8, 1892. President Cleveland appointed Ware as U.S. marshal for the Western District of Texas on May 11, 1893, and he served until replaced on January 26, 1898. Ware was appointed as an unpaid "Special Ranger" in "Volunteer Guards" in San Antonio on February 7, 1898, his purpose being to "protect my property in Texas and to aid and assist the civil authorities." He was described in 1898 as being 5' 9-1/2", blue eyes, brown hair, light complexion, and in another account he was reported to weigh two hundred pounds. He never married and died in Fort Worth of heart trouble on June 26, 1902. *Dallas Morning News*, 27 June 1902, 7; Tise, *Texas County Sheriffs*, 378; Texas State Library, General Service Records, Files 401-176, 401-216; Stephens, *Texas Ranger Sketches*, 151-52; Tyler, ed., *New Handbook of Texas*, Vol. 6, 824; 1880 Howard County, Texas, Census, 404 (32/32); *Austin Gazette*, as quoted in the *Lampasas Daily Times*, 31 July 1878.

14. Christian Razar Connor was born on April 11, 1850, in Alabama to Meriwether Lewis Connor and Sarah J. Razar. While his death certificate gives a birth date of February 24, 1846, that is inconsistent with his age given in census records, and the 1850 date given by Robert W. Stephens in *Texas Ranger Sketches* is more likely. The family moved to Madison County, Texas, in 1852 where they farmed. Because of his age he was turned down for service in the Confederate Army. A brief first marriage to Annie Randolph ended with her death. On July 11, 1876, he enlisted in Captain Neal Coldwell's Company A, then transferred into Lieutenant N.O. Reynolds' Company E on September 1, 1877, as a private. He mustered out of ranger service on November 30, 1878, and returned to Madison County where he married Belle Steele and served as a deputy sheriff while also farming. Connor died at Madisonville on January 23, 1916. Stephens, *Texas Ranger Sketches*, 39-43; 1860 Madison County, Texas, Census, 447 (176/176); 1870 Madison County, Texas, Census, 320 (122/125); 1880 Madison County, Texas, Census, 307 (248/248); Certificate of Death (Chris Razar Connor), Madison County, Texas, No. 2181; Texas State Library, Adjutant General Service Records, Frontier Battalion, Box 401-147.

15. George Herold was born on May 9, 1840, on the James River seven miles below Richmond, Virginia. Because he was illiterate and spelled his name a number of ways, detailing his life is somewhat difficult. Coming to Texas prior to the Civil War, he served in the Second Texas Field Artillery Battery which served in New Mexico, Texas and the Trans-Mississippi. He reportedly married Virginia Garcia about 1867 in San Antonio and she died in 1869. Ojinia Garza Herold claimed that she married him on April 21, 1873, at San Antonio and that they never divorced (she died on September 24, 1939, in Bexar County). However, he apparently abandoned her as Herold married Jesusita Saiz in 1884. There is an indication that he served in something called the "Frontier Force" in 1870 but then served as city marshal of Laredo. Herold enlisted as a private in Captain D.W. Roberts' Ranger Company D on October 16, 1877, and by May 1878 was serving in Lieutenant N.O. Reynolds' Company E. In November 1879 he was serving in Lieutenant George Baylor's Company D. He apparently mustered out of ranger service on December 26, 1879. It was reported that he served as a chief of police in Mexico then moved to El Paso about 1883. In approximately 1889 Herold became a member of the El Paso Police Department. He was involved in a gunfight with Mexican horse thieves in 1890. He divorced his third wife in El Paso about 1894, and on June 15 of that year he applied to be a "Special Ranger," an appointment recommended by famous Ranger Captain John R. Hughes. Herold was described as a "terror to thieves" and could speak Spanish fluently. However, because of his illiteracy he was often the butt of jokes, which he took

good-naturedly. He never talked about his days as a ranger or the killing of Bass. He was described as 5' 8-1/4" (5' 10" in another affidavit), 165 pounds, blue eyes, grey hair (in 1914), dark complexion, and three bullet hole scars. On August 8, 1899, Herold married a widow, Manuela Larroque Gallardo. In his marriages, he had a total of six children. He retired from the El Paso Police Department in 1916 and died in that city on December 11, 1917. Stephens, *Texas Ranger Sketches*, 59-61; Stephens, *Texas Rangers Indian War Pensions*, 44-45; 1880 Bexar County, Texas, Census, 240 (217/217) (shows a wife named Eugenia); 1900 El Paso County, Texas, Census, ED 20, Sheet 13, Line 24 (288/288); 1910 El Paso County, Texas, Census, ED 68, Sheet 5A, 250 (92/92); Texas State Library, General Service Records, File 401-154; Declaration for Survivor's Pension-Indian Wars (George Herold, 17 May 1914); Declaration for Widow's Pension-Indian Wars (Ojinia Garza Herold, 12 September 1922); *El Paso Morning Times*, 18 December 1917; *El Paso Times*, 21 August 1939.

16. *Galveston Daily News*, 24 July 1878, 1; *El Paso Herald*, 12 August 1902, as quoted in a publisher's note in Hogg, *Authentic History*, 186; Gard, *Sam Bass*, 204.

17. *El Paso Herald*, 12 August 1902, as quoted in a publisher's note in Hogg, *Authentic History*, 187; Leona Bruce, *Banister Was There* (Fort Worth, Texas: Branch-Smith, Inc., 1968), 34.

18. Charles L. Nevill was born on April 6, 1855, to Zach L. and Anne Lewis Nevill at Carthage, Alabama, and the family came to Fayette County, Texas, in 1858. He moved to Austin about 1870. On May 25, 1874, he was mustered into Lieutenant D.W. Roberts' Company D, but, because Nevill's father protested that his son was a minor, Major Jones discharged the young ranger on March 12, 1875. It was said that Zach Nevill refused to help his son enter the ranger service and the only weapon that the boy had with him was a butcher knife. After several weeks' service he was provided a horse and revolver on credit. Nevill again enlisted in Roberts' company as a private on September 9, 1875. A year later he was a member of Company A, and by November 1877 was a sergeant in N.O. Reynolds' Company E. He was promoted to lieutenant on August 25, 1879, and assumed command of Company E. By May 31, 1882, he was a captain and remained as such until he left the ranger service on November 25, 1882, having been elected sheriff of Presidio County on November 7. He was reelected twice and served as sheriff until November 6, 1888. Nevill married Sallie E. Crosson at Fort Davis in 1883, and they subsequently had eight children. Nevill moved his family to San Antonio in 1892, where he first worked in the Texas Abstract Office, then as Back Tax Collector for the city. He became Chief Deputy District Clerk for Bexar County then in 1904 was elected District Clerk. He died in San Antonio on June 13, 1906, his oldest daughter succeeding him as District Clerk. Stephens, *Texas Ranger Sketches*, 103-05; Texas State Library, Adjutant General Service Records, Frontier Battalion, Box 401-165; Certificate of Death (C.L. Neville), Bexar County, Texas, No. 4872; *San Antonio Daily Express*, 15 June 1906, 7, 10; Tise, *Texas County Sheriffs*, 424.

19. James B. Gillett, *Six Years With the Rangers* (Lincoln, Nebraska: University of Nebraska Press, 1976), 122-23; Bruce, *Banister Was There*, 33-35; Texas State Library, Frontier Battalion, Company E Minutes, Box 401-1180-23; *Results of Operations of State Troops*, Ledger 401-1082, p. 230; *El Paso Herald*, 12 August 1902, as quoted by publisher in Hogg, *Authentic History*, 186-88.

20. Holman T. Ham was born in Kentucky about 1854. He was married in Williamson County on December 6, 1877, to Ellen (Ella) J. Beverly. 1880 Williamson County, Texas, Census, 557 (12/12); Marriage Records, Williamson County, Texas, Book 4, 292 (License No. 583).

21. Texas State Library, Adjutant General Correspondence, Box 401-397-8.

22. Maurice B. Moore was listed in Lieutenant B.E. Foster's Ranger Company E on November 30, 1876, as a first sergeant, having been mustered in on October 1. He apparently married Julia Bell Eanes in Travis County on December 9, 1873.

The 1880 Travis County census lists farmer "Maurice D. Moore" who is thirty, born in Louisiana, married to Berty, twenty-seven, and they have three children, the oldest five. Texas State Library, Adjutant General Records, Frontier Battalion, Box 401-165; Lucie Clift Price, *Travis County, Texas, Marriage Records, 1840-1882* (Austin, Texas: Lucie Clift Price, 1973), 117; 1880 Travis County, Texas, Census, 141 (67/73).

23. *Galveston Daily News*, 24 July 1878, 1; 25 July 1878, 2.

24. *Galveston Daily News*, 24 July 1878, 1.

25. Henry Albert Highsmith was born on January 11, 1843, in Bastrop, Texas, to Samuel and Teresa Williams Highsmith. His brother, Maleijah Benjamin (Kige) Highsmith, had been a ranger under Captain John S. (Rip) Ford. He attended the Bastrop Military Institute then reportedly joined the ranger service at Salado in Bell County, although there is no record of his service with the rangers. He served in Parson's Twelfth Texas Cavalry as a regimental sergeant major during the Civil War, returning to Bastrop where he married Sarah A. McCutcheon on July 31, 1867, and they subsequently had seven children. Once more it is alleged that he was a Texas Ranger, although no records reflect this. In 1876 Highsmith moved his family to Round Rock in Williamson County, where he opened a feed store and livery stable. On January 20, 1881, a jury found him guilty of aggravated assault and fined him twenty-five dollars. Highsmith moved to the Williamson County town of Hutto in 1885, where he died on March 19, 1930, only ten days after the death of his wife. 1880 Williamson County, Texas, Census, 557 (19/19); District Court Minutes, Williamson County, Texas, *State v. Albert Highsmith*, Cause No. 1983, Vol. 1, 288-89; Certificate of Death (Albert H. Highsmith), Williamson County, Texas, No. 16270; Maude Wallis Traylor, "Two Famous Sons of a Famous Father," *Frontier Times*, Vol. 18, No. 7 (April 1941), 299-305; *Galveston Daily News*, 2 April 1878, 1; Tyler, ed., *New Handbook of Texas*, Vol. 3, 605.

26. *Galveston Daily News*, 24 July 1878, 1.

27. Gard, *Sam Bass*, 205.

28. Texas State Library, Adjutant General Correspondence, Box 401-397-8. "Creasy" is likely Ed Creary who was sheriff of Travis County from November 2, 1880, until November 7, 1882. Tise, *Texas County Sheriffs*, 494.

29. *Galveston Daily News*, 21 July 1878, 1; Interview with Scott Mayes by Alex Williams, 15 December 1930, Goodman-Williams Collection, Denton County Historical Museum.

30. Texas State Library, Adjutant General Correspondence, Box 401-397-8.

31. Texas State Library, Adjutant General Correspondence, Box 401-397-8.

32. *Life and Adventures of Sam Bass*, 79.

33. Dennis Corwin was born about 1835 in Canada. He was elected Travis County Sheriff on February 15, 1876, reelected once, and served until November 2, 1880, after which he became a civil engineer. In 1879 he was elected president of the Texas Sheriffs Association. 1880 Travis County, Texas, Census, 251 (43/53); Tise, *Texas County Sheriffs*, 494.

34. *Texas Capital*, 21 July 1878, 4; *Galveston Daily News*, 23 July 1878, 1.

35. Ahijah W. "Caige" Grimes was born in Bastrop, Texas, on July 5, 1850, to Robert H. and Elizabeth Highsmith Grimes. He was a member of a noted Texas family, having lost an uncle at the Alamo and having a grandfather who signed the Texas Declaration of Independence. Grimes initially worked as a printer in Bastrop, as well as the city's forty dollars-a-month marshal, marrying Lottie A. Lyman there on March 2, 1874, her twentieth birthday and Texas Independence Day. In January 1875 he was elected city tax collector and assessor, also continuing to serve as city marshal. Grimes was defeated in the 1876 election for county tax assessor, but in September was appointed by the commissioners court as constable in Bastrop County's Precinct Six.

Major Jones enlisted Grimes' service with the rangers on September 20, 1877, sending him to ride with Lieutenant Pat Dolan's Company F. Grimes' brother,

Albert, had enlisted only seventeen days earlier. However, Caige Grimes was shortly transferred to Company A at Rio Grande City, then discharged from the rangers the following December 13 by order of Jones after less than three months' service. By May 1878 he, his wife and three children were living in Williamson County, working first as a constable then as deputy sheriff in the Round Rock area. He stood 5' 10" tall, with dark hair, grey eyes and dark complexion. 1860 Bastrop County, Texas, Census, 288 (732/687); Stephens, *Texas Ranger Sketches*, 55-58; Mike Cox, *Texas Ranger Tales* (Plano, Texas: Republic of Texas Press, 1997), 53-57; Traylor, "Two Famous Sons," 305; *Galveston Daily News*, 21 July 1878, 1; Texas State Library, General Service Records, File 401-154; Muster Roll, Frontier Battalion, Company A, September 1877, 28 February 1878; Center for American History, University of Texas at Austin, Transcripts From the Office of the Adjutant General of Texas, 1877, File No. 2Q400, Vol. 9(B), pp. 106, 188; Evelyn Wolf, Loretta Leonhardt and Valerie Johnson, *Bastrop County Marriage Records, 1851-1881*, Vol. 1 (Bastrop, Texas: Baron de Bastrop Chapter, Daughters of the Republic of Texas, n.d.), n.p.; Commissioners Court Minutes, Williamson County, Texas, Vol. 1, pp. 162, 172; Grave Marker, Round Rock, Texas, Cemetery.

36. *San Antonio Daily Express*, 12 September 1895, 8; *Texas Capital*, 21 July 1878, 4; *Galveston Daily News*, 24 July 1878, 1. Hall recalled in a newspaper interview in 1895 that he rode horseback to Round Rock, taking with him Lieutenant John R. Armstrong, Jim Lucy, Netteville Devine, and his brother, R.M. Hall, leaving them to set up a camp outside New Round Rock while he went in to confer with Major Jones. It is clear from more reliable contemporary accounts that his memory was faulty and that Armstrong and the others did not arrive until after the shootout occurred.

37. Traylor, "Two Famous Sons," 303.

38. *San Antonio Daily Express*, 12 September 1895, 8.

39. The 1880 Williamson County census lists fifty-three-year-old "Wane" Graham, who had a wife and four children. 1880 Williamson County, Texas, Census, 570 (241/241).

40. Tobias B. "By" Asher was born on January 6, 1828, in Owen County, Indiana. He married his first wife, Miriam Davis, in Williamson County, Texas, on January 4, 1849, producing four children. He married his second wife, Mrs. Elizabeth Kinchloe Bowmer, in February 1864. Shroyer and Wood, eds., *Williamson County, Texas: Its History and Its People*, 56; 1870 Williamson County, Texas, Census, 407 (481/481); 1880 Williamson County, Texas, Census, 569 (226/226); Marriage Records, Williamson County, Texas, Book 1, 14 (License No. 23).

41. Traylor, "Two Famous Sons," 303.

42. *San Antonio Daily Express*, 12 September 1895, 8.

43. Henry Burkhardt was born about 1844 in Germany, and in 1880 was married to his wife, Christina, twenty-six. 1880 Williamson County, Texas, Census, 560 (60/60).

44. Traylor, "Two Famous Sons," 303; *Austin American-Statesman*, 14 August 1927, Supp. p. 11.

45. *Austin Daily Democratic Statesman*, 26 July 1878, 4.

46. *Galveston Daily News*, 25 July 1878, 2.

47. *Austin American-Statesman*, 1 May 1927, Sec. 3, 6; "Truest Story of Death of Sam Bass," *Frontier Times*, 91. Jefferson Dillingham was born in Texas about 1866 and lived in Williamson County in the Florence area with his parents, Brice Dillingham, a miller, and Sarah Dillingham. 1870 Williamson County, Texas, Census, 434 (844/844).

48. Hart Stilwell, "I Saw Them Kill Sam Bass," *Badman*, Vol. 1, No. 2 (Summer 1971), 33. Benjamin Warden was born in Virginia around 1834 and had studied medicine in New York, setting up a medical practice. When a flood destroyed a crop, he brought his family to Burnet County, Texas, in December

1873. Benjamin and his wife, Frances ("Fannie"), had at least eight children. James Bradley Warden was born on December 23, 1867, at Wardenville, West Virginia. A farmer and rancher in Burnet County, James married Rella Barton on February 22, 1899, and they subsequently had five children. James Warden died in Burnet on September 9, 1955. Darrell Debo, *Burnet County History* (Burnet, Texas: Eakin Press, 1979), Vol. II, 325-27; *Burnet Bulletin*, 15 September 1955, 5; 1880 Burnet County, Texas, Census, 143, (55/55).

49. Howard W. Peak, *A Ranger of Commerce* (San Antonio, Texas: Naylor Printing Co., 1929), 207-208. Adler Dieckmann was born in Prussia about 1839, and in 1880 lived with his young daughter, Gertrude. 1880 Williamson County, Texas, Census, 561 (90/90).

50. Gard, *Sam Bass*, 206-207. David H. Davis was born about 1868 in Williamson County to William F. and Ellen L. Davis, both from Tennessee. 1880 Williamson County, Texas, Census, 510 (3/3).

51. *Life and Adventures of Sam Bass*, 79; Hogg, *Authentic History*, 164-65.

52. *Galveston Daily News*, 25 July 1878, 2.

53. Traylor, "Two Famous Sons," 303; *Life and Adventures of Sam Bass*, 79-80.

54. 1880 Williamson County, Texas, Census, 557 (9/9); Thompson and Digesualdo, *Historical Round Rock*, 315-16.

55. *Galveston Daily News*, 2 April 1878, 1.

56. *Galveston Daily News*, 21 July 1878, 1.

57. 1880 Travis County, Texas, Census, 268 (66/79).

58. *Galveston Daily News*, 21 July 1878, 1; 25 July 1878, 2.

59. Gard, *Sam Bass*, 210.

60. Dr. A.F. Morris was born in Pennsylvania about 1819 and had been in Texas with his wife, Margaret, since the mid-1850s. 1880 Williamson County, Texas, Census, 557 (13/13).

61. *Galveston Daily News*, 25 July 1878, 2.

62. "Veteran Ostrander Writes," *Frontier Times*, Vol. 5, No. 8 (May 1928), 346-47. The 1880 Williamson County census lists a John C. Tubb, forty-eight, a farmer from Alabama, who lived with his wife and five children. 1880 Williamson County, Texas, Census, 461 (35/36).

63. *Galveston Daily News*, 2 April 1878, 1.

64. Frank L. Jordan was born in Georgia about 1848, and his wife, M.L. Searight Jordan, was a pianist in his saloon. They married on November 11, 1879. 1880 Williamson County, Texas, Census, 425 (4); Marriage Records, Williamson County, Texas, Book 5, 52, (License No. 103).

65. *Galveston Daily News*, 21 July 1878, 1; 24 July 1878, 1; 25 July 1878, 2; *Austin Daily Democratic Statesman*, 26 July 1878, 4; *Austin American-Statesman*, 14 August 1927, Supp. 11; *San Antonio Daily Express*, 6 September 1895, 4; 11 September 1895, 6; 18 September 1895, 5; 22 December 1901, 18; Traylor, "Two Famous Sons," 303; Hogg, *Authentic History*, 165; Capt. J.B. Gillett, "The Killing of Sam Bass," *Lloyd's Magazine*, May 1924, 37-38.

66. Gard, *Sam Bass*, 211; Thompson and Digesualdo, *Historical Round Rock*, 113. Anna Fahner was born about 1864 to French-born stonemason Paul and Barbary Fahner. 1860 Williamson County, Texas, Census, 49; 1870 Williamson County, Texas, Census, 400 (387/387); 1880 Williamson County, Texas, Census, 566 (171/171).

67. *Austin Daily Democratic Statesman*, 26 July 1878, 4; *Life and Adventures of Sam Bass*, 81.

68. *San Antonio Daily Express*, 18 September 1895, 5. There were three J. McCutcheons in the 1880 Williamson County census, all farmers. See 1880 Williamson County, Texas, Census, 532 (48), 553 (375/375), and 553 (383/383).

69. Traylor, "Two Famous Sons," 303-04; *Life and Adventures of Sam Bass*, 81-82.

70. *Galveston Daily News*, 24 July 1878, 1.

71. *San Antonio Daily Express*, 12 September 1895, 8.

72. *Galveston Daily News*, 24 July 1878, 1; Traylor, "Two Famous Sons," 304; Texas State Library, Results of Operations of State Troops, Ledger 401-1082, p. 230.

73. *Galveston Daily News*, 20 July 1878, 4.

74. Ewing E. Dunn was born April 15, 1835, in Kentucky to James Dunn and had moved to Texas in the mid-1850s. His first wife, from Mississippi, bore him several children, a second wife from Illinois bore him more, and his third wife, Mary E., from Alabama, ultimately survived him. He was elected Navarro County sheriff on February 15, 1876, reelected in 1878, 1880 and 1882, and served until November 4, 1884. He ultimately became a wealthy man, described as "a great character, full of charity and love for his fellow men, firm in his beliefs and honored by all who knew him." He died in Corsicana on November 9, 1917. 1860 Ellis County, Texas, Census, 6 (25/25); 1870 Navarro County, Texas, Census, 9 (129/129); 1880 Navarro County, Texas, Census, 493 (91/96); Certificate of Death (E.E. Dunn), Navarro County, Texas, No. 32323; *Corsicana Democrat and Truth*, 15 November 1917, 1; Tise, *Texas County Sheriffs*, 389.

75. Texas State Library, Adjutant General Correspondence, Box 401-397-8; Frontier Battalion, Box 401-1159-8; *Galveston Daily News*, 21 July 1878, 1.

76. *Williamson County Sun*, 25 July 1878, Center for American History, University of Texas at Austin, Walter Prescott Webb Collection, Box 2M275.

77. *Life and Adventures of Sam Bass*, 83; *Williamson County Sun*, 25 July 1878, Center for American History, University of Texas at Austin, Walter Prescott Webb Collection, Box 2M275; Hogg, *Authentic History*, 173; Gillett, *Six Years With the Texas Rangers*, 126. John and Semantha Sherman were both born in Texas, and the July 25, 1878, *Williamson County Sun* refers to her as Mrs. Sherman, but Williamson County marriage records indicate that they married on October 17, 1878, some three months after the incident. 1880 Williamson County, Texas, 567 (199/199); Marriage Records, Williamson County, Texas, Book 4, 367 (License No. 733).

78. Gard, *Sam Bass*, 214-15. Dudley Hiram Snyder, born about 1834, and his brothers, John Wesley and Thomas Shelton Snyder, came to Texas from Mississippi prior to the Civil War to join their maternal grandfather, Dr. Thomas Hail, who lived in Round Rock. They were involved in a variety of business ventures, including transporting apples from Missouri to Austin, horse trading and threshing wheat. After serving in the Confederate Army, they went into the cattle business, driving one of the first Texas herds to Omaha and Cheyenne. Dudley Snyder and his wife, Mary, whom he married on February 3, 1864, had at least seven children. He died in 1921. Shroyer and Wood, eds., *Williamson County, Texas: Its History and Its People*, 279; 1880 Williamson County, Texas, Census, 437 (245); Marriage Records, Williamson County, Texas, Book 2, 140 (License No. 125); *Index to Probate Cases Filed in Texas* (San Antonio, Texas: State-Wide Records Project, 1941), (No. 246, Williamson County 1848-1938), 64.

79. *The Texas Capital*, 21 July 1878, 4.

80. Olander C. Lane was born in 1848 to James Sterling Lane and Annie Clayborn Jones Lane. Lane married Annie Green and they had six children. On March 27, 1877, he was indicted in Williamson County for assault with intent to murder, but a jury acquitted him on April 4, 1877. He was on the Williamson County payroll as early as April 1878 for "riding bailiff." Shroyer and Wood, eds., *Williamson County, Texas: Its History and Its People*, 180; District Court Minutes, Williamson County, Texas, *State of Texas v. Orlando Lane*, Cause No. 1520, Vol. 5, pp. 554, 585; Williamson County Commissioners Court Minutes, Vol. 1, 155.

81. *San Antonio Daily Express*, 22 December 1901, 21 July 1902, 7.

82. C.P. Cochran, born about 1830 in Georgia, lived in the Florence area in Williamson County with his wife, Elizabeth E., and their four children. 1880 Williamson County, Texas, Census, 492 (38/38). Dr. Cochran was paid forty dollars by the state for visiting and dressing Bass' wounds. Texas State Library,

Adjutant General Records, Voucher to C.P. Cochran; Adjutant General Correspondence, Box 401-397-11.

83. *Galveston Daily News*, 24 July 1878, 1. Highsmith stated in 1927 that he hitched a team to an ambulance and conveyed Dr. Cochran to where Bass was located. Jeff Dillingham asserted that his future brother-in-law, C.P. Barnes, a vegetable salesman, took his vegetable wagon to ferry Bass back to town. Traylor, "Two Famous Sons," 304; *Austin American-Statesman*, 1 May 1927, Sec. 3, p. 6; "'Truest' Story of Death of Sam Bass," 90-91.

84. Texas State Library, Adjutant General Correspondence, Box 401-397-8.

85. *Life and Adventures of Sam Bass*, 83

86. Thompson and Digesualdo, *Historical Round Rock, Texas*, 326-27. Dr. Alexander McDonald was born about 1842, and he and his wife, Mary J. Wolfgin McDonald, whom he married on January 12, 1868, had at least six children. 1880 Williamson County, Texas, Census, 566 (167/167); Marriage Records, Williamson County, Texas, Book 3, p. 67 (License No. 146).

87. "'Truest' Story of Death of Sam Bass," *Frontier Times*, 90-91. August Gloeber, born about 1842 in Germany, and his wife, Johanna, would have at least six children. 1880 Williamson County, Texas, Census, 558 (26/26).

88. Center for American History, University of Texas at Austin, Adjutant General Records, Voucher from Major John B. Jones to Richard C. Hart, 22 July 1878; "Abilene Woman Saw Sam Bass Die at Round Rock," *Abilene Reporter*, as quoted in the *Denton Record-Chronicle*, 5 October 1911. Richard C. Hart was born about 1832 in Maryland. He married Ann E. Northington in Williamson County on August 5, 1861. A hotel keeper, he and his wife had at least three children. 1880 Williamson County, Texas, Census, 559 (37/37).

89. Thompson and Digesualdo, *Historical Round Rock*, 274; Gard, *Sam Bass*, 219; "Abilene Woman," *Denton Record-Chronicle*, 5 October 1911. Nancy T. Earle was born in Missouri about 1857. She was married at fifteen to William Earle, of South Carolina, and by 1880 they had five children. 1880 Williamson County, Texas, Census, 582 (445/445).

90. *Galveston Daily News*, 24 July 1878, 1. Jim Chatman was born about 1840 in Alabama. He and his wife, Easter, had at least four children. The family moved to Brazos County shortly after the Bass episode. 1880 Brazos County, Texas, Census, 357 (469/491).

91. *Austin Daily Democratic Statesman*, 21 July 1878, as quoted in the *Galveston Daily News*, 25 July 1878, 2; 21 July 1878, 4. Moore was up and about in Austin by August 1, and as of September was digging a well on his place nine miles west of Austin. *Texas Capital*, 4 August 1878, 3; *Waco Examiner and Patron*, 13 September 1878, 2.

92. Texas State Library, Adjutant General Correspondence, Box 401-397-8.

93. Texas State Library, Adjutant General Correspondence, Box 401-397-8; *Galveston Daily News*, 21 July 1878, 1.

94. Texas State Library, Adjutant General Records, Frontier Battalion, Box 401-1159-5.

95. Texas State Library, Results of Operations of State Troops, Ledger 401-1082, pp. 141-42; Monthly returns, Company B, August 1878, Box 401-1247-5.

96. *Galveston Daily News*, 24 July 1878, 1.

97. *Galveston Daily News*, 21 July 1878, 1.

98. *El Paso Herald*, 12 August 1902, as quoted in Hogg, *Authentic History*, 191; *Lloyd's Magazine*, May 1924, 38.

99. *Galveston Daily News*, 21 July 1878, 1; Bruce, *Banister Was There*, 37-38. In February 1926 a cartridge belt alleged to be that of Sam Bass was donated to the University of Texas by Sam A. Arnett of Lubbock, Texas. It was described at the time as being badly worn and containing thirteen .44 caliber cartridges in the forty-five loops on the belt. A search for this belt in 1997 revealed that the cartridge belt has been lost or stolen from the university. *Grand Saline Sun*, 26 March

1926; "Historical Relic," *Frontier Times*, Vol. 3, No. 8 (May 1926), 45.

100.   A descendant of early Dutch colonists in 17th century New York, the original family name had been Van Aten. Austin C. Aten was born in Ohio about 1833. He became a Methodist minister, marrying his wife Kate, then filling pulpits in Illinois. After the Civil War he came to Texas as a circuit rider for his church. Harold Preece, *Lone Star Man* (New York: Hastings House Publishers, 1960), 21-25. By 1880 he had four children in accordance with the 1880 Travis County, Texas, Census, 67 (301/301); As written in *An Aten Geneaology* by Alan Lamb (Alan J. Lamb Publications: 1997), the Rev. Aten had seven children. Several of the children were possibly too old to join the migration of the rest of the family to Texas in 1876. Three of his five sons, Ira, Cal and Eddie, would become rangers in Texas. Another son, Frank, claimed in the 1950s at age ninety-seven that he and his brother Ira went with their father to pray over the mortally wounded Sam Bass, that Bass did repent, and that Ira said, after seeing Major John Jones, "I'm gonna be a Ranger when I grow up."

101.   *Austin American-Statesman*, 14 August 1927, Supp. 11; Preece, *Lone Star Man*, 23-24.

102.   Traylor, "Two Famous Sons," 304.

103.   *Life and Adventures of Sam Bass*, 84; *Galveston Daily News*, 24 July 1878, 1. Charles Nevill later claimed that Bass had clotted blood in his throat that delayed his death. According to him, Bass turned on his side, loosened the clot, and died almost instantly. *San Antonio Daily Express*, 22 December 1901, 18.

XVI. AFTERMATH

1.   *El Paso Herald*, 12 August 1902, as quoted in Hogg, *Authentic History*, 191; Gillett, "Killing of Sam Bass," *Lloyd's Magazine*, 38; *Galveston Daily News*, 24 July 1878, 1; Texas State Library, *Results of Operations of State Troops*, Ledger 401-1082, p. 230.

2.   *San Antonio Daily Express*, 11 September 1895, 6; 12 September 1895, 8; *Galveston Daily News*, 25 July 1878, 2; Gillett, *Six Years With the Texas Rangers*, 126-27. Descendants of Moore claimed that the deputy's Colt .45 revolver was the one that inflicted Bass' fatal wound at Round Rock. *Austin American-Statesman*, 1 March 1995, B:1.

3.   Robert McNellis, "Is This the Gun That Killed Sam Bass?" *Arms Gazette*, Vol. 11, No. 2 (October 1974), 46-47.

4.   *Austin Daily Democratic Statesman*, 26 July 1878, 4.

5.   Traylor, "Two Famous Sons," 303; *Austin American-Statesman*, 14 August 1927, Supp. 11; *El Paso Herald*, 12 August 1902, as quoted in Hogg, *Authentic History*, 189-90.

6.   Texas State Library, Adjutant General Correspondence, Box 401-397-8; "Abilene Woman," *Denton Record-Chronicle*, 5 October 1911.

7.   The Rev. John W. Ledbetter was born December 23, 1829, in Tennessee, and his wife, Fannie, was born in North Carolina on August 6, 1835. They came to Texas prior to the Civil War and had at least three children, all born in Texas. Rev. Ledbetter died on January 19, 1890, and his wife on March 19, 1918. 1870 Williamson County, Texas, Census, 399 (375/375); 1880 Williamson County, Texas, Census, 567 (187/187); Thompson and Digesualdo, *Historical Round Rock*, 419.

8.   *Austin American-Statesman*, 14 August 1927, Supp. 11.

9.   *Galveston Daily News*, 24 July 1878, 1.

10.   *Galveston Daily News*, 3 August 1878, 2.

11.   Texas State Library, Adjutant General Correspondence, Box 401-397-8.

12.   *Galveston Daily News*, 26 July 1878, 1; 31 July 1878, 2.

13.   *Sherman Register*, as quoted in the *Denison Daily News*, 25 July 1878, 1;

ENDNOTES

Galveston Daily News, 28 July 1878, 1; 31 July 1878, 2.

14. Texas State Library, Adjutant General Correspondence, Box 401-397-8,9; Frontier Battalion Correspondence, Box 401-1159-3,4; *Galveston Daily News*, 6 August 1878, 1; Center for American History, University of Texas at Austin, Transcripts from Adjutant General's Office, File No. 2Q400, Vol. 10, p. 237.

15. *Austin Gazette*, as quoted in the *Lampasas Daily Times*, 31 July 1878, 1.

16. *Galveston Daily News*, 11 September 1878, 4.

17. Center for American History, University of Texas at Austin, Letter to Major John B. Jones from M.F. Leach, 27 July 1878.

18. Texas State Library, Frontier Battalion, Minutes of Company E Scouts & Etc., 20-26 July 1878, Box 401-1180-23.

19. *Galveston Daily News*, 27 July 1878, 1; 28 July 1878, 1; 10 August 1878, 1; *Dallas Herald*, as quoted in the *San Antonio Daily Express*, 16 August 1878, 1; *Austin Daily Democratic Statesman*, 27 July 1878, 4.

20. *Galveston Daily News*, 28 July 1878, 1; *Dallas Morning News*, 11 April 1926, Sec. 7, p. 5.

21. *Dallas Herald*, 7 August 1878, as quoted in the *San Antonio Daily Express*, 10 August 1878, 1.

22. District Court Minutes, Collin County, Texas, *State of Texas v. Thomas Spotswood*, Cause No. 1500; *Galveston Daily News*, 16 July 1878, 1; 18 July 1878, 1; 27 July 1878, 1.

23. Texas State Library, Adjutant General Records, Frontier Battalion, Box 401-1159-2.

24. *Sherman Register*, as quoted in the *Waco Examiner and Patron*, 23 August 1878, 8.

25. *Galveston Daily News*, 31 July 1878, 1.

26. Texas State Library, Adjutant General Records, Frontier Battalion, Box 401-1159-2.

27. Texas State Library, Adjutant General Correspondence, Box 401-397-9.

28. Texas State Library, Frontier Battalion Correspondence, Box 401-1159-8.

29. *Galveston Daily News*, 14 August 1878, 1.

30. *Galveston Daily News*, 20 August 1878, 1.

31. *The Frontier Echo*, 2 August 1878, 3.

32. *Fort Worth Daily Democrat*, 11 August 1878, 1.

33. *Denison Daily News*, 13 August 1878, 4.

34. *Fort Worth Daily Democrat*, 22 August 1878, 4.

35. *Denison Daily News*, 30 August 1878, 1.

36. Texas State Library, Frontier Battalion Correspondence, Box 401-1159-8.

37. *Dallas Daily Herald*, 17 November 1876, 1.

38. Henry H. Haley was born in 1846 at Mount Vernon, Missouri, to Kentucky-born parents. He served in the Confederate Army during the Civil War. He subsequently became a U.S. Deputy Marshal. Married, he died in Grayson County on July 4, 1911. Certificate of Death, Grayson County, Texas, No. 15742; *Confederate Veteran*, Vol. IX, No. 1 (January 1901), 8.

39. Sam Ball, City Marshal of Sherman, was in Austin on Friday evening, January 24, 1879, when Palo Pinto County Sheriff J.T. Wilson, overhearing Ball make a remark about him outside the Occidental Saloon, drew his pistol and the two exchanged gunfire, with others among the crowd joining in. Wilson was shot twice in the breast and killed, and Ball was wounded in a finger, another shot hitting a watch which spared him serious injury. *Austin Daily Democratic Statesman*, 24 January 1879, 4; 25 January 1879, 4; *Denison Daily News*, 25 January 1879, 1; 26 January 1879, 1. A year later, Marshal Ball, late in the evening of Tuesday, January 27, 1880, in Josie Belmont's bawdy house in Sherman's red light district, received a mortal gunshot wound at the hands of Alf Johnson, whom Ball also shot dead after being wounded. *Denison Daily News*, 29 January 1880, 4; 31 January 1880, 4.

40. The 1880 Grayson County census lists three George Bonds, one a thirty-

five-year-old saloon keeper in Sherman, born in Arkansas, and the second a sixty-three-year-old retired farmer from Tennessee with a twenty-one-year-old son, also named George, who is a bartender. 1880 Grayson County, Texas, Census, 88 (170/181), 91 (217/230).

41. William Erwin was born about 1850 in Missouri, and by 1880 he and his wife had two children. At one point before becoming a deputy sheriff, he was Sherman City Marshal. 1880 Grayson County, Texas, Census, 47 (220/265).

42. *Denison Daily News*, 28 August 1878, 4; 29 August 1878, 4; 31 August 1878, 1; 4 September 1878, 4; 5 September 1878, 4; *Dallas Commercial*, as quoted in the *Denison Daily News*, 30 August 1878, 1; *Galveston Daily News*, 28 August 1878, 1; 28 August 1878, 1; 29 August 1878, 1; 4 September 1878, 1.

43. Center for American History, University of Texas at Austin, Transcripts from the Adjutant General's Office, File No. 2Q400, Vol. 10, pp. 250, 261.

44. Texas State Library, Frontier Battalion Correspondence, Box 401-1159-7.

45. District Court Records, Williamson County, Texas, *State of Texas v. Frank Jackson*, Cause No. 1762.

46. *Denison Daily News*, 15 October 1878, 1; *Dallas Herald*, as quoted in the *Waco Examiner and Patron*, 18 October 1878, 2; *Dallas Commercial*, as quoted in the *Denison Daily News*, 16 October 1878, 1.

47. Williams, "Denton County Deputy Sheriff Tom Gerren."

48. *Galveston Daily News*, 10 November 1878, 1; 26 November 1878, 1; Monograph by Peter Kostiuk, Fort Pembina, North Dakota, Historical Society, taken from a 1934 account in the *Grand Forks Herald*, as told to Win V. Working by James R. Moorhead (courtesy Charles Walker, Pembina, North Dakota); Letter From Charles Walker, Pembina, North Dakota, to author, 1997.

49. Telegram to U.S. Attorney General, Washington D.C., from U.S. Marshal Stillwell Russell, 8 November 1878 (Courtesy Robert Ernst, Stillwater, Oklahoma).

50. Martin, *Sketch of Sam Bass*, 164.

51. George W. Waller was born about 1845-1848 in Tennessee. He enlisted on August 1, 1863, as a private in Company C, 15th (also 20th) Tennessee Cavalry, in the Confederate Army. He was reported as a deserter on May 23, 1864. Waller moved to Dallas County in Texas about 1870. He was a member of the Stonewall Grays militia unit in Dallas under the command of June Peak. He married Eliza Fletcher in Dallas on February 18, 1875. He and his brother, Henry, were bartenders at the Windsor Hotel, and he had at least one daughter, Emma. 1910 Dallas County, Texas, Census, ED 65, Sheet 9B, Line 69; *Dallas Weekly Herald*, 2 March 1878; Lu and Neumann, eds., *Dallas County Marriages*, 38; Texas State Library, Confederate Pension Applications, Reject File; *Gillespie & Work's Dallas Directory, 1881-1882*, 95.

52. *Galveston Daily News*, 10 November 1878, 1; 13 November 1878, 1; 16 November 1878, 1; 26 November 1878, 1.

53. *Galveston Daily News*, 27 November 1878, 1.

54. *Dallas Weekly Herald*, 15 December 1881, 4.

55. *Denton Monitor*, as quoted in the *Denison Daily News*, 17 January 1879, 2.

56. Interview of Scott Mayes by Alex Williams, 15 December 1930, Goodman-Williams Collection, Denton County Historical Museum.

57. *Dallas Herald-Commercial*, as quoted by the *Denison Daily News*, 11 June 1879, 1; *Galveston Daily News*, 8 June 1878, 1; Interview of John Hudson and Will Clark, Denton, Texas, by Alex Williams, 6 January 1931, Goodman-Williams Collection, Denton County Historical Museum.

58. Gard, *Sam Bass*, 235.

59. District Court Records, Collin County, Texas, *State of Texas v. Thomas Spotswood*, Cause Nos. 1500 and 1501; *Dallas Daily Herald*, 13 July 1880, 1.

60. 1880 Denton County, Texas, Census, 195 (445/447); Marriage Records, Collin County, Texas, Vol. 5, p. 95. William D. Spotswood, born in Missouri on February 17, 1853, lived in Aubrey, in Denton County, dying a widower on

February 1, 1925, from pneumonia only sixteen days shy of his seventy-second birthday. 1920 Denton County, Texas, Census, ED 67, Sheet 7, Line 70 (149/149); Deed Records, Collin County, Texas, Vol. 16, pp. 165-66; Vol. 65, 56; Deed Records, Denton County, Texas, Vol. 36, 226; Vol. 39, 107-113; Certificate of Death (William D. Spottswood), Denton County, Texas, No. 5779; *Denton Record-Chronicle*, 6 February 1925, 8. John Cleveland Spotswood was born at Calhoun, Missouri, on January 6, 1856. He was a defendant in a criminal case in Denton County in 1879, although the charge and the disposition are unknown. Spotswood married Mary Virginia "Mollie" Ashby in Denton County on April 20, 1887, and in 1889 he moved his family to Henrietta in Clay County, where he earned a living as a teamster and he and Mollie subsequently had four children. John Spotswood moved back to Denton County sometime after 1920, making his home with Mr. and Mrs. Arthur Thorne, and dying there on January 25, 1940. 1900 Clay County, Texas, Census, ED 14, Sheet 10, Line 31, p. 34A (199/199); 1910 Clay County, Texas, Census, ED 30, Sheet 13, Line 43 (254/265); 1920 Clay County, Texas, Census, ED 17, Sheet 3, Line 28 (53/61); Certificate of Death (John Cleveland Spotswood), Denton County, Texas, No. 1717; *Denton Record-Chronicle*, 31 January 1940, 3; Marriage Records, Denton County, Texas, Vol. 3, 136; Deed Records, Clay County, Texas, Vol. 57, 251.

61. Robert S. Erwin raised stock in Denton County, and was born about 1853 in Wisconsin. In 1880 he lived with his wife Lula. 1880 Denton County, Texas, Census, 12 (197/204).

62. Albert M. Cochran, born about 1825 in Alabama, lived on the farm adjacent to that of Robert Erwin. In 1880 he lived with his wife, Ella, and five children. They had lived in Mississippi, where their three oldest children were born, and came to Texas in the late 1860s or very early 1870s. Cochran took another wife, M.J. Goodwin, on December 28, 1892. 1880 Denton County, Texas, Census, 12 (196/203); Marriage Records, Denton County, Texas, Vol. 4, p. 370.

63. National Archives (Southwest Region, Fort Worth, Texas), U.S. District Court Records, Northern District of Texas, *United States v. Jim Tyler*, Cause No. 130; *Dallas Daily Herald*, 30 June 1880, 8; 27 July 1881, 1; 28 July 1881, 5.

64. *Dallas Herald*, as quoted in the *Denison Daily News*, 9 March 1880, 1.

65. *New York Times*, 19 February 1879, 2.

66. District Court Civil Minutes, Denton County, Texas, *State of Texas v. Scott Mays*, Cause No. 1688, Vol. B, pp. 395, 398, 430.

67. 1880 Cooke County, Texas, Census, 228 (165/172).

68. District Court Records, Cooke County, Texas, *State of Texas v. Scott Mayes*, Cause No. 1257; *Dallas Daily Herald*, 1 March 1881, 1.

69. Marriage Records, Cooke County, Texas, Vol. 4, p. 143.

70. District Court Records, Cooke County, Texas, *State of Texas v. Scott Mayes*, Cause No. 3061.

71. Probate Records, Cooke County, Texas, *Estate of E.S. Mayes, Deceased*, File No. 4529; Certification of Birth Record for Vernie Andrew Mayes, File No. 4842; 1900 Cooke County, Texas, Census, ED 27, Sheet 17, Line 31, p. 74A (355/366); 1910 Cooke County, Texas, Census, ED 47, Sheet 1 (11/12); 1920 Cooke County, Texas, Census, ED 30, Sheet 1B, Line 59 (12/13); *Gainesville Daily Register*, 19 June 1937, 6; 21 June 1937.

72. *Dallas Daily Herald*, 20 July 1881, 4; Tyler, ed., *New Handbook of Texas*, Vol. 3, 986.

73. 1880 Smith County, Texas, Census, 307 (178/212); National Archives, RG 60, Records Relating to the Appointment of Federal Judges, Marshals, and Attorneys, 1853-1901, Appointment Files for Judicial Districts 1853-1905; *Dallas Daily Herald*, 15-16 May 1882, 1; 5-7 July 1882, 1.

74. *Galveston Daily News*, 4 April 1883, 1; 12 April 1883, 1; *Waco Daily Examiner*, 26 April 1883, 4.

75. Grave Marker, Oakwood Cemetery, Denton, Texas.

76. *Dallas Daily Herald*, 21 October 1883; 29 August 1885, 8.

77. *Denton Record and Chronicle*, 24 November 1904, 4.

78. District Court Minutes, Denton County, Texas, *State of Texas v. T.E. Gerren*, Cause No. 3214, Vol. G, pp., 513, 577.

79. Interview with Sheriff W.S. Fry by Alex Williams, 11 September 1925; Interview with John Hudson by Alex Williams, 3 July 1930; Interview with Dick Cobb by Alex Williams, 11 June 1930; Goodman-Williams Collection, Denton County Historical Museum; Alex Williams, "Denton County Deputy Sheriff Tom Gerren."

80. 1880 Denton County, Texas, Census, 407 (177/178).

81. *Denton Record and Chronicle*, 24 November 1904, 4.

82. *IOOF Cemetery, Denton, Texas*, 75.

83. Robert W. Stephens, "Junius Peak, Texas Confederate," *Military Images*, Vol. 1, No. 6 (May-June 1980), 4-5; Stephens, *Texas Ranger Sketches*, 114-15; "Captain June Peak," *Frontier Times*, Vol. 4, No. 11 (August 1927), 6; Tyler, ed., *New Handbook of Texas*, Vol. 5, pp. 107-108; *Dallas Morning News*, 21 April 1934, Sec. II, 1.

XVII. EPILOGUE

1. *Denison Daily News*, 11 September 1878, 4.

2. 1880 Jennings County, Indiana, Census, 356 (56/56).

3. National Archives, RG 21, Records of the U.S. District Court, Southern District of Indiana, Indianapolis Division, Criminal Records, Criminal Case Files, *United States v. James K. Rittenhouse, William Jones, Isaac Haworth, and John F. Holloway*, Case Nos. 3362, 3372, and 3373 consolidated.

4. *Dallas Weekly Herald*, 17 April 1875; *Dallas Daily Herald*, 11 April 1875.

5. Indiana State Archives, Descriptive Lists of Convicts in the Indiana State Prison, Vol. G (1879-1883), 128.

6. National Archives, RG 21, Records of the U.S. District Court, Southern District of Indiana, Indianapolis Division, Criminal Records, Criminal Record Books, Vols. 1 and 2; Criminal Case Files, *United States v. James K. Rittenhouse, William Jones, Isaac Haworth, and John F. Holloway*, Cause No. 3362; *Indianapolis News*, 26 May 1881, 4; 27 May 1881, 3; 28 May 1881, 4.

7. Indiana State Archives, Descriptive Lists of Convicts in the Indiana State Prison, Vol. G (1879-1883), 128.

8. Indiana State Archives, Descriptive List of Convicts in the Northern Indiana State Prison, Near Michigan City, Vol. 3 (July 1877-May 1883), 231.

9. Gideon Underwood was born about 1841, married Martha Jane Burroughs in Jennings County, Indiana, on February 11, 1846, then married Julia Ann Twadell in Jennings County on December 8, 1849. In the 1880 census he was listed as living in Boone County with another wife, Eliza A., and seven children. Deed records reflect that Underwood was living in Boone County by April 1879. On January 20, 1884, his daughter Mary married Edward G. Silvers, and on April 5, 1884, his son William was mangled and killed while blasting tree stumps on the farm. Marriage Record Book, Jennings County, Indiana, No. 4, pp. 93, 456; Deed Records, Boone County, Indiana, Vol. 30, 118; 1880 Boone County, Indiana, Census, 151 (6/6); *Lebanon Patriot*, 20 January 1884; 12 April 1884, 1.

10. *Lebanon Patriot*, 17 December 1885, 1.

11. *Indianapolis Times*, 16 December 1885, 1; *Lebanon Pioneer*, 17 December 1885, 1 and 3; Indictment Book, Boone County, Indiana, *State of Indiana v. Gideon Underwood et al*, Cause No. 598, 402-405.

12. *Lebanon Patriot*, 17 December 1885, 1 and 3; 1880 Boone County, Indiana, Census, 44 (54/52).

13. *Lebanon Patriot*, 25 March 1886, 1.

14. *Lebanon Patriot*, 5 August 1886, 3; *Lebanon Pioneer*, 5 August 1886, 1.

15. Indiana State Archives, Descriptive Lists of Convicts in the Indiana State Prison, South, Vol. H (1883-1887), 191.

16. *Lebanon Patriot*, 15 July 1886, 1; 5 August 1886, 1; 3 February 1887, 1; *Lebanon Pioneer*, 15 July 1886, 1.

17. Indictment Book, Boone County, Indiana, *State of Indiana v. Gideon Underwood et al*, Cause No. 598, 402-405.

18. *Lebanon Pioneer*, 30 September 1886, 1; 14 October 1886, 1.

19. *Lebanon Pioneer*, 18 November 1886; *Indianapolis Sentinel*, 15 November 1886, 4. Charles Walker Hammond was born in Carroll County, Kentucky, in October 1846, his mother dying when he was six months old. He was raised by an aunt in Johnson County, Indiana, and then lived with her at Seymour. In 1861 he enlisted and served for a few months in a Kentucky regiment, then reenlisted in Company E of the 33rd Indiana Regiment. After discharge on August 4, 1865, he returned to Seymour. John and Simeon Reno, along with Frank Sparks, had pulled off the first train robbery in the United States at Seymour on October 6, 1866. On Saturday, September 28, 1867, Hammond and Michael Colleran attempted a copycat robbery at the same place but were arrested within weeks. Boley, *The Masked Halters*, 168-72.

Hammond was convicted of the train robbery in Jackson County on February 20, 1869, and sentenced to six years in prison. Described as 5' 9", with fair complexion, blue eyes and brown hair, he was discharged from prison on June 12, 1874. Indiana State Archives, Descriptive Lists of Convicts in the Indiana State Prison, South, Vol. E (1866-1876), 133. Out of prison Hammond became involved with Pete McCartney and other counterfeiters involved with James Rittenhouse and served another five years at the Joliet prison in Illinois. He and McCartney again tried their counterfeiting skills in Ohio and escaped when they were arrested in Dayton. Hammond then became affiliated with Tom Foster's gang of horse thieves when he met Henry Underwood. *Lebanon Patriot*, 17 February 1887, 1.

20. *Indianapolis News*, 12 January 1887, 3; 15 January 1887, 1; *Indianapolis Sentinel*, 13 January 1887, 8; 14 January 1887, 8; 15 January 1887, 4.

21. *Indianapolis Sentinel*, 16 January 1887, 8; 18 January 1887, 8.

22. *Indianapolis News*, 18 January 1878, 3; *Indianapolis Sentinel*, 20 January 1887, 3; 25 January 1887, 8.

23. *Lebanon Pioneer*, 27 January 1887; *Indianapolis Sentinel*, 26 January 1887, 8.

24. *Lebanon Patriot*, 3 February 1887, 1; *Lebanon Pioneer*, 3 February 1887, 1.

25. *Indianapolis Sentinel*, 7 February 1887, 4; *Lebanon Pioneer*, 10 February 1887, 1; *Lebanon Patriot*, 10 February 1887, 1.

26. *Lebanon Pioneer*, 5 October 1893; 12 October 1893; *Lebanon Patriot*, 5 October 1893.

27. *Lebanon Pioneer*, 17 February 1887, 1.

28. Indiana State Archives, Descriptive List of Convicts in the Northern Indiana State Prison, Near Michigan City, Vol. 4 (May 1883-Nov. 1887), 184.

29. Indiana State Archives, Descriptive List of Convicts in the Northern Indiana State Prison, Near Michigan City, Vol. 2 (Dec. 1869-June 1877), 184; *Lebanon Pioneer*, 10 February 1887, 1; 23 May 1889, 4.

30. National Archives, RG 15, Pension Records, Records of the Veterans Administration.

31. James "Doc" Phillips was born in Masschusetts in August 1840 and in 1893 married his wife who was almost twenty years younger than he. He had a daughter from a previous marriage who was born in Pennsylvania in June 1888. 1900 Vigo County, Indiana, Census, ED 98 (372/372, 373/373).

32. *Terre Haute Express*, 8 March 1901, 4; 9 March 1901, 4; 10 March 1901, 8; 11 March 1901, 8; 14 March 1901, 3; *Terre Haute Evening Gazette*, 8 March 1901, 2; 9 March 1901, 1, 2;

33. Circuit Court Order Book, Vigo County, Indiana, Vol. 8, 274, *State of*

Indiana v. Henry Underwood, Cause Nos. 4417 and 4418; p. 276, *State of Indiana v. James Phillips*, Cause Nos. 4419 and 4420; *Terre Haute Evening Gazette*, 15 March 1901, 2.

34. Circuit Court Order Book, Vigo County, Indiana, Vol. 8, 275-76, 279-80; *Terre Haute Evening Gazette*, 15 March 1901, 2; *Terre Haute Express*, 15 March 1901, 4; 16 March 1901, 3, 5.

35. Indiana State Archives, Prisoners Record, Indiana State Prison, Vol. A, No. 1979.

36. Certificate of Death, Boone County, Indiana, Department of Health (Henry Underwood), Book 20, p. 40.

37. *Jamestown Press*, 12 July 1907, 1. One nineteenth-century author incorrectly claimed that Underwood was really Dr. Henri Stewart, a physician who was convicted of murder on May 16, 1879, in Judge Isaac Parker's federal court at Fort Smith Arkansas and subsequently executed. S.W. Harman, *Hell on the Border* (Fort Smith, Arkansas: Phoenix Publishing Co., 1898), 223-24. Henry Underwood's brother, Nathan, who had been born on January 26, 1844, in Indiana, maintained his home in San Antonio after his outlaw days. On January 30, 1878, he purchased a tract on the east bank of the San Pedro Creek there. Nathan married Mary Susan Rabb on July 29, 1879, and they subsequently had six children. He became a civic and political leader in San Antonio, once even running for Bexar County Sheriff. He was a partner with Harry Tappan in the Underwood Polo Farm, which bred and trained polo ponies. His wife died in February 1930 and Underwood died on May 9, 1931, in the hospital on Fort Sam Houston. *San Antonio Daily Express*, 11 May 1931, 18; 1880 Bexar County, Texas, Census, 43 (158/158); 1900 Bexar County, Texas, Census, ED 89, Sheet 3, Line 57, p. 213B (51/52); 1910 Bexar County, Texas, Census, ED 28, Sheet 48, Line 71 (illegible); 1920 Bexar County, Texas, Census, ED 54, Sheet 13A, Line 45 (285/296); Marriage Records, Bexar County, Texas, Vol. G, 19 (No. 5847); Deed Records, Bexar County, Texas, Vol. 9, 11; Probate Records, Bexar County, Texas, *Estate of Nathan Underwood*, Cause No. 19427; Certificate of Death (Nathan Underwood), Bexar County, Texas, No. 21923.

38. *Indianapolis News*, 8 January 1929, 1.

39. Hall of Records, Albany County, New York, Record of Inmates 1873-1886, Albany County Penitentiary.

40. George R. Howell and Jonathan Tenney, *History of the County of Albany, New York* (New York: W.W. Munsell & Co., Publishers, 1886), 352.

41. National Archives II (College Park, Maryland), RG 204, Office of the Pardon Attorney, Pardon Case Files 1853-1946, Record J, pp. 93-118, Box 155.

42. *Dallas Weekly Herald*, 27 March 1884, 7.

43. National Archives II (College Park, Maryland), RG 204, Office of the Pardon Attorney, Pardon Case Files 1853-1946, Record J, pp. 93-118, Box 155; Hall of Records, Albany County, New York, Record of Inmates 1873-1886, Albany County Penitentiary.

44. *Dallas Morning News*, 2 March 1886, 5.

45. *Morrison & Fourmy's General Directory of the City of Dallas, 1888-1889* (Galveston, Texas: Morrison & Fourmy, 1888), 213 and 270.

46. *Dallas Morning News*, 7 January 1887, 8.

47. *Dallas Daily Times Herald*, 18 February 1889, 1; *Dallas Morning News*, 17 February 1889, 4; Darnell, Jamieson, and Lu, eds., *Dallas County Cemeteries*, Vol. I, 90.

48. Certificate of Death, Dallas County, Texas (Mrs. Sallie Z. Pipes), No. 20072; *Dallas Morning News*, 10 April 1929, 11.

49. *Dallas Daily Times Herald*, 8 December 1898, 8; *Dallas Morning News*, 9 December 1898.

50. Marriage Records, Lawrence County, Indiana, Vol. G, 94; Circuit Court Records, Lawrence County, Indiana, *Denton Bass v. Emma Bass*, Cause No. 3551;

Probate Records, Lawrence County, Indiana, File No. 3, *Estate of Denton Bass*, Cause No. 4226; *Mitchell Tribune*, 16 December 1948, 1.

51. Undated memorandum by Alex Williams, Williams-Goodman Collection, File No. 87.24.161, Denton County Historical Museum.

52. Letter to Adjutant General J.B. Jones from Thomas J. Goree, 25 May 1881 (Courtesy Gary Fitterer, Kirkland, Washington).

53. *Abilene Reporter-News*, 26 December 1927, as quoted in Frank Sweeney, "Survivor of Sam Bass Gang Seeking to Return," *Frontier Times*, Vol. 5, No. 5 (February 1928), 200.

54. "Where is Frank Jackson?" *Frontier Times*, Vol. 5, No. 5 (February 1928), 224.

55. Gober, *Cowboy Justice*, 279.

56. Capt. Thomas H. Rynning, *Gun Notches* (San Diego, California: Frontier Heritage Press, 1971), 326-30.

57. Bill O'Neal, *The Arizona Rangers* (Austin, Texas: Eakin Press, 1987), 150-53.

58. N. Howard (Jack) Thorpe, *Pardner of the Wind* (Lincoln, Nebraska: University of Nebraska Press, 1977), 138-39.

59. Letter to Alex Williams, Denton, Texas, from E.S. Key, Fort Worth, Texas, 17 August 1963 (Courtesy Jim Browning, Charleston, South Carolina).

60. *Dallas Daily Herald*, 29 March 1882, 5; 1 April 1882, 4; *The Evening Review* [Albuquerque, New Mexico], 30 March 1882, 1.

61. Letter to Alex Williams, Denton, Texas, from H.N. Graves, Georgetown, Texas, 6 October 1930 (Courtesy Jim Browning, Charlotte, South Carolina); Center for American History, University of Texas at Austin, *Austin American-Statesman*, undated clipping from the 1920s, Scrapbook No. 17, Daughters of the Republic of Texas, p. 7; Sampson Connell served as Williamson County Sheriff from November 6, 1888, until November 4, 1890, then again from November 8, 1898, until November 5, 1912. Tise, *Texas County Sheriffs*, 544-45.

62. John H. Jenkins and H. Gordon Frost, *I'm Frank Hamer* (Austin, Texas: Pemberton Press, 1968), 141-42.

63. William Warren Sterling, *Trails and Trials of a Texas Ranger* (William Warren Sterling, 1959), 491-95.

64. District Court Records, Williamson County, Texas, *State of Texas v. Frank Jackson*, Cause No. 1762.

65. Hogg, *Authentic History*, 178.

66. Gard, *Sam Bass*, 238; "Sam Bass Song," *Frontier Times*, Vol. 23, No. 9 (June 1946), 163-64.

67. Ed Bartholomew, *Money in the Ground* (Fort Davis, Texas: Frontier Book Co., 1974), 87-88.

68. Gard, *Sam Bass*, 238.

BIBLIOGRAPHY

BOOKS

Abandoned Cemetery Records. Denton, Texas: Benjamin Lyon Chapter, Texas Daughters of the American Revolution, 1996.

Acheson, Sam. *Dallas Yesterday.* Dallas, Texas: SMU Press, 1977.

At Home in Ellis County, Kansas, 1867-1992. Dallas, Texas: Taylor Publishing Co., 1991.

Bartholomew, Ed. *Money in the Ground.* Fort Davis, Texas: Frontier Book Co., 1974.

Bartholomew, Ed. *Wyatt Earp, The Untold Story.* Toyahville, Texas: Frontier Book Co., 1963.

Bates, Ed F. *History and Reminiscences of Denton County.* Denton, Texas: McNitzky Printing Co., 1918.

Biographical Souvenir of the State of Texas. Chicago, Illinois: F.A. Battey & Co., 1889.

Boley, Edwin J. *The Masked Halters.* Seymour, Indiana: Graessle-Mercer Co., 1977.

Bonner, Helen Francis. *Major John B. Jones: The Defender of the Texas Frontier* (Master's Thesis). University of Texas at Austin, 1950.

Brant, Marley. *Outlaws: The Illustrated History of the James-Younger Gang.* Montgomery, Alabama: Elliott & Clark Publishing, 1997.

Bridwell, J.W. *The Life and Adventures of Robert McKimie.* Houston, Texas: The Frontier Press of Texas, 1955.

Brown, Jesse, and Willard, A.M. (Milek, John T., ed.). *The Black Hills Trails.* Rapid City, South Dakota: Rapid City Journal Co., 1924.

Brown, John Henry. *History of Dallas County, Texas, From 1837 to 1887.* Dallas, Texas: Milligan, Cornett & Farnham, Printers, 1887.

Brown, John Henry. *Indian Wars and Pioneers of Texas.* Austin, Texas: State House Press, 1988.

Bruce, Leona. *Banister Was There.* Fort Worth, Texas: Branch-Smith, Inc., 1968.

Bushick, Frank H. *Glamorous Days.* San Antonio, Texas: The Naylor Co., 1934.

Castel, Albert and Goodrich, Thomas. *Bloody Bill Anderson.* Mechanicsburg, Pennsylvania: Stackpole Books, 1998.

Cates, Cliff D. *Pioneer History of Wise County.* Decatur, Texas: Wise County Historical Committee, 1975.

Clarke, Mary Whatley. *The Palo Pinto Story.* Fort Worth, Texas: The Manney Co., 1956.

Coke, Ben H. *The Underwood Family From Madison County, Virginia.* Utica, Kentucky: McDowell Publications, 1986.

Cowling, Mary Jo. *Geography of Denton County.* Dallas, Texas, Banks Upshaw and Company, 1936.

Cox, Mike. *Texas Ranger Tales.* Plano, Texas: Republic of Texas Press, 1997.

Cullum, George W. *Biographical Register of the Officers and Graduates of the U.S. Military Academy.* New York: Houghton, Mifflin & Co., 1891.

Cutrer, Thomas W. (Introduction). *Terry Texas Ranger Trilogy.* Austin, Texas: State House Press, 1996.

BIBLIOGRAPHY

Darnall, Rubyann Thompson; Jamieson, Adrienne Bird; and Lu, Helen Mason, eds. *Dallas County, Texas: Genealogical Data From Early Cemeteries.* Dallas, Texas: Dallas Genealogical Society, 1982.

Davis, Vinita. *Marriage Records Index, Denton County, Texas, 1875-1884.* Fort Worth, Texas: American Reference Publishing Co., 1972.

DeArment, Robert K. *Alias Frank Canton.* Norman, Oklahoma: University of Oklahoma Press, 1996.

DeArment, Robert K. *Bat Masterson.* Norman, Oklahoma: University of Oklahoma Press, 1979.

Debo, Darrell. *Burnet County History.* Burnet, Texas: Eakin Press, 1979.

Denton County Genealogical Society. *Denton County, Texas, Wills (1876-1940).* Decorah, Iowa: Anundsen Publishing Co., 1994.

Douglas, C.L. *Cattle Kings of Texas.* Austin, Texas: State House Press, 1989.

Durham, George. *Taming the Nueces Strip.* Austin, Texas: University of Texas Press, 1990.

Earle, J.P. *History of Clay County and Northwest Texas.* Austin, Texas: Brick Row Book Shop, 1963.

Ellsberry, Elizabeth Prater. *Marriage Records of Audrain County, Missouri, 1836-1879.* Chillicothe, Missouri: Elizabeth Prater Ellsberry, n.d.

Engebretson, Doug. *Empty Saddles, Forgotten Names.* Aberdeen, South Dakota: North Plains Press, 1984.

Gard, Wayne. *Sam Bass.* New York: Houghton Mifflin Co., 1936.

Gard, Wayne. *Fabulous Quarter Horse: Steel Dust.* New York: Duell, Sloan and Pearce, 1958.

Gillespie & Work's Dallas Directory, 1881-1882.

Gillett, James B. *Six Years With the Rangers.* Lincoln, Nebraska: University of Nebraska Press, 1976.

Gillett, James B. *Fugitives From Justice.* Austin, Texas: State House Press, 1997.

Gober, Jim. *Cowboy Justice.* Lubbock, Texas: Texas Tech University Press, 1997.

Goodrich, Thomas. *Black Flag.* Bloomington, Indiana: Indiana University Press, 1995.

Grammar, Norma R., and Mullins, Marion Day. *Cooke County, Texas, Marriages, 1849-July 1879.* n.p., 1957.

Gregg, Rosalie. *Wise County History: A Link With the Past.* n.p.: Nortex Press, 1975.

Haley, J. Evetts. *A Good Man With a Gun.* Norman, Oklahoma: University of Oklahoma Press, 1949.

Harman, S.W. *Hell on the Border.* Fort Smith, Arkansas: Phoenix Publishing Co., 1898.

History of Lawrence County, Indiana. Paoli, Indiana: Stout's Print Shop, 1965.

History of Texas Together With a Biographical History of Tarrant and Parker Counties. Chicago, Illinois: The Lewis Publishing Co., 1895.

History of The State of Nebraska. Chicago, Illinois: The Western Historical Co., 1882.

Hogg, Thomas E. *Authentic History of Sam Bass and His Gang.* Bandera, Texas: Frontier Times, 1932 (reprint of 1878 edition).

Horan, James D. *The Pinkertons.* New York: Bonanza Books, 1967.

Horan, James D., and Sann, Paul. *Pictorial History of the Wild West.* New York: Bonanza Books, 1954.

Howell, George R., and Tenney, Jonathan. *History of the County of Albany, New York.* New York: W.W. Munsell & Co., 1886.

BIBLIOGRAPHY

Hunter, J. Marvin, ed. *Trail Drivers of Texas.* Austin, Texas: University of Texas Press, 1985.

Index to Probate Cases Filed in Texas. San Antonio, Texas: State-Wide Records Project (No. 246, Williamson County 1848-1938), 1941.

Inventory Book, Precinct No. 1 for 1874. Denton, Texas: Denton Public Library, n.d.

IOOF Cemetery, Denton, Texas. Denton, Texas: Denton County Historical Commission, 1989.

Jackson, George. *Sixty Years in Texas.* n.p., n.d.

Jenkins, John H., and Frost, H. Gordon. *I'm Frank Hamer.* Austin, Texas: Pemberton Press, 1968.

Jennings, N.A. *A Texas Ranger.* Austin, Texas: The Steck Co., 1959.

Lake, Stuart N. *Wyatt Earp, Frontier Marshal.* New York: Houghton-Mifflin Co., 1931.

Life and Adventures of Sam Bass. Dallas, Texas: Dallas Commercial Steam Print, 1878.

Lu, Helen Mason, and Neumann, Gwen Blomquist, eds. *Marriages, Dallas County, Texas, Books A-3 (1846-1877).* Dallas, Texas: Dallas Genealogical Society, 1978.

Martin, Charles L. *A Sketch of Sam Bass, the Bandit.* Norman, Oklahoma: University of Oklahoma Press, 1968 reprint of 1880 edition.

McClintock, John S. (Senn, Edward L., ed.). *Pioneer Days in the Black Hills.* New York: J.J. Little and Ives Co., 1939.

McCormick, Edna Haynes. *William Lee McCormick, A Study in Tolerance.* Dallas, Texas: The Book Craft, 1952.

McCown, Leonard Joe. *Cemeteries of Indianola, Texas.* Irving, Texas: Leonard Joe McCown, 1979.

McCoy, Joseph G. *Historic Sketches of the Cattle Trade of the West and Southwest.* Lincoln, Nebraska: University of Nebraska Press, 1985.

McIntire, Jim. *Early Days in Texas.* Norman, Oklahoma: University of Oklahoma Press, 1992.

Meeks, Beth Thomas, and Speer, Bonnie. *Heck Thomas, My Papa.* Norman, Oklahoma: The Apache News, 1988.

Memorial and Biographical History of Dallas County. Chicago, Illinois: The Lewis Publishing Co., 1892.

Mesquite Historical Committee. *A Stake in the Prairie: Mesquite, Texas.* Dallas, Texas: Taylor Publishing Co., 1984.

Metz, Leon Claire. *John Selman, Texas Gunfighter.* New York: Hastings House, 1966.

Miller, Nyle H., and Snell, Joseph W. *Why the West Was Wild.* Topeka, Kansas: Kansas State Historical Society, 1963.

Miller, Nyle H., and Snell, Joseph W. *Great Gunfighters of the Kansas Cowtowns, 1867-1886.* Lincoln, Nebraska: University of Nebraska Press, 1973.

Miller, Rick. *Bounty Hunter.* College Station, Texas: Creative Publishing Co., 1988.

Moore, Euroda. "Recollections of Indianola." *Indianola Scrapbook.* Austin, Texas: Jenkins Publishing Co., 1974.

Morrison & Foumy's General Directory of the City of Dallas, 1888-1889. Galveston, Texas: Morrison & Fourmy, 1888.

Nolan, Frederick. *The Lincoln County War: A Documentary History.* Norman, Oklahoma: University of Oklahoma Press, 1992.

Oakwood Cemetery, Denton, Texas. Denton, Texas: Denton County Genealogical Society, 1989.

O'Neal, Bill. *The Arizona Rangers*. Austin, Texas: Eakin Press, 1987.

Parsons, Chuck. *"Pidge," A Texas Ranger From Virginia*. Wolfe City, Texas, Henington Publishing Company, 1985.

Patterson, Richard. *The Train Robbery Era*. Boulder, Colorado: Pruett Publishing Co., 1991.

Peak, Howard W. *A Ranger of Commerce*. San Antonio, Texas: Naylor Printing Co., 1929.

Penal Code of the State of Texas. Galveston, Texas: A.H. Belo & Co., 1879.

Petty, J.W. *History of Victoria*. Victoria, Texas: Book Mart, 1961.

Pitts, Alice; O'Roark, Wanda; and Posey, Doris. *Collin County (Texas) Cemetery Inscriptions*. Fort Worth, Texas: The Manney Co., 1975.

Preece, Harold. *Lone Star Man*. New York: Hastings House Publishers, 1960.

Price, Lucie Clift. *Travis County, Texas, Marriage Records, 1840-1882*. Austin, Texas: Lucie Clift Price, 1973.

Proud Heritage: Pioneer Families of Dallas County. Dallas, Texas: Dallas County Pioneer Association, 1986.

Ray, Worth S. *Down in the Cross Timbers*. Austin, Texas: Worth S. Ray, 1947.

Raymond, Dora Neill. *Captain Lee Hall of Texas*. Norman, Oklahoma: University of Oklahoma Press, 1982.

Records of Collin and Denton Counties, Texas. Plano, Texas: Mary Shirley McGuire Chapter, Daughters of the American Revolution, n.d.

Reed, Paula and Tate, Grover Ted. *The Tenderfoot Bandits*. Tucson, Arizona: Westernlore Press, 1988.

Report of the Adjutant General of the State of Indiana. Vol. VIII. Indianapolis, Indiana: Alexander H. Conner, State Printer, 1868.

Roberts, Dan W. *Rangers and Sovereignty*. San Antonio, Texas: Wood Printing & Engraving Co., 1914.

Rosa, Joseph G. *They Called Him Wild Bill*. Norman, Oklahoma: University of Oklahoma Press, 1974.

Rosa, Joseph G., and Koop, Waldo. *Rowdy Joe Lowe, Gambler With a Gun*. Norman, Oklahoma: University of Oklahoma Press, 1989.

Rynning, Capt. Thomas H. *Gun Notches*. San Diego, California: Frontier Heritage Press, 1971.

Selcer, Richard F. *Hell's Half Acre*. Fort Worth, Texas: Texas Christian University Press, 1991.

Shaw, James C. (Brayer, Herbert O., ed.). *North From Texas*. College Station, Texas: Texas A&M University Press, 1996.

Shirley, Glenn. *Heck Thomas: Frontier Marshal*. New York: Chilton Company, 1962.

Shroyer, Mrs. Jean, and Wood, Mrs. Hazel, eds. *Williamson County, Texas: Its History and Its People*. Austin, Texas: Nortex Press, 1985.

Sifakis, Stewart. *Compendium of the Confederate Armies: Texas*. New York: Facts on File, Inc., 1995.

Sifakis, Stewart. *Compendium of the Confederate Armies: Kentucky, Maryland, Missouri, the Confederate Units and the Indian Units*. New York: Facts on File, Inc., 1995.

Sillers, Florence Warfield. *History of Bolivar County, Mississippi*. Jackson, Mississippi: Hederman Brothers, 1948.

Sorenson, Al. *Hands Up! Or the History of a Crime*. College Station, Texas: Creative Publishing Co., 1982 reprint of 1877 edition.

Speer, Bonnie. *Portrait of a Lawman*. Norman, Oklahoma: Reliance Press, 1996.

BIBLIOGRAPHY

Spring, Agnes Wright. *The Cheyenne and Black Hills Stage and Express Routes.* Glendale, California: Arthur H. Clark Co., 1949.

Stambaugh, J. Lee, and Stambaugh, Lillian J. *A History of Collin County, Texas.* Austin, Texas: Texas State Historical Association, 1958.

Stephens, Robert W. *Texas Ranger Sketches.* Dallas, Texas: Robert W. Stephens, 1972.

Stephens, Robert W. *Texas Rangers Indian War Pensions.* Quanah, Texas: Nortex Press, 1975.

Sterling, William Warren. *Trails and Trials of a Texas Ranger.* n.p.: William Warren Sterling, 1959.

Street, James, Jr. "The Struggle for Tennessee." *Time-Life Civil War Series.* Alexandria, Virginia: Time-Life Books, 1985.

Stroud, Dorothy Alice. *My Legacy for Mitchell, Indiana.* Paoli, Indiana: The Print Shop, 1985.

Terrell, C.V. *The Terrells, Eighty-Five Years From Indians to Atomic Bomb.* Dallas, Texas: Wilkinson Printing Co., 1948.

Terrell, W.H.H. *Indiana in the War of the Rebellion.* n.p.: Indiana Historical Bureau, 1960 reprint of 1869 edition,

Thompson, Karen R., and Digesualdo, Jane H. *Historical Round Rock.* Austin, Texas: Eakin Press, 1985.

Thorpe, N. Howard (Jack). *Pardner of the Wind.* Lincoln, Nebraska: University of Nebraska Press, 1977.

Tise, Sammy. *Texas County Sheriffs.* Albuquerque, New Mexico: Oakwood Printing, 1989.

Tuttle, Albert B. and Mary T. *History and Heritage of Gove County, Kansas.* n.p.: 1982.

Tyler, Ron, ed. *New Handbook of Texas.* Austin, Texas: Texas State Historical Association, 1996.

Webb, Walter Prescott. *The Texas Rangers.* Austin, Texas: University of Texas Press, 1982.

Wise County Historical Commission. *Wise County History.* Austin, Texas: Eakin Publications, 1982.

Wolf, Evelyn; Leonhardt, Loretta; and Johnson, Valerie. *Bastrop County Marriage Records, 1851-1881.* Bastrop, Texas: Baron De Bastrop Chapter, Daughters of the Republic of Texas, n.d.

Wooster, Ralph A. *Texas and Texans in the Civil War.* Austin, Texas: Eakin Press, 1995.

ARTICLES

"Abilene Woman Saw Sam Bass Die at Round Rock," *Denton Record-Chronicle,* 5 October 1911.

Adair, W.S. "Holdups Recall Sam Bass Gang," *Dallas Morning News,* 23 January 1921.

Adair, W.S. "Civil War Repeated in Indian Territory," *Dallas Morning News,* 1 July 1923.

Ball, Larry D. "The United States Army and the Big Springs, Nebraska, Train Robbery of 1877," *Journal of the West,* Vol. 34, No. 1 (January 1995).

Cammack, Harry C. "Letter to Editor," *Frontier Times,* Vol. 5, No. 1 (October 1927).

Caperton, Benjamin Franklin. "Sam Bass Robbed My Train," *True West,* Vol. 11, No. 5 (May-June 1964).

BIBLIOGRAPHY

"Captain June Peak," *Frontier Times*, Vol. 4, No. 11 (August 1927).

Cook, Capt. J.H. "Early Days in Ogallala," *Nebraska History Magazine*, Vol. XIV, No. 2 (April-June 1933).

Cope, Millard L. "G.W. Smith of Sonora Chased Sam Bass," *Dallas Morning News*, 11 April 1926.

Dobie, J. Frank. "The Robinhooding of Sam Bass," *True West*, Vol. 5, No. 6 (July-August 1958).

[Fearn, George R.] *Confederate Veteran*, Vol. II, No. 4 (April 1894).

Foree, Kenneth. "Sam Bass Rides Right Up Main Street," *Dallas Morning News*, 3 March 1948.

Gillett, Capt. J.B. "The Killing of Sam Bass," *Lloyd's Magazine* (May 1924).

[Haley, Henry H.]. *Confederate Veteran*. Vol. IX, No. 1 (January 1901).

[Hogg, Thomas Elisha]. *Confederate Veteran*, Vol. 14, No. 10 (October 1906).

"Historical Relic," *Frontier Times*, Vol. 3, No. 8 (May 1926).

McNellis, Robert. "Is This the Gun That Killed Sam Bass?" *Arms Gazette*, Vol. 11, No. 2 (October 1974).

[Meaders, Berry B.]. *Confederate Veteran*, Vol. V, No. 4 (April 1897).

Parsons, Chuck. "A Sam Bass Pictorial," *The Westerner*, Vol. 7 (Fall 1987).

Pearce, Bennett R. "Night of Terror at Big Springs," *The West*, Vol. 14, No. 6 (May 1971).

"Sam Bass Song," *Frontier Times*, Vol. 23, No. 9 (June 1946).

"Sends Us a Good List," *Frontier Times*, Vol. 4, No. 10 (July 1927).

Stilwell, Hart. "I Saw Them Kill Sam Bass," *Badman*, Vol. 1, No. 2 (Summer 1971).

Stephens, Robert W. "Junius Peak, Texas Confederate," *Military Images*, Vol. 1, No. 6 (May-June 1980).

Sternberg, William A. "The Big Springs Robbery of 1877," *Union Pacific Magazine* (December 1923).

Sweeney, Frank. "Survivor of Sam Bass Gang Seeking to Return," *Frontier Times*, Vol. 5, No. 5 (February 1928).

Traylor, Maude Wallis. "Two Famous Sons of a Famous Father," *Frontier Times*, Vol. 18, No. 7 (April 1941).

"'Truest' Story of Death of Sam Bass," *Frontier Times*, Vol. 11, No. 2 (November 1933).

"Vernon Wilson," *Frontier Times* (April 1929).

"Veteran Ostrander Writes," *Frontier Times*, Vol. 5, No. 8 (May 1928).

Webb, Walter Prescott. "Sam Bass, Texas' Beloved Bandit," *Dallas Morning News*, 2 January 1927.

"Where is Frank Jackson?" *Frontier Times*, Vol. 5, No. 5 (February 1928).

Williams, Alex. "Denton County Deputy Sheriff Tom Gerren: The Bully of the Town", *Denton Enterprise*, 23 July 1972.

[Withers, Peter Clay]. *Confederate Veteran*, Vol. XI, No. 5 (May 1903).

NEWSPAPERS

CALIFORNIA

Tulare County Times, 15 September 1892.

Visalia Daily Delta, 14 September 1892.

ILLINOIS

Chicago Daily Sun, 2 October 1877.

BIBLIOGRAPHY

INDIANA

Indianapolis News, 26, 27, 28 May 1881; 16 December 1885; 12, 15, 18 January 1887; 8 January 1929.

Indianapolis Sentinel, 15 November 1886; 13, 14, 15, 16, 18, 20, 25, 26 January 1887; 7 February 1887.

Jamestown Press, 12 July 1907.

Lebanon Patriot, 20 January 1884; 12 April 1884; 17 December 1885; 25 March 1886; 15 July 1886; 5 August 1886; 3, 10, 17 February 1887; 5 October 1893.

Lebanon Pioneer, 17 December 1885; 15 July 1886; 5 August 1886; 30 September 1886; 14 October 1886; 18 November 1886; 27 January 1887; 3, 10, 17 February 1887; 23 May 1889; 5, 12 October 1893.

Mitchell Tribune, 16 December 1948.

Terre Haute Evening Gazette, 8, 9, 15 March 1901

Terre Haute Express, 8, 9, 10, 11, 14, 15, 16 March 1901.

KANSAS

The Commonwealth [Topeka], 27, 29 September 1877.

Hays City Sentinel, 6 September 1876; 28 September 1877; 5, 12, 19 October 1877.

Wichita Weekly Beacon, 3 October 1877.

MISSOURI

Callaway Weekly Gazette, 19, 26 October 1877.

Fulton Telegraph, 26 October 1877.

Mexico Ledger, 14, 18 October 1877.

St. Louis Missouri Republican, 17, 22 October 1877.

NEBRASKA

Black Hills [Deadwood] *Daily Times*, 28 July 1877; 3 August 1877.

Columbus Journal, 20 March 1878.

Kearney Daily Press, 23 March 1878.

Nebraska City News, 16 March 1878.

Omaha Daily Bee, 30, 31 December 1877; 2 January 1878; 18 March 1878.

Omaha Republican, 30 December 1877.

Omaha Weekly Herald, September-October 1877; 4 January 1878.

Omaha Weekly Republican, 5 January 1878.

Sidney Telegraph, 12 January 1878.

NEW MEXICO

Evening Review [Albuquerque], 30 March 1882.

NEW YORK

New York Times, 25 October 1877; 19 February 1879; 24 February 1895.

TEXAS

Austin American, 11 July 1927.

Austin American-Statesman, 1 May 1927; 14 August 1927; 1 March 1995.

Austin Daily Democratic Statesman, February-July 1878; 24, 25 January 1879.

Austin Daily Statesman, 12 October 1880.

Austin Weekly Democratic Statesman, 26 June 1873.

Brenham Banner, 10 March 1876; 19 May 1876.

Burnet Bulletin, 15 September 1955.

Colorado Citizen, 4 June 1874.

Corsicana Democrat and Truth, 15 November 1917.

Daily Dallas Herald, 4 October 1874.

Dallas Daily Commercial, 12 April 1874; 30 July 1874.

Dallas Daily Herald, 14, 22, 23 July 1874; 5, 19 August 1874; 10, 11 April 1875; 29

September 1875; 7 November 1875; 29 December 1875; 10, 12, 14, 16 March 1876; 18 May 1876; 13, 15 June 1876; 2 August 1876; 17 November 1876; 24, 25 January 1877; 17 April 1877; 22 December 1877; January-June 1878; 13, 24 February 1880; 30 June 1880; 13 July 1880; 1 March 1881; 17, 20, 27, 28 July 1881; 29 March 1882; 1 April 1882; 15, 16 May 1882; 5, 6, 7 July 1882; 9, 16 September 1883; 21 October 1883; 29 August 1885; 3 September 1885; 30 June 1887; 18 February 1889.

Dallas Daily Times Herald, 18 March 1895; 13 June 1897; 8 December 1898; 28 December 1930.

Dallas Herald, 10 August 1859; 7 November 1860; 23 November 1867; 14 March 1868; 20 November 1869; 4 December 1869; 1 January 1870; 14 May 1870; 23 July 1870; 20 May 1871; 16 March 1872; 21 December 1872; 4 January 1873.

Dallas Morning News, 1885, 2 March 1886; 7 January 1887; 1888; 15, 17 February 1889; 1890; 1892; 1894; 9 December 1898; Obituaries: 1899 through 1948.

Dallas Weekly Herald, 17 April 1875; 7 August 1875; 22 July 1876; 16 December 1876; 7 April 1877; 23 June 1877; 29 December 1877; 2 March 1878; 27 April 1878; 2,3 March 1881; 15 December 1881; 27 March 1884.

Denison Daily News, 24, 29 December 1875; 2, 9 March 1876; 21, 30 September 1877; 13 October 1877; 29 December 1877; January-October 1878; 17, 25, 26 January 1879; 11 June 1879; 29, 31 January 1880; 9 March 1880.

Denton Enterprise, 23 July 1972.

Denton Monitor, 19 March 1870, 3 December 1874, and as quoted in other sources.

Denton Record and Chronicle, 24 November 1904; 1905.

Denton Record-Chronicle, 5 October 1911; Obituaries: 1916 through 1964.

El Paso Morning Times, 18 December 1917.

El Paso Times, 24 April 1926; 21 August 1939.

Evening State Gazette [Austin], 11 July 1878.

Flake's Daily Bulletin, 20 April 1870.

Fort Worth Daily Democrat, 23 December 1877; January-August 1878.

Fort Worth Daily Democrat-Advance, 8 April 1882.

Fort Worth Democrat, 4 September 1875; 24 July 1875; 19 February 1876; 26, 29 January 1879.

Fort Worth Gazette, 30 January 1884.

Fort Worth Weekly Democrat, 10 June 1876.

Fort Worth Star-Telegram, 3 August 1967.

Frontier Echo [Jacksboro], 17 May 1878; 7 June 1878; 2 August 1878.

Gainesville Daily Register, 19, 21 June 1937.

Galveston Daily News, 18 June 1875; 9 March 1876; January-August 1878; 4, 11 September 1878; 10, 13, 16, 26, 27 November 1878.

Grand Saline Sun, 26 March 1926.

Lampasas Daily Times, 8, 15, 29 June 1878; 12, 14, 31 July 1878.

Luling Signal, 19 June 1878.

Norton's Union Intelligencer, 29 May 1875; 12, 26 June 1875.

San Antonio Daily Express, 26 March 1876; 1, 8, 9 April 1876; 3, 9, 10 October 1877; 8, 15 December 1877; 10, 16 August 1878; 6, 11, 12, 18 September 1895; 22 December 1901; 21 July 1902; 15 June 1906; 11 May 1931.

San Antonio Express, 18 March 1911; 13 November 1913.

Texas Capital, 28 October 1877; 9 December 1877; 14, 21 July 1878; 4 August 1878.

BIBLIOGRAPHY

Waco Examiner and Patron, 8 February 1878; 22 March 1878; 19 April 1878; 21 June 1878; 23 August 1878; 13 September 1878; 18 October 1878; 15 November 1878.

Weatherford Exponent, 21 April 1877; 2 February 1878.

Williamson County Sun, 25 July 1878.

WYOMING TERRITORY

Cheyenne Daily Leader, 26, 28 March 1877; June-October 1877; 30 January 1878; 20-22 February 1878.

Cheyenne Daily Sun, 23, 30 September 1877.

PUBLIC RECORDS

ALBANY COUNTY, NEW YORK
Record of Inmates 1873-1886, Albany County Penitentiary

ATASCOSA COUNTY, TEXAS
District Court Minutes: *State of Texas v. Joseph Collins,* Cause No. 202.
Record of Marks and Brands: Vol. 1, 62.

BEXAR COUNTY, TEXAS
Deed Records: Vol. T-1, 339; Vol. 2, 289-90; Vol. 4, 405-06; Vol. 9, 11.
Marriage Records: Vol. G, 19.
Probate Records: *Estate of Nathan Underwood,* Cause No. 19427.

BOONE COUNTY, INDIANA
Certificate of Death (Henry Underwood): Book 20, p. 40.
Deed Records: Vol. 30, 118.
Indictment Book: *State of Indiana v. Gideon Underwood et al,* Cause No. 598.

CALDWELL COUNTY, TEXAS
District Court Minutes:
State of Texas v. Joe Lowe, Cause Nos. 1250, 1276, 1419.
State of Texas v. Joel Collins, Cause Nos. 1266, 1292, 1410.
State of Texas v. Manning Clements, Cause No. 1262.

CALHOUN COUNTY, TEXAS
Assessment of Property, 1865-1867, 1869-1870.
Deed Records: Vol. F, 168; Vol. G, 498.
Final Probate Record: Vol. C, 125-26, 131-32, 468.

CALLAWAY COUNTY, MISSOURI
Probate Record: *Estate of James F. Berry,* Bundle 6, Box 77.

CLAY COUNTY, TEXAS
Commissioners Court Minutes: Vol. 1, 29, 33, 37.
Deed Records: Vol. 57, 251.
Marriage Records: Vol. 1, 67.

COLLIN COUNTY, TEXAS
Deed Records: Vol. 16, 165-66; Vol. 65, 56.
District Court Records: *State of Texas v. Thomas Spotswood,* Cause Nos. 1500, 1501.
Marriage Records: Vol. 5, 95.

COOKE COUNTY, TEXAS
Certification of Birth Record (Vernie Andrew Mayes): File No. 4842.
District Court Records: *State of Texas v. Scott Mayes,* Cause No. 1257.
State of Texas v. Scott Mayes, Cause No. 3061.
Marriage Records: Vol. 4, 143.
Probate Records: *Estate of E.S. Mayes,* Cause No. 4529.

BIBLIOGRAPHY

DALLAS COUNTY, TEXAS
  Dallas City Council Minutes: 1874-1896.
DENTON COUNTY, TEXAS
  Commissioners Court Minutes: Vol A.
  Deed Records: Vols. A, B, D, F, J, O, R, 36, 39.
  District Court Minutes:
      State of Texas v. John Ailer, Cause No. 1672.
      State of Texas v. T.E. Gerren, Cause No. 3214
      State of Texas v. Mathew Gray, Cause No. 2.
      State of Texas v. Scott Mays, Cause No. 1688.
      State of Texas v. John Skaggs, Cause Nos. 1532, 1533.
      State of Texas v. Thomas Spotswood, Cause Nos. 1362, 1363, 1405, and
        1406..
      State of Texas v. Henry Underwood, Cause No. 1480.
  Marriage Records: Vols. A, 1, 2, 3, 4.
  Tax Assessment Rolls:- 1874-1875, 1877
ELLIS COUNTY, KANSAS
  Deed Records: Vol. B, 219; Vol. C, 276.
  Probate Records: *Estate of Anna Lang*, Cause No. 1562, Vol. 3, 606.
FRIO COUNTY, TEXAS
  Deed Records: Vol. F, 458-59; Vol. H, 103-04; Vol. I, 67.
  District Court Minutes:
      State of Texas v. John E. Gardner, Cause Nos. 115, 148, 154.
  Records of Marks and Brands: Vol. 1, 115, 281.
GOLIAD COUNTY, TEXAS
  Deed Records: Vol. K, 351.
INDIANA STATE ARCHIVES
  Civil War Enrollment Records
  State Prison Records
JENNINGS COUNTY, INDIANA
  Deed Records: Vol. H, 28.
  Marriage Record Book: Vol. 4, 93, 456.
KARNES COUNTY, TEXAS
  Deed Records: Vol. W-2, 347, 523.
  District Court Minutes: *State of Texas v. Joseph Collins*, Cause Nos. 388, 595,
    886.
LABETTE COUNTY, KANSAS
  Criminal Appearance Docket: Vol. A, 130.
  District Court Records: *State of Kansas v. Nathan Underwood and Henry
    Underwood*, Cause No. 217.
  Marriage Records: Vol. A, 119.
LASALLE COUNTY, TEXAS
  District Court Minutes: *State of Texas v. John Gardner*, Cause No. 30.
LAWRENCE COUNTY, INDIANA
  Circuit Court Records: *Denton Bass v. Emma Bass*, Cause No. 3551.
  Deed Records: Vol. C, 1020.
  Marriage Records: Vols. B, C, D, E, F, G.
  Probate File: *Estate of Daniel Bass*, Box 29, File No. 6.
              Estate of Denton Bass, Cause No. 4226.
              (David Sheeks, Guardian), Court of Common Pleas, Box 59,
              File No. 30.

BIBLIOGRAPHY

Margaret Bass v. John L. Bass et al, Court of Common Pleas, Box 50, File No. 35.
    Probate Orders: Court of Common Pleas, Vols. F, H, I.
LLANO COUNTY, TEXAS
    Tax Assessment Rolls: 1857-1865
MONTAGUE COUNTY, TEXAS
    Death Records: C.M. Sterling, Vol. 2, 74.
    Marriage Records: Vol. B, 316.
    Probate Records: *Estate of C.M. Sterling*, Cause No. 2415.
PARKER COUNTY, TEXAS
    Commissioners Court Minutes: Vol. 1.
    Deed Records: Vol. 2.
TARRANT COUNTY, TEXAS
    District Court Minutes: *State of Texas v. Seaburn Barnes*, Cause No. 692.
TEXAS DEPARTMENT OF VITAL STATISTICS
    Various death certificates.
TEXAS STATE LIBRARY
    Adjutant General Correspondence
    Adjutant General Service Records, Frontier Battalion
    Confederate Pension Applications
    Correspondence, Gov. Richard B. Hubbard
    Correspondence, Special State Troops and Frontier Battalion
    Declarations for Survivor's/Widow's Pension (Indian Wars)
    Extradition Records
    "Lists of Fugitives," Frontier Battalion Records (Box 401-1160)
    Monthly Returns, Frontier Battalion
    Muster and Payroll Records, Frontier Battalion
    Probate Cases (Microfilm):
        Dallas County - *Estate of H. Barksdale.*
        Dallas County - *Estate of John W. Herndon.*
        Dallas County - *Estate of Elisha McCommas.*
        Dallas County - *Estate of W.P. Stone.*
        Dallas County - *Estate of Edwin D. Walton.*
    Results of Operations of State Troops Since August 1, 1876, to December 31, 1881, Vol. I.
UNITED STATES CENSUS RECORDS
    Albany County, Wyoming Territory, 1880
    Atascosa County, Texas, 1860
    Audrain County, Missouri, 1870, 1880
    Bastrop County, Texas, 1860
    Bell County, Texas, 1900, 1910, 1920
    Bexar County, Texas, 1880, 1900, 1910, 1920
    Boone County, Indiana, 1880
    Bowie County, Texas, 1880
    Brazos County, Texas, 1880
    Burnet County, Texas, 1860, 1880
    Caldwell County, Texas, 1880
    Calhoun County, Texas, 1860, 1870
    Callaway County, Missouri, 1850, 1860, 1870
    Carroll County, Arkansas, 1870
    Cass County, Texas, 1850

Clay County, Texas, 1880, 1900, 1910, 1920
Coleman County, Texas, 1880, 1900, 1910
Collin County, Texas, 1880
Cooke County, Texas, 1880, 1900, 1910, 1920
Dallas County, Texas, 1850, 1860, 1870, 1880, 1900, 1910
Denton County, Texas, 1850, 1860, 1870, 1880, 1900, 1910, 1920
Douglas County, Nebraska, 1880
El Paso County, Texas, 1900, 1910, 1920
Ellis County, Kansas, 1860, 1880
Fannin County, Texas, 1860
Galveston County, Texas, 1880
Goliad County, Texas, 1900
Gove County, Kansas, 1880
Grayson County, Texas, 1880, 1900
Harris County, Texas, 1880
Harrison County, Texas, 1880
Henry County, Missouri, 1860, 1870
Hood County, Texas, 1880
Howard County, Texas, 1840, 1880
Jack County, Texas, 1880
Jennings County, Indiana, 1850, 1860, 1880
Kaufman County, Texas, 1880
Labette County, Kansas, 1870
Laramie County, Wyoming Territory, 1880
LaSalle County, Texas, 1880
Lawrence County, Indiana, 1850, 1860, 1880
Llano County, Texas, 1860
Madison County, Texas, 1860, 1870, 1880
Montague County, Texas, 1900
Navarro County, Texas, 1870, 1880
Orleans Parish, Louisiana, 1870
Palo Pinto County, Texas, 1860, 1880, 1900
Parker County, Texas, 1880
Pennington County, Dakota Territory, 1880
Pettis County, Missouri, 1870
Pulaski County, Arkansas, 1850
Schuylkill County, Pennsylvania, 1850
Shackelford County, Texas, 1880
Smith County, Texas, 1880
Stephens County, Texas, 1880
Tarrant County, Texas, 1880
Tom Green County, Texas, 1900
Travis County, Texas, 1860, 1870, 1880
Van Zandt County, Texas, 1880
Vigo County, Indiana, 1900
Williamson County, Texas, 1860, 1870, 1880
Wise County, Texas, 1870, 1880
Yell County, Arkansas, 1850
Young County, Texas, 1880

BIBLIOGRAPHY

UNITED STATES NATIONAL ARCHIVES AND RECORDS SERVICE
Central Plains Region-Kansas City
United States Circuit Court Records, District of Nebraska, *Bardsley v. Union Pacific Railroad et al*, Cause No. 295D.
College Park, Maryland
Pardon Case Files (*Samuel Pipes, Albert Herndon*), Office of the Pardon Attorney.
Southwest Region - Fort Worth, Texas
United States District Court Records, Western District of Texas:
   United States v. Sam Bass et al, Cause No. 731.
   United States v. Jim Tyler, Cause No. 130.
Washington, D.C.
Compiled Military Service Records.
Muster Rolls, U.S. Army Military Post Returns.
Pension Records, Veterans Administration.
Records of the Adjutant General's Office.
Records of the U.S. Army Continental Commands.
Records Relating to the Appointment of Federal Judges, Marshals, and Attorneys, 1853-1901.
United States District Court Records, Southern District of Indiana:
   United States v. James K. Rittenhouse, William Jones, Isaac Haworth, and John F. Holloway, Cause No. 3372.
VICTORIA COUNTY, TEXAS
   District Court Minutes: *State of Texas v. Joel Collins*, Cause No. 913.
VIGO COUNTY, INDIANA
   Circuit Court Order Book: *State of Indiana v. James Phillips*, Cause Nos. 4419, 4420.
   State of Indiana v. Henry Underwood, Cause Nos. 4417, 4418.
WILLIAMSON COUNTY, TEXAS
   Commissioners Court Minutes: Vol. 1.
   District Court Minutes:
      State of Texas v. Albert Highsmith, Cause No. 1983.
      State of Texas v. Frank Jackson, Cause No. 1762.
      State of Texas v. Orlando Lane, Cause No. 1520.
      State of Texas v. P.G. Peters, Cause No. 1451.
   Marriage Records: Vols. 1, 2, 3, 4, 5.
WISE COUNTY, TEXAS
   Probate Docket: *Estate of G.W. Stevens, Dec'd*, Vol. 2, 632.

PRIVATE COLLECTIONS

Bass, Wayne E., West Baden, Indiana.
Bedford, Indiana, Public Library.
Browning, Jim, Charleston, South Carolina.
Callaway County, Missouri, Public Library
Center for American History, University of Texas at Austin:
   Adjutant General Records
   Daughters of the Republic of Texas Scrapbook Collection
   Walter Prescott Webb Collection
Dallas, Texas, City Secretary's Office
Dallas Historical Society, Dallas, Texas

BIBLIOGRAPHY

Dallas Public Library, Dallas, Texas
Denton County Historical Museum, Denton, Texas:
    Cemetery Records
    Genealogical Records
    Goodman-Williams Collection
Denton, Texas, Public Library
Elliott, Barbara Chapman, San Angelo, Texas
Ellis County Historical Society, Hays, Kansas
Ernst, Robert R., Stillwater, Oklahoma
Fort Worth Public Library, Fort Worth, Texas
Johnson, Warren, Allen, Texas
McCubbin, Robert G., Jr., El Paso, Texas
Nebraska State Historical Society, Lincoln:
    Union Pacific Railroad Collection
North Vernon, Indiana, Public Library
Parsons, Chuck, Yorktown, Texas
Schmidt, Mrs. Ruby, Granbury, Texas
Stephens, Robert W., Dallas, Texas
Walker, Charles, Pembina, North Dakota
Wilson, C.B., Dallas, Texas

CORRESPONDENCE AND INTERVIEWS

Donaly Brice, Texas State Library, Austin, Texas, 1 March 1997.
Beth P. Caruth, Lewisville, Texas, to Author, 1 December 1997.
Ruth Priest Dixon, Mitchellville, Maryland, to Author, 9 March 1997; 6 October 1997.
John Lynch, Lawrence County, Indiana. Interview with Author, 4 February 1997.
Barbara Tweedle, Deputy Chancery Court Clerk, Bolivar County, Mississippi. Interview with Author, 3 October 1997.
Ruby Schmidt, Granbury, Texas, to Author, 7 January 1997; 14 April 1997.
Nita C. Thurman, Denton, Texas, to Author, 22 December 1997.
Charles Walker, Pembina, North Dakota, to Author, 1997.

INDEX

INDEX

Cleveland, Grover, 297
Cobb, Richard E. "Dick", 21, 309
Cochran, A.M., 280, 383
Cochran, C.P., 258ff, 378-79
Cockrell, Alex, 148, 189ff, 213, 217, 218, 343-44
Coke, Richard, 243
Colbert, Superintendent, 288
Coldwell, Neal, 169, 176, 273
Cole, John H., 181, 211, 277, 278
Coleman, Tex., 175
Coleman Co., Tex., 115, 268-69
Coleman, Richard B., 218, 368
Colleran, Michael, 9, 385
Collin Co., Tex., 29, 125ff, 132, 231, 279-80
Collins, Albert Galvin, 35, 43, 178, 181, 185, 204, 211, 238, 272, 278, 313, 364
Collins, Billy, 35, 36, 42, 43, 145-46, 148, 149, 157, 158, 160, 185, 188, 192, 199, 204, 205, 211, 226, 236ff, 255-56, 271ff, 274ff, 278, 296, 313, 343
Collins, Hart, 162
Collins, Henry, 145-46, 158, 160, 178, 192, 194, 205, 212, 218, 223, 226ff, 269, 271ff, 278, 313
Collins, James, 313-15
Collins, Joe, 35, 38, 41, 43, 61, 313-15
Collins, Joel (cousin), 271
Collins, Joel, 2, 34ff, 38, 43, 45-48, 51ff, 61ff, 74ff, 84ff, 103, 113, 118, 260, 271-72, 313-15, 343
Collins, Permelia, 272, 313, 364
Collins, Sallie Z. (Pipes), 238, 298, 315, 371
Colquitt, Oscar B., 302
Comanche, Tex., 33, 205
Connell, Pat, 193
Connell, Sampson, 302, 387
Connor, Chris, 243ff, 258, 264, 373
Cook, Ed, 61
Cook, J.H., 63
Cooke Co., Tex., 39, 107, 131, 205, 278, 281
Coons, John T., 100ff, 104
Cornish, W.K., 131, 136, 140, 167, 338-39
Corwin, Dennis, 246, 375
Coryell Co., Tex., 196
Cottondale, Tex., 221
Courtney, Lieutenant, 136
Courtright, Timothy I. "Jim", 133, 214, 218, 220, 228
Cowart, Robert E., 145-46, 181
Cox, Morgan, 93
Craighead, James, 103
Creasy [Creary], 245, 375
Crook City, Dakota Territory, 59
Crook, George, 79

Cruger, William R., 207, 364
Crutchfield, L.L., 211, 365
Crystal, Garrett, 56
Cullen, Cicero, 232, 268
Cummings, J.F., 73
Cummings, Merrick, 68-69
Curley (Kerley), Spofford, 164ff, 232
Curry, James, 153ff, 346
Curry, Louis, 56

Dallas Co., Tex., 15, 35, 45, 133, 145, 153, 205, 226ff, 269, 281
Dallas, Tex., 22, 35, 36, 43, 121, 123, 128-29, 131, 136, 142-43, 149, 167, 171, 175, 179, 185-86, 284, 298, 301-302
Daniels, W.E., 181
Darling, F.M., 55-56
Darsey, R.C., 199, 354, 359
Davis, David H., 248, 250, 377
Davis, Edward J., 296
Davis, Hugh, 225, 370
Davis, Ira, 276
Davis, Jack, 43, 48, 51, 61ff, 81, 97, 106ff, 133, 260, 266
Davis, Joe, 268, 279
Davis, R., 274
Davis, Sam, 147
Davis, William, 191
Davis, Wirt, 80
Dawson, 219
Dawson Co., Neb., 118
Day, William, 195, 362
Deadwood, Dakota Territory, 45ff, 55ff
Dean, H.B., 182
Decatur, Tex., 194, 221, 222, 223
Delaney, John W., 162, 348
Denison, Tex., 126, 285
Denton Co., Tex., 14-15, 23, 25, 27ff, 39, 110-11, 114, 115, 119ff, 140, 153, 159, 170ff, 183, 185ff, 192, 193, 205, 211ff, 273-74, 280
Denton, Tex., 2, 15, 22, 121, 153, 157, 190, 191, 220
Denton Mare, 27-32, 34, 39-41
Derrick, William, 244ff
Dieckmann, Alf, 248, 251, 377
Dillingham, Jeff, 248, 376
Dillon, Sidney, 73
Dixon, 214
Dodge City, Kan., 45, 97
Dodson, John L., 8
Dolan, H.A., 303
Dolan, Pat, 114
Doliver, Hiram A., 81, 85, 92
Douglas Co., Wy., 74, 77
Downing, Israel, 286-87
Downing, William. *See* Jackson, Francis M. "Frank".
Drake (posse), 191
Drennan, George W., 131

405

INDEX

INDEX

INDEX